H. Schmidt
295 Lipton Street
Winnipeg — R3G 2H2
21, Jul. 77

WARPLANES
& AIR BATTLES
OF WORLD WAR 1

PHOEBUS, LONDON

WARPLANES
& AIR BATTLES
OF WORLD WAR I

PHOEBUS, LONDON

Introduction

The first fighting pilots, with their popular image as 'knights of the sky', have been invested with a romantic aura which obscures the harsher reality of the war in the air. There was chivalry and romance, it is true ; the first pilots tended to be unconventional, idealistic young men, attracted by the possibilities of a spectacular and untried weapon, and they often had more in common with their enemies in the sky than their allies on the ground. They fought individual opponents whom they could recognize and respect—yet the difference in a dog-fight between survival and sudden, flaming death rested on the skill, coldly and ruthlessly exercised, of the pilot, and the technical performance of his machine.

Under the stimulus of war, technical development was rapid, if often haphazard and unco-ordinated. The warplanes of 1918 were a far cry from their frail, unarmed, under-powered counterparts of 1914, and improvements in performance and capabilities were reflected in refinement of their use. No longer were they used purely for observation and artillery spotting, the role envisaged for them at the beginning of the war. Strategic bombing, aerial photography and ground support techniques were evolved which have shaped the use of aircraft ever since.

This book presents the whole fascinating story of the warplanes of World War One, and of the men who flew them. Technical developments, military application and combat techniques are described authoritatively and in detail, alongside accounts by the pilots themselves of what the war in the air was really like. It is lavishly illustrated throughout with action photographs and detailed colour drawings, and forms a readable and informative account of the birth of air power as a decisive factor in modern warfare.

Edited by Bernard Fitzsimons

Phoebus, London.

This edition © BPC Publishing Ltd.
1973

First published in Purnell's History of the First World War

First published in this form 1973

ISBN 0 7026 0000 8

Printed in Belgium - H. Proost & Cie p.v.b.a. Turnhout - Belgium

Contents

Aircraft:

In August 1914, the military use of aircraft was very much in its infancy, and only a few far-sighted men realised its potential. The majority of military or naval leaders controlling military aviation in most countries barely understood the new arm, intending basically to use it as third dimensional cavalry to carry out reconnaissance missions or to spot for the artillery.

Below: A modern reconstruction of a typical 1910 aircraft of the wire and canvas era — a Bristol Box-kite

a new factor in war

Here **Air-Marshal Sir Robert Saundby** details the growth of the new arm, from the days of ballooning to the first primitive bombings and reconnaissances.

During the First World War no one spoke or wrote of 'Air Power'. The phrase had not yet been invented and, with minor exceptions, aircraft were still regarded as ancillary weapons. It was their task to help navies and armies to gain their ends. Until the foundation of the Royal Air Force in April 1918 practically all operational sorties were employed in some form of naval or army co-operation, and even by the end of the war the proportion of co-operation to other types of sortie was still about 19 to 1. In these circumstances the belief grew up, and was strongly held by the armies and navies of all countries for very many years to come, that aircraft were of value only in so far as they could directly support and participate in naval and military operations.

Although the Wright brothers successfully flew a heavier than air aircraft in December 1903, balloons of various kinds had existed since de Rozier and d'Arlandes had made a successful flight at Annonay in a hot-air balloon in November 1783, and as early as 1901 the Brazilian engineer Santos-Dumont had developed a successful dirigible airship. But navies and armies the world over were very slow to see the war potential of aircraft, and generally took little interest in them. For a long time aviation had mainly peaceful uses, and even its first military applications were inoffensive and ancillary. Balloons were used during the siege of Paris in 1870 to carry messages and, on occasions, people in and out of the beleaguered city. The British, during the Boer War of 1899-1902, used man-lifting kites in order to see 'the other side of the hill'.

It seems likely that one of the curbs on the development of aviation was the fear of its misuse by the evilly-disposed. Francesco de Lana, a Jesuit monk who lived during the latter part of the 17th Century, gave a warning that an airship might be able to cause 'a ship to capsize by flinging down pieces of iron, kill the crew and set the ship ablaze with artificial fire, with bullets and with bombs. Not only ships, but also houses, castles, and towns might be served in this way, without risk to those who cast down such objects from immeasurable heights'. And in *Rasselas* the great Dr Johnson wrote that the security of the good would be gravely imperilled if the wicked were able to attack them from the air at will.

It must also be remembered that in the years before the First World War the conduct of warfare was still shackled by con-

ventions. It is true that the extremely rigid conventions of earlier warfare had been largely destroyed by Napoleon, with his *levée en masse,* but they had been replaced by new formalities. Armies still thought in terms of lines, fortifications and cavalry charges, and navies of long-range bombardment between lines of battleships.

Italy was first in the field of military aeronautics. An Army Aeronautical Section was formed as early as 1884, and balloons were used for reconnaissance during the Eritrean War of 1887-88. Five aeroplanes and two small airships took part in the army manoeuvres in Libya in 1911, with some degree of success. Towards the end of that year war broke out between Turkey and Italy, and on October 23, 1911 Captain Piazza, who bore the imposing title of 'Commander of the Air Fleet', took off for the first wartime flight. He flew over the Turkish troops, causing consternation in their ranks. On November 1 a further remarkable development occurred when Lieutenant Cavotti dropped four bombs on enemy targets. These bombs were apparently modified Swedish grenades weighing two kilograms each (4.4 pounds). During the next few days several more of these small bombs were dropped, and it was not long before the Turks protested that the Italian aircraft had bombed a

military hospital at Ain Zara. Independent inquiries could not establish the existence of a hospital at that place, though it is possible that some tents were used as a casualty clearing centre. The Italians pointed out that their warships had bombarded the camp at Ain Zara a few days previously with 152 heavy shells without drawing any protest from the Turks. There followed a prolonged discussion in the Italian, Turkish and neutral Press about the ethics of air bombardment—the first example of a long series of such controversies which has continued ever since. It is significant that the very first use of a few tiny aerial bombs resulted in a protest, suggesting that they were far more devastating and inhumane than a large number of heavy shells fired by naval guns.

By this time many other countries had formed small naval and military aviation corps. In the USA, on August 1, 1907 the Signals Corps established an Aeronautical Division, responsible for 'balloons, air machines, and kindred subjects'. At first the division possessed only balloons, but in 1908 it acquired a small dirigible airship. In August 1909 the first aeroplane was delivered to the US Army, but it was 18 months before it received another, lent to it by the generosity of Mr Robert F. Collier. In December 1913 an Aviation

An imaginative prewar German view of what air warfare would be like. With surprising candour the enemy is unmistakably identified as France, and German aircraft are seen attacking the Eiffel Tower. Few prewar tacticians dreamt of using aircraft as daringly as this

The considerable advance in aeronautics since 1909 is reflected in the **Bristol Scout A**, designed in late 1913. Astonishingly clean and trim for its day, it was able to attain 95 mph on the 80 hp of its Gnôme rotary engine

△ Based on the design for the 1914 'Round Britain' race, the military **Sopwith 'Folder'** was typical of civilian machines adapted by the armed forces

▽ The **Sopwith Tabloid** made its first appearance in 1913 as a sporting biplane. Apart from its very clean design, especially in the cowling of the rotary engine, it was remarkable in the placing of the two occupants side by side

The **Sopwith Gordon Bennett Racer,** pressed by the Admiralty on the outbreak of war, was one of the best prewar designs. Very clean, and with a fully cowled 80 hp Gnôme rotary engine, it was capable of 105 mph

School was set up at North Island, San Diego, but progress was still very slow, and at the outbreak of war in Europe in 1914 the Army Air Arm had only 20 aeroplanes on its strength. The Naval Air Arm was almost non-existent.

'Good sport – but useless'

In France there were many enthusiastic junior officers, but the navy and army chiefs were apathetic. By 1914 the army possessed an air arm, but so little thought had been given to the military uses of aviation that it would seem that the authorities had not grasped the importance of applied flying as distinct from pure flying. It is said that General Foch, an unusually progressive and open-minded man who had commanded the *École Supérieure de la Guerre,* remarked that 'Aviation is good sport, but for the army it is useless'.

The Germans had set up naval and military corps of aviation, but seemed equally uncertain as to their use. The Army Air Service was placed under the Inspector-General of Military Transport, suggesting that aeroplanes were mainly regarded as a means of conveyance. The German Naval Air Service, however, concentrated from an early date on large rigid airships. The first Zeppelin did its trial flights in 1900, but it was not until 1906 that a second ship was built to government orders. By 1914, the Germans possessed a considerable number of large airships, whose long range and great lifting power put them, in those days, in a class by themselves. As, however, their envelopes were filled with hydrogen gas, they were very vulnerable to anti-aircraft shells and incendiary bullets fired from aircraft.

In Britain, it was not until 1911 that the first step was taken by forming the Air Battalion of the Royal Engineers. This had one company of aeroplanes, one of small airships, one of balloons and one of man-lifting kites. Before the formation of this unit a number of enthusiastic young naval and army officers had learned to fly at their own expense, and when in 1912 the Royal Flying Corps was formed, they were naturally drawn into it. The RFC was a joint service, with Naval and Military Wings designed to meet the needs of both services. A Central Flying School was set up at Upavon on Salisbury Plain, staffed by officers and men seconded from the army and the navy. The Commandant was Captain Godfrey Paine, RN, and the second-in-command and chief instructor was Major H. M. Trenchard of the Royal Scots Fusiliers.

Unlike most other nations, the British had a clearly defined, though very limited, idea of the task of military aviation. It was to be reconnaissance, pure and simple. The navy hoped that their airships and aeroplanes would be able to search very rapidly great areas of sea, and keep a close eye on the whereabouts of the enemy's main naval forces. Thus they hoped to maintain always a favourable tactical position, and avoid being surprised. The army hoped that aeroplanes would be able to fly over the enemy's rear areas, reporting troop and traffic movements, and the location of depots, dumps, and railheads. The Intelligence Staff, using this and their other sources of information, would be well placed to locate the enemy's main forces and estimate his intentions.

Belgium, Austria and Turkey had very

The **Bristol Box-kite** was the first British mass-produced aircraft, and its importance lay in its use in the development of RFC tactics and in training — many military and civilian pilots learning to fly on this type.

The Box-kite is a classic example of the first consistently successful type of aircraft — a heavily-braced, multi-bay pusher biplane with no or a small nacelle, the elevator on the biplane tail being supplemented by a forward elevator. *Engine:* Gnôme rotary, 50 hp. *Maximum speed:* 40 mph. *Loaded weight:* 900 lbs. *Span:* 33 feet (46 feet 6 inches with top plane extensions). *Length:* 38 feet 6 inches

The **Albatros BII** was in service with the German air services from before the war well into 1915 as a first line aircraft. In common with other Albatros reconnaissance types, it had an immensely strong fuselage made up of plywood skinning on a basic wooden rectangular framework. Despite the exposed engine, it is clear that some thought has been given to streamlining in the design of the relatively pointed nose. *Engine:* Mercedes 6-cylinder in-line, 100 hp. *Maximum speed:* 66 mph. *Climb:* About 260 feet per minute. *Ceiling:* 9,840 feet. *Endurance:* 4 hours. *Loaded weight:* 2,356 lbs. *Span:* 42 feet. *Length:* 25 feet

The **Maurice Farman M.F.7 'Longhorn'**, although dating from 1913, exemplifies the pre-1910 design philosophy, particularly in the forward elevator and the complicated structure supporting the undercarriage and the forward elevator. Despite its low performance and not very good handling characteristics, the 'Longhorn' served in a training capacity well into the war, after starting it as a general duties and reconnaissance aircraft. *Engine:* Renault, 70 hp. *Speed:* 59 mph. *Ceiling:* 13,123 feet. *Endurance:* 3 hours 30 minutes. *Weight:* 1,885 lbs. *Span:* 51 feet. *Length:* 37 feet $2\frac{7}{8}$ inches (from leading edge of forward elevator to trailing edge of rudders)

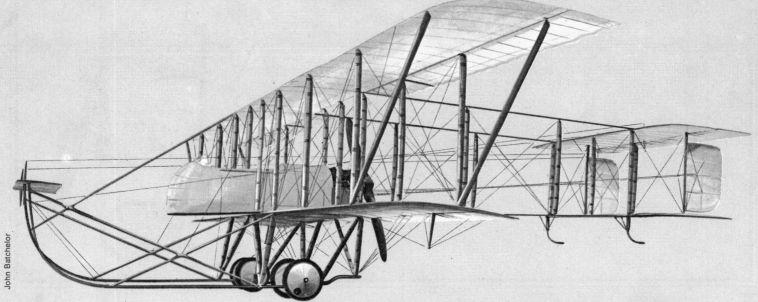

John Batchelor

The **Pfalz A I** reconnaissance machine in use during the first few months of the war was merely a German-built copy of the French Morane-Saulnier Type L

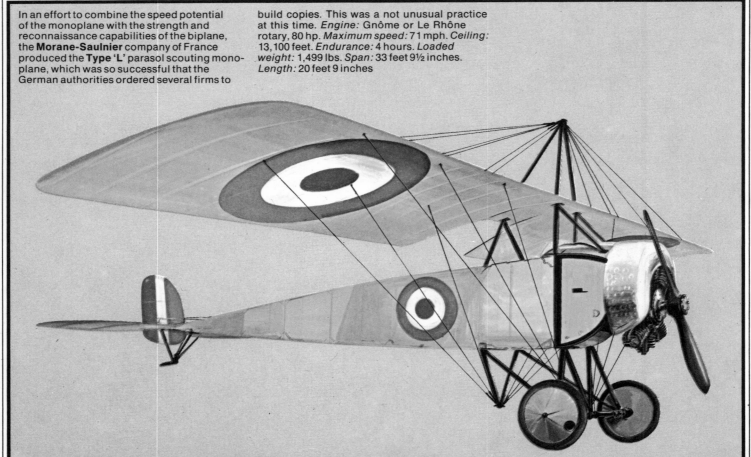

In an effort to combine the speed potential of the monoplane with the strength and reconnaissance capabilities of the biplane, the **Morane-Saulnier** company of France produced the **Type 'L'** parasol scouting monoplane, which was so successful that the German authorities ordered several firms to build copies. This was a not unusual practice at this time. *Engine:* Gnôme or Le Rhône rotary, 80 hp. *Maximum speed:* 71 mph. *Ceiling:* 13,100 feet. *Endurance:* 4 hours. *Loaded weight:* 1,499 lbs. *Span:* 33 feet 9½ inches. *Length:* 20 feet 9 inches

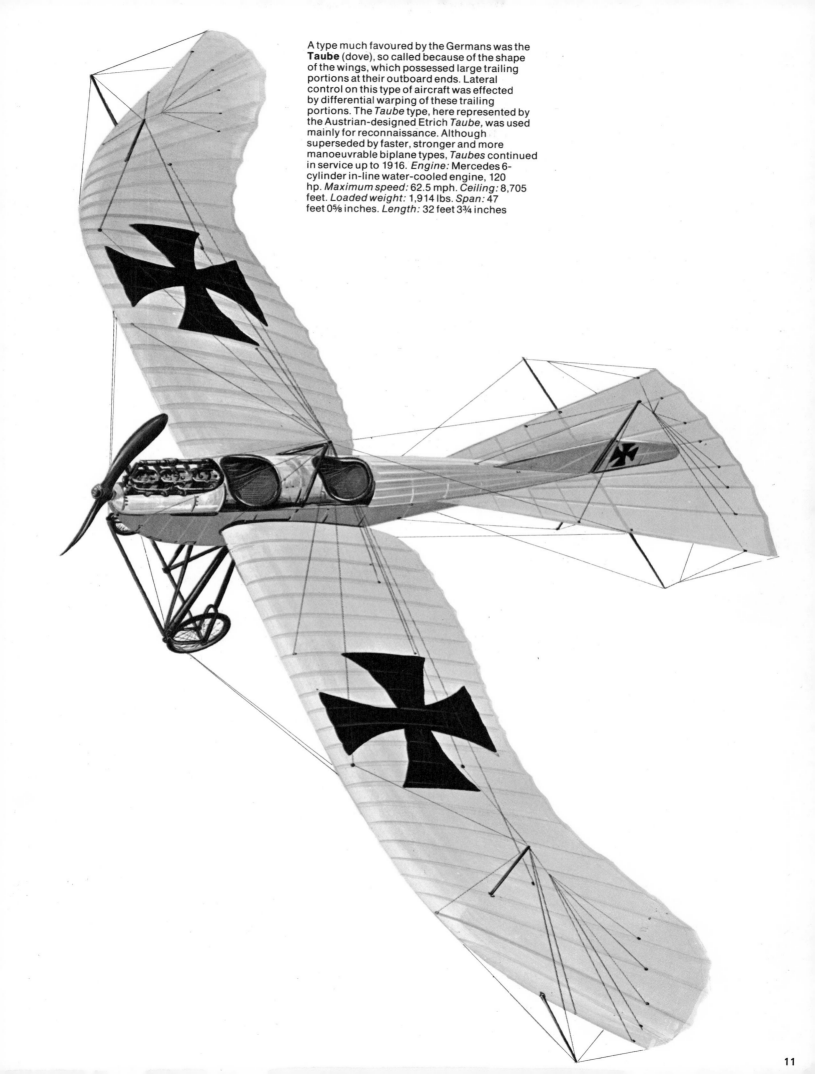

A type much favoured by the Germans was the **Taube** (dove), so called because of the shape of the wings, which possessed large trailing portions at their outboard ends. Lateral control on this type of aircraft was effected by differential warping of these trailing portions. The *Taube* type, here represented by the Austrian-designed Etrich *Taube,* was used mainly for reconnaissance. Although superseded by faster, stronger and more manoeuvrable biplane types, *Taubes* continued in service up to 1916. *Engine:* Mercedes 6-cylinder in-line water-cooled engine, 120 hp. *Maximum speed:* 62.5 mph. *Ceiling:* 8,705 feet. *Loaded weight:* 1,914 lbs. *Span:* 47 feet 0⅝ inches. *Length:* 32 feet 3¾ inches

Designed by the first Geoffrey de Havilland and built by the Royal Aircraft Factory, the **BE 2a** was the basic military aircraft of the RFC at the outbreak of war. It had been ineligible for the 1912 Military Trials on Salisbury Plain, but flying *hors concours* it had been clearly the best all-round performer at the trials, this being reflected in the orders placed for this type but not for the winner of the competition. This particular aircraft was the first RFC machine to land in France.

Engine: Renault V-8 in-line water-cooled engine, 70 hp. *Maximum speed:* 70 mph. *Climb rate:* 9 minutes to 3,000 feet. *Ceiling:* 10,000 feet. *Endurance:* 3 hours. *Loaded weight:* 1,600 lbs. *Span:* 38 feet 7½ inches. *Length:* 29 feet 9½ inches

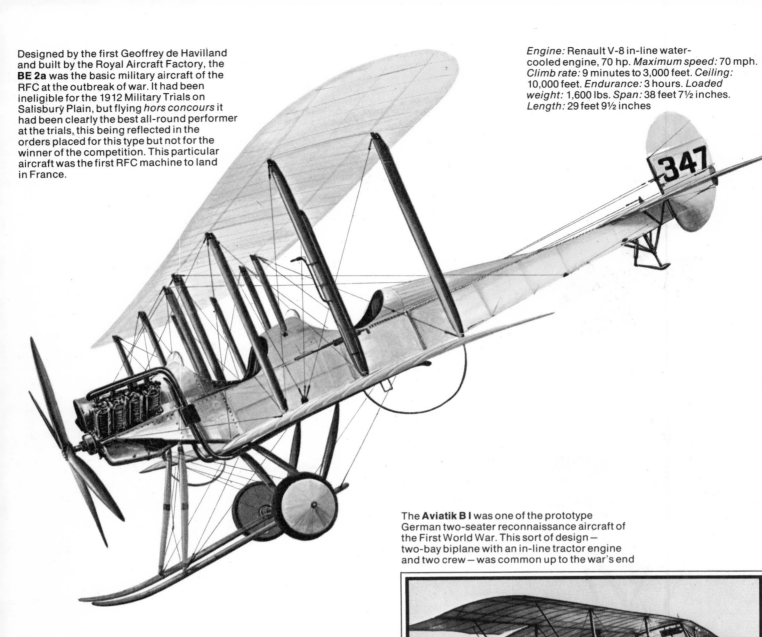

The **Aviatik B I** was one of the prototype German two-seater reconnaissance aircraft of the First World War. This sort of design — two-bay biplane with an in-line tractor engine and two crew — was common up to the war's end

Below: The **Caudron G III**, adopted by the French air force as a reconnaissance aircraft, was obsolescent by the beginning of the war and was soon reduced to training duties
Below right: The original version of the **SE2**, shown here, was built by the Royal Aircraft factory, Farnborough, and was a direct descendant of the first aircraft built for the single seat scouting rôle. It was capable of 92 mph

little in the way of military aviation. Belgium was overrun early in the war, and the air needs of Austria and Turkey were met by the Germans, chiefly by means of passing on aircraft superannuated from the Western Front.

The Russians, then as now, were highly secretive and unco-operative, and little is known about their military aviation at that time, but it is fairly clear that they had not made much progress.

Alone among the belligerent nations, Britain had created a unified air service, with naval and military wings. This sensible organisation did not, however, last long. The British Admiralty decided in July 1914, only some six weeks before the outbreak of the war, to break away and form its own air service. So the Royal Naval Air Service came into being, and the RFC reverted to the status of a corps of the army.

Thus we see that, in August 1914, the British had the RNAS and the RFC, trained for reconnaissance; the French had air services trained for nothing in particular but which were fairly large by the outbreak of war; the Germans placed their army aircraft under the control of military transport, while their naval air service had the largest and most advanced airships in the world; the United States had made an early start with an Aeronautical Division

of the Signals Corps, but had progressed incredibly slowly; the Italians had also started early, and at least had some war experience, both of reconnaissance and bombing; while Russia, Austria, Belgium and Turkey had made little or no progress.

It is fair to say that, on the outbreak of the war, the military and naval air forces of all countries were new and untried. It is also true that the generals and admirals had for the most part only the vaguest possible idea of the tasks which they expected aircraft to perform. It soon became obvious, however, that aircraft provided great opportunities for reconnaissance over land and sea, and at first this was their main employment. But air reconnaissance has its limitations as well as its advantages, and the danger of relying on negative reports was not fully realised. A famous instance of this was the failure of General von Kluck, commander of the German *First Army,* to keep in touch with and outflank the British Expeditionary Force during the retreat from Mons. He had relied on a report from an aircraft saying that all roads through the Forêt de Mormal were clear of troops. He took this to mean that there were no troops in the area, whereas in fact the forest contained a large British force. The troops, on hearing or seeing the approach of the aircraft, had moved off the roads under the trees, and so

nothing was seen. This incident, with others, did not encourage many senior officers of both services to rely on aircraft to give effective assistance to land or sea operations, and none of them had any faith in the offensive power of aircraft.

AIR-MARSHAL SIR ROBERT SAUNDBY KCB, KBE, MC, AFC, DL was born in 1896 and was educated at St Edward's School. He was serving with the Royal Warwickshire Regiment at the outbreak of the First World War and in 1915 was seconded to the Royal Flying Corps, with whom he won the MC for destroying the Zeppelin *L 48* in 1917. After the war he continued his career in the RAF in the Air Ministry, at Netheravon and in Aden, where he was awarded the DFC. After his service in Aden he became commander of a Training School in Egypt in 1926. After a spell at the Staff College he served in the Wessex Bomber Area staff, from which he went to the Air Ministry, the RAF Staff College, and back to the Air Ministry, where by 1939 he had become Director of Operational Requirements. He became Assistant Chief of the Air Staff in 1940 and in 1941 was promoted to Air Vice-Marshal. In 1944 he was knighted and in 1945 was promoted to Air-Marshal. In 1946 he was invalided out of the Service as a result of a spinal injury sustained in the First World War and received numerous awards. He became a member of the governing bodies of many societies, aeronautical and otherwise.

The **Breguet AG4,** nicknamed the 'Whitebait', was an example of the sometimes rather odd designs which were built in fairly large numbers and were developed quite considerably

The eyes of the German advance, and the Allied retreat

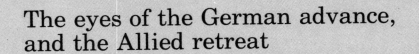

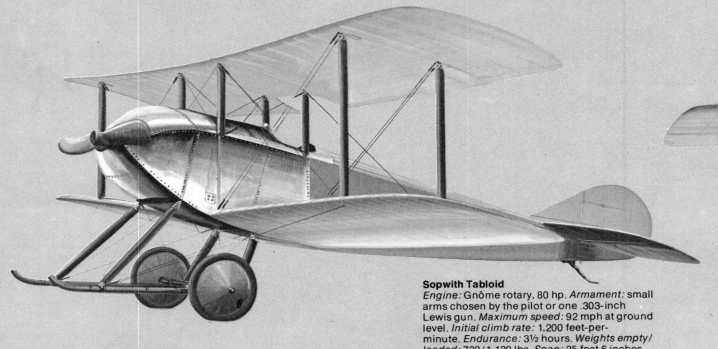

Sopwith Tabloid
Engine: Gnôme rotary, 80 hp. *Armament:* small arms chosen by the pilot or one .303-inch Lewis gun. *Maximum speed:* 92 mph at ground level. *Initial climb rate:* 1,200 feet-per-minute. *Endurance:* 3½ hours. *Weights empty/ loaded:* 730/1,120 lbs. *Span:* 25 feet 6 inches. *Length:* 20 feet 4 inches

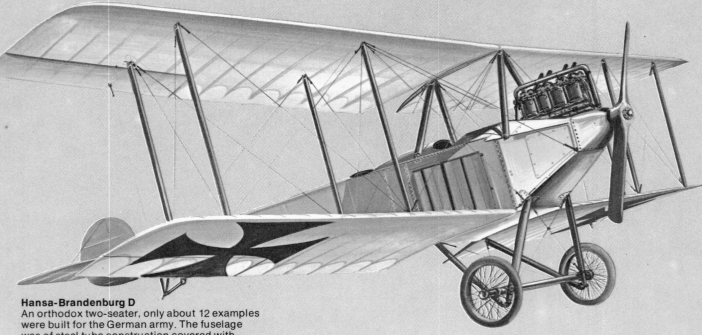

Hansa-Brandenburg D
An orthodox two-seater, only about 12 examples were built for the German army. The fuselage was of steel tube construction covered with ply, and the rest of the structure was of the normal wooden construction with fabric covering. *Engine:* Benz Bz II, 110 hp. *Span:* 43 feet 0⅞ inches. *Length:* 27 feet 8⅞ inches

Avro 504
Engine: Gnôme rotary, 80 hp. *Armament:* small arms as chosen by the pilot, one .303-inch Lewis gun or a few small bombs. *Maximum speed:* 82 mph at ground level. *Climb rate:* 7 minutes to 3,500 feet. *Endurance:* 3½ hours. *Weights empty/loaded:* 924/1,574 lbs. *Span:* 36 feet. *Length:* 29 feet 5 inches

Aviatik BI
This aircraft first appeared in 1914, and was derived from the prewar P 15A.'As it appeared originally, it lacked the fixed fin shown here, and possessed struts bracing the ends of the upper mainplane from the outer pairs of inter-plane struts. Its power was provided by a 100 hp Mercedes D I engine. The type was only produced in very small numbers

the making of a pilot

What was it like learning to fly in the early days of aviation? Initially, methods were crude, quite naturally. But the art progressed at a fairly quick pace, and by the time the war broke out many competent pilots had been

turned out by the schools. The war altered all this, however. More and more pilots were needed, and to produce the number required meant that training programmes had to be curtailed, and the standard thus fell. Moreover the arrival of the Fokker *Eindekker* proved that the type of training given had been of the wrong sort. The result was a very difficult and bloody period for the RFC; a period that continued until the arrival of Smith-Barry and his new school of flying. *C. M. Chant. Above:* One of the great training aircraft; the Bristol Boxkite

Jack Pia

17

Above: A Sopwith Pup. Tractable, delightful to fly and viceless, the Pup was relegated to training after it had become obsolete as a front line aeroplane. In training, its main use was as an advanced trainer, in which a pupil could learn the feel of the sort of aircraft used in combat after he had become proficient on the ordinary school machines.
Below: In 1918, the RFC started putting out diagrams such as this to help novice pilots get to know the sort of tactics they would meet on the front. All too often in the years before, pilots had been thrown into combat with no idea of what to expect

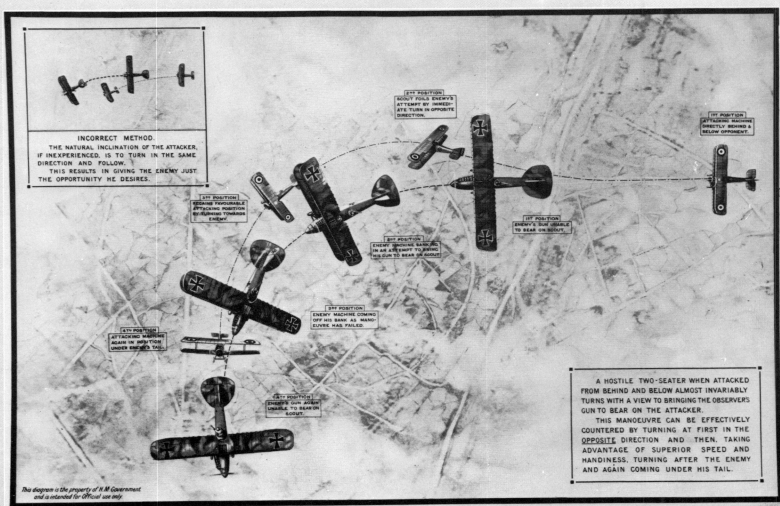

INCORRECT METHOD.
THE NATURAL INCLINATION OF THE ATTACKER, IF INEXPERIENCED, IS TO TURN IN THE SAME DIRECTION AND FOLLOW.
THIS RESULTS IN GIVING THE ENEMY JUST THE OPPORTUNITY HE DESIRES.

2ND POSITION
SCOUT FOILS ENEMY'S ATTEMPT BY IMMEDIATE TURN IN OPPOSITE DIRECTION.

1ST POSITION
ATTACKING MACHINE DIRECTLY BEHIND & BELOW OPPONENT.

3RD POSITION
REGAINS FAVOURABLE ATTACKING POSITION BY TURNING TOWARDS ENEMY.

2ND POSITION
ENEMY MACHINE BANKING IN AN ATTEMPT TO BRING HIS GUN TO BEAR ON SCOUT

1ST POSITION
ENEMY'S GUN UNABLE TO BEAR ON SCOUT.

3RD POSITION
ENEMY MACHINE COMING OFF HIS BANK AS MANOEUVRE HAS FAILED.

4TH POSITION
ATTACKING MACHINE AGAIN IN POSITION UNDER ENEMY'S TAIL.

4TH POSITION
ENEMY'S GUN AGAIN UNABLE TO BEAR ON SCOUT.

A HOSTILE TWO-SEATER WHEN ATTACKED FROM BEHIND AND BELOW ALMOST INVARIABLY TURNS WITH A VIEW TO BRINGING THE OBSERVER'S GUN TO BEAR ON THE ATTACKER.

THIS MANOEUVRE CAN BE EFFECTIVELY COUNTERED BY TURNING AT FIRST IN THE OPPOSITE DIRECTION AND THEN, TAKING ADVANTAGE OF SUPERIOR SPEED AND HANDINESS, TURNING AFTER THE ENEMY AND AGAIN COMING UNDER HIS TAIL.

This diagram is the property of H.M Government and is intended for Official use only.

OUTMANOEUVRED.

AIR TECHNICAL SERVICES
O.TS | 1686 | 21·5·18

The Wright brothers had made their first successful heavier-than-air, controlled and sustained aeroplane flight in December 1903. But not until 1906 was flight of a sort achieved in Europe, and it was only in 1908, at the first aerial race meeting, organised by the French champagne industry and held at Le Mans near Rheims, that European aviators realised the full extent of the progress made by the Wrights—they were far ahead of their European rivals. The appearance of Wilbur Wright at Le Mans was therefore a huge incentive to the fledgling European flying community, in a personal way because Wilbur Wright showed how patience and research could be used to achieve consistent advance in a new field, and in a technical way because Europe got the chance to see the most advanced flying machine in the world, the aeroplane its own flyers would have to beat.

In a way, then, 1908 should be looked upon as the date of the true birth of flight in the world—until that date only the Wrights knew how to fly, the other claimants to the title of flyer having made only the most insignificant and paltry hops in comparison. After the Rheims Aviation Week, the development of flight in Europe advanced with great speed and enthusiasm, while on the other side of the Atlantic it underwent a reversal, for too few were sufficiently interested to maintain a lively progress in the art.

In the early days of flight there was a fundamental difference of opinion on the form flying should take, in a way analogous to the use of the car and the horse. A majority of the flying community believed that the aeroplane should be an ordinary means of travelling, like the newly-triumphant car, and as such should be inherently stable. The pilot of this sort of aeroplane would be virtually nothing more than a chauffeur, directing the course of his vehicle but doing very little else, and leaving the actual flying to the machine itself. The main exponent of this form of flying was the Frenchman Gabriel Voisin, whose aeroplanes, for this reason, were great, lumbering, strongly-built and inherently stable machines which perambulated sedately around the skies in considerable numbers.

The other school of flight believed not only that the aeroplane should be fully controllable by the pilot (as were the majority of the aeroplanes built by the other school of thought), but also that this controllability should be used. The aim of this school was therefore to avoid inherent stability, so that the pilot might control his machine fully, as the rider does his horse. The adherents of this belief were the showmen of the skies, who were already thinking in terms of flying exhibitions and the like, where manoeuvrability would be a great asset. But in the infancy of flying, it was almost inevitable that the chauffeur approach should prevail, when it was still an achievement to get an aeroplane into the air, let alone having to worry about the problems of controlling an unstable machine.

The first aviators were, naturally enough, self-taught. There was no one to teach them, and so they had to learn to fly empirically. Casualties were few and far between because the aircraft were so underpowered and inadequate aerodynamically that even if they did crash, it was only from a few feet up and at a low speed, the pilot standing a good chance of surviving the misfortune. Learning by experiment, the pioneers of flight gradually taught themselves how to control their elementary machines once they had managed to get them into the air. First, the would-be flyer did straight runs across the aerodrome, without allowing the wheels to leave the ground, increasing the speed run by run until the aircraft was almost leaving the ground, in this way getting to know the feel of the aircraft and how the controls affected the run of the machine. Then came the first powered hop, just a few feet off the ground, and straight, so that the aircraft touched down further across the grass field used as an aerodrome. Once this had been mastered, the novice pilot could progress to gentle turns, circles, figure eights, vol-plane landings (landings with the engine off) and finally cross-country flights.

Once the first generation of pilots had learned to fly, things were much easier for the novice—he could now be told how he might control the machine, and what was likely to happen in given circumstances. But the process was still one that had to be learned by the novice on his own, for there were no such things as dual-control aircraft—indeed, aircraft of the early days were able to carry only one person, so that once the novice was aloft, he was on his own, with only his own skills and imagination to help him. Even if there were two seats, the controls were only arranged for one person to use them. A good description of this early empirical method of learning to fly appears in Graham Wallace's book *Claude Grahame-White,* about one of the great pioneers of British aviation. After working in the factory where his Blériot Type XII was being built, Grahame-White was too eager to wait for the arrival of the mechanics who were to assist

him in his first flight and started early practice one day with a friend. After high-speed runs across the aerodrome and a near accident, the two Englishmen had to try a flight.

For 20 exhilarating minutes they careered to and fro, until Grahame-White thought he had mastered the controls.

'It's a flying machine, isn't it?' he shouted above the roar of the engine. 'Then let's see if it can fly!'

Fleetwood Wilson nodded in speechless agreement.

Grahame-White recalled everything he had observed other pilots do on take-off. He checked the wind direction and taxied to a far corner of the parade-ground for the longest possible run. He opened the throttle wide, and the White Eagle bounded forward. Tentatively he eased back the cloche, *as the joy-stick was known, and with blood-quickening elation realised that the abrupt cessation of vibration meant the wheels had left the ground. They were airborne! With a reassuring grin at his companion he essayed a more positive movement of the elevators. The ground receded with a sickening rapidity, and he hastily levelled off. Only a few seconds —and now he had to land, the trickiest of manoeuvres, as he well*

The perpetual struggle: the chauffeur outlook and inherent stability against the rider view and full controllability

knew. More by luck than skill he brought off an impeccable touch-down.

They sat in breathless silence, overwhelmed by the sensations of flight.

'Ready?' asked Grahame-White when his pulse rate was back to normal. 'Let's try again.'

With mounting confidence he continued to fly from end to end of the parade-ground, consistently improving his handling of the White Eagle.

Thus the pioneers taught themselves to fly. But with the increasing popularity of aviation, it soon became clear that something better would have to be developed. Flying schools were springing up all over Western Europe, especially in France, and to make full use of their facilities competent pilots had to be turned out at the minimum expense, and novice pilots trained under the current methods were very prone to breaking the machines of the schools, with a consequent loss of revenue.

Dual control?

The next method was used most extensively by the flying schools run by the British and Colonial Aeroplane Company, at Brooklands and at Larkhill on Salisbury Plain. This development was a step towards full dual control, and was used on the schools' most common aeroplane, the Bristol Boxkite. This could carry two people, who had to sit in an exposed position over the leading edge of the lower wing. First of all, the pupil underwent a series of lectures explaining the theory of flight as it was understood at the time. Then he went for a series of short flights with the instructor, who would explain what he was doing as he flew the aeroplane. When the pupil was judged to have picked up sufficient knowledge to give him some likelihood of controlling the machine adequately, the instructor would allow him to take over the control column, which controlled the aeroplane in pitch and roll. Here, however, the Boxkite was an unfortunate machine, for the novice sat behind the instructor. So, in order to learn how to manoeuvre the machine in pitch and roll, the novice had to reach past his instructor and try to get the hang of this difficult stage of instruction when in an awkward and, more important, un-natural position. When the instructor thought the pupil could control the aeroplane with a fair degree of competence, the two would change positions and the pupil would have full control of the machine, for he could now use the rudder bar as well as the control column. In an emergency, the instructor hoped that he could reach across his pupil and regain control of the aeroplane himself. After a few flights with the instructor, the pupil was then sent off to do a short solo flight on his own, and if this proved satisfactory, he could then progress to the more difficult lessons of cross-country flights and the like.

An excellent description of this second stage in the evolution of flying training appears in the book *Recollections of an Airman*

by L. A. Strange, who learned to fly at a school at the London Aerodrome at Hendon run by Claude Grahame-White.

When I learned to fly, things had progressed greatly. We knew that the machines into which they put us would fly, and we had expert instructors who could tell us how to fly them. All we had to do, so to speak, was to obey the instructor's directions and fly, which, of course, sounds a good deal easier than it really was.

At any rate I never had any dual-control work before I took my 'A' Licence, which I succeeded in obtaining about three weeks after I started my course of instruction. This was about the average time it took in those days. I got a good deal of ground instruction, however, and in my opinion this is neglected in the majority of flying clubs today. It is so easy to impart when the weather is too bad for actual flying.

Our ground instruction consisted chiefly in sitting in a machine, which was put up on adjustable trestles—fore and aft and on the wing tips. In this we were shown the effect of the controls, and we had to learn thoroughly (by instinct rather than experience based on vision) what should be the machine's attitude in regard to the ground when taxying, how to get the tail up to the correct height to gain flying speed in the shortest possible distance and how to take off. We were also taught the proper angle of climb and how to make gentle turns, glide down, flatten out to land, etc.

Our instructor made quite sure that we knew almost instinctively the correct procedure for a wheel landing [landing with the tail up] and a proper three-point landing before he would even let us taxi the machine. Then we learned to control the machine on the ground, after which we were allowed to indulge in straight flights a few feet off the ground. Finally we passed onto half-circuits, circuits (first left-hand and then right-hand) and figures-of-eight. My actual flying time before taking my ticket was only three and a half hours, which shows the value of the ground instruction we got in those days.

It is perhaps wrong to describe Strange's training as belonging to the second stage of flying training, for he got no dual instruction in the air as the aeroplane he was using was a Caudron with only a 35-hp Anzani engine. This would have proved unequal to the task of taking off with two people aboard. His training, however, was very thorough and progressed gradually and methodically, and he benefited from all the experiences of the first stage. After he had learned to fly on the Caudron, Strange went on to finish his instruction on a Boxkite in the manner already described. His Boxkite instructor (Louis Noel, a Frenchman) had 'a forceful way of expressing himself (to pupils about to go solo):

"I have told you how to fly; you have understood? Yes? Well, I give you the last chance to say No. Very well, you can fly, do you hear? I, Louis Noel, say you can fly; I speak no more. I go to the bar; if you commit suicide, that is bad, but if you almost do that, it will be much, much worse for you."'

Throughout both these stages in the development of flying training, it must be remembered that the 'chauffeur' school of thought was dominant in flying circles. For the period up to the beginning of the war this view was entirely justified on the grounds of safety and aircraft capabilities, even if it was short sighted. In these early days of flight, the theory of flight was very imperfectly

Top: A Bristol Boxkite. This aeroplane formed a vital link in the development of training from the single-seat to dual control type. *Centre:* Claude Grahame-White, one of the great figures in the pioneer days of flying, especially in the promotion of safety and adequate training. *Above:* A Maurice Farman S 7 Longhorn. Together with its derivative, the Shorthorn, this was the premier early training machine

understood, and it was not realised what the various positions an aeroplane might get into in the course of aerobatics might do to the airflow round the machine, and consequently how control response might be affected. Moreover, in order to get the machines to fly on the small amount of horsepower available from early aeroplane engines, the whole machine had to be very light. The best place to economise in weight, indeed the only place on early aeroplanes, was in the airframe, and these were thus extremely flimsy. This did, however, have the beneficial side effect that the structure broke up in a crash, and this afforded the pilot some degree of protection. Louis Blériot is reported to have said: 'A man who keeps his head can never be injured through a fall. If one falls one must not try to save both the machine and oneself. I always throw myself upon one of the wings of my machine when there is a mishap, and although this breaks the wing, it causes me to alight safely.' Blériot was something of an authority on crashes—he was perpetually being pulled from the wreckage of his machines by his mechanics!

To return to the point, however. For reasons of weight economy, then, early aeroplanes had a flimsy structure. This, combined with the not very advanced state of stressing aeroplane structures, meant that early types were not suitable for aerobatics. Such aerobatics as were performed were done by daring men in especially strengthened machines.

Training continued along these lines up to the beginning of the war and indeed into the war. For in the first year of hostilities, the main use of the aeroplane was for reconnaissance, and here the chauffeur idea was quite reasonable, for the aeroplane was merely a means of getting an observer to the place from which he could see what the opposition was doing and back again after he had seen what he wanted. In this sort of war flying the pilot was nothing but a chauffeur, though the more adventurous were already beginning to see further ahead.

But in the late summer and autumn of 1915 the whole concept of war flying changed with the arrival of the Fokker *Eindekker*. To avoid being shot down, aeroplanes had to take evasive manoeuvres, and this pilots were not adequately trained to do. Those already at the front had to learn by experience how to avoid the Fokker (which, luckily, was not a very strong machine and could therefore not stand being thrown about) or be shot down. The lesson of manoeuvrability now had to be learnt by pilots and designers alike. The latter had to design machines that could be stunted without breaking up, so that the pilot could use the manoeuvrability now afforded him to avoid attack or to put himself in a good position to attack another aeroplane, while the former had to learn to make good use of his new-found agility.

The birth of aerobatics

This, of course, took time. The designers had to conduct much research into aerodynamics and aircraft controllability, especially the hitherto dreaded spin, which the brilliant Farnborough test pilot Frank Gooden had done so much to clear up. The pilots had to learn their new antics, but first they had to wait for first-hand accounts from the front to find out what were the best tactics to adopt and then ally these with the results of test flying by pilots at experimental stations and the companies producing aeroplanes to find out what they should learn. Aerobatics now had to come into the curriculum of flying training of all pilots, whether they were destined for scout squadrons or not. In fact, the ability of any pilot to perform aerobatics quickly and smoothly became the criterion of whether or not he went to a fighter squadron or to one operating bombers or reconnaissance machines.

No longer could the air forces of the world afford to select pilots in the way Cecil Lewis describes his own selection, at a time when he was below the age for enlistment. Arriving from school, Lewis was interviewed by Lord Hugh Cecil:

'Were you in the Sixth?'

'Yes, sir—Upper Sixth. Er—a year under the average, sir.'

'I see. How old are you?'

'Almost 18, sir.' (Liar! You were 17 last month.)

'Play any games?'

'Yes, sir, I got my School Colours at Fives, and captained the House on the river. I should have got my House Colours for Rugger this year if I'd stayed; but—'

'Fives, you say? You should have a good eye, then.'

'Yes, I suppose so, sir.' (Does Fives need a good eye? Well, he seems to think so. I'm getting on all right.)

'You're very tall.'

'Six foot three, sir.'

'I don't think you could get into a machine.'

'Why, sir?' (Oh Lord! He's going to turn me down. He mustn't turn me down!)

'Well, they're not built for young giants like you, you know.'

'Couldn't I try, sir?'

A slow smile, a pause, then: 'Yes, I suppose so. I'll write a note to the OC at Hounslow.'

There are exceptions to every rule, but what, basically, was needed in pilots was youth (reactions are quicker), good eyesight, excellent health, an average size (it is difficult to accommodate very large or very small people in the cockpit) and a lively intelligence (to weigh up conditions, and the tactics to be adopted in view of them, quickly and accurately).

Typical of the training still being received as airmen on the fronts were beginning to realise the full demands that were going to be made on their aerobatic skills is Cecil Lewis' first solo, made after he had had only one and a half hours' dual:

I had trundled around the aerodrome with Sergeant Yates, my instructor, doing left-hand circuits, and made a few indifferent landings.

'You'd better go solo this afternoon, if the wind drops.'

'Yes, sir.'

'Remember to take plenty of room to get off.'

'Yes, sir.' (Last week George had neglected that important point, caught the upper lip of the concrete, and gone arsy-tarsy down into the meadow on the other side.)

'Get your tail well up before you try to take her off. Don't climb under 45, and when you come down, keep her at 55 until you want to land. If you're at 300 feet over the Members' Bridge you'll get in all right.' (Sandy had misjudged it two days ago, and flown into the sewage farm! How we had laughed!)

'Yes, sir.'

Alone in the nacelle of the [Farman] Longhorn, the engine ticking over, the instructor leaning over the side. 'Run her up.' Stick back, throttle slowly forward. 1,200 [revolutions]. 'She'll do.' Chocks away. Taxi slowly. Away over the bumpy ground. How difficult to steer right down the aerodrome with a following wind! Give her a bit of throttle, rudder . . . round she comes. Throttle back. Take a deep breath. Try the controls. Rudder – Elevator – Ailerons . . . God! Who said they wanted to fly? How the heart pumps! Waiting for the pistol at the school races last year! Just the same – sick, heart pumping, no breath . . . Well, come on! Can't stay here all night! Throttle full open, elevator forward . . . We're hardly moving. The revs are all right. Why doesn't the tail lift? What's the speed? 30! . . . 40! . . . Ah! It's coming up! . . . She'll never get up, though . . . We shall soon fly into the track! . . . Steady now. Don't pull her off too soon! 45! 50! Now! Ease back the stick! Gently, gently . . . Bounce . . . Bounce . . . Bounce . . . She's lifting! She's away! 45! Keep her down, man! For god's sake keep her down, we shall stall! Easy does it. Ah! We'll clear the track after all . . . Steady now . . . There it goes, well underneath. Now I can breathe. Keep her at 50. That's it. Good . . . Now, what about a turn? Just a little left rudder. Bank. Ease her round . . . I'm getting on all right. What's the height? 500. That'll do. That's safe enough . . .

And so round the track, getting confidence, turning, turning, always left . . . Try a right turn now. Now . . . oh, she's shuddering. There's something wrong! Straighten! Quick! Straighten! . . . No, it's all right . . . Funny, that vibration. Must report it when I get down. When I get down! How the hell do I get down? (Young Johnson, a week or two back, was frightened to come down, flew round and round the aerodrome for an hour until his petrol gave out, and then crashed on landing.) The engine keeps me up. If I shut it off we shall fall . . . What did he say? Put your nose down before shutting off. Let's try it . . . God! Stomach in your mouth like a scenic railway! How I hate scenic railways! Horrible things. Try again. Throttle back and nose down together . . . That's better! That's it! Keep her at 55 . . . How quiet it is without the engine! Look out! 60, 65. Nose up a bit. Shall we get in? Yes. No. A bit more engine. That's it. There go the pines underneath. Lovely woods look from the air! Mossy. Now shut off again. Steady. Now . . . Now! Hold your breath. Ease her back. Gently . . . Quick! You're flying into the ground! Pull her up! Up! . . . Not too much . . . That's it. Now . . . why don't we land? We're stalling. Engine, quick! Bang! Bounce! Bounce! Bounce! Rumble! Rumble . . . rumble . . . We're down! Hurrah! We're down! I've done it! I haven't crashed! I've done it! . . .

Pause for a minute to get your breath. Good boy! You've done it! Phew! Thank God it's over! . . . Now, come on! Taxi up to the sheds in style. Confidence. That's the way! Show 'em. Good! Switch off.

Mechanics examine the undercarriage. 'Any damage?'

'Nao! These 'ere airioplanes 'll stand anything!'

And so flying training continued, inadequately. The demands of war made huge calls on the output of the various flying schools, now greatly augmented in number. Originally, all military pilots had been trained at civilian schools, but soon the navy and the army built their own schools, and these were greatly expanded and added to after the beginning of the war. Demands from the front were so great that pilots had to be sent out there with only a few hours solo to their credit. It was a lucky novice who had flown the type of machine used by his squadron before he had to fly it in combat. Consequently casualties were very high, especially among the new pilots, but the High Command correctly said that casualties must be accepted in the hour of crisis, the end of 1916 and the beginning of 1917, to maintain aerial superiority.

Training itself was also hit, for the squadrons about to go overseas were loathe to leave behind a competent pilot to become an instructor, in exchange for a novice pilot, who would be a liability to himself and his squadron. Thus instructors tended to be inferior pilots, who did not make able teachers, and wounded or resting front line pilots, whose heart was not in the job – they wanted to get back to the front. The same applied to the aerial gunnery and advanced flying schools, to which newly qualified pilots were posted to learn about fighting rather than just flying, always given the proviso that demands from the front did not preclude this.

Onto this not altogether fortunate scene now appeared a remarkable man, R. R. Smith-Barry, and his creation, the third stage in the evolution of flying training. In 1916 Smith-Barry was in command of an RE 8 squadron on the Western Front, and he was appalled by the quality of the new pilots posted to him. The basic material was good, but the standard of training given new pilots was no longer adequate to give new pilots even a fair chance of survival on the Western Front. He correctly diagnosed the basic faults in the training given these novices and concluded:

● Though more advanced aerodynamic theory was available, few pilots or instructors had taken the trouble to translate the findings of the test pilots into practical flying possibilities, so that events like spinning were still taking a heavy toll of less experienced pilots when there was a means of recovery. It just needed teaching, first to instructors and then to pupils.

● What was needed was a permanent, skilled, trained and dedicated corps of instructors to replace the present group of inferior pilots and those eager to get back to the front, though the latter could do much to aid novices by giving talks and keeping the schools of aerial gunnery and fighting fully posted on the latest fighting tactics.

● Proper training aeroplanes were needed to replace the obsolete and inefficient aeroplanes then used for training. It was wasted effort to teach a man to fly on a Farman Longhorn and then have to retrain him to fly something nearer a combat type. What was needed was something with a reasonable performance and handling characteristics approximating to current combat types. For this the Avro 504 was ideal. All that was needed was to turn it into a full dual-control aeroplane and devise some means of letting the instructor in the rear cockpit communicate with his pupil. This was done by fitting a tube to the machine. The instructor spoke into one end, and the pupil, who had the other end attached to his flying helmet, could hear.

● Training needed to be made much more systematic, starting with the instructors and then moving on to the pupils. The instructors must first be educated in a homogeneous system of training, and this had then to be taught to all pupils. The system was based on the latest scientific knowledge, the use of the best aeroplanes available and, most important, the instillation into the pupil of confidence – confidence to fly his aeroplane almost to the limit, at any height, relying on his ability to correct any position the machine might end up in, i.e. that he might be able to control the aeroplane in any altitude.

Smith-Barry pestered General Trenchard with letters to this effect while he was in France, and it is one of Trenchard's great achievements that he found the time to read and realise the value of Smith-Barry's suggestions. At the end of 1916, Smith-Barry was sent home to organise his scheme at Gosport, using No 1 Reserve Squadron as a nucleus. The scheme was an enormous success. Once Smith-Barry had collected his instructors and trained them, the first course of training produced its first batch of pilots in nine weeks instead of the usual 15, and the pilots were much better than average. Later in 1917, the Gosport School received its first Avro 504's and training got successively better.

Great credit must go to Smith-Barry's system for the way in which British pilots were to a great extent able to cope with better German machines later in the war by using their superior fighting abilities. The proof of the pudding is in the eating: when the effects of Smith-Barry's training made themselves felt, British aerial casualties declined. In addition, the system is the basis of nearly every flying training system in use all over the world today. Flying training started by showing the pilot how to take his machine wherever he wanted to go whenever the weather was reasonably good; Smith-Barry showed the pilot that he should and could control his machine in almost any circumstances and in conditions that would have grounded even the most courageous pilot of even a few years before his own time.

Further Reading
Any first hand accounts of the First World War in the air
Bishop, W. A., *The Courage of the Early Morning* (Heinemann 1966)
Cole, C., *McCudden VC* (Kimber 1967)
Douglas of Kirtleside, Lord, *Years of Combat* (Collins 1963)
Gould Lee, A., *No Parachute* (Jarrolds 1968)
Grinnell-Milne, D., *Wind in the Wires* (Hurst & Blackett 1966)
Lewis, C., *Sagittarius Rising* (Peter Davies 1936)
McCudden, J. T. B., *Five Years in the Royal Flying Corps* (Portway)
Raleigh, Sir Walter and Jones, H. A., *The War in the Air* (OUP)
Strange, L. A., *Recollections of an Airman* (Hamilton)
Taylor, J. W. R., *C.F.S.* (Putnam)
Wallace, G., *Claude Grahame-White* (Putnam 1960)
Yeates, V. M., *Winged Victory* (Cape 1934) [a novel]

CHRISTOPHER CHANT was born in Cheshire in 1945 and was brought up in Tanganyika in the twilight of the British Empire. He was educated at the King's School, Canterbury and at Oriel College, Oxford, where he took a degree in Literae Humaniores (Philosophy and Ancient History). He has been interested in and devoted to military history, in particular aviation history (especially the period up to 1914), for many years, and hopes to make his career in this field. He is a former Assistant Editor on Purnell's *History of the First World War*, concerned mostly with research on maps and statistics.

THE AIR WAR

In 1914 the tactics of air warfare had not even been thought of, and the pilots of both sides had to learn their lessons the hard way. Even the problem of arming aircraft had not been thought of seriously and many of the ideas on this subject were more eccentric than effective. *D. B. Tubbs. Above:* An early victim of air fighting. For one aircraft to shoot another down was more the exception than the rule in 1914

When war broke out between Britain, France and Germany in August 1914 the art and science of air warfare were not merely new, they were non-existent. It was only 11 years since the Wright brothers' first successful aeroplane flight at Kitty Hawk, and a bare five since Louis Blériot's crossing of the English Channel had destroyed the United Kingdom's island status, although the airships with which both France and Germany had been experimenting since the turn of the century had long been capable of making a return trip.

Prophets and scaremongers had long foreseen a 'Zeppelin menace'. Aeroplanes were taken less seriously. Although there had been many experimenters with heavier-than-air craft it was not until the arrival of Wilbur Wright at Le Mans in 1908 that European sportsmen—for flying was primarily a sport in those days—learned to make and fly properly controllable aeroplanes. The French learned fast, and although their experiments led at first in many directions it was not long before two main types of aeroplane became dominant: the 'tractor' which had a fuselage of more or less modern appearance, with the engine in front of the pilot and driving a propeller in the nose; and the 'pusher', in which the airscrew was mounted behind a bath-like nacelle for pilot and passenger, and the tail was carried on outrigger booms. Both types found a use in warfare; the pusher because pilot and observer, seated in the nose, had an excellent view of the ground, the tractor because its cleaner aerodynamic shape provided a better performance. Types were made in monoplane and biplane form, the former having the advantage of speed and the latter of structural strength.

The French army, although possessing a few airships, at once saw the value of aeroplanes for reconnaissance and built up a sizeable fleet. This frightened the Germans (hitherto secure in their superiority in airships) into emulation, and soon their machines, both in number and performance, had overtaken the French. By 1914 the German and Austro-Hungarian empires had many aeroplane factories and two main types had been more or less standardised: monoplanes known, from their back-swept wings and spreading tail, as *Tauben* (doves) and a biplane series also notable for a back-swept trailing edge known, for this reason,

as 'arrows'. The wing plan in each case was based on the work of Etrich and Wels in Austria, who had discovered that such a wing form produced inherent stability, providing a steady platform for aerial observation. The need for rapid manoeuvring in aerial combat had not been foreseen.

The Germans had only one 'pusher' type in service, the Otto biplane. They did, however, possess many excellent aero-engines, based on motor-racing engines. The *Kaiserpreis* race of 1907 for the Emperor's Cup, and the series of ostensibly sporting trials during 1909, 1910 and 1911 sponsored by Prince Henry, the Kaiser's brother, produced motorcars powered by remarkably efficient engines, made by Mercedes, Benz, Opel and Austro-Daimler. Water-cooled engines, on the motorcar principle, were popular because it was realised that a big, powerful engine could support a large airframe, thus fulfilling two of the army's demands: a high ceiling and long range. By the outbreak of war Germany held the altitude record at 27,500 feet, and the endurance record at 24 hours.

In aeronautics, as elsewhere, the French approach was directly opposed to the German. The French had been the first Europeans to fly, and because at first the problem had been to rise from the ground at all, they evolved relatively flimsy aeroplanes and the lightest possible engines. At the outbreak of war they had only one make of water-cooled engine, the Canton-Unné (Salmson) radial, but they had two kinds of air-cooled engine, based on the now forgotten rotary principle: the Gnôme and the Le Rhône. The rotary layout appears so improbable at this range in time that a short explanation is due. The crankshaft was held stationary and the rest of the engine—crank-case and radially disposed cylinders—revolved round it, carrying the airscrew with them. The 80 hp Gnôme was frail and temperamental, but it was the lightest of all for its power, and extremely compact. It was to make possible the first single-seater fighters—although anything so specialised as a fighter lies outside the period of this article. In 1914 all aeroplanes, of whatever type were used primarily for scouting.

Britain began late, and in a very small way. The authorities had always adopted a repressive and suspicious attitude to flying,

and, just as motor racing was forbidden on the roads (in sharp contrast with France, Germany and Italy) so pioneer aviators were 'warned off', A. V. Roe being threatened with prosecution if he persisted in trying to fly from Hackney Marshes. Enthusiasts like the Hon C. S. Rolls and J. T. C. Moore-Brabazon learned their flying in France, and until the government-owned Aircraft Factory at Farnborough undertook the design and development of aeroplanes, such few machines as the Royal Flying Corps possessed were French. The Royal Navy, too, took an interest in flying, but the Navy, in contrast to the army, who patronised the Factory, encouraged private constructors such as Avro, Sopwith and Short Brothers. The British authorities had done little to foster the design of indigenous engines, and apart from a Factory copy of the Renault which began to emerge by the end of 1914, most service engines were French. The Belgian air force, too, relied entirely on France for both airframes and engines. Only Russia cast her net wide, to include machines from France, Britain, Germany, Austria and the United States.

Airmen distrusted

Aerial reconnaissance flights could, with advantage, have begun before the war. France's Lebaudy airships could have discovered German mobilisation plans and troop concentrations. The air was a new dimension, however, and as events were quickly to show, senior officers on each side proved more ready to believe their own preconceptions than the reports of their aerial observers. It was, however, purely as long-range scouts that aeroplanes were regarded, a means of 'seeing over the hill'. This does not mean that the air arm was universally accepted. Cavalrymen thought it might frighten their horses, gunners resented the need for increased camouflage, soldiers of the old school distrusted airmen on principle and the infantry fired at everything that flew. Nor were airmen regarded as heroes; they were more often suspected of 'dodging the column'.

However, in the early months of the war German machines flew 200-mile reconnaissance flights over the French positions daily, bringing back valuable information to corps headquarters, as the Germans, unlike the French and the British, had aircraft

at corps level from the start, landing with their messages beside corps' HQs. In this they were wise; but in their handling of lighter-than-air craft they made serious mistakes in the first few days of the war. They should have kept their Zeppelins for high-level reconnaissance and long-range strategic bombing. Instead they squandered them on low-level missions. Zeppelin *L VI* was one of the first aerial casualties of the war, lost after bombing Liège on August 6. *L VII* and *L VIII* were employed on the tactical mission of surveying the extent of Joffre's counterattack in the Argonne, when aeroplanes would have done the job better. *L VII* was claimed by French gunners (and also by a French airman, Caporal Finck) on August 16 in the Argonne, and *L VIII* was mistaken for French and brought down by German troops at Badonvillers on August 23. Similarly a French Lebaudy airship was brought down at Rheims in August, amid great enthusiasm, by French troops. Airship crews may well have prayed 'Heaven preserve us from our friends'.

The French air force had been slow to mobilise, but by this time it was in action, having bombed the German airship sheds at Metz on August 14. The British Royal Flying Corps, meanwhile, had arrived at Amiens, and by the 17th its four squadrons were installed alongside General French's HQ at Maubeuge, a dozen miles south-west of Mons. Their aeroplanes were supposedly unarmed. Officially they were regarded purely as scouts, although it was suggested that should enemy aircraft be encountered it might be possible to drop hand-grenades upon them from above, or possible *fléchettes*, pointed steel darts which had been issued for anti-personnel bombing. Nobody took these weapons seriously, although a senior German officer, General von Meyer, was to be fatally wounded by *fléchettes* from a French aeroplane on December 6. Far more effective were the weapons which pilots and observers improvised. Some carried service revolvers, some carbines, some the standard Lee Enfield rifle. Véry pistols were also employed, and sporting-guns firing chain-shot. A German aeroplane flew over Maubeuge on August 22, and amongst the machines unsuccessful in intercepting it was an Henri Farman of 5 Squadron in which Lieutenants L. A. Strange and Penn-Gaskell had rigged a Lewis machine gun on an improvised mounting, the first machine

The first aerial clashes were rarely fought to a conclusion, but when they were, the result could be grisly in the extreme

gun in the RFC. The same day the British army suffered its first casualty of the war, when an observer in 2 Squadron, Sergeant-Major Jillings, was wounded.

Riddled with bullets

'On the 23rd August,' wrote Major McCudden, VC, who at that time was an air mechanic, 'things began to hum.' It was the Battle of Mons. Continuous sorties were flown, and aeroplanes returned riddled with bullets, for everyone shot at anything that flew, friend or foe, and it was not until November, when the RFC adopted tricolour roundels like the French (but with colours reversed), that identification was more certain. It is thought that Blériots of 3 Squadron brought news of the German attempt to outflank the British army, which made possible the successful retreat from Mons. Infantry fire was the worst danger at this period, although the Germans already had effective 65-mm, 70-mm, 75-mm and 105-mm anti-aircraft guns on mobile mountings. Allied pilots returning from patrol made an easy mark when flying against the prevailing west wind; the maximum speed of a Farman or Blériot was barely 65 mph, so that ground speed against the wind could be very low indeed.

During the retreat RFC ground staffs managed every day to keep ahead of the Germans, although pilots sometimes returned from patrol to find the aerodrome from which they had taken off in German hands. Air mechanics flew on with their pilots, servicing engine and aircraft before sleeping under a wing; McCudden and one other fitter kept four machines in the air, using only the tools carried on board. At this time the armament of the single-seater Blériot Parasol flown by Captain Conran, a pilot of McCudden's squadron, was made up as follows: 16 hand grenades, two shrapnel bombs, each in a rack outside the fuselage, to be thrown by hand, and a 26-pound Melinite bomb (made from a French shell) tied to an upper fuselage longeron, to be dropped by cutting the string. 'Pilots landed,' wrote Maurice Baring, General Henderson's Intelligence officer at RFC HQ, 'with their maps showing long black lines of German troops on every road.' Message-dropping was tried but landing was better. In addition, wireless was being developed and was to prove very useful for directing artillery fire once the lines became stabilised. It was used, sparingly, at the Battle of the Marne but increasingly at that of the Aisne and during the First Battle of Ypres, when the RFC advanced once more to take up permanent quarters at Saint-Omer.

Much had been learned during the first three months. Reconnaissance machines, competing with the enemy in the same air space, had to fight for their information, and here the 'pusher' machines had the advantage because the observer had a clear field of fire forward, unmasked by the propeller. Until 1915 neither side developed a means of firing a machine gun forwards through the propeller-disc and aiming the machine as a whole. The nearest they came to it was rigging carbines on a Bristol Scout to fire obliquely forwards at 45 degrees, missing the propeller. This did not make an effective fighter but it was the best the RFC had, as the Bristol, with its 80 hp Gnôme, was one of the fastest machines in France, with a maximum speed of over 90 mph. The Vickers FB 5 'Gun Bus', the first *ad hoc* fighter aeroplane, was not operational before 1915.

The first few weeks did indeed provide a war of movement. Apart from incessant scouting, pilots evolved incendiary bombs made from streamlined petrol tins, 5 Squadron's Lewis Gun was used for effective 'ground strafing', and ordinary hand-grenades caused havoc amongst cavalry. Several German machines were 'driven down' by unarmed combat—that is to say RFC pilots harried them with aggressive tactics until they preferred to land. Economically, too, life was unconventional: Maurice Baring and the CO of 3 Squadron drove to Paris on August 25 to purchase a new Blériot and Gnôme engine; Baring had stayed awake all the previous night guarding a suitcase full of gold.

Between August 16 and the final halt at Melun on September 4, the RFC occupied ten separate aerodromes, most of them improvised. Machines were pegged out in the open, and when stormy weather blew up, at Fère-en-Tardenois on the Aisne, after the return northward had begun, McCudden recalls seeing a Blériot 'absolutely stand vertically on its tail, poise for a second and then fall over on its back with a resounding crash'. An Henri Farman also blew over, and 5 Squadron had four Farmans completely wrecked. From Fère-en-Tardenois the RFC moved north, with the BEF, to what Raleigh, the official historian, calls their 'natural' position near the Channel ports, at St Omer, where they took up permanent quarters on October 12, in time for the First Battle of Ypres, in which the Belgian air force, after escaping the German invaders, played a useful part.

The light-hearted clublike atmosphere which united all ranks in the RFC was notably lacking in the French *Aviation Militaire*. Aerial reconnaissance was regarded as an Intelligence matter, and observers were therefore staff officers, billeted at army HQ, and having no social contact with the squadrons. Many non-commissioned pilots were used, by France and also by Germany. These were at a disadvantage *vis à vis* their observers and, indeed, their maintenance crews. It was hard for pilots holding the rank of private to reason with a technical NCO. In some units observers regarded the pilot as a mere chauffeur, and this was especially true in the German air force, as Manfred von Richthofen recorded in his memoirs *The Red Air Fighter*; indeed, a ludicrous incident took place during the first Battle of Ypres when the officer observer of a German two-seater driven down by the RFC, whose life had been saved by a brilliant forced landing, was seen to belabour his pilot for his incompetence!

Prying airmen

In the French service all aerial reconnaissance reports were forwarded by army HQs to the *Deuxième Bureau* for analysis; this was a clumsy arrangement. Sometimes observers' reports were disbelieved, and sometimes they were simply pigeon-holed. This also happened to a German dispatch reporting the presence of the BEF at Mons; but *coups* there were in plenty, both tactical and strategic. It was an aerial report that told the size of the German forces massing against Belgium, and which pointed the gap between the armies of Generals von Bülow and Kluck at the Marne. Ground forces, especially the gunners, learned to mislead the prying airman. False tracks were laid and imitation guns put out, with fireworks to add verisimilitude. This confused the other side and gave friendly aircraft an opportunity to plot enemy batteries when the latter fired on supposed positions.

Some excellent bombing was done by the French, as, for example, when the destruction of a railway tunnel at Soissons kept an ammunition train from the front and thus halted a barrage; the same pilot and observer, Roeckel and Châtelain, in the course of ten hours' artillery spotting near Vaubécourt on September 8, silenced half the artillery of the German *XVI Corps* during the First Battle of the Marne. By the end of the year the French, like the British, were using wireless-equipped aeroplanes, and had inspired the British to follow their lead in aerial photography. Both sides were using observation balloons, and the French had a section of man-carrying kites under Captain Saconney, which made a notable five-hour artillery observation on December 1. It was not until October 5, however, that the French claimed their first victim in aerial combat, an Aviatik biplane brought down by Sergeant Frantz and his mechanic in a Voisin pusher. They used a Hotchkiss *mitrailleuse* as their offensive weapon.

The German air force, meanwhile, found respite from unrelieved corps duties in sporadic propaganda raids. Single aeroplanes overflew the 'Entrenched Camp' of Paris, defended only by a few school aeroplanes and pilots under training. On September 1 a Taube dropped bombs on Montmartre and near the Gare Saint-Lazare, killing four civilians. Next day propaganda leaflets were dropped urging the French to give in. On October 11 two bombs fell on the cathedral of Notre Dame, and next day the target was the Gare du Nord. Paper streamers were also released over Nancy: *Nantzig, ville à bientôt allemande* (Nancy, soon to be German). More effective were French raids during December on Metz, Mulhouse and Freiburg-im-Breisgau.

The earliest examples of true 'strategic bombing' were carried out by the Royal Naval Air Service. Regarding the Zeppelin as its most important naval target, the RNAS sent four machines from Antwerp to bomb the airship sheds at Düsseldorf and Cologne on October 8. Balked by thick mist, they returned, and only two tiny Sopwith Tabloid single-seater biplanes with 80 hp Gnômes got out of Antwerp as the city was being evacuated. Squadron Commander Spenser Grey failed to find the Cologne sheds, but bombed the central station instead; Flight Lieutenant Marix did find the Düsseldorf hangar and scored a direct hit, subsequent flames showing that a Zeppelin had been inside.

Two other raids were flown by the RNAS. Having convinced the French that Zeppelin's were the Royal Navy's legitimate prey, they were granted permission to operate from Belfort, in the Vosges, only five miles from the German frontier. Their target was the Zeppelin factory at Friedrichshafen, on Lake Constance.

Three Avro biplanes took off carrying four 20-pound Melinite bombs apiece, and, flying across the Black Forest and avoiding (in theory) the Swiss town of Schaffhausen, they covered the 125 miles in two hours. Two bombs hit the main hangar, destroying an airship and blowing up the gas-generating plant. One pilot was taken prisoner and the other two returned.

The fourth raid was a seaborne operation. Working closely with Short Brothers, manufacturers of balloons and seaplanes, the RNAS had developed sea-going biplanes with a three-float undercarriage and (in two cases) folding wings, for stowage aboard seaplane-carriers. Escorted by two light cruisers, eight destroyers, and with a further two destroyers and ten submarines in attendance, the three seaplane-carriers, each with three Short biplanes powered by Canton-Unné engines, set sail for Heligoland Bight. The purpose of the raid was to bomb the Zeppelin sheds at Cuxhaven and report if possible on the German warships at Wilhelmshaven, in the Schillig Roads and at the mouth of the Elbe. Seven seaplanes took off after being hoisted overboard, and although the airship sheds were not found, an immensely valuable survey was made of the German naval bases, and bombs were dropped on the dockyard. Three seaplanes returned safely and were hoisted aboard; the other four pilots came down in the sea but were picked up, one by a Dutch trawler, the rest by one of the waiting British submarines. While the Royal Navy was cruising in German waters two Zeppelins and several seaplanes came to investigate. A salvo of 6-inch shells fired at full elevation from a range of 11,000 yards discouraged the airships, and it was realised that Zeppelins were less of a menace to the Fleet than had been thought. The very same day a Zeppelin raided Nancy, dropping 14 bombs. The date was December 25, arguing that all was not fraternisation on the first Christmas Day of the war. Two solitary German aeroplanes visited England at the same season, one on December 24, the other on December 27. No harm was done.

There was no organised air warfare in the Mediterranean between August and December 1914. Austrian aeroplanes and seaplanes, however, made regular reconnaissance flights over Allied shipping blockading the Dalmatian coast. A few bombs were dropped but no damage was done.

Ramshackle equipment

Imperial Russia cannot be said to have taken aviation very seriously. By 1913 she is said to have purchased about 250 miscellaneous aeroplanes, of which 150 were still optimistically described as modern. They included aircraft of the following makes: Albatros, Aviatik, Bristol, Curtiss, Deperdussin, Farman, Nieuport and Rumpler. To these in 1914 were added a few experimental machines by Sikorsky. Flying schools existed at Moscow, Odessa, Omsk and Tashkent, but when the Russian armies advanced upon East Prussia almost simultaneously with the German invasion of Belgium, she could muster only 72 military pilots, plus a reserve of 36 qualified civilians. Bad roads and overloaded railways made support an almost impossible task.

A German artillery observation 'sausage balloon' and its launching equipment, in France

On the German side aeroplanes made valuable reconnaissance flights, as they were doing on the Western Front, and there were some casualties. Russian gun-fire brought down a German machine during the Battle of Lemberg on September 5, while on the following day the Germans made the mistake they had already made twice in the West: they employed a Zeppelin on low-level tactical work. Airship *L V* was brought down and captured, complete with its crew of 30. During the same fighting the Russians lost their most brilliant and picturesque pilot, Nesterov, the first man to loop the loop. This feat Nesterov achieved while the better known Pégoud was still nerving himself for the attempt; he was court-martialled for hazarding military property and sentenced to the equivalent of a month's confinement to barracks. His death was heroic but unnecessary. Encountering a German aeroplane and having no guns, he deliberately rammed the enemy and brought both machines down in flames.

Some Russian units remained operational, for they were bombing German trains at Rava in December 1914. German bombing was quite widely used, and the Austrians made a leaflet raid on Belgrade.

At the end of 1914 air warfare was still at the 'experimental' stage. The initiative in making developments in tactics was still in the hands of the individual pilots. During the bad weather of the winter months there was bound to be a certain slackening of air activity, and not until the spring of 1915 were the lessons of 1914 to bear fruit.

Further Reading
Baring, M., *R.F.C. H.Q.* (Blackwood 1968)
Cole, C., *McCudden, VC* (Kimber 1967)
Cuneo, J. R., *The Air Weapon, 1914-1916* (Harrisburg: Military Service Publishing Company, 1947)
L'Aeronautique Pendant la Guerre Mondiale (Paris: De Brunoff, 1919)
Lafon, C., *Les Armées Aeriennes Modernes* (Paris: Lavauzelle, 1916)
Lafon, C., *La France Ailee en Guerre* (Paris: Lavauzelle)
McCudden, J. T. B., *Five Years in the RFC* (Hamilton 1930)
Mortane, J., *Histoire de la Guerre Aerienne* (Paris: l'Edition Francaise Illustree)
Raleigh, Sir Walter, *The War in the Air Volume I* (OUP 1922)
Strange, L. A., *Recollections of an Airman* (Hamilton)

D. B. TUBBS was born in Chelsea. He had his first flight in a Le Rhône-engined Avro 504K as a small boy and has been interested in that sort of flying ever since. He has written various books on motoring history and also a guide to Kent pubs. His interests are vintage and Edwardian motoring, horology, pistol shooting, antique firearms and wine. He is married and has three small daughters.

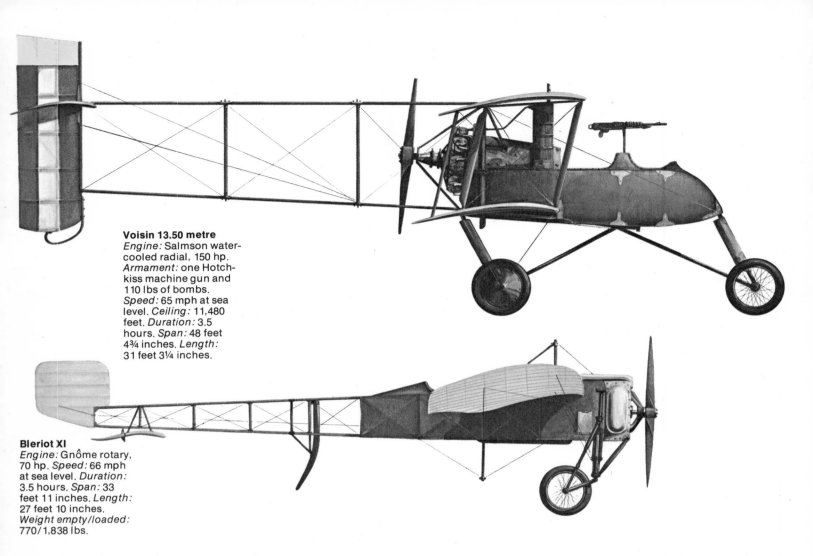

Voisin 13.50 metre
Engine: Salmson water-cooled radial, 150 hp. *Armament:* one Hotchkiss machine gun and 110 lbs of bombs. *Speed:* 65 mph at sea level. *Ceiling:* 11,480 feet. *Duration:* 3.5 hours. *Span:* 48 feet 4¾ inches. *Length:* 31 feet 3¼ inches.

Bleriot XI
Engine: Gnôme rotary, 70 hp. *Speed:* 66 mph at sea level. *Duration:* 3.5 hours. *Span:* 33 feet 11 inches. *Length:* 27 feet 10 inches. *Weight empty/loaded:* 770/1,838 lbs.

	Great Britain	France	Russia	Belgium	Germany	Austria-Hungary
Aeroplanes						
Airships and dirigibles						

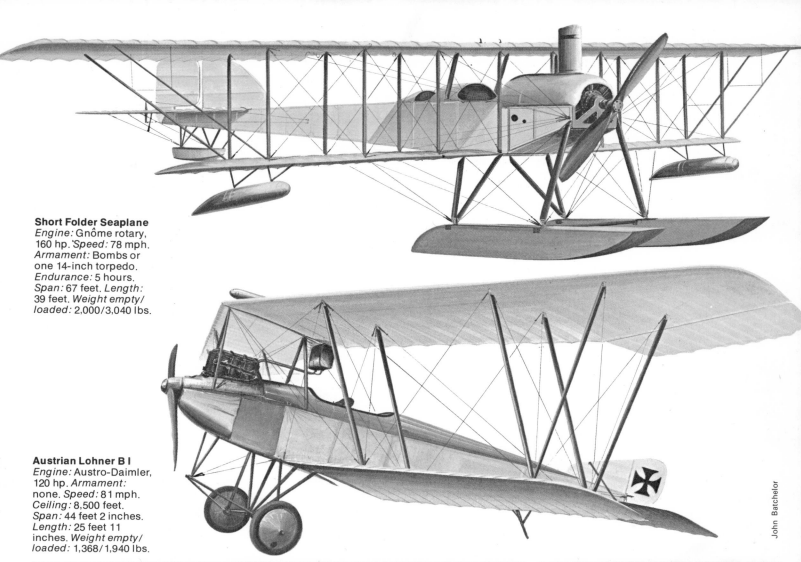

Short Folder Seaplane
Engine: Gnôme rotary, 160 hp. *Speed:* 78 mph. *Armament:* Bombs or one 14-inch torpedo. *Endurance:* 5 hours. *Span:* 67 feet. *Length:* 39 feet. *Weight empty/loaded:* 2,000/3,040 lbs.

Austrian Lohner B I
Engine: Austro-Daimler, 120 hp. *Armament:* none. *Speed:* 81 mph. *Ceiling:* 8,500 feet. *Span:* 44 feet 2 inches. *Length:* 25 feet 11 inches. *Weight empty/loaded:* 1,368/1,940 lbs.

John Batchelor

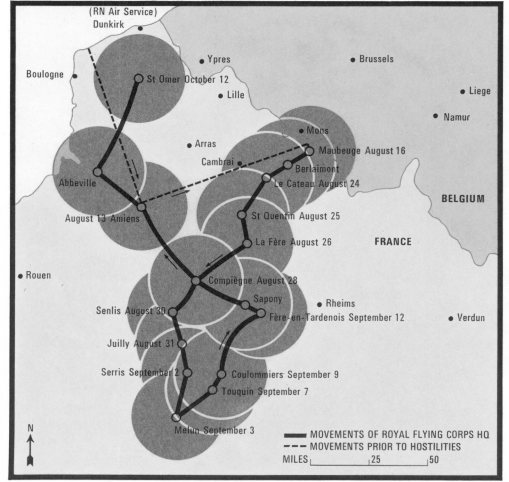

(RN Air Service)
Dunkirk

Boulogne

● Ypres
● Brussels

○ St Omer October 12
● Lille
● Liege

● Namur

● Mons

● Arras
○ Maubeuge August 16

Cambrai ●
○ Berlaimont
○ Le Cateau August 24

BELGIUM

Abbeville

August 13 Amiens
○ St Quentin August 25

○ La Fère August 26

FRANCE

● Rouen

○ Compiègne August 28

○ Sapony
● Rheims

Senlis August 30
○ Fère-en-Tardenois September 12
● Verdun

Juilly August 31

Serris September 2
○ Coulommiers September 9

Touquin September 7

N

Melun September 3

━━━ MOVEMENTS OF ROYAL FLYING CORPS HQ
- - - MOVEMENTS PRIOR TO HOSTILITIES

MILES |_____|25|_____|50

Far left: The aerial balance of forces at the beginning of the war. In many cases, for example Russia, a seemingly large air force lacked adequate backing and was composed of obsolete aircraft. *Left:* The movements of the RFC up to the end of 1914. *Above:* An improvised high angle mounting for a German machine gun in use as a primitive form of anti-aircraft defence.

AIR WAR:
THE FIRST FIGHTER PLANES

Early 1915 saw important innovations in the techniques of air warfare. Inspired by a French attempt, Fokker invented for the Germans an interrupter gear which permitted a machine gun to fire forward through the airscrew, and at the same time the French took the lead in strategic bombing attacks and originated organised air fighting. *D. B. Tubbs. Below:* The charred remains of an Albatros and its pilot

On April 18, 1915, an event which was to have extreme importance in the history of aerial fighting took place. A well-placed rifle bullet fired by a rifleman named Schlenstedt, defending Courtrai railway station, fractured the petrol pipe on a Morane-Saulnier monoplane in which the well-known French pilot Roland Garros (who had been the first to cross the Mediterranean by air, from Bizerta to St Raphael) was attacking the line. Garros landed, but before he could set fire to his machine it was captured by the Germans. The secret was then out: Garros, who had destroyed several German aircraft in the previous few weeks, was found to have a machine gun able to fire forwards through the airscrew.

The propeller, which was armoured with steel deflectors to avoid damage from the aircraft's own bullets, was shown to the Dutchman, Anthony Herman Gerard Fokker, whose M 5 monoplane was then undergoing service trials, and within 48 hours Fokker was claiming to have invented an interrupter gear to prevent bullets hitting the screw. But then Fokker's brilliance as a demonstration pilot was equalled only by his unscrupulousness and his flair for public relations. The irony in the situation lies in the fact that Fokker's new monoplane, which went into service as the E1 (*Eindekker* – monoplane), had been designed only after Fokker had acquired and analysed a Morane. Furthermore, Saulnier of Morane-Saulnier had himself invented

and tried an interrupter gear but had discarded it because of the unreliable performance of service ammunition. He saw steel deflector plates as an improvement, and he may have been right in the early war years. 'Bad rounds' continued to bedevil machines with interrupter and synchronising gears on both sides throughout the war. This, rather than official stupidity, could possibly be the reason why the notion of using the airscrew to

fire a gun had not been adopted before, though it is unlikely. Several patents existed besides that of Franz Schneider, the Swiss aeronautical engineer working first for the French Nieuport and later for the German LVG companies, whose device not only closely resembled Fokker's new 'invention' but had already been flown operationally in an LVG E VI monoplane which, according to one account, was shot down by rifle fire from the Morane two-

Top: The fabric with which the wings were covered was very susceptible to damage, and repairs, such as the German ground crew above are carrying out, were a common but necessary chore. *Above:* The Russian Sikorsky Ilya Mourometz, the world's first four-engined bomber

A Short seaplane dropping a torpedo. The idea of using aircraft to drop torpedoes eventually proved sound, but aircraft engines of the period were not powerful enough to give the required lift or impetus. Nevertheless, limited successes were to be achieved

Imperial War Museum

seater of the French Sergeant Gilbert in December 1914. It is more likely, however, that it crashed as a result of structural failure. Drawings of the gear had also been published in *The Scientific American*.

The 'Fokker Scourge'

If, however, the Fokker monoplane and its gun were not new, they were certainly *ben trovato*. They came at a time when the German air service was being remodelled and liberally dosed with 'offensive spirit' by a new *Chef des Feldflugwesens* (Chief of Field Operations), following a period of dreadful docility during which French Voisin and Farman bombers had raided the Fatherland unmolested, inflicting damage which had inspired notices on Rhineland walls saying *'Gott strafe England—und unsere Flieger!'* (God smite England—and our own airmen!) The outcry which followed the 'Fokker Scourge', so richly dramatised in the House of Commons during 1915/16, therefore had its German counterpart many months before. In the face of unarmed two-seater Type B reconnaissance biplanes and a German air service then forming part of an amorphous, largely 'chairborne' transport command, the machine gun carrying Voisins of the *1ère Groupe de Bombardement* (GB 1) had had things all their own way. It is arguable therefore that the seminal aircraft of 1915 was not a Fokker monoplane at all, but Gabriel Voisin's *type treize-cinquante* (13·50 metre) which could not only bomb but shoot down defenceless *B-Flugzeuge*. The reason the Fokker caused such a stir when Immelmann scored his first victory on August 1, 1915, is very simple: the Germans had begun to shoot back.

The French, along with the highly combative and enterprising Royal Naval Air Service, realised that aeroplanes were no mere substitute for cavalry vedettes and quickly explored their offensive possibilities. General Joffre himself was keen, and his liaison man at GHQ, the ex-pilot *Commandant* Barès, saw the importance of strategic bombing as opposed to squandering aircraft on tactical missions. Orders to carry out a mass bombing attack on the Kaiser's personal HQ at Mézières in September 1914, had been countermanded—for some reason—but a potent instrument existed in the *1ère Groupe de Bombardement* under Commandant Goÿs, who had worked out theory and practice for long-range sorties, albeit rather elementary. This *groupe*, comprising three six-machine *escadrilles* (an *escadrille*, like a German *Fliegerabteilung*, was smaller than a British squadron) was armed with Voisins. It took part in the fighting in Champagne and at one stage moved close to Ypres; it was quickly joined by the *2ème Groupe*, operating most notably from Dunkirk in co-operation with the British, and the *3ème Groupe*.

French bombing aeroplanes included various types of Farman, Breguet and Caudron, but as the Voisin 13.50 was both original and typical of its species, the two-seater pusher biplane, it is described here.

Aeronautical engineers like Geoffrey de Havilland were right on aerodynamic grounds in regarding 'pusher' machines as crude and archaic; but the occupants of a pusher, sitting in a nacelle like a boot slung forward of the mainplanes did enjoy a fine view forwards, sideways and downwards for observation and, in the Voisin's case, later the use of a Hotchkiss machine gun or 37-mm cannon. Pushers were 'blind' to the rear, but in the absence of hostile fighters this mattered little. Gabriel Voisin chose the powerful (for 1914) 130 hp Salmson (alias Canton-Unné) engine for the Type 3 13.50, which was unusual in being a water-cooled radial, and believed that strength was more-important than speed. He chose a wingspan of 13.50 metres, which gave the machine its type name.

This powerful clodhopper (*'ce rustre puissant'* as a friend of Voisin's called it) was tough enough to operate without hangars and was designed to take off from the roughest ground. Its landing run was short because one axle of the four-wheeled undercarriage was fitted with motorcar brakes, and the machine was easy and not unduly heavy to fly. As normally used, the 13.50 could carry two men plus 220 pounds of useful load for three hours. Its maximum speed was given variously as 90 or 95 kph, i.e., 55 mph or so.

Early French raids

As 1915 opened the French launched frequent raids to relieve the pressure on the Russians on the Eastern Front. From St Pol-sur-mer (Dunkirk) they co-operated with the British, and targets in Champagne, Lorraine and the Argonne were attacked. Here MF 25 (a Maurice Farman *escadrille* as the initials imply) attacked German industrial targets opposite Ste Ménéhould, west of Verdun. From Intelligence and other sources—even picture-postcards—target dossiers were compiled, and crews set about learning to drop bombs, first with the aid of three nails knocked into the cockpit as a guide for high, medium and low-level attacks, but later with the aid of a Triplex glass panel in the floor, stopwatches, spirit-levels and other less crude bomb-sights: the Dorand sight appeared in February, the Lafay in April. The British too had a sight, evolved at the Central Flying School by Lieutenant Bourdillon.

At first it proved true that 'the bombers always get through'. One of the most spectacular sorties was a reprisal raid for the

The world's first fighter aircraft

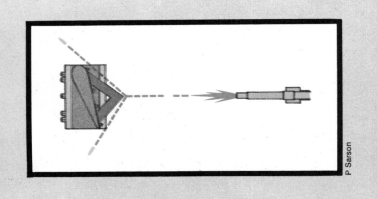

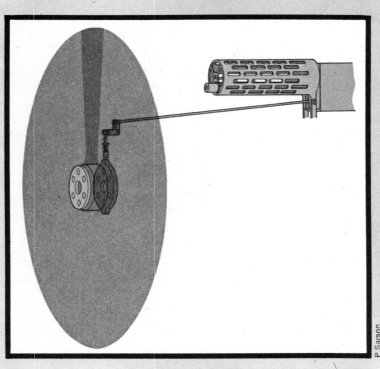

Top left: The Morane-Saulnier deflector gear. Its object was not to interrupt the stream of bullets from the machine gun, but to deflect those few which would otherwise have struck the propeller rather than passing between its blades. *Top: right:* A **Morane-Saulnier N** fitted with the deflector gear. (Contrary to popular belief, Garros was flying a Type L Parasol when he was shot down.) *Engine:* 80 hp Gnôme rotary. *Armament:* One Hotchkiss machine gun. *Speed:* 102 mph at 6,500 feet. *Ceiling:* 13,000 feet. *Length:* 21 feet 11¾ inches. *Left:* The Fokker synchroniser gear. In this gear, the cam aligned with the propeller blade stops the gun firing when blade is in front of the muzzle. *Above:* The **Fokker E 1**, fitted with the interrupter gear. *Engine:* 80 hp Oberursel UO rotary. *Armament:* LMG .08 machine gun. *Speed:* 80 mph. *Weight loaded:* 1,239 pounds. *Span:* 29 feet 3 inches. *Length:* 22 feet 1¾ inches.

John Batchelor

▽ An unarmed Albatros B-type taking off from an airfield in France: easy prey for any armed plane

Bapty

Without a good interrupter gear, efficient armament could only be mounted at the expense of aerodynamic efficiency. This French Farman F40 used a pusher engine and a boom-mounted tailplane

German poison-gas attack of April 22. Great care was taken in preparing the attack, which was launched from Malzéville, near Nancy, HQ of GB 1. The target, involving an out-and-home flight of five hours led by Commandant Goÿs in person, proved to be the *Badische Anilin- und Soda-Fabrik,* Ludwigshafen, near Mannheim. The Voisins were loaded with Canton-Unné bombs—90-mm and 155-mm shells, supplied with fins and impact fuses by the Canton-Unné engine firm. These were France's standard aerial missiles. The three *escadrilles* took off at 0300 hours on May 26. Two 155-mm and 47 90-mm bombs were dropped on Ludwigshafen and a further two 155-mm and 36 90-mm bombs on a secret establishment at Oppau nearby, with highly satisfactory results. Chlorine and acid factories were damaged, fires started and lead storage-chambers breached, releasing clouds of poison gas into the lower town of Mannheim. The only Voisin which failed to return was that of Commandant Goÿs, which force-landed with ignition trouble. Goÿs eventually escaped from captivity, but his temporary loss was a serious blow to French bombing. Before this, in April, effective raids had been made on the Thyssen factories, on blast furnaces at Thionville, on an electric power station at Rombach and on an explosives factory at Buss in the valley of the Moselle. No opposition was encountered, but the end of this tranquil period was in sight.

It must not be thought that the Germans had no bombers. As early as September 1914, a bomber-force of 36 aeroplanes had been set up at Ghistelles, 11 miles south-south-west of Bruges, by Major Wilhelm Siegert, a keen private owner and balloon pilot of prewar days. This force, officially known as the *Fliegerkorps des Obersten Heeresleitung* (GHQ Air Corps) comprised two wings, code-named 'carrier-pigeon units' *(Brieftaubenabteilungen)*—BA Ostende (BAO) and BA Metz (BAM). As a start, Siegert himself, flying as observer in an Aviatik BI biplane, led *BAO* in a night bombing raid on Dunkirk on January 28/29. Flying at 3,500 feet, they dropped 123 bombs as a dress rehearsal for raiding England; but before big British raids could take place *BAO* was posted to the Eastern Front, where the unit assisted greatly in the breakthrough at the battle of Gorlice-Tarnow in March.

Meanwhile at home, Major Siegert was appointed second in command to the new *Feldflugchef,* a very able 48-year-old staff officer of wide experience named Major Hermann von der Lieth-Thomsen. Thomsen's cry was: 'We've got the men, now give us machines!' The *Inspektion der Fliegertruppen, Idflieg* for short, was gingered up, industry organised and communications between Berlin and all fronts streamlined in every way. The German and Austrian motor car industries, drawing upon prewar racing experience, had already doubled the horse power of their 1914 designs, the specification of which had called for 80-100 hp. Mark II engines had been giving 120 hp reliably, and the Mark IIIs were now emerging, mainly in overhead-valve water-cooled six-cylinder-in line form, offering 150, 160 or even a claimed 180 hp, to power a new generation of greatly improved airframes.

The A-class monoplanes were already dead, and the B-class of unarmed two-seater biplanes was ripe for replacement by the *C-Flugzeuge* which would not only have more power and consequently a greater speed, higher ceiling and better climb, but in most cases the tremendous advantage of a 'sting in the tail', namely a defensive Parabellum MG14 light machine gun developed by DWM, makers of the famous infantry Luger automatic pistol. This armament had been under development since November 1914, and the C-class began to emerge, complete with an effective gun-ring for the observer's cockpit: the Rumpler C I (160 hp Mercedes D III), Albatros C I (160 hp Mercedes D III or 150 hp Benz Bz III) and Aviatik C I (Mercedes D III). The most important of these, perhaps, was the Albatros, for it was while flying aircraft of this type that Oswald

Boelcke began to evolve the first techniques of air fighting. The Aviatik was less satisfactory, for in it the observer was still encaged beneath the centre section, as in the obsolete B-class machines, and virtually unable to use his gun. The 'standard' British observation machine of the period, designed at the Royal Aircraft Factory, Farnborough, and produced by innumerable sub-contractors, never lost its archaic 'B-class' layout: a BE2c pilot sat in the rear seat, while his observer struggled helplessly in the front seat, hedged about by wings, fuselage, wires and struts.

First fighter units

As has been seen, however, before there could be a 'Fokker Scourge' there had to be a Morane and a Garros. Morane-Saulnier monoplanes had been used for racing before the war, when their clean monoplane lines and rounded fuselage cross-section made them highly competitive, despite the drag of cabane, bracing and the external wires by which the wings were warped.

Late in 1914, J. B. McCudden had used a rifle while flying as observer with Captain Conran of No 3 Squadron RFC on private offensive patrols; in January he reported that the squadron had received two Lewis machine guns for its Moranes, and the latter were being fitted with 'machine gun racks'. Similar offensive patrols were flown in Sopwith Tabloid, Martinsyde Scout, Bristol Scout and other fast single-seaters by picked pilots in the RNAS and RFC. A 'scout' or two was attached to each squadron, rather as riding-schools kept a hunter for the use of star pupils. It is surprising indeed that the term 'hunter' was not coined by the British, for the French already spoke of *avions de chasse,* and it was they who really originated organised air fighting.

Escadrilles de chasse were formed, one for each army. Their duties were to protect

Allied reconnaissance machines and to escort bombers. With such practitioners as Garros, Vedrines and Pégoud flying Moranes the results could not be in doubt. Three famous escadrilles flying Moranes were MS 3, under *Commandant* Brocard, MS 23, under *Commandant* de Vergette, and MS 12, whose commander, *Commandant* Tricornot de Rose, did much to evolve the tactics of aerial combat. Passengers were given *mitrailleuses* for offence and defence and single-seater pilots often had aircraft armed with a fixed machine gun to fire through an armoured propeller. Hardened steel deflector plates impaired the efficiency of the airscrew, but the tactical surprise of bullets coming from an apparently impossible direction brought many victims. Many types of Morane were used, with mid-wing, shoulder wing or a wing mounted above the fuselage, the last-named being known, for obvious reasons, as a 'parasol'. British Morane pilots included Flight-Sub-Lieutenant Warneford, VC, RNAS who brought down a Zeppelin while flying a Morane (he also flew a single-seater with deflectors), and Captain L. A. Strange, whose inventions included an offset Lewis gun-mounting for the pilot.

Garros force-landed his Morane on April 18 but his colleagues continued to score while the Fokker E I was incubating, using not only the single-seater 'Bullet', as the British called the Type N Morane, but also the L-type Parasol two-seater, which Brocard, Guynemer and others often flew solo on offensive patrols.

It may be wondered, in view of the chanciness of using a deflector propeller, and the non-availability of interrupter gears, why somebody did not bring out a fighter with a pusher engine. The answer is that several people had thought of it, and several effective pusher fighters eventually came into service. Two excellent two-seater pushers were in fact flying be-

fore the outbreak of war. Vickers exhibited a biplane, the 'Gun-bus', in 1913, and laid down a batch of 50 on their own initiative. Unfortunately the Wolseley engine chosen proved a failure, and the *Monosoupape* Gnôme rotary was not yet available. A rather similar machine with an even more dilatory history was the Royal Aircraft Factory's Farman Experimental (later called Fighting Experimental) FE2b.

The FE2b was easy to arm and made a useful fighting aeroplane. Orders were placed for it on the outbreak of war, but the six-cylinder Green engine chosen proved too heavy and the Beardmore, developed from a prewar Austro-Daimler, took some time to arrive. Two excellent single-seater pusher scouts were also on the stocks well before Immelmann first scored on August 1. The DH2, designed by Captain Geoffrey de Havilland, had undergone flight trials by July 1915 and the FE8, a Farnborough design by J. Kenworthy, had been started at the Factory in May. Contrary to aviation folklore neither of these aircraft was called into being by the Fokker; they were probably seen as an improvement on the Morane. All the same, the central feature which made the Morane and Fokker so effective was not appreciated at the time. The first DH2 had a Lewis gun on a moveable mounting controlled by the pilot. It was not realised that success lay in aiming the aircraft as a whole. This fact renders all the more remarkable the feat brought off by Major Lanoe G. Hawker, of No 6 Squadron RFC on July 25, just six days after another great pilot, Guynemer, had drawn first blood. That evening Hawker brought off a treble. He drove down one German C-class two-seater; another he forced down with a damaged engine; and the third he shot down in flames. All three were armed with machine guns: Hawker's Bristol Scout had one hand-loaded cavalry carbine on the star-

Anthony Fokker, the brilliant Dutchman who contributed so much to German aviation

board side firing obliquely forward to miss the propeller. He was awarded the VC.

An oblique mounting of this sort, adopted, also for the Strange Lewis gun for BE2c pilots was indeed one solution. Another, adopted on Strange's own Martinsyde scout was a Lewis on the centre section inclined upwards so as to miss the propeller. A quadrant mounting for such a gun was devised by Sergeant Foster of No 11 Squadron RFC. The oddest resolution of the tractor/pusher controversy was adopted by the Royal Aircraft Factory for its experimental BE9, which was basically

An RNAS Voisin LA on Imbros. This type was more than a match for any aircraft the Turks had

Hier sehen Euch
feindliche Flieger!
Hier dürfen
Fahrzeuge nicht halten.

An early German exhortation to the army on the need for camouflage against prying aircraft

The gunner of a German C-class aircraft. Early experience had shown that it was vitally important to have a gun covering the tail

a BE2c with the engine moved back and a nacelle for the observer rigged forward of the airscrew. Similar arrangements were adopted on the Spad A2.

In 1915 engines were too scarce and too unreliable for the Allies to attempt a twin-motor layout, which would have provided high performance together with fore-and-aft shooting for pilot and observer. The Germans, however, evolved an effective three-seater *Kampfflugzeug* (bomber/escort aircraft) early in 1915 mainly for the Eastern Front. Designed to use a pair of the obsolete Mercedes D I 100 hp engines, the AEG GI *grossfleugzeug* had a span of 16 meters (52 feet 6 inches). It could carry its load at a maximum speed of 125 kph (78 mph), and thanks to the overhead-valve water-cooled engines in which the German industry specialised, possessed a useful ceiling.

The rotary engine
The rotary engines used so widely by the French and British (and also by Fokker) during 1914-1916 had the advantage of compactness and a good power-to-weight ratio, but because of their atmospheric inlet valves (long since discarded in automobile practice) performance fell off badly at altitude and in hot weather. A note on the working of the early rotaries may be of interest.

The Gnôme engine was invented by Laurent Séguin in 1907. The cylinders were disposed radially like the spokes of a wheel and were finned for cooling like those of a motorcycle engine. In contrast with the latter, however, in which the main body of the engine remained stationary while the crankshaft rotated, the cylinders and crankcase of a rotary revolved about a stationary crankshaft, carrying the airscrew with them. The usual number of cylinders was seven or nine and all the pistons acted upon a single crankpin; one 'master' connecting-rod mounted on ball-bearings embraced the crankpin direct, while around the periphery of its big end were arranged plain bearings for the big ends of the other connecting-rods. A simple single-jet carburettor, stationary of course, supplied petrol via the hollow crankshaft

into the crankcase, where movement of the engine turned it into vapour. This combustible mixture was drawn into the cylinders by an automatic mushroom valve in the crown of each piston and exhausted after a normal four-stroke cycle through a pushrod operated valve in the cylinder-head. Wipe contacts carried current from a stationary magneto to a sparking-plug in each head via plain brass wires. It is thought that all magnetoes were obtained from Germany via neutral sources during the early months of the war as neither Britain nor France had developed this branch of the industry.

The *Monosoupape* Gnôme, as the name implies, had one valve only, a mechanically-operated poppet valve situated in the cylinder head. This functioned not only as exhaust valve, but also admitted plain air during the first part of the induction stroke to mix with the rich mixture entering the cylinder through a ring of ports in the cylinder wall, uncovered by the piston at the bottom of its stroke, and communicating with the crankcase, which was pressure-fed from the carburettor. The *Mono* was an improvement upon the ordinary Gnôme, but both were superseded by the Le Rhône, in which both inlet and exhaust valves were mechanically operated. The Oberursel used by Fokker was a copy of the Le Rhône, as was the Austrian version made in the Steyr arsenal. British Le Rhône engines were made in quantity by W. H. Allen Son & Co Ltd. Better than the Oberursel was the Swedish-built Thulin version of the Le Rhône, which reached German in considerable quantity. All rotary engines, however, made one demand which proved embarrassing for Germany: to avoid dilution of lubricant in the vapour-filled crankcase they required pure castor oil, which does not mix with petrol. Castor oil in Germany was very scarce.

From the start of the war until January 1915, Austro-Hungarian squadrons were not uniformly equipped, having a selection of Etrich *Taube* monoplanes and Lohner *Pfeil* arrow-wing biplanes with various in-line and rotary engines, together with Albatros BIs made under licence by

Phönix. These aeroplanes were designed by Ernst Heinkel, who was to have a great influence on Austrian design. Just before the war, the Trieste magnate, Camillo Castiglione, had bought up the *Brandenburgischen Flugzeugwerke* at Brandenburg/Havel and the *Hanseatische Flugzeugwerke,* afterwards known as Hansa-Brandenburg, and Heinkel became chief engineer. Austria's most important contributions, however, were the Austro-Daimler and Hieronymus (Hiero) engines, on which Dr Ferdinand Porsche worked.

Frustrated bombing attacks
When Italy declared war on May 24, 1915, the Austrian air forces found the Alps somewhat hampering. The Italian air forces were at a high state of readiness, but were very under-equipped and lacking in modern aircraft. Italy had also five airships. A French naval squadron went to Venice to assist, and the U-boat *U11* was damaged on July 1 by *Enseigne* de Vaisseau Roulier. Attempts to bomb the Austrian arsenals at Trieste and Pola were frustrated by the Italian aircraft's insufficient performance and the prevailing Austrian *C-Flugzeuge*.

Equipment for 'side-show' operations was seldom of the best, as the British found in East Africa. A German commerce-raider, the light cruiser *Königsberg* had taken refuge in the Rufiji River in October 1914. Unsuccessful operations by Short Folder seaplanes, a Curtiss flying-boat and two Sopwith 807 seaplanes located and photographed but could not destroy the raider. Two Henri Farmans and two Caudron G IIIs arrived in June, and on the 11th of that month, shellfire directed by a Farman and a Caudron put an end to the *Königsberg*. As an example of a Middle-Eastern side-show may be cited the bombing of El Murra on April 16, 1915, by two Maurice Farmans and a BE2a from the Ismailia Flight of the RFC in Egypt.

The amphibious operations in the Dardanelles provided scope for both the RNAS, under the dashing Commander C. R. Samson, and also the French, operating from the islands of Imbros and Tenedos. Two seaplane carriers, HMS *Ark Royal,* a con-

An Albatros two-seater dropping bombs. By this time (mid-1915) the value of bombing from aircraft was being increasingly exploited

verted merchant ship, and the Isle of Man packet, HMS *Ben-My-Chree,* made the operations sea- and airborne. Turkish flourmills and other ration targets on the Gallipoli peninsula were bombed, the Turkish troops visited regularly at mealtimes, and highly effective attacks made on shipping. 'The British,' wrote a French historian, 'had an ineluctable vocation for bombing.' Squadron-Commander C. H. Edmonds (Short 184 Seaplane, 225 hp Sunbeam) sank an enemy merchant ship off Injeburnu, and a Turkish ammunition ship off Ak-Bashi-Liman, and Flight-Lieutenant J. B. Dacre sank a tug off Nagara, using an air-launched 1,000-pound Whitehead locomotive torpedo. During 1915 the RNAS made 70 attacks on shipping. In addition to their coastal patrol, anti-submarine and anti-Zeppelin activities, naval squadrons also joined the RFC in Flanders.

Following a nomadic existence during the retreat and occupation of so much of their country, the Belgians reorganised their air service early in 1915. In April the *Aviation Militaire* took up quarters at Coxyde and Houthem. Five *escadrilles* of Voisin, Henri Farman and Maurice Farman pusher biplanes were formed to support the Belgian divisions in the field.

When General Ludendorff was a mere colonel in October 1910 he took the opportunity of going up in an aeroplane with *Hauptmann* de le Roi and expressed himself 'delighted'. Ludendorff's appreciation of the possibilities of aerial reconnaissance received confirmation on both Fronts. In August 1914, *Feldfliegerabteilungen Nos 14, 15, 16, 17* and *29,* together with four *Festungsfliegerabteilungen* (fortress defence flights) went to the Eastern Front. Aerial reconnaissance certainly paid dividends: news of Russian troop movements brought back by *Leutnant* Canter and his observer, *Leutnant* Mertens, proved of vital importance for the Battle of Tannenberg. Landing where they could, and proceeding to General von François's headquarters by cycle, cart and commandeered motor car, they made possible a great German victory. As Hindenburg himself remarks in his memoirs, '*Ohne Flieger,*

kein Tannenberg': 'Without airmen there would have been no Tannenberg.'

Among the junior officers on this front was the cavalry subaltern Manfred von Richthofen, lately transferred to the air service, having decided that cavalry warfare was no occupation for an officer of the *1st Regiment (Emperor Alexander III) Uhlans.* Richthofen was posted to the East as an observer in June 1915. He had not applied for training as a pilot, being convinced the war would be over too soon, and took part during June, July and August in the Central Powers' advance from Gorlice to Brest Litovsk. His Albatros B I was brought down by infantry machine gun fire, but was able to land on ground which had just been taken from the Russians, a matter of yards only.

The Russian air services, through faulty organisation and widely stretched communications, made no great showing. Technically, however, they had much of interest to contribute, apart from French aeroplanes made under licence, the most advanced being some Sikorsky Ilya Mourometz four-engined bombers produced by the Russo-Baltic Wagon Works. An Anatra two-seater copy of the Voisin was fairly successful, but structurally weak, and Russo-Baltic produced the armoured RBVZ S17 and S20. In the armaments field they did even better. A Sikorsky S16 (80 hp Renault, later 100 hp Gnôme) was fitted with a machine gun synchronising interrupter gear invented by Lieutenant Poplavko, whose experiments with Maxim guns had been proceeding since 1913, while news of another Russian interrupter gear was brought to London late in 1914 by Lieutenant-Commander V. V. Dybovski of the Imperial Russian Navy, who, with Engineer Smyslov, was its co-inventor. Later, Dybovski was to co-operate fruitfully on such matters with Warrant-Officer Scarff, RNAS.

On the lunatic fringe of the aircraft armament world may be mentioned a Russian pilot named A. A. Kazakov, who tried conclusions with an Albatros biplane near the village of Guzov on March 18, 1915. Having endeavoured unsuccessfully to entangle his enemy's propeller with a trailing cable and grapnel, he rammed it with his undercarriage. It is of interest that a trailing bomb was tried from a BE2c of No 6 Squadron.

Further Reading
Baring, M., *RFC HQ* (Bell 1920)
de Havilland, Sir Geoffrey, *Sky Fever* (Hamilton 1961)
Gray, P. and Thetford, O., *German Aircraft of the First World War* (Putnam 1962)
Joubert de la Ferte, Sir Philip, *The Fated Sky* (Hutchinson 1952)
Lamberton, W. A., *Fighter Aircraft of the 1914-1918 War* (Harleyford 1960)
Lamberton, W. A., *Bomber and Reconnaissance Aircraft of the 1914-1918 War* (Harleyford 1962)
Lewis, C., *Sagittarius Rising* (Davies 1966)
Longmore, Sir Arthur, *From Sea to Sky* (Bles 1946)
Robertson, B., *Air Aces of the 1914-1918 War* (Harleyford 1962)
Weyl, A. E., *Fokker, the Creative Years* (Putnam 1965)

THE AIR WAR
tactics and technology

The first half of 1916 had led to the development of the Fokker *Eindecker*, and the second saw it become the dominant factor in the skies. But naturally the introduction of the new weapon led to new countertactics on the part of the Allies. These were the beginnings of the 'dogfighting' technique and its protagonists, the 'aces'. Meanwhile, the less glamorous but basically more important tasks of artillery observation and reconnaissance were developing apace, as were the infant bombing forces of the warring powers. *D. B. Tubbs. Below:* A DFW C V armed reconnaissance machine, which went into production towards the middle of 1916

The period from August 1, 1915 to June 30, 1916 opens with the first successful use of a synchronised machine gun and closes on the eve of the Battle of the Somme. On August 1 nine Royal Flying Corps two-seaters, flown solo to increase the bomb-load, raided Douai aerodrome, home of the newly introduced Fokker E I single-seater monoplanes. Oswald Boelcke, enjoying his Sunday morning sleep when the raiders first appeared, failed to score owing to his gun jamming, but his pupil, Max Immelmann, firing a machine gun for the first time in anger, wounded a British pilot in the left elbow and forced him to land. The 'Fokker Scourge' so richly advertised by publicists on both sides, had begun.

So great was the agitation during the next six months in the British press and Parliament, and so elaborate the glorification of Boelcke and Immelmann in Germany, both of them receiving the *Pour le Mérite* order, a decoration whose nearest British equivalent would be a GCB (not a VC as is often imagined), that it is tempting to see the whole period in terms of a Fokker syndrome. In fact the new armed C-Class two-seaters, which also started coming into service during the summer of 1915, seemed at first to have been quite as formidable as Tony Fokker's *Eindekker*. The important thing was that at last, after almost a year of unarmed docility, the German air force had begun to shoot back.

The effect of this was felt immediately by the French Bomber Groups based on the Malzéville plateau, near Nancy, who had previously had things all their own way. The extent of these operations is not usually appreciated. The French had been regularly visiting the Saar valley and South Germany, with particularly devastating effect on the explosives plant at Rothweil. When, therefore, on August 9, GB 4 (No. 4 Bomber Group) lost four aircraft, including one of the escorting Voisin *avions-canons* to 'particularly offensive Aviatiks', it came as a shock. However, operations continued on a very large scale. On August 25 a French formation of no less than 62 bombers attacked the steelworks and blast furnaces at Dilligen, dropping converted 155-mm artillery shells, the standard heavy bomb of the period. Great damage was caused by molten metal, and considerable loss of life. Four of the bombers were damaged by AA fire and two shot down. German 'Archies' were quite good. At the beginning of September one group (GB 2) was posted to Humières in the Pas de Calais, but the remaining three pressed on with their raiding, with missiles both old and new: on September 6 they dropped 93 90-mm bombs and 8 155-mm, as well as a 580-mm Cheddite torpedo. A week later they flew up the Moselle Valley to Trèves railway junction, causing three days' interruption to rail communications. The risks to the fragile Maurice Farman and Caudron biplanes, and to the strong but cumbersome steel-built Voisins were very substantial. The Parabellum guns on the rear ring-mountings of the Albatros, Aviatik and LVG CIs were better than the Hotchkiss, and it was now admitted that the 37-mm *canon*, designed for train-busting, was of little use in air-to-air fighting. Furthermore the French biplanes were desperately slow when laden, and their pusher layout provided a large blind spot which German two-seater and scout pilots quickly learned to exploit. By the end of September daylight bombing from Malzéville had been discontinued and the bomber groups dispersed to other sectors, where losses continued to mount and the morale of crews to decline. For a month or so bombing was carried on from Humières against medium-range (Cambrai) and short-range (Lens) targets, but in December the Group's Voisins were taken off daylight operations. GB 3 returned to Malzéville for training in formation flying, at which the French were pioneers, and night-bombing, which this group began in earnest on April 10, 1916.

During the French Champagne offensive of October 1915, GB 1, GB 2 and GB 4 mounted some heavy attacks, 62 aircraft raiding the German HQ town of Vouziers on October 2 as part of the plan to clear the Paris-Nancy railway line and liberate Châlons-sur-Marne. They were met by armed German two-seaters and lost two machines. Outclassed and demoralised, the Voisin crews asked for an escort of Nieuport fighters. This offensive equipment was successful in keeping attackers at bay, but seriously curtailed the bombers' range, and after a 19-bomber raid on Bozancourt on the 12th, escorted by three Nieuports, the rest returned to Malzéville for formation and night-flying training.

The need for true formation flying, which was to become compulsory in the British RFC in January 1916, was first realised by that remarkable fire-eater, *Capitaine* Happe of *Escadrille* MF 29, who drilled his Maurice Farman pilots to fly in 'V' formation, led by the centre machine, while he himself held a roving commission to drive off attackers and, from greater altitude plot the position of each bomb-burst. He raided the Roessler poison-gas works at Dornach on August 26, 1915, and bombed the Aviatik factory at Freiburg-im-Breisgau so effectively that the works

were transferred to Leipzig. On September 25 the Germans placed a price of 25,000 marks on his head. 'Splendid!' wrote Happe, in a note dropped behind the lines. 'You will know my machine by its red wheels. Don't bother to shoot at anyone else.' This was after a three-machine raid on Rothweil from which only Happe returned, having managed in a Maurice Farman to ward off Boelcke flying a two-seater Albatros. Another favourite target was the German aerodrome at Habsheim, from which long-range reconnaissance aircraft kept a constant watch above the *départements* adjoining the German border, it being a recurrent nightmare to the High Command that French armies might one day burst through the Belfort Gap and overrun south Germany. It was Happe who modified the poor old 80-hp rotary-engined Farman by fitting a 130-hp water-cooled Canton-Unné, providing in this 'Type Happe' or 'camel-backed' Farman better performance and longer range. He was to continue day bombing, undaunted, until October 12, 1916.

France was the only Power to possess a true bomber force, apart from the two 'Carrier Pigeon Units' attached to German GHQ, which were more in the nature of general purpose squadrons. If most of the French bombers retired from the fray they could hardly be blamed. The shortcomings of the Maurice Farman and Voisin have been noted. The twin-engined Caudron G IV was a failure because the observer could hardly shoot backwards because of the pilot, and its two engine nacelles made deadly blind spots on the flank. Supplies of Bréguet-Michelin IV were held up because of the failure of a promised 220-hp Renault engine and the type was powered by the 130-hp Canton-Unné which gave it a top speed of about 70 mph and a ceiling of 13,000 feet, with a useful load of 650 pounds. Pilots did not like it. It stalled easily, was liable to spin without warning, had a long take-off run and was difficult to land; also, they disapproved of the armament and criticised the forward and downward view. Fortunately, when it came to escort and fighter aircraft the French had the best in the world, thanks to Morane-Saulnier and the Nieuport *Bébé* designed by Gustave Delage. Fortunately, too, there were enough of them to arm some of the RFC.

Fighters or Scouts?

France, long before Britain and Germany, saw the need of specialised fighter units. She was fortunate in a tradition of sporting flying which dated back to the first European aviation meets of 1908-10. A French engineer, Séguin, had invented the rotary type of air-cooled engine around which all the most manoeuvrable aeroplanes were built, and the Staff early saw the wisdom of attaching an *escadrille de chasse* to each army. These units had been harrying German two-seaters, notably in Artois and Champagne, since January 1915. There were those in the Royal Flying Corps, including General Henderson, commanding the RFC in the field, who shared this view, but they were overruled by those who believed that one or two single-seater 'Scouts'—the term is significant—should be attached to each squadron for the use of the CO or other selected pilots when routine duties permitted. Additionally two-seater 'fighting machines' should be apportioned as available for patrol and escort duties.

The Germans thought the same. The Fokker monoplane, when it appeared in July 1915, equipped with that most famous of all German 'secret weapons', a machine gun synchronised to fire through the revolving airscrew, was issued to selected *Feldflieger-abteilungen* (general purpose squadrons) including *FlAbt 62*, Douai. Here it was flown by Lieutenant Oswald Boelcke, recently distinguished by having shot down an Allied aeroplane from his new C-class biplane, and his pupil, *Fähnrich* Max Immelmann.

Before discussing fighter aircraft and the tactics worked out by their pilots, it is logical to glance at aerial warfare as a whole, as it stood in the autumn of 1915. On both sides the General Staff now realised the importance of the air arm. Army units brought back strategic information based on long reconnaissance while corps' squadrons patrolled the lines, photographing the trenches, spotting for the artillery, locating hostile batteries, attacking observation balloons, bombing enemy aerodromes, and foiling the attempts of enemy aircraft to carry out similar duties. An ingenious 'clock' code now enabled RFC observers to pinpoint the range and direction of their battery's shooting to within a few yards by means of a two-digit wireless signal (for example A3 would signify a shot falling 50 yards due east of the target). Photographic equipment, although still fairly primitive, was improving, and on the German side, a photographic expert, Lieutenant Fricke, was soon to win the *Pour le Mérite* for organising this branch of the service.

When General H. M. Trenchard took over from General Henderson just in time for the Battle of Loos in September 1915, the

'The knights of the sky' — new heroes for the sensation seeking masses at home — and some of the weapons which they used

Left and right: A French pilot (based on a picture of Lieutenant Nungesser), and a German pilot (right). The choice of flying clothing was conditioned by the time of year and the altitude at which the pilot expected to fly. In winter or at height the cold is intense, and privately purchased fur-lined clothing was warmer. *Below:* Aircraft armament. **1.** The old style — an unsynchronised Hotchkiss on a Deperdussin, aerodynamically appalling and also inefficient. **2.** The British .303-inch Lewis gun, sometimes seen without the casing around the barrel and gas cylinder. **3.** The German standard flexible gun for rear defence, the 7.92-mm Parabellum, a lighter version of the 'Spandau' and usually seen with a fretted water jacket. **4.** The Austrian Schwarzlose 8-mm machine gun. When adapted for aircraft use the gun was not very successful as its range was short and its rate of fire low. **5.** The standard British fixed gun, the .303-inch Vickers, also used by the French. **6.** A German 7.92-mm LMG 08/15 twin machine gun mounting. (These guns are known popularly as Spandaus after their place of manufacture.) This gun was the standard fixed armament on German aircraft, twin mountings starting in the middle of 1916

Julian Allen

Julian Allen

Roger Viollet

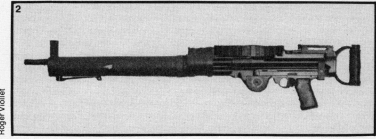

Jack Pia

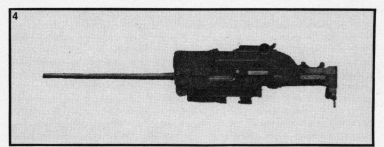

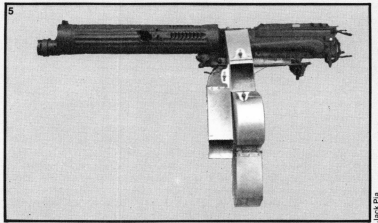

Jack Pia

Jack Pia

43

Royal Flying Corps comprised three Wings and a Headquarters squadron—a very fully employed force, for whereas the land forces of the BEF had increased from four to some 30 divisions, the strength of the RFC had grown only from four squadrons to 12 (equipped with a highly miscellaneous collection of aeroplanes to the number of 189 serviceable aircraft in France, and four Kite Balloon sections manned by the RNAS).

In view of the Parliamentary outcry in the spring of the following year, it is often assumed that re-equipment of the RFC with manoeuvrable two-seater combat aircraft and the first armed single-seater scouts, came about directly as a result of the Fokker *Eindekker,* and that Allied interrupter-gears were copied from the Germans. A glance at the Order of Battle before Loos will show that several of the 'replies' were already in service, although not yet in sufficient quantity. For example, No 5 Squadron possessed a Flight of Vickers FB 5 'Gun Bus', and No 11 was fully equipped with this type. The first FE 2b had been flown to France on May 20, 1915; by September No 6 Squadron had four. Supplies of this Royal Aircraft Factory design were slow in coming through, but by the end of the year 32 were in service. Nearly every squadron owned its tractor scout, but at first the lack of an interrupter-gear made these difficult to arm. Local experiments were made, however, and a number of gun-mountings evolved, ranging from a 45-degree horizontal Lewis firing abeam to miss the airscrew, to the most effective, found on Captain L. A. Strange's Martinsyde S I biplane as early as May 1915, which comprised a Lewis gun on the upper centre section, high enough to clear the propeller. This was the layout adopted on the Nieuport *Bébé,* used first by the French and later by the RNAS and RFC, and which was to bring such success to Georges Guynemer and Albert Ball. Of the two British pusher single-seaters which were to deal so stoutly with the Fokker threat during preparations for the Somme battle (the DH 2 and FE 8) both were on the drawing-board before Immelmann's initial victory on August 1. In the meanwhile pilots made do with the two most numerous two-seaters, namely the Morane Parasol and the BE 2c, which in design and conception could not have been more different. Of the Parasol, a well-known Morane pilot, Captain Cecil Lewis, has remarked that there was 'only one position to which it automatically reverted and that was a vertical nosedive'. The aircraft was 'ropey, treacherous, dangerous to fly, permitted no liberties and needed attention every second she was in the air'. In short very much a 'pilot's aeroplane', and it is no coincidence that famous French pilots often flew the Parasol solo on offensive patrol. It was in a Morane L-type of No 3 Squadron that J. B. McCudden had a successful brush with Immelmann's Fokker, holding it at bay with short bursts from a Lewis gun fired from the shoulder. A great advantage of the Morane was that the observer sat behind the pilot close enough for shouted conversation, and with an excellent field of fire upwards, sideways and behind. This was very different from the BE 2c, the type chosen by the RFC for quantity production.

The BE would have made an excellent civil aircraft—in fact it looked surprisingly like the same designer's DH Moth biplane of the late 1920s, as used by Amy Johnson and others. One trouble was that the observer sat in front, tucked away below the centre-section and hedged about with wires and struts. His armament was a Lewis gun which could be fired from the shoulder or plugged into any of several spigot mountings disposed about the cockpit. Another drawback was the machine's 'inherent stability', which made it a steady observation-platform but discouraged rapid manoeuvring. One wonders why, with a mounting casualty-list as prompter, the authorities never revised the seating of the BE, placing the observer behind to guard the tail, as the Germans did when the C-class two-seaters replaced the B-class in the summer of 1915.

A 'joyous scrap'

At first, however, BE pilots quite held their own, even against the Fokker E III. One such 'joyous scrap' is documented from both sides. On December 29 Lieutenant Sholto Douglas (later Marshal of the RAF Lord Douglas of Kirtleside) made a reconnaissance to Cambrai and St Quentin escorted by another BE of No 8 Squadron. Near Cambrai, says Douglas's report: 'We were set upon by six Huns. Glen, my escort, was shot down, followed by two of the Huns. I was then set upon by the remainder. Child, my observer, downed one Hun. We fought the remaining three for half an hour. Petrol began to get low and engine sump was hit. So, relying on the stability of the BE 2c as against the Fokker, I came down in steep spiral to 10 feet above the ground.' This fight is described from the German side as well, for one of the Fokkers was flown by Lieutenant Oswald Boelcke, who in one of his letters home describes Douglas as 'a tough fellow who defended himself stoutly'. Boelcke forced the BE down from 6,500 feet to 3,000 feet when, he says, it should have been an easy matter to shoot the Englishman down because he had mortally wounded his observer, but Boelcke had been in two previous fights and now ran out of ammunition. The two continued to circle round one another but neither could do the other any harm. 'Finally Immelmann came to the rescue and the fight began all over again. We managed to force him down to 300 feet and waited for him to land.' Fortunately Immelmann's gun jammed, as machine guns of all makes did at that time, and Douglas was able to land just behind the French lines.

There is more about this encounter in Lord Douglas's book *Years of Combat,* published in 1963. He comments on his lucky

escape, and explains that Child, his observer, was not in fact killed. 'Oswald Boelcke was led into believing that he had killed my observer because Child, who was facing backwards and firing over my head, became so physically sick through the violence of the way in which I was having to toss our aircraft about that he finally fell over and threw up all over me.' So much for the story that BE 2cs were too inherently stable to be thrown about. It should be noted, too, that in this fight Lieutenant Child shot down one of the Fokkers and Douglas records that Glen, his escort, had shot down another a few days before.

In the early days of the Fokker menace there was controversy amongst BE pilots as to the best thing to do. Some, including Douglas, advised turning in under the Fokker as it dived to attack, thus getting out of the way, others, of whom Glen was one, believed in holding a steady course to provide one's observer with a steady gun-platform. It is interesting to note that the RFC (and especially the Third Wing) were sending at least one escort with each reconnaissance aircraft, while Boelcke and Immelmann were still stalking on their own, not as a pair. Tactics were still highly personal. The usual Fokker method was to attack in a dive; it is uncertain whether the famous 'Immelmann turn', in which the pilot pulls up into the first half of a loop to gain height then stall turns to face his adversary again, was Immelmann's own invention or that of the Bristol Scout pilot Gordon Bell during a brush with an *Eindekker*. It was certainly effective. So was a ploy used by the peacetime actor and Gun Bus pilot Robert Loraine of No 5 Squadron, obeying his CO's injunction to be 'more aggressive'. 'I had asked Lubbock (the observer) to hold his fire until I gave him the order, for I meant to engage at the closest possible quarters. As we drew near to the German, approaching each other nose to nose, I pretended to outclimb him. He opened fire at about 400 yards, and I stood my machine almost on its tail to lure him on. As he came, I quickly dived, passing just below him with about five feet between my upper plane and his wheels, firing from both guns meanwhile, continuous fire with the enemy pilot as target.' The Albatros fell 20 yards behind the British front-line trenches; Loraine, having over-revved his engine in a dive, force-landed neatly in a ploughed field. At this time the Gun Bus was employed on *ad hoc* tactical duties, for example, to drive away aircraft interfering with wire-cutting near Ypres. After Loraine had fitted experimentally a 110-hp Le Rhône engine and coarse-pitch propeller in place of the 80-hp Monosoupape Gnôme, the Vickers was found to be 4 mph faster than a BE 2c. Individual aircraft varied enormously, a fact which must be borne in mind when assessing published figures for speed and climb. For example, Loraine tested a BE 2c, taking one hour to reach 6,300 feet and one hour 30 minutes to reach 8,200 feet. With a similar engine

Above left: Oswald Boelcke, the greatest figure in the early German air force. *Above right:* Immelmann, Boelcke's pupil and rival, with the wreckage of one of his victims, a BE 2. *Below left:* German floatplanes, mostly Friedrichshafen types, used for coastal reconnaissance

in the same airframe he reached 8,700 feet in an hour.

Until January 1916 air warfare was a very personal matter, not only in the dropping of messages over the lines, but in the picturesqueness of individual incidents: Guynemer, one Sunday morning after shooting down a German over Compiègne, where he lived, spotted his father coming out of church, landed beside the road and asked Papa to 'please find my Boche'. Another time, when the non-commissioned Guynemer landed beside an artillery battery, having shot down a German in flames, the battery commander fired a salvo in his honour and, stripping the gold braid from his own cap, presented it to the victorious pilot bidding him 'wear it when you, too, are promoted captain'.

However, aerial fighting was becoming ever more organised. During the French Champagne offensive of October, the Germans wisely decided to group their single-seaters, forming small *Kampfeinsitzerkommando* or Single-seater Detachments. Immel-

The 'Fokker Scourge'

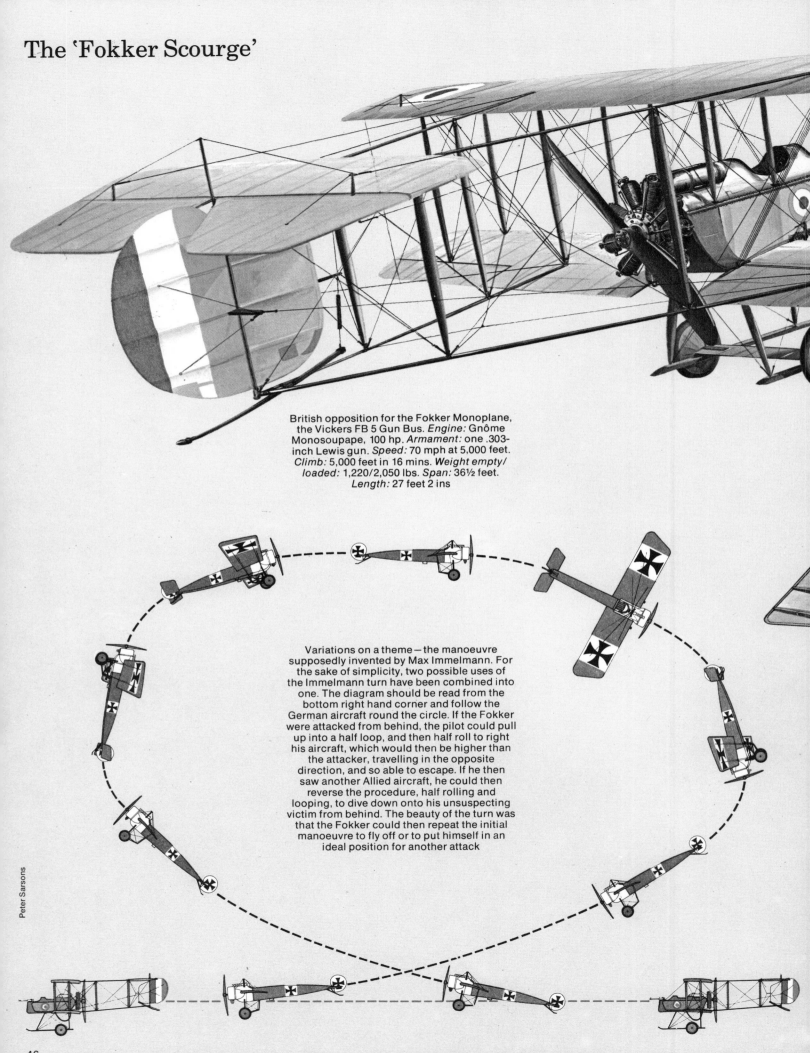

British opposition for the Fokker Monoplane, the Vickers FB 5 Gun Bus. *Engine:* Gnôme Monosoupape, 100 hp. *Armament:* one .303-inch Lewis gun. *Speed:* 70 mph at 5,000 feet. *Climb:* 5,000 feet in 16 mins. *Weight empty/loaded:* 1,220/2,050 lbs. *Span:* 36½ feet. *Length:* 27 feet 2 ins

Variations on a theme—the manoeuvre supposedly invented by Max Immelmann. For the sake of simplicity, two possible uses of the Immelmann turn have been combined into one. The diagram should be read from the bottom right hand corner and follow the German aircraft round the circle. If the Fokker were attacked from behind, the pilot could pull up into a half loop, and then half roll to right his aircraft, which would then be higher than the attacker, travelling in the opposite direction, and so able to escape. If he then saw another Allied aircraft, he could then reverse the procedure, half rolling and looping, to dive down onto his unsuspecting victim from behind. The beauty of the turn was that the Fokker could then repeat the initial manoeuvre to fly off or to put himself in an ideal position for another attack

Peter Sarsons

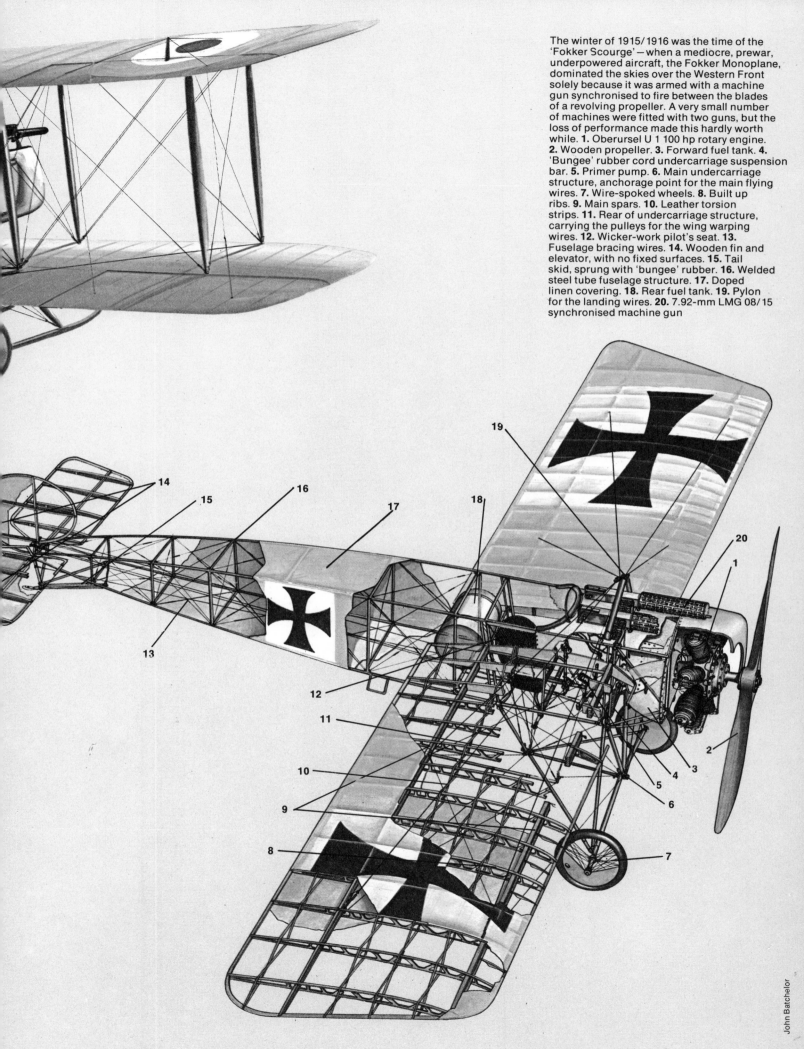

The winter of 1915/1916 was the time of the 'Fokker Scourge' — when a mediocre, prewar, underpowered aircraft, the Fokker Monoplane, dominated the skies over the Western Front solely because it was armed with a machine gun synchronised to fire between the blades of a revolving propeller. A very small number of machines were fitted with two guns, but the loss of performance made this hardly worth while. **1.** Oberursel U 1 100 hp rotary engine. **2.** Wooden propeller. **3.** Forward fuel tank. **4.** 'Bungee' rubber cord undercarriage suspension bar. **5.** Primer pump. **6.** Main undercarriage structure, anchorage point for the main flying wires. **7.** Wire-spoked wheels. **8.** Built up ribs. **9.** Main spars. **10.** Leather torsion strips. **11.** Rear of undercarriage structure, carrying the pulleys for the wing warping wires. **12.** Wicker-work pilot's seat. **13.** Fuselage bracing wires. **14.** Wooden fin and elevator, with no fixed surfaces. **15.** Tail skid, sprung with 'bungee' rubber. **16.** Welded steel tube fuselage structure. **17.** Doped linen covering. **18.** Rear fuel tank. **19.** Pylon for the landing wires. **20.** 7.92-mm LMG 08/15 synchronised machine gun

John Batchelor

47

mann remained at Douai but Boelcke left for an advanced landing ground near Rethel to fly what became known as 'barrage patrols' against French fighter, corps and reconnaissance aircraft. He returned to Douai in December and continued, almost alone amongst German pilots, to patrol behind the Allied lines where Fokker pilots were not encouraged to venture owing to the secrecy of the synchronising gear and the unreliability of the engine.

The concept of barrage patrols was more fully worked out at Verdun, where the great German offensive was launched along a nine-mile front on February 21, 1916. Here too, Boelcke fought his own private war, *'alles ganz auf eigene Faust'*. Bored with escorting observation machines, he obtained permission to leave the rest of the KEK and establish a private landing-ground beside the Meuse, only seven miles from the front with one other pilot, an NCO and 15 men, after discharging himself from hospital to shoot down a Voisin which bothered the neighbourhood. Here was the true 'offensive spirit' so dear to Trenchard and the RFC.

At first the idea of barrage patrols worked well. The aim was to drive the French air force out of the sky, and every available aircraft was concentrated above the lines, except for those giving close support to the infantry, forerunners of the contact patrol machines employed on the Somme. The French, in their slow Farmans, Caudrons and Voisins were quickly downcast, but the defensive thinking of the German High Command soon proved a costly mistake. Not only did the barrage fail to keep out all intruders, but the concentration of so many pilots on this task meant that vital jobs were left undone. Counterbattery work was neglected, to the great damage of German ground forces, and, most important of all, reconnaissance machines did not fly where they should. Had they done so, the High Command would have learned that the Verdun citadel was largely dependent upon one road for its supplies, a road used by some 8,000 lorries a day. Had they known this and bombed the convoys, Verdun might have proved a rout for the French. Instead, the French underwent a change of heart. Pétain took over and demanded from his fliers offensive tactics. Hurriedly moved in from other sectors the *escadrilles de chasse* were regrouped under *Commandant* de Rose, *Chef d'Aviation* of the Second Army. Among them came Brocard and the rest of his Storks, brought from the Sixth Army in Champagne. They found no lack of targets. The nimble Nieuport single-seater 'sesquiplanes' (for the lower plane was almost too small to count) found new German fighters against them, including the Halberstadt D I biplane (100-hp Mercedes), Pfalz monoplanes (which were almost indistinguishable from Fokkers and later marks of the Fokker

itself, which was now feeling its age. The extremely 'clean' LFG Roland C III had a useful turn of speed (103 mph), far higher than the other current German two-seaters such as the Rumpler C I (95 mph) and the LVG C II, whose maximum was 81 mph.

The Storks suffered severely. Guynemer was shot down, wounded in the face and arm; Brocard, his CO, wounded, Lieutenant Deullen wounded, Lieutenant Peretti killed. But the French had regained the offensive, and to foster this spirit *Commandant* de Rose took a leaf from the German book and instituted the 'ace' system, announcing the score as follows: Chaput 7, Nungesser 6 and a balloon, Navarre 4, Lenoir 4, Auger and Pelletier d'Oisy 3, and several pilots with two apiece. Guynemer's tally, counting his work on two-seaters, was five.

Meanwhile in the British sector flying hours mounted fast. In July 1915 the hours flown were 2,100, in August 2,674. In September, with the opening of the Battle of Loos they leapt to 4,740. New squadrons were continually being formed, trained — after a fashion — and flown to France. By the end of June, 1916 there were 27 operational squadrons with BEF, flying 421 aeroplanes, together with 216 aeroplanes at aircraft depots, and four kite balloon squadrons now handled by the RFC. The RNAS Dunkirk were also most active, not only against shipping, docks, submarines and Zeppelins, but also on bombing raids, working closely with the French, with whom they shared the aerodrome at St Pol, Dunkirk. They had also obtained some Nieuport fighters.

From the RFC communiqués it is clear that 'Offensive Spirit' was never lacking: nothing could be more 'offensive' than the action of the BE 2c of No 2 Squadron which, 'on artillery registration', climbed to engage an LVG 4,000 feet above although armed only with a rifle. By late December, however, BEs were better armed, and to make up for it the Germans had learned to make multiple attacks. Fokkers were numerous and aggressive, often attacking three at a time. Casualties were numerous amongst the inexperienced new crews until, profiting from Third Wing lessons, HQ RFC issued an order on January 14 that every reconnaissance aircraft must be accompanied by at least three other machines, in the closest possible formation. At the same time the growth of the RFC made necessary the adoption of larger units than the Wing, and Brigades were established, each comprising a Corps Wing and an Army Wing, one brigade being assigned to each army. The Army Wings took over most of the long-range and high-performance aircraft, and the policy of arming each squadron with a single type of aircraft became standard as supplies improved. Single-seater and two-seater fighter machines were no longer scattered throughout the service. The first homogeneous fighter squadron, No 11, had arrived in France on July 25, 1915, armed with Vickers Gun Bus two-seaters. The first single-seater Fighter Squadron to go into action reached France on February 14, 1916, No 24, under Major L. G. Hawker, VC. No 29 followed on March 25 and No 32 on May 28. These neat little pusher biplanes were fitted either with 100-hp Gnôme Monosoupape or 110-hp Le Rhône. Once their habits were understood they proved popular

Manoeuvrable, and with the same firepower as the *Eindekker*, the DH2 retained a pusher layout

in the RFC, and highly unpopular with Fokker pilots, who had now met their match. The new formation tactics, too, preserved formations from harm. The provision of escorts was by no means easy; but it was now realised on both sides, that a pilot cannot fight and keep the whole sky under observation at the same time. He needs a second pair of eyes.

Between them the Vickers Gun Bus, the FE 2b, and the DH 2 regained the mastery of the air. The Fokker Scourge may be said to have lasted six months. It was exceedingly tough while it lasted, especially to under-trained and inexperienced crews, who now formed a large proportion of the RFC. As Maurice Baring, Trenchard's ADC, wrote at the end of October, the RFC 'had been so used to doing what it wanted without serious opposition that not enough attention was paid to this menace, and the monoplane, in the hands of a pilot like Immelmann, was a serious, and for us a disastrous, factor. But the point is that our work never stopped in spite of this. The work of the armies was done, Fokker Scourge or no Fokker Scourge'.

The original Fokker E I, 80-hp monoplane, underwent several changes. With clipped wings and a 100-hp Oberursel it was known as the E II; redesigned with 31' 2¾" wings this became the most famous *Eindekker* of all, the Fokker E III. A captured 80-hp Le Rhône engine (which had mechanically operated valves, not atmospheric inlet valves like the Oberursel) performed better. Experiments were made with the 160-hp two-row Le Rhône radial from a special French Morane, and by November 1915 a prototype E IV was flying with a two-row 160-hp Oberursel. Armament and synchronising gears also progressed. The classic dive-and-shoot approach required concentrated fire for very short periods. Boelcke asked for and got a twin-Spandau installation. Immelmann asked for three, with the big Le Rhône to carry the extra load. He also had his guns tilted upward at an angle of 15 degrees. Boelcke said they should be aligned in the direction of flight. He reported that the 160-hp E IV was outclimbed by the Nieuport and that performance at height was unsatisfactory. Also, he said the engine quickly lost tune, and that fast turns in the E IV could only be made by blipping the engine off. He recommended the development of a new fighter, preferably a biplane.

Ironically, the worst point of the Fokker was the very feature that had brought it fame. The mechanical synchronising gear linkages gave perpetual trouble, and instances of pilots shooting away their own airscrews were very frequent. It happened to Boelcke, and it is recorded that Anthony Fokker himself put 16 shots through his own propeller. This happened to Immelmann twice,

and a third such accident may have occasioned his death during a fight with an FE 2b of No 25 Squadron on June 18, 1916. The British naturally claimed a victory, for a bogey was laid. Immelmann's score at this time stood at 15, Boelcke's at 18. The latter's remarks on his colleague's death are convincing. 'Immelmann met his death by the most stupid accident,' he wrote home. 'The newspaper stories about an airfight are nonsense. Part of his propeller flew off, and the broken flying-wires, whirling round, ripped the fuselage apart.' There will always be argument, but at least the 'stupid accident' was not uncommon.

With the exception of the Nieuport Scout, with Lewis gun on the upper plane fired by Bowden cable, the most effective anti-Fokker aircraft were pushers, whose rear-mounted engine and propeller allowed a clear cone of fire in a forward direction. The work started by the slow but effective Vickers FB 5 Gun Bus was carried on by another successful two-seater, the FE 2b. The single-seater DH 2 was also a pusher, and it was pushers which largely put an end to the Scourge. Meanwhile Allied types of interrupter-gear had been developed, and contrary to rumour they were not copied from the Germans. The first German example was captured on April 8, 1916; the first British aeroplane armed with synchronising mechanism to arrive in France was a Bristol Scout which landed exactly two weeks before. Operationally, however, only the Sopwith 1½ Strutters of No 70 Squadron and two squadrons of the unsatisfactory BE 12 received synchronised machine guns in time for the Battle of the Somme. The story of aircraft development during the crucial year 1916 will form the subject of a later article.

It is appropriate to close the present chapter with an account of Oswald Boelcke's movements during June. Shortly before Immelmann's funeral (which he attended) Boelcke had a brush with American pilots of the *Escadrille* Lafayette over Verdun, and his ideas for larger formations of fighters than his own little outfit at Sivry were adopted by the aviation Staff. He was promoted captain and posted to the command of a new, all Fokker unit of six aircraft. Now, however, with Immelmann dead, it was decided that Boelcke was too valuable to lose, and he was, to quote his own expression 'put in a glass case'. Evading the grounding order for a day or two, he flew to Douai, where he gave the new Halberstadt D II biplane scout its first battle-flight. Then, flying up to Sivry to pack his kit, he managed to shoot down a final Frenchman before departing on a combined rest-cure and propaganda tour to Turkey and the Eastern Front. Thus it was that, as the preliminary barrage for the Battle of the Somme burst forth, Germany's best and most influential airman departed in the opposite direction. His heart remained at Douai, and had Boelcke's personal leadership been available it is possible that the German air forces would have put up a better performance during the opening months of the Somme battle.

Left: France's premier fighter, the Nieuport 11 *Bébé. Engine:* Le Rhône rotary, 80 hp. *Max speed:* 97 mph at sea level. *Ceiling:* 15,000 feet. *Endurance:* 2½ hours. *Armament:* one .303-inch Lewis gun. *Weights empty/loaded:* 774/1,058 pounds. *Span:* 24 feet 9 inches. *Length:* 19 feet 0½ inches. *Below:* German-designed but used only by the Austrians — the Hansa Brandenburg C I

The second half of 1916 witnessed an
enormous stride in the development of
aircraft. Designers and theoreticians
had, of course, been working to their
full capacity since the beginning of the
war, and now their efforts were beginning
to bear fruit. Though much still remained
to be learned, the days of haphazard
design and flimsy structures had gone.
This advance took practical form in a
dramatic increase in speeds and climb rates
for fighters, and sheer size for bombers.
D. B. Tubbs. Below: An Albatros C X

AIRCRAFT
HIGHER
FASTER
LIGHTER

The six months between the opening of the Battle of the Somme and New Year's Day 1917 can be viewed as a kind of watershed in the history of aeroplane design, for while such archaisms as the Vickers FB 5 Gun Bus were still operational, many of the war's most famous and advanced aircraft were also being flown, if only in prototype form. These included the Sopwith Triplane, the Sopwith Camel and the SE 5 single-seater fighters, advanced two-seat fighter/day-bombers such as the DH 4 and Bristol Fighter, heavy bombers from Handley Page, Gotha and Zeppelin Staaken and a variety of seaplanes and flying-boats. Equally striking was the range of engines. Simple rotaries still formed the basic motive power of most British fighters, while in Germany an intriguing 'bi-rotary'

contra-rotating design was being tried by Siemens Halske, although cooling problems had largely killed the two-row engines developed by Gnôme and Oberursel. Water-cooled engines also made great advances during the period. Little more had been heard of the Salmson/Canton-Unné water-cooled radial developed by the French in the early days, but almost every other configuration was to be seen: straight six, eight-cylinder Vee, 12-cylinder Vee and even straight eights were tried, some with water cooling, others with air cooling, the more sophisticated having overhead camshafts to operate the valves, instead of the more ponderous pushrod-and-rocker system. Rotational speeds were already high enough to require reduction-gearing between crankshaft and propeller, and one

constructor at least had taken advantage of the offset propeller thus provided to experiment with a cannon in the Vee between the cylinder-blocks, firing through the propeller hub. Growing use was being made of light alloys and two constructors (Hispano-Suiza and BHP) had gone over to 'wet liners'—steel sleeves screwed into an aluminium cylinder block, used in conjunction with light-alloy pistons. Cast-iron for pistons was still the rule, but steel was also being used for strength and lightness.

As regards airframes, almost every arrangement of single- and twin-engined machine was being tried, from monoplane to quadruplane, while the pusher layout (rendered necessary on the Allied side by the lack of gun-synchronising gears) was obsolescent but not quite dead. Structural methods and materials ranged from the conventional wire-braced wooden box-girder covered with fabric, to Fokker's welded steel tubing and a couple of most interesting experimental all-metal designs, on the Allied side the Bristol MR 1, a sort of aluminium-clad steel-tube Bristol Fighter, and in Germany the Junkers 'Tin Donkey' types J 1 and J 2. A more promising material in the 1916 context was plywood, used either for reinforcement as in Britain and France, or as a means of fabricating a 'semi-monocoque' fuselage as used by Albatros and LFG Roland.

The temporary supremacy earned for Germany by the Fokker monoplane was at an end. 'July and August 1916 were the blackest days in the history of German military aviation,' wrote Oswald Boelcke's biographer. 'Large formations of enemy aircraft disported themselves unhindered behind our lines. The enemy had gained

A crashed Austrian-built Albatros D III. Note the plywood fuselage and sesquiplane wings

With the increase in quality went increase in quantity: above is an RE 8 production line

complete command of the air.' The Fokkers had been defeated by their own obsolescence. Even when armed with three machine guns (as on Max Immelmann's mount) and powered by a 160 hp Oberursel two-row rotary, the Fokker E IV was seen for what it was: a metal-built copy of a pre-war Morane. A new generation of fighters was now taking the air and, what is more important, the Allied supply position had improved.

On the British sector pusher aircraft still held sway, led by the Royal Aircraft Factory's FE 2b (six-cylinder Beardmore, 120 or 160 hp) and FE 2d (225 hp Vee-12 Rolls-Royce Eagle) two-seaters and the Airco DH 2 single-seater scout (80 hp Le Rhône). All these were formidable because of the unencumbered forward view from the boot-like nacelle and the quick rate of fire from their unsynchronised guns. Heavy escorts of these machines kept the Fokkers at bay while reconnaissance and artillery machines went about their work; a further pusher scout, the FE 8 (80 hp Le Rhône), an already obsolete Royal Aircraft Factory design, joined the RFC during the Somme. More formidable, because they were faster, were the French Nieuport and Spad tractor single seaters.

'Bloody April'
Before describing these and examining the new German scouts which brought about the rapid reversal of Allied fortunes which culminated in 'Bloody April' 1917, it is interesting to see what Captain Boelcke's *Staffel* had to say about the opposition in autumn 1916, shortly after the death, in a collision with one of his own men, of Oswald Boelcke himself.

In unconscious tribute to the old FB 5 Gun Bus, the German air force referred to all British pushers as 'Vickers'. Thus: Vickers single-seater biplane [DH 2]: *Very manoeuvrable. Slightly slower than the Albatros* [D I and D II]. *Loses height during combat, especially at high altitudes. Usual armament one machine gun movable in the vertical plane—can shoot obliquely upwards. Sometimes two parallel guns. Unprotected from rear, and pilot's view restricted. Best attacked from behind, preferably in a zoom from below.* Vickers two-seater biplane [FE 2b and 2d]: *Not so handy and fast. Two movable machine guns, one on a high telescopic mounting. Good field of fire forwards, sideways and upwards, blanketed only by the pusher propeller. Attack from behind on same level or slightly*

below . . . Both Vickers can take a lot of punishment because the crew are shielded by the engine. Nieuport Scout: *Very manoeuvrable and fast. Armament and fire-power as in German single-seaters. Tends to lose height in combat, especially up high. Get on its tail, preferably at short range.*

The main peculiarity of the new Nieuport 16 and 17 (110 hp Le Rhône), a peculiarity which they shared with the 13 square metre *Bébé* (Nieuport 11), the French aces' mount at Verdun, was the *sesquiplan* (sesquiplane) layout. To improve the pilot's view the lower wing was reduced both in chord and span, to become little more than a fairing round the single wood box spar which formed the anchorage for a pair of Vee struts. The top wing had no dihedral and, as in the Moranes and the Fokker

A captured French Spad VII. The type's main virtues were its speed and extreme strength

Bayer, Hauptstaatsarchiv/Munich

monoplanes, a balanced rudder was provided, but no fin. The Nieuport had no need of interrupter gear because a single Lewis gun was mounted above the upper plane, controlled by Bowden cable like the throttle and clutch of a motor cycle. A quadrant mounting devised by Sergeant Foster and Captain H. A. Cooper of 11 Squadron RFC allowed the gun to be pulled down for loading, and also for shooting almost vertically upwards, a method of attack used very successfully by Albert Ball against LFG Roland two-seaters. An optional extra on the Nieuport were electrically-fired Le Prieur rockets launched from the interplane struts. The rockets were intended for use against balloons.

So successful was this scout that copies of the Nieuports were ordered from the German aircraft industry, resulting finally in the famous 'Vee-strutter' Albatros, first the D III, then later the V and Va.

The first generation of German biplane scouts, produced in response to a recommendation from Boelcke, proved disappointing. Fokker tried two series, using modified *Eindecker* fuselages and warping two-bay wings, but neither with 100 or 160 hp Oberursel rotaries nor with 120 or 160 hp Mercedes stationary six-cylinders, was performance good enough; rather better were the Halberstadt D II and D III (120 hp Mercedes or Argus) two-bay scouts which impressed Allied pilots by their ability to dive steeply away from combat. More modern were the Albatros D I and very similar D II that had greeted Boelcke and his new *Jasta 2* on his return to operations in September after the long leave and eastern tour upon which he had been sent following Immelmann's death in June. The Albatros, although not a pretty aeroplane, had a shark-like grace, thanks to the smoothly rounded semi-monocoque fuselage, the basis of which was ⅜-inch ply formers with six spruce longerons, to which was pinned and screwed a plywood skin. With a span of just under 28 feet and single-bay wings this was a reasonably compact aeroplane, and powerful enough with its 150 hp Benz or 160 hp Mercedes engine to carry twin Spandau machine guns in the D II version, a formidable advance. The D III model followed quickly, using a high-compression Mercedes up-rated to 170 hp, and the sesquiplane wing arrangement of the Nieuport.

These Albatros scouts make an interesting comparison with a trio of Sopwith scouts all of which saw the light, either operationally or experimentally, before Christmas 1916. The first was the Pup biplane, always described as one of the most delightful aeroplanes ever made. It certainly looked right. The span was a mere 26 feet 6 inches and although the engine was no more than an 80 hp Le Rhône, which gave the Pup a military load of 80 pounds (one machine gun, ammunition and some Verey cartridges), its light wing-loading made the Pup an excellent gun platform at high altitudes. It could also climb from ground level to 4,500 feet in the same time an Albatros D II took to reach 3,280—but then the Albatros, empty, weighed as much as a Pup fully laden. When it came to manoeuvring, wrote McCudden, the Pup 'could turn twice to an Albatros' once'.

Design methods in the days of wooden aircraft were often empirical. The Sopwith Pup inherited the fuselage profile, wing

chord and stagger from a previous single-seater, the Tabloid. No sooner had the Pup begun scoring for the RNAS than a new Sopwith scout left the drawing-board, and this used the same datum lines again; but to improve the climb and give the pilot more visibility, triplane wings were adopted, with the same span as the Pup's, and with the same overall stagger—although naturally a narrower chord. A Clerget 130 hp rotary was fitted, inherited from the successful two-seater Sopwith 1½-Strutter fighter/bomber, slightly senior to the Pup, which gave the 'Tripehound', as it was nicknamed, ample power.

A third Sopwith, perhaps the most famous fighter of the war, the two-gun Sopwith Camel, designed by R. J. Ashfield, took the air just after Christmas. It would accept any of the more powerful rotaries—Le Rhône, Monosoupape, 130 hp Clerget and eventually the 150 hp BR 1 designed by W. O. Bentley of the navy. Oddly enough a machine which might have been the most successful scout of the period, and was certainly the fastest, never went into squadron service on the Western Front. This was Frank Barnwell's Bristol Monoplane M 1, which was started in July and was flying by September 1916. The unexcelled pilot's view in all directions, a top speed of 128 mph at 5,400 feet and a climb to almost 10,000 feet in 10 minutes, would have put it far in front of all opposition. Such performance on a mere 110 hp Clerget was a tribute to clean design. Handling, too, was delightful.

The Allies, although largely committed to rotary engines for their fighting scouts, possessed one stationary water-cooled engine that was to have a great effect on war in the air. This was the Hispano-Suiza Vee-8 already mentioned as being made largely of aluminium, with wet liners and overhead camshafts. The result of this layout, as might be expected, was an excellent power to weight ratio. Figures published for the high-compression 200 hp Hispano, dimensionally the same as the early 140 hp, give the weight as 442 pounds. Contemporary straight sixes like the 160 hp Beardmore and 160 hp Mercedes weighed 600 pounds or more. The exotic name, already famous in motoring, meant 'Spanish-Swiss'; the company, now largely French, was based on Barcelona and its chief engineer, Birkigt, was Swiss.

The first machine using Marc Birkigt's masterpiece was the Spad S VII designed by Béchereau for Louis Blériot's Société Pour l'Aviation et ses Dérivés (SPAD), successors to Deperdussin. This biplane had first appeared late in 1915. On the Somme, the S VII, now fully developed, became the mount for Guynemer and Fonck, whose personal scores were advancing rapidly. The Spad looked as pugnacious as it was, having a hunched, muscular stance even on the ground, brought about by the design of the wings, which had little gap, no dihedral and no stagger—a French fashion evident also in the Morane biplanes, some of which were still in use by No 3 Squadron RFC. The wings were of one-bay construction with a light supplementary strut at the cable intersections, and the machine was famous for its strength. One day Guynemer was brought down by a 75-mm shell which damaged his radiator and stripped the fabric from the port upper main plane. Hitting the ground at 100 mph, the Spad

shed various bits, slewed through 45 degrees and finally planted itself in the ground like a post. Guynemer was unhurt, except for concussion, some delayed shock and a gash on the knee from the magneto. Every cockpit in those days was filled with such protuberances. Fireproof bulkheads, too, had yet to be invented.

Negotiations for purchase and licence to manufacture the Hispano in England started in 1915, but Anglo-Franco-Spanish talks moved slowly. However, many aeroplanes were designed round the engine, in particular the SE 5 (Scouting Experimental 5) at Farnborough, prototypes of which were flying by the end of 1916 with 150 hp ungeared and 200 hp geared Hispanos.

The world of two-seaters also saw many changes and much progress during these six months. The British at last acquired some tractor two-seaters designed, like the German C-Class, with the pilot in front

and the observer-gunner behind, although two RFC squadrons already enjoyed this advantage in their somewhat antiquated Moranes. In the 1½-Strutter (named from the appearance of its interplane struts) the Sopwith company had a winner, for it was defended behind by a Lewis and by a synchronised Vickers in front using either Sopwith-Kauper or Scarff-Dibovsky interrupter gear. Production was hampered by strikes, but eventually 1½-Strutters were built in huge quantities and made over to the French and other Allies for reconnaissance, fighting and day-bombing. They were delightful aeroplanes to fly and beautiful to look at, says Captain Norman Macmillan who flew them with 45 Squadron, but the 110 hp Clerget was overtaxed, and their maximum speed with full war load at 10,000-12,000 feet was a mere 80 mph. The family likeness between 1½-Strutter and Pup was unmistakable.

Top: A crashed Sopwith 1½-Strutter. The Sopwith was the mainstay of the British aerial forces of the time. *Above:* A Sopwith Triplane. The arrangement of the wings gave good visibility, great climb rate and manoeuvrability and considerable strength. The idea was widely copied

Higher and faster, but there were still many defects in the designs of some of the aircraft

The Gnôme Monosoupape rotary, 80 hp model Advantages: Good power-to-weight and size-to-power ratios and relative mechanical simplicity. **Disadvantages:** Fine tolerances required in maintenance, tendency to shed cylinders and no proper throttle (the only way of controlling the engine was by cutting the ignition to a number of cylinders). Unlike more conventional engines, the rotary had a stationary crankshaft, around which rotated the cylinders and crankcase, with the propeller bolted to their front. The crankshaft itself **(1)** is bolted to the aeroplane's structure. Into the crankshaft are led three inlets (only two are visible) **(2)** for air, fuel and lubricant

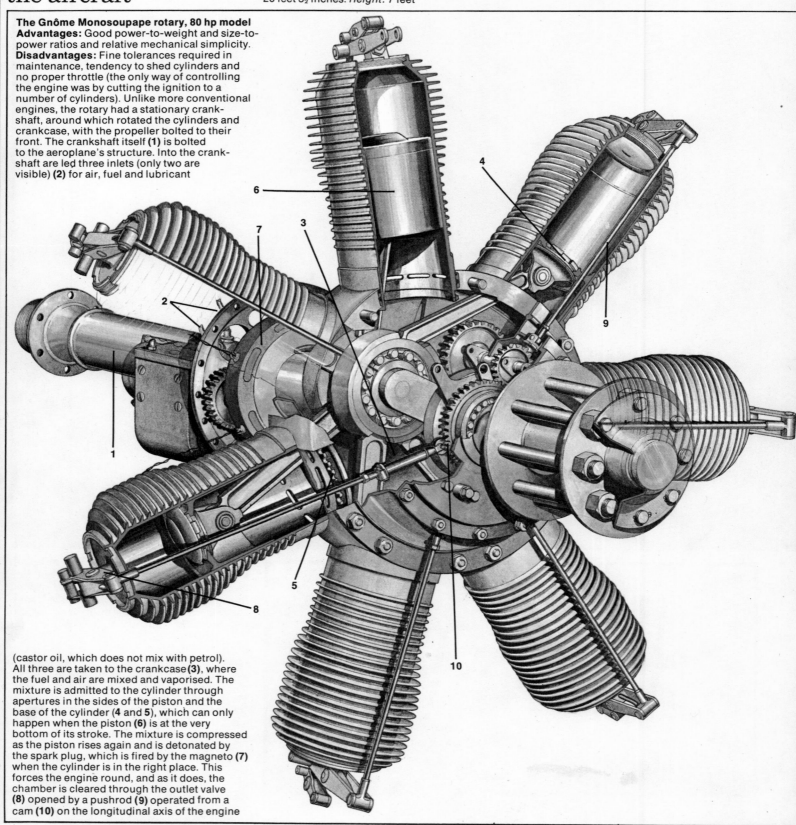

(castor oil, which does not mix with petrol). All three are taken to the crankcase **(3)**, where the fuel and air are mixed and vaporised. The mixture is admitted to the cylinder through apertures in the sides of the piston and the base of the cylinder **(4 and 5)**, which can only happen when the piston **(6)** is at the very bottom of its stroke. The mixture is compressed as the piston rises again and is detonated by the spark plug, which is fired by the magneto **(7)** when the cylinder is in the right place. This forces the engine round, and as it does, the chamber is cleared through the outlet valve **(8)** opened by a pushrod **(9)** operated from a cam **(10)** on the longitudinal axis of the engine

Below: The British **RE 8** artillery spotter and reconnaissance machine. The type was introduced late in 1916 and remained in service in large numbers until the armistice despite its many shortcomings. **Advantages:** None. **Disadvantages:** The type was too stable, had weak upper wing extensions, was prone to spinning, and sometimes developed a dangerous 'air cushion' when landing. The engine was also unreliable when first introduced. *Engine:* RAF 4a, 150 hp. *Speed:* 103 mph at 5,000 feet. *Armament:* one .303-inch Vickers and one .303-inch Lewis gun plus up to 224 pounds of bombs. *Ceiling:* 13,500 feet. *Endurance:* 4¼ hours. *Weight empty/loaded:* 1,803/2,869 lbs. *Span:* 42 ft 7 in. *Length:* 27 ft 10½ in.

Above: The German **LFG Roland C II** escort and reconnaissance machine. The type was marked by the very great care taken to ensure aerodynamic cleanliness. This care was reflected in the machine's good turn of speed. **Advantages:** A strong and capacious fuselage and an excellent view, particularly upwards as there was no wing above the crew to obstruct their view as in most biplanes. The view downward was also good as a result of the careful arrangement of the wing root cut-outs and the wings' stagger. **Disadvantages:** The wings were too thin and tended to distort in service, with the result that climb and ceiling were affected adversely. *Engine:* Mercedes D III, 160 hp. *Armament:* one 7.92-mm Spandau for the pilot and one 7.92-mm Parabellum for the observer. *Speed:* 103 mph at sea level. *Climb:* 12 minutes to 6,560 feet. *Ceiling:* 13,100 feet. *Endurance:* 4 to 5 hours. *Weight empty/loaded:* 1,681/2,825 pounds. *Span:* 33 feet 9½ inches. *Length:* 25 feet 3¼ inches. *Right:* The development of reconnaissance aircraft from 1914 to 1916 (BE 2a to Albatros C VII) and comparative fighter performance at the end of 1916. Note that although every other aspect of performance has improved, climb rate has stayed at the 1914 level. In the fighter performance part of the chart, note that very little divides the types in speed and ceiling, but that the difference in climb rate is marked.

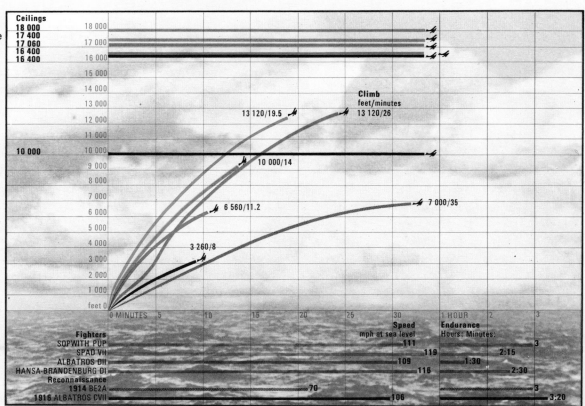

Ceilings		
18 000	13 120/19.5	13 120/26 Climb feet/minutes
17 400		
17 060		
16 400		
16 400	10 000/14	
10 000	6 560/11.2	7 000/35
	3 260/8	

Fighters	Speed mph at sea level	Endurance Hours: Minutes:
SOPWITH PUP	111	3
SPAD VII	119	2:15
ALBATROS DII	109	1:30
HANSA-BRANDENBURG DI	116	2:30
Reconnaissance		
1914 BE2A	70	3
1916 ALBATROS CVII	106	3:20

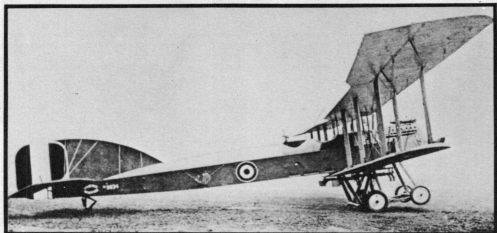

Top: The Zeppelin-Staaken R VI, the most famous type of German 'Giant' aircraft. The Germans devoted much effort to the development of 'Giant' types. *Above:* A Short Bomber, used mostly by No. 3 Wing, RNAS. *Below:* Albatros D IIIs, Germany's fighter mainstay in 1917 and 1918

Far less graceful was the Royal Aircraft Factory's RE 8, in which, at last, the observer sat behind the pilot. Initially, many crashes were caused by inadequacies in the design of the tail, and the drag was such that observers were advised not to stand up while landing as the extra wind resistance of their bodies might cause a stall. The engine was the Factory's 150 hp RAF 4a Vee-12 of Renault inspiration, an engine whose air cooling in the RE 8 was assisted by an aerodynamically disastrous metal scoop. The RE 8, like the BE 2c before it, was put into mass production and was to suffer heavy losses in 1917. Another Farnborough effort, the BE 12, a fixed-gun single-seater based on the BE 2c, two-bay wings and all, provoked General Trenchard, commanding the RFC in France, to write: 'I realise I shall lose two squadrons if I stop using the BE 12 . . . but I cannot do anything else but to recommend that no more be sent to this country.' The BE 12, like the Martinsyde G 100 and G 102 Elephant, another oversize single-seater, was quickly diverted from fighting to other duties. The most effective British two-seaters were still pushers—the FE 2d, especially when fitted with the water-cooled Vee-12 Rolls-Royce of 225 hp, whose overhead-camshaft drive and welded steel water-jackets were inspired by prewar Mercedes automobile practice. This Eagle series was later developed to produce 360 hp, and a smaller Vee-12 the 190-250 hp Falcon proved the Hispano's most serious rival, being used in the Bristol F2B Fighter, flown experimentally during 1916. This was a biplane whose mid-gap location of the fuselage gave both pilot and gunner an excellent view, and which could be fought and stunted like a single-seater.

The Bristol two-seater fighter was matched in excellence by the de Havilland DH 4 day-bomber, a two-bay biplane which out-performed many contemporary single-seaters. The prototype was flying at Hendon in August 1916, powered by the new BHP (Beardmore-Halford-Pullinger) 220 hp engine that had its origins in the 160 hp Beardmore but differed from it in having a larger cylinder bore (145-mm instead of 143-mm), an aluminium block and wet liners inspired by Hispano-Suiza, an overhead camshaft instead of pushrods and a piston stroke of 190-mm, this last factor making the engine very tall. This did not affect early production DH 4s, which were given the Rolls-Royce Eagle. Supplies reached the RFC early in 1917, and the Rolls-DH 4 was voted the finest machine of its kind on either side. Its qualities as a fighting machine were marred, however, by the long distance separating pilot and observer, which made communication virtually impossible.

Better firepower

Various twin-engined and pusher aeroplanes contemplated in mid-1916 were shelved as synchronising gears had become available, and the tractor layout offered better performance, and the twin-engined layout was too cumbersome.

German reconnaissance machines, in marked contrast to the Factory's two-seaters, presented a clean and often fish-like appearance, spoilt only by clumsy exhaust manifolds and radiators in several instances. The majority employed one or other of the 150-160 hp vertical six-cylinder engines which the industry produced in such profusion, or, in later cases, the 200 hp Benz Bz IV or the interesting but underdeveloped Mercedes D IV 220 hp straight-eight. Aesthetically the most advanced aeroplane on the Somme front was the LFG Roland C II, whose semi-monocoque fuselage earned it the nickname of *Walfisch* (Whale). Constructionally too it was interesting. Around the shape dictated by plywood formers and longerons a skin of thin plywood was wrapped in spiral strips pinned and glued in place, the whole structure then being covered with fabric and doped. The Roland's fuselage filled the entire gap between the sharply staggered upper and lower planes, which were joined by a single wide I-section strut on each side, faired to streamline form with two layers of plywood and connected to each wing by a ball-and-socket joint. The crew position was no less unorthodox than the rest. The pilot sat well forward, his eyes level with the top plane; his observer was immediately behind, with a commanding view all round. Downward vision was helped by cut-outs at the wing roots and by transparent panels in the sides of the fuselage. The observer was armed with a Parabellum machine gun on ring mounting, and later machines also carried a fixed gun firing through the propeller. Its thin wings tended to distort, however, and this affected climb adversely. Rolands were met in large formations, photographic machines being escorted by others; Albert Ball's approach was to close on the Roland from below, unseen, and fire almost vertically at shortest range possible with his Foster-mounted Lewis. Perhaps because they proved easy, Ball described the Rolands as the best aeroplane the Germans had. Top speed, thanks to the clean shape, was 103 mph.

Larger, later and more orthodox was the Deutsche Flugzeug Werke DFW C V (200 hp Benz Bz IV) introduced towards the end of 1916, a slab-sided but graceful two-bay biplane that was still fighting well a year later. In common with many German aeroplanes it had a wooden, plywood covered fuselage which could absorb a good deal of punishment. Albatros, after early disappointments with their C V/16 two-seater, developed it during the year into a comfortable, formidable aeroplane with good flying characteristics let down by the unreliability of the straight-eight Mercedes' crankshaft. It was then redesigned using the proven 200 Benz Bz IV engine and embodying characteristics of both C V series. This model, designated C VII, proved very popular in 1916/17. Simultaneously a larger machine, the C X, with 47 feet 1½ inches span (7 feet more than the C VII and with loaded weight increased from 3,410 pounds to 3,669 pounds) was being developed to accept a six-cylinder Mercedes replacement, the D IVa of 260 hp, the German equivalent of the Rolls-Royce Falcon as used in the Bristol Fighter.

The rôle of heavy bomber is so familiar today that it is surprising to remember how little it was regarded during the first two years of the war. However, the Admiralty and RNAS with typical enterprise did during 1916 develop a Short Bomber based on the well-known Short 184 seaplane. Production Bombers resembled the seaplane in having three-bay wings with long overhang to the upper planes, braced from kingposts, and an extremely long fin. The undercarriage comprised an upward tilted four-wheeled chassis, and the engine could be either a 225 hp Sunbeam as fitted to 184 Seaplanes, or the 250 hp Rolls-Royce later known as the Eagle.

The pattern is set: Allied numbers and enterprise against German quality

Südd Verlag

With a wing span of 85 feet this very large single-engined aeroplane had an all-up weight of 6,800 pounds and a maximum speed of 77 mph. The bomb load could be four 230-pound bombs or eight 112-pounders, carried on racks under the wings. Four Short Bombers of No 7 Squadron RNAS, Coudekerque, took part in a raid on Ostend on the night of November 15, each dropping four 65-pound bombs.

First British giant

Admiralty influence, in the person of Commodore Murray F. Sueter, was also responsible for Britain's big twin-engined bomber. He told Frederick Handley Page to build a 'bloody paralyser'. The Handley Page 0/100 took shape during the course of 1916 after official trials at Eastchurch beginning in January, and deliveries to the RNAS began in September. The 0/100 was by far the largest aeroplane to go into action on the British side, having a wing span of 100 feet on the overhanging upper planes, braced, as in the Short, from king-posts. There were two sets of interplane struts outboard of the engines, which were mounted tractor-wise in nacelles supported on structures of steel tube. The streamlined nacelles also housed the main fuel tanks, but experiments with armour plating were discontinued. In planning the big bomber Handley Page and his assistant George Volkert put their faith in a so-far undeveloped engine; but a big (4·5″ × 6·5″ bore and stroke, 20½ litre, 900 pound) Rolls-Royce Vee-12 had shown 300 hp on test at 2,000 rpm and derated to 250 hp and 1,600 rpm it gave promise of reliability —which was amply fulfilled.

Two of these Rolls-Royce Eagle Mk II engines were installed, driving left- and right-handed airscrews. Built-up hollow wooden spars were used wherever possible to save weight, and for easier handling the fuselage was constructed in four sections and the wings were made to fold. A biplane tail was chosen for reduced span and to give the gunners a clearer field of fire. There were three machine gun positions: in the extreme nose and behind the wings, both above and below the fuselage. The aeroplane was supported on the ground by a massive but fairly orthodox two-wheeled undercarriage below each engine nacelle, with a shock-absorber for each wheel. The work required of the four tyres was considerable. The 0/100 prototype weighed 8,480 pounds empty and 14,022 fully loaded: 2,830 pounds for fuel and oil, 760 pounds for crew, and almost 2,000 pounds for military load. Up to 16 112-pound bombs could be carried. The first two 0/100s arrived safely at Dunkirk before Christmas, 1916.

Twin-engined Gotha and Friedrichshafen day bombers appeared in autumn 1916, just in time to replace the vulnerable Zeppelin airships. Although differing in construction, both machines were biplanes of about 77 feet span, powered by a pair of pusher engines (Mercedes D IVa) giving 260 hp each, and able to operate at 15,000 feet—a ceiling which placed them beyond the range of any contemporary fighter sent up specially to intercept. The normal bomb load for raids on England was six 50-kg (112-pound) bombs, but up to 1,120 pounds could be taken on shorter raids.

Basic design for the giant multi-engined aeroplanes had been going on since 1915, first in the Gothaer Waggonfabrik, Gotha-Ost, and from 1916 onwards in the Zeppelin Werke Staaken, at Staaken near Berlin.

There can be no denying that these huge aircraft were prettier and more modern in appearance than the Handley Page, because the upper main planes had no overhang and their cabin and nacelles were neater. Development followed a logical pattern as more powerful engines became available. The original prototype, known as VGO I (for *Versuchs* (Experimental) Gotha Ost) set the pattern, being of fairly orthodox wood and fabric braced box-girder construction. Three Maybach 240 hp Mb IV engines were used. One in the nose drove a tractor airscrew and there was a pusher engine in the rear half of each nacelle, the front of which housed a machine gunner. Then two more Maybachs were installed in each 'power egg', coupled in tandem to a pusher screw, making five in all. The gun emplacements remained. Empty weight was now 16,390 pounds. Power was still lacking, as it took an hour to reach 10,000 feet; so next a machine was built with six 160 hp Mercedes D IIIs, two in the nose and a pair in each nacelle: the weight empty of this VGO III was 18,920 pounds. The model known as R IV retained the two nose Mercedes but more powerful 220 hp Bz IVs replaced those in the nacelles. Empty weight was 19,298 pounds. The R V reverted to a single nose engine, and there was a general cleaning up of design as well as increased efficiency through making the tandem engines drive tractor screws. The machine gun positions were transferred to the rear of the nacelles and an extra machine gunner installed in a plywood 'crow's nest' above the top wing. The production R VIs which raided London in the summer of 1917 (and were therefore building during the period of this article) discarded the nose engine, and were fitted with a tandem pair of engines in each nacelle driving tractor and pusher propellers. They carried two pilots, a radio operator, a navigator, a mechanic and two gunners. A gun position was provided in the extreme nose, ahead of the spacious cabin, and the bomb-aiming gear was also in the nose. A large gunners' cockpit amidships allowed defenders to shoot both upwards and downwards, through a ventral slot. The huge biplane tail, which like that of the Handley Page had been called 'as big as a single-seater fighter', was unusual for the wide use of aluminium in its construction. An undercarriage to carry the loaded weight of 26,066 pounds—more than 11½ tons—was a problem solved by placing four of the contemporary thin-section aircraft wheels and tyres on each hub of the two main vee undercarriages. An extra pair of wheels was located below the nose, making 18 wheels in all. Maximum speed was given as 84 mph, with climb to 3,000 metres (10,000 feet) in 43 minutes. Ceiling was 14,170 feet and endurance up to 10 hours.

Great advances in performance

From the R VI weighing almost 8 tons unladen to the Sopwith Pup's 746 pounds is a far cry indeed. Equally striking was the contrast in performance between elderly operational aircraft still in service during July 1916 and the powerful prototypes already on test at the end of the year. The Fokker-slaying DH 2 scout had a top speed at 10,000 feet of 77 mph; a Hispano SE 5 would do 114 mph at the same height, an improvement of 47%. The contrast was equally striking among two-seaters: a BE 2c with RAF 1a 90 hp engine at 10,000 feet would do only 69 mph. The prototype DH 4 with a 220 hp BHP attained a speed at the same height, carrying bombs, of 109 mph, which means that a BE pilot who found himself posted to DH 4s would benefit from a 70% improvement in speed.

Speed can be measured. Scientific progress is harder to assess, and wartime discoveries receive little publicity. However, the second half of 1916 was a time of lively experiment, especially in matters affecting controllability, and the controls themselves. The behaviour of balanced rudders and ailerons was being studied, and new, thicker aerofoil sections investigated. Sopwith patented a variable-incidence tailplane on the 1½-Strutter, and this soon became a common feature. Cowlings for rotary engines were the subject of considerable experiment, although arrangements for directing a draught to the air-cooled cylinders of Factory aircraft seem to have been peculiarly haphazard, as was the manner in which extra equipment of all kinds was attached to service aircraft, with no regard for handling or aerodynamics. The Germans, especially, were a prey to complicated exhaust manifolds, although these grew simpler towards 1917. They also evolved progressively neater radiator installations, the Windhoff *Ohrenkühler* ('ear' radiator) on the side of the fuselage giving way, in later marks of Albatros D II scout, for instance, to a Teeves und Braun radiator of aerofoil shape let into the centre section. The Allies increasingly went over to the flat, car type of radiator, in the Spad, SE 5 and DH 4. Conical 'spinners' surrounding the airscrew hub were much used by German designers although seldom provided on Allied aeroplanes except by keen pilots intent on improving performance, as witness F. T. Courtenay's Bristol Scout D fitted with a Morane type spinner and McCudden's SE 5 which had the spinner from an LVG he had shot down.

Throughout the period every factory accumulated 'know-how' in the handling of woods and metals. Mention may be made of the unbraced semi-monocoque construction in Germany, the use of built-up hollow spars by Handley Page, Sopwith's ingenious sockets and junction plates made from folded sheet metal, and a growing awareness that flat and circular sections, such as axles and bracing wires, should be made or adapted to a reasonably streamlined shape. The central months of the war were indeed a productive period. Perhaps never before or since the final six months of the year 1916 has aeroplane design proved so interestingly diverse.

Further Reading

Bruce, J. M., *British Aeroplanes 1914-1918* (Putnam 1969)
Gray, P. and Thetford, O., *German Aircraft of the First World War* (Putnam 1962)
Jones, H. A., *The War in the Air Volume II* (OUP)
Lamberton, W. M., *Fighter Aircraft of the 1914-1918 War* (Harleyford 1961)
Lamberton, W. M., *Bomber and Reconnaissance Aircraft of the First World War* (Harleyford)
Penrose, H., *British Aviation: The Great War and Armistice* (Putnam 1969)

In the autumn of 1916 the Zeppelin appeared for the last time in a significant rôle as a strategic bomber. Always in the forefront of the air war against England, the Imperial Navy's airship division was inspired by the advent of still larger craft, called 'super-Zeppelins' by the British, to mount a final offensive against London.

The first of these new giants, *L 30*, had made her maiden flight from Friedrichshafen on May 28, 1916. With double the volume of the craft produced a year earlier, *L 30* displaced 1,949,600 cubic feet and had a gross lift of 141,200 pounds. With better streamlining of the hull, and a total of six Maybach engines, the new Zeppelin was slightly faster than her predecessors, achieving 62.2 mph on trials. Her combat ceiling, however, was still only about 13,000 feet. A useful lift of 61,600 pounds (improved in later ships of the class) allowed for a heavier bomb load in English raids —*L 31* on the night of September 23, 1916, carried 9,250 pounds of bombs to England, the largest amount in any attack of the war. *L 31* herself was commissioned on July 14 by Heinrich Mathy, *L 32* on August 7 by Werner Peterson, and *L 33* on September 2 by Alois Böcker. Yet the Germans were unaware that their opponents were at this time equipping their aircraft with machine guns firing incendiary ammunition, which could turn the hydrogen-filled Zeppelins into blazing funeral pyres.

Strasser, optimistic as ever, wrote to Admiral Scheer on August 10, after a few preliminary attacks on the north of England that 'the performance of the big airships has reinforced my conviction that England can be overcome by means of airships, inasmuch as the country will be deprived of the means of existence through increasingly extensive destruction of cities, factory complexes, dockyards, and harbours'. Wishing to make a 'big effort' against England during the waning moon from August 20 to September 6, Strasser augmented the North Sea Zeppelins with two of the despised Schütte-Lanz craft brought from the Baltic. Thus, 13 naval airships set out on August 24; but the only result was that Mathy, for the first time in ten months, reached London, doing £130,000 worth of damage in a swift onslaught against Deptford, Plumstead and Eltham.

The end of 1916 marked a transition in strategic bombing: the vulnerable Zeppelins were bowing out and aircraft began to take over. *Douglas Robinson.* *Below:* The German naval airship *L 32*, one of the new 'super-Zeppelins'

A bad landing at Ahlhorn grounded Mathy until September 21; but on the night of September 2, 12 other naval airships set out for London, while four army craft joined them from sheds in the Rhineland. It was the largest airship armada sent against England during the war, and the only time army and navy airships attacked the same target simultaneously. The military ships had the shortest journey, and were therefore the first to approach London. *LZ 98*, coming up from Dungeness, dropped all her bombs on Gravesend in the belief that she was over the London docks. One of the three Royal Flying Corps officers patrolling at the time, Second-Lieutenant William Leefe Robinson, sighted the Zeppelin, but she escaped into the clouds at 60 mph before he could attack. A second army Zeppelin, *LZ 90,* got no nearer to London than Haverhill, and accidentally dropped her sub-cloud car near Manningtree before going out to sea. A third military ship, the new Schütte-Lanz *SL 11* under *Hauptmann* Schramm, came inland via the River Crouch and made a determined attempt to attack London from the north. At Finsbury Park, however, Schramm turned back in the face of very heavy gunfire from the centre of London. Unknown to him, three aeroplanes were converging on the giant raider, lit up in the beams of searchlights, and Leefe Robinson was the first to arrive. Two drums of the new Brock and Pomeroy ammunition distributed along the airship's hull had no effect. The third, concentrated on one spot aft, produced a bright glow within the

THE BOMBING WAR

envelope and suddenly there was a monstrous burst of flame which illuminated the countryside for miles around. One of the naval Zeppelins, *L 16*, barely a mile distant, was revealed to one of the RFC pilots by the conflagration aboard *SL 11*, but the illumination gave out before he could close the range. The wooden-framed army ship fell burning at Cuffley; all 16 on board were killed.

The fate of the Schütte-Lanz ship understandably disheartened the personnel of the navy ships, still making their approaches to London via Norfolk, Suffolk and Cambridgeshire. Four of them, *L 14*, *L 16*, *L 21* and *L 32*, saw the disaster to Schramm's ship from north of London and turned back, claiming later to have attacked the capital. Viktor Schütze in *L 11*, over Harwich, witnessed the catastrophe from above the clouds 50 miles away. Three Zeppelins had been carried north by the wind and attacked targets in the Midlands. One, *L 13*, burned out three gas holders in East Retford near Nottingham. No important targets were bombed and the big attack was a failure, with only four dead and 12 injured, while the damage toll amounted to only £21,000. The credit was Leefe Robinson's, and in the opinion of the public, he thoroughly deserved the Victoria Cross which was awarded to him.

Despite the loss of the army Schütte-Lanz, Strasser continued to be confident that his Zeppelins, particularly the big 'thirties', were still superior to the London defences, even though several of his commanders had seen an aeroplane attacking

the *SL 11*. On September 23, 1916, 12 ships were sent out in two groups—eight older ones via the North Sea, and four 'thirties' via the Rhineland and Belgium, to approach London with the south wind behind them.

L 33 brought down

L 30, commanded by Buttlar, claimed an attack on London as early as 2235 hours, but no bombs fell on southern England at this early hour, and *L 30's* whereabouts cannot be traced. It was Böcker in *L 33* who first reached London. Coming up the north side of the Thames Estuary, he was fired on, but blinded the searchlights by dropping magnesium parachute flares. Between midnight and 0040 hours, *L 33* released 'two bombs of 300-kg, eight of 100-kg, 32 of 50-kg, and 20 incendiaries' over the eastern end of London. These started serious fires in an oil depot and a timber yard, and demolished many dwellings, including a popular public house, the 'Black Swan'. But Böcker was exposing his ship to a heavy artillery barrage over the strongest portion of the London defences. One shell burst inside Cell 14 abaft the control car, destroying the cell. Other gas cells were riddled in many places by shell splinters. Leaking hydrogen and sinking steadily, *L 33* turned away from the capital, only to encounter Second-Lieutenant Albert de Bathe Brandon, who had unsuccessfully attacked *L 15* six months earlier. Again, Brandon failed to set the super-Zeppelin afire with his incendiary ammunition, but *L 33* was too badly damaged to get home. At 0120

hours Böcker brought his damaged ship down in a field at Little Wigborough in Essex and set her on fire. The crew, marching to the coast to look for a boat, were 'taken in charge' by a special constable.

Next came Mathy in *L 31*. Coming down Channel from Belgium with *L 32*, he had aimed ten bombs at the Dungeness Lighthouse to lighten the ship for the attack on London. Beyond Tunbridge Wells he had confidently followed the railway from Eastbourne into Croydon. Here searchlights picked up his Zeppelin, but clever use of parachute flares blinded the searchlight crews as he dropped the bulk of his heavy cargo on Brixton and Streatham. Crossing the heart of the capital, Mathy dropped his last bombs on Lea Bridge Road and Leyton, and above a blanket of mist in the Lea Valley got away unscathed. How he missed bombing the City remains a mystery; his War Diary states that ten 128-pound bombs fell on it.

Peterson in *L 32* had circled near his landfall for over an hour, and then, heading towards London, deviated to the east. South of the Thames his ship was shrouded in mist, but on crossing the river at Erith she came into clear air and was picked up by the searchlights and came under gunfire. A BE 2c biplane flown by Second-Lieutenant Frederick Sowrey overhauled *L 32* at 13,000 feet and set her afire; the flaming wreck, shedding parts for miles, crashed to earth near Great Burstead.

Of the ships that crossed the North Sea, *L 17* did considerable damage in Nottingham. The others failed to reach the Mid-

land cities, and two of them saw *L 32's* fall, *L 23* from 150 miles away near Lincoln.

The loss of two new super-Zeppelins, together with Peterson and Böcker—two commanders who could not be adequately replaced—signalled the end of Strasser's dream of 'the quick and effective conquest of England' by his strategic bombers. Yet Strasser's only concession to the improved defences, when he sent out his raiders on the afternoon of September 25, was to order 'caution in case of clear weather'. Mathy was out that night, but finding a cloudless sky at Dungeness, he proceeded down the Channel to bomb Portsmouth. His navigation as usual was impeccable and he reported dropping 8,000 pounds of bombs as he crossed the dockyard; but they must have been released prematurely and were not traced by the British. Again, seven older craft headed for the Midlands via the North Sea. Martin Dietrich in *L 22* caused some damage to the Sheffield armament works; others were frustrated by the blackout and by increased anti-aircraft defences in their attempt to bomb the Midlands industrial centres.

One week later, on the night of October 1, Heinrich Mathy's *L 31* returned to England with ten other Zeppelins. While most of them wandered over Lincolnshire and Norfolk, *L 31*, coming inland at Lowestoft, steered a straight course for London. At Ongar, with the searchlights of the London defences converging on him, Mathy turned aside, but not to give up the raid. Circling around to the north of the capital, Mathy evidently intended to make a high-speed

Left: Reconnoitring above a Helgoland class battleship, the *L 31*, one of the giant Zeppelins introduced in autumn 1916. But the days of the super Zeppelins were soon over: the Allies were equipping their aircraft with machine guns firing incendiary ammunition, one round of which could turn the hydrogen-filled Zeppelins into funeral pyres

Top right: Manoeuvring a Zeppelin into its hangar, northern France. *Above:* Heinrich Mathy, the boldest and most successful airship commander of the war. His *L 31* was shot down on the night of October 1; Mathy jumped out and was still breathing when found, but died immediately. *Right:* Werner Peterson. He was killed when his *L 32* was shot down on September 12

65

run across the city with the stiff north wind behind him—his bomb sight was later found set for a ground speed of 89 mph. But as he opened up his engines for the run-up, four defence pilots started across London to attack him. Undoubtedly Mathy saw them closing in, for he dropped his bombs over Cheshunt and climbed away to the west. At this point Second-Lieutenant Wulstan J. Tempest dived on him and set *L 31* afire at 12,700 feet. The wreckage fell at Potters Bar; Mathy, who had jumped out, was still breathing when found but died almost immediately.

Such was the end of the boldest and most successful airship commander of the war, admired by friend and foe alike; and such was the end of the last deliberate airship attack on London. The mood back in Ahlhorn and Nordholz was one of depression and discouragement, particularly among the ratings. Two months passed before the naval Zeppelins returned to England, and this time avoiding London, they went to the Midlands. The new super-Zeppelin *L 34* was, however, promptly shot down in flames by an RFC pilot when she bombed West Hartlepool. Next morning, as dawn was breaking, *L 21,* which had spent nine hours over England and had gone as far west as Newcastle-under-Lyme, was shot down in flames off Lowestoft.

One of the first decisions of Ernst von Hoeppner, appointed General Commanding the *Luftstreitkräfte,* on October 8, 1916, was to downgrade the rôle of the Zeppelin as a strategic bomber, at least in the West, and to substitute heavier-than-air craft.

Following the shooting down in flames of the *SL 11* at Cuffley, no more army airships were sent to England. Having already been forbidden to cross the Western Front, the only possible mission for the army airships in the west was to proceed down-Channel to attack ports and bases in northern France, such as Rouen, Etaples and Boulogne. A few successes were claimed, but the final attack of this series, by *LZ 107* on Boulogne on February 16, 1917, was actually the last successful raid by an army airship. Ironically, it was just at this time that the army finally received its first super-Zeppelins, *LZ 113* and *LZ 120*; they went to the Eastern Front.

The army airship service's last attempt to intervene in the war was during the campaign against Rumania, which started with a declaration of war on August 27, 1916, and ended with the German occupation of Bucharest, the capital, on December 6. In preparation for the campaign, *LZ 101* had replaced *SL 10* in Jamboli on August 3, and *LZ 86* had been sent to Temesvar on August 24. Bucharest was their target as soon as war broke out, and *LZ 101* made her first attack on the capital on the night of August 28 with 4,000 pounds of bombs. She was back over the city again on the nights of September 4 and 25. The Temesvar Zeppelin was slower off the mark, making her first attack on the oil refinery town of Ploeşti on the night of September 4. Attempting to land next morning, she crashed at high speed outside her base and was wrecked, most of the crew being killed, including her commander, *Oberleutnant*

Wolff. She was promptly replaced by *LZ 81,* but in her second attack on Bucharest on the night of September 26, this Zeppelin was so badly shot up by the defending artillery that she force-landed short of her base and had to be dismantled. *LZ 97* replaced her, and she and *LZ 101* made some attacks after the fall of Bucharest.

In June 1917, Hoeppner decided to abolish the army airship service. The surviving airships were withdrawn to Germany and in July and August they were broken up at Jüteborg, Schneidemühl, Dresden and other bases. Only the two 'super-Zeppelins' *LZ 113* and *LZ 120* were turned over to the navy for service in the Baltic.

For the Germans, a strategic aeroplane bombing force already existed in embryo, and required only improved and larger aircraft to have long range capability. In November, 1914, while the Western Front was still fluid, the Army High Command assembled some 36 aircraft, manned by the most experienced flight crews, at Ghistelles in Belgium under the camouflage designation 'Ostend Carrier Pigeon Section' *(Brieftauben Abteilung Ostende)*. The mission, however, was strategic bombing raids on England, as soon as the German armies should have captured Calais. While awaiting this development, the *BAO* practised with attacks on Dunkirk, Nieuport, Furnes and La Panne. When it became clear that Calais would not be available, the *BAO* was transferred early in 1915 to the Eastern Front. In any case, it would have accomplished little against England, for most of its aircraft were Aviatik B Is, unarmed

two-seaters with 100 hp engines and able to carry only a few small bombs. For the next year and a half the *BAO* and a companion unit, the *Brieftauben Abteilung Metz*, served as a mobile tactical bombing force, the fact that the entire unit was housed in railway trains making it easy to switch them from one front to another.

Following the Battle of the Somme, the *BAO*, now renamed *Kampfgeschwader 1* (Battle Wing 1), at last received some big bombers—the twin-engined AEG G III— and left for Bulgaria to participate in the Rumanian campaign. Before its departure, however, as a result of a decision of Hoeppner's, it released three of its six squadrons, or *Staffeln*, to form the nucleus of *Kampfgeschwader 3*. Sent back to Belgium, the new wing trained and waited for the delivery of suitable aircraft—the famous Gothas— to commence operations against England.

Whereas Germany's military leaders had early appreciated the value of strategic bombing attacks on the Allies' industrial facilities and transportation system, French and British military men saw the bombing aeroplane as an extension of the artillery in the immediate zone of combat. Until forced to follow the German example, the Allied air forces carried out only sporadic strategic attacks under the influence of certain imaginative leaders who in the end were unable to prevail against the military system. This explains why the French, the first in the air with a strategic bombing plan, abandoned their first effort when the war was only a year old. But during the autumn of 1916 the Allies

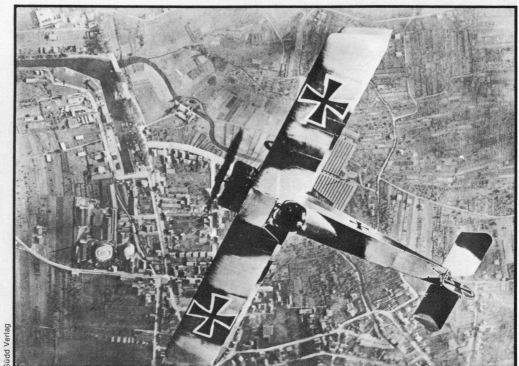

Top right: Photographed from directly above, a Fokker D II fighter on the way to the front. *Right:* The pilot of the RNAS No 3 Wing Sopwith 1½-Strutter poses beside his aircraft before raiding into Germany. *Below:* The wreckage of the *L 33*. Badly damaged by shell fire while raiding London on September 12/13, *L 33* limped out into the Essex countryside where her commander brought her down and set her on fire. The crew, marching to the sea to find a boat, were 'taken in charge' by a special constable

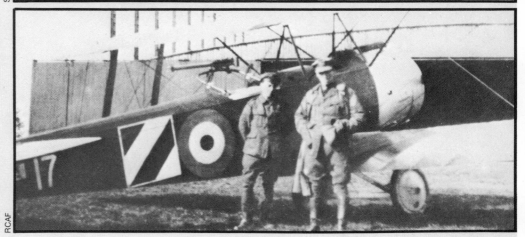

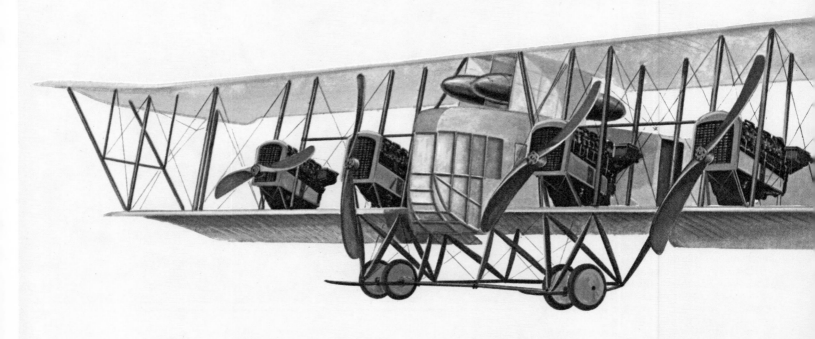

Above: The world's first four-engined bomber, the Russian **Sikorsky RBVZ *Ilya Mouromets* (IM-G1).** *Engines:* Sunbeam Cossacks, 170 hp each. *Armament:* five .303-inch Lewis guns and up to 1,500 lbs of bombs. *Speed:* 74 mph. *Endurance:* six hours. *Ceiling:* 14,100 feet. *Weight empty/loaded:* 8,378/12,125 lbs. *Span:* 113.19 feet. *Length:* 55.77 feet. *Below:* Britain's first effective bomber/fighter-bomber, the **Sopwith 1½-Strutter,** with forward and rearward firing machine guns. It was also the first British aircraft to have a variable incidence tailplane and air brakes—hinged on the inboard portions of the rear spars of the lower wings. *Engine:* Clerget rotary, 130 hp. *Armament:* one .303-inch Vickers and one .303-inch Lewis gun plus up to 224 lbs of bombs. *Speed:* 100 mph at 6,500 feet. *Endurance:* 4 hours.

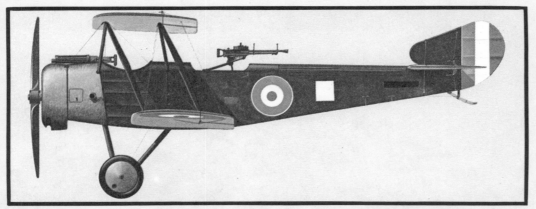

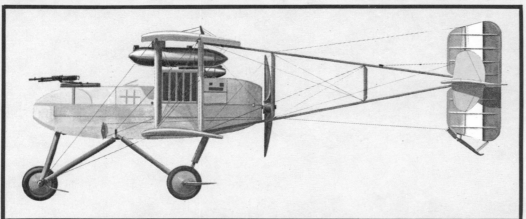

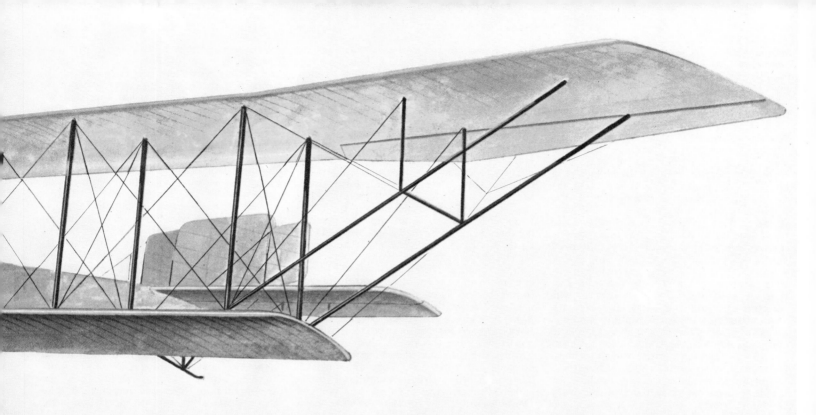

Ceiling: 15,000 feet. Weight empty/loaded: 1,305/2,150 lbs. Span: 33 feet 6 inches. Length: 25 feet. Bottom left: The French **Breguet-Michelin 4** bomber. Engine: 220-hp Renault inline. Armament: one 7.62-mm Hotchkiss machine gun and up to 640 lbs of bombs. Speed: 84 mph at sea level. Span: 61 feet 9 inches. Left centre: RFC uniforms, 1916. On the left is a pilot wearing typical flying clothing, and on the right a private. Below: An early German fighter, the **AEG G III**. Engines: Mercedes D IV, 220 hp. Armament: two 7.92-mm Parabellum machine guns plus up to 660 lbs of bombs. Speed: 99 mph at sea level. Range: 450 miles. Ceiling: 13,100 feet. Weight empty/loaded: 4,268/6,633 lbs. Span: 60 feet 6 inches. Length: 30 feet 2¼ inches. The type was too slow and ponderous

staged a series of joint strategic bombing operations which culminated in a spectacular large-scale attack on October 12 on the *Mauser Waffenfabrik* at Oberndorf, which was the chief supplier of rifles for the German army.

A new weapon

The initiative for this operation came from the British Admiralty, which is said to have decided early in 1916 to mount a bombing campaign against the steel industry in the Saar to interfere with the production of raw materials for U-Boats. Captain W. L. Elder, RN, was ordered to reactivate No 3 Wing RNAS, and since he had recently procured several hundred volunteers for naval flight training during a tour of Canada, he was instructed to use these Canadian trainees in his organisation. A new and advanced aircraft was selected to equip the wing—the Sopwith 1½ Strutter, a two-seater biplane powered by the 110 hp Clerget rotary engine, and equipped for the first time with a synchronised Vickers gun firing forward through the propeller, together with a Lewis on a revolving mount handled by the rear observer. Against contemporary German aircraft this was a formidable weapon. The majority of the Sopwiths of No 3 Wing were delivered, however, as single seaters, with cells for four 56-pound bombs taking the place of the observer's cockpit. The 49 aircraft on the establishment of the wing were intended to operate in flights of seven, and in each flight the five lead aircraft were to be single seater bombers, while the two in the rear would be two seaters acting as fighter escorts. Since they had fuel for four hours, the same as the bombers, they could accompany the latter all the way to the target and back.

The French, on their part, withdrew the *4ème Groupe de Bombardement* under *Capitaine* Happe from army control and sent them to a base at Luxeuil in the Vosges, some 65 miles south of Malzéville. Unfortunately the equipment of Happe's three squadrons was little better than the Voisins flown by de Goÿs a year earlier. Two squadrons were again of Farman 42s, two-seater pushers, underpowered with only 130 hp engines, and possessing a top speed of about 85 mph. The third squadron, equipped with Breguet-Michelin 4 bombers, was even slower despite having 220 hp engines. Both types were completely defenceless against attack from the rear. The French, impressed with the performance of the new Sopwith 1½ Strutters, had undertaken to manufacture them under licence, and 15 of the fighter version were available by October 1.

The French bomber *escadrilles* started warming up with an attack on Karlsruhe on June 22, which killed 120 civilians and injured 150. The British 3rd Wing's build-up was slow, many of its aircraft being handed over to the RFC to replace losses in the Somme fighting. Three Sopwith bombers joined six French in an attack on Mülheim on July 30, but no further missions were attempted until the attack on Oberndorf. Even then, No 3 Wing had only seven Sopwith fighters and 13 bombers on hand, and had to take over six Breguets from the French.

The Oberndorf mission made unusual demands on the untried Canadian pilots of No 3 Wing. Over 100 miles east of Luxeuil, beyond the Rhine, then across the Black Forest to the valley of the Neckar, the round trip would take 2½ hours for the Sopwiths, and longer for the slow French pushers. Furthermore, the Germans, after repeated Allied attacks on their cities, had set up anti-aircraft guns and fighter formations. One of these units was at Colmar, half-way between Luxeuil and Oberndorf on the direct route, and another was at Habsheim, a few miles south of Colmar.

The squadrons were late in getting away, the first, one of the Farman formations, taking off at 1315 hours. There followed the second Farman squadron, then the French Breguets. Escorting the French bombers were 12 French Sopwiths and four agile Nieuport 17 fighters of the newly formed *Escadrille Américaine*, not yet renamed the *Escadrille Lafayette*. The short-ranged Nieuports could not go all the way to the target. Next came the British aircraft—13 Sopwith bombers, seven Sopwith fighters and six Breguets. Several turned back for various reasons before reaching the lines, with the result that only nine French aircraft reached and bombed Oberndorf, as did nine of the British Sopwiths. The six English Breguets deviated to the south after crossing the lines and bombed Donaueschingen by mistake for Oberndorf.

The German fighters had been alerted by ground observers at the front, and while the first squadron of Farmans got to the target and back, the fighters—Fokker E III monoplanes and D II biplanes, and twin-boomed Ago C I pushers—had a field day with the succeeding formations. The leader of the second Farman squadron was shot down and killed with his observer near Colmar; another machine was shot down a few miles farther into Germany. Of the French Breguets, four never made it home. Two were damaged and forced down by German fighters, and a third was shot down in flames *en route* to the target, while another was shot down with the crew dead *en route* home. The cumbersome British Breguets also had their losses, one being brought down by anti-aircraft fire and one by a German fighter, both crews being captured. Remarkably, only one Sopwith of the total of 32 participating was lost over the German lines—an RNAS bomber forced down on Freiburg aerodrome with its pilot shot through the neck. The *Escadrille Américaine* lost one of its original members when Norman Prince struck a power line landing at dusk and was fatally injured. Three of the four Nieuport pilots claimed victories over German aircraft, and three more were claimed by the other escorts. The Germans denied any losses.

Senior officers at the time realised that the raid was a failure, in that a disproportionately small fraction of the force committed actually bombed the target. The Germans in Oberndorf counted only 153 bombs from 12 attacking aircraft. Several buildings in the rifle works were badly damaged and work was partially disrupted for two days. Numerous buildings in town were destroyed or damaged; five people were killed, two of them prisoners of war. The French discontinued daylight raids with the vulnerable and clumsy Farman and Breguet pushers, though continuing to bomb with them at night. The 3rd Wing made a few more attacks on Hagendingen, Volkingen and Dillingen with small numbers of aircraft. By early 1917 the British bombing wing was disbanded and its pilots were transferred to single-seater fighter squadrons on the British front in Northern France. The *4ème Groupe de Bombardement* also reverted to tactical bombing in support of the armies.

Italy, which declared war on Austria-Hungary on May 24, 1915, already had a three-engined bomber prototype of native design, the Caproni 32. Under development since early 1914, this machine had three 100 hp Fiat engines and a crew of three. The first bombing unit equipped with this aircraft assembled at Pordenone, and made their first raid on August 20, 1915. Improved Caproni bombers with higher-powered engines were developed, including the huge Ca 40 triplane, with a span of 98 feet and a bomb load of 3,000 pounds, which appeared in 1916. The Caproni squadrons however did not constitute a strategic bombing force in the sense that they attacked distant industrial centres of the Central Powers. Most of their bombing was in the Austrian Army's back areas and on cities around the head of the Adriatic—Trieste, Durazzo, Ljubljana.

Last comes the Russian contribution to stragetic air warfare—the first four-engined aircraft in the world. This, the dream of Igor Sikorsky and named 'The Grand', made its first flight on May 13, 1913. A larger version named 'Ilya Mourometz', with a span of 102 feet and four Argus 100 hp engines, was completed in January 1914 and on February 11 carried 16 passengers aloft for five hours. The Russo-Baltic Wagon Works received contracts for a military version after war broke out, and in December 1914 the 'Squadron of Flying Ships' was set up to operate the big bombers. Based at Jablonna in Eastern Poland, an 'Ilya Mourometz' made the first raid on February 15, 1915, with 600 pounds of bombs. Seventy-three were built altogether, the 'C' type being the first to have a gunner's cockpit at the rear of the fuselage behind the tail. Strongly built and defended, the Russian bombers were tough opponents and only one was shot down. Individual flights lasted up to 7½ hours.

1916 had witnessed the eclipse of the airship as a strategic weapon and the tentative introduction of the aeroplane as its successor in this rôle. Its introduction had not progressed very smoothly, but what completely new weapon has ever entered service with no teething troubles at all, technical or operational? But the main lessons had been learnt, and the advocates of the strategic bomber looked forward into the future with high hopes.

Further Reading
Cross and Cockade Journal Volume 4 No 1, Volume 4 No 2 and Volume 5 No 4
Cuneo, J. R., *The Air Weapon 1914-1916* (Harrisburg, Pa: Military Service Publishing 1947)
Gladisch, W., *Der Krieg in der Nordsee Band VI* (Berlin: E. S. Mittler & Sohn 1937)
Hoeppner, E. von, *Deutschlands Krieg in der Luft* (Leipzig: Hase & Koehler 1921)
Jones, H. A., *The War in the Air Volume III* (OUP 1931)
Neumann, G. P. (ed.), *Die deutschen Luftstreitkräfte im Weltkrieg* (Berlin: E. S. Mittler & Sohn 1920)
Robinson, D. H., *The Zeppelin in Combat* (Foulis 1962)
Sikorsky, I., *The Story of the Winged S* (New York: Dodd, Mead & Co. 1943)

Spring 1917: the twilight of the Zeppelin and dawn of the strategic bomber. First came the Gothas, but these were soon followed by the German 'Giants' — none of which was ever shot down over England. Their aim was strategic, but directed more against morale than military targets. The losses they incurred in combat and in accidents far exceeded any moral effect, however. *Dr Douglas Robinson. Below: A German Intelligence photograph of the July 17 raid. Note St Paul's Cathedral and the plume of smoke (marked '15') rising from the Central Telegraph Office*

STRATEGIC BOMBING

By January 1917, the reign of the Zeppelin as a strategic bomber was over. Though sporadic attacks continued on the north of England, the Zeppelin only appeared once more over London during the war, and then by accident. In its place there came the first unit of large bombing aeroplanes especially organised by the Germans to bomb London by day. Here was foreshadowed the burning of Hamburg and Dresden, and the holocausts of Hiroshima and Nagasaki. The immediate consequences also were far-reaching: the British responses to the pioneering efforts of the 36 Gothas of *BOGOHL 3* were the formation of the Royal Air Force and the doctrine of strategic bombing of civilian centres which remains with us today, more than 50 years later.

The *England Geschwader* (England Squadron) was under the direct control of the *Oberste Heeresleitung* (OHL), or Supreme Command of the German Army. The chief aim, as set forth by General Ludendorff, was to score a propaganda success which would intensify the effect on the British population of the economic strangulation by the U-Boat blockade. Conceivably, bombs in the heart of London could so arouse the English population that the government might be forced out of office and replaced by one that would sue for peace. Disruption of war industry, of communications between London and the coast and of transportation across the Channel were secondary objectives. Lastly, it was hoped that the activities of the England Squadron would force the withdrawal from the Western Front of men and weapons out of all proportion to the German forces engaged. As will be seen, the last objective was more than realised, while the initial daylight attacks on London at least had a seriously disturbing effect on home front morale.

As related earlier, the German army had proposed the bombing of England as early as the autumn of 1914, but the lack of suitable long range aircraft had rendered this goal unattainable then and later. In the year 1916, however, the aircraft department of the *Gothaer Waggonfabrik AG,* builders of railway rolling stock, produced in the G II and G III twin-engine bombers, machines with the range sufficient to attack southern England from Belgian bases. In the autumn of 1916 it was the intention of General Ernst von Hoeppner, commanding the German *Luftstreitkräfte,* to commence attacks on London with 30 of these aircraft by February 1, 1917. In the event, the twin-engine bombers were not ready until May 1917, but preparations and training for the attack on London proceeded through the winter and spring of 1917. *Bombing Wing 3,* consisting of the three *Staffeln* (flights) *1, 4* and *6,* at this time operating single-engined C-type machines, had been concentrated at Ghistelles near Ostend. In order to improve their over-water navigation, their personnel were attached to naval air stations on the islands of Heligoland and Sylt. In mid-March the wing was renamed *Kampfgeschwader 3 OHL* or *Bombing Wing 3 of the Supreme Command,* while the *Staffeln* were renumbered *13, 14* and *15.* The name *England Geschwader* was, however, the favourite colloquial designation.

Also in March the first Gothas of the series production type, the G IV, were delivered and training with them commenced. These aircraft were destined to become a household word on the other side of the Channel. The power plant was a pair of Mercedes 260 hp D IVa six cylinder inline water-cooled engines. The biplane wings, spanning 77 feet 9¼ inches, comprised a lower wing centre section covered with plywood, on which were mounted the two engines driving pusher propellers, outboard lower panels covered with fabric and a pair of fabric-covered upper wings meeting on the centreline, the whole stoutly braced with steel tube struts and wire. The fuselage, some 35 feet long, was built on spruce longerons and spacers, plywood-skinned. Right forward, in a cockpit circled by a gun ring mounting a single 7.62-mm Parabellum machine gun, rode the aircraft commander (not a pilot), who also acted as bombardier. Much of the space in his cockpit was taken up by the Görz precision bomb sight with a telescopic tube over three feet long. A few feet to the rear sat the pilot on the port side of a roomy cockpit. Usually he was an officer inferior in rank to the aircraft commander; sometimes he was an NCO. Abaft the wings, and separated from his fellow crew members by the main fuel tanks, which filled the entire fuselage, was the rear gunner, always an NCO, armed with a Parabellum on a ring mount. This did not cover the traditional 'blind spot' behind and beneath the tail, from where a skilled fighter pilot could attack at close range without fear of retaliation. Hence, it was a sensation when the British discovered that the rear gunner could shoot downward under the tail through a plywood tunnel leading down and aft from the rear cockpit. The bombs were carried horizontally under the fuselage and centre section. The usual bomb load by day was 660 pounds; at night, when the Gothas flew at lower altitudes, 1,100 pounds could be carried.

As so often happens, the early products of the parent company had the best performance; later 'improvements', modifications and overloading with equipment lowered the original performance, particularly rate of climb and ceiling. The contract called for Gotha G IV to reach 18,000 feet in one hour with full load; actually, maximum altitude in the first raid on England was 16,700 feet, and as low as 12,500 in later daylight raids. Cruising speed was about 80 mph, 'much too little'. Manoeuvrability was considered excellent for so large an aircraft, and an asset in defeating the attacks of Allied fighters. On the other hand, light construction and poor stability with empty tanks caused many landing accidents, the operational losses throughout the campaign (37) exceeding the combat losses (24).

Along with the first of the big bombers there arrived in March the commanding officer of *KAGOHL 3, Hauptmann* Ernst Brandenburg, destined to lead the wing in its earliest triumphs, and to leave his mark on the personnel. An observer (most German pilots in the two-seater squadrons were NCOs), he had had no flight training, but it was for him to determine the doctrine, tactics and operational procedures for the first strategic bombing squadrons. He planned to attack London by day, to ensure precision bombing of specific targets, and in close formation to exploit the massed defensive firepower of his aircraft against British fighters. As the G IV's arrived, he put his crews to work in training flights with war loads, at first singly, then in formation.

Many other operational problems had to be anticipated and provided for at this time. Good weather over England was all-important to the success of the bombing attacks, while bad weather at the bases on return, considering that the Gothas had no radio or blind flying instruments, could lead to disaster. Although the most able meteorologists in Germany were assigned to the *England Geschwader,* their job was made almost impossible by the lack of necessary data. Typically, the weather over north-west Europe is made in the vastness of the North Atlantic, and sweeps in over the British Isles before arriving on the coast of Belgium; and weather data in England was of course classified information.

Navigation without sophisticated radio tracking equipment, such as exists today, was a matter of dead reckoning, in which the evaluation of wind direction and velocity was all important. In practice, the navigator-observer attempted to establish the winds at altitude during the climb-out from the bases to the coast, determining from landmarks below the amount of drift and retardation or acceleration of the bomber's progress over the ground as a result of the wind. He then gave his pilot a compass heading to hold in order to make good the course for England, and an estimated time of arrival. Over England navigation was visual from landmarks and the map, the River Thames and the sprawling mass of London being unmistakable by day. At night, as with the Zeppelin crews, errors were frequent.

The equipment of each day bomber included compressed oxygen in cylinders, each crew member using a pipe stem mouthpiece rather than a mask. Later this was replaced by liquid air in insulated flasks. No doctrine on the use of oxygen existed, and flight crews preferred to do without it even though the day raids were made well above 12,000 feet, the altitude at which nowadays its use is obligatory. Personal equipment included fur-lined boots, coat and gloves, helmet and goggles, but no parachutes.

The spectre of drowning in the North Sea in case of engine failure over water was always with the flight crews. Carrier pigeons were carried with which to send off distress messages, and the bomber itself was advertised as being able to float on the water for at least eight hours, as it had watertight compartments in its plywood fuselage. This may be doubted; but the claim undoubtedly improved morale.

Objective evaluation of the results of raids was difficult for the Germans, and there was a tendency to exaggeration and wishful thinking not unknown in later bombing operations. The crews' attack reports were highly coloured and overestimated the degree of destruction of military targets, particularly at night. Newspaper reports, as a result of strict British censorship, provided no information of operational value. There was a mass of Intelligence forthcoming from German agents residing in London, and from neutral travellers passing back and forth between London and Holland or the Scandinavian countries. These gentlemen seem to have been unable to resist the temptation (probably financial) to tell any German agent what he wanted to hear, for their reports of military damage in particular were wildly exaggerated, if not completely fabricated.

Finally, towards mid-May, the three *Staffeln* were at last fully equipped with six Gothas each. These were assigned to fields around Ghent as follows: *Staffeln 13* and *14* at St Denis Westrem and *Staffel 15* and the headquarters unit at Gontrode. In June,

Staffel 16 was added at Gontrode, and in July, *Staffeln 17* and *18* at Mariakerke.

With about 25 Gothas available in the three *Staffeln,* plus his headquarters aircraft, Brandenburg was ready for his first attempt on England. But the initial attack, on May 25, 1917, failed to reach London. Twenty-three Gothas set out from the bases around Ghent. One force-landed at Thielt, another turned back over the North Sea with a failing starboard engine. The remaining 21 came inland north of the River Crouch, but at Gravesend towering clouds barred the way to the capital. Disappointed, Brandenburg turned south, crossing Kent to the Channel at Hythe. Once more changing course to the east, the formation salvoed its bombs on the hapless coastal resort of Folkestone, then passed close to Dover on its way back to Belgium.

While British Intelligence might have been expected to be well informed about the *England Geschwader,* with its aerodromes set down among a hostile population, responsible commands had not been alerted to the imminence of daylight aeroplane attacks in force. With no warning system, the 74 aircraft which rose in pursuit from English aerodromes with no advance notice had to climb after a retreating opponent and attacked without co-ordination or concentration. None of them achieved any success, but the Germans lost one Gotha over the sea, possibly to Royal Naval Air Service pilots from Dunkirk. Another crashed near Bruges on the return flight.

The Gothas had with one blow killed and wounded more English civilians than in any one Zeppelin raid of the war. There were 95 dead and 195 wounded: the highest concentration of casualties was in Folkestone, where most of the bombs fell on a busy street lined with shops. There was much anger and resentment in Folkestone, but in London, which had been spared because of the weather, the reaction to the death and destruction in 'a coastal town to the south-east' was more one of curiosity.

Nor did Londoners take alarm from the second Gotha onslaught. On the evening of June 5, 22 of the big bombers appeared over Sheerness. In a five-minute attack eight soldiers and three civilians were killed, and 25 soldiers and nine civilians injured. The local anti-aircraft guns damaged one of the raiders, which ditched in the Thames off Barton's Point. Sixty-six British aircraft took off; only five got within range of the German formation, and none scored successes. Newspapers however claimed that ten out of 20 bombers had been destroyed. Londoners were understandably complacent.

Brandenburg and his crews now felt ready to tackle London, and after anxiously awaiting the right weather, they finally received the signal from their meteorologist on June 13. Twenty bombers took off; their number, however, steadily decreased as they approached England. Two turned back soon after take-off with engine trouble, and a third aborted near the English coast and dropped its bombs on Margate before heading home. Three more left the formation over the English coast, one bombing Shoeburyness and another dropping its cargo on Greenwich. Only 14 remained, in a loose diamond formation which appeared over London about 1130 hours. Attacking from 15,000 feet, they were clearly visible in the clear air, but many of the civilian spectators on the streets of the capital took them to be British.

A few aircraft released their bombs on the way in – five missiles falling in East Ham. These killed eight people and caused some damage. Fifteen more fell along the north side of the river in Blackwall, Poplar and Limehouse. One of these, a 110-pounder, caused the first major tragedy of the raid. Descending on the Upper North Street School, Poplar, it exploded in a crowded classroom, killing 18 small children and injuring 30 more, together with four adults.

Brandenburg's intention was to bomb the heart of the city, whose large buildings – St Paul's Cathedral, Tower Bridge, the Tower itself and others – stood out below as on a relief map. Liverpool Street Station and the surrounding area were the main target. At 1140 hours the lead aircraft fired a white flare. The Gothas scattered to bomb individual targets, and within two minutes, 72 bombs crashed down within a radius of a mile of Liverpool Street Station. Only three hit the station, but these, falling on and around a loading passenger train, killed 16 people and injured 15. Other bombs fell close to Fenchurch Street Station, killing 19 people and injuring 14 in a building at No 65 Fenchurch Street, while 13 were killed and 11 injured by another bomb landing in Central Street, Finsbury. The Royal Mint was struck and damaged. The formation then divided, some dropping bombs in Southwark, others going north to Dalston. Altogether the casualties reached the shocking total of 162 dead and 432 injured – higher than necessary because many people, not realising the aircraft were German, had failed to seek cover.

The defenders again replied bravely but without co-ordination, while the Gothas, once more flying in tight formation as they withdrew, gave better than they got. A Bristol Fighter, caught in the crossfire of many Parabellums, was driven off with the observer mortally wounded. The British airmen made no claims, and none of the Gothas was lost over England or in landing.

Triumph and disaster

For the Germans it was a triumph loudly proclaimed the length and breadth of the *Reich*. 'According to our observation,' reported Brandenburg, 'a station in the City, and a Thames bridge, probably Tower Bridge, were hit. Of all our bombs it can be said that the majority fell among the Docks, and among the city warehouses.' The doughty *Hauptmann* was summoned to Supreme Headquarters to receive Germany's highest decoration, the *Ordre Pour le Mérite*. This nearly proved his undoing, for on departure from Kreuznach, his two-seater Albatros crashed, killing the pilot and sending the leader of the *England Geschwader* to hospital for many months.

For Londoners, here at last was a new menace which could not be dismissed lightly – a formation of large German aircraft free to circle at leisure over the capital in broad daylight, distributing their lethal loads where they desired. The home defence squadrons, intended to attack Zeppelins, were equipped with slow, stable variants of the BE 2c observation aircraft – quite incapable of climbing up to and pursuing the Gothas or of facing their heavy defensive armament. Over the objections of Sir Douglas Haig, his best fighter squadron, No. 56, equipped with SE 5's, was brought back to Bekesbourne in Kent, while No 66 Squadron, with Sopwith Pups, was relocated at Calais. More long range measures contemplated doubling the Royal Flying Corps, and the possibility of retaliatory raids across the Western Front against Mannheim and other German cities.

The successor of the popular Brandenburg was *Hauptmann* Rudolf Kleine, an experienced airman who, unlike other senior officers of *KAGOHL 3,* was a qualified military pilot. His first attempt against England was on July 4, when 25 Gothas started for Harwich, though only 18 made it to the target. The Royal Naval Air Station at Felixstowe was considerably damaged. Since the attackers did not come inland, the aircraft based in England made no interceptions, but some Camels from Dunkirk attacked the homeward-bound raiders and claimed – erroneously – to have shot one down in flames.

The next day No 56 Squadron returned to France.

On July 7 (though not in consequence of this event) the *England Geschwader* was back for a second daylight blow against London. Twenty-four Gothas set out; two turned back with engine failure, but one first succeeded in dropping three bombs on Margate, where three were killed and three wounded. The remaining 22 Gothas came inland north of the Crouch, and proceeded to the northwest of London, thence turning to cross the capital against the wind. Their bombs, falling in the City and the East End, caused some spectacular damage, including a smoky fire visible for miles which destroyed a temporary shelter on the roof of the General Post Office in St Martin's-le-Grand; and very severe injury to Ironmongers' Hall in Fenchurch Street, caused by a bomb which detonated inside the enclosed court. Many bombs fell in the vicinity of Cannon Street Station without striking the terminal itself. Casualties were much lower than in the June 13 raid, but still totalled 54 killed and 190 injured.

Once again the unco-ordinated and impromptu attacks of isolated aircraft ascending from home defence and training stations were ineffective. Seventy-eight RFC and 17 RNAS machines ascended, including 30 of the new Camel fighters, but the only success was won by an intrepid pair in a slow Armstrong-Whitworth two seater who brought down a straggler in the sea off the North Foreland. Two young RFC pilots, one from a training squadron, were shot dead in the air when they made headlong attacks single handed on the tight German formation. On the other hand, Kleine lost four more of the big bombers in crash landings in gusty winds at St Denis Westrem and Gontrode.

Despite the lower death and damage toll, the July 7 attack produced a far more intense reaction among the London public than the earlier raid of June 13. The first had been a surprise; the second seemed to prove that the Germans could come whenever they pleased and bomb at leisure, and nothing was going to stop them. There were riots in the East End in which the shops of foreigners, not always German, were smashed and looted. Angry questions were asked in Parliament, where Lloyd George, the Premier, astonished members and newspaper readers alike by admitting that 'complete protection in the air would never be secured'. The army in France, he insisted, must come first.

But public pressure for more defensive aircraft, and for reprisal raids against German cities, could not be resisted, and thus the menace of Kleine's 30-odd Gothas produced a far larger diversion of aircraft from the war effort in France. At the Cabinet meeting of July 11, it was resolved to set up a committee to examine the defence arrangements against raids and the air organisation generally and the higher direction of aerial operations. The work was done by the farsighted former Boer leader, Lieutenant-General Jan Christiaan Smuts, now a member of the War Cabinet.

His first report argued that the defence of London, the political and economic heart of the Empire, demanded 'exceptional measures'. He recommended that three home defence squadrons of modern single seater fighters be formed, a defensive anti-aircraft barrage system be developed to bar the Germans' path to London, and the entire 'London Air Defence Area' be placed under a single commander. This appointment was given on August 5, 1917, to an experienced airman brought home from France, Brigadier-General E. B. Ashmore.

Smuts' second report on the air organisation generally is not germane to the immediate subject, but since it called for the use of aviation after the German example as 'an independent means of war operations', with the Royal Flying Corps and Royal Naval Air Service amalgamated into a third and co-equal arm, it is evident what effects the two daylight raids on the capital had had on the astute military leader. 'Air supremacy may in the long run become as important a factor in the defence of the Empire as sea supremacy' – a prophetic vision for 1917, but one for which the Gothas had provided the inspiration. Unpopular with the conventional military and naval leaders, Smuts' second report was taken up by the politicians, egged on by agitation among their constituents in favour of forming a British air striking force. The result was the establishment of the RAF on April 1, 1918.

Rarely has a single event such as the July 7 daylight raid had such far reaching consequences. Yet Kleine had been greatly impressed by the strength of the London gun barrage and the aggressiveness of attacking British aircraft. Crews which had taken part in the June 13 raid warned that the defences had been greatly strengthened. Unacceptable losses seemed inevitable if daylight attacks continued on the capital. But Kleine was stubborn, and persisted with peripheral daylight raids with diminishing numbers of Gothas.

On July 22, 21 Gothas bombed Harwich and Felixstowe. Considerable damage was done at the naval air station at Felixstowe, with 13 killed and 26 injured – mostly service men. A hundred and twenty-one aircraft ascended from British aerodromes; but the Gothas had been over land so briefly that the former stood no chance of intercepting them.

Strong west winds delayed the next attack until August 12. The target was the British naval base at Chatham. Only 13 bombers departed the bases around Ghent; two turned back shortly with engine trouble. A third, experiencing engine trouble over the English coast, dropped four bombs on Margate from 12,000 feet and was lucky to make it back to the beach at Zeebrugge. Carried north by a stiff south-west wind, the remaining ten Gothas reached the coast near Felixstowe. From here the leader set course for Chatham. En route they passed over Rochford, where one of the three new fighter squadrons called for by Smuts – No 61, equipped with Sopwith Pups – was based. As bombs fell from the German formation, the Pups madly scrambled and gained altitude. The sky in fact seemed to be filling with unfriendly aircraft – 132 in all ascended this day – and the Gotha formation turned back, dropping its bombs on Southend, where 32 were killed and 46 wounded. A naval pilot shot down one of the fleeing bombers over the sea; four more were written off in crash landings.

Only 15 Gothas were serviceable on August 22 for the last daylight attack on England. Four dropped out with engine trouble before reaching the English coast at Margate. The remaining 11 were too few for effective self-defence. A gun barrage brought down one in flames near Margate; another spun into the sea after an attack by a naval fighter. Harried and hunted down the coast, the remaining black-crossed bombers hurriedly dropped 34 bombs on Ramsgate, where eight were killed and 12 injured. Some more bombs fell on Dover, where a fighter shot down another Gotha into the sea. Altogether, 137 aircraft ascended from English aerodromes, and had the Germans persisted in their advance inland, it is certain that few of them would have escaped. It was clear even to Kleine that the day bombers had been mastered by the defences, and a switch to night attacks was imperative.

The Gotha crews were given a hasty course in night flying, and arrangements were made to illuminate the runways at St Denis Westrem, Gontrode and Mariakerke with petrol flares and search-lights. Formation flying was of course out, and the big bombers would now fly individual courses to England by compass. Larger bomb loads could be carried as it was safe to fly at lower altitudes, and the rear gunner was often left at home. On the night of September 3, Kleine led four of the more experienced crews towards England, the target being the naval base at Chatham. Here 131 naval ratings were killed and 90 injured by a 110-pound bomb exploding among them as they slept in a crowded drill hall. The Gotha crews felt themselves protected by darkness against British guns and aircraft. But three officers of No 44 Squadron succeeded on this night in taking off and landing in their Camel fighters, though they saw nothing of the raiders. Immediately all squadrons commenced training in night flying.

Encouraged by this initial success, Kleine sent out 11 bombers manned by volunteers on the following night, September 4. Two turned back with motor trouble; one fell in the sea off Sheerness, possibly a victim of the guns. The handful of Gothas kept Londoners awake from 11 pm to 1 am as they crossed the capital singly, scattering their bombs. It was in this raid that a bomb on the Embankment scarred Cleopatra's Needle and left holes in one of the bronze sphinxes, visible to this day. The British believed that 26 bombers had attacked London; actually only five had gone the whole distance. Casualties were correspondingly light – 19 dead, 71 injured. Eighteen British aircraft ascended, but only two caught brief glimpses of the Gothas, which by now were painted in dark mottled camouflage.

In the ensuing night raids at the end of the month, the Gothas were joined by the remarkable and little known *Riesen* (Giant) aircraft, which after three years of experiment were at last ready for operational testing on the Western Front. Several large German industrial firms had taken contracts to build these huge machines, intended to supplement the Zeppelin as a long-range strategic bomber, but only the products of the Zeppelin Werke at Staaken near Berlin saw action against England. In August 1917 *Riesenflugzeugabteilung 501*, commanded by *Hauptmann* Richard von Bentivegni, arrived at St Denis Westrem; it reported to the newly renamed BOGOHL 3, the *England Geschwader*, and was expected to co-ordinate its operations with Kleine's Gothas. The six aircraft of *Rfa 501* were Staaken R VI's, the largest aircraft to fly over England in two world wars. Their huge wire-braced biplane wings measured 138 feet 5½ inches across. Between the wings were two nacelles, each housing two Maybach or Mercedes engines of 260 hp driving tractor and pusher propellers. In each nacelle, between the engines, was a cockpit for a mechanic, who was expected to repair breakdowns in flight.

The massive enclosed fuselage measured 72 feet 6 inches in length. Right forward was an open observer's cockpit with bomb sight and gun ring. Just to the rear was a glassed-in cabin occupied by the two pilots and the aircraft commander. Instruments included a practical artificial horizon. Unlike the Gothas, the Giants had a radio transmitter and receiver for Morse code, and parachutes for the crew. Abaft the wings was a gunner's cockpit where one or two machine gunners handled two upper guns and a lower one firing under the tail. 660 gallons of fuel were carried in the tanks in the fuselage. Racks accommodated 18 220-pound bombs. Sometimes three 660-pound bombs were carried, and occasionally a single monster 2,200-pounder.

Sixteen Gothas led the offensive against London opening on September 24; three reached the capital. A bomb landing in front of the Bedford Hotel in Southampton Row killed 13 people and injured 26. More bombs fell in Dover. One bomber crash landed at its base. Thirty English aircraft ascended but did not encounter the Germans. On the night of September 25, out of 15 Gothas only one reached London; more damage was done by three which bombed Camberwell and Bermondsey. One British pilot found and fired on a Gotha, pursuing it for ten minutes; the Germans admitted one aircraft missing.

For the first time, two of *Rfa 501's* Giant bombers joined the Gothas against England on the night of September 28. Twenty-five of BOGOHL 3's aircraft set out, but the night sky over the North Sea was full of towering clouds. On this account, 15 Gothas turned back, plus one more due to engine trouble. The remainder flew a short distance inland, scattering their bombs in poor visibility on Essex and Kent. Three were claimed by anti-aircraft gunners along the Kentish coast; in fact, the Germans had three Gothas missing, while six more crashed on landing at the bases in Belgium. Nor did the two Giants bomb London, though they succeeded in reaching England, and received the congratulations of General von Hoeppner.

On the next night, September 29, Kleine, for various reasons, was able to send out only seven Gothas, which were joined by three Giants. Three Gothas and one Giant (probably Bentivegni

himself in *R 39*) reached London, and their bombs damaged Waterloo Station. One Giant bombed Sheerness and bombs fell in various places in Kent. One Gotha was shot down in flames by anti-aircraft gunners at Dover. This was the last raid by the Giants for more than two months, but they had already shown several advantages over the Gothas—greater bomb carrying capacity, greater reliability as a result of having four or more power plants, superior navigation due to being fitted with radio and gyro instruments for blind flying and, as the future would show, greater resistance to attack. No Giant was ever brought down over England.

September 30 saw 11 Gothas dispatched to London. The air crews thought they had hit the Admiralty, warehouses on the docksides and the City, but most of the damage was to houses in East London. By now, however, Kleine's handful of aircraft were achieving a significant effect on morale, totally disrupting the nightly repose of millions of Londoners, many of whom were spending the night in the Underground. Further, a recent innovation by General Ashmore—blind barrage firing—was causing an enormous expenditure of shells, fragments of which caused nearly as much damage as the bombs.

Although everyone else, including Britain's leaders, had written off the Zeppelin as a bombing weapon, the indomitable Leader of Airships, *Korvettenkapitän* Strasser, still believed in them—as did his chief, Admiral Scheer. At a conference in Berlin on January 26, 1917, Strasser proposed that the Zeppelins be lightened to attain altitudes of 16,500 feet or more with war load, and with ships built to these specifications, raids continued during this period. London was not attacked, though still ordered as a target; in practice, the raiders dropped their bombs ineffectively in the eastern counties and the Midlands. Strasser recognised that little material result could be expected, but pleaded that the raids be continued for their morale effects and to tie down defending guns and aircraft in the Midlands and the North, which the Gothas and Giants could not reach. The high altitude operations brought new problems—loss of engine power as a result of the thin air at altitude, and winds which at times carried the big airships incontinently over France—together with much misery for their crews. Oxygen was carried, but not used steadily as it should have been, while the men suffered terribly from cold, frostbite, fatigue and exposure. One painful loss occurred over England when on the night of June 16, 1917, the new *L 48* was shot down in flames over Suffolk by an RFC pilot. Among those lost was Strasser's deputy, *Korvettenkapitän* Viktor Schütze. A frozen compass had led his flagship north inside the coast as dawn was breaking, while her commander believed he was already over the sea.

As for the Allies, this period saw only the petering-out of the strategic bombing effort from Luxeuil. Operations early in 1917 were hampered by bitter winter weather. Not until January 23 did ten naval Sopwiths bomb blast furnaces at Burbach. There was one small raid in February, and two in March, again on Burbach. A single Handley Page 0/100 joined the wing in April and made a few night attacks. On April 14, 21 British and French bombers, escorted by 15 fighters, made a day raid on Freiburg im Breisgau, dropping leaflets announcing that it was in reprisal for German submarine attacks on hospital ships. This was the swan song of the naval strategic bombing squadrons, which were being broken up and sent north to replace the RFC's heavy losses in the Battle of Arras. A far louder cry for reprisals arose after the daylight Gotha attacks on London, but the activities of the 41st Wing, established in October for reprisal bombing of German cities, belong to the next chapter.

Further Reading

Aschoff, Walter, *Londonflüge 1917* (Potsdam: Ludwig Voggenreiter Verlag, 1940)
Bülow, Hilmer von, *Die Angriffe des Bombengeschwader 3 auf England* (in *die Luftwacht,* 1927)
Fredette, Raymond, *The Sky On Fire* (New York: Holt, Rinehart & Winston, 1966)
Haddow, G. W., and Grosz, Peter, *The German Giants* (Putnam 1962)
Jones, H. A., *The War In The Air Vols V and VI* (OUP 1935 and 1937)
Morison, Frank, *War on Great Cities* (Faber & Faber 1937)

Above: The engineer's compartment in the port engine nacelle of a Staaken R IV. One of the many remarkable requirements for the German 'R' types was that the engines had to be serviceable in flight. *Below:* German bombs. These are of the type designed by the Test Establishment and Workshop of Aviation Troops to replace the earlier Carbonit type

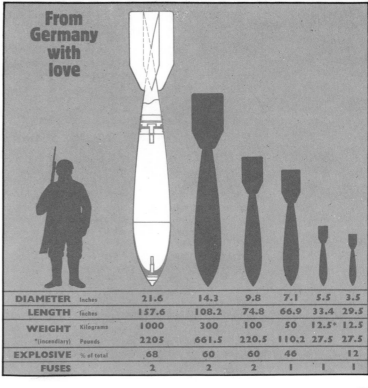

From Germany with love

DIAMETER	Inches	21.6	14.3	9.8	7.1	5.5	3.5
LENGTH	Inches	157.6	108.2	74.8	66.9	33.4	29.5
WEIGHT	Kilograms	1000	300	100	50	12.5*	12.5
*(incendiary)	Pounds	2205	661.5	220.5	110.2	27.5	27.5
EXPLOSIVE	% of total	68	60	60	46		12
FUSES		2	2	2	1	1	1

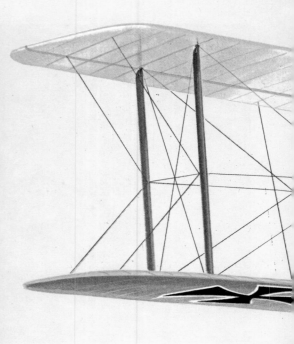

Right: A precarious position: the port upper wing gunner of a Staaken R IV *en route* to his post. The pusher propeller of the port nacelle is just in front of him. Gun positions on the upper wings were common features on the Giants as they gave excellent fields of fire.
Below: Bombing up a Gotha G V, a development of the G IV which saw service in 1918. *Far right bottom:* The major daylight Gotha raids over England

Above: The **Zeppelin Staaken R VI**. *Engines:* Four Maybach Mb IVa (245 hp) or Mercedes D IVa (260 hp) inlines. *Armament:* Up to 4,400 lbs of bombs over very short distances (increased range meant more fuel and therefore less bomb-load) and up to four Lewis or Parabellum machine guns. *Speed:* 84 mph. *Climb:* 9,843 feet in 43 minutes (with Mb IVa engines). *Ceiling:* 14,174 feet. *Endurance:* 7-10 hours. *Weight empty/loaded:* 17,465/26,125 lbs. *Span:* 138 feet 5½ inches. *Length:* 72 feet 6 inches.
Right: The **Gotha G IV**. *Engines:* Two Mercedes D IVa inlines, 260 hp each. *Armament:* Up to 1,100 lbs of bombs and two Parabellum machine guns. *Speed:* 87.5 mph at 12,000 feet. *Climb:* 9,840 feet in 28 minutes. *Ceiling:* 21,320 feet. *Endurance:* 6 hours. *Weight empty/loaded:* 5,280/7,997 lbs. *Span:* 77 feet 9¼ inches. *Length:* 38 feet 11 inches

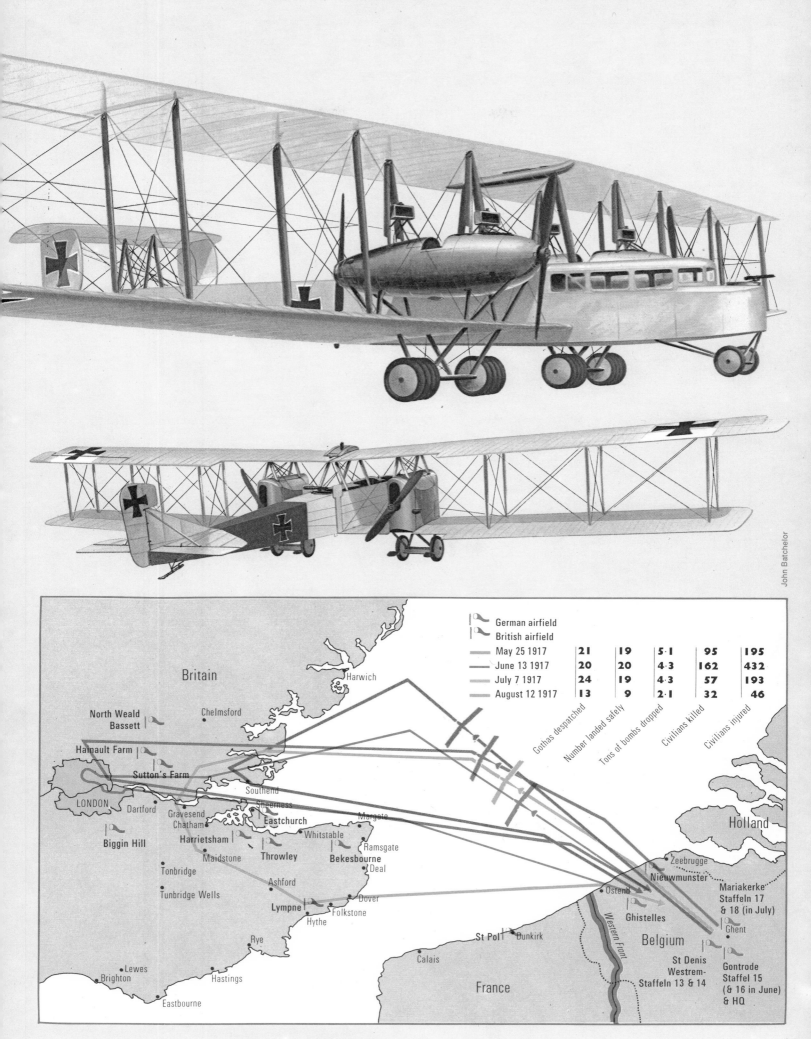

John Batchelor

BOMBS BY NIGHT

Although the Germans led the way with strategic bombing, the Allies also produced large bombing aircraft and towards the end of the war started to launch large-scale night raids — with few practical results. *Below:* A Caproni Ca 3 bomber caught in the searchlights

It is a quarter to eight. Eight thousand feet above the coast near Dunkirk we move. My pilot is a senior officer, and I have never flown with him before, so I sit quietly and do not talk, as I watch carefully the dials of my petrol instruments, and also keep a careful eye on the country below. The pilot looks at the engines with a satisfied glance, and the machine swings round and points east.

Soon the dim pattern of the Dixmude floods lie below, reflecting the gleam of a quivering star-shell. In the sky above Thorout appears a dazzling Verey light which drifts and dies—German machines are abroad in the darkness also. Far below now lies Thorout, and for a minute or two its pale beam waves vainly and impotent in the moonlit sky, its strength so dissipated that it is useless. Soon south of Ghent we move, and see to our right the landing lights of the huge Gotha aerodrome of Gontrode.

I stand up and look across the pilot, and count the lights.

'Eight on each side—two red at the west!' I say.

'I make it more,' he comments. 'Count again!'

I make sure of my accuracy, and draw in my notebook a detailed sketch of the landing arrangements.

'Look!' suddenly cried the pilot. 'We've been heard!'

I peer down once more and see only the two red lights glowing on the ground. The two lines of white electric lamps have been switched off, for the drone of our engines has been heard high above the aerodrome.

Suddenly I realise that we will be heard through the whole of our long journey. The absence of searchlights and shell fire in these undefended regions makes one forget that from town to town, from village to village, the report of our progress is sent to 1,000 military centres in a vast radius. Already our passage into virgin territory (for not for years has country east of Ghent been bombed at night) must be causing a sensation. Brussels must be apprehensive: Aix-la-Chapelle is feeling anxiety: Cologne is uneasy. . . .

Far ahead I can see a light flashing and flashing in a regular code. I presume it to be near Brussels, and point it out to the pilot. In a few minutes through the slight haze of the distance appears a great number of twinkling lights, and soon to our left I see a vast sea of glittering, shimmering gems, with lines of lights radiating outwards from it like the tentacles of an octopus. I suddenly realise that it is Brussels, and with a cry of utter delight stand up to look down more clearly at it. It is a wonderful spectacle. There, in one wide sweep before my eyes, lies the whole city, triumphantly blazing out into the night. I can see the long lines of the boulevards stretching through the mass of lights, on the outskirts of which glitter little villages, from which also radiate the lines of street lamps, as though illuminated starfish lay here and there across the country.

Brussels passes. Road and forest and village flow beneath us in a regular and expected stream. Slowly the minutes go by. Ten minutes to ten says the watch. For over two hours we have been in the air, and our engines show no signs of wavering. On them alone now depend our chances of return. Soon I see far ahead of me the silver ribbon of the Meuse shining in the haze of the horizon, and then the lights of Namur, cold and sparkling, appear by the side of the river. I examine every tiny landmark on the ground below, and check it with my map. There is no doubt. There lie the lights of the town—there lies the forest on its outskirts—there lie the two bridges, from one of which the thin black line of the railway trails off into the distance.

'Namur!' I say to the pilot.

He looks down and flies round in a wide circle in order to examine every point, and to ensure for himself that no doubt whatever exists as to the identity of the place. He is quite satisfied, and turns the machine towards the south-east. We cross the river south of the town as I explain to him my intentions. I want him to turn north-west, against wind, and to throttle the engines. We will glide down parallel to the railway line, which will help me to get a good line. We will reach the bridge at a low altitude, and I will drop my bombs. We will turn quickly down wind to escape.

Before I crawl into the back I point out to him some very bright lights in the direction of the Namur Zeppelin sheds, which seem to confirm my supposition of the activity of German airships tonight. Then, with a final word of explanation, I stoop through the door behind my seat and lie on the floor of the machine. I slide open the little trap-door beneath the pilot's seat, and see a small square picture of moonlit country. Ahead there is just visible the curve of the river, and the black line of the bridge across it. Beneath me runs the railway track which is to be my guide. To my joy I can see, at one place upon this thin dark line, the intermittent red glowing of an engine's fire-box. In a swift moment I realise the actuality of the country below. For a second it ceases to be a map and becomes peopled with busy human beings. Oh, Namur (think I), ablaze with lights, you enjoy this moonlight night of late September, far, far from the turmoil of war, little conscious that overhead this very moment lies a fur-clad airman peering down at you, preparing to drop his terrific missiles, packed with fierce explosive! Laugh on in your cafés, you exquisitely-clad German *embusqués*! For me this moment is rich and ecstatic. Then the difficulty of the task absorbs my mind. The noise of the engines has ceased. Through the machine sounds the faint rush of wind hissing and sighing round the tight-strung wires and planes as we sink lower and lower. My bomb-sight draws nearer and nearer to the bridge. Pressing the buttons of the direction indicator I steer the machine to right and left, as green or red glow the lights before the eyes of the pilot. The direction bar touches the bridge and drifts off to the left. I swing the machine round quickly, again the bar crosses the bridge, again it drifts off. We are flying slightly side to wind, and I can

The largest wartime bomber used by the British in any numbers: a Handley Page 0/400 in flight over Germany with an SE 5a escorting it

scarce keep the head of the machine on a straight course. The pale-glowing range-bars draw nearer and nearer, with a slow progression, to the black edge of the silver river. Again I press the right button; again a green light glows; again the machine swings towards the bridge. The range-bars cross the base of it. I press over the bomb handle quickly . . . and again. Clatter-click-clatter-click-click-clatter sound the opening and closing bomb doors behind me as bomb after bomb slides out into the moonlight depths below. For a moment I see the fat yellow shapes, clear-let in the pale light beneath me, go tumbling down and down towards the dim face of the country.

I hurry back to my seat beside the pilot.

'Half dropped, sir. 'Fraid they will not get it. Oh! I am sorry, sir! We drifted!'

The first salvo misses

One, two, three red flashes leap up in the water of the river some hundred yards to the south of the bridge. One, two more flashes, more rapid and brilliant, leap up on the moonlight embankment, leaving large white clouds of smoke.

'Jolly good! You didn't miss by much! he says encouragingly.

Boom-boom-Boom-boom-BOOM! sound the five explosions as we turn. It is strange to look at Namur—still sparkling beauti-fully with a wealth of light under the stars—still unchanged, though we know that the thundering clamour of these five un-expected explosions must have stirred up the placid life of the little tranquil town till it is seething like an ant-hill upset by the wayside. In the squares must run the alarmed population, rushing to and fro aimlessly, utterly terrified. In the military headquarters the telephones and tele-graphs must have burst into a sudden activity. The vibrant roar of the explosions must have been heard for a great distance. Even in remote Aix-la-Chapelle the stroll-ing Germans must have wondered at the far-away sound drifting to them under the stars.

Again we fly to the south: again we turn and start on our second 'run' over the target: again I crawl into the back, steeled this time by a great anxiety and a great determination, for I realise the enormous responsibility which is mine. With this sense of responsibility weighing heavily on me I lie down, peering through the little square hole. My face is wet with the pers-piration of anxiety in spite of the intense cold of the biting wind: my hands shake with excitement. I decide to take the machine to the river along the railway line, and slightly to the east of it, and then to judge the wind drift so that the machine is turned by it to the left, when I will press the starboard signal button and swing the machine at an angle across the bridge, and then drop my bombs. It is a great risk, and unless I judge exactly I will not succeed.

In a fever of apprehension, and with my whole being concentrated on the relation of the fine wires and bars of my bomb-sight with the black thread of the railway far below me, I lie on the varnished strips of wood on the floor of the machine, my legs flung wide apart behind me, my bare hands and face frozen with the icy blast of wind, my uncovered eyes running with water. Nearer and nearer to the bridge draw the two range-bars. Gently and rarely do I touch the starboard signal button, to swing

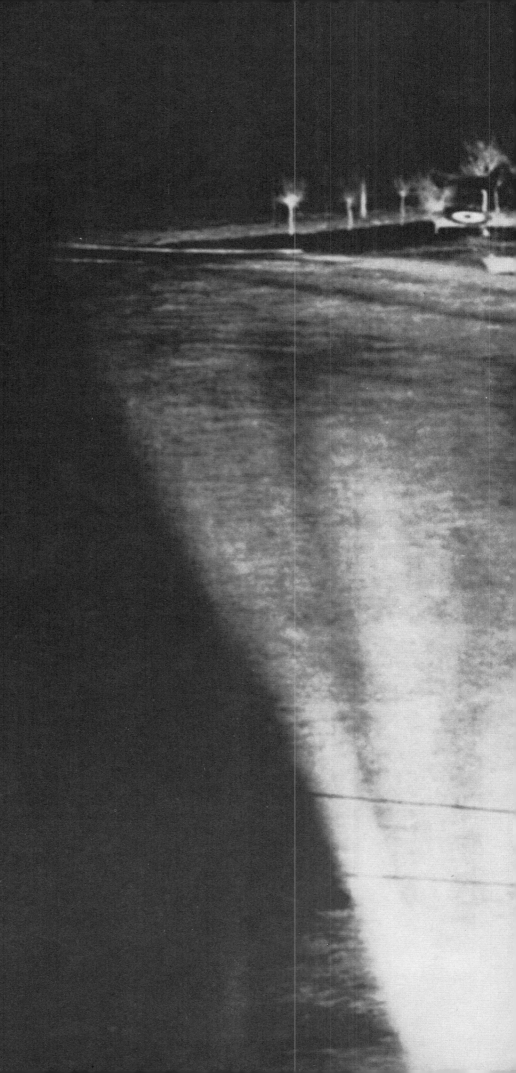

A night bomber airfield. The most dangerous moments in flight occur at take-off and landing, and the primitive facilities of First World War flying fields made these moments doubly dangerous, particularly when landing.

the machine again and again to the right as the wind drifts it to the left. We are near the bridge—we are almost over it. I press the starboard button determinedly, and I see the glow of green light illuminate the dashboard. To the right swings the machine. White glows a light as I press the central button. I look below quivering with anxiety. The machine ceases its leftward drift and swings to the right, and the two luminous range-bars are in line with the bridge. I grasp the bomb-handle and once, twice press it over. I look behind—the bombs are all gone. It is all over! The irrevocable deed has been done! The failure or success of the long raid is sealed. I climb clumsily to my feet and look through the door beside the pilot.

'All gone, sir, I . . . Oh! look, look!'

Upon the thin black line of the bridge leap out two great flashes leaving a cloud of moonlit smoke which entirely obscures one end of it.

'Oh—damn good—damn good!' yells out the pilot excitedly. 'Hit it! Hit it! You've hit it! Oh—priceless—priceless!'

'Good—oh, sir! I am glad. It is hit, isn't it, sir? Two of them. I am bucked!'

'Something for you for this when we get back!' he says. 'Oh! damn good—damn good, Paul. Priceless—priceless!'

I look round, and in the back of the machine I see a sight which left the clearest image of this raid in my mind. There stands the moonlit figure of the tall good-humoured gunlayer, and with a characteristic gesture I see him put out his arms with the thumbs pointing upwards—the most sincere expression of congratulation he can deliver. My heart goes out in gratitude to this solitary man who already, for nearly three hours, has stood alone on a thin platform in the back of the machine, watching and eager, knowing that he has no control over his destiny, that his life lies in the hands of the little figure whose black head he can see so far away from him in the nose of the machine.

Now we turn at once and start on our long homeward trail . . . Charleroi sparkles on our left. Near it at La Louvière flashes an aerial lighthouse, whose presence I record on my notebook. Having found our way to Namur by map, we seem to return by a kind of curious homing instinct. We know where we are as if by second nature. Indeed so little do I trouble that I mistake Courtrai for Roulers, but it makes but little difference. Such confidence have I in our safety, so lively is the moon-drenched night, so friendly are the undefended skies, that we fly on and on as in a stupor of utter bliss. We know that if we return we are famous, and we know that we will return. Song and laughter, and rich thoughts of far-distant London and its proffered glories when next comes leave, fill my drowsy brain. I hug the pilot's arm affectionately. At twelve o'clock he was at Dover, now scarcely 11 hours after he is coming back from Namur. How wonderful it is—how wonderful he is!

Ypres flickers to the left with its ever uneasy artillery fire. In our ease we do not even trouble to cross the lines as soon as possible, but fly on parallel to them, some five miles on the German side. At last we turn and cross slowly over the white blossoms of the ever-rising, ever-drooping star-shells.

[*Reprinted from* Green Balls *by Paul Bewsher, published by Blackwood.*]

The Aces

The introduction of effective armament did much more than produce the fighter aeroplane — it led to the emergence of the aces, morale boosters for the home front and inspiration for the other pilots. At first these men were individualists — they had to be, for they were the pathfinders. But as their skill grew and was passed on to others, their outstanding light was eclipsed by the 'packs', whose very numbers could overwhelm the peculiar talents of the lone flyers. *Thomas G. Miller. Above:* Albert Ball's last fight on May 17, 1917, by Norman Arnold

Left: Max Immelmann, the so-called 'Eagle of Lille'. Though he achieved a victory score of 15 by the time of his death on June 18, 1916, his real importance lay in developing the art of aerial fighting and in boosting the morale of the German people. He and his mentor, Oswald Boelcke, were the first two German aviators to be awarded the *Pour le Mérite*. *Right:* Immelmann and his mount, a Fokker *Eindekker*. Again, the importance of the Fokker was not that it was a good fighter, which it was not, but that it was the first true fighter and thus showed the way to the more efficient weapons of the future. *Far right:* Immelmann's end: the collected remnants of his *Eindekker*. It is still uncertain how Immelmann died, for the Germans claim that he crashed as a result of a structural failure in his aircraft, while the British claim that he was shot down by an FE 2b, which before a synchronising gear, was the backbone of the RFC's fighting forces

Airborne armament of a fashion came almost immediately in the war of 1914. In most two-seater aircraft on both sides the observer managed to carry at least a cavalry carbine, and, as early as September 1914, such relatively powerful aircraft as the Voisins of the French *Escadrilles* V14 and V21 began to mount Hotchkiss machine guns. It was only a question of time before someone brought down a hostile aircraft.

The occasion came at 1005 hours on October 5, 1914, when a Voisin of V24 flown by *Sergent* Joseph Frantz with *Sapeur* Quenault as his mechanic/gunner encountered an Aviatik B-type of *Feldfliegerabteilung 18*: Quenault put 47 rounds into the Aviatik which dived into the ground and burned, killing *Vizefeldwebel* Wilhelm Schlichting and *Leutnant* Fritz von Zangen, the very first names on the long list of those who have died in air combat.

Frantz' and Quenault's victory was typical of dozens of random encounters between opposing aircraft that followed. Airmen of all the armies were killed and captured as a result of such combats during the autumn of 1914 and the winter of 1914/15. But it rapidly became obvious to the flyers that fighting was a specialised task requiring manoeuvrable single-seat aircraft, not the clumsy and underpowered two seaters with which both the Allies and Central Powers were almost completely equipped. Efforts to produce such a machine began about the same time in Britain, France and Germany. The problem was to devise a means whereby a machine gun could be aimed and fired by the pilot without undue distraction from his primary duties of controlling the aircraft.

Roland Garros, the famous prewar French flyer, helped by the expertise of Raymond Saulnier of the Morane-Saulnier firm, developed a steel deflector plate, wedge-shaped in cross-section, to be attached to each blade of the monoplane's propeller at the point where it was intersected by the fire from a Hotchkiss mounted on the cowling. After several unsuccessful tests, Garros and Saulnier perfected their device so that it would reliably deflect bullets striking the propeller, without harming it; the majority of the bullets fired passed between the blades. Garros now had a machine with an easily sighted gun that he could aim by controlling his direction of flight. The fighter aircraft had been born.

Garros first used his invention in combat on April 1, 1915. He flew up behind a German aircraft and opened fire from a range of only 30 feet. The German aircraft burst into flames and crashed behind the French lines, killing its crew. This grim event was to be repeated many thousands of times in the next four years.

Twice more in the next three weeks Garros repeated his feat. Then on the 19th his Morane Parasol was forced down by ground fire while returning from a pointless bombing raid. He was captured and his secret fell into German hands.

Garros' Morane was examined by Anthony Fokker who, according to his story, returned to his factory and within less than a week conjured up a synchronising mechanism that would enable a Spandau machine gun to be fired between the propeller blades of his M5K single-seater monoplane, an aircraft based on the Morane layout. Later research has turned up the fact that work had been in progress on this device at the Fokker works for some months, but Tony Fokker never missed an opportunity to cast himself in a starring rôle. At any rate when tested and demonstrated in the M5K the mechanism worked and the German army promptly placed an order for a number of the Fokker monoplanes, which received the military designation of E I. Late in May Fokker started on a combined demonstration and instruction tour of German operating units on the Western Front during which a small number of the best pilots in various *Feldfliegerabteilungen* learned to fly the machine. By the time he returned to Schwerin in mid-July, 11 pilots had received Fokker E I's, which were now in full production.

Immelmann, the 'Eagle of Lille'

Max Immelmann was not only one of Germany's first aces, but his character and combat tactics might almost be regarded as typical of a good fighter pilot. Called back up as a reserve NCO upon the outbreak of the war, he applied almost immediately for aviation training and was ordered to flight school early in November 1914. He proved to be a slow pupil, but reached the front in mid-April and was then assigned to the newly formed *Feldfliegerabteilung 62,* another of whose original members was the veteran *Leutnant* Oswald Boelcke.

Immelmann was, in psychological terms, 'other-directed'; the impression he made on his peers and superiors was very important to him and he wanted their opinions to be favourable. Somewhat envious of Boelcke's sole stewardship of the section's Fokkers, he persuaded the more experienced pilot to take him up in one and give him a bit of dual instruction. After the first landing, Immelmann asked Boelcke to step out and made five good landings in succession. Three days later, on August 1, both went up to intercept an RFC bombing raid on their aerodrome, and Immelmann

forced down an unarmed BE 2c, its sole occupant wounded. He was awarded the Iron Cross, First Class and received the congratulations of Boelcke, not unmixed with envy and incredulity at such luck. Thus started a more-or-less friendly rivalry that lasted almost a year. The two shared a victory on September 18 (which was Boelcke's third—he had rapidly caught up with his chief competitor). Five more followed in that autumn; then on a memorable day for both Immelmann and Boelcke, January 12, 1916, each shot down his eighth opponent and received the *Pour le Mérite,* the first award of this decoration to aviators. The era of the 'ace' had dawned.

During these few months of the autumn of 1915 and early winter, the classic tactics of fighter aircraft evolved, still unchanged in their essentials more than half a century later. As first worked out by Immelmann and Boelcke and their contemporaries, they may be summarised as follows:

● The ultimate position desired in aerial combat is that where one can shoot at one's enemy at a range from which he cannot be missed while he remains unable to shoot at one. In combat, with aircraft having guns firing forward, this position is directly behind and slightly above one's opponent. If he has guns firing aft, the preferred position is directly behind and below, out of his line of fire;

● The basic defensive manoeuvre for an aircraft attacked from forward of the beam is to turn directly toward the opponent, thus presenting as small a target as possible and, by maximising the relative speed of the two aircraft, minimising the time he can keep one in his gunsight;

● The basic defensive manoeuvre for an aircraft attacked from aft of the beam is to enter and maintain as tight a turn as possible in order to make it difficult for one's opponent to get on one's tail and keep one in his gunsight;

● The basic offensive manoeuvre is to turn more tightly than one's opponent, thus flying in a circle of smaller radius and eventually into a position on his tail; and

● The initial approach to an enemy should be from a superior altitude, and from such natural cover, such as the sun or clouds, as is available. By using a higher altitude, the patrol area may be better surveyed, and one may convert altitude to airspeed by diving in order to overtake an opponent and the airspeed back to altitude to withdraw from combat and regain position for another attack.

The most important characteristics of a fighter aircraft thus are a high ratio of thrust to weight and low wing loading for manoeuvrability. The manoeuvres most used in combat are the simple steep turn, dive and zoom climb, and combinations of the three. More elaborate acrobatics are seldom used and almost never effective.

A peculiar individualism

The scarcity of fighter aircraft and their initial dispersion among observation units accustomed the first aces to flying and fighting alone. However, they probably would have done so in any case. The qualities of daring and aggressiveness that characterised the best fighter pilots were likely to be accompanied by such traits as extreme individualism, impatience with authority, egotism that could easily turn into selfishness and a taste for the fruits of military glory—decorations and popular adulation. One must remember that most of them were very young men, some scarcely out of boyhood.

The few months that followed the emergence of Immelmann and Boelcke have been called 'the Fokker era' by two generations of British historians. They accurately perceived that with the Fokker E I and its principal successor, the E III, the German air forces gained a temporary material and moral ascendancy over their opponents. Interestingly enough, though, the Germans were largely unaware of the existence of this 'era'. They were too conscious of the very small number of fighter aircraft actually available to them. German records show 55 Fokker E-machines at the front on October 31, 1915 and only 86 at the year's end. The difficulty lay in the slow production of rotary engines.

The Allies were no faster off the mark. Gustave Delage's classic Nieuport 11 appeared in the summer of 1915, almost simultaneously with the Fokker E I. This little sesquiplane, nicknamed *Bébé,* was generally superior to the German fighter in performance, its only critical deficiency being its inadequate armament of a single Lewis gun mounted on the top wing and firing over the propeller. However, the Nieuport factory was no more capable of going into large-scale production than was the Fokker. The same slow hand-building craftsmen's methods used before the war were still the norm, and by February 1916, only 210 Nieuports of all types had reached the front, mostly two-seaters.

The Royal Flying Corps was still largely equipped with the products of the Royal Aircraft Factory in mid-1915, and these had not been designed with air combat in mind. The prewar Bristol and Martinsyde single-seater 'scouts' were made into makeshift fighters, although the original designs had not been produced with any notion of later arming the types. The first British single-seater fighter designed for the purpose, the Airco DH2, arrived in France in ones and twos as early as December 1915, but not in squadron strength until the following February. Like the Germans, the RFC's initial disposition was to disperse its fighters as protection machines to the observation squadrons.

The most marked superiority of the Fokker lay not in its performance, which was no better than those of its chief contemporary adversaries the Nieuport 11 and DH2, but in its armament. Here the British and French clearly had been out-thought and out-engineered. While their fighters had to make do with shakily mounted Lewis guns fed from 47-shot drums, the German machines had fixed Model 08/15 'Spandau' machine guns fed with 500-round continuous belts. Allied pilots had to change drums every 47 shots while in combat and with their guns located in the windstream, and in any case only had room to carry a maximum of four extra drums.

The next step in the evolution of fighter aviation followed almost immediately upon the emergence of Boelcke and Immelmann. It came during the Verdun campaign, which opened on February 21, 1916. The importance of that epic series of battles to both the French and the Germans led to concentrations of aircraft on an unprecedented scale. Instead of a few dozens of machines being available to each side, now it was a few hundred, but only a very few of them were fighters.

The Battle of Verdun was to be the crucible of French fighter aviation and out of that desperate fighting came her first aces. When the German offensive started, only one fighter *escadrille* was located in that sector. Within three weeks five more had arrived and were concentrated into a group at Behonne, just outside Bar-le-Duc, a nominal total of 36 fighter aircraft. Opposing them were 21 Fokkers attached to the German *Fifth Army*, divided into three groups located at Bantheville, Jametz and Anvillers. The latter group was commanded by Oswald Boelcke, sent down from the British front.

Boelcke, quiet but aggressive
The few Fokkers were used singly, mostly on escort missions, except for Boelcke's two-plane *Kommando*. The quiet but aggressive Saxon continued the tactics that had brought him success and fame, patrolling over the lines for the unwary. His first partner having been killed in an accident, he was joined at Sivry by the young Baron Erich von Althaus. It had not yet occurred to Boelcke to fly and fight in co-operation with another aircraft, and the two Fokker pilots operated independently over Verdun. On the French side, attempts were made to substitute some order for the flamboyant individualism of their 30-odd fighter pilots, but the shortage of Nieuport 11's and the heavy losses suffered by the *escadrilles* would have prevented them from being carried out even had the pilots been willing—which they emphatically were not.

As early as February 29, 1916 before the age of the aces was much more than six weeks old, *Commandant* du Peuty, commanding the French air forces at Verdun, issued an order that began its end. The order specified that the mission of the fighter *escadrilles* was offensive patrols by several aircraft flying in formation, the objective of which was to find, fight and destroy German aircraft. This was a real innovation for the time, but it left unspecified whether or how aircraft were to fight in formation. In the event, the French *escadrilles*, when they obeyed the order at all, flew together without any idea of fighting co-operatively and combats invariably degenerated into duels between individual pilots.

For the Germans the heroes of the air fighting over Verdun were the peerless Boelcke, who brought down a further ten aircraft, and Althaus, whose five victories brought him up to a total of nine, for which he was awarded the *Pour le Mérite*. The French had many more, chief among them in actual accomplishment being Jean Navarre who brought down seven, Charles Nungesser six, and Jean Chaput and Maxime Lenoir with four each. Navarre and Nungesser, both flamboyant figures, were the ones who caught the imagination of the public. Navarre was the first French ace. The son of a wealthy paper manufacturer, whose natural intolerance of authority was heightened by financial independence, he had been a military pilot since 1914 and had already been credited with two victories when the Battle of Verdun started. He shot down two within the French lines on February 26, and a further five during the next few months when his red-striped and skull and crossbones-marked *Bébé* became well-known to the soldiers. Navarre was reckless to the point of insanity. He claimed a distaste for killing, but took the most meticulous care to ensure that his victims did not escape. His method of attack was to fly

Roger Viollet

up to within a few feet below and behind a German aircraft, then stand up in his cockpit to sight his Lewis gun, trusting to the dubious stability of the Nieuport. It was a technique suited only to combat with unhandy, poorly armed two-seaters and utterly suicidal given any kind of competent opposition. As might have been expected, he was severely wounded in June and never fought again. Nungesser, crippled and battered in a bad crash in 1915, flew indomitably for four months at Verdun, with only will power keeping him alive. His particular technique, the same as Navarre's, was based on point-blank shooting. He once confessed to a curious general that before pulling the trigger he closed his eyes: 'when I open them, sometimes my opponent is falling, sometimes I am in a hospital!' Charles Nungesser, with his jingling medals, his huge car and his Paris binges the archtype of the public image of the ace, held a roving commission in the French air service. Despite an endless succession of wounds and crashes, he survived the war, credited with 45 victories.

The struggle for the ancient citadel of Verdun cost the French almost 100 aircraft and the Germans around 30. Most of the French losses were inflicted by two-seater 'combat' biplanes, of which the LVG C II was the best. Proportionately more of the German losses were due to the French fighter pilots. The tactics were based on the individual pilot seeking targets of opportunity.

The fighter's influence grows
The lessons of Verdun now were to be applied on a larger scale as the centre of gravity on the Western Front shifted to the Somme. The aviation buildup for this campaign was even more impressive than for Verdun. The Royal Flying Corps concentrated 185 aircraft, the French around 201 against 129 German machines. The RFC, recognising almost as soon as the French and long before the Germans the need for concentrating fast single-seater fighters into specialised squadrons, fielded four of them, Nos 24, 29, 32 and 60. Unfortunately their equipment was not adequate to the concept: the first three operated the flimsy, underpowered DH2, No 60 the treacherous Morane Bullet. The Germans were cursed with heterogeneous equipment, *Kampfeinsitzer-Kommando Nord*, one of their two fighter units, being composed of two new Halberstadt D II's, six Fokker E III's, one Fokker E IV and one Pfalz E IV. However, their major handicap was the fact they were grossly outnumbered. Not only did they have the aggressive, confident RFC to deal with, but the French concentrated six

Roger Viollet

Above right and above: Charles Nungesser, France's third highest scoring ace, who achieved 45 victories. He is seen here in the cockpit of his Voisin 10 of VB 106, before his rise to fame as a fighter ace. It was while flying the lumbering Voisins of VB 106 that Nungesser first gave evidence of the pugnacious spirit that was to lead him to flying fighters. He revelled in macabre individual markings, skull and crossbones, coffins and candles, perhaps in the hope that being surrounded by so many unlucky markings would ward off the real thing. In fact, Nungesser's career in the air was punctuated by a series of crashes, in both cars and aeroplanes, but he survived the war only to die in an attempt to fly across the Atlantic in 1927. An impulsive and daredevil pilot, he did not hesitate to plunge into the most dangerous situations if he thought that there was even the most remote chance of success. Had he not been so impetuous, he might have ended the war with a score very near that of René Fonck, the Allied ace-of-aces, who reached a total of 75 victories and with whom at one time Nungesser had a great rivalry. *Above left:* Jean Navarre, an ace with 12 victories, was the first French ace to achieve widespread fame. It was the concentration of German aircraft around Verdun in the early days of 1916 which gave Navarre his chance, but soon after this he was shot down and severely wounded, and did not fly again during the war. He habitually wore a lady's silk stocking as a flying helmet, a bizarre but functional and warm headgear

escadrilles of Nieuports at Cachy. Thus on July 1, the day the Battle of the Somme opened, only 19 German fighter aircraft faced 66 British and about 72 French.

The result of the Allied superiority was predictable; the few German fighters were simply brushed aside, and British and French aircraft, although they suffered considerable losses, had effective command of the air. During July and August the Germans lost 51 aircraft in combat. No German fighter pilots achieved prominence during this first phase of the air battle. Although the Germans began the regular use of co-operative tactics, their numerical and material inferiority rendered them completely ineffective.

Max Immelmann had been killed on June 18, the British claiming that he had been shot down by an FE 2b, the Germans asserting that a fault in his synchronising gear had caused him to shoot off his own propeller. The truth of the matter will probably never be known with certainty. At any rate his death was a blow to the morale of the German public, and the authorities did not care to risk another one. Boelcke, recently promoted to *Hauptmann* (Captain), was now worth more as a national hero than as a soldier, and by order of the Kaiser he was grounded and despatched on a tour of Germany's forces in the East. However, the events of July and August on the Somme overtook officialdom's attempt to preserve Boelcke under glass. *Oberstleutnant* (Lieutenant-Colonel) Hermann Thomsen, the *de facto* chief of the German army's flying forces, had decided to organise seven *Staffeln* (squadrons) of single-seat fighters, and Germany's most successful fighter pilot now was hastily recalled to command one.

The new units were to be equipped with D-class machines (D-class denotes armed single-seater), largely the radical new Albatros D I and D II, with a scattering of Fokker D III's and Halberstadt D II's. The Albatros machines were sturdy streamlined biplanes with two synchronised machine guns, 1,000 rounds of ammunition and almost twice the horsepower of the Nieuport and DH2. Four of these *Jagdstaffeln* were assigned to the *First* and *Second Armies* on the Somme, and Oswald Boëlcke's *Jagdstaffel 2* was one of them. Boelcke returned from Russia with two pilots from his brother's unit, both recommended as potentially good air fighters. One of them was a 37-year-old colonial called Erwin Böhme. The other was a lieutenant of Lancers, Manfred, *Freiherr* von Richthofen. These two were the only pilots he recruited personally. Otherwise he took whoever was sent to

Below: Richthofen's *Jasta 11* at Douai early in 1917. Richthofen's Albatros D III is second from the front, without a prominent cross on the fuselage. *Right:* A German postcard of Boelcke and his last victory. Boelcke was the real father of disciplined air fighting. *Far right:* Undefeated in the air, Boelcke lost his life in a mid-air collision with his friend Erwin Böhme, who succeeded him as leader of *Jasta 2. Opposite page left:* The ace of aces, Manfred von Richthofen, who shot down 80 Allied aeroplanes, most of them the vital two-seater reconnaissance and artillery spotter types. Not a brilliant pilot, Richthofen achieved his successes by superb shooting. *Opposite page right:* A morbid hobby—his victims' serial numbers as Richthofen's wallpaper

FLIEGER HAUPTMANN BOELCKE

Boelckes letzter Sieg
Das 40. Flugzeug abgeschoßen!

The new age of chivalry, with knights like Guynemer, or the cold ruthlessness of hunters like Manfred von Richthofen?

him. In a frantic two weeks he trained his eager fledglings to fly as a homogeneous unit rather than in the random individual patrols hitherto used, and to sacrifice individual scores for *Staffel* scores through teamwork. He whetted their appetites during their training period by going out alone every morning before breakfast, 1915-style, running his victories up to 25. *Jagdstaffeln 1* and *3* had already been in action when Boelcke's pilots finally got their new Albatros machines and Boelcke judged them ready. On September 17 *Jagdstaffel 2* burst on the startled RFC like an avalanche.

The Allies outclassed

During the months of September-November 1916 *Jagdstaffel 2* shot down 76 British aircraft for the loss of seven of its own. Together with the other two fighter *Staffeln* it completely reversed the air situation on the Somme. The new German aircraft completely outclassed the new Nieuport 17 and the primitive DH2, and Boelcke's tactical leadership and personal example gave to German aviation an *élan* it had never before possessed. In October German losses fell from 27 the previous month to 12, while Allied losses were 88. However, one of the 12 was Oswald Boelcke. In a combat on the 20th, he and Erwin Böhme collided lightly, but it was enough to make his Albatros uncontrollable. His pilots last saw him diving ever more steeply into the clouds. So died the chivalrous Oswald Boelcke, at the height of his fame. But he left German fighter aviation a legacy it was never to lose, and which was to cost many British and French lives.

While Boelcke was the outstanding German hero of the Somme campaign, the British and French each produced rivals. In the RFC it was Albert Ball, in the French service, Georges Guynemer.

Albert Ball was the first British ace to achieve a service-wide reputation as an air fighter and the first to become well known to

the public. A shy charming boy of 20, he was at first an indifferent pilot, a characteristic he shared with many other famous fighter pilots, including Richthofen. But his individualistic nature rebelled at the dull, hazardous routine of the observation pilot and he seized the opportunity to fly a Nieuport fighter that was assigned to No 11 Squadron. In this machine he began his fighting career in May 1916. Like all the early aces, his tactics started with the simple ambushing of careless or indifferently defended two-seaters. However, as he acquired experience and confidence he began to make single-handed attacks on formations of German aircraft, which at that time were mostly LVG and LFG Roland C II armed two-seaters. His preferred position was a few yards directly beneath his opponent, who he would then shoot by tilting up his single wing-mounted Lewis gun. Ball attacked, shot and escaped very quickly, taking advantage of the preoccupation of a close formation with stationkeeping. In late August he went to No 60 squadron, which had just been pulled out of the line and re-equipped with Nieuports after having suffered disastrous losses. In the congenial atmosphere provided by No 60's understanding CO, Major Smith-Barry, the temperamental Ball thrived. During the last week of August and in the following month, Albert Ball became the most successful British fighter pilot of the period. His service with 60 Squadron overlapped the arrival of the first *Jagdstaffeln* on the British front by only about three weeks, during which his solitary patrol habits and the wariness of experience prevented him from falling victim to the new German equipment. Indeed he shot down two aircraft of Boelcke's *Jagdstaffel 2* in a week. When Ball was sent back to England on October 4, he was recorded as having crashed 10 German aircraft and 'forced to land' another 20, plus one 'out of control'. The vague categories of victory used by the RFC inflated his score far beyond the actual accomplishment, which was that he had shot down nine German aircraft. But the importance of Albert Ball did not lie in the material achievement, but in his effect on RFC morale at a time when it was being outfought by a numerically inferior enemy as a result of superior equipment and more intelligent tactics. Ball proved by example the eternal importance of aggressiveness and daring and he did so when it was of particular value to Britain.

The incomparable Guynemer

The aces often are compared to the knights of the Middle Ages, and the simile is not a bad one. It is particularly apt when applied to Georges Guynemer. The impetuosity, fierce pride and immensely strong personality of this tall, dark youth found its natural outlet in air fighting. A schoolboy in 1914, he was a legend to his countrymen when he was killed three years later. Admitted reluctantly to aviation upon his peremptory demand, he went to *Escadrille* MS3, where he and his gunner scored a victory on July 19, 1915. The unit, converting to Nieuports, was sent to Verdun, but Guynemer was shot down and severely wounded before he could make a name for himself on that front. He entered his heroic period during the Battle of the Somme, shooting down his ninth victim on July 16 and his 23rd in November, as that dreadful campaign was in its final throes. In tactics Guynemer, like Immelmann, used no tricks. He flew sometimes alone or, more often, with another aircraft. He rarely hesitated to attack a German formation, and his attacks were usually deadly because he was a superb shot. From the Somme he went on from success to success. By the end of April 1917, he was the leading Allied ace, credited with 36 victories; most of these can be verified by historical research because so many of them were shot down within the French lines. Even when commanding his *escadrille* he was an enigma, a distant figure who would not lead but fought his own solitary battles. Like some hero in a myth he was doomed and knew it. But while he lived he personified the classic French warrior.

As November 1916 came, both sides were approaching exhaustion. With the exception of Guynemer and a relatively few others, the concentration of French fighters at Cachy lost its effectiveness with the appearance of the *Jagdstaffeln*. The single- or two-aircraft patrols that the pilots insisted upon flying were unable to cope with the formation tactics of the Germans. The campaign that had begun so brightly ended with the French quiescent and the British fighter pilots struggling ineffectively against superior equipment and tactics. The plight of the RFC was epitomised on November 23 when Major L. G. Hawker, VC, the brilliant CO of No 24 Squadron, encountered Manfred von Richthofen in single combat and was shot down after a most gallant fight. Hawker, a veteran fighter pilot from the old Bristol Scout days of 1915, was almost certainly Richthofen's superior in piloting skill and was no less brave; the outcome depended solely on the immense superiority of the Albatros D II over the DH2.

More or less by unspoken mutual agreement, the air fighting over the Somme drew to a close by the end of the month. During this respite the Germans continued the expansion and re-equipment of their fighter arm. The original seven *Jagdstaffeln* grew to 37, 36 of which were stationed on the Western Front. The Albatros D III followed hard on the heels of its predecessors and by early spring equipped many of the German units. This expansion was difficult for the older organisations, who found themselves stripped of all their veterans to command the new *Jagdstaffeln*.

The RFC received nine new fighter squadrons during the winter: however, the older fighter squadrons continued to operate the types that had been found inadequate during the Battle of the Somme. Many of the best British pilots had been lost or fought to exhaustion during that campaign, and most of the new arrivals were insufficiently trained and without combat experience. The RFC was not ready to fight another major offensive action. However, this was precisely what it had to do. Sir Douglas Haig had been directed to support Nivelle's French offensive on the Aisne, and thus was forced to undertake a large-scale attack on his front. The situation of the RFC was almost a guarantee of disaster in the air, and this was what in fact occurred.

The RFC and RNAS had 385 fighter aircraft on the front for the Battle of Arras, opposed by only 114 German machines. However, the Germans were superior in every other aspect: their aircraft were better, they combined a defensive strategy with aggressive tactics, and they had high confidence in themselves and their equipment. During the month of April, 1917 – 'Bloody April' – they shot down 151 RFC and RNAS aircraft for the loss of about 70 of their own. No less than 88 of these aircraft fell to *Jagdstaffel 11*, commanded by Boelcke's pupil Manfred von Richthofen. He gained 21 of these victories himself, and by the end of the month had a total of 52. Other notable aces of April were Kurt Wolff of *Jagdstaffel 11* with 21 victories, Lothar von Richthofen (Manfred's brother) and Karl Emil Schaefer of the same unit with 15 each, Otto Bernert of *Jagdstaffel Boelcke* with 11, and Sebastian Festner of *Jagdstaffel 11* with 10.

It was the combination of tactical skill and better aircraft that brought a victory of such magnitude to the Germans. Their tactics were the sophisticated opportunism of the true military professional: when their fast-moving formations encountered groups of aircraft of smaller size or inferior performance, they attacked persistently until all their opponents were shot down. When they found themselves dealing with superior numbers or with aircraft of better performance (only the Sopwith Triplane matched the Albatros D III at this time), they would hit and run.

On May 7, 1917 another symbolic tragedy occurred, underlining

April 1917: the end of the solitary hunter's day in the air with the arrival of the packs — the colourful German 'circuses', the élite French *groupes* and the constant and aggressive British patrol flights

the lessons of the previous months' air fighting. A German infantry unit saw a British SE 5 emerge inverted from a low-hanging cloud and fly into the ground. Its pilot was Albert Ball, returned to France only to die. Neither he nor his aircraft showed any signs of combat injuries; without much doubt he succumbed to vertigo in the overcast and crashed before he had time to recover. It was perhaps as well that one of the supreme exponents of individual air fighting passed on at the end of the age of individualism. The surviving aces of the early period would fight on, most to die in their turn, some to adapt to the new methods and survive the war; other free spirits would emerge to fly and fight alone. But after April, 1917 the emphasis in air combat changed from the solitary ace to the tactics of interdependence and prudence.

Further Reading
Cross and Cockade Journal
Cuneo, J., *The Air Weapon 1870-1916* (Harrisburg, Penn.: Military Service Publishing Co, 1947)
Hawker, *Hawker, VC* (The Mitre Press 1965)
Hervouin, *Guynemer. Heros Légendaire* (Paris: Monceau 1944)
Hoeppner, Gen. von, *Deutschlands Krieg in der Luft* (Leipzig: Koehler 1921)
Immelmann, *Max Immelmann, The Eagle of Lille* (Hamilton)
Kiernan, R. H., *Captain Albert Ball, VC* (Aviation Book Club 1939)
La Doctrine de l'Aviation Française de Combat 1915-1918
Mortane, *Carre d'As* (Paris: Baudiniere 1934)
Raleigh, Sir Walter and Jones, H. A., *The War in the Air* (OUP 1922-1937)
Richthofen, Manfred von, *The Red Air Fighter* (Aeroplane and General Publishing Co. 1918)

THOMAS G. MILLER JR was born in Philadelphia, Pennsylvania in 1926 and educated at the William Penn Charter School and the United States Naval Academy. He completed pilot training at Pensacola in 1952 and flew carrier-based attack and fighter aircraft as a regular and reserve officer until 1961. For the last ten years he has been employed by a research and management consulting firm in Massachusetts. He is one of the editors of the *Cross and Cockade Journal* of First World War Aero Historians, and has written several articles for that magazine and for the *Journal of the American Aviation Historical Society*. He is the author of *The Cactus Air Force,* an account of the pilots who flew from Guadalcanal in the critical days of 1942.

Below left: The members of *Jasta 11* in March 1917. From left to right, standing, are: unknown, *Leutnant* Hintsch, *Vizefeldwebel* Festner, *Leutnant* Emil Schaefer, *Rittmeister* Manfred von Richthofen (in the cockpit of his Albatros D III), *Oberleutnant* Kurt Wolff, *Leutnant* Georg Simon, *Leutnant* Otto Brauneck and, sitting, *Leutnant* Esser, *Leutnant* Krefft and *Leutnant* Lothar von Richthofen (on the ground), Manfred's brother. The known total of Allied aircraft destroyed by this group of men is 204. *Below:* Part of the opposition: the personnel of 56 Squadron, RFC. Though the British did not in general band together their best pilots into special units, as did the French and Germans, 56 Squadron was one of the exceptions. From left to right, standing, are Lieutenants Gerald Maxwell, W. Melville, H. Lehmann, C. Knight, L. M. Barlow and K. J. Knaggs. Sitting are Lieutenants C. A. Lewis and J. O. Leach, Major R. G. Blomfield, Captain Albert Ball and Lieutenant R. T. C. Hoidge. The total victory scores of the aces in this group amounted to 124. The normal British practice was to allocate pilots, regardless of any skill they might possess as fighter pilots, to any squadrons in need of replacements. The result of this practice was that the influence and example of the better pilots was more evenly spread, and this raised the general standard of fighter squadrons. On the German side, the posting of pilots of above average ability to special units meant that the remaining *Staffeln* were deprived of their example

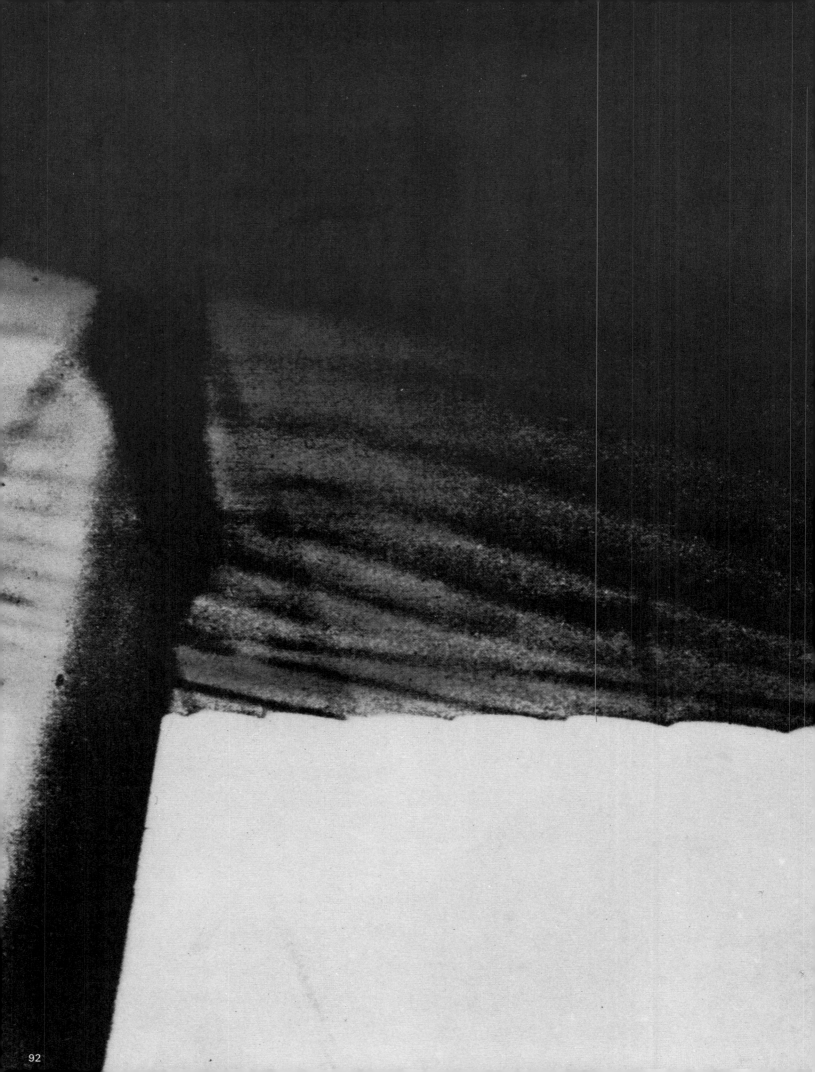

ECP Armées

BLOODY APRIL

'Bloody April' 1917 marked both the high and low water points of the Allied struggle for mastery of the air over the Western Front. The Germans, though inferior in numbers, were introducing superior machines, and the Allies' pilots had to exert all their courage and tenacity to match and then beat the German effort. *D. B. Tubbs. Above:* Allied fighters, such as this Nieuport, were still handicapped by inadequate armament. *Below:* Shepherd and charge: a Nieuport seen from the Farman it is escorting

The four months which culminated in 'Bloody April', 1917, taught one very important lesson: numerical superiority in the air cannot make up for technical inferiority. The preparations for the Battle of Arras and the battle itself came at a time when the Royal Flying Corps was suffering from a preponderance of obsolete aeroplanes, inadequate training for pilots and slow delivery of new types. The German air force, on the other hand, had recently been reorganised, new fighter aircraft were in production and, most important of all, morale, thanks largely to the inspiration of Oswald Boelcke, recently killed in an accident on the Somme, was higher than it had ever been. It is significant that when General Nivelle was discussing his proposed big push at a London conference in January, Sir Douglas Haig expressed the view that the Royal Flying Corps would not be ready for an offensive by April 1. At the same time Nivelle's plans greatly extended the front for which the British armies were responsible—they were to relieve the French as far south as the Roye-Amiens road, so that the French C-in-C could concentrate his forces and deal the Germans a tremendous blow on the Aisne, a blow which was supposed to rupture their line 'within 24 or at most 48 hours'.

However, in February Allied grand strategy was neatly upset by the German High Command. Instead of waiting for the pincer movement which was to have nipped off the salient created by the Somme fighting, the German armies moved back to the Hindenburg Line defences they had been building throughout the winter. After much bad weather had hindered flying, a patrol of RFC Sopwith Pup single-seaters returned from offensive patrol to report large dumps burning and villages in flames: the salient was being evacuated and the country between the old and the new front lines laid waste in a 'scorched earth' policy. Complete plans for the German withdrawal were captured on March 14 and a British advance accordingly planned for March 17. For the first time since 1914 there would be something approaching open warfare as the British Fourth and Fifth Armies moved steadily forward for the next two weeks. There was little air opposition because on March 3 the Germans in their turn had captured General Nivelle's strategic plans for the great thrust on the Aisne and were massing their air forces to the north and south of the fighting around the Hindenburg Line, knowing that no important offensive could be launched from the now fluid British front line. The Aisne/Champagne sector was the affair of the French, and the main RFC concentration, supported by RNAS fighter squadrons, was on the Third Army front near Arras, and opposite the German fighter station at Douai, once the home of Immelmann and Boelcke, now HQ of Manfred von Richthofen's new *Jagdstaffel 11,* with V-strutter Albatros D IIIs (160/175-hp Mercedes D IIIa in-line water-cooled 'six').

During the British advance to the Hindenburg Line, 'Contact Patrol' techniques learned on the Somme were put into effect, Aeroplanes co-operated closely with infantry and cavalry, carrying messages (dropped in message-bags), and sending out W/T 'zone calls', identifying tactical targets for the gunners and discovering (usually by drawing infantry fire) the German strongpoints. In practice aircraft were little needed, since opposition was slight and ground communications (cavalry and field telephone) reasonably effective. For long-distance reconnaissance of and behind the Hindenburg Line the army wings of the Fourth and Fifth Brigades, RFC, made some use of single-seater fighters—a return to the original idea of 'scouts'. Photographic maps of the line were made by FE 2bs of No 22 Squadron escorted by No 54's Sopwith Pups (80-hp Le Rhône rotary).

The Battle of Arras began for the ground forces on Easter Monday, April 9, for the airmen five days before that. Their job was to clear the air of German machines so that corps aircraft of the First Army (holding a line roughly from the Béthune-La Bassée road south to the village of Angres, opposite Loos) and the Third Army (concentrated opposite Vimy Ridge and down to the Scarpe) could get on with their work of trench-mapping, artillery ranging and counterbattery work.

The German air force, well equipped with tractor single-seaters—Halberstadt and Albatros scouts, each armed with a pair of LMG 08/15 machine guns synchronised to fire through the propeller, in contrast with Allied machines' one gun, had profited by the lull between the Battle of the Somme and the Battle of Arras to train the hand-picked pilots of which the new *Jagdstaffeln* (fighter squadrons) were composed. A steady procession of sitting targets was provided by the BEs of the RFC on corps work or long-range reconnaissance, when head-winds often reduced cruising speed to a snail's pace.

The RFC now learned the dangers of standardising and keeping in service an obsolete machine. A formation of six BE bombers, each virtually unarmed, required an escort of six FE 2b fighter-reconnaissance aircraft plus an 'umbrella' of six Sopwith Pups —an expensive way indeed of delivering six 112-pound bombs or a shower of 20-pound Cooper bombs from 6,000 feet with primitive bomb-sights. But Major-General Trenchard, commanding the RFC in France, and his French opposite number, *Commandant* du Peuty, in charge of the *Groupement de combat* on the Aisne, believed firmly that an offensive policy must be maintained whatever the cost. The aeroplane, they held, could not be used defensively because the sky was too vast. 'Victory in the air,' de Peuty announced in a note from GQG on April 9, 'must *precede* victory on land.' Again, 'Your task is to seek out, fight and destroy *l'aviation boche.*' The constant presence of Allied aircraft far behind the German lines not only worried the civilian population but pinned down quantities of fighters and AA gunners who could otherwise have been employed against 'corps aircraft' engaged in vital mapping, artillery spotting and counterbattery work above the trenches. Furthermore, reasoned Trenchard, if his airmen managed to retain the initiative when poorly equipped, there would be absolutely no holding them when equipment improved. Events were to prove him right.

April 1917 started early upon its 'Bloody' reputation. In the five days before the infantry attack, in a snow-storm, on April 9, 75 British aeroplanes were shot down with a loss of 105 crew (19 killed, 13 wounded and 73 missing). Wastage too was very high: 56 aeroplanes crashed and written off. Pilots were being posted to squadrons with as little as 10 hours solo to their credit and often with no experience whatever of the type they were to fly in combat. The average expectation of life for a British airman on the Western Front during the month of April 1917 was 23 days. The 25 squadrons, one third of which were single-seater units, lost 316 airmen killed in action from an establishment of 730 aircrew, a casualty rate of over 40% not counting those wounded, missing and grounded.

A magnificent exploit on the credit side, however, was a raid on Douai aerodrome by FE 2ds of 100 Squadron during the night of April 5/6. Two days later the FE 2ds made another raid on Douai, bombing the aerodrome and railway station twice. Meanwhile the squadron's two FE 2bs, whose armament of Vickers one-pounder pom-pom guns had arrived only that day, attacked trains and other ground targets.

The worst piece of news reaching RFC HQ during the opening week concerned the Bristol Fighters, of which so much had been expected. Six F2As led by Captain W. Leefe Robinson, VC, of Zeppelin fame, had been 'jumped' by Manfred *Freiherr* von Richthofen and four of his *Staffel* in Albatros D III single-seaters from Douai. Richthofen shot down two, and two more fell to his comrades; the remaining two reached home, one badly damaged. From the wreckage the Germans could learn only that the unidentifiable engine was a V-12 of considerable power. The lesson drawn belatedly by the RFC was that the Bristol should be flown like a scout, using the synchronised Vickers as main armament, the observer's Lewis being a heaven-sent bonus to protect the tail. Flown thus, the Bristol was a most formidable fighting machine, and was to make a great name for itself later in the war.

In the opening days of the Battle of Arras air fighting ran through the gamut of aerial tasks: unsuccessful attacks on kite balloons, artillery shoots to flatten German wire, photography, bombing and fighting. As infantry moved forward through unseasonable Easter snow, contact patrol aeroplanes, using Klaxon horn and Verey pistols, kept track of the advance. Zone calls were sent out to indicate special targets, and the gunners' response proved so prompt and accurate in counterbattery work that aircraft were able to turn upon infantry targets—the 'trench-strafing' which was to become a permanent and hazardous feature of squadron life. On the 10th, Nieuports of 60 Squadron went on tactical photographic reconnaissance, an unusual job for single-seaters. On the 11th Richthofen equalled Boelcke's score of 40 by shooting down a BE 2c of No 13 Squadron which lost a wing as it dived. Miraculously the crew escaped with bruises.

Unwilling to leave the front for a spell of celebration—and propaganda—leave, the *Jasta* commander insisted upon adding one more to his score. In fact he added two: on April 13, the first fine day of the battle, an RE 8 shortly after 0830 hours and an FE 2b at mid-morning. The former was one of six RE 8s, in which four were escorting the other two. All six were shot down, because the slow and cumbersome biplane was no match for a single-seater and by a series of misfortunes the OPs of three Spads, six FE 2ds and a flight of Bristol Fighters which were supposed to escort them past Douai failed to appear. Richthofen was allowed to remain at the front. British 'Offensive Patrols' met few HA (Hostile Aeroplanes), which were all joining in the battle, but RFC bombers were active all day, and that evening's mission against

Front Line Strength
April 9 1917

British   German
        (v. British alone)

754   **264**

(**385** single-seater   (**114** single-seater
fighters)   fighters)

Losses
Whole of April 1917

316   **119**

Aircrew killed & missing

151   **66**

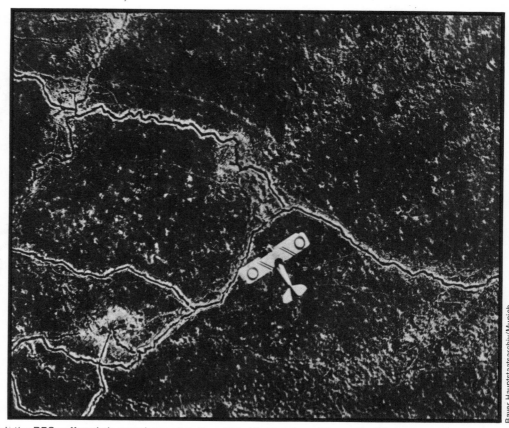

Left: The credit and debit of 'Bloody April', in which the RFC suffered air crew losses totalling 40%. *Right:* A Spad VII over the Hindenburg Line

Henin-Liétard railway station shows the scope and complication of such missions. Six 230-pound bombs and seven 112-pounders were dropped, the force comprising 12 Martinsyde G 102 'Elephants' escorted by five Spads and six Sopwith Pups, plus nine FE 2d pusher bombers with an escort of six Nieuports. Only one Martinsyde was lost, but on the way home the FE leader mistook a patrol of V-strutter Albatros for friendly Nieuports, and *Jasta 11* claimed three more victims.

It was a high time for the great individualists, the *as* (aces) as the French called them. The activities of the great fighter pilots are dealt with in another article, but it may be noted here that Boelcke's record score of 40 was being challenged not only by his pupil, Richthofen, but also by the Frenchmen Georges Guynemer and René Fonck, and the young Englishman Alfred Ball. Guynemer and Ball, particularly, believed in hunting alone and attacking unseen from extremely close range, although they took part also in Flight and Squadron patrols.

Thanks largely to Boelcke, whose *Jagdstaffel* had practised full squadron take-offs and patrols as early as September 1916, much had been learned about fighter tactics. Acting at first in pairs as Boelcke and Immelmann had done in the Fokker *Eindekker* days, single-seater pilots had learned to operate in flights of three, or, preferably, four (two pairs), under a flight commander. After trying line-ahead, line abreast and echelon formations, both sides hit upon the Vee ('vic') and diamond, with the leader in front where his view was clear and his Verey light or 'wing waggling' signals could be seen. Pilots picked their own targets when the signal to attack was given, and reformed afterwards at a prearranged rendezvous. Four machines were regarded as the maximum for one leader to control, and when larger formations were used these were built up from several groups each under its own flight commander.

Into the battle the High Command of the *Luftstreitkräfte* moved reinforcements comprising two *Jagdstaffeln* (fighter squadrons), four *Abteilungen* of corps aircraft, and two *Schutzstaffeln* of armoured close-support biplanes with downward-firing guns, the new AEG J I two-seaters (200-hp Benz water-cooled six-cylinder engine). Their appearance coincided with the withdrawal of No 3 (Naval) Wing from Luxeuil, the base from which Sopwith 1½-Strutters had been engaged in strategic bombing of Germany. This enterprise, very much to the taste of RNAS pilots, was not relished politically by the French, who feared damage to the property of loyalists in Alsace-Lorraine and lived in dread of reprisals against French towns including Paris, which lay alarmingly close to the front.

The second phase of the Battle of Arras opened on April 16,

when General Nivelle launched his widely publicised offensive on the Aisne. The fighters were commanded by *Commandant* du Peuty, the able ex-cavalryman whose 'offensive thinking' had early influenced Trenchard. Du Peuty was still under 40, a fact which did not endear him to certain senior officers. Under his command came *Groupes de combat* 11, 12 and 14, plus three *escadrilles* of Nieuport and Caudron machines — on paper four *groupes*, or 200 aeroplanes. In fact he had 131 machines on April 16, and only 153 by April 21, his maximum, to which could be added 30 machines from the Paris defences. Staff arrangements were woefully, and it seems almost wilfully, muddled. Pilots were sent to Le Bourget on ferry duty who should have been in action, and the front of the *Groupe des Armées de Reserve* was divided geographically, not according to commands. The staff had also decreed, on April 1, that each army must file its expected air requirements by 2000 hours the previous day.

German supremacy
There were to be six standing patrols along the whole front, three for each sector comprising:
● two patrols (one offensive, one defensive) at 6,000-8,000 feet (corps aircraft height); and
● one high patrol.
There was no zone call system, and often fighter *escadrilles* were not warned of local attacks or changes of plan.

German fighter supremacy was such that on April 13 it was requested that zero hour for the offensive on the 16th should be advanced to first light, as German dawn patrols would otherwise discover all. German fighters did, in fact, harry the front line during the attack, driving away French artillery and contact patrols. There was a continual cry for close, that is defensive, fighter support, notably from General Mangin, and in fact during the Verdun attack low patrols did operate at 2,000-3,000 feet between 0500 and 0615 hours to drive off marauding HA and to attack balloons. Bad weather limited du Peuty's long-range offensive patrols ('fortunately', said his detractors), and when these did go out, in patrols of six, 'never less than five', the Germans avoided combat, thus giving unconscious support to du Peuty's opponents on the French staff, who were quick to speak of 'wasting petrol', 'shadow-boxing' and the like. Theirs was to be the last word. *Commandant* du Peuty eventually resigned, and despite his cavalry background joined an infantry unit in the trenches, where he was killed.

In machines, too, France was weak. The Spad S VII (150-hp Hispano-Suiza) was a good fighter, as witness the scores of Guynemer and other aces, but the pusher Voisins and Farmans were

hopelessly outclassed. Only slightly better able to defend itself was the Caudron 4, a twin-engined three-seater (two 130-hp Hispano-Suizas) which lasted until replaced by the Letord I (two Hispano-Suiza V-8s). The *Aviation Militaire* also possessed for some reason the Paul Schmitt 7, an extraordinary biplane of great span, minimal performance and no fewer than 12 sets of interplane struts. The PS 7 (265-hp Renault) was unique in that the angle of incidence of the entire biplane cellule could be varied to give either maximum speed or maximum lift, but the drag was so great that neither speed nor lift was sufficient. The Paul Schmitt was armed with two machine guns and proved extremely unhandy in the air. Strangely, all documents relating to its adoption are missing from the French archives. The French also used Sopwith 1½-Strutters in two-seater and single-seat bomber form. Criticising it, with some justification, as more of a touring machine than a combat aeroplane, they applauded its *'exploits sportifs'* with the 240-pound bomb. French aviation, so brilliant during the early war years, was far from happy in spring 1917, despite the gallantry of individual airmen.

The new German tactics of ignoring offensive patrols the better to concentrate above the trenches were employed also on the Arras front, where the Germans, said General Trenchard, were 'undoubtedly slipping underneath our high patrols without being seen by them'. Even when a force of Bristol Fighters and RNAS Sopwith Triplanes trailed their coats above Douai itself *Jasta 11* failed to rise. Richthofen preferred to meet Nieuports in the air, which he did on April 16. Six Nieuports met four Albatros and four Nieuports went down.

Economical of aeroplanes, the Germans made few fighter sweeps behind the British lines, and because in their 1914 retreat they had prudently dug in on high ground affording a view over the plains, they had less need of aerial reconnaissance than had the RFC. Strangely, they made no sustained bombing attack on Calais, Boulogne and Dieppe, where disembarkation could have been severely hindered.

As the ground forces prepared for a new assault in the Arras sector to take some of the sting out of Nivelle's failure further south, bad weather kept most machines on the ground. The four days from the 16th to the 20th were virtually 'washed out'. On the 21st a preliminary bombardment flattened German wire and sorties were made against the balloons directing counterbattery fire. Two were shot down on the Third Army front and one on that of the Second Army. Three others were damaged but hauled down in time because the Germans had discovered a method far quicker than the winch: the cable was passed under a pulley and hitched to a lorry which then drove away, towing the balloon rapidly to the ground. The counter to this, invented by Major L. Tilney, CO of No 40 Squadron (Nieuports), was a hedge-hopping fighter attack at ground level. The Nieuport 17 sesquiplane was still the favourite mount of Captain Ball, the RFC's top-scoring pilot. He preferred it to his new SE 5, which was now operational after No 56 Squadron's CO had improved upon the Royal Aircraft Factory's design of the cockpit. W. A. Bishop, another future VC, also cherished his Nieuport 17 although clearly it was outperformed,

Could the agility of the Triplane match the heavier armament of the Albatros?

and its single Lewis doubly outgunned, by the Albatros V-strutters it had inspired. A further four Nieuports were lost to *Jasta 11* pilots on April 21, but the RFC was past its bad time. The factory strikes at home which had halted production had now largely been settled and supplies of vital new aircraft were reaching the front. The SE 5 was in action, Sopwith Pups and Triplanes were more than a match for the German fighters, and the Sopwith Camel was on its way. Admittedly the SE was in trouble with its Hispano engine and with a new and secret gun-synchronising device for its Vickers but there was a Lewis on the centre-section and these teething troubles would soon be overcome.

The new synchronising gear had the great advantage that it could be fitted quickly to any type of engine. Invented by George Constantinesco, a Rumanian mining-engineer and developed by him with Major C. Colley, Royal Artillery, the device was known in the RFC as the CC gear, and must count as one of the simplest and most useful inventions of the war. It worked on the same principle as a modern car's hydraulic brakes, and may be described diagrammatically as a column of liquid in a pipe sealed by a plunger at each end. Pressure exerted at one end, by an engine cam, could not fail to reach the other and exert a similar and simultaneous pressure on, for example, the trigger of a gun. Tested on a BE 2c in August 1916, the design was adopted forthwith. The first squadron so equipped, No 55 (DH 4s), landed in France on March 6, 1917. Meanwhile obsolete machines like the BE 2c, FE 2b, 'Strutter' and the early marks of Spad continued to suffer, and occasionally to mistake Albatros for the friendly though outmoded Nieuport.

Left: Leutnant Werner Voss' Albatros D III fighter. The D III had double the armament of contemporary Allied fighters, but its wings were relatively weak and water from the centrally-placed radiator was likely to scald the pilot if it were punctured in combat. *Engine:* Mercedes D IIIa inline, 160/175 hp. *Armament:* two Spandau machine guns. *Speed:* 103 mph at sea level. *Climb:* 3.3 minutes to 3,280 feet. *Ceiling:* 18,050 feet. *Endurance:* 2 hours. *Weight empty/loaded:* 1,454/1,949 lbs. *Span:* 29 feet 8¼ inches. *Length:* 24 feet.

Left: A Sopwith Triplane of No. 1 Naval Squadron. This type took the Germans completely by surprise, for though its fire-power was only half that of the Albatros, its manoeuvrability, climb and altitude perform-ance left the Albatros standing. *Engine:* Clerget 9Z rotary, 110 hp. *Armament:* one Vickers machine gun. *Speed:* 113 mph at 6,500 feet. *Climb:* 9 minutes 25 seconds to 10,000 feet. *Ceiling:* 20,500 feet. *Endurance:* 2 hours 45 minutes. *Weight empty/loaded:* 1,100/1,500 lbs. *Span:* 26 feet 6 inches. *Length:* 18 feet 10 inches.

John Batchelor

Haig's second offensive opened on April 23, St George's Day, on a 9-mile front, Croisilles-Gavrelle. Fortunately two Triplanes of Naval 1 had, two days before, dispersed an unusually powerful German reconnaissance formation of 14 DFW C Vs and escorting Albatros, disappointing them of vital information. Tiny, compact and with the masses of engine, pilot and tanks closely concentrated, the 'Tripehound' was immensely manoeuvrable and in its element at 16,000 feet, where this engagement took place.

Over the lines on St George's Day, German fighters from a variety of units harried the unfortunate corps aircraft as they wheeled in figures of eight spotting for the guns, while army squadrons gave what support they could. In an area bounded by Lens, Henin-Liétard, Bullecourt, Sains and the battle line itself 48 British scouts and Bristol Fighters plus 20 two-seater fighter-reconnaissance machines were on Offensive Patrol, while the number of famous names figuring in the day's engagements read like 'Who's Who': Ball, Bishop, Hermann Göring, Lothar von Richthofen (brother of Manfred) and of course Richthofen himself. That evening a bombing raid on Epinoy by six FEs of 18 Squadron escorted by five Pups was attacked by two formations of Albatros and Halberstadt fighters and there developed one of the first big 'dog-fights' of the war, as British Fighters, Triplanes and Nieuports hastened to join in a fight, which lasted for an hour. Later FE 2d night bombers of 100 Squadron overflew Douai to bomb Pont à Vendin station, also machine gunning troop trains whereby desperately needed German reinforcements arrived late and almost too tired to relieve their comrades in the trenches.

During daylight fighter opposition was intense. New German

two-seaters were also in service, including the Albatros C V (220-hp Mercedes D IV straight-eight) and C VII (200-hp Benz IV six) which would outperform an SE 5 at 10,000 feet. Whatever motives had led the *Jagdstaffeln* to avoid combat earlier in the month, they were now deployed in full force and full of spirit. On the morning of April 29, picturesquely, the Richthofen brothers each shot down a Spad before entertaining their father, Major Albrecht *Freiherr* von Richthofen, to lunch in the mess. At 1600 hours Manfred destroyed an FE after a stiff fight over Inchy, while on yet another sortie the two brothers scored again, against a pair of BE 2ds. In a final combat of the day, when *Jasta 11* was involved with 11 Triplanes of Naval 8 and one Nieuport of 60 Squadron, Manfred secured his 52nd victim, but only after Captain F. L. Barwell's Nieuport, absurdly underpowered and under-armed in comparison with the Albatros, had defended itself magnificently for almost half an hour. Not all Manfred von Richthofen's victims were easy ones, though it must be pointed out that although without so many defenceless BEs and antiquated pushers in the sky his score would undoubtedly have been smaller.

The Red Baron

Quantity production of factory-designed BE 2, FE 2 and RE 8 biplanes made up to some extent for the Allies' lack of high ground. It was therefore essential for the Germans to shoot them down. With so many targets the German rate of scoring was high—four times (and on some sectors even five times) the RFC rate; but the RFC fighters were usually matched against fighters, either on offensive patrol or while driving the predatory Albatros from its

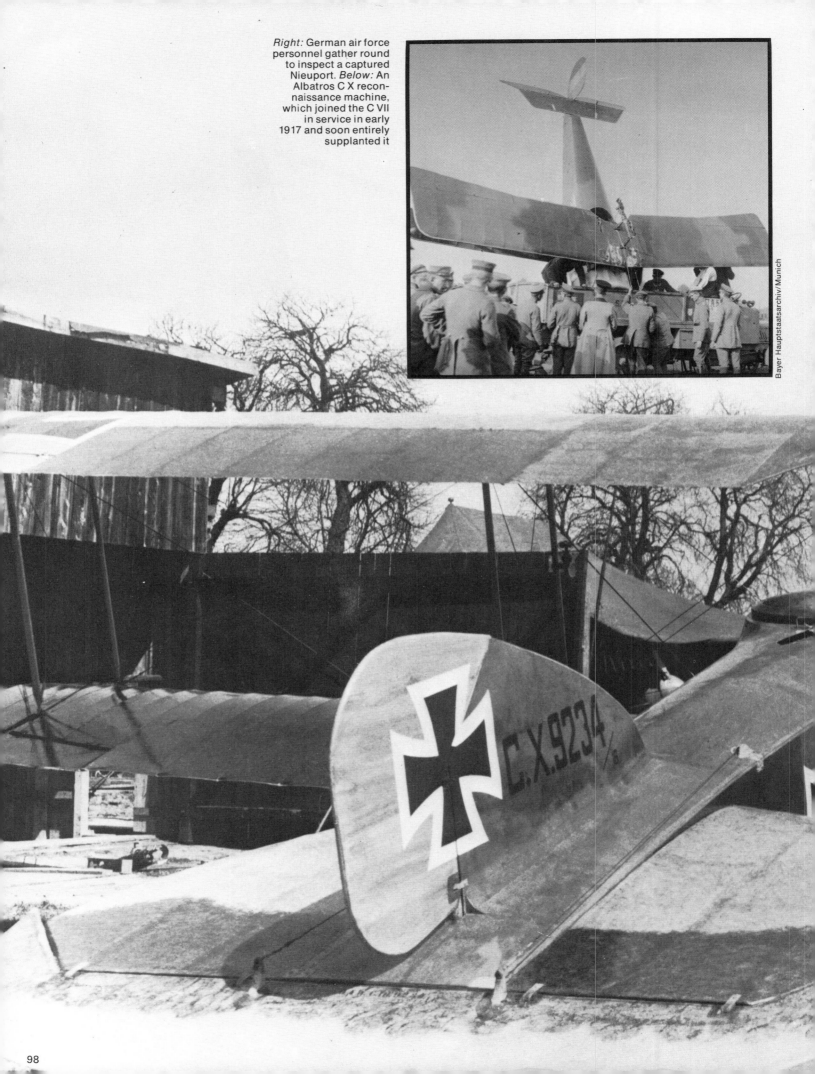

Right: German air force personnel gather round to inspect a captured Nieuport. *Below:* An Albatros C X reconnaissance machine, which joined the C VII in service in early 1917 and soon entirely supplanted it

Bayer. Hauptstaatsarchiv/Munich

prey. Their antagonists, the *Jagdstaffeln* invented by Boelcke in 1916 and efficiently developed by Richthofen, had done well, thanks to good equipment, good training—and plentiful targets. There was also the *panache* that characterised the elder Richthofen. It was a master stroke to paint the aeroplanes of his squadron in brilliant colours—quite against German army regulations—while reserving the only almost totally red machine for himself, a return to the personal style of the mediaeval knight, with his crest and coat of arms. No better publicity device has ever been invented than the blood red aircraft of 'the Red Knight'.

Further to raise the rate of scoring it was now decided to increase the local striking power of the *Jagdstaffeln* by banding together four of them into a larger group. *Jasta 11* was combined with numbers *3, 4* and *33* into an independent fighter wing called *Jagdgruppe 1* which first went into action, rather clumsily, on April 30, the day on which *Rittmeister* Manfred von Richthofen went on leave to celebrate his 52 victories. Reorganised on his return, and now comprising *Jagdstaffeln* numbers *11, 10, 6* and *4*, this unit became the true 'Richthofen Circus', a private army of mobile trouble-shooters known after July as *Jagdgeschwader 1*.

'Bloody April' was over. The supply of new machines from England improved and new types came into service capable of outfighting the Albatros D III and Halberstadt scouts which had taken such toll during the worst month in the history of British air fighting overseas. French airmen too had taken a terrible beating during the ill-fated 'push' of General Nivelle, now fortunately superseded.

In the RFC casualties would have been lighter if those responsible for supply had been more flexible in outlook. It would have been perfectly possible to update the Royal Aircraft Factory's series of helpless BE two-seaters so that pilot and passenger changed places, giving the observer a clear field of fire. Frederick Koolhoven of Armstrong-Whitworth had refused to build BEs and the result was the FK 8, the 'Big Ack', a far more robust and effective machine. The lack of British engines, a result of blind trust in the French aviation industry, led to many casualties, for a rotary Le Rhône or Clerget of 110-hp or 130-hp, although marginally sufficient for a single-seater fighter, was woefully inadequate in two-seaters like the Sopwith 1½-Strutter. The Factory's air-cooled stationary engines, based on Renault designs, lacked smoothness, power and reliability, while the cooling scoops devised by Factory designers had a disastrous effect on the performance of BE and RE aeroplanes.

Technical inferiority must always mean a high casualty rate. Machines already proved obsolete against the Fokker monoplane in 1915 could not be expected to hold off an Albatros D III, and it is not surprising that some squadrons during Bloody April lost more aircrew than there were chairs in the Mess. Perhaps Trenchard's policy of 'offensive at all costs' was unduly robust for the machines under his command. But the Royal Flying Corps did all he required of it during both periods of German air supremacy, and the fact that RFC pilots never lost their offensive spirit was to prove decisive during the coming struggles with the 'Circus', and the tremendous ground-strafing days of 1918.

Bayer Hauptstaatsarchiv/Munich

THE AIR BATTLE

The first phases of Ludendorff's offensive were
preluded and accompanied by intense air activity.
Careful strategy was matched against daring
and aggressive individualism, and a heavy toll
of British aircraft against a disproportionate
lowering of German morale. *Thomas G. Miller, Jr.*
Below: RFC pilot ready for take-off in an
RE 8 artillery observation aircraft

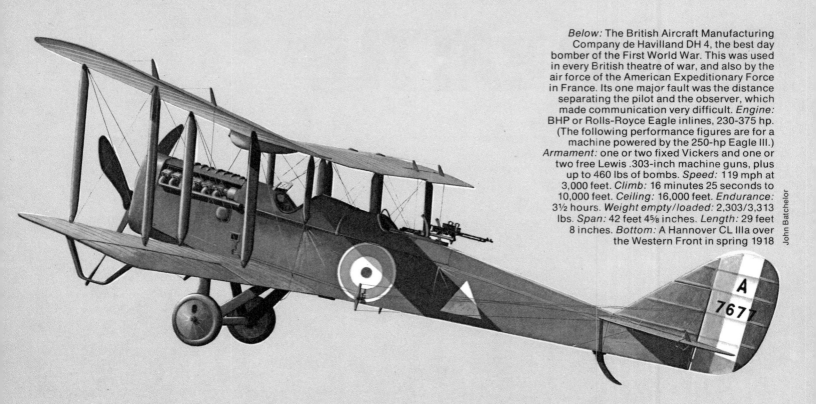

Below: The British Aircraft Manufacturing Company de Havilland DH 4, the best day bomber of the First World War. This was used in every British theatre of war, and also by the air force of the American Expeditionary Force in France. Its one major fault was the distance separating the pilot and the observer, which made communication very difficult. *Engine:* BHP or Rolls-Royce Eagle inlines, 230-375 hp. (The following performance figures are for a machine powered by the 250-hp Eagle III.) *Armament:* one or two fixed Vickers and one or two free Lewis .303-inch machine guns, plus up to 460 lbs of bombs. *Speed:* 119 mph at 3,000 feet. *Climb:* 16 minutes 25 seconds to 10,000 feet. *Ceiling:* 16,000 feet. *Endurance:* 3½ hours. *Weight empty/loaded:* 2,303/3,313 lbs. *Span:* 42 feet 4⅝ inches. *Length:* 29 feet 8 inches. *Bottom:* A Hannover CL IIIa over the Western Front in spring 1918

John Batchelor

In summer 1917 the German *Luftstreit-kräfte* started on a major programme of expansion as part of Ludendorff's plan to defeat the Allies on the battlefield before the power of America could be deployed. Sardonically dubbed the 'Amerikapro-gramm', the expansion resulted in a field strength by March, 1918 of 153 *Flieger-abteilungen*, 38 *Schlachtstaffeln*, 80 *Jagd-staffeln*, and seven *Bombengeschwader* totalling 24 *Staffeln*.

Generalleutnant von Hoeppner and *Oberstleutnant* Thomsen planned aviation's participation in the coming spring offen-sives with great thoroughness. By early March the stealthy buildup of German air strength in *Second, Seventeenth* and *Eighteenth Armies* was complete. Ever since the Battle of the Somme in 1916 the Germans had kept the bulk of their air forces facing the RFC which they considered to be far more skilful and aggressive than the numerically superior French. But for almost the first time the Germans would have numerical superior-ity over the British. Incorporated into the three attacking armies were no less than 49 *Fliegerabteilungen*, 27 *Schlachtstaffeln*, 35 *Jagdstaffeln* and four *Bombengesch-wader*. As was true of German aviation dur-ing most of the war, these units operated a wide variety of aircraft makes and models. The *Jastas* were mostly equipped with the Albatros DV and DVa, by now obsolescent, but some also had the Fokker DrI, the Pfalz D III and D IIIa and the Roland D VIa. The *Schlachtstaffeln* were equipped with the excellent Hannoveraner C II and Halberstadt CL II, and the *Fliegerabtei-lungen* a motley of LVG, DFW, Rumpler, Junkers and Albatros models.

The Royal Flying Corps had a total of 60 squadrons on the Western Front in March, and 31 of these were with Third and Fifth Armies. The III Brigade had four squadrons of RE 8's, one each of DH 4's and FE 2b's, and seven fighter squadrons, three operat-ing SE 5a's, three Camels and one Bristol Fighter. The V Brigade's Corps Wing had five observation squadrons; the Army Wing had two bombing squadrons (DH 4 and FE 2b), two of SE 5a's, and one each of Camels, Spads and Bristols. The Ninth Wing, normally attached to HQ, RFC as a general reserve, had been moved up behind Fifth Army front in early March in ac-curate anticipation of the German offen-sive. Its six squadrons included two of DH 4's, two of Camels, one of Bristols and one with the new Sopwith Dolphin. In all, 579 serviceable British aircraft, of which 261 were single-seater fighters, faced 730 German, 326 of which were fighters.

Outnumbered and outfought

The RFC was thoroughly prepared for the time and place of the German offensive, if not its scale. Instructions had been drawn up in detail as early as January specifying the basic tactics to be followed by each squadron. A number of the fighter squad-rons were assigned to fly low level bombing missions against specific targets, mostly bridges and roads that would be used by the advancing German infantry. Early in March the British began to organise bombing attacks against German airfields opposite Third and Fifth Army fronts. The bombing missions were supplemented by offensive fighter patrols which started the air battles over a week before the German ground offensive actually began.

These culminated on March 18 in one of the largest air battles of the First World War, the 'Battle of Le Cateau'. From the German side, virtually every fighter squad-ron on the front of *Second Army* rose to meet a British force of five bombers and 24 fighters. Manfred von Richthofen led a formation of some 30 Fokker Triplanes,

Below: The German Hannover CL IIIa escort fighter and ground attack aircraft. This compact and manoeuvrable two-seater was introduced in 1918, and was often, and disastrously, taken for a single-seater. The biplane tail was adopted so that tail surfaces of a sufficient area could be packed into as small a space as possible, to give the gunner an excellent field of fire. *Engine:* Argus As III inline, 180 hp. *Armament:* one fixed Spandau and one free Parabellum machine gun. *Speed:* 103 mph at 16,400 feet. *Climb:* 5 minutes 18 seconds to 3,280 feet. *Ceiling:* 24,600 feet. *Endurance:* 3 hours. *Weight empty/loaded:* 1,577/2,378 lbs. *Span:* 38 feet 4¾ inches. *Length:* 24 feet 10½ inches

John Batchelor

Left: Soon to depart the scene—the last photograph of Richthofen, with his dog Moritz. *Above:* A German fighter passes over the troops it is supporting. *Below:* The inevitable conclusion—the remains of a hopelessly obsolete BE 2e, which should have been replaced by the end of 1916. *Right:* A Hannover CL IIIa (foreground), one of Germany's best strafing aircraft

Albatros and Pfalz of *Jagdgeschwader I*; eight other *Staffeln* also took part. The RFC was outnumbered and outfought. Five of No 54 Squadron's Camels were shot down, plus two SE 5's and two of the bombers. The total loss to the Germans was one Albatros.

The air preliminaries to the German offensive are most instructive in retrospect. The RFC undertook an aggressive policy, as was its wont, evidently with the expectation that the results necessarily would be favourable. They most certainly were not. Several British squadrons were severely mauled at a trifling cost to the Germans. The RFC genuinely believed it outfought its opponent upon almost every occasion they met, or at least its High Command behaved as if they did, for the strategy followed by the RFC was apparently based on implicit assumptions of individual superiority. The outcome unfortunately failed to support the assumption. Once again, intelligent defensive tactics, professionally overseen, carried the day, and the British suffered unnecessarily high losses to no good purpose.

Air fighting subsided after Le Cateau. The next event of note came early in the morning of March 21 when the German onslaught was unleashed on Fifth Army. Fog throughout the morning prevented the carefully-rehearsed air attacks of both the Germans and the defending British, but shortly after noon the aircraft of both sides took off. There was intense and chaotic air fighting, and great numbers of aircraft flying low altitude bombing and strafing missions. On Fifth Army front such attacks were made by Nos 23, 24, 48, 54 and 84 Squadrons while the 27 German *Schlachtstaffeln* were all in action ahead of their advancing infantry. Although the RFC Corps aircraft suffered losses at the hands of the German fighters, most of the latter were flying patrols high above the front and did very little to impede the British low-level attacks, a fact upon which German regimental histories comment with some asperity. Despite the scale of the air activity, losses were

moderate: the Germans lost eight aircraft and the RFC seven.

Intense air activity

The gallantry and intense activity of the RFC squadrons against the German advance were of course of little avail. Aircraft weakly armed with a few small bombs and machine guns were capable at best of exercising sharp but essentially transient material impact upon widely scattered units of infantry; on the other hand the effect on morale of such attacks was cumulative and doubtless considerable. Nevertheless, the German onrush was inexorable. Early in the afternoon, No 5 Naval Squadron was shelled out of its aerodrome and Major Sholto Douglas, OC of No 84, took his squadron out only hours before its field was overrun. By that night it was obvious that all Fifth Army squadrons and some of Third Army's would have to fall back, and the necessary orders were issued.

The morning of the 22nd was almost exactly like that of the previous day, thick fog and no flying until around 1300 hours, after which intense air activity started. Fifth Army's squadrons were pulled back to airfields further behind the lines that afternoon, the pilots taking off from the old field, flying their patrols and landing at the new one. Virtually all the air activity was at low altitudes, most of it consisting of attacks on the retreating British and advancing German infantry. At the end of the day the RFC had lost 19 aircraft and the Germans 11.

The weather improved considerably on March 23 and air activity was almost continuous during the daylight hours from then to March 28. The aircraft of both sides concentrated on low-level bombing and strafing attacks. The German *Schlachtstaffeln,* although ubiquitous, were not particularly effective; their Halberstadts and Hannoveraners normally flew at around 200 feet and their principal weapons were 7.62-mm machine guns and 'potato-masher' hand grenades. The logic for so weak an armament apparently was

that aircraft attacking infantry required nothing more than infantry weapons, but in so doing they failed to avail themselves of the ability of aircraft to carry and deliver more lethal payloads. The RFC fighter pilots, being unencumbered by any tactical doctrine, generally attacked from very low altitudes; indeed one German company commander was run over by a strafing Camel even though he had thrown himself flat on the ground! As a result of this superb daring, commented upon many times in German regimental histories, the British pilots exacted a mental toll from the Germans out of proportion to their slight material impact.

Throughout March 24, squadrons supporting Third Army attacked German troops advancing against the Bapaume-Peronne road. Air fighting greatly increased, almost all of it taking place over Bapaume below 5,000 feet. By the morning of the 25th, Third Army's front had begun to crumble between Montauban and Urvillers, and Major-General Salmond sent the following order to the OC 9th Wing (Lieutenant-Colonel Wilfred Freeman): '. . . send out your scout squadrons and those of No 27, No 25 and No 62 Squadrons that are available on to the line Grevillers-Martinpuich-Maricourt. These Squadrons will bomb and shoot up everything they can see. . . . Very low flying is essential. All risks to be taken. Urgent.'

Further Reading
Bodenschatz, K., *Jagd in Flanderns Himmel* (Verlag Knorr & Hirth 1935)
Hoeppner, Gen. E. von, *Deutschlands Krieg in der Luft* (Koehler 1921)
Kirtleside, Lord Douglas of, *Combat and Command* Volume 1 (Collins 1963)
Martel, R., *L'Aviation Francaise de Bombardment* (Paul Hartmann 1939)
Raleigh, Sir Walter, & Jones, H.A., *The War in the Air* Volumes I-VI (OUP 1922/23)
Voisin, Gen., *La Doctrine de L'Aviation Francaise de Combat, 1915-1918* (Berger-Levrault 1932)

The Air Battle over Lys

During the Battle of the Lys, the German ground support tactics were further refined. All was overshadowed by the death of Richthofen, however. *Thomas G. Miller. Below:* A Halberstadt CL II is 'bombed up'

Ten squadrons from I Brigade, five of them corps observation units, plus two from V Brigade augmented the efforts of Freeman's wing and III Brigade. Salmond shortly lost communication with all but one of his brigades, and the battle now devolved onto the squadron commanders and pilots, who flew so low and in such numbers over the threatened portion of the front that the danger of collision was almost constant. SE 5's, Camels, Dolphins, even lumbering RE 8's and 'Ack W's' were in action continuously through the daylight hours. By the early dawn of March 26, 37 of the 60 RFC squadrons on the Western Front were flying support for Third Army to the west of Bapaume. This crisis was effectively at an end by the afternoon of the 26th, but a new threat arose as the Germans redirected the weight of *Michael* back to Fifth Army front towards Roye and Montdidier. This thrust in turn became the centre of gravity of the air effort on the 27th, although low-level air attacks were continued on Third Army front through the day. RFC losses were extremely severe, with 13 aircraft missing and 26 shot down or wrecked. *Jagdgeschwader 1*, patrolling the skies over Albert, shot down 13 British aircraft without loss. The *Schlachtstaffeln* of *Second Army* also were active during the day, attacking Vaux, Vaire, Morcourt and Bouzincourt. However, they had suffered considerable losses from British ground fire since March 21, losing five aircraft on the 26th, and by now the pace of the German advance had placed their airfields far from the action. The attitude of the senior German staffs toward their flying forces appeared to be 'out of sight, out of mind'. Communications were intermittent, few definite orders were sent out and even those attacks ordered were poorly coordinated with the ground action. By contrast, the RFC daily became more

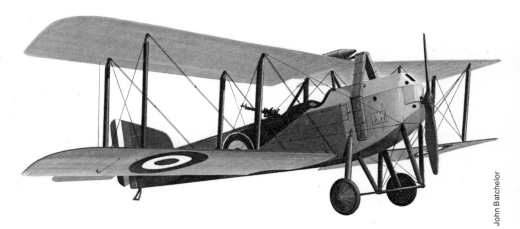

John Batchelor

Aeroplanes, *top to bottom:*
One of the machines that began to bomb Paris again in 1918 after an interval of three years, the **Friedrichshafen G III**. Although better known as builders of a superb series of seaplanes, the Friedrichshafen concern also produced a series of good long range bombers, of which the G III and IIIa, the former's twin-tailed version, were the best. *Crew:* 2 or 3. *Engines:* Two Mercedes D IVa inlines, 260 hp each. *Armament:* Two or three Parabellum machine guns and up to 3,300 lbs of bombs. *Speed:* 87½ mph at 3,280 feet. *Ceiling:* 14,800 feet. *Endurance:* 5 hours. *Weight empty/loaded:* 5,929/8,646 lbs. *Span:* 77 feet 9¼ inches. *Length:* 42 feet. Next, the extraordinary all-metal **Junkers J I** armoured close support aircraft. Although underpowered and therefore slow and tricky at take off and landing, the J I soon endeared itself to its crews by virtue of its extreme strength and the ample protection of the armoured crew area. A last unusual feature was the cantilever structure of the thick, high-lift section wings. The type was very successful in 1918. *Crew:* 2. *Engine:* One Benz Bz IV inline, 200 hp. *Armament:* Two fixed Spandau and one flexible Parabellum machine gun. *Speed:* 97 mph at sea level. *Climb:* 32 minutes to 6,560 feet. *Endurance:* 2 hours. *Weight empty/loaded:* 3,885/4,787 lbs. *Span:* 52 feet 6 inches. *Length:* 29 feet 10⅜ inches. Lastly, the British **Armstrong Whitworth FK 8** light bomber and reconnaissance machine, nicknamed 'Big Ack' to distinguish it from the FK 3. The FK 8 was an excellent combat type. *Crew:* 2. *Engine:* One Beardmore inline, 120 or 160 hp. *Armament:* One fixed Vickers and one flexible Lewis machine gun. *Speed:* 98½ mph. *Climb:* 11 minutes to 5,000 feet. *Endurance:* 3 hours. *Weight empty/loaded:* 1,916/2,811 lbs. *Span:* 43½ feet. *Length:* 31 feet

The shell of the village of Kemmel, part of the Lys battlefield, seen from the air

Sudd Verlag

The brunt of long range bombing on the Western Front was borne by Gothas and the type illustrated here, the Friedrichshafen G III. Note the later pattern of markings

active, and, although its losses were heavy, it secured command of the air from the Germans and kept it.

The *Michael* offensive as such effectively came to an end with the German assault on Arras on March 28. The weary, horribly dangerous routine of low-level attacks continued throughout the day, at a cost to the RFC of 17 aircraft missing and 35 wrecked; seven German aircraft were shot down. The attack was a complete failure, and following this severe rebuff, Ludendorff realised his chance of breaking through on the Somme had gone. The air fighting slowly lost its intensity and the huge concentration of aircraft put together for *Michael* now began to be dispersed.

One further event on the Somme front must be recorded, the death on April 21 of Manfred von Richthofen. Although remembered as the foremost air fighter of the First World War, he was even more valuable to the Germans as an inspiration to the *Luftstreitkräfte* and the people and as a tactical leader of large fighter units. The manner of his death will never be fully settled. Conflicting claims were made by several Lewis gunners of an Australian machine gun battery and by Captain A. R. Brown of No 209 Squadron. The latter claim obviously was more acceptable to the RAF (the Royal Flying Corps and Royal Naval Air Service were combined into the Royal Air Force on April 1); the former was preferred by the army and, incidentally, the Germans. The preponderance of evidence carefully compiled in recent years suggests that Richthofen in fact was killed by ground fire. Almost alone among the famous pilots of the First World War his name is still widely familiar more than half a century later.

The German preparations for the *Georgette* attack on the Lys were quite similar to those for *Michael*. Local air superiority for the period of the initial assault and breakthrough was assured by a heavy concentration of aircraft. *Fourth* and *Sixth Armies* had 25 *Jagdstaffeln*, 17 *Schlachtstaffeln*, 28 *Fliegerabteilungen*, and two *Bombengeschwader*, totalling 492 aircraft. Thirty-eight RAF squadrons of I, II and IX Brigades opposed these units, 17 of which were single-seat fighters, four day-bombing, three two-seater reconnaissance,

two night-bombing and 12 corps observation. It is a measure of the extent to which *Michael* strained the *Luftstreitkräfte's* resources that many of the *Staffeln* assigned to *Georgette* were borrowed from the armies actively engaged on the Somme.

Grounded by fog

The air fighting in April was uncannily like that of the previous month. Even the first day was almost an exact replica of March 21. The thick fog that on the morning of April 9 shielded the shattering assault on the Portuguese 2nd Division also effectively kept both sides from flying until the early afternoon. After 1400 hours the Camels of 203 and 210 Squadrons and No 40 Squadron's SE 5's carried out intermittent bombing and strafing attacks against the Germans. Air opposition was light, both sides concentrating on low-level work. As in March, hasty evacuation of many British airfields was made necessary by the speed of the German advance, and the commanding officer of No 208 Squadron, unable to fly his aircraft out in the fog, burned 18 Camels in the middle of his airfield and evacuated the squadron's personnel by motor transport.

The next day the battle spread to cover most of the region between Ypres and Béthune. Once again fog kept the aircraft on the ground until the afternoon, when both the RFC and the Germans were out in force. On First Army's front, Nos 203, 4 Australian, 210, 19, 40 and 18 Squadrons carried out extensive attacks against German infantry advancing in front of Merville, while the SE 5's of No 1 carried almost the entire burden for Second Army. Losses, which on the previous day had been only one British and four German aircraft, now began to mount, as a result of machine gun fire from the ground for the most part; four RAF aircraft and seven German were shot down on April 10. The same weather and air combat patterns were repeated on the 11th, with the losses on both sides (five British, four German) also about the same as previously. However, this was the last day on which the Germans were able to use their *Schlachtstaffeln* and low-flying fighters to assist the advance of their infantry. As had been the case in the *Michael*

offensive, the rapid pace of the ground battle apparently bewildered staffs grown slow-thinking in almost four years of siege warfare, and hitherto unaccustomed to thinking in terms of close co-ordination between ground and air. The German squadrons found themselves miles behind the front, seemingly forgotten. Communications with higher headquarters were poor and orders, when they came, bore little relation to current needs of the battlefield. The infantrymen, who then (and have ever since) regarded aviators as light-hearted swaggerers, understandably perceived the failure of their own staffs as the failure of the air force.

The critical day for *Georgette* came on April 12. For the first time since the offensive began, the morning dawned fine and clear and the RAF began a maximum effort to help stem the German rush toward Hazebrouck. One hundred and thirty-seven aircraft from I Brigade attacked German troops and transport around the important junction of Merville between 0600 and 1900 hours. They were joined by the tireless No 1 Squadron and two day-bomber squadrons of II Brigade. Air fighting was continuous and German aircraft were encountered at all altitudes; ten British aircraft were shot down during the day for the loss of five German. Perhaps the climax was an attack at 1305 hours by Nos 210 and 40 Squadrons on German balloons near Merville, five of which were shot down. Four days after the German attack started, the RAF was in disputed but firm control of the air. So weak was the effect of air control in those days, though, that the Germans took no notice of the fact. Although the 12th was the last day of heavy air activity along the Lys, the German ground advance continued until the 18th. Then it too was held, just short of Hazebrouck.

But the last had not yet been heard of *Georgette*. The main thrust gradually shifted from *Sixth Army* to *Fourth Army* and this organisation built up a strong concentration of aircraft for the assault on Kemmel Hill. Fourteen *Jagdstaffeln* under the tactical command of *Oberleutnant* Bruno Loerzer, *Kommandeur* of *Jagdgeschwader III*, were to provide air cover over the battlefield, while four *Schlachtgeschwader* and three *Jagdstaffeln* were assigned to direct support of the three attacking corps. Twelve *Fliegerabteilungen* handled artillery spotting and reconnaissance for the attacking army.

At 0600 hours on April 25 the assault on Kemmel Hill marked the first large scale use of tactical aircraft from the outset of an offensive battle. The attacking German divisions were preceded by 16 *Schlachtstaffeln* flying in a long sawtooth formation that swept over No-Man's Land like a mowing machine. These 96 aircraft fired over 60,000 rounds of machine gun ammunition and dropped 700 bombs; they then split up into units of two or three aircraft which proceeded independently, attacking targets of opportunity behind the British and French lines. Loerzer's fighter *Staffeln* maintained absolute control over the battlefield, shooting down four British aircraft for no losses of their own. Indeed only one *Fourth Army* aircraft was lost during the entire day.

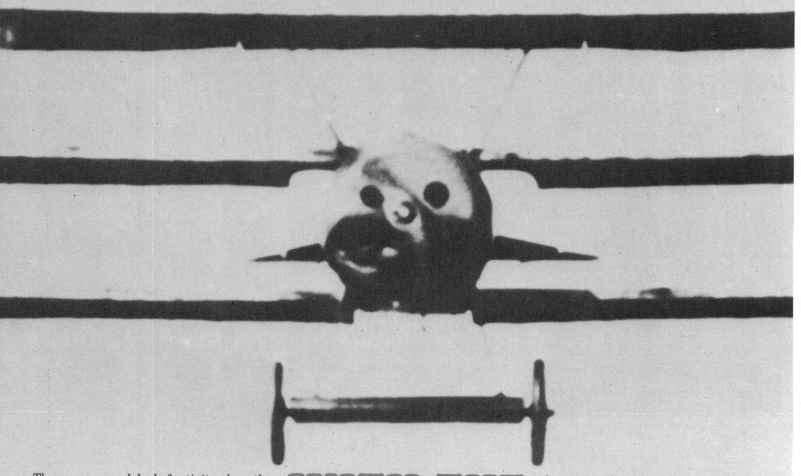

WITH THE RED BARON

At the time of which he was writing, Ernst Udet was a novice, but he went on to be Germany's second greatest ace, with 62 victories. *Above:* The master — Richthofen and his Dr I

There was a good deal of activity along the fronts, and it was rumoured that a big offensive was being prepared on the other side. Every day we saw long rows of captive balloons, which, against the summer sky, looked like' a string of over-sized sausages. These balloons annoyed us and we decided that something would have to be done about them.

So one morning I started out early, at a time when I should have the sun at my back as I made my dive at the enemy balloon. I flew very high, higher, I think, than I had ever flown before. The altimeter showed 15,000 feet, the air was thin, and it was very cold.

The world below me looked like a huge aquarium. Above Lierval, where Reinhold had fallen, I sighted a hostile machine. From a distance it looked like a minute water beetle.

Then, from the west, a small object rapidly approached. Small and black at first, it quickly grew in size and I soon recognised it as a Spad, an enemy fighter on the lookout for trouble-seekers like myself. I braced myself in my cockpit, for I knew that there was going to be a fight.

We met at the same altitude. As the sun caught it, I saw the other man's machine was painted light brown. Soon we were circling round each other playing for an opening. Below we probably looked like two great birds of prey indulging in springtime frolics, but we knew that it was a game of death. The first man to get behind the other's back was the winner. In the single-seater fighters you could only shoot forward, and if your opponent got on your tail you were lost.

Sometimes we passed so near to each other that I could see every detail of my opponent's face — that is, all that was visible of it below his helmet. On the machine's side there was a Stork and two words painted in white. The fifth time that he flew past me — so close that I could feel the draught from his propeller — I managed to spell out a word, *V-i-e-u-x*. And *Vieux Charles* was Guynemer's insignia.

And, indeed, there could only have been one Frenchman who handled a machine with the skill that he showed. He was a man, who like all the really dangerous beasts of prey, always hunted alone. Guynemer it was who made a practice of diving at his victims from out of the sun,

destroying them in a few seconds. In this way he had shot down my friend Puz. He had some 30 victories to his credit and I knew that I was in for the fight of my life.

I threw a half loop, with the object of getting at him from above but immediately he grasped my purpose, and half rolled out of the way. I tried another manoeuvre but again Guynemer forestalled me, and the jockeying for position continued.

Once, as I was coming out of a turn, he had advantage of me for a few seconds, and a regular hailstorm of bullets rattled against the wings of my 'plane.

I tried every trick I knew — turns, loops, rolls, sideslips — but he followed each movement with a lightning speed and gradually I began to realise that he was more than a match for me. Not only had he a better machine, but the man in it was a superior duellist. But I had to fight on, or turn away. To turn away would be fatal.

I went into a steep turn, and for a moment I had him at the end of my sights. I pressed the trigger . . . there was no response . . . my gun had jammed!

Holding the stick in my left hand, I hammered at the gun with my right. My efforts were unavailing.

For a moment I had considered the possibilities of escaping by diving away from him. But with such an opponent that would have been inviting disaster. In a few seconds he would have been on my tail, and could have shot me down with the utmost ease.

We still flew in circles round each other. It was a wonderful flying experience — if one could forget that one's life was at stake. I have never had to deal with a more

Above: The Richthofen 'Circus' prepares to take off. The photograph, which features Fokker Dr I fighters, must have been taken after April 15, 1918, as the aeroplanes have 'Greek' crosses rather than 'Iron' crosses as their national markings. *Top right:* Ernst Udet in the days of his successes. *Right:* Another of the great 'circuses'—*Jagdgeschwader Nr 2* near Laon

skilful opponent, and for a while I completely forgot that he was Guynemer, my enemy. It seemed to me, rather, that I was having some practice over the aerodrome with an old friend. This feeling, however, did not last for very long. For eight minutes we had been flying round each other in circles, and they were the longest eight minutes that I have ever experienced.

Suddenly Guynemer looped, and flew on his back over my head. That moment I relinquished hold of the stick, and hammered with both hands at the machine gun. It was a primitive remedy but it sometimes worked.

Guynemer had observed my actions and now knew that I was his helpless victim.

He again passed close over my head, flying almost on his back. And then, to my great surprise, he raised his arm and waved to me. Immediately afterwards he dived away towards the west.

I flew back home, stupefied.

There are some people who believe that Guynemer himself had a machine gun stoppage at the same time. Others claim that he feared that I, in desperation, might ram him in the air. I do not believe any of them. Rather do I believe that Guynemer gave proof that even in modern warfare there is something left of the knightly chivalry of bygone days. And, accordingly, I lay this belated wreath on Guynemer's unknown grave.

I reported for duty to the new squadron at ten o'clock one day, and at 12 o'clock on the same I made my first flight with *Jagdstaffel 11*. In addition, *Staffeln 4, 6* and *10* belonged to the squadron. Richthofen himself led *No 11 Flight*. I was

made a member of it because he liked to have all new-comers where he could keep an eye on them.

There were five of us. The *Rittmeister* took the lead, then came Just and Gussmann, then Scholz and myself brought up the rear. It was the first time that I had piloted a Fokker Triplane.

We flew at an altitude of about 1,500 feet, setting a westerly course. Above the ruins of Albert we saw, just below the clouds, an RE 8, a British artillery co-operation machine that was evidently spotting for the guns. Although he was somewhat higher than ourselves, he apparently did not observe our approach, and continued to fly in circles.

I exchanged a quick glance with Scholz, who nodded. I left the flight, and went in to challenge the Briton.

I attacked from the front and opened fire at such close quarters that his engine was positively riddled with bullets. He at once crumpled up and the burning wreckage fell close to Albert.

A minute later I had rejoined the flight and continued with them towards the west. Scholz signalled his pleasure by waving to me. And Richthofen, who seemed to have eyes everywhere, also turned his head, and nodded to let me know that he had witnessed the incident.

Below, to our right, we saw the Roman road. The trees were still bare, and the columns of troops marching along the road looked as though they were moving behind iron bars. They were proceeding towards the west, English troops who had been beaten back by our offensive.

Flying low over the tops of the trees were

several Sopwith Camels. These British single-seaters had the task of protecting the Roman road, which was one of the main arteries of their communications' system.

I had no time for further observations, for Richthofen set the nose of his red Fokker towards the ground and dived, with the rest of us following close on his tail. The Sopwiths scattered like chicks from a hawk, but one of them was too late —the one in the *Rittmeister's* sights.

It happened so quickly that one could hardly call it an aerial fight. For a moment I thought that the *Rittmeister* would ram him, so short was the space that separated them. I estimated it at 30 feet at the most. Suddenly the nose of the Sopwith tilted downwards and a cloud of white smoke shot from the exhaust. The ill-fated machine crashed into a field close to the road and burst into flames.

Richthofen, instead of changing direction as we expected, continued to dive until he was close above the Roman road. Tearing along at a height of about 30 feet from the ground, he peppered the marching troops with his two guns. We followed close behind him and copied his example.

The troops below us seemed to have been lamed with horror and apart from the few men who took cover in the ditch at the roadside, hardly anyone returned our fire. On reaching the end of the road the *Rittmeister* turned and again fired at the column. We could now observe the effect of our first assault: bolting horses and stranded guns blocked the road, bringing the column to a complete standstill.

[*Reprinted from* Ace of the Black Cross *by Ernst Udet, published by Newnes.*]

ARRAS FROM THE AIR

'Billy' Bishop finished the war with 72 victories, but here he describes the extraordinary sensations of ground strafing

Dawn was due at 5.30 on Easter Monday, and that was the exact hour set for the beginning of the Battle of Arras. We were up and had our machines out of the hangars while it was still night. The beautiful weather of a few hours before had vanished. A strong, chill wind was blowing from the east, and dark, menacing clouds were scudding along low overhead.

We were detailed to fly at a low altitude over the advancing infantry, firing into the enemy trenches, and dispersing any groups of men or fatigue parties we happened to see in the vicinity of the lines. Some phases of this work are known as 'contact patrols', the machines keeping track always of the infantry advance, watching points where they may be held up and returning from time to time to report just how the battle is going. Working with the infantry in a big attack is a most exciting experience. It means flying close to the ground and passing through our own shells and those of the enemy.

The shell fire this morning was simply indescribable. The bombardment which had been going on all night gradually died down about 5 o'clock, and the Germans must have felt that the British had finished their nightly 'strafing', were tired out and going to bed. For a time almost complete silence reigned over the battlefield. All along the German lines starshells and rocket-lights were looping through the darkness. The old Boche is always suspicious and likes to have the country around him lighted up as much as possible so he can see what the enemy is about.

The wind kept growing stiffer and stiffer and there was a distinct feel of rain in the air. Precisely at the moment that all the British guns roared out their first salvo of the battle, the skies opened and the rain fell in torrents. Gunfire may or may not have anything to do with rainmaking but there was a strange coincidence between the shock of battle and the commencement of the downpour this morning. It was beastly luck, and we felt it keenly, but we carried on.

The storm had delayed the coming of day by several minutes, but as soon as there was light enough to make our presence worthwhile, we were in the air and braving the elements just as the troops were below us. Lashed by the gale, the wind cut the face as we moved against the enemy. The ground seemed to be one mass of bursting shells. Farther back, where the guns were firing, the hot flames flashing from thousands of muzzles gave the impression of a long ribbon of incandescent light. The air seemed shaken and literally full of shells on their missions of death and destruction. Over and over again one felt a sudden jerk under a wing-tip, and the machine would heave quickly. This meant that a shell had passed within a few feet of you. As the battle went on the work grew more terrifying, because reports came in that several of our machines had been hit by shells in flight and brought down. There was small wonder of this. The British barrage fire that morning was the most intense that the war had known. There was a greater concentration of guns than at any time during the Somme. In fact, some of the German prisoners said afterwards that the Somme seemed a paradise compared with the bombardments we carried out at Arras. While the British fire was at its height, the Germans set up a counterbarrage. This was not so intense, but every shell added to the shrieking chorus that filled the air and made the lot of the flying man just so much more difficult. Yet the risk was one we could not avoid; we had to endure it with the best spirit possible.

The waves of attacking infantry as they came out of their trenches and trudged forward behind the curtain of shells laid down by the artillery were an amazing sight. The men seemed to wander across No-Man's Land, and into the enemy trenches, as if the battle was a great bore to them. From the air it looked as though they did not realise that they were at war and were taking it all entirely too easily. That is the way with clockwork warfare. These troops had been drilled to move forward at a given pace. They had been timed over and over again in marching a certain distance and from this timing the 'creeping' or rolling barrage had been mathematically worked out. And the battle, so calmly entered into, was one of the tensest, bitterest of the whole world war.

For days the battle continued, and it was hard work and no play for everyone concerned. The weather, instead of getting better, as spring weather should, gradually got worse. It was cold, windy and wet. Every two or three hours sudden snowstorms would shut in, and flying in these squalls, which obliterated the landscape, was very ticklish business.

On the fourth day of the battle I happened to be flying about 500 feet above the trenches about an hour after dawn. It had snowed during the night and the ground was covered with a new layer of white several inches thick. No marks of the battle of the day before were to be seen; the only blemishes in the snow mantle were the marks of shells which had fallen in the last hour. No-Man's Land, so often a filthy litter, was this morning clean and white.

Suddenly over the tops of our parapets a thin line of infantry crawled up and commenced to stroll casually towards the enemy. To me it seemed that they must soon wake up and run; that they could not realise the great danger they were in. Here and there a shell would burst as the line advanced or halted for a minute. Three or four men near the burst would topple over like so many tin soldiers. Two or three other men would then come running up to the spot from the rear with a stretcher, pick up the wounded and the dying, and slowly walk back with them. I could not get the idea out of my head that it was just a game they were playing at; it all seemed so unreal. Nor could I believe that the little brown figures moving about below me were really men—men going to the glory of victory or the glory of death. I could not make myself realise the full truth or meaning of it all. It seemed that I was in an entirely different world, looking down from another sphere on this strange, uncanny puppet show.

Suddenly I heard the deadly rattle of a nest of machine guns beneath me, and saw that the line of our troops at one place was growing very thin, with many figures sprawling on the ground. For three or four minutes I could not make out the concealed position of the German gunners. Our men had halted, and were lying on the ground, evidently as much puzzled as I was. Then in a corner of a German trench I saw a group of about five men operating two machine guns. They were slightly to the flank of our line, and evidently had been doing a great amount of damage. The sight of these men thoroughly woke me up to the reality of the whole scene below me. I dived vertically at them with a burst of rapid fire. The smoking bullets from my gun flashed into the ground, and it was an easy matter to get a good aim on the German automatics, one of which turned its muzzle towards me.

Hateful bullets

But in a fraction of a second I had reached a height only 30 feet above the Huns, so low I could make out every detail of their frightened faces. With hate in my heart I fired every bullet I could into the group as I swept over it, then turned my machine away. A few minutes later I had the satisfaction of seeing our line again advancing, and before the time had come for me to return from my patrol, our men had occupied all the German positions they had set out to take. It was a wonderful sight and a wonderful experience. Although it had been so difficult to realise that men were dying and being maimed for life beneath me, I felt that at last I had seen something of that dogged determination that has carried British arms so far.

The next ten days were filled with incident. The enemy fighting machines would not come close to the lines, and there was very little doing in the way of aerial combats, especially as far as I was concerned, for I was devoting practically all of my time

to flying low and helping the infantry. All of our pilots and observers were doing splendid work. Everywhere we were covering the forward movement of the infantry, keeping the troops advised of any enemy movements and enabling the British artillery to shell every area where it seemed concentrations were taking place. Scores of counterattacks were broken up before the Germans had fairly launched them. Our machines were everywhere back of the enemy lines. It was easy to tell where the Germans were amassing for a counterstroke. First of all our machines would fly low over the grey-clad troops, pouring machine gun bullets into them or dropping high explosive bombs among them. Then the exact location point of the mobilisation would be signalled to the artillery so that the moment the Germans moved our guns were on them. In General Orders commending the troops for their part in the battle, Field-Marshal Sir Douglas Haig declared that the work of the Flying Corps, 'under the most difficult conditions', called for the highest praise.

We were acting, you might say, as air policemen. Occasionally one of our machines would be set upon by the German gangsters—they were 'careful' fighters and seldom attacked unless at odds of four to one—and naturally we suffered some casualties, just as the ordinary police force suffers casualties when it is doing patrol duty in an outlaw country. The weather was always favourable to the German methods of avoiding 'open-air' combats. Even the clearer days were marked by skies filled with clouds sufficiently large and dense enough to offer protection and hiding places to the high winging Hun machines.

I had several skirmishes, but did not succeed in bringing down another machine until April 20, when I was fortunate enough to begin another series of extremely interesting and successful fights. I was promoted to be a Captain about this time and thought I was very happy; but the promotion was followed by another incident which really made me proud. The sergeants

De Havilland light bombers above No-Man's Land. DH 4's and 9's played a great part in destroying German morale by harassing their front line troops constantly

of my squadron had made me a round 'nose' for my machine. It fitted on the propeller head and revolved with it. I had it painted a brilliant blue, and from that time on my machine was known as 'Blue Nose'. It was given to me, the Serjeant-Major explained, as a sign that I was an 'Ace' — that I had brought down more than five machines. I was so pleased with this tribute from the men that I took old 'Blue Nose' visiting several other squadrons, where I exhibited my new mark of distinction to many of my friends and flying companions.

The machine I got on April 20 was the first I ever destroyed in flames. It is a thing that often happens, and while I have no desire to make myself appear as a blood-thirsty person, I must say that to see an enemy going down in flames is a source of great satisfaction. You know his destruction is absolutely certain. The moment you see the fire break out you know that nothing in the world can save the man, or men, in the doomed aeroplane. You know that there is no 'camouflage' in this, and you have no fear that the enemy is trying any kind of flying trick in the hope that he will be left alone.

I was flying over a layer of white clouds when I saw a two-seater just above me. We generally met the enemy in force during these days, but this German machine was all alone. Neither the pilot nor the observer saw me. They flew along blissfully ignorant of my existence, while I kept carefully underneath them, climbing all the time. I was only ten yards behind the Hun when I fired directly up at him. It had been an exciting game getting into position underneath him, carefully following every move he made, waiting, hoping and praying that he would not see me before I got into the place I wanted. I was afraid that if he did see me I would be at a distinct disadvantage below him. My hand must have been shaky, or my eye slightly out, because, although I managed to fire ten rounds, I did not hit anything vital. Even in this crucial moment the humour of the situation almost got the better of me. My machine seemed so little, carefully flying there under the big, peaceful Hun, who thought he was so safe, so far from any danger. Suddenly, from just beneath him, he heard the 'tat-tat-tat-tatter-tatter' of my machine gun almost in his ear, the range was so close. Then he must have seen my smoking bullets passing all around him. Anyway, there was consternation in the camp. He turned quickly, and a regular battle in the air began between the two of us. We manoeuvred every way possible, diving, rolling, stalling; he attempting to get a straight shot at me, while my one object was to get straight behind him once again, so as to have a direct line of fire right into him.

Twice I dived at him and opened fire from almost point-blank range, being within two lengths of him before I touched the lever which set my gun to spouting. But there was no success. The third time I tried a new manoeuvre. I dived at him from the side, firing as I came. My new tactics gave the German observer a direct shot at me from his swivel gun, and he was firing very well too, his bullets passing quite close for a moment or two. Then, however, they began to fly well beyond my wing-tips, and on seeing this I knew that his nerve was shaken. I could now see my own bullets hitting the right part of the Hun machine, and felt confident that the battle would soon be over.

I pulled my machine out of its dive just in time to pass about five feet over the enemy. I could see the observer evidently had been hit and had stopped firing. Otherwise the Hun machine seemed perfectly all right. But just after I passed I looked back over my shoulder and saw it burst into flames. A second later it fell a burning mass, leaving a long trail of smoke behind as it disappeared through the clouds. I thought for a moment of the fate of the wounded observer and the hooded pilot into whose faces I had just been looking — but it was fair hunting, and I flew away with great contentment in my heart.

[*Reprinted from* Winged Warfare *by Major W. A. Bishop, VC, DSO and MC, published by Hodder and Stoughton, 1918.*]

Imperial War Museum

The cockpit of an SE 5a fighter. Though it was not as manoeuvrable as the Sopwith Camel, the SE 5a had a distinct advantage in its extreme strength and its good turn of speed

LONE HUNTER'S DAY

While Bishop's squadron was active over the Battle of Arras itself, Cecil Lewis' unit was flying behind the German lines

On the first Offensive Patrol (in April 1917), with two others, we attacked five German scouts: four bright red and one green. I chose one and dived, got him in the sights, and pressed the trigger of the Vickers. Not a shot! I continued in the dive, trusting to the Lewis gun to do the trick: it fired two shots and jammed! Damnation! I zoomed away, trying frantically to clear the Vickers jam. Nothing would shift it, so I pulled the Lewis down its sliding quadrant to clear it and reload. The spade grip of the gun knocked down the hinged wind-screen, and the blast of a 100-mph wind nearly blew my head off. This was a pretty state to be in surrounded by five enemy scouts!

I was a sitter for any Hun, so I turned west and climbed away, working all the time to get my screen up and clear the Lewis jam. At last I managed it; but then, try as I would, I could not force the gun up the quadrant back into place on the top plane. The slide was twisted. I came home fed up, my gun pointing straight up into heaven. Nevertheless, that day the squadron got four Huns: a good start Ball accounted for two of them . . .

In 1917 co-operative tactics in single-seater fighting were rudimentary. A combat was a personal matter. In a fight no pilot has time to watch others: he is too occupied in attempting to down his own man or in avoiding an enemy intent on downing him. Tactics apart, the vital question is that of performance. A machine with better speed and climbing power must always have the advantage.

During the next ten days Offensive Patrols were carried out daily, and unfortunately it soon became clear that, good as the SE 5 was, it was still not equal to the enemy. Scrapping at high altitudes, 15,000 to 18,000 feet, the Huns had a marked superiority in performance. This naturally tended to make us cautious, since we knew that, once we came down to their level, we should not be able to get above them again. Height, apart from its moral superiority, means added speed for the one above, who in his dive and zoom away has gravity on his side. Since machine guns in a scout are fixed, firing forward in the line of flight, it follows that the pilot aims the whole machine at his adversary. If that adversary is above him, he will be forced to pull his machine up on its tail to get him in the sights. That means loss of speed, manoeuvrability and, if carried to an extreme, a stall, and wandering about at stalling speed is asking for trouble when there are enemy guns about. This inferiority of performance was an initial difficulty. Later, when the SE5 got a larger motor, things looked up.

Single combat, a duel with another machine, was, performance apart, a question of good flying. Two machines so engaged would circle, each trying to turn inside the other and so bring his guns into play. Ability to sustain such tight vertical turns is the crucial test of a fighting pilot. Once the balance of the controls is lost, the machine will slip, lose height, and the enemy will rush in. Then, by all the rules of the game, you are a dead man.

But when a number of machines had closed and were engaged in a 'dog-fight', it was more a question of catch-as-catch-can. A pilot would go down on the tail of a Hun, hoping to get him in the final burst; but he would not be wise to stay there, for another Hun would almost certainly be on his tail, hoping to get him in the same way. Such fights were really a series of rushes, with momentary pauses to select the next opportunity – to catch the enemy at a disadvantage . . .

But, apart from fighting, when 20 or 30 scouts were engaged, there was always a grave risk of collision. Machines would hurtle by, intent on their private battles, missing each other by feet. So such fighting demanded iron nerves, lightning reactions, snap decisions, a cool head and eyes like a bluebottle, for it all took place at high speed and was three-dimensional.

At this sort of sharpshooting some pilots

Below left: James McCudden, who rose from the ranks and scored 54 victories before he met his death in an accident in 1918. *Below:* A weapon whose bark was worse than its bite – the explosion of a British anti-aircraft shell

Imperial War Museum

Ullstein

excelled others; but in all air fighting (and indeed in every branch of aerial warfare) there is an essential in which it differs from war on the ground: its absolute cold-bloodedness. You cannot lose your temper with an aeroplane. You cannot 'see red', as a man in a bayonet fight. You certainly cannot resort to 'Dutch' courage. Any of these may fog your judgement – and that spells death.

Often at high altitudes we flew in air well below freezing point. Then the need to clear a jam or change a drum meant putting an arm out into an icy 100-mph wind. If you happened to have bad circulation (as I had), it left the hand numb, and since you could not stamp your feet, swing your arms, or indeed move at all, the numbness would spread to the other hand, and sometimes to the feet as well.

In this condition we often went into a scrap with the odds against us – they usually were against us, for it was our job to be 'offensive' and go over into enemy country looking for trouble – coldbloodedly in the literal sense; but nonetheless we had to summon every faculty of judgement and skill to down our man, or, at the worst, to come out of it alive ourselves. So, like duelling, air fighting required a set steely courage, drained of all emotion, fined down to a tense and deadly effort of will. The Angel of Death is less callous, aloof and implacable than a fighting pilot when he dives.

Below: An Albatros D Va, increasingly the main opposition for Allied fighters from the middle of 1917 onwards. Note the auxiliary strut from the leading interplane strut to the leading edge, to prevent flutter

There were, of course, emergency methods, such as standing the machine on its tail and holding it there just long enough to get one good burst into the enemy above you; but nobody would fight that way if he could help it, though, actually, an SE 5 pilot could do the same thing by pulling his top gun down the quadrant. He could then fire it vertically upward while still flying level.

Hedgehopping over Hunland
This was how Beery Bowman once got away from an ugly situation. He had been scrapping a couple of Huns well over the other side of the lines. He managed to crash one of them but in so doing exhausted the ammunition of his Vickers gun: his Lewis was jammed. The other Hun pursued him and forced him right down on to the 'carpet' – about 100 feet from the ground. There was nothing to do but to beat it home. The Hun, out to avenge the death of his friend, and having the advantage of speed and height over Beery, chivvied him back to the lines, diving after him, bursting his gun, zooming straight up again, hanging there for a moment in a stall, and falling to dive again.

He repeated this several times (he must have been a rotten shot) while Beery, with extraordinary coolness and presence of mind, pulled down his Lewis gun and managed to clear the jam. The next time the Hun zoomed, Beery throttled right down and pulled back to stalling speed. The result was that when the Hun fell out of his zoom, Beery was not ahead of him as before, but beneath him. As the

Hun dropped into his dive Beery opened fire with his Lewis gun, raking the body above him with a long burst. The Hun turned over on his back, dived, and struck the ground, bursting into flames. Beery laconically continued his way home. He was awarded the DSO.

With the exception of Ball, most crack fighters did not get their Huns in dogfights. They preferred safer means. They would spend hours synchronising their guns and telescopic sights, so that they could do accurate shooting at, say, 200 or 300 yards. They would then set out on patrol, alone, spot their quarry (in such cases usually a two-seater doing reconnaissance or photography), and carefully manoeuvre for position, taking great pains to remain where they could not be seen, below and behind the tail of the enemy. From here, even if the Hun observer did spot them he could not bring his gun to bear without the risk of shooting away his own tail plane or rudder. The stalker would not hurry after his quarry, but keep a wary eye to see he was not about to be attacked himself. He would gradually draw nearer, always in the blind spot, sight his guns very carefully and then one long deadly burst would do the trick.

Such tactics as those were employed by Captain McCudden, VC, DSO (killed in an accident in July 1918, having accounted for more than 50 German machines), and also by the French ace Guynemer (killed without trace in September 1917).

The squadron was doing well in Huns. Ball came back every day with a bag of one or more. Besides his SE 5 he had a Nieuport scout, the machine in which

Bayer Hauptstaatsarchiv, Munich

he had done so well the previous year. He had a roving commission, and, with two machines, was four hours a day in the air. Of the great fighting pilots his tactics were the least cunning. Absolutely fearless, the odds made no difference to him. He would always attack, single out his man and close. On several occasions he almost rammed the enemy, and often came back with his machine shot to pieces.

One morning, before the rest of us had gone out on patrol, we saw him coming in rather clumsily to land. He was not a stunt pilot, but flew very safely and accurately, so that, watching him, we could not understand his awkward floating landing. But when he taxied up to the sheds we saw his elevators were flapping loose — controls had been completely shot away! He had flown back from the lines and made his landing entirely by winding his adjustable tail up and down! It was incredible he had not crashed. His oil tank had been riddled, and his face and the whole nose of the machine were running with thick black oil.

He was so angry at being shot up like this that he walked straight to the sheds, wiped the oil off his shoulders and face with a rag, ordered out his Nieuport, and in two hours was back with yet another Hun to his credit.

Ball was a quiet, simple little man. His one relaxation was the violin, and his favourite after-dinner amusement to light a red magnesium flare outside his hut and walk round it in his pyjamas, fiddling! He was meticulous in the care of his machines, guns and in the examination of his ammunition. He never flew for amusement.

The only trips he took, apart from offensive patrols, were the minimum requisite to test his engines or fire at the ground target sighting his guns. He never boasted or criticised, but his example was tremendous . . .

The squadron sets out 11 strong on the evening patrol. Eleven chocolate-coloured, lean, noisy bullets, lifting, swaying, turning, rising into formation — two fours and a three — circling and climbing away steadily towards the lines. They are off to deal with Richthofen and his circus of red Albatroses.

The May evening is heavy with threatening masses of cumulus cloud, majestic skyscrapers, solid-looking as snow mountains, fraught with caves and valleys, rifts and ravines — strange and secret pathways in the chartless continents of the sky. Below, the land becomes an ordnance map, dim green and yellow, and across it go the lines, drawn anyhow, as a child might scrawl with a double pencil. The grim dividing lines! From the air robbed of all significance.

Steadily the body of scouts rises higher and higher, threading its way between the cloud precipices. Sometimes, below, the streets of a village, the corner of a wood, a few dark figures moving, glides into view like a slide into a lantern, and then is hidden again.

But the fighting pilot's eyes are not on the ground, but roving endlessly through the lower and higher reaches of the sky, peering anxiously through fur-goggles to spot those black slow-moving specks against land or cloud which mean full throttle, tense muscles, held breath and

the headlong plunge with screaming wires — a Hun in the sights, and the tracers flashing.

Ambush from above

A red light curls up from the leader's cockpit and falls away. Action! He alters direction slightly, and the patrol, shifting throttle and rudder, keep close like a pack of hounds on the scent. He has seen, and they see soon, six scouts 3,000 feet below. Black crosses! It seems interminable till the 11 come within diving distance. The pilots nurse their engines, hard-minded and set, test their guns and watch their indicators. At last the leader sways sideways, as a signal that each should take his man, and suddenly drops.

Machines fall scattering, the earth races up, the enemy patrol, startled, wheels and breaks. Each his man! The chocolate thunderbolts take sights, steady their screaming planes, and fire. A burst, 50 rounds — it is over. They have overshot, and the enemy hit or missed, is lost for the moment. The pilot steadies his stampeding mount, pulls her out with a firm

Collision courses, and then the steady circling, waiting for the other man to grant you even the smallest chance

hand, twisting his head right and left, trying to follow his man, to sight another, to back up a friend in danger, to note another in flames.

But the squadron plunging into action had not seen, far off, approaching from the east, the rescue flight of red Albatroses patrolling above the body of machines on which they had dived, to guard their tails and second them in the battle. These, seeing the maze of wheeling machines, plunge down to join them. The British scouts, engaging and disengaging like flies circling at midday in a summer room, soon find the newcomers upon them. Then, as if attracted by some mysterious power, as vultures will draw to a corpse in the desert, other bodies of machines swoop down from the peaks of the cloud mountains. More enemy scouts, and, by good fortune, a flight of Naval triplanes.

But, nevertheless, the enemy, double in number, greater in power and fighting with skill and courage, gradually overpower the British, whose machines scatter, driven down beneath the scarlet German fighters.

It would be impossible to describe the

Below left and right: The war from the air. From altitude, all that could be seen were the front line dispositions, but from lower down the chaos that reigned in No-Man's Land during the first stages of an attack could be seen all too clearly—infantry held up in front of strong points and casting around for a way to circumvent these horribly costly obstacles. There was little that a pilot could do to help directly, however. His real use lay in keeping up the morale of the infantry by strafing the opposition and in keeping HQ informed of the front line situation, so that new plans to keep the advance moving could be worked out

action of such a battle. A pilot, in the second between his own engagements, might see a Hun diving vertically, an SE 5 on his tail, on the tail of the SE another Hun, and above him again another British scout. These four, plunging headlong at two hundred miles an hour, guns crackling, tracers screaming, suddenly break up. The lowest Hun plunges flaming to his death, if death has not taken him already. His victor seems to stagger, suddenly pulls out in a great leap, as a trout leaps on the end of a line, and then, turning over on his belly, swoops and spins in a dizzy falling spiral with the earth to end it. The third German zooms veering, and the last of that meteoric quartet follows bursting . . . But such a glimpse, lasting perhaps ten seconds, is broken by the sharp rattle of another attack.

Two machines approach head-on at breakneck speed, firing at each other, tracers whistling through each other's planes, each slipping sideways on his rudder to trick the other's gun fire. Who will hold longest? Two hundred yards, 100, 50, and then, neither hit, with one accord they fling their machines sideways, bank and circle, each striving to bring his gun on to the other's tail, each glaring through goggle eyes, calculating, straining, wheeling, bent only on death or dying.

But, from above, this strange tormented circling is seen by another Hun. He drops. His gun speaks. The British machine, distracted by the sudden unseen enemy, pulls up, takes a burst through the engine, tank and body, and falls bottom uppermost down through the clouds and the deep unending desolation of the

twilight sky.

The game of noughts and crosses, starting at 15,000 feet above the clouds, drops in altitude engagement by engagement. Friends and foes are scattered. A last SE, pressed by two Huns, plunges and wheels, gun jammed, like a snipe over marshes, darts lower, finds refuge in the ground mist, and disappears.

Now lowering clouds darken the evening. Below, flashes of gun fire stab the veil of the gathering dusk. The fight is over! The battlefield shows no sign. In the pellucid sky, serene cloud mountains mass and move unceasingly. Here where guns rattled and death plucked the spirits of the valiant, this thing is now as if it had never been! The sky is busy with night, passive, superb, unheeding.

Of the 11 scouts that went out that evening, May 7, only five of us returned to the aerodrome.

The Mess was very quiet that night. The Adjutant remained in his office, hoping against hope to have news of the six missing pilots, and, later, news did come through that two had been forced down, shot in the engine, and that two others had been wounded.

But Ball never returned. I believe I was the last to see him in his red-nosed SE going east at 8,000 feet. He flew straight into the white face of an enormous cloud. I followed. But when I came out on the other side, he was nowhere to be seen. All next day a feeling of depression hung over the squadron. We mooned about the sheds still hoping for news. The day after that hope was given up. I flew his Nieuport back to the Aircraft Depot. [*Cecil Lewis.*]

AIR BATTLE OVER THE AISNE

The Germans again used their well-tried ground attack formula during the Aisne offensive. At first they had things their own way as the heavily mauled Allied squadrons pulled back to regroup. But once the Allies threw these units back into the battle, the Germans were halted in savage fighting over the now-worn-out infantry divisions below. *Thomas G. Miller Jr. Below:* A Halberstadt CL II about to set off on a mission. Note the grenades in the rack on the fuselage side and the signal gun cartridges over the fuselage's rear decking

Süddeutscher-Verlag

Twice Ludendorff had succeeded in achieving tactical surprise despite ample warning of his intentions, in furnishing which the RAF had played a most creditable part. The third of his hammer blows now fell on a sector of the front where British aviation had very limited strength and responsibility. The battle-shattered IX Corps had only one squadron to fly its reconnaissance missions. The French Tenth Army had assigned to it 14 *Escadrilles* of fighters and observation aircraft, and the French *Division Aérienne,* a powerful strategic air reserve of 18 day-bombing and 24 fighter *Escadrilles,* was stationed around Clermont, behind the front of the neighbouring Third Army. The German *Seventh Army* had two of the crack 'flying circuses', *Jagdgeschwader I* (Reinhard) and *III* (Loerzer), five additional *Jagdstaffeln,* 14 *Schlachtstaffeln* (organised into three *Gruppen*), 23 *Fliegerabteilungen* and two *Bombengeschwader.*

French air reconnaissance failed to discover the concentration of assault units by *Seventh Army* and on May 27 its strength fell thunderously against the Chemin des Dames between Rheims and Soissons. The *Schlachtstaffeln* flew in group strength, attacking the retreating British and French troops on all the roads behind the front. Continuous attacks by the grenades and machine guns of these low-flying aircraft prevented the evacuation or destruction

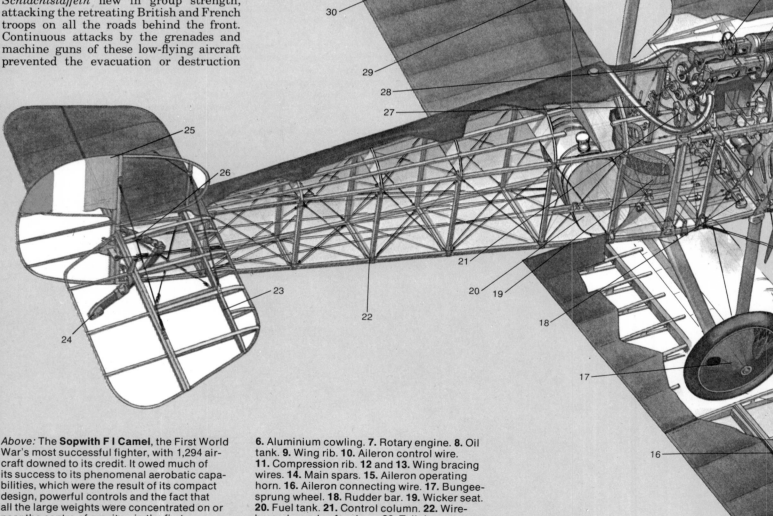

Above: The **Sopwith F I Camel**, the First World War's most successful fighter, with 1,294 aircraft downed to its credit. It owed much of its success to its phenomenal aerobatic capabilities, which were the result of its compact design, powerful controls and the fact that all the large weights were concentrated on or near the centre of gravity — in the first seven feet of the fuselage. The considerable torque of the rotary engine on the small frame was a vital factor in the Camel's lightning fast turn to the right, but it also meant that it was impossible to fly the Camel 'hands off'. Because of this difficulty, the type got an undeserved reputation as a killer, but all that was needed was great care, especially at take off and landing. The Camel was the first British fighter to have twin Vickers guns. **1.** Upper wing cutout for visibility. **2.** Ring sight. **3.** Vickers gun. **4.** Ammunition tank. **5.** Wooden propeller. **6.** Aluminium cowling. **7.** Rotary engine. **8.** Oil tank. **9.** Wing rib. **10.** Aileron control wire. **11.** Compression rib. **12 and 13.** Wing bracing wires. **14.** Main spars. **15.** Aileron operating horn. **16.** Aileron connecting wire. **17.** Bungee-sprung wheel. **18.** Rudder bar. **19.** Wicker seat. **20.** Fuel tank. **21.** Control column. **22.** Wire-braced wooden fuselage. **23.** Tailplane structure. **24.** Iron-shod skid. **25.** Fin and rudder. **26.** Bungee skid spring. **27.** Throttle and mixture controls. **28.** Instrument panel. **29.** Flying wire. **30.** Landing wire. **31.** Incidence bracing wires. *Engine:* Clerget (130-hp), Le Rhône (110-hp) or Bentley 1 (150-hp) rotaries. *Armament:* two Vickers guns. *Speed:* 122 mph at sea level. *Climb:* 16 minutes 50 seconds to 15,000 feet. *Ceiling:* 24,000 feet. *Endurance:* 2½ hours. *Weight empty/loaded:* 889/1,422 lbs. *Span:* 28 feet. *Length:* 18 feet 8 inches. Performance figures are as with the Le Rhône engine

Above: The **Fokker D VII**, Germany's best fighter
of the war, designed by the little-known
Reinhold Platz, who also designed the Dr I.
Originally a welder, Platz began designing with
little or no training. He possessed an enormous
flair for designing strong but light structures
(the fuselage was of metal tube) and had a
superb intuitive eye for line. The D VII was
noted for its great strength, good manoeuvrability and excellent performance at altitude.
It had the remarkable ability of being able to
hang on its propeller and fire upwards. The
aircraft illustrated is that of Georg von
Hantelman of *Jasta 15* of *Jagdgeschwader II.*
Engine: Mercedes D III or BMW III inlines, 160-
or 185-hp. *Armament:* two fixed Spandau
machine guns. *Speed:* 116½ mph at 3,280 feet.
Climb: 16,400 feet in 31½ minutes (Mercedes) or
16 minutes (BMW). *Ceiling:* 22,900 feet.
Endurance: 1½ hours. *Weight empty/loaded:*
1,540/1,870 lbs. *Span:* 29 feet 3½ inches.
Length: 22 feet 11⅝ inches. *Below:* 'The Blind
Spot' by N. G. Arnold — A Camel closes up in
the blind spot under a Hannoveraner's tailplane

John Batchelor

RAF Staff College

121

Below: Crews board their Friedrichshafen G III's for a bombing mission. *Left:* A gunner tests his weapon. *Bottom:* A mixed fighter unit of Fokker D VII's, Dr I's and an Albatros D V

of the French airfield at Magneux, near Fismes, and it was overrun on the 28th with all its aircraft, hangars and fuel intact. *Bombengeschwader 2's* attacks on the marshalling yards at La Fère-en-Tardenois contributed further to the confusion of the Allied armies. There was relatively little air fighting for the first four days of the offensive, most of the 19 German aircraft lost having fallen victim to ground fire. On the 31st, however, the *Division Aérienne* was committed to battle and savage combats were fought in the vicinity of their objective of Fismes. *Escadre* 12's Breguets were twice intercepted by *Jagdgeschwader I* and five of them were lost, as were two of the pilots of that stout German unit. The day's fighting cost 12 German and 17 French aircraft.

On the last day of May the Germans reached the Marne at Château-Thierry. In reaching it the men of the *Luftstreitkräfte* played their full part, and some of them remembered their parts well. Baron Wolfram von Richthofen was an apprentice fighter pilot in the unit once led by his famous cousin, and a huge, bemonocled *Hauptmann* named Hugo Sperrle directed all the air units of *Seventh Army.* Twenty-two years later both were to be made Field-Marshals for applying again the lessons learned in 1918 over the battlefields of the Somme, the Lys and the Marne. Many of their opposite numbers of course also rose to high command in the RAF.

Further Reading

Bodenschatz, K., *Jagd in Flanderns Himmel* (Munich: Verlag Korr & Hirth, 1935)
Die Deutschen Flieger in den Letzten Angriffsschlachten (Die Luftmacht, 1935)
Hoeppner, Gen. E. von, *Deutschlands Krieg in der Luft* (Leipzig: J. F. Koehler, 1921)
Raleigh, Sir Walter and Jones, H. A., *The War in the Air* (OUP, 1922-1936)
Résumé des Operations Aériennes Octobre 1917 — Novembre 1918
RFC — RAF HQ War Diary, March-May 1918
Voisin, General, *La Doctrine de l'Aviation Française de Combat* (Paris: Berger-Levrault, 1932)

CAMEL SCRAP

A remarkable but frequent occurrence in dogfighting was that the fight could break up and leave each pilot completely alone

Top: A typical cockpit. The pilot had less in the way of struts and wires to contend with compared with earlier types, but he now has a gun butt just in front of his face. This would damage his face in any crash. *Above:* 'The end of a German aeroplane over Arras' by Bertram Sandy

On September 10 I led five Camels of 'A' Flight on the north offensive patrol, which covered an area to the north of Ypres. We had not been long over the lines, and were flying at 14,000 feet, when I saw below us over Houthulst Forest a formation of enemy planes, made up of two DFW two-seaters protected by five Albatros Scouts. I had previously arranged that, in the event of encountering escorted aeroplanes, I should attack with one Camel, while the deputy leader and the other Camels were to remain above to protect our tails from attack. On my left was a new pilot; 2nd-Lieutenant R. J. Brownell, MM, a Tasmanian, who is now in the Royal Australian Air Force. I had told him that, until he got used to flying over the lines and rapidly spotting enemy craft as distinct from friendly, he must keep right alongside my 'plane and do whatever I did, maintaining formation station in all attitudes. Lieutenants Crossland, Moody and Smith made up the remainder of the formation.

The enemy 'planes were flying south about 1,000 feet below and ahead of us well east of their lines, and probably climbing to gain height before crossing the trench-lines upon reconnaissance. I swung our formation round above them from the north-easterly course we followed and dived for the two-seaters. Brownell came down in station. He had seen nothing. He simply knew that I had dived and that he had to keep position. The remaining three Camels maintained their height.

Down I rushed through the crisp, cold air, watching my Hun through the sights, holding my control stick with both hands, thumbs resting on the double gun-triggers within the spade-shaped stick-top. The observer in my opponents' bus saw me and I saw him swing his gun to bear. I saw the double flash of his shots even as he grew to personality in my sights and I pressed the fateful triggers. At the very first burst he crumpled up and fell backwards into the cockpit. My streams of lead poured into the fuselage of the 'plane around the pilot's cockpit and the DFW tipped up and over sideways and fell tumbling down.

I looked round for Brownell and saw him close beside me on my level. Following me down in the dive without knowing why we dived, he suddenly found himself squarely on the tail of the second DFW. He pressed his triggers instinctively in a long burst. The Hun's tail rose upward. A curl of smoke came from his fuselage and he fell headlong, plunging like a flaming comet.

Above us the three Camels kept the five Albatros Scouts engaged, and, after seeing the two-seaters go down, Smith dived on the tail of one of the scouts and shot 100 rounds into it, until it fell out of control.

Next day, in misty weather, with a patrol of seven, I saw a concentration of enemy planes, some 21 strong, flying below us east of Langemarck. There were three of the new Fokker triplanes, while the remainder were Albatros Scouts. They greatly outnumbered our strength. I could not determine whether they had observed us or not, but in any case I decided to attack. I dived on one of the triplanes, closed right in and as my burst went home I saw him falling down below his own formation. I knew that the Hun formation was so strong that it would be but to court disaster to follow him down. As I pulled forward from among the Huns for breathing space to review the situation I saw that one of my formation who had followed me had done just the thing I knew was wrong. Engrossed on the shooting of an Albatros he had passed right through the Hun level.

Instantly a Fokker pounced upon his tail. A burst of bullets caused the Camel pilot to look round and swerve away from the Albatros he followed. I saw the triplane close in upon the Camel's tail and I dived instantly upon it. As I dived I fired a short burst, before my sights were centred, because I knew that most Huns answered to the warning of bullets flying near. This fellow, however, was of a different breed. He looked round at me and, as I saw his begoggled face above his shoulder, he swerved slightly to one side, then followed on the Camel's tail.

I think the Camel pilot was wounded by the triplane's very first burst, because he did not use the Camel to manoeuvre as he might.

I increased speed and pulled closer to the triplane. Then I heard the splatter of Hun bullets rattling round my own ears. Glancing upward I saw two Albatros Scouts coming down upon me, but above them was another little Camel treating them the same.

I was almost dead upon the triplane's tail when the pilot looked around again. The range was so close that I could almost read the man's expression. I gave him another burst and saw the stream of tracer miss his head by inches as he swerved outward from my line of sight. The Camel was below him falling steeply in a gentle curve. When my burst ceased the German pilot looked again ahead.

Damn him! I thought. I'll get him next time. Each time I had fired a trifle earlier than I might have done, in the desire to shake him off the Camel's tail. And all the time we fell downward, losing height, fighting earthward from 14,000 feet along a pathway inclined at 60 degrees, rushing through the misty air towards the ground behind the German lines. From behind me came another burst of flying bullets.

Out of the corner of my eye I saw a solitary RE 8 heading towards us. I followed the swerving triplane and got squarely on his tail. Before I could fire he got out of my sights once more. Again I registered on him, dead. I pressed the triggers and saw my bullets flying home. His head did not look round this time. His angle of dive suddenly steepened. I increased my own to vertical, barely 20 feet behind him. Suddenly the RE 8 flashed in front of me between the German and my bus. I saw the wide-open mouth of the horror-struck observer. The wings passed across my vision as the pilot vainly strove to turn away.

For a fleeting instant of time I looked into the face of the observer and the cockpit in which he stood. He thought that I would hit him head on and wipe him from existence, torn to fragments with the whirring engine and propeller that I carried. So did I. For a fragment of time I hung in space, mentally, already dead. The observer and I saw each other as souls already hurled into the eternal cosmos.

There was but one thing to do.

'My God,' I breathed in prayer, even as I did it. I yanked the Camel's stick hard into my stomach and flashed between the two-seater's wings and tailplane as my gallant little Camel answered to the pull. By a miracle we missed collision, by a miracle my Camel held together. I flat spun upside down on top of a loop and fell out sideways. I had lost height so rapidly in my downward rush from 14,000 feet that the pressure in my fuel-tank had not had time to stabilise to meet the higher atmospheric pressure, and my engine ceased to run. Not certain of the cause I tried her on the gravity tank and she picked up. I turned west and scanned the sky. High overhead I saw 'planes pass between the mist and sky like goldfish in a bowl held up against a curtained window. Around me and on my level there was nothing to be seen, no aeroplanes, enemy or friendly, except the RE 8 fast disappearing westward in the mist, westward towards the lines. The triplane and the Camel both had vanished. The ground below was free from shell-holes, but indistinct on account of mist. I climbed upward as I travelled west and found some Camels of the squadron. Our patrol time was finished, and we returned to our aerodrome in formation. And as I went I cursed the damn-fool pilot of the British RE 8.

[*Reprinted from* Into the Blue *by Norman Macmillan, published by Duckworth.*]

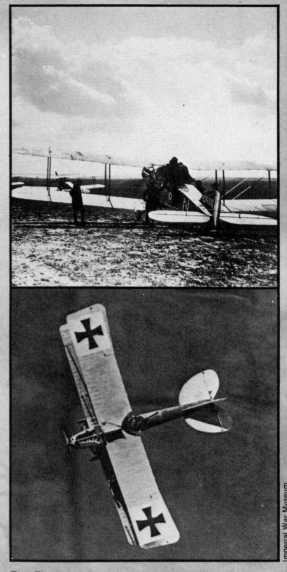

Top: The ground crew wait as the pilot and observer make their final preparations for a reconnaissance flight in their Bristol Fighter on a wintry day. *Above:* A fine air-to-air photograph of an Albatros C III 2-seater. Note the excellent field of fire for the observer

Imperial War Museum

DOG FIGHTING: FACT AND FICTION

These celebrated photographs, first produced in the anonymous autobiography of an RFC officer in the 1930's, are claimed to be authentic, but are more probably 'faked'. The author claimed that they were taken with a camera fitted to his aircraft's cabane struts and operated auto-

matically each time the machine gun trigger was pressed. Fact or fiction, they give a good impression of what First World War air fighting must have been like. The original captions are given in inverted commas.
1. 'Must have broken up at instant I pressed the trigger' (a Nieuport breaking up after being hit by a German being shot at by the author).
2. 'God, what a sight' (a Fokker D VII and a Bristol Fighter colliding).
3. 'His wings suddenly collapsed and floated past me' (an LVG breaking up). **4.** 'A dogfight' (a typical confused *mêlée* at very close range).
5. 'Have got the camera pointed off at an angle' (a Pfalz D III chasing an SE 5, taken with the camera facing backwards and outwards, rather than aligned along the line of fire of the machine guns). **6.** 'They got there first' (Albatros D V's pouncing on a straggling DH 4).

As 1918 witnessed Germany's last desperate struggles on the ground, so did it in the air as the Germans tried to force Britain and France out of the war by bombing their capital cities. The effort was in vain, however, as the defences had caught up with the bombers Germany could muster. But 1918 contained a far more important event, an augury for the future — the formation of the world's first truly independent strategic bomber force, the Independent Force, RAF

STRATEGIC BOMBING

Douglas Robinson

Below: The defences—searchlights on one of London's bridges. *Right:* A Handley-Page V/1500, potentially the best bomber of the war

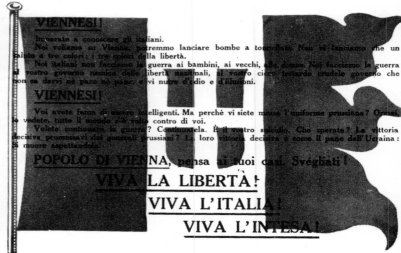

Left: The famous Gabriele d'Annunzio in the front cockpit of a Farman in 1915. *Right:* The leaflet dropped on the Austrian capital, Vienna

When Italy declared war on Austria-Hungary on May 24, 1915, there already existed an aircraft of Italian design well suited to the long-range bombing rôle. The creation of Gianni Caproni, the Ca 1 exemplified the basic design of all the large Caproni aircraft of the war period. A biplane with wings 72 feet 10 inches in span, it accommodated its crew in a central nacelle – an observer-bombardier-gunner right forward and two pilots side by side immediately behind him. At the rear of the nacelle was a 100-hp Fiat water-cooled engine. Two long 'outrigger' fuselages to right and left had Fiats in their noses, and at their after ends carried a broad horizontal tailplane on which were mounted three rudders. The maximum speed was 72 mph, the ceiling 13,100 feet with a load of approximately 1,000 lbs of bombs. One hundred and sixty-six of these aircraft were built. The later Ca 3 of 1917 was almost identical, but had three 150-hp Isotta-Fraschini engines. Some 250 of these were completed. Most impressive to the layman was the huge Ca 4 triplane, with a span of 98 feet and an all-up weight of 16,500 lbs including 3,000 lbs of bombs. The engines were Fiats, Isotta-Fraschinis or American Liberties of 200- to 400-hp. With all the struts and wires bracing the triplane wings, maximum speed was no more than 87·5 mph. Not more than 35 were built during 1918 (six of which wore the markings of the Royal Naval Air Service, but apparently never left Italy) and the type was used only for night bombing. Subsequently, Caproni returned to the biplane design, and the Ca 5, of which 252 were built in 1918, had three Isotta-Fraschinis or Fiats of 200- to 250-hp.

The Italians also used semi-rigid airships for bombing right to the end of the war. The 'M' class craft in use late in the war were 269 feet long, had a gas volume of 441,000 cubic feet of hydrogen, and were powered by two Itala Maybach engines of 225-hp. These craft could carry a ton of bombs, and could reach altitudes above 15,000 feet. High altitude night raids were made on depots and railway stations in the rear areas of the Austrian armies, and on occasion, across the Adriatic.

The Capronis were similarly used for tactical bombing of railway stations and junctions, ammunition and supply depots, aerodromes and troop concentrations in the Austrian rear areas, and at no time during the war did the Italian army set aside any part of its bombing force for strategic operations. To the flamboyant soldier-poet Gabriele d'Annunzio, who was 52 years old on the outbreak of war, must go much of the credit for the long-range missions of the Italian bombing force. Passionately dedicated to the recovery of the 'lost territories', as early as July 1915 he was participating in flights intended to show the Italian tricolour to fellow countrymen chafing under the Austrian yoke in Trieste, Trento (Trent), Zara (Zadar) and Pola.

From these propaganda flights the next step was to carry bombs to Austrian cities. Massed behind the active front along the Isonzo, east of Venice, even the Capronis could not reach Vienna, 260 miles distant, or Buda-Pest, 340 miles away. But across the Adriatic, not much more than 100 miles distant, were a number of important Austrian cities and bases: Pola, the main base of the Austrian battle fleet; Trieste, the largest and busiest port of the Austro-Hungarian Empire with steel mills and the big *Stabilimento Tecnico* shipyards; and Fiume (Rijeka), site of the Whitehead torpedo factory and of the Danubius shipyard. Cattaro (Kotor), farther south, was a fleet base and the home of the German U-Boats operating in the Mediterranean.

The first Capronis to enter service at the front assembled in August 1915, at Pordenone. On August 20 they made their first bombing raid, on the Austrian flying field at Asiovizza. By the date of the Third Battle of the Isonzo, in October 1915, four squadrons of Capronis were in service. The first long-distance mission was flown on February 18, 1916, when in reprisal for an Austrian attack on Milan nearly 4,000 lbs of bombs were dropped on Laibach (Ljubljana). Four tons of bombs on the Whitehead torpedo factory in Fiume on August 1, 1916, caused extensive fires and damage. These long-range daylight attacks had been made in formation without escorts, but when 22 Capronis went to Trieste on September 13, 1916, they were escorted by two squadrons of Italian-built Nieuports.

At the instigation of d'Annunzio a series of raids was made on Pola in 1917. In the first one, by 36 Capronis on the night of August 2/3, 1917, 20 aircraft reached the target; eight tons of bombs fell on the naval base. Ten aircraft were damaged by anti-aircraft fire, but all returned to their home fields. Twenty-eight Capronis returned to bomb Pola on the night of August 8/9. Yet the strategic campaign against Pola had to give way a few days later to the requirements of the Ninth Battle of the Isonzo, in which 85 Capronis bombed the Austrian rear areas.

An outstanding – but isolated – accomplishment was the raid on the naval base at Cattaro. Because the target was far to the south on the Dalmatian coast, two squadrons of Caproni Ca 3's based at Milan first flew south to Gioia del Colle in the province of Puglia on September 25. Fourteen aircraft set out from there for Cattaro on the night of October 4, but two turned back with engine trouble. The remainder made the 280-mile round trip across the open sea, claiming hits on the submarine base, the torpedo store, seaplane hangars and a petrol dump at Kumbor.

With the Caporetto disaster in October and November 1917, such strategic missions became an unjustifiable luxury; while the Caproni squadrons, caught up in the turmoil of the retreat to the Piave, were able to make only 18 bombing attacks on the Central Powers' troop concentrations. Early in 1918 the emphasis still was on tactical operations, Austrian airfields being the prime target.

In February 1918 a new aircraft came forward to participate in long-range missions – a fast single-seater, the SVA-5, which had been designed as a fighter but had been rejected because of lack of manoeuvrability. Its power and speed – 136 mph at sea level with a 220-hp SPA-6A water-cooled engine – made it ideal for long-range strategic reconnaissance. The 87th *Squadriglia,* 'La Serenissima', made the aircraft famous. On May 21, 1918 two of its pilots flew all the way to Friedrichshafen and returned with photographs of the Zeppelin works, a round trip of 440 miles. It also made bombing raids on Zagreb, Bolzano and Innsbrück, all long distance flights over high mountains. The greatest day in the history of 'La Serenissima' squadron, and perhaps in the life of d'Annunzio, was on August 9, 1918, when the poet, a passenger in a two-seater version of the SVA-5, was flown to Vienna escorted by seven single seaters, a round trip of 625 miles. The aircraft were heavily loaded with fuel, and dropped only leaflets over the Austrian capital. For the Capronis, however, there were few long-range missions, as the 11 squadrons equipped with them bombed railway stations and junctions, important highways and enemy aerodromes in preparation for the final victory at Vittorio Veneto.

Having turned to night bombing raids in the autumn of 1917, the Gothas of the *Englandgeschwader,* together with the Giant bombers based with them around Ghent, attempted to continue the campaign into the winter. On the night of October 1/2, 1917, 18 Gothas were sent out, but only eight reached London. Eighteen British aircraft ascended, but only one even saw any of the raiders. The anti-aircraft guns fired 10,532 rounds with no successes, while one person was killed and 13 injured by fragments.

On the night of October 31/November 1, 22 Gothas set out from Belgium. The weather was cloudy and most of the raiders scattered their bombs over Kent and Essex. Eighty-five bombs fell on London. Fifty defending aircraft ascended but no German machines were lost over England. One Gotha caught fire after landing in Belgium, and four more were damaged in crashes.

In the first December raid, on the night of the 6/7th, the 19 Gothas participating had hopefully loaded 10,300 lbs of a new type of incendiary bomb, and only 870 lbs of explosives. The two Giants participating loaded 1,660 lbs of explosive and 2,430 lbs of incendiary bombs. Many of the aircraft, including at least one of the Giants, dropped their bombs on Sheerness, Ramsgate, Margate and Dover. Between 4.30 and 5.30 am – an unusually late hour – six Gothas reached London, their incendiaries starting fires in Finsbury, Kennington and Whitechapel. The crews on their return, however, were very disappointed and reported that only a few fires had been seen. Two Gothas, damaged by anti-aircraft fire, made forced landings in England and were destroyed. A third went missing, probably at sea on the way home, while two Gothas, damaged by anti-aircraft fire, crash-landed outside their bases in Belgium. Still another was damaged in landing at its own aerodrome.

In the next attack, on December 18/19, the 15 Gothas loaded only high explosive bombs. One Giant accompanied them, carrying 2,200 lbs of mixed bombs. Reaching London, one of its 660-pounders fell near Eaton Square and damaged many homes. As usual, many bombs fell in Kent, and only six Gothas reached London. Three Royal Flying Corps pilots found and attacked Gothas, and one, shot up by Captain G. W. Murlis-Green in a Camel, fell in the sea off Folkestone. Back in Belgium, one Gotha crashed and four were damaged, two of them in crash landings outside their bases.

Thus, only a meagre 13 Gothas were dispatched in the next raid on January 28/29, 1918, of which six reached England and only three arrived over London. One, attacked by two Camels, crashed in flames at Wickford. One Giant was out, carrying 2,420 lbs of explosive bombs, including two of 660 lbs – the *R 39,* commanded by the redoubtable *Hauptmann* von Bentivegni, the commanding officer of *Reisenflugzeugabteilung 501.* Shooting up a Bristol Fighter which dared to attack, the Giant arrived over London, where one of its 660-lb bombs caused a memorable tragedy. Piercing a street level pavement light, the bomb exploded in the basement of Messrs Odhams' Printing Works in Long Acre. This was jammed with more than

500 people using it as an air raid shelter. The bomb blast and subsequent fire killed 38 persons and injured 85.

Four more Gothas were demolished in crash landings in Belgium, and because of the heavy losses, the *Englandgeschwader* was withdrawn for reorganisation, re-equipment and training of new personnel. When it was ready once more in March, it found itself committed to the support of the great drive which started on the 21st of the month. In the interval it was the Giants of *Rfa 501,* totalling six at the most, which alone continued the raids on southern England.

Four of the Giants were out on the night of January 29/30, and while they had little success against the capital, they demonstrated their ability to give and take punishment. Seventy-three British aircraft ascended, and one, a BE 12, encountered a Giant over Essex and stayed with it until it reached western London. Repeated attacks by the British pilot caused no apparent damage, while his own machine was badly riddled. The Giant's bombs fell on Kew, Brentford and Richmond; *en route* home it was attacked near Gravesend by another pilot who fired 100 rounds without effect. Another Giant was pursued by four aircraft which were unable to bring it down, though they forced it to dump its entire bomb load on Wanstead.

Five Giants set out on the night of February 16/17. Bentivegni's *R 39* was carrying for the first time a single 2,200-lb bomb, the largest used by either side in the war. Aiming at Victoria Station, the doughty *Kommandeur* instead blew up the North Pavilion of Chelsea Hospital. *R 12* also reached the capital, and survived with little damage a hair-raising encounter with the cables of a balloon barrage extending between Woolwich Arsenal and the West India Docks. Suddenly brought up short, it fell 1,000 feet before the pilot could regain control. The Giant went on to drop two 660-pounders in Woolwich Arsenal.

On the following night, *R 25,* flying alone, penetrated to the heart of the capital. The bulk of her bomb load was accurately aimed at St Pancras Station; here 20 were killed and 22 injured. One Camel pilot found the *R 25* but was forced to break off the engagement after firing 50 rounds. The R-plane commander remarked on the fact that a single machine could arouse the defences over a large area; guns 20 miles away 'were firing blindly into the air'.

Not until March 7 did the Giants return, all six of *Rfa 501's* machines being sent out that night. Again *R 39* was carrying a 2,200-lb bomb, which fell on Warrington Crescent, totally destroying four houses and damaging 140 to a greater or lesser degree. *R 27,* after dropping its cargo in Battersea, had all four engines fail simultaneously *en route* home when water in the petrol froze in the fuel lines; it just managed to glide to the Belgian coast, where it crash-landed. Still another unidentified Giant crashed in Belgium.

Only three Giants took part in the last raid on England, on May 19/20. The bulk of the attacking force was 38 Gothas from *BOGOHL 3,* whose commander had pleaded to have this attack sandwiched in between raids across the Western Front. The consequences were disastrous, for the British night fighter pilots had many engagements, three of which were successful. Three more Gothas were shot down by anti-

aircraft fire. Nineteen Gothas were supposed to have reached London, along with one Giant, but the damage was not impressive. Bombs fell in Kent and Essex, particularly at Dover and Folkestone.

More than the losses in this raid, the demands of the German offensives in France tied down both the Gothas and the Giants. Actually, as early as January 31, 1918, *BOGOHLs 1* and *2* had opened a series of attacks on Paris, designed together with the bombardment by the long-range guns to cause a collapse of French morale behind the fighting line. Plans were drawn to attack both London and Paris with a diabolically effective 'Elektron' or magnesium bomb weighing only 2·2 lb, but early in August the High Command decided 'on political grounds' against any further attacks on the capitals.

For the German navy's Zeppelins the last year of the war was marked by heavy losses. The last big raid, the 'Silent Raid', on October 19/20, 1917, resulted in most of the 11 participating airships being blown from the Midlands far into France by a 40-knot northerly gale above 15,000 feet. Four ships descended in France, another crash-landed in southern Germany. It was during this attack that one Zeppelin, *L 45,* found herself driving across London and released three 660-lb bombs which killed 33 people and wounded 49. Three months later, on January 5, 1918, four of the latest Zeppelins were destroyed at the Ahlorn base by a series of explosions which also demolished the four huge double hangars in which they were housed.

Three raids were made on the Midlands in the spring of 1918 by four or five airships carrying over 6,000 lbs of bombs and flying at 20,000 feet, where they were immune to the defences. Then came the last raid of the war, on August 5, 1918. Five Zeppelins, led by Strasser in the new *L 70,* set out for the Midlands, with the possibility that London might be bombed by his express order. Instead, as the raiding squadron approached England in twilight at a mere 16,000 feet, *L 70* was shot down in flames by a British aeroplane.

Bombing the Reich

Strategic bombing by the British Royal Flying Corps, and later by the Royal Air Force, on German cities, industry and communications resulted directly from the desire of the War Cabinet to retaliate for the raids on London by German Gothas. That astute politician, David Lloyd George, knew that the public was thirsting for revenge; but he had to battle the opposition of senior commanders in France. Sir Douglas Haig insisted on having the maximum number of aircraft to co-operate with the army in the Passchendaele battles; while Marshal Ferdinand Foch, the future generalissimo, rejected strategic bombing in pursuit of his obsession with winning the war through ground attack alone.

At the beginning of October 1917 Major-General Hugh Trenchard, then commanding the Royal Flying Corps in France, was instructed to commence attacks on German targets which could be reached from the area around Nancy in eastern Lorraine. Ochey was initially selected as the aerodrome for this bombing force. From here, it was theoretically possible to bomb by day and night not only the towns of the Saar but also such important German cities as Karlsruhe, Mannheim-Ludwigshafen (the huge Badische Anilin factory, manufacturing poison gas, was always a high priority target), Trier, Mainz, Coblenz and even such distant goals as Cologne, Frankfurt and Stuttgart, roughly 125 miles from Ochey. On October 11, Lieutenant-Colonel Cyril Newall was placed in command of the 41st Wing.

The force under Newall's command was pitifully small. The day bombing squadron was No 55, equipped with de Havilland DH 4's with Rolls-Royce Eagle engines of 250-hp. No 55 had taken the first 'Fours' to France in March 1917, and had had much practice in flying day bombing missions above 14,000 feet far into the German rear areas. The second squadron, No 100, was equipped with FE 2b's, lattice-tailed pushers obsolete for the day-fighting rôle for which they had been designed; but the squadron had come to France in March 1917, trained for night bombing and ground strafing. The big punch at night was to come from the Handley-Pages of Naval 'A' Squadron (later numbered No 16 Naval). At the time the Admiralty possessed, in the Handley-Page 0/100, the only large multi-engined bomber in British service. Designed originally for daylight overseas patrols, the 0/100 had two Rolls-Royce Eagles, a span of 100 feet, a crew of three, and carried up to 16 112-lb bombs. By contrast, the DH 4's carried only four 112-lb bombs; but Trenchard favoured day attack, even with lighter bomb loads, for its greater accuracy and supposed morale effect.

Initially the three units practised on nearby targets, the closest of which was the complex of railway junctions around Metz (Metz-Sablons, Metz-Woippy, Thionville, Longuyon), through which iron ore from the captured Lorraine fields passed daily to Germany. Not much farther were the Saar industrial towns—Saarbrücken, Pirmarsens, Bous, Volkingen, Dillingen and Merzig. The first daylight raid was by No 55 against the Burbach steel works near Saarbrücken. Four days later No 55 suffered its first loss when German fighters shot down one DH 4 during an attack on Bous. At this time home defence against daylight bombing attacks on the *Reich* was in the hands of scattered single seater formations known as *Kestn (Kampfeinsitzer Staffeln)* which neither in training nor equipment matched the fighter *Jagdstaffeln* on the Western Front. The first night raid was by nine Handley-Pages and 14 FE 2b's against the Burbach works on October 24/25. The weather was poor and two Handley-Pages and two FE's were lost.

Weather continued poor in November and December and what attacks could be made were on nearby targets. An ominous sign for the future was two night bombing attacks by German aircraft on Ochey during November. In time, much of the strategic bombing force would be diverted to attacks on German airfields at Metz-Frescaty, Morhange, Bühl, Volpersweiler, Boulay and others. Here the FE's of No 100 Squadron were in their element.

The first long-distance raid came on December 24, 1917, when ten de Havillands bombed Mannheim and Ludwigshafen from 13,000 feet. Minor attacks continued during the winter when the weather permitted, in conditions of appalling hardship for the flight crews. Despite fur-lined leather helmets, flying coats, trousers, boots and gauntlets, the icy blast of the 100-mph slipstream in open cockpits chilled the body and froze faces, fingers and toes. Electrically-heated flight suits were provided but were unreliable. Oxygen was issued to the high-flying day bombers, but the masks were prone to freezing.

Early in February, Newall's headquarters were given a new title—VIII Brigade. Several attacks were made on Trier during the month, the ideal of 'round the clock' bombing being attained on February 19, when the de Havillands bombed the town by day and the Handley-Pages followed by night. Nervous German civilians, and particularly their mayors, now began crying out in anguish and even urging that German air raids should stop—only to get short shrift from the Chief of the General Staff, *Feldmarschall* von Hindenburg.

With better weather in March, deeper raids were made by day—to Mainz on March 9, to Stuttgart on March 10, Coblenz on March 12, Freiburg on March 13, Mannheim on March 18, and again on March 24. Six de Havillands were lost to No 55 Squadron over Germany during these raids. Alarm was widespread, and the Germans added to the anti-aircraft guns around the threatened cities. The first attack on Cologne since October, 1914, was made on the night of March 24/25 by a Handley-Page. April was a month of high winds and fog, and strategic targets were not bombed.

May brought reinforcements for the thinly-spread day bombers—No 99 Squadron arriving on May 3, and No 104 on May 20. Unfortunately their aircraft were de Havilland DH 9's, modifications of the well-tried DH 4, and supposed to be improvements on the earlier craft, but actually inferior to it in performance. The fault was not in the airframe, but in the engine. Supplies of the excellent Rolls-Royce Eagle were falling far short of demand, and the DH 9 was intended to take a new mass-produced engine, the Siddeley Puma, originally expected to develop 300-hp, but de-rated after many failures to 230-hp. As a result of the unreliability of the Puma, the DH 9 squadrons were cursed with many aircraft falling out of formation before reaching the lines. Its low power limited the ceiling with bombs to about 12,000 feet, where the 'Nine' could easily be overtaken by German fighters.

With the formation of the Royal Air Force on April 1, 1918, the new Air Council decided to expand the strategic air war against Germany. Trenchard accepted on May 8 the command of the enlarged force, which was to be directly under the Air Ministry. The first members of the new organisation were of course the VIII Brigade squadrons. On June 6, 1918, they were again rechristened with the provocative title of Independent Force, RAF. The name grated on the ears of French generals, one of whom sarcastically posed the famous question, 'Independent of whom? Of God?'

Trenchard's first concern was to find space for a large number of additional squadrons in the region around Nancy; he had been promised a total of 40 by the end of August 1918. In fact, the Air Ministry's intentions embraced more than a solely British force, and its representatives had discussed before the Supreme War Council at Versailles the establishment of an Inter-Allied Independent Air Force which was to include at least one French *Groupe de Bombardement*; the Italian 18th Group, consisting of three Caproni squadrons, which arrived in France in February 1918; and whatever American squadrons might be established for the long distance bombing of Germany. The Inter-Allied Force never materialised (though many American officers were assigned to the British squadrons for operational training), nor did Trenchard's units exceed nine squadrons at the Armistice. The reason for this deficiency was the failure of engine and aircraft manufacture both in England and the United States to match extravagant expectations; but constant French army opposition to the whole concept of an 'independent' force occupying French soil played a more subtle rôle.

Trenchard saw himself having a choice of 'a sustained and continuous attack on one large centre after another until each centre was destroyed', or 'to attack as many of the large industrial centres as it was possible to reach with the machines at my disposal'. He adopted the latter alternative, as the former was not attainable with the meagre forces at his disposal, while the moral effect of widespread bombing was much greater than concentrated attack on a few cities.

Preferring day bombing, Trenchard sent out the untried DH 9 squadrons together with the veterans of No 55. It was their misfortune to meet the augmented *Kestn,*

now employing a fast-climbing interceptor, the Siemens-Schuckert D III, along with the familiar Albatros D Va's and Pfalz D III's. In a raid on Karlsruhe on June 26, No 104 lost two aircraft (one interned in Switzerland); four had dropped out before reaching the target, while five of No 99's had similarly aborted. Nine day bombers went missing during the month. In July the toll increased sharply. Bad weather frustrated many long range attempts in July, but raids were made on Coblenz (three times) and Stuttgart once by night. Fifteen day bombers were lost in combat. A massed assault by 40 German fighters on No 99 Squadron on July 31 knocked it out of the war for two weeks. Twelve aircraft set out for Mainz, but three of them turned back before reaching the trenches with engine trouble. The remaining nine came under such heavy attack that the leader abandoned the raid on Mainz and decided to bomb Saarbrücken. Four of the DH 9's were shot down before reaching the town, and three more were shot down on the return to the lines, the squadron losing altogether five officers killed and nine prisoners. The same fate was meted out to the other DH 9 squadron, No 104, in a flight to Mannheim on August 22. Two bombers were shot down by fighters near Karlsruhe on the way in, and five more were destroyed after bombing the target. Clearly the day bombers, par-

Opposite page top:
Major E. Cadbury,
who brought down the
*L 70. This page below
left:* The Zeppelin *L 70.
Below:* The ill-fated
Peter Strasser, lost
on the last Zeppelin
raid over Britain
in the war.
Bottom: A flight of
Handley-Pages sets
off at dusk for a night
raid on Germany

Imperial War Museum

Top: An experimental version of the Handley-Page 0/100 with four 200-hp Hispano-Suiza engines. *Above:* The inferior DH 9 day bomber. *Below:* The monstrous Caproni Ca 4 triplane bomber. *Bottom:* A Caproni Ca equipped as a torpedo bomber. *Above right:* Great Britain's first successful multi-engined bomber, the **Handley-Page 0/100**. *Engines:* two Rolls-Royce Eagle II inlines, 250/266-hp each. *Armament:* three to five flexible Lewis guns and up to 16 112-lb bombs. *Speed:* 85 mph at sea level. *Ceiling:* 7,000 feet. *Range:* about 700 miles. *Weight empty/*

loaded: 8,300/14,000 lbs. *Span:* 100 feet. *Length:* 62 feet 10¼ inches. *Below right:* Italy's best heavy bomber of the war, the **Caproni Ca 5**. *Engines:* three Fiat A 12 *bis* or Liberty inlines, 300- or 400-hp each. *Armament:* two Revelli machine guns and up to 2,000 lbs of bombs. *Speed:* 100 mph. *Climb:* 5½ minutes to 3,280 feet. *Ceiling:* 15,000 feet. *Range:* 400 miles. *Weight empty/loaded:* 6,620/11,700 lbs. *Span:* 77 feet. *Length:* 41 feet 4 inches. *Crew:* 2 for day- and 4 for night-bombing. Performance with Liberty engines was superior to the above figures

134

ticularly the DH 9 with its lamentable performance, could not reach the targets without long-range fighter escort.

There were compensations. Frankfurt-am-Main was reached for the first time by DH 4's of No 55 in an operation which saw 12 of the squadron's aircraft bombing the city from 14,000 feet. Twenty-five German fighters attacked the retreating day bombers near Mannheim but failed to break their tight formation; two German Albatroses were shot down, while all the 'Fours' made it back, one with a dead observer. The same crack squadron made the first attack on Darmstadt on August 16, with three aircraft lost to defending fighters *en route* home.

Of the four squadrons joining the Independent Force in August, three (nos 97, 215 and 115) flew Handley-Pages, while No 100 at this time was being re-equipped with the same machine. The fourth squadron, No 110, had been equipped by the gift of the Nizam of Hyderabad with a worthy replacement for the Puma 'Nine', the DH 9a with American Liberty engine of 400-hp. Here was a near sister of the 'Four' with more power and the ability to carry two 230-lb bombs to 16,750 feet, where it could still attain 102 mph.

On the night of August 25, two Handley-Pages of No 215 made a daring attack on the Badische Anilin plant at Ludwigshafen; one descending to 200 feet, the other to 500 feet to place their bombs accurately. Seven of the large bombers were lost in one night, however, on September 16/17, one force-landing in Holland after bombing Cologne, while others were shot down by anti-aircraft fire while attacking Saar-brücken and Trier.

During September, the Independent Force day squadrons, by order of Marshal Foch, were employed in tactical bombing in support of the American army's offensive at St Mihiel. Distant raids continued before and afterwards. On September 7,

Nos 99 and 104 went to Ludwigshafen; but 104 lost five of its DH 9's. No 110 flew to Mannheim on September 16 for its first raid, bombing from 17,000 feet. It lost one aircraft, but in a raid on Frankfurt on September 25 this same squadron, attacked by 50 German fighters, lost four machines.

Bad weather during October hampered the daylight raiders. Heavy losses in a raid on Cologne on October 21 ended No 110's effectiveness for the remaining days of the war. Four of the 11 DH 9a's which crossed the lines were shot down by defending fighters after the formation had broken up in heavy cloud, while others crash-landed on the Allied side of the lines. The augmented Handley-Page squadrons began using this month the 1,650-lb SN bomb, one of which on the night of October 21 demolished a munitions factory in Kaiserslautern. Two nights later another of the huge bombs wrecked a whole street of houses in Wiesbaden.

Without doubt, the Independent Force would have been greatly augmented, with even more devastating effect on the towns of south-west Germany, had the war continued into 1919. At Bircham Newton in Norfolk, three giant bombers were secretly being prepared for the first attack on Berlin — Handley-Page V/1500's, with a wing span of 126 feet, grossing more than 12 tons fully loaded, and powered by four Rolls-Royce 375-hp Eagles. Up to 30 250-lb bombs could be carried. They were ready to go to Berlin on November 11, when the Armistice stopped them. More would have joined this force, and in addition, Trenchard had a 'shuttle bombing' scheme for the giants, whereby they would proceed from Norfolk via Berlin to Prague, and return via Essen

or Düsseldorf to England, or via Regensburg or Munich to the fields around Nancy. All the DH 9's would have been replaced by 9a's, and at the Armistice, the Independent Force was testing two fast twin-engined day bombers, the de Havilland DH 10 Amiens and the Vickers Vimy. Long-range Sopwith Snipe fighters would have escorted them, and later would have been supplemented by the 140-mph Martinsyde Buzzard. And more and more American squadrons, equipped with American-built DH 4's and Handley-Pages, would have flocked to the Inter-Allied Independent Air Force.

During 13 months of strategic bombing, the Independent Force and its predecessors dropped 665 tons of bombs on German targets. Two hundred and twenty tons of this, however, fell on airfields. The Independent Force, after June 8, 1918, dropped 558 tons, 390 of them at night. Thus, the heaviest tonnage was transported by the night-flying Handley-Pages. It was the day bombers, however, which paid the price in blood—the four de Havilland squadrons losing 25 killed, 178 missing and 58 wounded, with 103 aircraft missing over the lines and 201 wrecked in crashes in friendly territory. The five night bombing squadrons had 87 killed or missing, and 11 wounded, while 34 aircraft were missing and 114 wrecked.

The effect of the Independent Force's penetrations into Germany was moral rather than material. To the war-weary

civilians of the Saar and the Rhineland, the threat of death from the skies was demoralising and undoubtedly war production suffered. Works managers, however, found the infrequent attacks with small bombs merely 'annoying'. The true significance of the Independent Force's operations was that they established a doctrine of defeating the enemy by aerial attack on his industrial base and civilian population, rather than by direct assault on his armies in the field, which had proved so costly and futile in the First World War.

Further Reading

Bülow, Hilmer von, *Die Angriffe des Bomben-geschwader 3 auf England (Die Luftwacht* 1927)

Caproni, Gianni, *Gli Aeroplano Caproni* (Museo Caproni 1935)

Fredette, Raymond, *The Sky on Fire* (New York: Holt, Rhinehart & Winston 1966)

Haddow, G. W. and Grosz, Peter, *The German Giants* (London: Putnam 1962)

Jones, H. A., *The War in the Air, Vol VI* (Oxford: Clarendon Press 1937)

Morris, Alan, *The First of the Many* (London: Jarrolds 1968)

Porro, Generale A. A. Felice, *La Guerra nell' Aria* (Milan: Corbaccio)

Below: Damage to the railway marshalling yards at Thionville on February 18, 1918 caused by bombers of the Independent Force. *Right:* A divided aim. A burning building in Paris after a Gotha raid. For a short period in 1918 the effort of the shorter ranged German bombers was switched to Paris to coincide with the bombardment of the 'Paris gun'

Imperial War Museum

The Allemanders have been getting rather uppish lately; and there has been another wail from the Gunners that our artillery machines are being unduly interfered with. Things are also boiling up for another fight round Passchendaele, and so it is particularly important to prevent the enemy from carrying out reconnaissances which might betray the movements of our troops. Talking of which, the contrast presented to the eyes of an airman between the areas immediately behind our own trench lines and those of the Germans is quite extraordinary.

Our own support and reserve areas are chockablock with troops, bivouacs, huts, horse-lines, lorry parks and every conceivable adjunct of an army in the field. Only the batteries seem to be well camouflaged. Whereas behind the German lines one sees practically nothing. Curious, isn't it?

Last week a reconnaissance in force of enemy scouts and two-seaters had the audacity to cross the lines! They got as far as Ypres. As luck would have it, one of my flights happened at that moment to be climbing to get their height over Poperinghe before going off on an offensive patrol, and spotted the Huns.

There were only four Bristol Fighters against some 16 EA (enemy aircraft), but they went straight in among them; and McGrath, one of my observers, got an Albatros down in flames. It crashed near Vlamertinghe on our side of the lines. McGrath, who is a Canadian and was on his last patrol before going home on leave, came back literally dancing with delight, as it does not often fall to our lot to get a machine down in our own territory. As soon as his report was made out, he begged for the squadron car to take him to the scene of the crash so that he might collect a souvenir before the infantry in the neighbourhood — Australians, who are notorious as having no peers in the art of scrounging — had collared everything worth having.

Off he went, and came back with a badly damaged aneroid — the Australians had been there first all right — which was the best he could procure. I expect that the aneroid will go down as a treasured heirloom in some distant British Columbian homestead.

The German formation was severely handled, as McCudden and his Flight of SEs came up shortly afterwards and accounted for at least two more of them, after which the remainder thought better of it and turned tail for home.

In spite of a very fair toll exacted from the enemy, we received a rude letter from GHQ asking what the devil we meant by allowing the Germans to cross the lines at all, and would we kindly see to it that this sort of thing should be stopped forthwith. We humbly expressed our regret at the occurrence and glibly promised that it should never happen again.

After that we felt in honour bound to pass on our 'strafing' from the GOC to our friends the enemy, the original instigator of the trouble. So, three days ago we took the air, six Bristol Fighters, eight SE 5s and two flights of Camels. I led my own contingent.

It was a perfect morning. Rarely have I seen the atmosphere so clear as we climbed to get our height behind the lines. The map of north-west Europe spread out below us precise in every detail. To the westward

DEATH OF AN ACE

Werner Voss, fourth on the list of German aces with 48 victories, was a superlative aerobatic pilot, but was finally brought down after an epic fight against several British aces

the French coastline ran back past Dunkirk to Calais and turned down towards Boulogne, from out whose harbour mouth were moving two slim ships, black upon the silver Channel waters . . . the leave-boat probably, and her accompanying destroyer. . . . The leave-boat, with 2,000 happy souls aboard her, homeward bound to England, for a few days' rest and comfort. Pigmy craft they looked, those two black boats, one tiny and one tinier . . .

To the southward lay the fair land of France, Picardy and Artois; the long straight files of trees which guard the roads marching ever onwards till lost to sight on the horizon. Dimly in the distance rose the spire of Amiens Cathedral. To the eastward, Lille, Douai, Courtrai, Tournai, Valenciennes . . . French towns held in bondage in the iron grip of war. Then Belgium . . . one narrow flooded strip of whose territory remained to her as a barrier against the foe. Ypres . . . the white stones of her ruins shining in the sunlight; Ypres, immortal in the annals of our race.

Far up the coast to the north-east one could distinguish the mouth of the Scheldt, the frontier of Holland; with Bruges and Ostend in the middle distance.

Then to the northwards — England! From 20,000 feet above the earth how lovely and alluring are the 'white cliffs of Dover'. I could see Dover Castle, Folkestone, Lympne, and Dungeness . . . round the foreland to Chatham and the mouth of the Thames . . . the river winding up to London . . . the City hidden in the haze; in my mind's eye I could see the street, the house we live in, you and I. I could see you, too . . . A wave of temptation swept over me. How easy to leave my formation and to fly on to the northwards! Within a few hours I could have been with you . . . back with you in England . . . Suddenly I felt every fibre of my being revolt against the whole idea of war! Why was I here? What were we all doing? What was the meaning of this mad, ruinous gamut into which we had precipitated ourselves?

Then a red flare from the leader of the SEs, indicating that he had sufficient height and was now making for the lines, brought me back to realities. The thoughts of a moment since fell away like a dream. No more doubts assailed me. Why this war indeed? Britain and her Allies were fighting for right! Victory was essential; and we of the Flying Corps could be deemed lucky that the part which we had been called upon to play in the great struggle was less exacting than that of many of our comrades in arms, in that it was a clean fight, novel, exciting and romantic.

The multi-hued 'Circus'
I altered my course eastward and opened up the throttle. Once more we were off to join in a tourney with the Allemander. We were to sweep him from the sky, 'larn' him to cross the line, in fact! But the worst of it was that there were no

Allemanders in the sky that morning! It was unthinkable that on so jolly a day these incredible Huns should be still lying abed instead of disporting themselves in the upper air. Where were Woolf, Voss, Richthofen and the rest? We knew them all by sight by this time. We knew them by the way they flew. Each had some little trick in flying by which we could identify him; and they painted their machines with a medley of gay colours (a form of extravagance which is denied to us by the unimaginative and parsimonious denizens of the Air Board). Richthofen himself flew a red Albatros; Voss affected checkers of black and white. Another sported green and silver, another blue, and so forth . . . They make a gallant showing.

As I said, the heavens were devoid of Huns, which, taking our resolve 'to do a big thing' into account, was most annoying!

There is nothing so unutterably boring as parading about the sky in undisputed possession of that empty space. It is not only boring, but intensely chilly.

Well, we roamed about in search of adventure for quite an hour and a half, affording the German anti-aircraft batteries a good excuse for blazing off their ammunition. For the first time I was able to look down in uninterrupted contemplation upon the towns of Ledeghem, Iseghem, and Englebelmer — names which daily appeared in operation orders as the line which we were to patrol — and satisfy myself that they were not the fiction of the Intelligence officer's restless brain.

A red flare again flickered up from the leader of the SE 5s. There were enemy in sight! But search as I might I could see nothing. Then, of a sudden, I espied the Hun . . . a solitary, lonely Hun in a Fokker triplane. This triplane was a *rara avis* on the Ypres front. Two of them had been seen at close quarters during the previous week farther to the south by a British pilot who had thought to recognise Voss as one of the pilots, and had further reported that in his opinion the machine was fitted with a Le Rhône engine taken from one of our machines which had been forced down in enemy territory.

In the light of after-events the pilot in question was probably right . . . Anyway, I was just about to become an eye witness to one of the finest individual efforts of the war in the air. Completely undismayed by the strength of the British formation arrayed against him in four tiers, one above the other, the German aviator flew straight to the attack.

Bald-headed he went for the SEs, guarded though they were by the Bristols from above and the Camels from below; and single-handed he fought them, the whole eight of them, though accounted in their number were several of the crack pilots of the day: Bowman, Rhys-Davies, Maxwell, and some more. For eight minutes on end he fought the eight, while I sat 1,000 feet above, watching with profoundest admiration this display of skill.

The dexterity of his manoeuvring was quite amazing. He was in and out and round about our scouts, zigzagging like forked lightning through the sky. None of our men could get at him. Then he broke off the fight and darted off to join a flight of Albatri which had appeared upon the scene—and were hanging about some distance away as if hesitating to take part. Placing himself at the head of this formation, he again wheeled to the attack. But the Albatri proved themselves unworthy of their would-be leader. They followed him to just within range of our machines, and then they turned and fled.

The triplane came on alone; again he flew to the attack; but, as was bound to happen in the end, the heavy odds against him told their tale. Rhys-Davies got in a short, straight burst and the triplane crashed in No-Man's Land, between the trenchlines. When they returned home, bullet holes in the wings and fuselage showed that not one of the SE 5s had escaped unscathed. PS—It has been officially announced in 'Comic Cuts' that Lieutenant Voss had met with a hero's death fighting single-handed against terrific odds. He thoroughly deserved the tribute paid to him; and the RFC were the gainers by the disappearance of a very skilful and gallant foe.

[*Rothesay Stuart-Wortley, MC.*]

Left: Werner Voss. *Top:* A Fokker Triplane coming in to land. By the time of Voss's death, the type was obsolete, despite its fantastic manoeuvrability. *Above:* A. P. F. Rhys Davids, 23 victories. *Below:* A crashed Triplane

Ullstein

139

Left: 'Panorama of the Western Front' by W. G. Wyllie. *Below:* 1918 aircraft. **1.** The Italian Savoia-Verduzio-Ansaldo 5 bomber and reconnaissance machine, of the 87° *Squadriglia (La Serenissima)*. The SVA 5 had good climb and range, and an odd fuselage marked by a change from rectangular to triangular section aft of the cockpit. *Engine:* SPA 6A inline, 205-220 hp. *Armament:* two Vickers guns. *Speed:* 143 mph at sea level. *Climb:* 12 mins 50 secs to 13,120 feet. *Endurance:* 4 hours. *Weight empty/loaded:* 1,500/2,315 lbs. *Span:* 29 ft 10¼ ins. *Length:* 26 ft 7 ins. **2.** The French Spad S XIII, in the markings of a pilot of the US 94th (Hat in the Ring) Squadron. The S XIII was an improved version of the VII. *Engine:* Hispano-Suiza 8, 220-235 hp. *Armament:* two Vickers guns. *Speed:* 138 mph at 6,560 ft. *Climb:* 12 mins 10 secs to 13,124 ft. *Ceiling:* 21,800 ft. *Endurance:* 2 hours. *Weight empty/loaded:* 1,245/1,807 lbs. *Span:* 26 ft 6¾ ins. *Length:* 20 ft 4 ins. **3.** The German Albatros D Va, an up-engined version of the D III. The one illustrated was flown by *Leutnant* von Hippel of *Jasta 5*. *Engine:* Mercedes D IIIa, 170-185 hp. *Armament:* two 'Spandau' machine guns. *Speed:* 116 mph at 3,280 ft. *Climb:* 22.8 mins to 13,120 ft. *Ceiling:* 20,500 ft. *Endurance:* 2 hours. *Weight empty/loaded:* 1,511/2,061 lbs. *Span:* 29 ft 8¼ ins. *Length:* 24 ft 0⅝ ins. **4.** The French Nieuport 17, this machine being flown by Charles Nungesser. *Engine:* Le Rhône rotary, 110 hp. *Armament:* one Vickers gun. *Speed:* 107 mph at 6,500 ft. *Climb:* 9 mins to 10,000 ft. *Ceiling:* 17,500 ft. *Weight empty/loaded:* 825/1,232 lbs. *Span:* 26 ft. *Length:* 19 ft 7 ins

Royal R.A.F. Staff College

John Batchelor

AIR OBSERVATION

The military importance of air power is the freedom it confers to oversee, and harass, the dispositions and activities of an opponent. Around this core all the elaborations of air fighting have been built. *Christopher Chant*

For two generations now we have grown accustomed to the use of 'air power' as a strategic weapon, and it is consequently difficult to imagine that in the First World War there was no such thing as air power as an independent strategic force—it was only a tactical adjunct of the army and of the navy. That the air forces of the fighting powers should be relegated to a secondary position, albeit an important one with a decisive influence in the outcome of tactical affairs, is inevitable, as aviation was too new an art to have developed machines capable of carrying a load sufficiently great to make the machines strategic offensive weapons in their own right.

As tactical weapons, therefore, aircraft had to be geared to the needs of the forces they were supporting. In the First World War, the main use of aeroplanes supporting the armies was as a means of observation. This took the form of optical spotting for the artillery, or photographic and optical reconnaissance for army and corps headquarters.

These two rôles fulfilled by the air forces, then, were the prime *raison d'êtres* of the Royal Flying Corps and its companion services on both sides. Though more attention is given usually to the exploits of the fighter (or scout) pilots, as the legatees of the 'tradition of chivalry' and as the memorable individualists of the air war, this is somewhat unfair to the pilots and crews of artillery spotting and reconnaissance squadrons on two counts: their bravery was no less (indeed, it could be argued that it was greater as they flew aircraft which were less combat-worthy in many instances) and their utility to the ground forces was greater. Fighter pilots were cast in an essentially negative rôle, their purpose being to deny the enemy the benefit of the information that their reconnaissance and photographic machines could provide. Thus, although it was less 'glamorous' and less dangerous than engaging other single-seater machines, a fighter pilot could far more profitably employ himself in shooting down artillery and reconnaissance machines than fighters. (Of the 80 machines shot down by Manfred von Richthofen, 47 were of the artillery and reconnaissance variety.)

It had been realised before the war by certain enthusiasts, notably in No 3 Squadron RFC, that aircraft would play an important part in the future conflict as eyes for the artillery, and a certain amount of work had been done in the development of means of communicating with the ground forces, principally by means of coloured lights fired from the aircraft and messages dropped near the guns. These were too inefficient to be practical, however, and the problem remained unsolved until the advent of wireless. This was at first clumsy and short in range, but the exigencies of war soon provided the stimulus to ensure rapid progress. The first truly successful artillery-spotting flights took place during the Battle of the Aisne in September 1914, when BE 2's spotted for the BEF. It is worth noting here that throughout the war the Germans had less need for artillery-spotting aircraft than the RFC or the French air force as they held the higher ground for most of the length of the Western Front. In many places, forward observation officers were sufficient to spot the fall of shot. This is not to say that they had no need for spotter aircraft and balloons, but merely a lesser need.

The practice of artillery spotting grew in scope and in sophistication throughout the war, but its principal elements had been decided by the beginning of 1915, and the only major changes were in the aircraft and the wireless equipment, which became lighter, more reliable and possessed of longer range. Though experiments with wireless telephony had proved fairly successful, the continuation of the war into 1919 would have seen little improvement in spotting. Let us, therefore, examine the techniques of spotting. The aim was for a particular aircraft to register the fire of one gun in a battery onto a specific target. When the aircraft could see the shells from this gun landing on the target, it could inform the battery commander that all his guns could now fire on the same laying as the registered one, hit the target and presumably destroy it. The target in most instances was a fixed one such as a hostile gun battery, strong point in the line, or, in the event of an offensive, the whole of the enemy's defence system. The recipients of the very heavy guns' attention were usually further behind the lines, targets such as supply and ammunition dumps and railway junctions.

On being ordered out, the aircraft would take off and fly to the vicinity of the shoot, and there identify the battery for which it was to spot and the target upon which it was to register the guns. Having done this, the spotter aircraft's observer, who was responsible for the registering of the shoot, would identify his aircraft to the battery and order a shot to be fired at a designated moment. As this moment approached, the pilot, who throughout the shoot had to fly a course between the guns and the target, turned so that his observer could see the gun as it fired. As he saw it

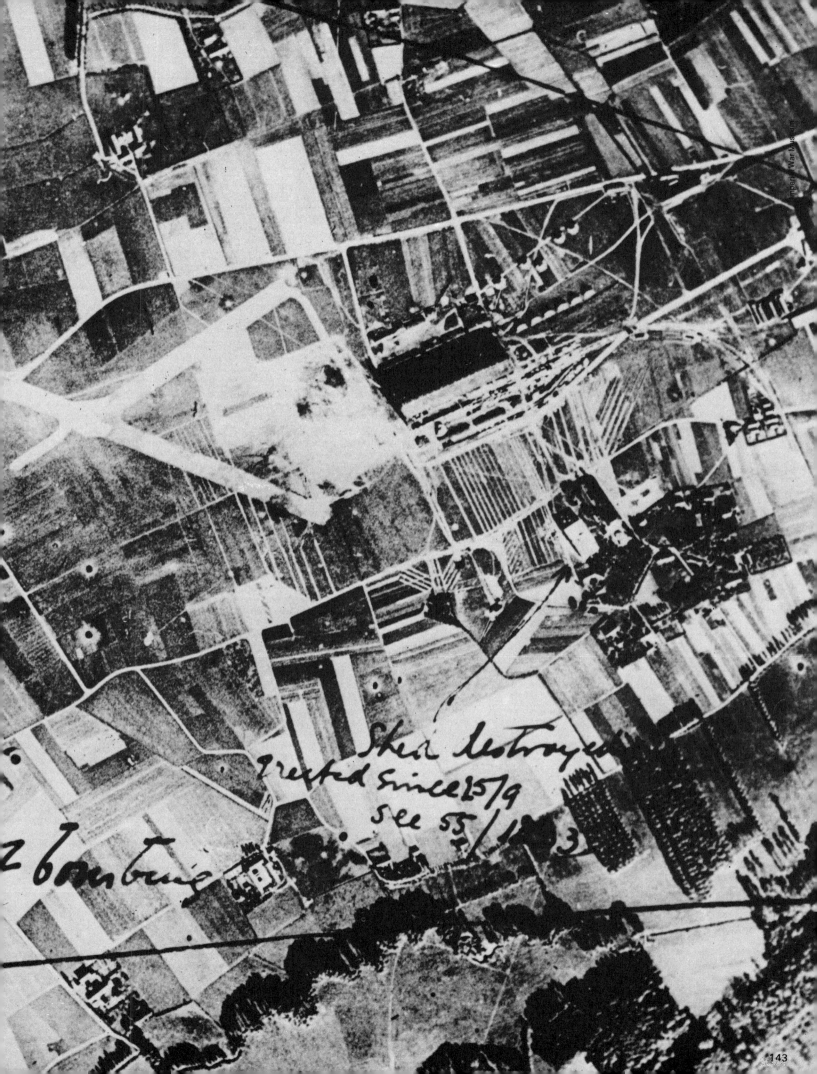

Shed destroyed
erected since 25/9
see 55/... 3

2 bombing

do so, the observer started his stopwatch and instructed the pilot to turn so that he (the observer) could see the target. As he knew the approximate range, and the ballistic characteristics of the gun for which he was spotting, he could glance at the stopwatch and predict the arrival of the shell in the vicinity of the target. The use of the watch was essential, for without it the observer might take the fall of shot of other batteries for his own and thus signal false corrections. After this first shot, the observer now had to correct the fire of the gun. Up until the early part of 1915, this had been done by signalling for the gun to vary its fire slightly around its original laying, until the target was hit, whereupon the observer would signal to this effect. Early in 1915, however, the 'clock code' was introduced. This marked the beginning of the day of scientific artillery spotting, economically much superior in shell and time over the earlier haphazard system. The clock code was virtually foolproof. It had as its two bases true north and the dial of a clock. The target was considered to be at the centre of the dial, and 12 o'clock due north of it, with the other hours in their standard positions relative to this. This part of the system, therefore, gave the direction from the target of the position where the shell had landed. Thus a shell that landed due east of the target was reported as having fallen at 3 o'clock. The other component of the system was of course range. Apart from knowing where, relative to the target, the shell had fallen, the battery commander needed to know how far in that direction from the target it had fallen. For this, the observer and the battery commander had to visualise a series of concentric circles around the target, at fixed intervals. These were at ranges of 10, 25, 50, 100, 200, 300, 400 and 500 yards from the target and were denoted by the letters Y, Z, A, B, C, D, E and F respectively. So if the shell landed 400 yards south-south-east of the target, the observer would transmit, in Morse, the code 'E 5'. The battery commander could then work out exactly where his shot had landed and make corrections to the laying of the gun accordingly. The process continued until the gun was firing in exactly the right direction and at exactly the right range, whereupon the rest of the guns in the battery would join in, firing on the same laying.

Hazardous work

Artillery observation was extremely hazardous work, for apart from the danger from hostile fighters, the need for the pilot to fly an even and regular course at a relatively low altitude in the vicinity of the front line made his aircraft a tempting and good target for AA guns. There was also the danger from one's own shells, for the aircraft flew at the height reached by howitzer shells at the top of their trajectories. Several aircraft are known to have been lost as a result of being hit by shells from their own side, and there are many recorded instances of pilots catching sight of shells. Imagine flying at about 5,000 to 6,000 feet and suddenly hearing a sound 'like an express train' moving towards you, then sighting the ghostlike grey form of an enormous howitzer shell tumbling ever more slowly up towards you, jelling into crystal solidity for the brief moment it is stationary at the apex of its

trajectory and then tumbling away with increasing speed into invisibility again and the ground.

The other means of artillery spotting was from balloons. The rows of these, about one every three miles along each side of the front, were one of the characteristic features of the Western Front. Intrinsically very vulnerable, as they were filled with hydrogen as their lifting agent, these were extraordinarily heavily defended with machine guns on the ground. As few aces were noted for their readiness to attack balloons, but most pilots gave them a wide berth – at the first sign of a hostile aircraft, the high-speed mooring winches for each balloon would haul down their charges, leaving the machine guns a clear and ranged field of fire in which to give the attacker a hot reception. The only real chance of success lay in using cloud cover to surprise the balloon crew. In an emergency situation such as this, the occupants of the balloon's basket, who had been equipped with parachutes from an early stage of the war, usually abandoned their craft.

The great advantage of using balloons was that they were stationary relative to the guns and their targets, and could communicate by telephone with the battery,

whereas aircraft were restricted to one-way wireless. The battery had to communicate with the aircraft by means of pre-arranged signals in the form of strips of cloth laid out on the ground. Britain had entered the war with only man-lifting kites, which required a strong wind and were very unstable, and with spherical balloons, which were useless in any but the calmest weather. The French and Germans were much better off, with the Caquot and the *Drachen* types respectively (both used the term *Drachen* for tethered observation balloons), and the Italians also had a good balloon. The Italian type was adopted by the British, but this had been replaced by the French type by the end of the war. These balloons were able to fly and to give their occupants a stable enough platform in winds up to about 50 mph. The actual practice of artillery spotting did not differ very much from that used by aircraft, except inasmuch as the balloon was stationary.

The other important tactical rôle fulfilled by aircraft in the First World War, as explained above, was that of reconnaissance. This fell into two parts: short range over the trenches for corps purposes and long range behind the lines for army purposes. Short-range reconnaissances were

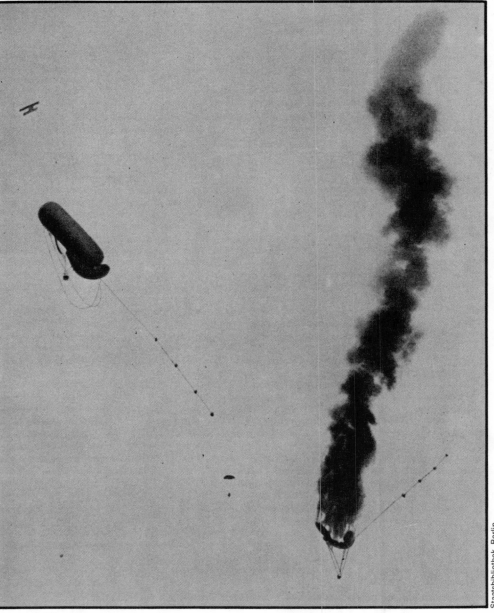

usually photographic, so that corps and divisional Intelligence officers could build up photographic maps of the front line for the purposes of planning attacks and raids. Long-range reconnaissances were different, usually visual, the observer marking down on a map the positions of any items that might interest army Intelligence officers (items that might have long-term ramifications or show a major build-up in strength, portending a large-scale offensive.

The Major difficulty in short-range reconnaissances lay in the fact that they were over the front line, the prowling ground of enemy fighters and the home of some of the heaviest anti-aircraft defences. Aircraft on such a mission had to fly straight and level for some distance to take the necessary overlapping series of photographs, and such aircraft were all the more easily surprised by fighters, as well as providing the AA guns with a good target. The difficulties of long-range reconnaissance machines, however, were different. AA fire and fighters had to be braved on the way out and back over the front lines, but more important was the problem of navigation and the reliability of the engine, both considerable factors in the still primitive days of the First World War. A German machine with engine trouble stood a better chance of

Left: Balloons; stable observation platforms, but vulnerable. *Top:* Instruction in aerial photography for the RFC. *Above:* Wireless tuition. Air to ground wireless was late in coming, but was vital to many observation tasks

gliding over the lines than an Allied machine, however, as the prevailing wind was usually a westerly one.

But let one who flew long-range reconnaissance missions at the time of the Battle of the Somme speak for himself, and describe the sensation of being on a 'long reconnaissance'. The following extract is from *An Airman's Outings* by 'Contact', published by Blackwood:

For 30 hours the flight had 'stood by' for a long reconnaissance. We were dragged from bed at 4.30 of dawn, only to return gratefully beneath the blankets three-quarters of an hour later, when a slight but steady rain washed away all chance of an immediate job. The drizzle continued until after sundown, and our only occupations throughout the day were to wade from mess to aerodrome, aerodrome to mess, and to overhaul in detail machines, maps, guns, and consciences.

Next morning again we dressed in the half-light, and again went back to bed in the daylight. This time the show had been postponed because of low clouds and a thick ground-mist that hung over the reeking earth. It was a depressing dawn—clammy, moist and sticky.

But by early afternoon the mist had congealed, and the sheet of clouds was torn to rags by a strong south-west wind. The four craft detailed for the reconnaissance were therefore lined outside their shed, while their crews waited for flying orders. I was to be in the leading bus, for when C.'s death left vacant the command of A Flight, the good work of my pilot had brought him a flight-commandership, a three-pipped tunic and a sense of responsibility which checked his tendency to over-recklessness. He now came from the squadron office with news of a changed course.

The plan

'To get the wind behind us,' he explained, 'we shall cross well to the south of Péronne. Next, we go to Boislens. After that we pass by Nimporte, over the Foret de Charbon to Siègecourt; then up to Le Recul and back by Princebourg, St Guillaume, and Toutprès.

'As regards the observers, don't forget to use your field-glasses on the rolling stock; don't forget the precise direction of trains and motor transport; don't forget the railways and roads on every side; don't forget the canals; and for the Lord's and everybody else's sake, don't be surprised by Hun aircraft. As regards the pilots—keep in close formation when possible; don't straggle and don't climb above the proper height.'

The pilots ran their engines once more, and the observers exchanged information about items such as Hun aerodromes and the number of railway stations at each large town. An air reconnaissance is essentially the observer's show; its main object being to supply the 'I' people at headquarters with private bulletins from the back of the German front. The collection of reconnaissance reports is work of a highly skilled nature, or ought to be. Spying out the land is much more than a search of railways, roads and the terrain generally. The experienced observer must know the German area over which he works rather better than he knows Salisbury Plain. The approximate position of railway junctions and stations, aerodromes, factories and depots should be familiar to him, so that he can without difficulty spot

any new feature. Also he must be something of a sleuth, particularly when using smoke as a clue. In the early morning a thin layer of smoke above a wood may mean a bivouac. If it be but a few miles behind the lines, it can evidence heavy artillery. A narrow stream of smoke near a railway will make an observer scan the line closely for a stationary train, as the Boche engine-drivers usually try to avoid detection by shutting off steam. The Hun has many other dodges to avoid publicity. When Allied aircraft appear, motor and horse transport remain immobile at the roadside or under trees. Artillery and infantry are packed under cover; though, for that matter, the Germans very rarely move troops in the daytime, preferring the night or early morning, when there are no troublesome eyes in the air.

To foil these attempts at concealment is the business of the observers, who gather information for Army Headquarters and GHQ. For observers on corps work the detective problems are somewhat different. This department deals with hidden saps and battery positions, and draws and photographs conclusions from clues such as a muzzle-blast, fresh tracks, or an artificial cluster of trees. All reconnaissance observers must carry out a simultaneous search of the earth for movement and the sky for foes, and in addition keep their guns ready for instant use. And should anything happen to their machines, and a forced landing seem likely, they must sit tight and carry on so long as there is the slightest hope of a safe return.

A nos moutons. I made a long list in my note-book of the places where something useful was likely to be observed, and tried my gun by firing a few shots into the ground. We hung around, impatient at the long delay.

'Get into your machines,' called the Squadron-Commander at last, when a telephone message had reported that the weather conditions toward the east were no longer unfavourable. We took to the air and set off.

V. led his covey beyond Albert and well south of the river before he turned to the left. Then, with the strong wind behind us, we raced north-east and crossed the strip of trenches. The pilot of the emergency machine, which had come thus far to join the party if one of the other four dropped out, waved his hand in farewell and left for home.

Archie barked at us immediately, but he caused small trouble, as most of his attention was already claimed by a party of French machines half a mile ahead. Anyhow we should have shaken him off quickly, for at this stage of the journey, with a 40-mile wind reinforcing our usual air speed of about 95 mph, our ground speed was sufficient to avoid lingering in any region made unhealthy by AA guns. The water-marked ribbon of trenches seemed altogether puny and absurd during the few seconds when it was within sight. The winding Somme was dull and dirty as the desolation of its surrounding basin. Some 4,000 feet above the ground a few clouds moved restlessly at the bidding of the wind.

Passing a few small woods, we arrived without interruption over the railway junction of Boislens. With arms free of the machine to avoid unnecessary vibration, the observers trained their glasses on the station and estimated the amount of rolling stock. A close search of the railway arteries only revealed one train. I grabbed pencil and note-book and wrote: 'Boislens, 3.5 P.M. 6 R.S., 1 train going S.W.' [*Boislens, 3.05 pm, 6 Rolling Stock, 1 train going south-west.*]

Just west of our old friend Mossy-Face [*a wood*] were two rows of flagrantly new trenches. As this is one of the points where the Germans made a stand after their 1917 spring retreat, it can be assumed that even as far back as last October they were preparing new lines of defence, Hindenburg or otherwise. Not far west of these defence works were two troublesome aerodromes at Bertincourt and Velu, both of which places have since been captured.

The aerial 'Hun'

A hunt for an aerodrome followed. V., who knew the neighbourhood well, having passed above it some two-score times, was quick to spot a group of hitherto unnoted sheds north of Boislens, towards Mossy-Face. He circled over them to let me plot the pin-point position on the map and sketch the aerodrome and its surroundings. The Hun pilots, with thoughts of a possible bomb-raid, began to take their machines into the air for safety.

'Got 'em all?' Thus V., shouting through the rubber speaking-tube, one end of which was fixed inside my flying-cap, so that it always rested against my ear.

'Correct. Get on with the good work.'

The good work led us over a region for ever associated with British arms. Some of the towns brought bitter memories of that anxious August three years back. Thus Nimporte, which saw a desperate but successful stand on one flank of the contemptible little army to gain time for the main body; Ventregris, scene of a cavalry charge that was a glorious tragedy; Làbas, where a battery of horse-gunners made for itself an imperishable name; Siègecourt, where the British might have retired into a trap but didn't; and Le Recul itself, whence they slipped away just in time.

In the station at Nimporte a train was waiting to move off, and two more were on their way to the military base of Plusprès. Both attempted to hide their heads by shutting off steam immediately the drone of our engines made itself heard; but we had spotted them from afar, and their presence was duly noted.

The next item of interest was activity at a factory outside a little town. Black trails of smoke stretched away from the chimneys; and surely, as we approached a minute ago, a short column of lorries was passing along a road towards the factory. Yet when we reached the spot there was no sign of road transport. Nevertheless, I was certain I had seen some motor vehicles, and I entered the fact in my note-book. Likewise I took care to locate the factory site on my map, in case it deserved the honour of a bomb attack later.

Our bus led the way across the huge unwieldy Foret de Charbon, patterned in rectangular fashion by intersecting roads, and we arrived at Siègecourt. This is at once a fortress and an industrial town. There are several railway stations around it, and these added greatly to the observers' collection of trains and trucks. The Huns below, with unpleasant memories of former visits from British aircraft, probably expected to be bombed. They threw up at us a large quantity of high-explosive shells,

but the shots were all wide and we remained unworried. To judge by the quality of the AA shooting each time I called there, it seemed likely that half-trained AA gunners were allowed to cut their active service teeth on us at Siègecourt.

Having squeezed Siègecourt of all movement, we headed for Le Recul. Here the intricate patchwork of railway kept the observers busy, and six more trains were bagged. Then, as this was the farthest point east to be touched, we turned to the left and travelled homeward.

It was soon afterwards that our engine went dud. Instead of a rhythmic and continuous hum there was at regular intervals a break, caused by one of the cylinders missing explosion at each turn of the rotary engine. The rev counter showed that the number of revolutions per

minute had fallen off appreciably. Decreased revs meant less speed, and our only chance to keep with the others was to lose height continuously. We were then nearly 50 miles from the lines.

I noticed the gap in the engine's drone as soon as it began. An airman is accustomed to the full roar of his engine, and it never distracts his attention, any more than the noise of a waterfall distracts those who live near it. But if the roar becomes noncontinuous and irregular he is acutely conscious of the sound.

When the machine began to lose height I knew there was a chronic miss. V. looked round and smiled reassuringly, though he himself was far from reassured. He tried an alteration in the carburettor mixture, but this did not remedy matters. Next, thinking that the engine might have been

Top: Final briefing—a German observation officer receives his last orders before ascending in his balloon. *Above:* Jack of all trades—the observer of a German reconnaissance machine, surrounded by the paraphernalia of his tasks, observation and self defence

Ullstein

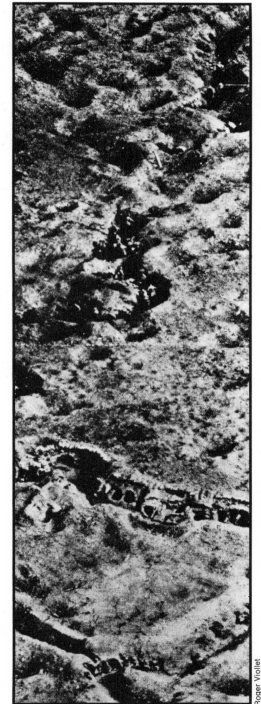

Top: Ground crew prepare an Albatros for a sortie. *Above:* Bird's eye view of the Battle of the Somme—information for the corps

Roger Viollet

slightly choked, he cut off the petrol supply for a moment and put down the nose of the machine. The engine stopped, but picked up when the petrol was once more allowed to run. During the interval I thought the engine had ceased work altogether, and was about to stuff things into my pocket in readiness for a landing on hostile ground.

We continued in a westerly direction, with the one cylinder still cutting out. To make matters worse, the strong wind that had been our friend on the outward journey was now an enemy, for it was drifting us to the north, so that we were obliged to steer almost dead into it to follow the set course.

As we passed along the straight canal from Le Recul to Princebourg many barges were in evidence. Those at the side of the canal were taken to be moored up, and those in the middle to be moving, though the slowness of their speed made it impossible to decide on their direction, for from a height of 10,000 feet they seemed to be stationary. About a dozen Hun machines were rising from aerodromes at Passementerie, away to the left, but if they were after us the attempt to reach our height in time was futile.

Between Le Recul and Princebourg we dropped 1,500 feet below the three rear machines, which hovered above us. Though I was far from feeling at home, it was necessary to sweep the surrounding country for transport of all kinds. This was done almost automatically, since I found myself unable to give a whole-hearted attention to the job, while the infernal motif of the engine's ragtime drone dominated everything and invited speculation on how much lower we were than the others, and whether we were likely to reach a friendly landing-ground. And all the while a troublesome verse chose very inopportunely to race across the background of my mind, in time with the engine, each cut-out being the end of a line. Once or twice I caught myself murmuring:

'In that poor but honest 'ome,
 Where 'er sorrowin' parints live,
 They drink the shampyne wine she sends,
 But never, never can forgive.'

The stalker

Slightly to the east of Princebourg, a new complication appeared in the shape of a small German machine. Seeing that our bus was in difficulties, it awaited an opportunity to pounce, and remained at a height slightly greater than ours, but some distance behind the bus that acted as rearguard to the party. Its speed must have been about 10 mph more than our own, for though the Hun pilot had probably throttled down, he was obliged to make his craft snake its way in short curves, so that it should not come within dangerous range of our guns. At times he varied this method by lifting the machine almost to stalling point, letting her down again, and repeating the process. Once I saw some motor transport on a road. I leaned over the side to estimate their number, but gave up the task of doing so with accuracy under the double strain of watching the Hun scout and listening to the jerky voice of the engine.

As we continued to drop, the German evidently decided to finish us. He climbed a little and then rushed ahead. I fired at him in rapid bursts, but he kept to his course. He did not come near enough for a dive, however, as the rest of the party, 2,000 feet above, had watched his movements, and as soon as he began to move nearer two of them fell towards him. Seeing his game was spoiled the Boche went down steeply, and only flattened out when he was low enough to be safe from attack.

Near St Guillaume an anti-aircraft battery opened fire. The Hun pilot then thought it better to leave Archie to deal with us, and he annoyed us no more. Some of the shell-bursts were quite near, and we could not afford to lose height in distance-dodging, with our machine in a dubious condition 25 miles on the wrong side of the trenches.

Toutprès, to the south-west, was to have been included in the list of towns covered, but under the adverse circumstances V. decided not to battle against the wind more than was necessary to get us home. He therefore veered to the right, and steered due west. The south-west wind cut across and drifted us, so that our actual course was north-west. Our ground speed was now a good deal greater than if we had travelled directly west, and there was no extra distance to be covered, because of a large eastward bend in the lines as they wound north. We skirted the ragged Forêt de Quand-Même, and passed St Guillaume on our left.

The behaviour of the engine went from bad to worse, and the vibration became more and more intense. Once more I thought it would peter out before we were within gliding distance of British territory, and I therefore made ready to burn the machine—the last duty of an airman let in for the catastrophe of a landing among enemies. But the engine kept alive, obstinately and unevenly. V. held down the nose of the machine still farther, so as to gain the lines in the quickest possible time.

Soon we were treated to a display by the family ghost of the clan Archibald, otherwise an immense pillar of grey-white smoky substance that appeared very suddenly to windward of us. It stretched up vertically from the ground to a height about level with·ours, which was then only 5,500 feet. We watched it curiously as it stood in an unbending rigidity similar to that of a giant waxwork, cold, unnatural, stupidly implacable, half unbelievable and wholly ridiculous. At the top it sprayed round, like a stick of asparagus. For two or three months similar apparitions had been exhibited to us at rare intervals, nearly always in the same neighbourhood. At first sight the pillars of smoke seemed not to disperse, but after an interval they apparently faded away as mysteriously as they had appeared. What was meant to be their particular branch of frightfulness I cannot say. One rumour was that they were an experiment in aerial gassing, and another that they were of some phosphorus compound. All I know is that they entertained us from time to time, with no apparent damage.

Archie quickly distracted our attention from the phantom pillar. We had been drifted to just south of Lille, possibly the hottest spot on the whole Western Front as regards anti-aircraft fire. Seeing one machine 4,000 to 5,000 feet below its companions, the gunners very naturally concentrated on it. A spasmodic chorus of barking coughs drowned the almost equally spasmodic roar of the engine. V. dodged steeply and then raced, full out, for the lines. A sight of the dirty brown jig-saw of trenches heartened us greatly. A few minutes later we were within gliding distance of the British front. When we realised that even if the engine lost all life we could reach safety, nothing else seemed to matter, not even the storm of shell-bursts.

Suddenly the machine quivered, swung to the left, and nearly put itself in a flat spin. A large splinter of HE had sliced away part of the rudder. V. banked to prevent an uncontrolled side-slip, righted the bus as far as possible, and dived for the lines. These we passed at a great pace, but we did not shake off Archie until well on the right side, for at our low altitude the high-angle guns had a large radius of action that could include us. However, the menacing coughs finally ceased to annoy, and our immediate troubles were over. The strain snapped, the air was an exhilarating tonic, the sun was warmly comforting, and everything seemed attractive, even the desolated jumble of waste ground below us. I opened a packet of chocolate and shared it with V., who was trying hard to fly evenly with an uneven rudder. I sang to him down the speaking-tube, but his nerves had stood enough for the day, and he wriggled the machine from one side to the other until I became silent. Contrariwise to the last, our engine recovered slightly now that its recovery was not so important, and it behaved well until it seized up for better or worse when we had landed.

From the aerodrome the pilots proceeded to tea and a bath, while we, the unfortunate observers, copied our notes into a detailed report, elaborated the sketches of the new aerodromes, and drove in our unkempt state to Headquarters, there to discuss the reconnaissance with spotlessly neat staff officers. At the end of the report one must give the height at which the job was done, and say whether the conditions were favourable or otherwise for observation. I thought of the absence of thick clouds or mist that might have made the work difficult. Then I thought of the cylinder that missed and the chunk of rudder that was missing, but decided that these little inconveniences were unofficial. And the legend I felt in duty bound to write was: 'Height 5,000-10,000 ft. Observation easy.'

Further Reading

Cuneo, J., *The Air Weapon* (Harrisburg: The Military Service Publishing Co, 1947)
Lamberton, W. M., *Reconnaissance and Bomber Aircraft of the 1914-1918 War* (Harleyford 1958)
McCudden, J. T. B., *Five Years in the RFC* (The Aeroplane & General Publishing Co)
Neumann, G. P., *The German Air Force in the Great War* (Chivers 1969)
Raleigh, Sir Walter, and Jones, H. A., *The War in the Air* (Oxford University Press)
Saunders, H. St G., *Per Ardua* (Oxford University Press 1945)

Imperial War Museum

Above: A British aircraft camera. Development of aerial cameras received an enormous extra impetus after the Western Front had stabilised. *Right:* A photograph taken over Nieuwe Stade in September 1917 showing shell damage

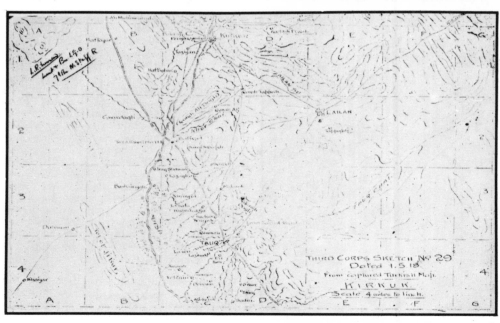

Though the British possessed fairly good maps for the areas in which they were fighting in Europe, the same could not be said for the Mesopotamian theatre. Consequently, maps of any description and provenance were invaluable. Above is a British sketch map based on a captured Turkish map, invaluable (as are all captured maps) for any military information in the way of dispositions or numbers. But, on the other hand, Intelligence officers in possession of captured material can never be sure that it is not 'planted' material rather than the genuine article on which they are basing their work. Therefore aerial confirmation of the information is vital, in addition to updating it and providing geographical knowledge as well

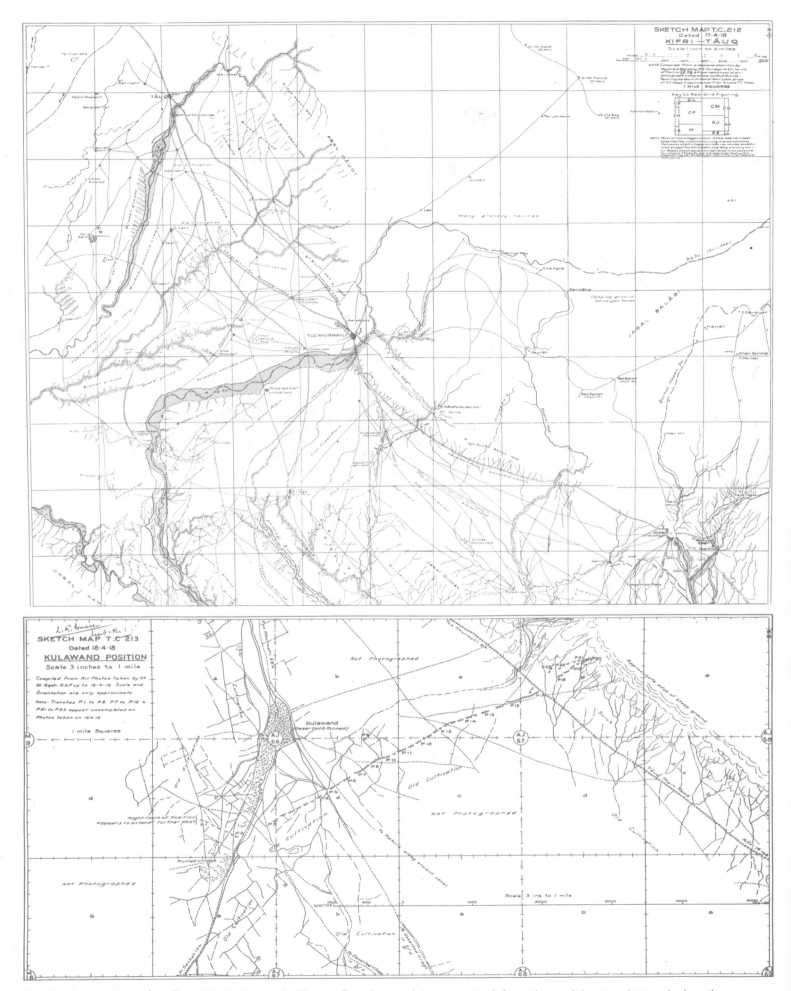

The art of aerial map making. Though important on the Western Front for strategic and tactical information, aerial reconnaissance had another rôle to fulfil in areas such as Mesopotamia, that of surveying the terrain. *Top:* The Kifri-Tauq area, a geographical map compiled from photographs in April 1918. *Above:* The Kulawand area, a simpler map showing the Turkish front line trenches in the area and the basic terrain

Two of the best general purpose and reconnaissance aircraft to operate over the Western Front. *Top:* The French Salmson **2A 2**. The two most notable features of this machine were the absence of any fixed fin or tailplane and the provision of a water-cooled radial engine. 3,200 of the type were built. *Engine:* Salmson-Canton-Unné radial, 260 hp. *Armament:* one fixed Vickers gun and two flexible Lewis guns. *Speed:* 115 mph at 6,560 feet. *Ceiling:* 20,500 feet. *Endurance:* 3 hours. *Weight empty/loaded:* 1,676/2,954 lbs. *Span:* 38 feet 8½ inches. *Length:* 27 feet 10⅔ inches. *Crew:* 2. *Above:* The German **LVG C VI**, a development of the CV, which had been hampered by inferior handling characteristics and visibility. The C VI was much improved in these. *Engine:* Benz Bz IV inline, 200 hp. *Speed:* 106 mph at sea-level. *Climb:* 15 minutes to 9,840 feet. *Ceiling:* 21,350 feet. *Endurance:* 3½ hours. *Weight empty/loaded:* 2,046/3,058 lbs. *Span:* 42 feet 7¾ inches. *Length:* 24 feet 5¼ inches. *Crew:* 2. *Right:* The ill-fated **Bristol M 1C**, one of the best fighters produced in Great Britain during the First World War, but relegated to service in the Middle East. It was not mass-produced as it was claimed that its landing speed was too high at 49 mph. It seems more likely, however, that it was suffering from the War Office's prewar prejudice against and ban on monoplanes. It was very fast and manoeuvrable, and would have made a significant difference to the RFC during 'Bloody April'. *Engine:* Le Rhône rotary, 110 hp. *Armament:* one fixed Vickers gun. *Speed:* 130 mph at sea-level. *Climb:* 10 minutes 25 seconds to 10,000 feet. *Ceiling:* 20,000 feet. *Endurance:* 1¾ hours. *Weight empty/loaded:* 896/1,348 lbs. *Span:* 30 feet 9 inches. *Length:* 20 feet 5½ inches

Above: The Halberstadt **CL IV**, in Turkish markings. This, like the LVG C VI on the opposite page, was a development of an earlier type, in this instance the CL II. The improvements achieved with the CL IV lay in the field of handling, rather than absolute performance. This was achieved by repositioning the wing, shortening the fuselage and altering the size and shape of the tail surfaces extensively. After these modifications, the CL IV made an excellent escort and ground attack fighter in 1918. *Engine:* Mercedes D III, 160 hp. *Armament:* one or two fixed Spandau machine guns and one flexible Parabellum machine gun, plus anti-personnel grenades and four or five 22-lb. bombs. *Speed:* 103 mph at 16,400 feet. *Climb:* 32 minutes to 16,400 feet. *Ceiling:* 16,700 feet. *Endurance:* 3½ hours. *Weight empty/loaded:* 1,602/2,350 lbs. *Span:* 35 feet 2⅞ inches. *Length:* 21 feet 5½ inches. *Crew:* 2. Crew communications were especially good

John Batchelor

THE EYES OF THE FLEETS: seaplanes of the 1st World War

Opposite page, top: The **Franco-British Aviation Type H** flying boat. Despite its name, the FBA concern was almost entirely French, and built a series of excellent flying boats for the air services of the Allies, starting with the Type B in 1915 and culminating with the Type S in 1918. Illustrated is the first model to be powered with an inline engine, the Type H anti-submarine and coastal patrol flying boat. This model was built in great numbers (at least 982) in Italy, and had the distinction of being produced in larger quantities than any other such machine in the First World War. *Engine:* Hispano-Suiza inline, 150- or 170-hp, Lorraine inline, 160-hp or Isotta-Fraschini inline, 180-hp. *Armament:* one machine gun (Lewis or Revelli) and a small bomb load. *Crew:* 3. *Speed:* 90 mph at sea level. *Climb:* 3,280 feet in 8 minutes. *Ceiling:* 16,000 feet. *Range:* 373 miles. *Weight empty/loaded:* 2,170/3,218 lbs. *Span:* 46 feet 7 inches. *Length:* 33 feet 2 inches. *Centre:* The Italian **Macchi M 7** fighter flying boat of 1918. Only three had been delivered before the Armistice, but they would have been more than a match for the Austro-Hungarian fighters of the same configuration. *Engine:* Isotta-Fraschini V-6B, 250-hp. *Armament:* two Fiat machine guns. *Speed:* 130 mph at sea level. *Climb:* 16,400 feet in 22 minutes. *Ceiling:* 16,400 feet. *Range:* 522 miles. *Weight empty/loaded:* 1,710/2,381 lbs. *Span:* 32 feet 8 inches. *Length:* 26 feet 7 inches. *Bottom:* The **Porte-Felixstowe F 3,** one of Britain's best boats of the war, developed from a Curtiss design by Commander J. Porte RN. The design was for an anti-submarine and patrol bomber, and was built mainly in 1918. *Engines:* two Rolls-Royce Eagle VIII, 345-hp each. *Armament:* four Lewis guns and four 230-lb bombs. *Crew:* 4. *Speed:* 93 mph at 2,000 feet. *Climb:* 10,000 feet in 24 minutes 50 seconds. *Ceiling:* 12,500 feet. *Endurance:* up to 9½ hours. *Weight empty/loaded:* 7,958/13,281 lbs. *Span:* 102 feet. *Length:* 49 feet 2 inches. *This page, below:* The German **Hansa-Brandenburg FB** patrol flying boat. Only six were built for the German navy, though the type was used in some numbers by the Austro-Hungarian navy in the Adriatic between 1915 and the end of the war. *Engine:* Austro-Daimler inline, 165-hp. *Armament:* one Parabellum machine gun. *Crew:* 3. *Speed:* 87 mph at sea level. *Climb:* 3,280 feet in 8½ minutes. *Range:* 683 miles. *Weight empty/loaded:* 2,513/3,571 lbs. *Span:* 52½ feet. *Length:* 33¼ feet

JOHN BATCHELOR, after serving in the RAF, went into the aircraft industry as a technical artist where he worked for three firms before establishing himself in the same line on the boys' magazine *Eagle,* and many other allied and technical magazines on a freelance basis. Later, he started what was to be a marathon task of over 1,000 technical paintings for Purnell's *Histories of the Second World War* and *First World War.* He is responsible for illustrations in the Purnell's Ballantine WW II pocket books and several Continental part works where his work is in demand.

After the success of the first of his series of illustrated books, "*Tank" History of the Armoured Fighting Vehicle,* in which 370 of his illustrations appear, he is working on six more books for an American publisher.

THE CALCULATING ACE

René Fonck was the doyen of Allied aces with 75 victories. He survived the war and attained his pre-eminence by means of careful tactics and unsurpassed marksmanship

The month of September 1918 saw the very characteristic symptoms of Boche agony appear. We were grounded in a clearing at Noblette north of Châlons, and for a few days none of us had flown. It was, in fact, a question of not letting our location be known too soon, for we were on the verge of dealing a staggering blow to the enemy.

Finally, on September 26, I obtained permission to take off. That date marks one of the toughest days of my fighting career.

I remained in the air from morning to night, and if my machine gun had not jammed, I would have added eight planes to my credit. Nevertheless, that day I repeated my sextuple exploit of the month of May. Our infantrymen had advanced several kilometres and menacing Boche patrols were flying above them. The first patrol that I attacked consisted of five Fokkers. Without giving them the time to work out by signals their plan to attack me, I dived into them at full speed, guns blazing. Letting myself then fly on my wing, I turned over completely in order to rocket up behind one of the planes which had already fired at me. But I also had fired, and two of the German aircraft crashed to earth in the vicinity of Somme-Py. The others, fearing for their safety, had thought it more prudent to take to their heels.

I then gained altitude and saw in the direction of Suippes an enemy plane being fired at by our own anti-aircraft artillery. I headed there at full speed and reached it at an altitude of 18,500 feet above Perthes-les-Hurlus. With the first burst that I fired at 30 yards, the observer was killed. The defenceless pilot became frightened, and his verticle dive was so sudden and steep that his companion, whom I had just sent off to join his ancestors, toppled overboard and almost fell on me at the moment of me finishing my loop, when I was going to climb in order to attack the two-seater again.

I had at that moment, I must admit, an odd feeling at suddenly seeing a body falling in space. The corpse, like a sack, dropped down and little by little seemed to shrink as it approached the ground — but I did not have time to analyse my feelings; It was necessary to fight and win. Without further delay I charged again. Through a sudden bank, I caught the enemy plane under the tail and sent a few incendiary bullets through his fuselage. A little later, while I expected to see him in flames, one of his wings broke off and the plane came crashing down to the ground.

Towards evening I was patrolling with *Lieutenant* Fontaine. We were accompanied by *Adjutants* Loup and Brugère. The Boches were out in force. Facing us were eight enemy planes ready to fight.

I awaited the attack confidently, and would have willingly provoked it when a Spad came in unexpectedly to lend us a hand. I immediately recognised *Capitaine* de Sevin and the *Cicognes* of the 26th. It was a formidable array, and without hesitating any longer, I launched the assault, followed by my comrades. I dived at full speed into the middle of our enemies. The fusillade crackled and the Boches were not hesitant to withstand the blow.

Adjutant Brugère was hemmed in close by two Fokkers and, to relieve him, I brought down one of his adversaries. During this time *Capitaine* de Sevin was going through a very risky acrobatic manoeuvre in order to shake off a Boche who had come to grips with him, and who seemed to me to be rather a bold devil. Only the captain's skill as a pilot permitted him to escape, for his motor had conked out. He was pursued to within 300 feet from the ground.

I too had difficulty in defending myself. I fired bursts at any Boches who passed in my line of fire, while disengaging myself by taildives. Moreover, my aim was true, since a plane against which I was firing came tumbling down with broken wings. Meanwhile, five Albatroses came to the rescue. I dived into their midst with wide-open throttle, and with my first volley I shot down the plane in the most favourable position. Two others owed their skins to the jamming of my machine gun, and despite the cold, which perpetually reigns in this high altitude, I must confess I felt drenched with perspiration upon returning to the field. But, for me, the day had been excellent. I now had 66 official victories to my credit.

That was the end of my great victories. The enemy still, at times, tried to regain the initiative by pitting his best squadrons against us. During the month of October I succeeded again in some good kills, but the story does not offer anything particularly exciting to recount. My last victory took place on November 1, 1918. At 1420 hours, exactly, I brought down on the outskirts of Vouziers my 75th official plane. It was one of those numerous two-seater planes whose mission it was to drop into the trenches propaganda leaflets designed to discourage our *poilus*.

That cost the Boches who were flying that sortie dearly, for coming at them, in a few seconds I sent them to join their papers, while my brave comrades below were advancing magnificently.

Those who read these pages are perhaps astonished at the number of my aerial victories. Others will believe that I was lucky when I claim to have passed uninjured under the fire of several machine guns criss-crossing at short distance. Upon reflection, however, my readers will better appreciate my situation. I studied the methods and techniques of my opponents at great length, and I acquired, little by little, a thorough knowledge of the strategy of the enemy fighter, reconnaissance and range-intelligence (artillery observation) pilots. Furthermore, I enjoy keen sight and know how to use it. My aim is legendary among my comrades, and it resulted in my achieving many advantages.

Even in 1915 I wanted to put a machine gun on my Caudron G III. The one on the twin-engined Caudron, which I had later, was stationary, and when I used my Spad I sent my bullets into the target as though directing them by hand. This is not an easy thing to do, however. You must consider that hunter and hunted are moving at full speed and keep at variable altitudes. You must estimate at a glance the speed of the adversary, correct your speed in comparing it with his, and foresee the deviations of the trajectories produced by the angle of fire. The resistance of the air also intervenes as an important factor, and this resistance varies a great deal according to the altitude of the plane.

The corrections, depending on circumstances, cancel each other out or complement each other, and to give you a less abstract example, I must tell you that one day, finding myself only 600 feet away from a Boche, I had to aim 60 feet ahead of him in order to shoot him down.

The speed of our planes sometimes reaches 200 mph, which gives us an average speed of about 150 feet per second. As it is necessary to fire at a distance of 300 to 600 feet in order to reduce the correction to a minimum, it is easy to see that the person who fires has only a few seconds of effective firing at his disposal. The margin of time is so slight that, in using a machine gun, I succeed most often by sending off a burst of only five or six cartridges — but in general that is enough for me.

I know how to position myself in an actual duel. Guynemer fought differently and faced fire regularly, but this strategy is very dangerous. It places the pilot at the mercy of the jamming of his gun. I always utilise the blind spots, and because of that, am forced to fire from whatever position my Spad might be in. But I have been doing this for a long time. My bursts are from eight to ten bullets at the maximum and I often do not use more than three. Besides the advantage of economising on ammunition, this method has also the advantage of facilitating my aim and reducing the chance of jamming or damaging my machine gun.

I should also like to add that, to obtain good results, you must also know how to control your nerves, how to have absolute self-mastery, and how to think coolly in difficult situations. I have had to duel with a great many Boche aces and have had the patience, while fighting, to wait for the moment my adversaries give way to nervous irritation — the fatal mistake — and I have profited a great deal from their errors. I always believed that it is indispensable to maintain absolute confidence in ultimate success, along with the most complete disdain for danger.

These are the necessary qualities for a fighter pilot. And I should like to repeat that, in order to become a great ace, the period of apprenticeship is long and difficult, strewn with disappointments and repeated setbacks during the course of which our lives are risked hundreds of times.

[*Reprinted from* Ace of Aces *by René Fonck, published by Doubleday.*]

Above: René Fonck practises his art on his airfield with a carbine. Only by dint of constant practice, and care lavished on the guns themselves, did Fonck become the great marksman that he was. *Below:* Fonck in the cockpit of his Spad XIII of the *Cicognes*

THE «CAT'S WHISKERS»
The Ultimate Aircraft of WWI

Had the war continued into 1919, there would have doubtless been great advances in the technology of war, but none so much as in aeronautics. By 1918, the Germans and the Allies had made enormous strides in basic design, engine power and in structures and materials

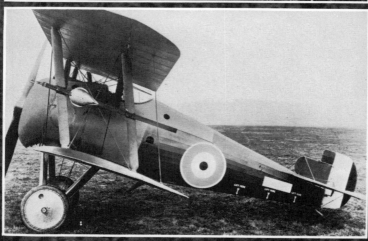

Double page, top: The classic two-seater of the First World War, the Bristol F2B fighter. The photograph shows four F2B's of 22 Squadron taking off in France in June 1918. *This page, top:* The Vickers FB 27 Vimy bomber, destined for a great future in 1919. *Centre left:* The Pfalz D XII fighter. Though overshadowed by the remarkable Fokker D VII, the D XII was nevertheless an excellent machine. *Above:* The Junkers CL I ground attack fighter, whose advanced features included cantilever monoplane wings and a metal skin. The gunner had a good field of fire and the pilot two machine guns, compared with the more standard one of most such machines. *Left:* The ultimate in the Sopwith stable of rotary-engined fighters, the 7F I Snipe. *Opposite page, top left:* The Junkers D I fighter, of which the CL I was a scaled-up version. This was the world's first all-metal service warplane, and proved very nimble and strong. *Top right:* The Pfalz D XV was fast and scheduled for large production in 1919. Note the fuselage mounted between the wings and the lack of exterior wires. *Centre left:* The Nieuport 29C 1 fighter. It was very fast (143 mph at sea level) and the first Nieuport fighter to have a stationary engine. *Centre right:* The Siemens-Schuckert D VI experimental fighter, featuring a parasol wing and a jettisonable belly tank for its fuel. *Bottom:* The Martinsyde F 4 fighter, the fastest Allied fighter of the war at 145 mph

Top: The **Bristol F2B** reconnaissance fighter. *Engine:* Rolls-Royce Falcon III, 275 hp. *Armament:* one fixed Vickers and one or two free Lewis guns plus 12 20-lb bombs. *Speed:* 123 mph at 5,000 ft. *Climb:* 11 mins 15 secs to 10,000 ft. *Ceiling:* 21,500 ft. *Endurance:* 3 hours. *Weight empty/loaded:* 1,934/2,779 lbs. *Span:* 39 ft 3 ins. *Length:* 25 ft 10 ins. *Above:* The **Siemens-Schuckert D IV** fighter, which had an incredible rate of climb. *Engine:* Siemens-Halske Sh IIIa, 200 hp. *Armament:* two Spandau machine guns. *Speed:* 119 mph. *Climb:* 13 mins to 16,400 ft. *Ceiling:* 26,240 ft. *Endurance:* 2 hrs. *Weight empty/loaded:* 1,190/1,620 lbs. *Span:* 27 ft 4¾ ins. *Length:* 18 ft 8½ ins

THE «CAT'S WHISKERS»
The Ultimate Aircraft of WWI

Above: The **Fokker D VIII** fighter, possessed of good performance and quite outstanding manoeuvrability. *Engine:* Oberursel U II, 110 hp. *Armament:* two Spandau machine guns. *Speed:* $127\frac{1}{2}$ mph at sea level. *Climb:* $10\frac{3}{4}$ mins to 13,120 ft. *Ceiling:* 19,680 ft. *Endurance:* $1\frac{1}{2}$ hours. *Weight empty/loaded:* 893/1,334 lbs. *Span:* 27 ft $4\frac{3}{8}$ ins. *Length:* 19 ft $2\frac{3}{4}$ ins.
Below: The **Handley Page V/1500** heavy bomber. *Engines:* four Rolls-Royce Eagle VIII, 375 hp each. *Armament:* up to five Lewis guns and 7,500 lbs of bombs. *Speed:* 97 mph at 8,750 ft. *Climb:* $18\frac{1}{2}$ mins to 6,500 feet. *Ceiling:* 10,000 ft. *Endurance:* 14 hours. *Weight empty/loaded:* 16,210/29,230 lbs. *Span:* 126 ft. *Length:* 62 ft. By the end of the war, only three of these huge 'Berlin bombers' had been built, with three more by the end of the year

John Batchelor

ECCE ROMANI

A LATIN READING PROGRAM

II·A

HOME AND SCHOOL

THIRD EDITION

ECCE ROMANI
A LATIN READING PROGRAM

II·A
HOME AND SCHOOL

THIRD EDITION

PEARSON
Prentice Hall

Needham, Massachusetts
Upper Saddle River, New Jersey

This North American edition of *Ecce Romani* is based on *Ecce Romani: A Latin Reading Course,* originally prepared by The Scottish Classics Group © copyright The Scottish Classics Group 1971, 1982, and published in the United Kingdom by Oliver and Boyd, a division of Longman Group.

Photo Credits appear on page 242, which constitutes an extension of this copyright page.

Cover illustration: Yao Zen Liu
Text art: Yao Zen Liu
Maps: Laszlo Kubinyi

Program Contributors

Audio Program:
David J. Perry
Rye High School
Rye, NY

ExamView® **Test Bank**
Anthony L. C. Hollingsworth
Roger Williams University
Bristol, RI

Companion Web Site Activities:

Timothy S. Abney
Marquette High School
Chesterfield, MO

Joan Jahnige
Kentucky Educational Television
Lexington, KY

Caroline Switzer Kelly
Covenant Day School
Charlotte, NC

Teacher Guide Notes and Standard Activities:
Sally A. Murphy
Winsor School
Boston, MA

ISBN: 0-13-116381-7

7 8 9 10   V056   13 12

REVISION EDITOR: GILBERT LAWALL
University of Massachusetts, Amherst, Massachusetts

AUTHORS AND CONSULTANTS

Peter C. Brush
Deerfield Academy
Deerfield, Massachusetts

Sally Davis
Arlington Public Schools
Arlington, Virginia

Pauline P. Demetri
Cambridge Ridge & Latin School
Cambridge, Massachusetts

Jane Hall
National Latin Exam
Alexandria, Virginia

Thalia Pantelidis Hocker
Old Dominion University
Norfolk, Virginia

Glenn M. Knudsvig
University of Michigan
Ann Arbor, Michigan

Maureen O'Donnell
W.T. Woodson High School
Fairfax, Virginia

Ronald Palma
Holland Hall School
Tulsa, Oklahoma

David J. Perry
Rye High School
Rye, New York

Deborah Pennell Ross
University of Michigan
Ann Arbor, Michigan

Andrew F. Schacht
Renbrook School
West Hartford, Connecticut

Judith Lynn Sebesta
University of South Dakota
Vermillion, South Dakota

The Scottish Classics Group
Edinburgh, Scotland

David Tafe
Rye Country Day School
Rye, New York

Rex Wallace
University of Massachusetts
Amherst, Massachusetts

Allen Ward
University of Connecticut
Storrs, Connecticut

Elizabeth Lyding Will
Amherst College
Amherst, Massachusetts

Philip K. Woodruff
Lake Forest High School
Lake Forest, Illinois

v

CONTENTS

REFERENCE MATERIALS

MAPS

INTRODUCTION

Welcome to the second level of *ECCE ROMANI*! At the beginning of the book, the family of Cornelius is making preparations for an elaborate dinner. The mother of the family, Aurelia, and her daughter, Cornelia, go shopping for delicacies to serve at the dinner, but when they arrive at the shop that they were seeking they find that a nearby apartment house is going up in flames, endangering both its occupants and those in the street. They must go on to the Forum to purchase their delicacies. The day before, Pseudolus, a clever slave in the household, had gone shopping for a pig to be roasted for the dinner party and had made a bargain with the butcher that he craftily planned to turn to his own advantage. With one minor mishap, preparations are completed for the party, and all goes well until Uncle Titus overdoes his after-dinner drinking. Late that night Eucleides, returning from a visit to his brother, barely stumbles into the house, having been mugged and robbed by thieves in the streets of Rome. The next day Cornelia writes a letter to her friend Flavia and tells her both about the dangers of life in Rome and about a letter that her father has just received from a young man named Valerius, who has just returned from Bithynia and will soon arrive in Rome.

While in Rome, Marcus and Sextus go off to school, accompanied by Eucleides, now recovered from being mugged. At school the boys learn about the great epic poet Vergil and his poem about Aeneas, the ancestor of the Romans. Sextus does not do well at school, and he writes a plaintive letter to his father who is stationed in the province of Asia. Cornelia receives dramatic news from a slave of Valerius who arrives in Rome ahead of his master and tells of a nearly fatal encounter with pirates on Valerius' return voyage. Cornelia listens attentively because of a special interest she has in Valerius.

While following this story of the life of our family in Rome, you will encounter interesting aspects of the cultural life of the Romans—their hairstyles and their dwellings, what they ate at dinner, the various levels of their educational system, their modes of writing, their books, and the dangers of pirates on the high seas. By reading the passages from Latin authors in *The Romans Speak for Themselves* that accompany Chapters 29, 30, 34, 35, and 38 in *ECCE ROMANI*, you will communicate directly with the Romans and hear what they themselves had to say about their city houses, their fire-fighters, excessive drinking, violence in the streets, and education. You will make comparisons with the very different life of Romans on the frontiers of their empire in further glimpses of Helge, as she spins and weaves for her husband Lucius. You will follow the course of Roman history through the tumultuous years of the late Republic, the civil wars, and the establishment of a new order under Augustus. You will expand your awareness of the connections between Latin and English through ongoing study of the ways in which Latin words were constructed and passed into English and also through study of Latin legal and medical terms that have come into English.

Italy

The Roman Empire, A.D. 80

CHAPTER 28

Go Online
For: Additional Practice
Visit: PHSchool.com
Web Code: jgd-0001

PREPARING TO GO SHOPPING

Māne erat. Aurēlia in cubiculō sedēbat. Crīnēs eius cūrābant duae ancillae, quārum altera speculum tenēbat, altera crīnēs pectēbat. Phrygia, quae crīnēs neglegenter pectēbat, dominam vexābat; Syra, quod manus tremēbat, speculum nōn bene tenēbat. Aurēlia igitur, neglegentiā eārum vexāta, subitō, "Quam neglegentēs estis!" clāmāvit. "Abīte! Abīte! Vocāte Cornēliam! Eam mēcum in urbem dūcere volō." 5

Statim exiērunt ancillae.

Mox in cubiculum iniit Cornēlia. "Cūr mē vocāvistī, māter?"

Aurēlia respondit, "Pater tuus amīcōs quōsdam, in quibus sunt senātōrēs praeclārī, ad cēnam hodiē invītāvit. Porcum servus iam ēmit, sed ego in animō habeō ipsa in urbem īre ad mercātōrem quendam cuius taberna nōn procul abest, nam glīrēs optimōs ille 10 vēndere solet. Sī tū vīs mēcum īre, mē in ātriō exspectā! Intereā servōs iubēbō sellās ad iānuam ferre."

1	**crīnēs, crīnium,** m. pl., *hair*	9	**porcus, -ī,** m., *pig*
2	**speculum, -ī,** n., *mirror*	10	**cuius,** *whose*
	neglegenter, adv., *carelessly*		**glīs, glīris,** gen. pl., **glīrium,** m.,
4	**vexātus, -a, -um,** *annoyed*		*dormouse*
8	**in quibus,** *among whom*	11	**sella, -ae,** f., *sedan chair*

2 **pectō, pectere, pexī, pexus,** *to comb*
11 **vēndō, vēndere, vēndidī, vēnditus,** *to sell*

Exercise 28a
Respondē Latīnē:

1. Quid faciēbant duae ancillae?
2. Quam ob causam Phrygia Aurēliam vexābat?
3. Quam ob causam Syra speculum nōn bene **Quod...** tenēbat?
4. Quōcum Aurēlia in urbem īre vult?
5. Quōs ad cēnam Cornēlius invītāvit?
6. Quid servus iam ēmit?
7. Quid Aurēlia emere vult?
8. Quid Aurēlia servōs facere iubēbit?

Quam ob causam...? *For what reason...?* Answer:

BUILDING THE MEANING
Relative Clauses I

A very common type of subordinate clause is the *relative clause*. Relative clauses are descriptive clauses that modify nouns. You have seen clauses of this sort since the very first chapter of this course:

> Cornēlia est puella Rōmāna **quae** <u>in Italiā habitat</u>. (1:1–2)
> *Cornelia is a Roman girl <u>**who** lives in Italy</u>.*

The relative clause (underlined) gives information about the noun phrase **puella Rōmāna**, describing this Roman girl as one who lives in Italy. Relative clauses are introduced by *relative pronouns* (e.g., **quae**, *who*), which relate or connect the statement made in the subordinate clause to a noun or noun phrase (e.g., **puella Rōmāna**, *a Roman girl*) in the main clause. This noun or noun phrase in the main clause is called the *antecedent* because it goes (Latin **cēdere**) before (Latin **ante-**) the relative clause.

FORMS
Relative Pronouns

Here are all the forms of the relative pronoun:

	Singular			
	Masc.	**Fem.**	**Neut.**	**Meanings**
Nom.	quī	quae	quod	*who, which, that*
Gen.	cuius	cuius	cuius	*whose, of whom, of which*
Dat.	cui	cui	cui	*to whom (which), for whom (which)*
Acc.	quem	quam	quod	*whom, which, that*
Abl.	quō	quā	quō	*(see note below)*

	Plural			
	Masc.	**Fem.**	**Neut.**	**Meanings**
Nom.	quī	quae	quae	*who, which, that*
Gen.	quōrum	quārum	quōrum	*whose, of whom, of which*
Dat.	quibus	quibus	quibus	*to whom (which), for whom (which)*
Acc.	quōs	quās	quae	*whom, which, that*
Abl.	quibus	quibus	quibus	*(see note below)*

Be sure to learn these forms thoroughly.

NOTE:
Translation of forms of the relative pronoun in the ablative case will depend on the function of the ablative case in the clause. For example, **quibuscum** means *with whom*, and **quō** could be ablative of means or instrument and mean *with which* or *by which*.

Exercise 28b

On the chart of relative pronouns locate the following forms that appeared in the story at the beginning of this chapter. Some of the forms appear more than once on the chart. Identify all the possibilities that each form could be. Then identify the gender, number, and case of the pronoun as used in the story:

1. quārum (line 1)
2. quae (line 2)
3. quibus (line 8)
4. cuius (line 10)

BUILDING THE MEANING
Relative Clauses II

The form of the relative pronoun that introduces a relative clause depends on two things:

1. the *gender* and *number* of its antecedent
2. the *case* required by the function of the relative pronoun in its own clause

The following passages from the story at the beginning of this chapter illustrate these points:

...duae ancillae, **quārum** altera speculum tenēbat.... (28:1–2)

The fact that **quārum** is feminine in gender and plural in number relates it to its antecedent, **duae ancillae** (feminine plural). The fact that **quārum** is genitive shows how it functions in its own clause, namely as a partitive genitive (see Chapter 25) with **altera,** thus *one of whom*.

Phrygia, **quae** crīnēs neglegenter pectēbat.... (28:2–3)

Here the relative pronoun is feminine singular because of its antecedent **Phrygia,** and it is nominative because it serves as the subject of the verb of its own clause, **pectēbat.**

...amīcōs quōsdam, in **quibus** sunt senātōrēs praeclārī.... (28:8)

Here the relative pronoun is masculine plural because of its antecedent **amīcōs quōsdam,** and it is ablative because of its use with the preposition in its own clause.

...ad mercātōrem quendam **cuius** taberna nōn procul abest.... (28:10)

Here the relative pronoun is masculine singular because of its antecedent **mercātōrem quendam,** and it is genitive to indicate possession in its own clause (*whose shop*).

Exercise 28c

Here are sentences with relative clauses. Read aloud and translate.
Then explain the gender, number, and case of each relative pronoun:

1. Sextus est puer strēnuus **quī** saepe in agrīs et in hortō currit.
2. Dāvus omnēs servōs in āream **quae** est prope vīllam venīre iubet.
3. Aurēlia et Cornēlia spectābant rūsticōs **quī** in agrīs labōrābant. *nom. m. pl.*
4. Marcus pede vexābat Cornēliam **quae** dormīre volēbat.
5. "Lectīcāriī, **quōs** vōbīs condūxī, vōs domum ferent," inquit Titus. *acc. m. pl.*
6. "Hic est arcus," inquit Titus, "**quem—**"
7. Sextus iam cōgitābat dē omnibus rēbus **quās** Titus heri nārrāverat. *f. pl. acc.*
8. Bovēs lapidēs quadrātōs in plaustrō trahēbant ad novum aedificium **quod** Caesar cōnficit.
9. Sunt multī hominēs scelestī **quī** bona cīvium arripiunt. *m. nom. pl.*

Exercise 28d

In the following sentences first decide the gender, number, and case required to make a Latin pronoun correspond to the English pronoun in italics. Then locate the correct form of the Latin pronoun on the chart on page 4. Read the sentence aloud with the Latin pronoun and translate:

1. Aurēliae crīnēs, *(which)* duae ancillae cūrābant, pulchrī erant. *quae*
2. Syra, *(whose)* manus tremēbat, speculum nōn bene tenēbat.
3. Ancillae, *(whose)* neglegentia Aurēliam vexāverat, ignāvae erant.
4. Mox in cubiculum iniit Cornēlia, *(whom)* Aurēlia vocāverat.
5. Servus, *(to whom)* Aurēlia pecūniam dederat, porcum ēmit. *to send out*

pulcher, pulchra, pulchrum, *beautiful, pretty*

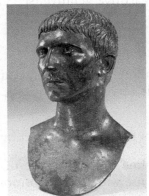
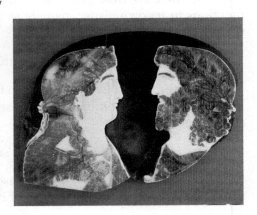

The hairstyles of both men and women varied greatly over time. Men's beards went in and out of fashion. Compare the cameo of Emperor Julian and his wife with the bronze busts of some earlier Romans.

Bronze heads, Louvre, Paris, France; sardonyx cameo, British Museum, London, England

HAIRSTYLES OF ROMAN GIRLS AND WOMEN

Roman girls and women let their hair grow long. Girls tied it in a bun at the back of the head or wound and knotted it in tresses on the top of the head. Straight hairpins of ivory, silver, or gold were used to hold the hair in place. Woollen fillets (**vittae**) were woven into the tresses as a sign of chastity. Mirrors of polished metal, not glass, were used, and slaves were specially trained to be expert hairdressers (**ōrnātrīcēs**). During some periods and especially at the imperial court and on special occasions some women went to great lengths to arrange their hair in different levels on the top of the head and to supplement their own hair with false hair. Bleaches and dyes were used, as well as

Relief sculpture of a hairdresser, circa A.D. 50
Bas relief, Landesmuseum, Hesse, Germany

A nineteenth-century artist's rendition of one hairdo a Roman girl could have worn

Oil on canvas, "A Roman Boat Race" by Sir Edward John Poynter, The Maas Gallery, London, England

lotions to make the hair softer. Styles varied greatly. The poet Ovid recommended that each woman should choose the style that best suited her, and he describes some of them as follows:

> An oval face prefers a parting upon the head left unadorned. Round faces want a small knot left on top of the head, so that the ears show. Let one girl's locks hang down on either shoulder. Let another braid her hair. It is becoming to this one to let her waving locks lie loose; let that one have her tight-drawn tresses closely confined; this one is pleased with an adornment of tortoise-shell; let that one bear folds that resemble waves. I cannot enumerate all the fashions that there are; each day adds more adornments.

> Ovid, *Art of Love* III.137–152

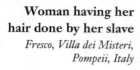

Woman having her hair done by her slave

Fresco, Villa dei Misteri, Pompeii, Italy

The poet Martial describes how a petulant woman named Lalage punished the slave who was dressing her hair because of one curl that went astray:

> A single curl of the whole concoction of hair had strayed, badly fixed in place with an insecure pin. This crime, which she noticed, Lalage avenged with her mirror and Plecusa fell wounded because of these cruel locks of hair. Stop, now, Lalage, to arrange your dire locks and let no maid touch your ill-tempered head.
>
> Martial, *Epigrams* II.66.1–4

GOING TO THE MARKET

Cornēlia summā celeritāte sē parāvit. Brevī tempore māter et fīlia ā servīs per urbem ferēbantur. In viīs erat ingēns multitūdō hominum. Concursābant enim servī, mīlitēs, virī, puerī, mulierēs. Onera ingentia ā servīs portābantur, nam interdiū nihil intrā urbem vehiculō portātur.

Omnia quae videt Cornēlia eam dēlectant. Nunc cōnspicit poētam versūs recitantem, 5
nunc mendīcōs pecūniam petentēs, nunc lectīcam ēlegantissimam quae ab octō servīs portātur. In eā recumbit homō obēsus quī librum legit.

Subitō Cornēlia duōs servōs per viam festīnantēs cōnspicit, quōrum alter porcum parvulum portat. Eō ipsō tempore ē manibus effugit porcus. "Cavēte!" exclāmant adstantēs, sed frūstrā. Homō quīdam, quī per viam celeriter currit, porcum vītāre nōn 10
potest. Ad terram cadit. Paulisper in lutō iacet gemēns. Deinde īrā commōtus servum petit ā quō porcus aufūgit. Est rixa.

Fīnem rixae nōn vīdit Cornēlia quod servī iam sellās in aliam viam tulerant. Tandem advēnērunt ad eam tabernam quam petēbant. Dē sellīs dēscendērunt. Tum Aurēlia, "Vīdistīne," inquit, "illam lectīcam in quā recumbēbat homō obēsus? Ūnus ē lībertīs 15
Caesaris ipsīus—Sed quid accidit? Fūmum videō et flammās."

1	**summā celeritāte**, *with the greatest speed, as fast as possible*	6	**mendīcus, -ī**, m., *beggar*
	ā servīs ferēbantur, *were being carried by slaves*		**ēlegantissimus, -a, -um**, *most elegant*
2	**concursō, -āre, -āvī -ātus**, *to run to and fro, run about*	10	**adstantēs, adstantium**, m. pl., *bystanders*
4	**portātur**, *is (being) carried*	12	**rixa, -ae**, f., *quarrel*
5	**dēlectō, -āre, -āvī, -ātus**, *to delight, amuse*	13	**fīnis, fīnis**, gen. pl., **fīnium**, m., *end*
		15	**lībertus, -ī**, m., *freedman*
		16	**ipsīus**, gen. sing. of **ipse, ipsa, ipsum**
			fūmus, -ī, m., *smoke*

7 **recumbō, recumbere, recubuī**, *to recline, lie down*
12 **aufugiō, aufugere, aufūgī**, *to run away, escape*

Exercise 29a
Respondē Latīnē:

1. Quōmodo Cornēlia sē parāvit?
2. Quid in viīs vidēbant?
3. Cūr onera ā servīs portābantur?
4. Quid faciēbat poēta?
5. Quī festīnābant per viam?
6. Quid portābat alter servōrum?
7. Quis ad terram cadit?
8. Cūr Cornēlia fīnem rixae nōn vīdit?
9. Quō advēnērunt Aurēlia et Cornēlia?
10. Quid ibi vīdit Aurēlia?

The Center of Ancient Rome

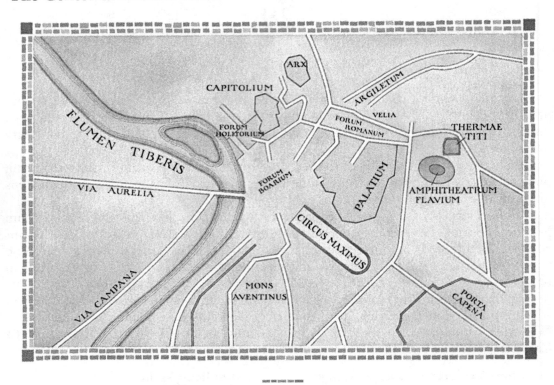

Malum est cōnsilium quod mūtārī nōn potest. *It's a bad plan that can't be changed.* (Publilius Syrus 403)

Hominēs id quod volunt crēdunt. *Men believe what they want to.* (Julius Caesar)

Quī vult dare parva nōn dēbet magna rogāre. *He who wishes to give little shouldn't ask for much.*

Exercise 29b
In the story on page 11, locate eight relative pronouns and explain why the particular gender, number, and case are used. Note that **quīdam, quod,** and **quid** in this passage are not relative pronouns (see below).

Exercise 29c
Read aloud and translate:

1. Servī, quī cistās portābant, hūc illūc concursābant. Cistae, quās servī portābant, plēnae erant vestium.
2. Ancillae, quae Aurēliae crīnēs cūrābant, dominam timēbant. Aurēlia, quae multīs rēbus sollicita erat, ancillās neglegentēs abīre iussit.
3. Servus, ā quō onus portābātur, gemēbat. Onus enim, quod portābat, ingēns erat.

4. Homō obēsus, cuius lectīca erat ēlegantissima, librum legēbat.
5. Porcī, quōs servī portābant, grunniēbant. Adstantēs, quī eōs audiēbant, rīdēbant.

   vestis, vestis, gen. pl., **vestium,** f., *clothing, garment*

Exercise 29d
Give the Latin for the relative pronoun (in parentheses) and then read the sentence aloud and translate it:

1. Homō, (*who*) per viam currēbat, ad terram cecidit.
2. Ancilla, (*who*) crīnēs neglegenter pectēbat, Aurēliam vexābat.
3. Homō obēsus, (*whom*) servī portābant, librum legēbat.
4. Aurēlia, (*whom*) ancillae vexābant, speculum ēripuit.
5. Duo servī, (*whom*) Cornēlia cōnspexit, per viam festīnābant.
6. Brevī tempore māter et fīlia in sellās, (*which*) servī tulerant, ascendērunt.
7. Puella, (*to whom*) librum dedī, erat Cornēlia.
8. Servus, (*whose*) dominus erat īrātus, statim aufūgit.

   ēripiō, ēripere, ēripuī, ēreptus, *to snatch (from)*

BUILDING THE MEANING

Many important Latin words begin with the letters *qu-*. Here are some examples:

1. relative pronouns, which you have studied extensively in Chapters 28 and 29:

   Omnia **quae** videt Cornēlia eam dēlectant. (29:5)
   *All the things **that** Cornēlia sees please her.*

2. the indefinite adjective **quīdam,** *a certain;* pl., *some.*

   Homō **quīdam,**... (29:10)
   *A **certain** man,...*

3. the interrogative pronouns **Quis...?** *Who?* **Quid...?** *What...?*

   Sed **quid** accidit? (29:16)
   *But **what** is happening?*

4. the causal conjunction **quod,** *because.* *

   ...**quod** servī iam sellās in aliam viam tulerant. (29:13)
   *...**because** the slaves had carried the sedan chairs into another street.*

*Note that **quod** may also be a relative pronoun. When it is, it is preceded by a neuter singular antecedent, e.g., **cisium, quod appropinquābat,**...

5. the exclamatory adverb **Quam...!** *How....!*

> **"Quam** neglegentēs estis!" (28:4)
> *"How careless you are!"*

You have seen all of these words a number of times in the readings. There is another important **qu-** word that you will meet, the *interrogative adjective:*

> **Quī** vir est ille?
> *What man is that?*

> **Quae** fēmina est illa?
> *What woman is that?*

> **Quem** virum vīdistī?
> *What man did you see?*

> **Cui** fēminae illud dedistī?
> *To which woman did you give that?*

The interrogative adjective modifies a noun and introduces a question. It has exactly the same forms as the relative pronoun.

FORMS
Indefinite Adjectives

The forms of the indefinite adjective **quīdam,** *a certain;* pl., *some,* are the same as those of the relative pronoun plus the letters *-dam,* except for the letters in boldface:

Number / Case	Masc.	Fem.	Neut.
Singular			
Nominative	quīdam	quaedam	quoddam
Genitive	cuiusdam	cuiusdam	cuiusdam
Dative	cuidam	cuidam	cuidam
Accusative	quendam	quandam	quoddam
Ablative	quōdam	quādam	quōdam
Plural			
Nominative	quīdam	quaedam	quaedam
Genitive	quōrundam	quārundam	quōrundam
Dative	quibusdam	quibusdam	quibusdam
Accusative	quōsdam	quāsdam	quaedam
Ablative	quibusdam	quibusdam	quibusdam

Interrogative Pronouns

In the singular the interrogative pronoun has identical forms in the masculine and feminine; in the plural it is the same as the relative pronoun (see page 4). We give only the singular forms here:

	Singular		
	Masc.	Fem.	Neut.
Nominative	quis	quis	quid
Genitive	cuius	cuius	cuius
Dative	cui	cui	cui
Accusative	quem	quem	quid
Ablative	quō	quō	quō

Learn the forms in the charts above thoroughly.

Exercise 29e

Read aloud and translate. Identify relative pronouns, **quod** causal, **quam** exclamatory, indefinite adjectives, interrogative adjectives, and interrogative pronouns:

1. Aurīgae, quōrum equī sunt celerrimī, nōn semper vincent.
2. Cui mercātōrī Aurēlia pecūniam dabit?
3. Mercātōrī, quī glīrēs vēndit, Aurēlia pecūniam dabit.
4. Quam ingēns est Circus! Quis tantum aedificium umquam vīdit?
5. Hī amīcī, quibuscum ad amphitheātrum crās ībimus, fēriātī erunt.
6. Ancillae quaedam crīnēs Aurēliae cūrābant.
7. Aurēlia īrāta erat quod ancillae neglegenter crīnēs cūrābant.
8. Cīvēs, quōrum clāmōrēs audīvimus, aurīgās spectābant.
9. Quam obēsus est homō quī in lectīcā librum legit!
10. Hanc urbem, in quā habitāmus, valdē amāmus.

   celerrimus, -a, -um, *fastest, very fast*

Exercise 29f

Using stories 28 and 29 as guides, give the Latin for:

1. The bedroom, in which the slave-women were taking care of the hair of their mistress, was not large.
2. Syra, whose hand was trembling, was annoying her mistress.
3. No one was able to catch the pig that escaped from the hands of the slave.
4. The fat man, whose litter was most elegant, was reading a book.
5. Aurelia, to whom the merchant sold dormice, was carrying much money.

TOWN HOUSE AND APARTMENT

The town house (**domus**) of a wealthy Roman was self-contained and usually built on one level with few, if any, windows on its outside walls. It faced inwards and most of its light came from the opening in the roof of the main hall (**ātrium**) and from the open-colonnaded garden (**peristȳlium**). Grouped around these open areas were the purpose-built rooms of the house: bedrooms (**cubicula**), study (**tablīnum**), kitchen area (**culīna**), and dining room (**trīclīnium**). Decoration and furniture in the **domus** were as splendid as its owner's pocket allowed and in some cases a second story was added. The domus-style house can be identified in towns throughout the Roman world.

A wealthy Roman would normally possess, in addition to his town house (**domus**), at least one country house (**vīlla rūstica** or **vīlla urbāna**). Cicero had several, where he could get away from the city din and summer heat, but even a **domus** provided considerable privacy and seclusion.

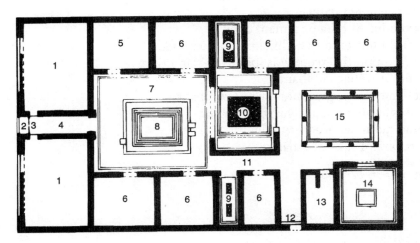

Plan of a domus

1. **tabernae** (shops)
2. **vestibulum** (entrance outside iānua)
3. **iānua** (double door)
4. **faucēs** (entrance passage)
5. **cella** (room for doorkeeper)
6. **cubicula** (bedrooms)
7. **ātrium** (hall)
8. **compluvium/impluvium** (roof opening and tank)
9. **āla** (alcove)
10. **tablīnum** (study)
11. **andrōn** (passage)
12. **postīcum** (servants' entrance)
13. **culīna** (kitchen)
14. **trīclīnium** (dining room)
15. **peristȳlium** (garden)

Rooms at the front or the side of a town house (**domus**) often housed shops, in which the owner of the house could conduct his business or which could be rented out. There were bakeries, butcher shops, barber shops, shoe shops, goldsmith shops, textile shops, and fast-food shops where you could get hot and cold food and drink of various sorts. There were also shops for many other kinds of activities such as washing clothes and tanning leather and for many other kinds of merchandise such as olive oil, wine, and knives. Merchants did not restrict themselves to their shops but tended to take over the street in front as well. Martial complained that there were only footpaths left in the middle of the street, that barbers endangered pedestrians with their razors as they shaved their clients, and that the grimy owners of cook-shops took over the whole street. He was happy when the emperor Domitian handed down a ruling requiring shop keepers to limit their activities to their shops. Now, Martial felt, the old Rome had been restored, which previously had become one **magna taberna,** one *huge shop* or shopping mall!

Where building space was at a premium, as in a city like Rome or a commercial town like Ostia, houses tended to grow upwards to accommodate the majority of the inhabitants. These apartment-type houses were called **īnsulae.** Sometimes they stood four or five stories high, and restrictions were introduced as early as the time of the Emperor Augustus to prevent their height exceeding 70 feet or approximately 20 meters.

Brick and concrete were commonly used in their construction, and they often had large windows and doorways enhancing their external appearance. The same rooms in the building tended to serve various functions, and there was a uniformity about the plan of each apartment in the building. Wooden shutters or canvas screens kept out the elements. Running water was rarely available above ground level, so heating and cooking often proved a hazard. Ground floor accommodation in the **īnsulae** was usually the most desirable.

While **īnsulae** could be very attractive and were often built around large central courts, some were less presentable. Often single rooms were let and conditions were cramped. Excessive reliance on wood and plaster construction led to the risk of fire or collapse, and after the fire of A.D. 64 the Emperor Nero introduced tighter control of building materials in the **īnsulae.**

On the ground floor of the **īnsula** in which Seneca, a Roman philosopher and writer, had his apartment there was a small public bath (**balneum**), and he describes some of the noises that disturbed him: the great splash made by the swimmer who likes to dive in as noisily as he can; the slapping sounds as people are being rubbed down; the noises of the man who likes to hear his own voice in the bath; the shouts of the pastrycook and the sausage-maker trying to sell their wares. Martial tells us of a schoolmaster who began shouting at his pupils in the early morning and kept his neighbors from sleeping.

ADDITIONAL READING:
The Romans Speak for Themselves: Book II: "Buildings for Different Ranks of Society," pages 1–11.

FORMS
Prefixes: Compound Verbs II

Some prefixes may undergo a change (often for ease of pronunciation) when they are added to verbs that begin with certain consonants:

1. Prefixes **ad-, con-, dis-, ex-, in-,** and **sub-** may change the final consonant of the prefix to the consonant that follows it. This process is called *assimilation*:

<table>
<tr><td>afferō (ad- + ferō)</td><td>differō (dis- + ferō)</td></tr>
<tr><td>attulī (ad- + tulī)</td><td>effugiō (ex- + fugiō)</td></tr>
<tr><td>allātus (ad- + lātus)</td><td>immittō (in- + mittō)</td></tr>
<tr><td>commoveō (con- + moveō)</td><td>succurrō (sub- + currō)</td></tr>
</table>

Note that **in-** and **con-** become **im-** and **com-** before *b* or *p*:

importō (in- + portō)   **compōnō (con- + pōnō)**

2. Prefix **ab-** becomes **au-** in front of verbs beginning with *f*:

aufugiō (ab- + fugiō)   **auferō (ab- + ferō)**

Exercise 29g
Read aloud and translate:

1. Geta effugere nōn potest.
2. Caupō Cornēliam et mātrem ad cubiculum addūxit.
3. Servī cistās in raedam impōnunt.
4. Servī onera ingentia ad vīllam apportābant.
5. Cibum ē vīllā aufert.
6. Aurēlia in cubiculum Marcī subitō irrumpit.
7. Cornēlia librum ē manibus Sextī celeriter abstulit et in hortum aufūgit.
8. Duo canēs ad Cornēliōs subitō accurrunt.
9. Viātōrēs multās fābulās dē caupōnibus scelestīs ad omnēs partēs Italiae differunt.
10. "Nōnne ēsurītis?" inquit caupō. "Mēnsās statim appōnam."

mēnsa, -ae, f., *table*   **rumpō, rumpere, rūpī, ruptus,** *to burst*

3. Sometimes the verb undergoes a change when a prefix is added:

facere, *to do*　　　　　　　　　**perficere,** *to do thoroughly, accomplish*
tenēre, *to hold*　　　　　　　　**continēre,** *to hold together, contain*
rapere, *to snatch*　　　　　　　**ēripere,** *to snatch from, rescue*
capere, *to take*　　　　　　　　**accipere,** *to take to oneself, receive*
iacere, *to throw*　　　　　　　　**conicere,** *to throw* (emphatic)
claudere, *to shut*　　　　　　　**inclūdere,** *to shut in*

4. Note that some verbs change conjugation when a prefix is added:

sedeō, sedēre, *to sit*　　　　　　**cōnsīdō, cōnsīdere,** *to sit down*
dō, dare, *to give*　　　　　　　　**reddō, reddere,** *to give back*

Exercise 29h

Read aloud and translate. Then tell what the uncompounded verb would be:

1. Servī raedam reficiēbant.
2. Sextus ad terram dēcidit.
3. Subitō Sextus librum arripuit et retinuit.
4. Domina ancillās ā cubiculō īrāta exclūdit.
5. Herculēs multōs labōrēs perfēcit.
6. Servī cistam repetent quod Cornēlia aliam tunicam addere vult.
7. Cornēlius pecūniam caupōnī trādit.
8. Flāvia epistulam ā Cornēliā accipiet.
9. Illī praedōnēs pecūniam surripuērunt.
10. Caupō Cornēliōs cum rīsū excēpit.

FIRE!

Cōnspexerat Aurēlia ingentem īnsulam ē quā ēmittēbātur magna vīs fūmī ac flammārum. Cornēlia iam ad id aedificium summā celeritāte currēbat, cum Aurēlia eī clāmāvit, "Cavē, Cornēlia! Eī incendiō appropinquāre est perīculōsum."

Mox fūmus omnia obscūrābat. Cornēlia aedificium ipsum vix vidēre poterat. Multī hominēs hūc illūc concursābant. Ab incolīs omnia simul aguntur; īnfantēs ex aedificiō ā 5
mātribus efferuntur; īnfirmī ē iānuīs trahuntur; bona ē fenestrīs ēiciuntur; in viā pōnuntur cistae, lectī, ōrnāmenta.

Cornēlia spectāculum tam miserābile numquam anteā vīderat. Lacrimābant mulierēs et līberōs parvōs tenēbant; lacrimābant līberī quī parentēs suōs quaerēbant; clāmābant parentēs quī līberōs suōs petēbant.   10

Via erat plēna eōrum quī ad spectāculum vēnerant. Aliī ex adstantibus aquam portābant; aliī in īnsulam intrābant et auxilium incolīs miserīs ferēbant. Multī tamen nihil faciēbant. "Nōs certē nihil facere possumus," inquiunt. "In hāc urbe solent esse incendia quae exstinguere nōn possumus. Neque hoc aedificium neque hōs incolās servāre possumus. Ecce! In tertiō tabulātō huius īnsulae est māter cum duōbus līberīs. Hī 15
miserī flammīs paene opprimuntur. Sī incolae sē servāre nōn possunt, quid nōs facere possumus?"

(continued)

1 **īnsula, -ae,** f., *island, apartment building*	**fenestra, -ae,** f., *window*
vīs, acc., **vim,** abl., **vī,** f., *force, amount*	7 **ōrnāmenta, -ōrum,** n. pl., *furnishings*
ac, conj., *and*	8 **tam,** adv., *so*
3 **incendium, -ī,** n., *fire*	9 **parvus, -a, -um,** *small*
5 **incola, -ae,** m./f., *inhabitant, tenant*	15 **tabulātum, -ī,** n., *story, floor*
omnia...aguntur, *everything is being done*	16 **paene,** adv., *almost*
6 **īnfirmus, -a, -um,** *weak, shaky, frail*	**opprimuntur,** (they) *are being overwhelmed*

6 **ēiciō, ēicere, ēiēcī, ēiectus,** *to throw out*
9 **quaerō, quaerere, quaesīvī, quaesītus,** *to seek, look for, ask (for)*
16 **opprimō, opprimere, oppressī, oppressus,** *to overwhelm*

Exercise 30a
Respondē Latīnē:

1. Quae ex īnsulā ēmittēbantur?
2. Cui appropinquāre est perīculōsum?
3. Quid agunt incolae?
4. Quid faciēbant līberī?
5. Quid faciēbant parentēs?
6. Quī incolās adiūvērunt?

Subitō exclāmāvit ūnus ex adstantibus, "Cavēte, omnēs! Nisi statim aufugiētis, vōs omnēs opprimēminī aut lapidibus aut flammīs."

Tum Cornēlia, "Ēheu, māter!" inquit. "Ego valdē commoveor cum hōs tam miserōs 20 līberōs videō. Quis eīs auxilium feret? Quōmodo effugient? Quid eīs accidet?"

Cui respondit Aurēlia, "Id nesciō. Sine dubiō iam mortuī sunt. Sed cūr tū ita commovēris? Nōs nihil hīc facere possumus. Nisi statim fugiēmus, nōs ipsae vix servābimur. Satis tamen hodiē vīdistī. Age! Ad Forum ībimus ac glīrēs emēmus."

Illō ipsō tempore parietēs īnsulae magnō fragōre cecidērunt. Nihil manēbat nisi 25 lapidēs ac fūmus.

19	**opprimēminī,** *you will be crushed, overwhelmed*	23	**commovēris,** *you are upset*
20	**commoveor,** *I am upset*	24	**servābimur,** *we will be saved*
22	**dubium, -ī,** n., *doubt*	25	**pariēs, parietis,** m., *wall (of a house or room)*

20 **commoveō, commovēre, commōvī, commōtus,** *to move, upset*

Respondē Latīnē:

1. Cūr Cornēlia "Ēheu, māter!" inquit?
2. Quid Aurēlia facere vult?
3. Quōmodo parietēs īnsulae cecidērunt?

Flamma fūmō est proxima. *Flame follows smoke.* (Plautus, *Curculio* I.i.53)
Ubi fūmus, ibi ignis. *Where there's smoke, there's fire.*
Adversus incendia excubiās nocturnās vigilēsque commentus est. *Against the dangers of fires, Augustus conceived of the idea of night guards and watchmen.* (Suetonius, *Life of Augustus* 30)

The danger of fire had prompted Rome's first emperor, Augustus, in A.D. 6 to set up a fire brigade, armed with buckets, axes, and pumps. The effectiveness of this brigade was limited, however, and fire remained a constant threat in Rome. The great fire in A.D. 64 during the reign of Nero devastated half of the city, and a fire raged in the city for three days in A.D. 80, the time of our story, during the reign of Titus.

Life in the city could be dangerous:

> We live in a city largely propped up by slender poles; for this is how the inspector stops the houses falling down and, plastering over old cracks, he bids us sleep secure with disaster hanging over us. We should live where there are no fires, no alarms in the night. By the time the smoke has reached you who are still sleeping on the third floor, Ucalegon on the ground floor is already calling for water and removing his bits and pieces of furniture. For if there is an alarm on the ground floor, the last to burn will be the one protected from the rain only by the tiles where the gentle pigeons lay their eggs.

Juvenal, *Satires* III.193–202

BUILDING THE MEANING
The Vivid or Historic Present

In the story at the beginning of this chapter, the verbs in lines 5–7 switch to the present tense although they describe past events. The effect of this is to make the reader feel personally involved in Cornelia's experience.

This use of the present tense is called the *vivid* or *historic present*, and it adds vividness (as in this story) and, where the story requires it, speed and excitement. Written English normally uses a past tense to describe such actions.

Notice that in the next paragraph, where the narrative resumes, the writer returns to the past tense.

Look back in story 29 and notice how there, too, in the second and third paragraphs the writer switches to the vivid or historic present.

FORMS
Verbs: Active and Passive Voice

Compare the following sentences:

Incolae omnia **agunt.**
*The tenants **are doing** everything.*

Ab incolīs omnia **aguntur.**
*Everything **is being done** by the tenants.*

Mātrēs īnfantēs **efferunt.**
*The mothers **carry out** the babies.*

Īnfantēs ā mātribus **efferuntur.**
*The babies **are carried out** by the mothers.*

Servī onera **portābant.**
*Slaves **were carrying** the loads.*

Onera ā servīs **portābantur.**
*The loads **were being carried** by slaves.*

Flammae vōs **oppriment.**
*The flames **will overwhelm** you.*

Vōs flammīs **opprimēminī.**
*You **will be overwhelmed** by the flames.*

The verbs in the left-hand column are in the *active voice*; in the right-hand column the verbs are in the *passive voice*.

In the active voice the subject performs the action of the verb. In the passive voice the subject receives the action of the verb.

	Singular		Plural
1	mítto**r**, I am (being) sent	1	mítti**mur**, we are (being) sent
2	mítte**ris**, you are (being) sent	2	míttí**minī**, you are (being) sent
3	mítti**tur**, he, she, it is (being) sent	3	míttú**ntur**, they are (being) sent

The following table gives the forms and meanings of the present passive of **mittere:**

The personal endings above (in bold italics) should be learned thoroughly; they are used on all the passive forms that follow.

The following tables give the forms of the present, imperfect, and future passive of each conjugation. Be sure to learn these forms thoroughly.

Present Passive

		1st Conjugation	2nd Conjugation	3rd Conjugation		4th Conjugation
Singular	1	pórto*r*	móveo*r*	mítto*r*	iácio*r*	aúdio*r*
	2	portá*ris*	mové*ris*	mítte*ris*	iáce*ris*	audí*ris*
	3	portá*tur*	mové*tur*	mítti*tur*	iáci*tur*	audí*tur*
Plural	1	portá*mur*	mové*mur*	mítti*mur*	iáci*mur*	audí*mur*
	2	portá*minī*	mové*minī*	mittí*minī*	iací*minī*	audí*minī*
	3	portá*ntur*	mové*ntur*	mittú*ntur*	iaciú*ntur*	audiú*ntur*

Imperfect Passive

		1st Conjugation	2nd Conjugation	3rd Conjugation		4th Conjugation
Singular	1	portá*bar*	mové*bar*	mittē*bar*	iaciē*bar*	audiē*bar*
	2	portā*báris*	movē*báris*	mittē*báris*	iaciē*báris*	audiē*báris*
	3	portā*bátur*	movē*bátur*	mittē*bátur*	iaciē*bátur*	audiē*bátur*
Plural	1	portā*bámur*	movē*bámur*	mittē*bámur*	iaciē*bámur*	audiē*bámur*
	2	portā*báminī*	movē*báminī*	mittē*báminī*	iaciē*báminī*	audiē*báminī*
	3	portā*bántur*	movē*bántur*	mittē*bántur*	iaciē*bántur*	audiē*bántur*

Future Passive

		1st Conjugation	2nd Conjugation	3rd Conjugation		4th Conjugation
Singular	1	portá*bor*	mové*bor*	mítta*r*	iácia*r*	aúdia*r*
	2	portá*beris*	mové*beris*	mittéris	iaciéris	audiéris
	3	portá*bitur*	mové*bitur*	mitté*tur*	iacié*tur*	audié*tur*
Plural	1	portá*bimur*	mové*bimur*	mitté*mur*	iacié*mur*	audié*mur*
	2	portā*bíminī*	mové*bíminī*	mitté*minī*	iacié*minī*	audié*minī*
	3	portā*búntur*	mové*búntur*	mitté*ntur*	iacié*ntur*	audié*ntur*

N.B.: The irregular verbs **esse, posse, velle,** and **nōlle** do not have passive forms. The passive forms of **ferre** are as follows:

		Present	Imperfect	Future
Singular	1	féro*r*	ferē*bar*	féra*r*
	2	fér*ris*	ferē*báris*	feré*ris*
	3	fér*tur*	ferē*bátur*	feré*tur*
Plural	1	féri*mur*	ferē*bámur*	feré*mur*
	2	ferí*minī*	ferē*báminī*	feré*minī*
	3	ferú*ntur*	ferē*bántur*	feré*ntur*

Compare the passive forms of **ferre** to the passive forms of **mittere**.

Exercise 30b
Write out in sequence and translate the seven sentences in story 30 that contain passive verbs.

Exercise 30c
Read aloud and translate:

1. Adstantēs auxilium ferēbant; auxilium ab adstantibus ferēbātur.
2. Parentēs nōs ex hōc aedificiō efferunt; nōs ā parentibus ex hōc aedificiō efferimur.
3. Amīcī incolās servābunt; incolae ab amīcīs servābuntur.
4. Flammae tē opprimunt; tū flammīs opprimeris.
5. Lapidēs tē oppriment; tū lapidibus opprimēris.
6. Incolae ōrnāmenta ē fenestrīs ēiciēbant; ōrnāmenta ē fenestrīs ab incolīs ēiciēbantur.
7. Hī līberī miserī mē commovent; ego ab hīs miserīs līberīs commoveor.
8. Ā parentibus servāminī; ab adstantibus servābāminī; ā mātribus servābiminī.
9. Numquam audiar; vix audior; tandem audiēbar.
10. Illō spectāculō commovēbāris; tālibus spectāculīs semper commovēris; crās memoriā commovēberis.
11. Adstantēs removēbuntur; iānuae aperientur; līberī excitantur; nihil agēbātur; fūmus ēmittitur; aqua portābitur.

Exercise 30d
Change each verb from active to passive voice, keeping the same tense, person, and number; translate both verbs:

1. commoveō	4. fers	7. spectāmus
2. ēicit	5. dūcis	8. custōdiēbant
3. quaerēbam	6. trahēs	9. servābis

Exercise 30e
Using story 30 and the charts of passive verb forms as guides, give the Latin for:

1. Everything was being done by the inhabitants at the same time.
2. Their goods were being thrown out of the windows.
3. Water was being brought to the apartment house.
4. The miserable children will be overwhelmed by the flames.
5. Cornelia is very moved when she sees the miserable children.

Trahimur omnēs studiō laudis. *We are all attracted by the desire for praise.* (Cicero, *Pro Archia poeta* XI.26)

ADDITIONAL READING:
The Romans Speak for Themselves: Book II: "The Vigiles," pages 13–21.

DEADLY STRUGGLES WITHIN THE ROMAN REPUBLIC

When Tiberius Sempronius Gracchus, a tribune of the people, was clubbed to death by a mob of rioters in 133 B.C., Rome witnessed the first of a long series of violent events that marked the conflict between the old guard who ruled the Roman Senate and ambitious individuals who sought to advance their positions in the senatorial aristocracy by courting popular favor through reforms that benefitted different groups within the **populus Rōmānus.**

During the second century B.C., the Roman upper class acquired wealth that many invested in large-scale farming. As their profits grew, they added smaller farms to their holdings. Slaves replaced peasants as the workforce on these large estates. The peasants were driven into the cities where, faced with homelessness and hopeless poverty, they grew desperate and dangerous. Popular reformers, **populārēs,** gathered political strength, especially by seeking to provide displaced farmers and poor urban citizens with land and programs designed to help them. The established leaders, the **optimātēs**, who controlled the Senate, feared and opposed these rival aristocrats, who were trying to gain power at their expense through institutions outside of the Senate. The struggles between **populārēs** and **optimātēs** were marked by much blood and violence. The terms **populārēs** and **optimātēs** did not refer to political parties. They were labels like "leftist" or "right-winger," which were applied to individual aristocrats who tried to gain or retain power in either nontraditional or traditional ways.

THE GRACCHI

The Gracchi brothers became two famous **populārēs**. They were trying to reverse the decline of their family's prestige in the Senate after their father's death. Tiberius Gracchus, as tribune, disregarded the custom of presenting pending legislation to the Senate for review and obtained passage in the popular assembly of a bill distributing portions of public lands to landless peasants. His opponents in the Senate tried to block his plan by refusing to allocate money to put it in operation.

At this same time King Attalus III of Pergamum, a kingdom in Asia Minor, died and in his will bequeathed his kingdom to Rome. At Tiberius' instigation, the popular assembly passed another law that ignored the Senate's traditional control of financial matters and provided that the king's wealth be used to finance the distribution of land to the landless. Then, Tiberius boldly stood for re-election for an unprecedented second consecutive term as tribune so that he could oversee the distribution of lands. To rid themselves of this popular tribune who was undermining their wealth and power in the Senate, his opponents organized a mob that murdered him and 300 of his followers on the Capitoline Hill.

Ten years later Gaius Sempronius Gracchus, Tiberius' younger brother and an eloquent orator, was elected tribune in 123 B.C. Backed by strong popular favor, he expanded his brother's program of land allotments and instituted a program to supply grain at subsidized prices to the poor citizens in Rome. He also engineered a change in the courts that weakened the grip that those who controlled the Senate maintained on the Roman court system: juries were drawn from the class of wealthy non-senators, the equestrian order (**equitēs**), rather than from the Senate. Next, Gaius Gracchus proposed the radical concept of extending Roman citizenship to other Italian cities. Those new citizens would then have become powerful supporters of Gaius in Roman politics. Violent street clashes between supporters of Gaius and mobs incited by his opponents gave his enemies within the Senate an opportunity to declare martial law to keep the peace. One of the consuls surrounded him with a contingent of archers, and he committed suicide with the help of his slave.

GAIUS MARIUS

Gaius Marius, elected consul in 107 B.C., was the next important leader to follow a **populāris** path. A rich equestrian from Arpinum, Marius was a "new man" (**novus homō**), one of the very few Romans who succeeded in senatorial politics without the usual qualification of birth into one of the families of senatorial nobility. His base of power was the military and discontented elements in the populace. He had recruited his legions from the citizenry at large by promising his soldiers pensions of land allotments and a share in the

Marius triumphs over the Cimbri
Oil on canvas by Saverio Altamura, Museo e Gallerie Nazionali di Capodimonte, Naples, Italy

Marius amid the ruins of Carthage

Oil on canvas by John Vanderlyn, Albany Institute of History and Art, Albany, New York

spoils of war. Leading this new kind of army into Africa, Marius was victorious by 105 B.C. over Rome's enemy in North Africa, King Jugurtha.

Next, Marius and his volunteer professional army beat back the Cimbri and Teutones, Germanic tribes threatening Italy's northern borders. But when Marius returned victorious to Rome, many in both the Senate and the popular assembly balked at providing his soldiers the choice lands in Gaul and the western provinces that they had been promised. Marius' soldiers resorted to armed intimidation to get their land grants.

Over the next several years, violent unrest rocked all of Italy, and in Rome bloody power struggles continued between various aristocrats. In 87 B.C. Marius and his **populārēs** seized Rome and conducted a reign of terror against their political enemies, murdering or exiling them and confiscating their property. That reign ended with Marius' death early in his seventh consulship in 86 B.C.

LUCIUS CORNELIUS SULLA

Lucius Cornelius Sulla had become Marius' greatest rival after serving as one of his officers in the war against Jugurtha. He obtained the support of leading **optimātēs** and was elected a consul for 88 B.C. In that year, King Mithridates of Pontus, a land on the south shore of the Black Sea, seized territories under Roman control in Greece and Asia Minor and massacred thousands of Italians and Romans living in those lands. Sulla's supporters in the Senate obtained for him command of the war to punish Mithridates. Marius, however, used popular tribunes to get the command away from Sulla. Sulla unexpectedly captured Rome with his army, drove Marius into exile, killed many of his supporters, and regained the command against Mithridates. While he was gone, Marius returned with an army of his veterans, seized Rome, and was elected to his seventh consulship, during which he died.

Sulla, on his victorious return to Rome, trounced the Marian forces still holding sway there and instituted his own government by terror, as he eliminated his political enemies by a process called proscription. Routinely Sulla posted in the Forum lists of names of his opponents and also of some wealthy equestrians, whose estates might increase the bonus he had promised his troops. Romans who had been thus proscribed were outlaws: a cash reward was paid the murderers who brought in the heads of the proscribed, and Sulla took possession of their property. The Senate granted Sulla the title "dictator for stabilizing the constitution." In exchange, Sulla's reforms did away with the tribunes' power to introduce legislation and thus returned power to his supporters, who had traditionally controlled the Senate. Once he had eliminated his opponents and set in place policies that he believed would assure that **optimātēs** who had supported him would retain firm control of the government, Sulla retired from his dictatorship. He died the next year, 78 B.C., at his villa in Campania.

GNAEUS POMPEIUS

Gnaeus Pompeius (Pompey the Great) had begun his rise to favor and power by lending Sulla the support of his private army of clients for the seizure of Rome in 83 B.C. and then by suppressing Marian forces in Sicily and Africa. For these actions, Sulla reluctantly honored Pompeius with the **cognōmen** "The Great" (**Magnus**). In 77 B.C. the Senate sent Pompey to Spain to put down a rebellion of Marians there. On his triumphant return from that expedition, Pompey's army arrived in Italy in time to cut off any escape for the last of the 70,000 rebellious slaves in the army of the Thracian gladiator Spartacus. For three years (73–71 B.C.), Spartacus had terrorized the wealthy Italian landowners as the leader of a spectacular slave uprising. Pompey's timely arrival ensured the Roman army's victory over Spartacus. Pompey claimed the honor of victory at the expense of Marcus Licinius Crassus, who had done most of the work in defeating Spartacus' uprising. Despite their mutual jealousy, they cooperated on their re-entry to Rome in order to be elected consuls in the face of optimate opposition to their ambitions in the Senate. The co-consuls agreed to support a law rescinding Sulla's removal of the tribune's right to initiate legislation.

In 67 B.C., a tribune proposed a law authorizing Pompey to command a fleet and to suppress the pirates who were at that time disrupting trade in the Mediterranean Sea, a feat he completed in three months. In the following year, a praetor, Marcus Tullius Cicero, the successful orator and an ardent supporter of Pompey, spoke strongly in favor of another tribune's proposal. That one granted Pompey extraordinary powers for tightening Roman control in Asia Minor and meeting the renewed threat of Mithridates. From 66 to 62 B.C. Pompey's military campaigns succeeded in defeating Mithridates once and for all and consolidated Roman domination of the East so that it provided a solid frontier for Rome's empire.

Go Online
For: Additional Practice
Visit: PHSchool.com
Web Code: jgd-0004

PSEUDOLUS

Quīnta hōra est. Marcus et Sextus per ātrium ambulant, cum subitō ē culīnā cachinnus maximus audītur. Statim in culīnam puerī intrant, ubi Syrum et aliōs servōs vident.

Sextus, "Cūr vōs omnēs rīdētis?" inquit. "Iocumne audīvistis?"

Cui Syrus, "Iocō optimō dēlectāmur, domine. Est in culīnā servus quīdam cui nōmen 5
est Pseudolus. Nōn servus sed mercātor esse vidētur. Heri māne in urbem ad laniī tabernam dēscendit, nam carnem emere volēbat. 'Quantī,' inquit Pseudolus, 'est illa perna?' Ubi pretium audītur, laniō respondet, 'Ego numquam dabō tantum pretium. Praedō quidem mihi vidēris, nōn lanius. Nēmō nisi scelestus tantum petit. Ad aliam tabernam ībō neque umquam—' 10

"'Procāx es, Pseudole,' interpellat lanius. 'Per iocum sine dubiō hoc dīcis. In hāc viā nēmō carnem meliōrem habet, ut bene scīs. Hoc pretium nōn est magnum. Sī autem multum emēs, pretium fortasse minuētur. Dominus tuus, ut audīvī, crās cēnam amīcīs suīs dabit. Nōnne porcum emēs?'

"Cui Pseudolus, 'Quem porcum mihi vēndere vīs? Ille est pinguis. Da mihi illum!' 15

(continued)

2 **cachinnus, -ī**, m., *laughter*	9 **quidem**, adv., *indeed*
5 **optimus, -a, -um**, *best, very good, excellent*	10 **umquam**, adv., *ever*
6 **lanius, -ī**, m., *butcher*	11 **procāx, procācis**, *insolent*; as slang, *pushy*
7 **carō, carnis**, f., *meat*	12 **autem**, conj., *however, but*
Quantī...? *How much...?*	13 **multus, -a, -um**, *much*
8 **perna, -ae**, f., *ham*	15 **pinguis, -is, -e**, *fat*
pretium, -ī, n., *price*	

13 **minuō, minuere, minuī, minūtus**, *to lessen, reduce, decrease*

Exercise 31a
Respondē Latīnē:

1. Quota hōra est?
2. Ā quibus cachinnus audītur?
3. Quid servōs dēlectat?
4. Cūr Pseudolus ad tabernam laniī dēscendit?
5. Quālis homō lanius vidētur esse?
6. Quid Pseudolus faciet?
7. Estne pretium pernae magnum?
8. Minuēturne pretium?
9. Quālem porcum Pseudolus emere vult?

"'Ille porcus heri in meīs agrīs pascēbātur, meā manū cūrābātur. Nūllum porcum meliōrem in hāc urbe emēs. Senātōrī Rōmānō illum vēndere volō. Itaque tibi decem dēnāriīs eum vēndam.'

"'Decem dēnāriīs? Immō quīnque!'

"'Octō!'

"'Octō, sī ille lepus quoque additus erit grātīs. Sī nōn, nihil emam et ad aliam tabernam ībō.'

"'Nōn sine causā tū vocāris Pseudolus. Vōs servī, nōn nōs laniī, rēctē praedōnēs vocāminī.'

"Multum et diū clāmat lanius, sed Pseudolus nihil respondet. Tandem lanius octō dēnāriōs invītus accipit; porcum et leporem Pseudolō trādit. Iam Pseudolus noster rediit et tōtam fābulam nōbīs nārrāvit. In animō habet leporem amīcō vēndere et pecūniam sibi retinēre."

"Minimē vērō!" clāmāvit Aurēlia, quae ā Forō redierat et omnia audīverat. "Syre, da mihi leporem! Pseudolus ad vīllam rūsticam mittētur. Vōs quoque puniēminī omnēs."

18 **dēnārius, -ī**, m., *denarius (silver coin)*
19 **immō**, adv., *rather, on the contrary*
21 **lepus, leporis**, m., *hare*
additus erit, *(it) will have been added, is added*

grātīs, adv., *free, for nothing*
23 **rēctē**, adv., *rightly, properly*
29 **vērō**, adv., *truly, really, indeed*

16 **pāscō, pāscere, pāvī, pāstus**, *to feed, pasture*
21 **addō, addere, addidī, additus**, *to add*
26 **accipiō, accipere, accēpī, acceptus**, *to receive, get*

Respondē Latīnē:

1. Ubi porcus pascēbātur?
2. Ā quō porcus cūrābātur?
3. Quid faciet Pseudolus sī lepus grātīs nōn additus erit?
4. Quid Pseudolus in animō habet facere?
5. Quis omnia audīverat?

A Roman butcher shop
Stone frieze, 2nd century B.C., Musée de la Civilisation, Paris, France

Exercise 31b

Take parts, read aloud, and translate:

In trīclīniō: Pseudolus, Syrus, aliī servī

SYRUS: Eho! Domina sine dubiō īrāta est hodiē. Ad vīllam mittēris, Pseudole. Ēheu! Nōs quoque puniēmur omnēs.

PSEUDOLUS: Ego nōn commoveor. Sī ad vīllam mittar, multōs leporēs ipse in agrīs capere poterō. 5

SYRUS: Minimē vērō! In vīllā enim servī semper custōdiuntur neque errāre possunt. Id nescīre vidēris.

PSEUDOLUS: Sine dubiō vōs puniēminī sī nōn statim hōs lectōs movēbitis. Fortasse domina mē ad vīllam mittī iubēbit. Estō! Hīc labōrāre nōlō. Vōs lectōs movēte! Ego fābulam vōbīs nārrābō. 10

SYRUS: Tacē, Pseudole! Fābulīs tuīs saepe delectāmur, sed sī cachinnus audiētur—

PSEUDOLUS: Nōlīte timēre! Domina fortasse mē reprehendit sed Cornēlius mē ad vīllam mittī nōlet. Hīc certē mē retinērī volet. Saepe enim dominus mē ad Forum mittit ubi aliquid parvō pretiō emī vult.

 1 **trīclīnium, -ī,** n., *dining room*   **retinērī,** *to be held back, kept*
13 **mittī,** *to be sent*   14 **emī,** *to be bought*

    12 **reprehendō, reprehendere, reprehendī, reprehēnsus,** *to blame, scold*

FORMS
Verbs: Present Passive Infinitives

Compare these sentences:

1. Aurēlia Pseudolum ad vīllam **mittere** volet.
   *Aurelia will want **to send** Pseudolus to the country house.*

2. Aurēlia Pseudolum ad vīllam ***mittī*** iubēbit.
   *Aurelia will order Pseudolus **to be sent** to the country house.*

In sentence 1, **mittere** is the present *active* infinitive; in sentence 2, **mittī** is the present *passive* infinitive. The table below shows the present active and passive infinitives of each conjugation:

1st Conjugation	2nd Conjugation	3rd Conjugation		4th Conjugation
port**áre**, *to carry*	mov**ére**, *to move*	mítt**ere**, *to send*	iác**ere**, *to throw*	aud**íre**, *to hear*
port**árī**, *to be carried*	mov**érī**, *to be moved*	mítt**ī**, *to be sent*	iác**ī**, *to be thrown*	aud**írī**, *to be heard*

Exercise 31c

Select, read aloud, and translate:

1. Incolae magna incendia (exstinguī, exstinguere, exstinguit) nōn possunt.
2. Incolae miserī lapidibus et flammīs (opprimere, opprimī, opprimunt) nōlunt.
3. Interdiū nihil intrā urbem vehiculō (portās, portārī, portātur) licet.
4. Cornēliī nūllum vehiculum intrā urbem (vidērī, vident, vidēre) poterant.
5. Syrus cachinnum ā dominā (audīvit, audīre, audīrī) nōn vult.

BUILDING THE MEANING
The Ablative Case (Consolidation)

In Chapter 12, the following uses of the ablative case were formally presented:

1. Ablative of Time When:

   Illō ipsō tempore parietēs īnsulae cecidērunt. (30:25)
   At that very moment the walls of the apartment building fell.

2. Ablative of Time within Which:

   Brevī tempore māter et fīlia ā servīs per urbem ferēbantur. (29:1–2)
   In a short time the mother and her daughter were being carried through the city by slaves.

3. Ablative of Instrument or Means (with active verbs):

   Cornēlia Flāviam **complexū** tenet. (9:20)
   Cornelia holds Flavia in an embrace.

4. Ablative of Manner:

   Parietēs īnsulae **magnō (cum) fragōre** cecidērunt. (30:25)
   The walls of the apartment building fell with a great crash.

In Chapter 24, the following use of the ablative case was formally presented:

5. Ablative of Cause:

   Tuā culpā raeda est in fossā. (14:7)
   Because of your fault the carriage is in the ditch.
   It's your fault that the carriage is in the ditch.

In recent chapters you have seen the following uses of the ablative case:

6. Ablative of Price:

   Itaque tibi **decem dēnāriīs** eum vēndam. (31:17–18)
   Therefore I will sell it to you for ten denarii.

7. **Ablative of Personal Agent with Passive Verbs:**

> Māter et fīlia **ā servīs** per urbem ferēbantur. (29:1–2)
> *The mother and her daughter were being carried through the city **by slaves**.*

> **Ab incolīs** omnia simul aguntur. (30:5)
> *Everything is being done at the same time **by the tenants**.*

Note that when the action of the passive verb is carried out by a person (*personal agent*) the preposition **ā** or **ab** is used with the ablative case.

N.B. The ablative of instrument or means is used with both active verbs (see 3 above) and passive verbs (see 8 below).

8. **Ablative of Instrument or Means (with passive verbs):**

> Interdiū nihil intrā urbem **vehiculō** portātur. (29:3–4)
> *During the day nothing is carried **by/in a vehicle** within the city.*

> **Iocō optimō** dēlectāmur. (31:5) *We are amused **by an excellent joke**.*

Note that when the action of the passive verb is carried out by a thing (*instrument* or *means*) a preposition is not used with the ablative case.

Exercise 31d

Select the appropriate verb, read aloud, and translate:

1. (a) Puerōs Rōmānōs patrēs saepe _____.
   (b) Puerī Rōmānī ā patribus _____.
   (verberant/verberāmus/verberantur)

2. (a) Uxōrēs Rōmānae ā virīs semper _____.
   (b) Uxōrēs virī Rōmānī semper _____.
   (amābant/amābantur/amātis)

3. (a) Hic liber ā mē tibi _____.
   (b) Hunc librum tibi _____.
   (dabitur/dabit/dabō)

4. (a) Omnēs convīvae cibō magnopere _____.
   (b) Omnēs convīvās cibus magnopere _____.
   (dēlectant/dēlectat/dēlectantur)

5. (a) Mercātor ipse manū porcum _____.
   (b) Porcus manū mercātōris _____.
   (cūrābās/cūrābātur/cūrābat)

6. (a) Lepus ā mercātōre grātīs _____.
   (b) Mercātor leporem grātīs _____.
   (addētur/addent/addet)

7. (a) Domina Pseudolum ad vīllam _____.
   (b) Pseudolus ad vīllam ā dominā _____.
   (mittētur/mittet/mittent)

8. (a) Flammae incolās miserōs _____.
   (b) Incolae miserī flammīs _____.
   (opprimēbantur/opprimēbant/opprimēbātis)

9. (a) Vehicula onera ingentia _____.
   (b) Onera ingentia vehiculīs _____.
   (portantur/portant/portārī)

10. (a) Cornēlia incendiō _____.
    (b) Incendium Cornēliam _____.
    (commovētur/commovēre/commovet)

convīva, -ae, m., *guest (at a banquet)*   **magnopere,** adv., *greatly*

Exercise 31e

In Exercise 31d, locate the sentences that contain:

1. ablative of personal agent
2. ablative of means or instrument or cause

Laudātur ab hīs, culpātur ab illīs. *He's praised by these and blamed by those.* (Horace)
Avārus animus nūllō satiātur lucrō. *A greedy mind is satisfied with no (amount of) gain.* (Publilius Syrus 55)

FORMS
Demonstrative Adjectives and Pronouns

In Chapter 26 the demonstrative adjectives and pronouns **hic** *this* and **ille** *that* were formally presented. Review them, using the charts at the back of this book. In Chapter 27 the forms of **is, ea, id** were formally presented as a pronoun meaning *he, she,* and *it*. Review the forms of this pronoun, using the chart at the back of this book. The forms of **is, ea, id** may also function as adjectives meaning *this* or *that* according to the context, e.g., **eō ipsō tempore**, *at <u>that</u> very moment.*

You have met two other words that may function as either demonstrative adjectives or pronouns:

> **ipse, ipsa, ipsum**, intensive, *himself, herself, itself, themselves, very*
>
> **īdem, eadem, idem**, *the same*

The forms of these demonstrative adjectives and pronouns are as follows. They should be learned thoroughly:

Number Case	Masc.	Fem.	Neut.
Singular			
Nominative	ipse	ipsa	ipsum
Genitive	ipsīus	ipsīus	ipsīus
Dative	ipsī	ipsī	ipsī
Accusative	ipsum	ipsam	ipsum
Ablative	ipsō	ipsā	ipsō
Plural			
Nominative	ipsī	ipsae	ipsa
Genitive	ipsōrum	ipsārum	ipsōrum
Dative	ipsīs	ipsīs	ipsīs
Accusative	ipsōs	ipsās	ipsa
Ablative	ipsīs	ipsīs	ipsīs

Compare the forms of **ipse, ipsa, ipsum** above with those of **ille, illa, illud**.

The forms of **īdem, eadem, idem** are the same as those of **is, ea, id** plus the letters -*dem*, except for the letters in boldface:

Number Case	Masc.	Fem.	Neut.
Singular			
Nominative	īdem	eadem	idem
Genitive	eiusdem	eiusdem	eiusdem
Dative	eīdem	eīdem	eīdem
Accusative	eundem	eandem	idem
Ablative	eōdem	eādem	eōdem
Plural			
Nominative	eīdem	eaedem	eadem
Genitive	eōrundem	eārundem	eōrundem
Dative	eīsdem	eīsdem	eīsdem
Accusative	eōsdem	eāsdem	eadem
Ablative	eīsdem	eīsdem	eīsdem

Exercise 31f

IN VIĀ SACRĀ

A great man in Rome would normally have men of lower rank (**clientēs**) who looked upon him as their patron (**patrōnus**) and attended him on public occasions. Clients who came along unbidden with their master to a **cēna** were referred to scornfully as **umbrae**, *shadows*. In this conversation, the brothers Vibidius and Servilius discuss how to get Gaius to invite them to his dinner party as members of Messalla's retinue.

Take parts, read aloud, and translate:

VIBIDIUS: Ecce, mī frāter! Vidēsne hanc domum? Est ea dē quā tibi saepe dīxī. Ibi enim multae et optimae cēnae dantur. Eae cēnae sunt per tōtam urbem celebrēs. Hodiē, ut dīcunt omnēs, dominus huius domūs multōs convīvās ad cēnam accipiet. Optima cēna ab illō dabitur. Ab omnibus multum vīnum bibētur et multae fābulae nārrābuntur. Ego et tū invītābimur? Mox sciē- 5 mus. Ecce enim appropinquat dominus ipse, Gaius Cornēlius, quī ā quattuor servīs in lectīcā maximā portātur.

SERVĪLIUS: At nōs eī dominō nōn nōtī sumus. Quōmodo ab eō ad cēnam invītābimur?

VIBIDIUS: Sine dubiō is ad Forum portābitur et extrā Cūriam dēpōnētur. Tum in Cūriam intrābit sōlus. Eōdem tempore quō ē lectīcā dēscendet, nōs eī oc- 10 currēmus et dīcēmus, "Nōnne tū es Gaius Cornēlius, amīcus nostrī patrōnī Messallae, cuius clientēs fidēlissimī sumus? Numquam sine nōbīs ad cēnam venit Messalla."

SERVĪLIUS: Tum Gaius nōs invītābit ad cēnam?

VIBIDIUS: Fortasse. 15

SERVĪLIUS: Fortasse? Minimē vērō! Nōs vocābit umbrās, nōn clientēs Messallae.

3 **celeber, celebris, celebre,** *famous*
8 **nōtus, -a, -um,** *known*

12 **fidēlissimus, -a, -um,** *most faithful*

5 **bibō, bibere, bibī,** *to drink*

Exercise 31g

In the story in Exercise 31f above, locate and translate all sentences that contain examples of the demonstrative adjectives and pronouns **hic, haec, hoc; ille, illa, illud; is, ea, id; ipse, ipsa, ipsum;** and **īdem, eadem, idem.** State whether the word is being used as an adjective or a pronoun, and if it is used as an adjective tell what word it modifies.

Exercise 31h

Using story 31 as a guide, give the Latin for:

1. Very loud laughter was heard from the kitchen by the children.
2. The slaves were amused by a very good joke.
3. If Pseudolus buys/will buy a lot, the price will be reduced by the butcher.
4. You slaves are rightly called robbers.
5. That pig and this hare are handed over to Pseudolus.

DINNER PREPARATIONS

The most substantial meal of the day was the dinner (**cēna**), eaten in the late afternoon, while it was still daylight; the richer classes, who could afford lamps or torches, sometimes began later or prolonged the dinner farther into the evening.

Earlier in the day the Romans ate little; in the early morning they took only a drink of water or wine and a piece of bread; this was called **iēntāculum**, and was similar to the "continental" rolls and coffee of the present day. The midday meal (**prandium**) would also be cold, possibly something left over from the previous day's **cēna**; this also was merely a snack.

In the early days of Rome, the dinner was eaten in the **ātrium,** but as manners became more sophisticated, a special room was set aside as a dining room. From the second century B.C., the adoption of the Greek custom of reclining at meals demanded a special arrangement of couches and tables that was called in Greek *triklinion* (tri-klin-ion, "three-couch-arrangement"), a word borrowed into Latin as **trīclīnium**. In this arrangement three couches (Latin **lectī**) were set around a table or several small tables, and the name **trīclīnium** came to be used for the dining room itself. At the time of our story, the male diners reclined. The wives who attended the dinner party would sit and not recline. Slaves cut up the food before serving so that the diners could eat with one hand. Though the Romans had spoons and knives, food was generally conveyed to the mouth by the fingers. Napkins (**mappae**) were sometimes provided by the host; guests often brought their own napkins and carried away with them any food they did not eat from their own portions.

Preparations for a banquet

*Fragment of mosaic pavement from
Carthage, Louvre, Paris, France*

Abhinc trēs diēs amīcī quīdam ā Gaiō Cornēliō ad cēnam invītātī erant. Quā dē causā Aurēlia in Forō glīrēs ēmerat. Porcus quoque ā Pseudolō ēmptus erat. Iam diēs cēnae aderat. Māne servī in Forum missī sunt et ibi comparāvērunt holera, pānem, pullōs. Ōva quoque et māla et multa alia comparāta sunt, nam cum senātor Rōmānus amīcōs ad cēnam invītāvit, cēna optima parārī dēbet. 5

Iam hōra cēnae appropinquābat. Dum in culīnā cibus coquēbātur, ancillae trīclīnium parābant. Mēnsa ā servīs in medium trīclīnium iam allāta erat; trēs lectī circum mēnsam positī erant.

Trīclīnium Cornēliī erat pulcherrimum atque ōrnātissimum. In parietibus erant pictūrae pulcherrimae. In aliā pictūrā canis Cerberus ē rēgnō Plūtōnis extrahēbātur, in 10 aliā Mercurius ad Charōnem mortuōs addūcēbat, in aliā Orpheus ad īnferōs dēscendēbat.

Cornēlius servōs festīnāre iubēbat, nam iam erat nōna hōra. Aurēlia, semper sollicita, ancillās vehementer incitābat. Subitō ancilla quaedam, quae Aurēliam magnopere timēbat, hūc illūc festīnāns ūnum ē candēlābrīs cāsū ēvertit. Candēlābrum in lectum dēiectum est; statim effūsum est oleum in strāta; haec celeriter ignem cēpērunt. Aurēlia 15 īrāta ancillam neglegentem reprehendēbat, sed Cornēlius celeriter palliō ignem exstīnxit.

"Bonō animō es!" inquit Cornēlius. "Ecce! Ignis iam exstīnctus est!" Tum aliae ancillae ab illō vocātae sunt: "Syra! Phrygia! Strāta alia ferte! Necesse est omnia statim reficere, nam convīvae mox aderunt." Omnia Cornēliī iussa facta sunt. *(continued)*

1 **invītātī erant,** *(they) had been invited*
   quā dē causā, *for this reason*
3 **comparō, -āre, -āvī, -ātus,** *to buy, obtain, get ready*
   holus, holeris, n., *vegetable*
   pānis, pānis, gen. pl., **pānium,** m., *bread*
4 **pullus, -ī,** m., *chicken*
   ōvum, -ī, n., *egg*
   mālum, -ī, n., *apple*
7 **allāta erat,** *(it) had been brought in*
   circum, prep. + acc., *around*
9 **pulcherrimus, -a, -um,** *most/very beautiful*

10 **rēgnum, -ī,** n., *kingdom*
11 **īnferī, -ōrum,** m. pl., *the underworld*
14 **candēlābrum, -ī,** n., *candelabrum, lamp-stand*
   cāsū, *by chance, accidentally*
15 **oleum -ī,** n., *oil*
   strātum, -ī, n., *sheet, covering*
   ignis, ignis, gen. pl., **ignium,** m., *fire*
16 **pallium, -ī,** n., *cloak*
17 **Bonō animō es!/este!** *Be of good mind! Cheer up!*
19 **iussa, -ōrum,** n. pl., *commands, orders*

6 **coquō, coquere, coxī, coctus,** *to cook*
7 **afferō, afferre, attulī, allātus,** irreg., *to bring, bring to, bring in*
14 **ēvertō, ēvertere, ēvertī, ēversus,** *to overturn, upset*
15 **dēiciō, dēicere, dēiēcī, dēiectus,** *to throw down;* pass., *to fall*
   effundō, effundere, effūdī, effūsus, *to pour out;* pass., *to spill*

Exercise 32a Respondē Latīnē:

1. Quī ad cēnam invītātī erant?
2. Quid servī in Forō comparāvērunt?
3. Quid ancillae faciēbant?
4. Quae pictūrae in parietibus trīclīniī erant?
5. Quid Aurēlia faciēbat?
6. Quid fēcit ancilla quaedam?
7. Quō īnstrūmentō Cornēlius ignem exstīnxit?

Adveniēbant convīvae, in quibus erant complūrēs clientēs quī ad cēnam invītātī erant. 20
Convīvae mappās sēcum ferēbant, nam cum cēna cōnfecta erit, in mappīs cibum auferre
eīs licēbit. Paulisper in ātriō stābant, Cornēlium exspectantēs. Tandem ā Cornēliō ipsō
cōmiter salūtātī sunt.

Aberat nēmō nisi Titus Cornēlius, patruus Marcī. Paulisper eum exspectābant
omnēs; sed tandem, quamquam ille nōndum advēnerat, convīvae in trīclīnium ductī sunt. 25
Soleae dēpositae ā servīs ablātae sunt. Omnēs in lectīs accubuērunt et cēnam
exspectābant.

20 **complūrēs, -ēs, -a**, *several*
21 **cōnfecta erit**, *(it) is/will have been*
     finished

23 **cōmiter**, adv., *courteously, graciously, in*
     a friendly way
26 **solea, -ae**, f., *sandal*

21 **auferō, auferre, abstulī, ablātus**, irreg., *to carry away, take away*
26 **accumbō, accumbere, accubuī, accubitūrus**, *to recline (at table)*

Respondē Latīnē:

1. Quid convīvae sēcum ferēbant?
2. Cūr convīvae in ātriō stābant?
3. Quid tandem Cornēlius fēcit?

4. Quis aberat?
5. Quō convīvae ductī sunt?

FORMS
Verbs: Perfect, Pluperfect, and Future Perfect Passive

Look at these sentences with verbs in the passive voice:

Perfect Passive:

Trīclīnium **parātum est**.

*The dining room **was prepared/has been
prepared**.*

Amīcī **invītātī sunt**.

*Friends **were invited/have been invited**.*

Pluperfect Passive:

Porcus **ēmptus erat**.
Trēs lectī **positī erant**.

*A pig **had been bought**.*
*Three couches **had been placed**.*

Future Perfect Passive:

Cēna **cōnfecta erit**.
Māla **comparāta erunt**.

*Dinner **will have been finished**.*
*Apples **will have been bought**.*

It is obvious from these examples that the *passive* forms of the *perfect*, *pluperfect*, and *future perfect* tenses are very different from their corresponding active forms. Here are passive forms of these tenses for **portāre**:

		Perfect Passive		Pluperfect Passive		Future Perfect Passive	
Singular	1	portátus, -a	sum	portátus, -a	éram	portátus, -a	érō
	2	portátus, -a	es	portátus, -a	érās	portátus, -a	éris
	3	portátus, -a, -um	est	portátus, -a, -um	érat	portátus, -a, -um	érit
Plural	1	portátī, -ae	súmus	portátī, -ae	erámus	portátī, -ae	érimus
	2	portátī, -ae	éstis	portátī, -ae	erátis	portátī, -ae	éritis
	3	portátī, -ae, -a	sunt	portátī, -ae, -a	érant	portátī, -ae, -a	érunt

Be sure to learn these forms thoroughly.

NOTES

1. Verbs of all four conjugations and the irregular verb **ferre** follow the same patterns in the perfect, pluperfect, and future perfect passive. They all use forms of the verb **esse** plus the *perfect passive participle*, which you learned in Chapter 20 and which is the fourth principal part of a transitive verb, e.g., **portō, portāre, portāvī, portātus**.

    a. To form the *perfect passive*, use the *present* tense of **esse**, e.g., **portātus *sum*, portātus *es***.

    b. To form the *pluperfect passive*, use the *imperfect* tense of **esse**, e.g., **portātus *eram*, portātus *erās***.

    c. To form the *future perfect passive*, use the *future* tense of **esse**, e.g., **portātus *erō*, portātus *eris***.

2. The perfect passive participle in these verb forms agrees with the subject in gender and number and will always be nominative in case:

Puer laudā*tus* est.	*The boy was/has been praised.*
Māter laudā*ta* est.	*The mother was/has been praised.*
Aedificium laudā*tum* est.	*The building was/has been praised.*
Puerī laudā*tī* sunt.	*The boys were/have been praised.*
Mātrēs laudā*tae* sunt.	*The mothers were/have been praised.*
Aedificia laudā*ta* sunt.	*The buildings were/have been praised.*

Exercise 32b
Read aloud and translate:

1. Servus, nōmine Pseudolus, in Forum missus est.
2. Glīrēs ab Aurēliā ēmptī erant.
3. Cum trīclīnium parātum erit, convīvae intrābunt.
4. Servī iocō optimō dēlectātī sunt.
5. Ē culīnā magnus cachinnus audītus erat.
6. Cum lepus ab Aurēliā inventus erit, Pseudolus pūniētur.
7. "Tū, Pseudole," inquit Aurēlia, "leporem emere nōn iussus es."
8. "Ego illō spectāculō miserābilī," inquit Cornēlia, "valdē commōta sum."
9. Octō dēnāriī ā laniō acceptī sunt.
10. "Cum ā Cornēliō salūtātī erimus," inquit ūnus ē convīvīs, "servī eius nōs ad trīclīnium addūcent."

Exercise 32c
Select, read aloud, and translate:

1. _____ ā mātre vocāta erat.
   Ancilla/Līberī/Eucleidēs
2. _____ ex īnsulā ēmissae sunt.
   Fūmus/Ōrnāmenta/Flammae
3. _____ in mēnsā positus erat.
   Pānis/Glīrēs/Mappa
4. _____ ā laniō minūtum est.
   Dēnāriī/Pretium/Porcus
5. _____ in Forō comparātī erant.
   Ōva/Glīrēs/Porcus
6. _____ ā servō allāta erunt.
   Māla/Mappa/Mulier
7. _____ in hāc tabernā ēmpta est.
   Carō/Holera/Lepus
8. _____ ā līberīs petītae sunt.
   Adstantēs/Auxilium/Mātrēs

Exercise 32d
Change each verb from active to passive voice, keeping the same tense, person, and number; translate both verbs. You may use masculine, feminine, or (if appropriate) neuter endings on the perfect passive participles:

1. dūxit
2. portāvistī
3. posuerat
4. oppressimus
5. commōvī
6. accēperit
7. mīserāmus
8. audīverātis
9. tulērunt

Mythological scenes dealing with the underworld, such as those adorning the walls of the Cornelii dining room, have remained popular subjects of art through the ages to this day. Pictured: Charon the Ferryman, who brought souls to the underworld for a fee.

"Psyche and Charon," oil on canvas by John Roddam Spencer-Stanhope, Roy Miles Gallery, London

Exercise 32e
Using story 32 and the chart on page 43 as guides, give the Latin for:

1. Vegetables had been bought in the Forum by the slaves.
2. The food was cooked in the kitchen.
3. The table has been brought by the slaves into the middle of the dining room.
4. Cerberus had been dragged from the kingdom of Pluto.
5. When the dinner is finished/will have been finished, the guests will carry food away in napkins.

━ ━ ━ ━ ━
Ālea iacta est. *The die has been cast.* Said by Julius Caesar at the
Rubicon River. (Suetonius, *Caesar* 32)
━ ━ ━ ━ ━

WORD STUDY VIII

4th Declension Nouns

Many 4th declension nouns are formed from the stem of the fourth principal part of verbs. For example, **adventus, -ūs,** m., *arrival*, is made from the stem of **adventūrus**, the fourth principal part of **adveniō**. English words are often derived from this kind of 4th declension noun by dropping the *-us* ending e.g., *advent*, "an arrival."

Exercise 1

Give the Latin 4th declension noun (nom. sing., gen. sing., and gender) that may be formed from the fourth principal part of each of the following verbs, and give the meaning of the noun:

1. prōcēdere
2. trānsīre
3. habēre
4. agere
5. audīre
6. exīre
7. colere
8. trahere

Exercise 2

Give the English words derived by dropping the *-us* ending from each 4th declension noun formed in Exercise 1 above, and give the meaning of each English word.

Exercise 3

Give the Latin verb to which each of these nouns is related, and give the meanings of both verb and noun:

1. **rīsus, -ūs,** m.
2. **lātrātus, -ūs,** m.
3. **reditus, -ūs,** m.
4. **gemitus, -ūs,** m.
5. **cursus, -ūs,** m.
6. **discessus, -ūs,** m.
7. **cōnspectus, -ūs,** m.
8. **aditus, -ūs,** m.
9. **cāsus, -ūs,** m.

More Compound Verbs

The following exercise on compound verbs uses the principles of word formation discussed in Chapter 27, Word Study VII, and Chapter 29.

Exercise 4

After each Latin verb is a group of English words that are derived from compounds of that simple verb. Give the present active infinitive of the compound Latin verb from which each English word is derived, and give the meanings of both the compound Latin verb and the English word:

mittō, mittere, mīsī, missus

1. commit
2. submit
3. remit
4. transmit
5. admit
6. emit
7. permit
8. promise

iaciō, iacere, iēcī, iactus

1. project
2. reject
3. subject
4. eject
5. inject
6. interject
7. conjecture
8. trajectory

faciō, facere, fēcī, factus

1. effect
2. affect
3. defect
4. perfect
5. infect
6. confection
7. suffice
8. affection

trahō, trahere, trāxī, tractus

1. abstract
2. attract
3. contract
4. detract
5. distract
6. extract
7. retract
8. subtract

AT DINNER

Cornēlius ancillīs signum dat. Prīmum aqua ab ancillīs portātur et convīvae manūs lāvant. Dum hoc faciunt, omnibus convīvīs mulsum datur. Deinde fercula ē culīnā efferuntur, in quibus est gustātiō—ōva et olīvae nigrae, asparagus et bōlētī liquāmine aspersī. Intereā ā convīvīs multae fābulae nārrantur, multa dē rēbus urbānīs dīcuntur: alius dē incendiīs nārrat, alius dē pestilentiā in urbe, alius dē amphitheātrō, aedificiō 5
ingentī quod mox dēdicābitur. Aliquid novī audīre omnēs dēlectat. Dum convīvae haec et multa alia nārrant, gustātiō editur, mulsum bibitur.

Tum servī gustātiōnem auferunt; deinde ab eīsdem servīs magnum ferculum in trīclīnium fertur, in mediā mēnsā pōnitur. In eō est porcus ingēns et circum porcum glīrēs quōs Aurēlia ēmerat. Ab aliīs servīs pōcula convīvārum vīnō optimō complentur. 10
Dum convīvae haec spectant, extrā trīclīnium magnus tumultus audītur. Subitō in trīclīnium magnō cum strepitū irrumpit Titus Cornēlius.

Mussant convīvae, "Cūr Titus noster sērō venīre solet neque sē umquam excūsat?"

At Titus, ad locum suum lentē ambulāns, "Salvēte, amīcī omnēs!" inquit. "Salvē, mī frāter! Amīcō cuidam in popīnā occurrī."

(continued) 15

2 **mulsum, -ī,** n., *wine sweetened with honey*
  ferculum, -ī, n., *dish, tray*
3 **gustātiō, gustātiōnis,** f., *hors d'oeuvre, first course*
  niger, nigra, nigrum, *black*
  bōlētus, -ī, m., *mushroom*
  liquāmen, liquāminis, n., *garum (a sauce made from fish, used to season food)*

4 **aspersus, -a, -um,** *sprinkled*
  rēs urbānae, rērum urbānārum, f. pl., *affairs of the city/town*
5 **pestilentia, -ae,** f., *plague*
10 **pōculum, -ī,** n., *cup, goblet*
14 **locus, -ī,** m., *place*
15 **popīna, -ae,** f., *eating-house, bar*

7 **edō, ēsse, ēdī, ēsus,** irreg., *to eat*
10 **compleō, complēre, complēvī, complētus,** *to fill*
12 **irrumpō, irrumpere, irrūpī, irruptus,** *to burst in*

Exercise 33a
Respondē Latīnē:

1. Quid prīmum ad convīvās portātur?
2. Quid prīmum ē culīnā effertur?
3. Quibus dē rēbus nārrant convīvae?
4. Quās rēs edunt convīvae dum mulsum bibunt?
5. Quid in mediā mēnsā pōnitur post gustātiōnem?
6. Quōmodo intrat Titus in trīclīnium?
7. Cūr Titus sērō vēnit?

Gaius, quamquam īrātissimus erat, nihil tamen dīxit quod hōc tempore frātrem reprehendere nōlēbat. Statim signum servīs dedit. Tum aliī ex eīs porcum scindēbant, aliī carnem ad convīvās portābant. Nōn omnibus dē porcō datum est: clientibus quidem data sunt pullōrum frusta.

Gaius servō, "Puer," inquit, "da frātrī meō quoque frusta pullī! Nōlī eī dē 20 porcō dare!"

Nunc omnēs cibum atque vīnum habēbant. Omnēs cēnam laudābant. Etiam clientēs, quamquam frusta modo habēbant, ūnā cum cēterīs clāmābant, "Euge! Gaius Cornēlius cēnam optimam dare solet. Nēmō meliōrem coquum habet. Nōnne coquum ipsum laudāre dēbēmus?" 25

Itaque coquus vocātus ab omnibus laudātus est.

Tandem fercula ā servīs ablāta sunt. Simul Gaius servōs iussit secundās mēnsās in trīclīnium portāre. Servī, quamquam dēfessī erant, hūc illūc currēbant. Ūvae, māla, pira in trīclīnium portāta sunt. Passum quoque in mēnsā positum omnibus est datum.

16 **īrātissimus, -a, -um,** *most/very angry*
18 **dē porcō datum est,** *some pork was given*
19 **frustum, -ī,** n., *scrap*
23 **ūnā,** adv., *together*
    cēterī, -ae, -a, *the rest, the others*
    Euge! *Hurray!*

24 **coquus, -ī,** m., *cook*
27 **secundae mēnsae, -ārum,** f. pl., *second course, dessert*
28 **ūva, -ae,** f., *grape, bunch of grapes*
    pirum, -ī, n., *pear*
29 **passum, -ī,** n., *raisin-wine*

17 **scindō, scindere, scidī, scissus,** *to cut, split, carve*

Respondē Latīnē:

1. Cūr Gaius nihil dīxit?
2. Quibus convīvīs data sunt frusta pullōrum?
3. Quae Titō data sunt?
4. Cūr coquus vocātus est?
5. Quās rēs convīvae postrēmō edunt?

BUILDING THE MEANING
Perfect Passive Participles I

Look at the following sentence:

    Coquus **vocātus** ab omnibus laudātus est. (33:26)

In Chapter 32 you learned that perfect passive participles are used with forms of **esse** to produce the passive voice of the perfect, pluperfect, and future perfect tenses, e.g., **laudātus est.**

A different use of the perfect passive participle is shown at the beginning of the sentence above. Here the participle **vocātus** modifies a noun and indicates an action that took place before the action of the main verb: the cook was first summoned and then praised. The sentence can be translated in various ways. The most literal translation is:

*The cook, **having been summoned**, was praised by everyone.*

Any of the following translations might make better English:

After being summoned, the cook was praised by everyone.
When summoned, the cook was praised by everyone.
When the cook had been summoned, he was praised by everyone.
The cook was summoned and praised by everyone.

Similarly, the following sentence can be translated in a variety of ways:

Aurēlia neglegentiā eārum **vexāta** speculum ēripuit.
***Having been annoyed** by their carelessness, Aurelia snatched away the mirror.*
 (literal translation)
Annoyed by their carelessness, Aurelia snatched away the mirror.
Because/Since Aurelia was annoyed by their carelessness, she snatched away the mirror.
Aurelia, who was annoyed by their carelessness, snatched away the mirror.

Note from the translations offered above that perfect passive participles can often be translated into English as relative clauses or as clauses introduced by conjunctions such as *when*, *after*, *because*, *since*, or *although*.

The perfect passive participle is a verbal adjective that has the endings of an adjective of the 1st and 2nd declensions (like **magnus, -a, -um**). Therefore, it must agree in gender, case, and number with the noun or pronoun it modifies:

Soleae **dēpositae** ā servīs ablātae sunt. (32:26)
*The sandals **having been set down** were carried away by the slaves.*
The sandals, which had been set down, were carried away by the slaves.

Exercise 33b
Give two translations for each of the following sentences: one in which the perfect passive participle is translated literally and the other in which it is translated using a relative clause or a clause introduced by *when*, *after*, *because*, *since*, or *although*:

1. Convīvae ad cēnam invītātī ā Cornēliō ipsō cōmiter salūtātī sunt.
2. Ancillae festīnāre iussae aquam ad convīvās lentē portāvērunt.
3. Convīvae in trīclīnium ductī in lectīs accubuērunt.
4. Magnum ferculum ā servīs ē culīnā lātum in mediā mēnsā positum est.
5. Servī ā Gaiō iussī frusta pullī frātrī eius dedērunt.
6. Porcus ā servīs scissus ad mēnsam portātus est.
7. Ūvae in trīclīnium portātae omnibus convīvīs datae sunt.
8. Cēna optima ā Cornēliō data ab omnibus laudāta est.
9. Coquus ab omnibus laudātus laetus erat.
10. Titus in trīclīnium ductus, "Salvē, mī frāter!" inquit.

Exercise 33c

During the course of Cornelius' dinner party, the guests would have exchanged news or gossip and entertained one another with stories. The Romans enjoyed stories of magic like the following, an adaptation of a tale told by Niceros, a guest at Trimalchio's dinner party in Petronius' *Satyricon*.

Read aloud and translate:

Ubi adhūc servus eram, in urbe Brundisiō habitābāmus. Illō tempore Melissam amābam, ancillam pulcherrimam quae in vīllā rūsticā habitābat. Forte dominus meus ad urbem proximam abierat; ego igitur Melissam vīsitāre cōnstituī, sōlus tamen īre nōluī. Erat autem mihi amīcus quīdam, quī mēcum īre poterat. Mīles erat, homō fortis et temerārius. 5

Mediā nocte discessimus. Lūna lūcēbat tamquam merīdiē. Vēnimus ad sepulcra prope viam sita. Mīles meus inter sepulcra iit; ego cōnsēdī et stēlās numerābam. Deinde rem mīram vīdī: omnia vestīmenta ab amīcō meō exūta in terrā prope viam dēposita sunt. Dī immortālēs! Nōn per iocum dīcō! Ille subitō lupus factus est! Ego stābam tamquam mortuus. Lupus tamen ululāvit et in 10 silvam fūgit.

Prīmum perterritus eram. Anima mihi in nāsō erat! Deinde ad stēlās prōcessī quod vestīmenta eius īnspicere volēbam. Vestīmenta dēposita tamen lapidea facta erant. Paulisper ibi stābam immōbilis. Gladium tamen strīnxī et umbrās cecīdī dōnec ad vīllam rūsticam pervēnī. Melissa mea ad portam vīllae mihi occurrit. 15 "Dolēmus," inquit, "quod nōn prius vēnistī; auxiliō tuō caruimus. Lupus enim vīllam intrāvit et omnia pecora tamquam lanius necābat. Nec tamen dērīsit. Servus enim noster eum gladiō vulnerāvit."

Ubi haec audīvī, perterritus eram. Neque dormīre neque in vīllā manēre potuī, sed summā celeritāte aufūgī. Postquam vēnī in illum locum in quō 20 vestīmenta lapidea facta erant, invēnī nihil nisi sanguinem. Ubi domum pervēnī, iacēbat mīles meus in lectō tamquam bōs; ā medicō cūrābātur. Tum scīvī mīlitem esse versipellem! Neque posteā potuī aut cum illō pānem esse aut illum amīcum meum vocāre.

2 **forte**, adv., *by chance*

3 **proximus, -a, -um**, *nearby*

6 **lūna, -ae**, f., *moon*
tamquam, conj., *just as if*
merīdiē, adv., *at noon*

7 **situs, -a, -um**, *located, situated*
inter, prep. + acc., *between, among*
stēla, -ae, f., *tombstone*

8 **numerō, -āre, -āvī, -ātus**, *to count*
vestīmentum, -ī, n., *clothing*; pl.,
clothes

9 **Dī immortālēs!** *Immortal gods! Good
heavens!*

10 **ululō, -āre, -āvī, -ātus**, *to howl*

12 **anima, -ae**, f., *soul, "heart"*
nāsus, -ī, m., *nose*

13 **lapideus, -a, -um**, *of stone, stony*

14 **umbra, -ae**, f., *shadow, shade
(of the dead)*
cecīdī, *I slashed at*

15 **donec**, conj., *until*

16 **prius**, adv., *earlier*

17 **pecus, pecoris**, n., *livestock, sheep
and cattle*

18 **vulnerō, -āre, -āvī, -ātus**, *to wound*

21 **sanguis, sanguinis**, m., *blood*

22 **medicus, -ī**, m., *doctor*

23 **versipellis, versipellis**, gen. pl.,
versipellium (**vertō**, *to
change* + **pellis**, *skin*), m., *werewolf*
posteā, adv., *afterward*

8 **exuō, exuere, exuī, exūtus**, *to take off*

12 **prōcēdō, prōcēdere, prōcessī, prōcessūrus**, *to go forward*

16 **careō, carēre, caruī, caritūrus** + abl., *to need, lack*

17 **dērīdeō, dērīdēre, dērīsī, dērīsus**, *to laugh at, get the last laugh*

Roman
tableware

RECIPES AND MENUS

The following are recipes from a Roman cookbook of the fourth century A.D. by Apicius.

STUFFED DORMICE

Stuff the dormice with minced pork, the minced meat of whole dormice, pounded with pepper, pine-kernels, asafetida (a kind of garlic), and fish sauce.* Sew up, place on tile, put in oven, or cook, stuffed, in a small oven.

SALT FISH WITHOUT FISH

Cook liver, grind and add pepper and fish sauce or salt. Add oil. Use rabbit, kid, lamb, or chicken liver; shape into a fish in a small mold, if liked. Sprinkle virgin oil over it.

HOMEMADE SWEETS

1. Stone dates, stuff with nuts, pine-kernels, or ground pepper. Roll in salt, fry in cooked honey, and serve.
2. Remove the crust from wheaten loaf, break up in largish morsels. Steep in milk, fry in oil, pour honey over, and serve.

*A staple of Roman cooking, fish sauce (**liquāmen** or **garum**) was made from a mash of finely chopped fish, which had been placed in the sun to ferment.

While menus must have varied very much between rich and poor people, and even between the day-to-day fare and the banquet for a special occasion, all Latin references to the **cēna** suggest that a basic menu was as follows:

1. **gustātiō** (hors d'oeuvre): egg dishes, eaten with **mulsum** (wine sweetened with honey)
2. **cēna** (the main course or courses): fish, game, poultry, pork, with wine
3. **secundae mēnsae** (dessert): usually fruit, with wine

Clientēs were sometimes invited to fill up spare places, but they were not given as good food and wine as the more important guests. Here a "client" expresses his indignation at this treatment:

> If you are asked to dinner by the great man, this is his way of paying you in full for all your services. So if after a couple of months he takes it into his head to invite you, his overlooked client (he can't leave that third place on the lowest couch unoccupied!), you're meant to feel your dearest prayer has been answered.
>
> Oh dear me! what a meal! You are given wine that fresh-clipped wool wouldn't soak up. The great man himself drinks a brand bottled in the days when consuls wore their hair long.
>
> The cup your host is holding is studded with beryl. No one trusts you with gold, or if you are given a precious cup, there's a slave watching you, and all the gems on it have been counted.

Even the water is different for clients; and it will be given you by the bony hand of a fellow you'd rather not meet at midnight among the tombstones of the Via Latina.

All the big houses are full of insolent slaves these days. Another one will grumble as he hands you a morsel of bread you can hardly break, or lumps of dough gone moldy. For your host meanwhile there is kept a tender loaf, snow-white and made from the choicest flour.

You see that huge lobster he's getting now! You'll get a tiny little crab with half an egg around it.

He is served a lamprey. For you—an eel, first cousin to a water-serpent; or maybe a pike that's made its way to Rome up the sewers.

Before the host a huge goose's liver is placed, and a boar piping hot, then truffles. All you can do is sit and watch.

Before the guests will be set some dubious toadstools; before the host a fine mushroom.

Is it the expense he grudges? Not a bit! What he wants is to see you squirm. There's nothing on earth so funny as a disappointed belly!

Juvenal, *Satires V* (extracts)

In Petronius' novel, the *Satyricon*, we are given a glimpse of an elaborate **cēna** given by the wealthy and ostentatious Gaius Trimalchio. The following excerpt illustrates the lengths to which a host might go in order to impress and entertain his dinner guests. A huge roast pig is brought into the dining room, and Trimalchio, eyeing it critically, suddenly becomes angry:

"What? Hasn't this pig been gutted? I swear it has not. Call the cook in here!" The poor cook came and stood by the table and said that he had forgotten to gut it. "What? Forgotten?" shouted Trimalchio. "Off with his shirt!" In a moment the cook was stripped and stood sadly between two torturers. Then everyone began to beg him off, saying: "These things will happen; do let him go; if he does it again none of us will say a word for him." But Trimalchio's face softened into smiles. "Well," he said, "if your memory is so bad, clean him here in front of us." The cook put on his shirt, seized a knife, and carved the pig's belly in various places with a shaking hand. At once the slits widened under the pressure from within, and sausages and black puddings tumbled out. At this the slaves burst into spontaneous applause and shouted, "God bless Gaius!"

Petronius, *Satyricon* 49–50 (abridged)

REVIEW VII: CHAPTERS 28–33

Exercise VIIa: Relative Pronouns
Give the Latin for the relative pronoun in italics, and then read the sentence aloud and translate it:

1. Aurēlia, (*whose*) crīnēs Phrygia neglegenter pectēbat, vexāta erat.
2. Līberī, (*whose*) clāmōrēs ab Aurēliā et Cornēliā audiēbantur, flammīs oppressī sunt.
3. Sextus, (*to whom*) Syrus iocum Pseudolī nārrāvit, dēlectābātur.
4. Servī, (*whom*) Aurēlia in urbem mīserat, holera, pānem, pullōs ēmērunt.
5. Magnus tumultus, (*which*) Titus extrā trīclīnium fēcit, ā convīvīs audītus est.
6. Coquus vocātus ā convīvīs (*who*) cēnāverant laudātus est.
7. Pseudolus, ā (*whom*) porcus ēmptus est, mercātor esse vidēbātur.
8. Cēnae (*which*) Cornēlius dare solet optimae sunt.
9. Convīvae, (*whom*) Cornēlius invītāverat, iam domum intrābant.
10. Iocus, (*by which*) servī dēlectābantur, ā Pseudolō nārrātus est.

Exercise VIIb: *is, ea, id*
Supply the correct form of **is**, **ea**, **id** to substitute as a pronoun for the italicized word(s), read aloud, and translate:

1. Audīvistīne *iocum* Pseudolī? _____ nōn audīvī.
2. *Pseudolīne* iocum audīvistī? _____ iocum nōn audīvī.
3. Vīdistisne *flammās* in tertiō tabulātō īnsulae? _____ vīdimus.
4. Trāditne lanius porcum et leporem *Pseudolō?* _____ trādit.
5. Quid post cēnam *convīvīs* licēbit? _____ cibum auferre licēbit.
6. In ferculō erant *olīvae nigrae*. _____ ā convīvīs eduntur.

Exercise VIIc: *hic, haec, hoc*
Supply the correct form of **hic**, **haec**, **hoc**, read aloud, and translate:

1. Aurēlia glīrēs in (*this*) tabernā ēmit.
2. Aurēlia et Cornēlia flammās in tertiō tabulātō (*of this*) īnsulae vīdērunt.
3. Pseudolus octō dēnāriōs (*to this*) laniō dedit.
4. (*This*) magnum ferculum porcum ingentem et multōs glīrēs habet.
5. Ab (*these*) servīs holera, pānis, pullī feruntur.

Exercise VIId: Other Adjectives
In the sentences in Exercise VIIc, supply the correct forms of the following where you previously supplied forms of **hic**, **haec**, **hoc**; then read each new sentence aloud, and translate it:

1. quīdam, quaedam, quoddam
2. ipse, ipsa, ipsum
3. īdem, eadem, idem

Exercise VIIe: Passive Forms of Verbs

Give the requested forms of the following verbs in the present, imperfect, future, perfect, pluperfect, and future perfect. Give all forms in the passive voice:

	Present	Imperfect	Future	Perfect	Pluperfect	Future Perfect
1. ferō *(3rd sing.)*	_____	_____	_____	_____	_____	_____
2. commoveō *(1st pl.)*	_____	_____	_____	_____	_____	_____
3. scindō *(infinitive)*	_____					
4. capiō *(2nd sing.)*	_____	_____	_____	_____	_____	_____
5. audiō *(2nd pl.)*	_____	_____	_____	_____	_____	_____
6. commoveō *(infinitive)*	_____					
7. incitō *(1st sing.)*	_____	_____	_____	_____	_____	_____
8. addō *(2nd sing.)*	_____	_____	_____	_____	_____	_____
9. inveniō *(infinitive)*	_____					
10. accipiō *(3rd pl.)*	_____	_____	_____	_____	_____	_____
11. dēmōnstrō *(infinitive)*	_____					
12. dēbeō *(3rd sing.)*	_____	_____	_____	_____	_____	_____

Exercise VIIf: Passive Forms of Verbs

Read aloud and translate:

1. Complūrēs clientēs ā Cornēliō ad cēnam invītātī erant.
2. Soleae ā servīs ablātae sunt.
3. Olīvae et asparagus ab omnibus edēbantur.
4. Coquus ab omnibus convīvīs laudātur.
5. Vīnum allātum omnibus datum est.
6. Illī bōlētī, sī liquāmine aspersī erunt, omnēs convīvās dēlectābunt.
7. Coquus inductus ab omnibus laudātus est.

Exercise VIIg: Passive Forms of Verbs

Complete the following sentences according to the cues provided:

1. Trēs porcī ā Pseudolō _____ _____. (had been bought)
2. Magnum incendium ā praedōnibus _____ _____. (was made)
3. Multae epistulae ā Flāviā _____ _____. (will have been sent)
4. Complūrēs convīvae ā Cornēliō _____ _____. (were invited)
5. Ancilla ab Aurēliā numquam _____ _____. (was praised)
6. Porcus _____ nōn poterat. (to be caught)
7. Coquus _____ vult. (to be praised)

Exercise VIIh: Ablative of Instrument or Means and Ablative of Personal Agent

Identify the phrases that would require the preposition **ā** or **ab**:

1. The first course was carried in by the slaves.
2. Pseudolus was not frightened by Aurelia.
3. The building was overwhelmed by a huge fire.
4. All the guests were delighted by the story.
5. The pig had been raised by the butcher.

Exercise VIIi: Prefixes

Add the given prefixes to the following verbs, and make any necessary changes in the prefix and the verb. Translate the resulting form:

	Compound Verb	Translation
1. re + facimus	_____	_____
2. ex + fūgistī	_____	_____
3. ab + ferēbat	_____	_____
4. in + mīserō	_____	_____
5. ad + capiēbam	_____	_____
6. ad + currēbant	_____	_____
7. con + tenēbās	_____	_____
8. ab + fugiunt	_____	_____
9. ad + tulimus	_____	_____
10. re + ībimus	_____	_____

Orpheus

*Roman mosaic, Blanzy,
Musée Municipal, Laon,
France*

Exercise VIIj: Reading Comprehension

Read the following passage and answer the questions below with full sentences in Latin:

ORPHEUS AND EURYDICE

　　Multae fābulae nārrantur dē Orpheō quī ā Mūsīs doctus erat citharā lūdere. In pictūrā in trīclīniō Cornēliī sitā Orpheus ad īnferōs dēscendit. Cūr? Dēscendit quod uxor eius Eurydicē morte abrepta iam sub terrā ā Plūtōne tenēbātur. Dolōre oppressus Orpheus cōnstituit Plūtōnī appropinquāre et uxōrem ab eō petere.

　　Iānua rēgnī Plūtōnis ā Cerberō, cane ferōcī quī tria habēbat capita, cus- 　5
tōdiēbātur. Orpheus, quod semper ēsuriēbat Cerberus, frusta cibī ad eum coniēcit et, dum cibus arripitur ā Cerberō, in rēgnum intrāvit. Per umbrās ībat Orpheus; uxōrem diū et dīligenter quaerēbat. Tandem Plūtō dolōre eius commōtus, "Licet tibi," inquit, "uxōrem tuam redūcere, sed hāc condiciōne: Eurydicē exībit ad lūcem tē sequēns; tū vetāris eam respicere. Sī tū respiciēs, ea 　10
retrahētur neque umquam iterum ad vīvōs remittētur."

　　Mox Eurydicē ex umbrīs dūcēbātur. Tum Orpheum sequēns ad lūcem lentē ascendēbat. Orpheus, quamquam uxōrem vidēre valdē dēsīderābat, ascendēbat neque respexit. Iam ad lūcem paene adveniēbant cum Orpheus amōre oppressus est. Respexit. Eurydicē revocāta ad Plūtōnem retracta est neque ad lūcem 　15
umquam reddita est.

1　**cithara, -ae,** f., *lyre*
　citharā lūdere, *to play (on) the lyre*
3　**dolor, dolōris,** m., *grief*
5　**ferōx, ferōcis,** *fierce*

9　**condiciō, condiciōnis,** f., *condition, stipulation*
11　**vīvus, -a, -um,** *living*
14　**amor, amōris,** m., *love*

3　**abripiō, abripere, abripuī, abreptus,** *to snatch away*
10　**respiciō, respicere, respexī, respectus,** *to look back (at)*

1. By whom was Orpheus taught to play the lyre?
2. What had happened to Eurydice?
3. Where was Pluto holding Eurydice?
4. Why did Orpheus decide to approach Pluto?
5. Who was guarding the kingdom of Pluto?
6. What was Cerberus doing when Orpheus entered the kingdom of Pluto?
7. Was Pluto moved by Orpheus' grief?
8. What was Orpheus forbidden to do?
9. What will happen to Eurydice if Orpheus looks back at her?
10. What overwhelmed Orpheus?

Translate the following groups of words taken from the story in Exercise VIIj:

1. ā Mūsīs doctus erat (1)
2. uxor eius Eurydicē morte abrepta (3)
3. dolōre oppressus (3–4)
4. Plūtō dolōre eius commōtus (8–9)
5. Eurydicē ex umbrīs dūcēbātur (12)
6. Orpheus amōre oppressus est (14–15)
7. Eurydicē revocāta (15)
8. retracta est (15)
9. reddita est (16)

Go Online

For: Additional Practice
Visit: PHSchool.com
Web Code: jgd-0007

THE COMMISSATIO

The Roman **cēna** was a major occasion in the daily routine. During the meal wine was drunk, usually mixed with water in the drinking-cup (**pōculum**) to suit the drinker's taste, for undiluted wine (**merum**) was thick and sweet.

Sometimes the dessert course (**secundae mēnsae**) was followed by a drinking party (**commissātiō**) for the male guests who were usually supplied with garlands (**corōnae**) to wear on their heads or around their necks. Originally these were worn not merely for ornament but in the belief that their perfume lessened the effect of the wine. Thus garlands were made with flowers (**flōrēs**), especially roses and violets, and also with herbs, such as parsley (**apium**), and with ivy (**hedera**). Later, and especially in winter, garlands were made with other materials such as copper foil or colored silks. Perfumes (**unguenta**) were also liberally provided at the **commissātiō**. These were applied to the hair and face and even mixed with the wine!

At the **commissātiō** a "master of the drinking" (**arbiter bibendī**) was appointed to determine the strength of wine to be drunk. He was often selected by throwing knucklebones (**tālī**) from a cylindrical box (**fritillus**). The **tālī** were oblong, rounded at the two ends, having four sides with the values 1, 3, 4, and 6, respectively. The highest throw was called **Venus**, when the four **tālī** came up all different; the lowest throw was **canis**—four "ones." Another poor throw was **sēniō**—a combination containing sixes.

The **arbiter bibendī** decided the number of measures (**cyathī**) of water to be added to the wine in the bowl. He might also determine the number and order of the toasts: the formula for the toast was **bene** followed by the dative case, as in a play by Plautus:

Bene mihi, bene vōbīs, bene amīcae meae.
Health to me, to you, and to my girlfriend.

**Dice and counting pieces
used by Romans in games**
*Musée Alesia,
Alise-Sainte-Reine, France*

ADDITIONAL READING:
The Romans Speak for Themselves: Book II: "The Commissatio," pages 23–31.

Cornelius' dinner party continues with a **commissātiō**:

Plūs vīnī est allātum, et omnibus convīvīs corōnae flōrum datae sunt. Aliī corōnās rosārum, aliī hederae corōnās induērunt. Gaius apiō modo sē corōnāvit, sed Titus et rosās et unguenta poposcit, nam in popīnā prope Forum multum vīnum iam biberat.

Ūnus ē convīvīs, cui nōmen erat Messalla, clāmāvit, "Quis creābitur arbiter bibendī?"

"Nōn tū certē, Messalla," inquit alter. "Aliī vīnum sine aquā bibunt, sed tū aquam 5 sine vīnō bibis."

Cui Messalla, "Cūr nōn Gaius ipse? Quis enim est prūdentior quam Gaius? Ille enim aquam et vīnum prūdenter miscēbit, neque sinet convīvās nimis vīnī bibere."

"Minimē!" interpellat Titus magnā vōce. "Hōc modō creāre arbitrum nōn licet. Fer tālōs! Nōn nisi tālīs rēctē creātur arbiter bibendī." 10

Paulisper tacēbant omnēs. Tum Gaius, "Estō! Fer tālōs! Necesse est omnia rēctē facere."

Statim igitur tālī cum fritillō allātī in mēnsā positī sunt. Ā Gaiō prīmō iactī sunt tālī. "Est sēniō!" ab omnibus clāmātum est. Deinde ūnus ē convīvīs tālōs mīsit. "Canis!" omnēs cum rīsū clāmāvērunt. Identidem tālī missī sunt, sed nēmō Venerem iēcit. 15

Tandem Titus tālōs arripit et in fritillō magnā cum cūrā pōnit. "Meum Herculem," inquit, "invocō." Tum fritillum vehementer movet. Omnēs Titum attentē spectant. Subitō mittuntur tālī.

"Est Venus!" exclāmat Titus. "Vīcī! Vīcī! Herculēs mihi favet! Nunc tempus est bibendī. Iubeō duās partēs aquae et trēs partēs vīnī." Prīmum tamen merum arripit et 20 pōculum suum complet. "Bene tibi, Gaī!" clāmat et pōculum statim haurit. "Bene tibi, Messalla!" clāmat et iterum pōculum haurit. Subitō collāpsus est.

"Non bene tibi, Tite!" inquit Gaius. "Ēheu! Nimis vīnī iam hausistī." Servī Titum vīnō oppressum auferunt. Titus erat bibendī arbiter pessimus omnium.

1	**plūs vīnī,** *more wine*	9	**modus, -ī,** m., *way, method*
4	**creō, -āre, -āvī, -ātus,** *to appoint*	16	**cūra, -ae,** f., *care*
7	**prūdentior,** *wiser*	17	**invocō, -āre, -āvī, -ātus,** *to invoke,*
	quam, adv., *than*		*call upon*
8	**prūdenter,** adv., *wisely, sensibly*	22	**collāpsus est,** *he collapsed*
	nimis, adv., *too much*	24	**pessimus, -a, -um,** *worst*

3 **poscō, poscere, poposcī,** *to demand, ask for*
8 **misceō, miscēre, miscuī, mixtus,** *to mix*
   sinō, sinere, sīvī, situs, *to allow*
21 **hauriō, haurīre, hausī, haustus,** *to drain*

Exercise 34a
Respondē Latīnē:

1. Quālēs corōnās convīvae induērunt?
2. Quid Titus in popīnā fēcerat?
3. Cūr est Gaius prūdentior quam aliī convīvae?
4. Quid Titus poscit?
5. Quis prīmum tālōs iēcit?
6. Quid Titus arripit?
7. Quem Titus invocat?
8. Quantum vīnī Titus hausit?

BUILDING THE MEANING
Adjectives: Positive, Comparative, and Superlative Degrees

Look at these sentences:

Positive:
Gaius est **laetus**.   *Gaius is **happy**.*

Comparative:
Messalla est **laetior** quam Gaius.   *Messalla is **happier** than Gaius.*

Superlative:
Titus est **laetissimus** omnium.   *Titus is **happiest** of all.*

Adjectives have *positive*, *comparative*, and *superlative degrees*. In the sentences above you can recognize the comparative by the letters *-ior* and the superlative by the letters **-issimus**.

The comparative can have several meanings; for example, **prūdentior** can mean *wiser*, *rather wise*, or *too wise*. In the first sense it is often followed by **quam**, *than*:

Nēmō est **prūdentior** quam Gaius.
*No one is **wiser** than Gaius.*

The superlative can also have several meanings; for example, **prūdentissimus** can mean *wisest* or *very wise*. In the first sense it is often used with a partitive genitive:

Gaius est **prūdentissimus** omnium.
*Gaius is **the wisest** of all.*

The ancient custom of drinking wine was connected to the religious mystery cult of Dionysus (god of the vine), the grape, and of vegetation in general. Pictured is a detail from a Roman fresco depicting followers of Dionysus.
Fresco, Villa dei Misteri, Pompeii, Italy

Exercise 34b

Locate comparative or superlative forms in the following stories or exercises
and translate the sentences in which they occur. Try some of the alternative
translations given above:

1. 29:5–7
2. 31f:11–12
3. 33:24
4. 34:7

FORMS

Adjectives: Positive, Comparative, and Superlative

1. Study these further examples of positive, comparative, and superlative adjectives:

Positive	Comparative	Superlative
1st and 2nd declension adjectives:		
molest*us*, -*a*, -*um*	molest*ior*, molest*ius*	molest*issimus*, -*a*, -*um*
3rd declension adjectives:		
brev*is*, -*is*, -*e*, *short*	brev*ior*, brev*ius*	brev*issimus*, -*a*, -*um*
fēlīx, fēlīc*is*, *lucky*	fēlīc*ior*, fēlīc*ius*	fēlīc*issimus*, -*a*, -*um*
prūdēns, prūdent*is*, *wise*	prūdent*ior*, prūdent*ius*	prūdent*issimus*, -*a*, -*um*

2. Note what happens with adjectives that end in -*er:*

1st and 2nd declension adjectives ending in -*er*:		
miser, miser*a*, miser*um*	miser*ior*, miser*ius*	miser*rimus*, -*a*, -*um*
pulcher, pulchr*a*, pulchr*um*	pulchr*ior*, pulchr*ius*	pulcher*rimus*, -*a*, -*um*
3rd declension adjectives ending in -*er*:		
celer, celer*is*, celer*e*, *swift*	celer*ior*, celer*ius*	celer*rimus*, -*a*, -*um*
ācer, ācr*is*, ācr*e*, *keen*	ācr*ior*, ācr*ius*	ācer*rimus*, -*a*, -*um*

3. Most 3rd declension adjectives that end in -*lis* form their comparatives and
superlatives regularly:

fidēl*is*, -*is*, -*e*, *faithful*	fidēl*ior*, fidēl*ius*	fidēl*issimus*, -*a*, -*um*

Exceptions: six 3rd declension adjectives that end in -*lis* form their superlatives
irregularly, as does **facilis**:

facil*is*, -*is*, -*e*, *easy*	facil*ior*, facil*ius*	facil*limus*, -*a*, -*um*

The other adjectives are **difficilis**, *difficult*; **similis**, *similar*; **dissimilis**, *dissimilar*, **gra-
cilis**, *slender*; and **humilis**, *humble*.

4. Note that you can usually recognize the superlative by the endings -*issimus*, -*rimus*,
or -*limus*.

Exercise 34c

Form the comparatives and superlatives of the following 1st and 2nd declension adjectives (meanings are given for adjectives you have not yet had):

1. longus, -a, -um
2. asper, aspera, asperum, *rough*
3. īrātus, -a, -um
4. scelestus, -a, -um
5. aeger, aegra, aegrum, *sick*

Exercise 34d

Form the comparatives and superlatives of the following 3rd declension adjectives (meanings are given for adjectives you have not yet had):

1. ēlegāns, ēlegantis
2. pinguis, -is, -e
3. celeber, celebris, celebre
4. difficilis, -is, -e, *difficult*
5. nōbilis, -is, -e, *noble*

Irregular Comparative and Superlative Adjectives

Some very common adjectives are irregular in the comparative and superlative:

Positive	Comparative	Superlative
bonus, -a, -um, *good*	melior, melius, *better*	optimus, -a, -um, *best*
malus, -a, -um, *bad*	peior, peius, *worse*	pessimus, -a, -um, *worst*
magnus, -a, -um, *big*	maior, maius, *bigger*	maximus, -a, -um, *biggest*
parvus, -a, -um, *small*	minor, minus, *smaller*	minimus, -a, -um, *smallest*
multus, -a, -um, *much*	plūs,* *more*	plūrimus, -a, -um, *most, very much*
multī, -ae, -a, *many*	plūrēs, plūra, *more*	plūrimī, -ae, -a, *most, very many*

*Note that **plūs** is not an adjective but a neuter substantive, usually found with a partitive genitive, e.g., Titus **plūs vīnī** bibit. *Titus drank **more (of the) wine**.*

Exercise 34e

Complete the comparison of the following adjectives by giving the missing items:

Positive	Comparative	Superlative
longus	_____	longissimus
_____	stultior	stultissimus
_____	melior	_____
multus	_____	_____
_____	_____	maximus
_____	ingentior	ingentissimus
_____	peior	_____
_____	pulchrior	pulcherrimus
_____	minor	_____

Adjectives: Case Endings of Comparatives and Superlatives

All superlatives have the same endings as the 1st and 2nd declension adjective **magnus, magna, magnum**, e.g., **laetissimus, laetissima, laetissimum**.

The comparatives have endings like those of 3rd declension nouns. Here are the forms of the comparative. Note in particular the neuter nominative and accusative singular form: **laetius:**

Number Case	Masc.	Fem.	Neut.
Singular			
Nominative	laetior	laetior	laetius
Genitive	laetiōris	laetiōris	laetiōris
Dative	laetiōrī	laetiōrī	laetiōrī
Accusative	laetiōrem	laetiōrem	laetius
Ablative	laetiōre	laetiōre	laetiōre
Plural			
Nominative	laetiōrēs	laetiōrēs	laetiōra
Genitive	laetiōrum	laetiōrum	laetiōrum
Dative	laetiōribus	laetiōribus	laetiōribus
Accusative	laetiōrēs	laetiōrēs	laetiōra
Ablative	laetiōribus	laetiōribus	laetiōribus

Compare these forms with those of 3rd declension nouns and adjectives. Note the differences from the endings of 3rd declension adjectives.

NOTE:

When given in vocabulary lists, comparatives will be listed as follows: **melior, melior, melius**, gen., **meliōris**, *better*.

Exercise 34f

Change the italicized adjectives to the comparative and then to the superlative. Translate the new sentences. Try some of the alternative translations given above:

1. Gaius, quamquam *īrātus* erat, frātrem nōn reprehendit.
2. Aurēlia, quod erat *sollicita*, ancillās festīnāre iubēbat.
3. Puerī ā Cornēliō vīsī ad cubiculum *parvum* rediērunt.
4. Senātor pecūniam servīs *ignāvīs* nōn dederat.
5. Omnēs convīvae in lectīs *magnīs* accubuērunt.
6. Cēna ā coquō *bonō* parāta ab ancillīs efferēbātur.
7. Ancillae quae hūc illūc currēbant vīnum ad convīvās *fēlīcēs* portāvērunt.
8. Aliī convīvae corōnās rosārum *pulchrārum* induērunt.
9. Plaustrum *novum* ā Cornēliō ēmptum ad vīllam rūsticam missum est.
10. Pater puerī *molestī* mussāvit, "Numquam puerum peiōrem vīdī!"

Exercise 34g

Using story 34 and the presentation of comparative and superlative adjectives as guides, give the Latin for:

1. Titus had already drunk too much wine.
2. No one had drunk more wine.
3. No one is wiser than Gaius, for he always mixes water and wine wisely.
4. Titus was the luckiest when he threw the knucklebones.
5. Titus was very miserable when he collapsed.

Exercise 34h

Take parts, read aloud, and translate:

REFLECTIONS AFTER DINNER

Postquam convīvae discessērunt, nē tum quidem cubitum iērunt Cornēlius et Aurēlia, nam multa dē convīviō inter sē dīcēbant.

AURĒLIA:	Placuitne tibi cēna, Gaī?
CORNĒLIUS:	Ita vērō! Tū quidem omnia optimē ēgistī. Coquus nōbīs cēnam parāvit optimam quae ab omnibus laudābātur. 5 Quam ingēns erat ille porcus! Maiōrem porcum numquam vīdī. Glīrēs quoque suāviōrēs numquam ēdī.
AURĒLIA:	Cūr tam sērō advēnit Titus? Quid eī acciderat?
CORNĒLIUS:	Nihil! Amīcō veterī in popīnā occurrerat!
AURĒLIA:	In popīnā? Ubi? 10
CORNĒLIUS:	Prope Forum Rōmānum.
AURĒLIA:	Omnēs popīnae sunt foedae, sed foedissimae omnium sunt popīnae prope Forum sitae.
CORNĒLIUS:	Ita vērō! Iam ēbrius erat cum in trīclīnium irrūpit. Omnēs convīvae erant īrātissimī. 15
AURĒLIA:	Fit in diēs molestior.
CORNĒLIUS:	Sed hāc nocte erat molestissimus.
AURĒLIA:	Quōmodo?
CORNĒLIUS:	Missī sunt tālī; arbiter bibendī creātus est ille; iussit duōs cyathōs aquae et trēs cyathōs vīnī! 20
AURĒLIA:	Paulātim igitur fīēbat magis ēbrius?
CORNĒLIUS:	Minimē! Statim factus est maximē ēbrius, nam nīl nisi merum bibit! "Bene tibi, Gaī!" clāmat et, "Bene tibi, Messalla!" tum collāpsus est vīnō oppressus. Hominem magis ēbrium quam Titum numquam vīdī. 25
AURĒLIA:	Quid tum accidit?
CORNĒLIUS:	Iussī servōs eum lectīcā portāre domum quam celerrimē.
AURĒLIA:	Fortasse crās fīet vir vīnō abstinentissimus!
CORNĒLIUS:	Fortasse!

1 **nē...quidem,** *not even*
2 **convīvium, -ī,** n., *feast, banquet*
3 **placeō, -ēre, -uī** + dat., *to please*
4 **optimē,** adv., *very well, excellently*
7 **suāvis, -is, -e,** *sweet, delightful*
9 **vetus, veteris,** *old*
12 **foedus, -a, -um,** *filthy, disgusting*
14 **ēbrius, -a, -um,** *drunk*
16 **in diēs,** *every day, day by day*

20 **cyathus, -ī,** m., *small ladle, measure (of wine)*
21 **paulātim,** adv., *gradually*
   magis, adv., *more*
22 **maximē,** adv., *very much, very*
   nīl, *nothing*
27 **quam celerrimē,** adv., *as quickly as possible*
28 **vīnō abstinēns,** *refraining from wine, abstemious*

16 **fīō, fierī, factus sum,** irreg., *to become, be made, be done, happen*

Exercise 34i

Here is a famous poem by Catullus (ca. 84–54 B.C.), in which he extends a dinner invitation to his friend Fabullus. This is a piece of original Latin that you can easily read at this stage with the help of the vocabulary given below. After reading the poem consider whether the invitation to dinner is serious or facetious.

Read aloud and translate:

> Cēnābis bene, mī Fabulle, apud mē
> paucīs, sī tibi dī favent, diēbus,
> sī tēcum attuleris bonam atque magnam
> cēnam, nōn sine candidā puellā
> et vīnō et sale et omnibus cachinnīs.   5
> Haec sī, inquam, attuleris, venuste noster,
> cēnābis bene: nam tuī Catullī
> plēnus sacculus est arāneārum.
> Sed contrā accipiēs merōs amōrēs
> seu quid suāvius ēlegantiusvest: 10
> nam unguentum dabo, quod meae puellae
> dōnārunt Venerēs Cupīdinēsque,
> quod tū cum olfaciēs, deōs rogābis,
> tōtum ut tē faciant, Fabulle, nāsum.

—Catullus 13

2 **paucī, -ae, -a,** *few*
4 **candidus, -a, -um,** *white, fair-skinned, beautiful*
5 **sal, salis,** m., *salt, wit*
6 **venuste noster,** *my charming fellow*
8 **sacculus, -ī,** m., *small bag (used for holding money)*
   arānea, -ae, f., *cobweb*
9 **contrā,** adv., *in return*
   merus, -a, -um, *pure*
10 **seu = sīve,** conj., *or if*

quid suāvius ēlegantiusvest
   (= ēlegantiusve est), *there is anything sweeter or more elegant*
   -ve, enclitic conj., *or*
12 **dōnō, -āre, -āvī, -ātus,** *to give*
   dōnārunt = dōnāvērunt
   Venus, Veneris, f., *Venus (the goddess of love)*
   Cupīdō, Cupīdinis, m., *Cupid (the son of Venus)*
14 **ut tē faciant,** *that they make you*

Go Online

For: Additional Practice
Visit: PHSchool.com
Web Code: jgd-0008

CRIME

Postquam Aurēlia cubitum iit, Cornēlius adhūc in ātriō manēbat sollicitus. Eucleidēs enim māne ierat domum frātris quī in colle Quirīnālī habitābat. Iam media nox erat neque Eucleidēs domum redierat. Quid eī acciderat?

Tandem intrāvit Eucleidēs, sanguine aspersus. Cornēlius, "Dī immortālēs! Quid tibi accidit?" clāmāvit. Eucleidēs nihil respondit; ad terram ceciderat. Statim servī ad ātrium 5 vocātī celerrimē concurrērunt. Eucleidēs in lectō positus est et vulnera eius lauta atque ligāta sunt. Diū iacēbat immōbilis. Tandem animum recuperāvit et lentē oculōs aperuit. Postquam aliquid vīnī bibit, rem tōtam explicāvit.

"Hodiē māne, dum in urbem dēscendō, poētae cuidam occurrī cui nōmen est Marcus Valerius Mārtiālis. Breviōre itinere mē dūxit ad eam īnsulam in quā habitat frāter meus. 10 Plūrima dē praedōnibus huius urbis mihi nārrāvit. Ego tamen vix eī crēdidī. Sed, ubi īnsulae iam appropinquābāmus, hominēs quōsdam in popīnam intrantēs cōnspeximus.

"'Cavē illōs!' inquit Mārtiālis. 'Illī sunt praedōnēs scelestissimī. Nocte sōlus per hās viās ambulāre nōn dēbēs.'"

(continued)

2 **collis, collis,** gen. pl., **collium,** m., *hill*	4 **deus, -ī,** m., *god*
Quirīnālis, -is, -e, *Quirinal (referring to the Quirinal Hill, one of the seven hills of Rome)*	6 **vulnus, vulneris,** n., *wound*
	7 **ligō, -āre, -āvī, -ātus,** *to bind up*

11 **crēdō, crēdere, crēdidī, crēditus** + dat., *to trust, believe*

Exercise 35a
Respondē Latīnē:

1. Cūr Cornēlius sollicitus in ātriō manēbat?
2. Quō māne ierat Eucleidēs?
3. Quid fēcērunt servī Cornēliī, postquam Eucleidēs cecidit?
4. Quid fēcit Eucleidēs, postquam tandem animum recuperāvit?
5. Cui occurrit Eucleidēs, dum in urbem dēscendit?

"Tōtum diem apud frātrem meum mānsī. Post cēnam optimam domum redīre 15
cōnstituī. Quamquam nox erat, nihil perīculī timēbam. Sēcūrus igitur per Subūram
ambulābam cum subitō ē popīnā quādam sē praecipitāvērunt duo hominēs quī fūstēs
ferēbant. Timōre affectus, celerius ambulābam. Facile tamen mē cōnsecūtī sunt. Ab
alterō percussus sum, sed baculō mē fortissimē dēfendī. Tum ā tergō ab alterō correptus
ad terram cecidī. Mihi est adēmptum baculum, adēmpta pecūnia. Abiērunt illī rīdentēs. 20
Diū prōnus in lutō iacēbam. Tandem surrēxī et summā difficultāte domum rediī."

Cornēlius, "Doleō quod vulnera gravia accēpistī. Stultissimus tamen fuistī."

Cui Eucleidēs, "Ita vērō, domine! Sed iam prūdentior sum. Nōn iterum nocte sōlus
per viās urbis ambulābō."

16 **sēcūrus, -a, -um,** *carefree, unconcerned*
Subūra, -ae, f., *Subura (a section of
Rome off the Forum, known for its
night life)*
17 **fūstis, fūstis,** gen. pl., **fūstium,** m.,
club, cudgel
18 **timor, timōris,** m., *fear*
affectus, -a, -um, *affected, overcome*

celerius, adv., *more quickly*
facile, adv., *easily*
cōnsecūtī sunt, *they overtook*
19 **fortissimē,** adv., *most/very bravely*
tergum, -ī, n., *back, rear*
21 **prōnus, -a, -um,** *face down*
summus, -a, -um, *greatest, very great*
22 **gravis, -is, -e,** *heavy, serious*

19 **percutiō, percutere, percussī, percussus,** *to strike*
corripiō, corripere, corripuī, correptus, *to seize, grab*
20 **adimō, adimere, adēmī, adēmptus** + dat., *to take away (from)*

Respondē Latīnē:

1. Quibus occurrit Eucleidēs, dum domum redit?
2. Quid fēcērunt praedōnēs, postquam Eucleidem cōnsecūtī sunt?
3. Quid est perīculōsissimum nocte facere?

BUILDING THE MEANING
Comparisons

Latin sentences in which a direct comparison is made may take one of two patterns:

Sextus est molestior **quam** Marcus.   *Sextus is more annoying **than** Marcus.*
Sextus est molestior **Marcō.**

In the first example, **quam** (*than*) is used with the same case on either side of it (i.e.,
molestior and **Marcus** are both nominative). In the second example, no word for "than"
is used, and **Marcō** is ablative.

Sometimes an ablative (e.g., **multō,** *much*; **paulō,** *a little*) is used with comparatives to
indicate the degree of difference. This is called the *ablative of degree of difference*:

Sextus est **multō** molestior quam   *Sextus is more annoying **by much** than
Marcus.*   *Marcus.*
Sextus est **multō** molestior Marcō.   *Sextus is **much** more annoying than Marcus.*

Exercise 35b

Using the following lists of names and comparative adjectives, make up pairs of sentences that express comparisons according to the patterns in the discussion above:

Marcus, Sextus, Aurēlia, Cornēlius, Cornēlia, Flāvia, Eucleidēs, Titus, Dāvus, Pseudolus
minor, maior, pulchrior, īrātior, laetior, miserior, scelestior, prūdentior, stultior, dīligentior

dīligēns, dīligentis, *diligent, painstaking, thorough*

Exercise 35c

Using the names and adjectives from Exercise 35b above, and changing each adjective to superlative, make one sentence for each name, according to the following examples:

Dāvus est dīligentissimus omnium.
Flāvia est miserrima omnium.

Exercise 35d

Read aloud and translate:

1. Hic servus est ignāvissimus omnium. Nūllum servum ignāviōrem habet Cornēlius.
2. Cornēliī coquus est optimus omnium. Nēmō meliōrem coquum habet quam Cornēlius.
3. Līberī laetissimī sunt quod crās fēriātī erunt.
4. Mārtiālis Eucleide est multō prūdentior.
5. Ego semper habeō multō minus pecūniae quam tū.
6. Marcus est maximus līberōrum, Sextus est minimus.
7. Flāvia est paulō minor Marcō, sed multō maior Cornēliā.
8. Ad amīcum epistulam longissimam mittam, ad frātrem breviōrem.
9. Dāvus est servus optimus. Sine dubiō nēmō est dīligentior.
10. Coquus plūs cibī in culīnā parābat.

▬▬▬▬

Exēgī monumentum aere perennius. *I have erected a monument more lasting than bronze.* (Horace, *Odes* III.30.1)
Fāmā nihil est celerius. *Nothing is swifter than rumor.* (adapted from Vergil, *Aeneid* IV.174)
Mea mihi cōnscientia plūris est quam omnium sermō. *My conscience is more to me than what the world says.* (Cicero, *Letters to Atticus* XII.28.2)

▬▬▬▬

Adverbs

In Chapter 13, adverbs were presented as words that expand the meaning of a sentence by modifying verbs, other adverbs, or adjectives. Sometimes adverbs are formed from adjectives, but many adverbs are not.

Exercise 35e

In story 35, locate the following adverbs that are not formed from adjectives, and tell what word each modifies:

1. 35:1, adhūc.
2. 35:2, māne.
3. 35:2, iam.
4. 35:4, tandem.
5. 35:5, statim.
6. 35:7, diū.
7. 35:9, hodiē māne.
8. 35:11, vix.
9. 35:14, nōn.
10. 35:23, iterum.

FORMS
Adverbs: Positive

1. Adverbs may be formed from adjectives of the 1st and 2nd declensions by adding *-ē* to the base of the adjective:

Adjective	Adverb
strēnu**us**, **-a**, **-um**	strēnu**ē**, *strenuously, hard*

   But note:

bon**us**, **-a**, **-um**	ben**e**, *well*
mal**us**, **-a**, **-um**	mal**e**, *badly*

2. Adverbs may be formed from adjectives of the 3rd declension by adding *-iter* to the base of the adjective or *-er* to bases ending in **-nt**:

brev**is**, **-is**, **-e**	brev**iter**, *briefly*
prūdēns, prūdent**is**	prūdent**er**, *wisely*

   But note:

facil**is**, **-is**, **-e**	facil**e**, *easily*.

Exercise 35f

Give the adverbs (and their meanings) that may be formed from these adjectives:

1. **ignāvus, -a, -um,** *lazy*
2. **fortis, -is, -e,** *brave*
3. **lentus, -a, -um,** *slow*
4. **neglegēns, neglegentis,** *careless*
5. **miser, misera, miserum,** *unhappy*
6. **ferōx, ferōcis,** *fierce*
7. **gravis, -is, -e,** *serious*
8. **laetus, -a, -um,** *happy*
9. **vehemēns, vehementis,** *violent*
10. **īrātus, -a, -um,** *angry*
11. **celer, celeris, celere,** *swift*
12. **pulcher, pulchra, pulchrum,** *beautiful*

Adverbs: Comparative and Superlative

Adverbs also have comparative and superlative forms.

The neuter singular comparative adjective (ending in *-ius*) is used as the comparative adverb.

The superlative adjective ends in *-us, -a, -um*; the superlative adverb ends in *-ē*. Study these examples:

laet*ē, happily*	laet*ius*	laet*issimē*
fēlīc*iter, luckily*	fēlīc*ius*	fēlīc*issimē*
celer*iter, quickly*	celer*ius*	celer*rimē*
prūdent*er, wisely*	prūdent*ius*	prūdent*issimē*

Note the following as well:

diū, *for a long time*	diūt*ius*	diūt*issimē*
saepe, *often*	saep*ius*	saep*issimē*
sērō, *late*	sēr*ius*	sēr*issimē*

Some adverbs are irregular. Compare these forms with their related adjectives:

bene, *well*	**melius,** *better*	**optimē,** *best*
male, *badly*	**peius,** *worse*	**pessimē,** *worst*
facile, *easily*	**facilius,** *more easily*	**facillimē,** *most easily*
magnopere, *greatly*	**magis,** *more*	**maximē,** *most*
paulum, *little*	**minus,** *less*	**minimē,** *least*
multum, *much*	**plūs,** *more*	**plūrimum,** *most*

Be sure to learn these forms thoroughly.

The comparative adverb, like the comparative adjective, can have several meanings; for example, **lentius** can mean *more slowly*, *rather slowly*, or *too slowly*. In the first sense it may be followed by a comparison using **quam** or the ablative without **quam** (cf. note on comparisons, p. 72):

> Eucleidēs lentius **quam** puerī ambulat.
> Eucleidēs lentius **puerīs** ambulat.
> *Eucleides walks more slowly **than** the boys.*

The ablative of degree of difference may be used with comparative adverbs:

> Eucleidēs **multō** lentius quam puerī ambulat.
> Eucleidēs **multō** lentius puerīs ambulat.
> *Eucleides walks **much** more slowly than the boys.*

The superlative adverb, like the superlative adjective, also has more than one meaning; for example, **lentissimē** can mean *most slowly* or *very slowly*. In the first sense it is often followed by a partitive genitive:

> Dāvus lentissimē **omnium** ambulat.
> *Davus walks most slowly **of all**.*

Exercise 35g
Study the forms in the completed columns and then fill in the other columns.
Be sure you can give the meaning of every form:

Adjectives			Adverbs		
longus	longior	longissimus	longē	_____	_____
lentus	_____	_____	lentē	lentius	lentissimē
pulcher	pulchrior	pulcherrimus	pulchrē	_____	_____
fortis	fortior	fortissimus	fortiter	_____	_____
brevis	brevior	brevissimus	breviter	_____	_____
facilis	_____	_____	facile	facilius	facillimē
certus	certior	certissimus	certē	_____	_____
fidēlis	_____	_____	fidēliter	fidēlius	fidēlissimē
rēctus	_____	_____	rēctē	rēctius	rēctissimē
ferōx	ferōcior	ferōcissimus	ferōciter	_____	_____

longē, adv., *far*
certus, -a, -um, *certain*
rēctus, -a, -um, *right, proper*

Exercise 35h

Read aloud and translate. Try some of the alternative translations suggested above:

1. Diūtius manēre mihi nōn licet. Necesse est mihi celerrimē ad urbem redīre.
2. Hic puer optimē omnium scrībit.
3. Nēmō celerius quam frāter meus currere potest.
4. Sextus paulō celerius Marcō currere potest.
5. Dē perīculīs viārum saepissimē audīvimus.
6. Per viās urbis lentē ambulāre volō.
7. Cornēlius īrātissimus erat quod frāter sērius advēnit.
8. Titus plūrimum bibit.
9. Eucleidī praedōnēs pecūniam adēmērunt atque quam celerrimē discessērunt.
10. Sextus in hortō quam diūtissimē lūdēbat.

> **quam** + a superlative adjective or adverb = *as…as possible*, e.g., **quam celerrimē**, *as quickly as possible*

Exercise 35i

Using story 35 and the presentation of adverbs as guides, give the Latin for:

1. Eucleides returned home very late.
2. He lay motionless a long time and regained his senses rather slowly.
3. Eucleides had walked through the Subura too bravely and had feared no danger.
4. When two men hurled themselves out of a bar, Eucleides ran as quickly as possible.
5. He lay in the mud a very long time.

Canis timidus vehementius lātrat quam mordet. *A timid dog barks more fiercely than he bites.* (adapted from Q. Curtius Rufus, *Exploits of Alexander* VII.4.13)

ALTIUS, CITIUS, FORTIUS *Higher, faster, stronger.* (Motto of the Olympic Games)

ADDITIONAL READING:
The Romans Speak for Themselves: Book II: "Violence in the Streets of Rome," pages 33–39.

CICERO, CAESAR, AND THE COLLAPSE OF THE REPUBLIC

Marcus Tullius Cicero reached the peak of his political career in 63 B.C., when he took office as one of the consuls. As an equestrian from Arpinum and a **novus homō**, he had plied his skills as an orator to fuel his rise to the top magistracy. His main opponent in the election had been the ruthless aristocrat Lucius Sergius Catilina, who conspired to assassinate Cicero as part of a plot to overthrow the government and seize power by force. In a series of actions that one can track in Cicero's four famous orations *Against Catiline (In Catilinam)*, the consul drove Catiline out of the city, publicized the details of his plot, and saw to the execution of a group of co-conspirators. Catiline attempted to continue his rebellion from his military base in Etruria. He died, however, in a battle with the Roman army in 62 B.C. Cicero thereafter earnestly advocated a "concord of orders" (**concordia ōrdinum**), the joining together of senators and equestrians to work in support of the republican constitution.

Cicero and the magistrates discovering the tomb of Archimedes
Oil on canvas by Benjamin West, Christie's, London, England

At this point in time, 62 B.C., Pompey returned from his successful campaigns in the East and, contrary to the fears of many, disbanded his army. But many Senators feared the growing power of the popular military hero and refused to approve land grants to Pompey's veterans. He formed a three-man political alliance (**factiō**) with Caesar and Crassus, whose own ambitions were being blocked by the same people. Their alliance is known as the First Triumvirate. Caesar, with the help of Pompey's armed veterans, won passage in 59 B.C. of the veterans' land bill. Caesar's reward for his key effort in this success was a five-year term as proconsular governor of the province of Cisalpine Gaul and Illyricum, which gave him the opportunity to conquer Transalpine Gaul. Crassus obtained financial concessions for wealthy equestrians who backed him.

During the first year of his proconsulship, Caesar led his legions to a rapid succession of victories. By 50 B.C., he had all of Transalpine Gaul under his legions' control and had annexed it as a new province of Rome's empire. Further, he crossed the English Channel and attacked Britain.

While Caesar was away campaigning in Gaul, the political scene in Rome grew violent as **populārēs** and **optimātēs** battled one another for power. One victim who survived physically was Cicero, but his career as a political leader and the moderate voice of the **optimātēs** was destroyed.

The death of Julia, Pompey's wife and Caesar's daughter, weakened the triumvirate in 54 B.C. In the following year, the **factiō** broke apart completely when Crassus was killed in battle against the Parthian Empire in Syria. Violence in the streets escalated as political mobs beset one another, armed factions scuffled, and mass riots erupted. In 52 B.C. the Senate authorized Pompey to quell the rioting in Rome by using his troops and then got him elected sole consul. Leading **optimātēs** in the Senate steadily pressed him to turn against the popular hero Caesar, whom Pompey increasingly viewed as his chief rival now that Crassus was dead.

In January of 49 B.C. the Senate issued a **senātūs cōnsultum ultimum** empowering Pompey to direct Caesar to disband his army. Caesar responded by leading his legions across the Rubicon River, the northern boundary of Italy, and beginning an advance toward Rome. Civil war erupted with Caesar fighting Pompey and the leading **optimātēs**, who were now backing him in the Senate.

As Caesar rapidly advanced toward Rome, Pompey and his allies fled to Greece, where Pompey could recruit and train a new army. His plan, apparently, was to be able to attack Caesar in Italy with both this eastern army and his troops stationed in Spain. Once Pompey had abandoned Italy, Caesar, with almost no opposition, became the master of Rome.

Caesar began to build a fleet so that he could go after Pompey. While his ships were being prepared, he crossed over land into Spain and quickly subdued Pompey's army there. Thus he removed the threat of being surrounded. Then he returned to Rome, secured the consulship, and set sail for Greece. After a nearly disastrous attempt to defeat Pompey in a siege at Dyrrhacchium, Caesar was forced to withdraw to Thessaly, with

Pompey in pursuit. On the plain of Pharsalus in August of 48 B.C., however, Caesar's battle-hardened legions routed Pompey's larger army. Pompey managed to escape and flee to Egypt, in hope of finding refuge there, but the agents of King Ptolemy XIII murdered him and sent his head to Caesar.

Caesar became dictator in October of the same year and followed Pompey's trail to Egypt, where he began a three-year series of campaigns that would finalize his victory as the head of the Roman state. In Alexandria, Caesar fought against King Ptolemy and deposed him. He then set Cleopatra on the throne to assure that Egypt would be friendly to Rome. From there Caesar advanced to Asia Minor and defeated Pharnaces, son of Mithridates, in a war that lasted only days. This victory, the story goes, prompted Caesar's dispatch to Rome, "I came, I saw, I conquered" (**Vēnī, vīdī, vīcī**). In 46 B.C. Caesar celebrated his Gallic, Alexandrian, Pontic, and African triumphs, all in the span of one month. Gigantic parades celebrated Caesar's achievements, displaying the rich spoils from conquered lands and famous prisoners of war and raised his popularity to new heights. The following year, Caesar went once more to Spain, where he wiped out the last of the resistance forces, which were under the command of Pompey's sons.

Territory of the Late Roman Republic

Julius Caesar
Compidoglio, Rome, Italy

In 44 B.C. Caesar was the unchallenged head of the Roman state. He accepted the title "dictator for life" (**dictātor perpetuus**). As dictator Caesar continued his program of reforms. He granted Roman citizenship to people in Gallia Narbonensis and sent Romans from the city to create colonies in the provinces, thus increasing his number of clients. There was also a public works program: expanding the Forum, building the Basilica Julia and the temple of Venus Genetrix, and rebuilding the Curia. Through the so-called Julian reform, Caesar adapted an Egyptian solar calendar, which we still use today in modified form, for use in Rome.

Caesar made it increasingly clear that he intended to rule Rome himself and not to bring back the Senate-dominated republican constitution. He weakened the old guard's power in the Senate by appointing a diverse group of new senators from the equestrian order and from cities in other parts of Italy. The **optimātēs** resented Caesar's evident desire to be king, especially when they saw him put on a purple robe and sit on a golden chair. Romans had hated the title "king" (**rēx**) since the ouster of Tarquinius Superbus and could not easily accept the thought that one man might change the government of the free city-state of Rome into a monarchy, although the old form of government was ill-suited for ruling an empire. On the Ides of March, 44 B.C., a group of Roman senators, armed with daggers and led by Gaius Cassius and Marcus Brutus, assassinated Caesar under the gaze of Pompey's statue. By their plot they hoped to rescue the Republic from the threat of the would-be tyrant.

WORD STUDY IX

Adjective Suffixes *-ōsus*, *-idus*, and *-bilis*

When added to the base of a Latin noun, the suffix *-ōsus*, *-ōsa*, *-ōsum* creates an adjective meaning *full of*…:

>   **fābula, -ae**, f., *story*
>   base: **fābul-** + *-ōsus* = **fābulōsus, -a, -um**, *"full of story,"* *legendary*

English words derived from these adjectives commonly end in *-ous* (sometimes *-ious*, *-eous*, or *-ose*), e.g., *fabulous*, which means "astonishing" (as in legend or myth).

Exercise 1
Give the Latin adjective ending in *-ōsus* for each of the nouns below and give its English derivative. Give also the meaning of the Latin adjective and its English derivative. Is the meaning of the English derivative the same as that of the Latin adjective?

1. **numerus, -ī**, m.
2. **onus, oneris**, n.
3. **pretium, -ī**, n. (*in the derivative* t *changes to* c)
4. **glōria, -ae**, f.
5. **cūra, -ae**, f.
6. **labor, labōris**, m.
7. **tumultus, -ūs**, m. (*add* u *to base:* **tumultu-**)
8. **iocus, -ī**, m. (*derivative begins with* j *and ends in* -ose)
9. **perīculum, -ī**, n. (*derivative drops* -cu- *from* **perīculum**)
10. **verbum, -ī**, n., *word*

The addition of the suffix *-idus*, *-ida*, *-idum* to the base of the present infinitive of a Latin verb (often of the 2nd conjugation) creates a Latin adjective meaning *tending to*… or *inclined to*…:

>   **timēre**, *to fear*
>   infinitive base: **tim-** + *-idus* = **timidus, -a, -um**, *"tending to fear,"* *afraid*

Exercise 2

For each Latin verb below, give the Latin adjective ending in *-idus* and give its English derivative. Use the English derivative in a sentence that illustrates its meaning:

1. **sordēre,** *to be dirty*
2. **stupēre,** *to be astonished*
3. **placēre,** *to please, to be agreeable*
4. **vīvere,** *to be alive, to live*
5. **valēre,** *to be strong*
6. **rapere,** *to seize, to tear away*
7. **lūcēre,** *to be light, to shine*
8. **frīgēre,** *to be cold*

The suffix *-bilis, -bilis, -bile*, when added to the base of the present infinitive (sometimes the perfect passive participial stem) of a Latin verb, creates an adjective that usually means *able to be*.... In adjectives formed from 1st conjugation verbs, the suffix is preceded by **-ā-**; in adjectives formed from verbs of other conjugations, the suffix is preceded by **-i-**:

> **laudāre,** *to praise*
> infinitive base: **laud-** + **-ā-** + *-bilis* = **laudābilis, -is, -e,** *"able to be praised,"*
>   *praiseworthy*

> **reprehendere,** *to scold*
> perfect passive participial stem: **reprehēns-** + **-i-** + *-bilis* = **reprehēnsibilis, -is,**
>   **-e,** *"able to be scolded," blameworthy*

English words derived from these Latin adjectives generally end in *-ble*, e.g., *laudable* and *reprehensible*.

Note that whether the English word ends in *-able* or *-ible* is usually determined by the conjugation of the original Latin verb: *-able* usually comes from a Latin verb of the 1st conjugation and *-ible* from a verb of one of the other conjugations.

Exercise 3

For each of the following Latin verbs, give the adjective ending in *-bilis*, and give the English derivative and its meaning. Use the infinitive base in Nos. 1–9, and the perfect passive participial stem in No. 10.

1. audīre
2. crēdere
3. excūsāre
4. habitāre
5. legere

6. portāre
7. revocāre
8. vincere
9. vulnerāre
10. vidēre

N.B.: On some Latin adjectives (and their English derivatives), the suffix *-bilis* means *able to....* rather than *able to be....* The following verbs produce adjectives of this type:

11. dēlectāre
12. stāre
13. terrēre

Latin in the Law

One of the greatest achievements of the Romans was the spread of the rule of law throughout their empire. From its first codification in the Law of the Twelve Tables in the fifth century B.C. to its ultimate expression in the *Corpus iuris civilis* of the emperor Justinian in the sixth century A.D., Roman law formed the foundation for the development of modern legal systems. The rights of inheritance, the notion of private property, the sanctity of contracts—these and many other common legal concepts have their origins in Roman law.

It is not surprising, therefore, that Latin words and phrases are still in use in the practice of law today. Some of these Latin legal expressions have been incorporated into everyday English. For example, an *alibi* (Latin for *elsewhere*) in law is a claim that the accused was not at the scene of the crime and is therefore not guilty; in everyday language, however, the word refers to any sort of excuse.

Exercise 4

Look up the italicized expressions in an English dictionary (or a law dictionary) and explain the meaning of each of the following phrases:

1. a *prima facie* case
2. a plea of *nolo contendere*
3. to serve a *subpoena*
4. the *onus probandi* of the prosecution
5. a writ of *habeas corpus*
6. the responsibility of the school *in loco parentis*
7. the necessary *corpus delicti*
8. an *ex post facto* law
9. a *bona fide* (*mala fide*) offer
10. an offense *malum in se* (*malum prohibitum*)
11. *de facto* (*de jure*) segregation
12. testimony of an *amicus curiae*
13. caught *in flagrante delicto*
14. a claim that the accused is *non compos mentis*

Exercise 5

Give an example to illustrate each of these Latin legal maxims:

1. Ignorantia legis neminem excusat. *Ignorance of the law is no excuse.*
2. Caveat emptor. *Let the buyer beware.*
3. Res ipsa loquitur. *The matter speaks for itself.*
4. De minimis non curat lex. *The law does not concern itself with trifles.*
5. Nemo est supra leges. *No one is above the law.*
6. Publicum bonum privato est praeferendum. *Public good is to be preferred over private.*
7. Potior est conditio possidentis. *Possession is nine-tenths of the law.*
8. Qui tacet consentire videtur. *Silence is taken as consent.*
9. Qui facit per alium, facit per se. *He who acts through another acts by himself.*
10. Nemo debet bis vexari pro una et eadem causa. *No one ought to be tried twice for one and the same reason.*

Go Online

For: Additional Practice
Visit: PHSchool.com
Web Code: jgd-0009

A LETTER

Cornēlia Flāviae S.D.

Hodiē Nōnīs Novembribus illam epistulam accēpī quam tū scrīpsistī Kalendīs Novembribus. Eam iterum iterumque lēgī, quod tē maximē dēsīderō. Quam celeriter tua epistula hūc advēnit! Quīnque modo diēbus! Herī aliam epistulam Brundisiī scrīptam accēpit pater meus. Haec epistula ā Valeriō prīdiē Īdūs Octōbrēs scrīpta Rōmam post vīgintī diēs advēnit! 5

Valerius, ut scīs, est adulēscēns pulcher et strēnuus quī cum patre suō diū in Bīthȳniā morātus est. Nunc in Italiam Brundisium regressus est. Brundisiō Īdibus Novembribus proficīscētur et Rōmam a.d. iii Kal. Dec. adveniet.

Quam libenter eum rūrsus vidēbō! Sānē tamen multō libentius tē vidēbō ubi tū Rōmam veniēs! Tum tē libentissimē nōs omnēs accipiēmus! 10

(continued)

Note that the Romans did not start a letter with "Dear So-and-So." They put the name of the person sending it (in the nominative case) followed by the name of the person to whom it was sent (in the dative case), and after that the letters **S.D.** (**salūtem dīcit,** *sends greetings*) or **S.P.D.** (**salūtem plūrimam dīcit,** *sends fondest greetings*). There was no signature at the end, but simply the word **valē.**

2 **Nōnīs Novembribus,** *on November 5*
   Kalendīs Novembribus, *on November 1*
3 **-que,** enclitic conj., *and*
4 **hūc,** adv., *here, to here*
   Brundisiī, *at Brundisium*
5 **prīdiē,** adv. + acc., *on the day before*
      prīdiē Īdūs Octōbrēs, *on October 14*
6 **vīgintī,** *twenty*
7 **adulēscēns, adulēscentis,** m., *young man*

8 **morātus est,** *he has stayed*
   regressus est, *he has returned*
   Īdibus Novembribus, *on November 13*
9 **proficīscētur,** *he will set out*
   a.d. iii Kal. Dec. = ante diem tertium Kalendās Decembrēs, *on November 29*
10 **libenter,** adv., *gladly*
   rūrsus, adv., *again*
   sānē, adv., *certainly, of course*

Exercise 36a
Respondē Latīnē:

1. Quō diē Cornēlia epistulam Flāviae accēpit?
2. Quis epistulam ad patrem Cornēliae mīsit?
3. Ubi nunc est Valerius?
4. Quem Cornēlia libentissimē vidēbit?

Vix: scarcly

In epistulā tuā multa rogābās dē perīculīs urbānīs. Abhinc trēs diēs in īnsulā quādam magnum incendium vīdimus. Nihil miserābilius umquam vīdī. Quamquam enim maior pars incolārum ē perīculō effūgit, māter et duo līberī quōs in tertiō tabulātō cōnspeximus effugere nōn poterant. Ēheu! Hī miserī flammīs oppressī sunt. Ubi dē illā mātre et līberīs 15 cōgitō, valdē commoveor.

Heri vesperī Eucleidēs noster, ab urbe domum rediēns, duōs hominēs ē popīnā quādam exeuntēs vīdit. Quī hominēs, ubi Eucleidem cōnspexērunt, statim eum secūtī sunt. Eucleidēs effugere cōnātus est, sed frūstrā. Quō celerius currēbat ille, eō celerius currēbant hominēs. Facile eum cōnsecūtī sunt. Ō miserrimum Eucleidem! Ā praedōnibus 20 correptus ac fūstibus percussus, gravissimē vulnerātus est. Vix quidem sē domum trāxit.

Sed dē perīculīs satis! Hodiē māter pulcherrimam mihi pallam ēmit, quae mihi valdē placuit. Sed trīstis sum quod lānam semper trahō. Trīstissima autem sum quod tē nōn videō. Fortasse tū Rōmam cum patre veniēs. Nōnne tū patrī hoc persuādēbis? Tē plūrimum dēsīderō. Scrībe, sīs, quam saepissimē. Valē! 25

18 **quī hominēs,** *which/those men*
 secūtī sunt, *(they) followed*
19 **cōnātus est,** *(he) tried*

quō celerius...eō celerius..., *the faster...the faster...*
23 **trīstis, -is, -e,** *sad*
25 **sīs = sī vīs,** *if you wish, please*

24 **persuādeō, persuādēre, persuāsī, persuāsus,** *to make something* (acc.) *agreeable to someone* (dat.); *to persuade someone of something*

Respondē Latīnē:

1. Dē quibus rēbus Flāvia in epistulā rogābat?
2. Quid Cornēlia in īnsulā quādam vīdit?
3. Quid Cornēliae placuit?
4. Cūr est Cornēlia trīstis?

FORMS
Dates

In each month there were three special days from which Romans calculated all dates:

The Kalends (**Kalendae, -ārum,** f. pl.) were always on the 1st of the month.
The Nones (**Nōnae, -ārum,** f. pl.) usually fell on the 5th of the month.
The Ides (**Īdūs, Īduum,** f. pl.) usually fell on the 13th of the month.

But in March, May, July, and October, the Nones were on the 7th and the Ides were on the 15th.

Actual dates were expressed in the following ways:

1. The ablative of time when indicates that the date coincides with one of the special days:

Kalendīs Aprīlibus, *on April 1*   **Nōnīs Februāriīs,** *on February 5*
Īdibus Mārtiīs, *on March 15*

Compare **eō diē,** *on that day.*

2. The word **prīdiē** + *accusative* indicates the day before one of the special days:

> **prīdiē Kalendās Maiās** (lit., *on the day before May 1*), *on April 30*
> **prīdiē Īdūs Octōbrēs**, *on October 14.*

3. A phrase beginning **ante diem** (**a.d.**) is used to express all other dates:

> **ante diem iv Kalendās Decembrēs** (lit., *on the fourth day before December 1*), *on November 28*. (When calculating, you should include the special day and count backwards, e.g., Dec. 1, Nov. 30, Nov. 29, Nov. 28.)

> **ante diem viii Īdūs Mārtiās** (lit., *on the eighth day before the Ides of March*), *on March 8.*

Here are the Latin names for the months, expressed as adjectives:

Iānuārius, -a, -um	**Iūlius, -a, -um**
Februārius, -a, -um	**Augustus, -a, -um**
Mārtius, -a, -um	**September, Septembris, Septembre**
Aprīlis, -is, -e	**Octōber, Octōbris, Octōbre**
Maius, -a, -um	**November, Novembris, Novembre**
Iūnius, -a, -um	**December, Decembris, Decembre**

4. The Romans designated years by the names of the consuls, the chief Roman magistrates, who were elected annually. The ablative case is used: **Antōniō et Cicerōne cōnsulibus** = 63 B.C.

> **cōnsul, cōnsulis**, m., *consul*

5. They also designated years by counting from the foundation of Rome, which was set at a year corresponding to 753 B.C. These dates were expressed with the initials A.U.C. (**ab urbe conditā**, *from the foundation of the city*).

> **condō, condere, condidī, conditus**, *to found*

To convert a Roman year to our system, follow these rules:

a. If the A.U.C. date is 753 or less, subtract it from 754 and you will obtain a B.C. date.
b. If the A.U.C. date is 754 or greater, subtract 753 from it and you will obtain an A.D. date.

Examples:

691 A.U.C. (less than 753)

$$754 - 691 = 63$$

63 B.C. (the year of Cicero's consulship)

833 A.U.C. (greater than 754)

$$
\begin{array}{r}
833 \\
-753 \\
\hline
80
\end{array}
$$
A.D. (the year of our story)

To convert a year designated according to our system to a Roman year, follow these rules:

a. If the year is B.C., subtract it from 754.
b. If the year is A.D., add it to 753.

Examples:

$$
\begin{array}{r}
754 \\
-63 \\
\hline
691
\end{array}
$$
B.C. (the year of Cicero's consulship)

691 A.U.C.

$$
\begin{array}{r}
753 \\
+80 \\
\hline
833
\end{array}
$$
A.D. (the year of our story)

833 A.U.C.

Exercise 36b
Give English equivalents for the following dates:

1. Kalendīs Iānuāriīs
2. Kalendīs Decembribus
3. Kalendīs Iūniīs
4. Nōnīs Augustīs
5. Nōnīs Octōbribus
6. Īdibus Mārtiīs
7. Īdibus Maiīs
8. Īdibus Septembribus
9. prīdiē Kalendās Februāriās
10. prīdiē Kalendās Iūliās
11. prīdiē Nōnās Augustās
12. prīdiē Īdūs Iānuāriās
13. prīdiē Īdūs Novembrēs
14. ante diem iv Kalendās Iūniās
15. ante diem iii Nōnās Iūliās
16. a.d. vi Kal. Apr.
17. a.d. xviii Kal. Maiās
18. a.d. xii Kal. Feb.
19. a.d. vi Nōn. Mārt.
20. a.d. iv Īd. Feb.

Roman girl reading a letter
"Neaera Reading a Letter from Catullus," oil on canvas by Henry J. Hudson, Bradford Art Galleries and Museums, England

Exercise 36c
Give Roman equivalents for the following dates:

1. Today's date
2. Your own birthday
3. The foundation of Rome (April 21)
4. Cicero's birthday (January 3, 106 B.C.)
5. The date of the assassination of Julius Caesar (March 15, 44 B.C.)
6. Martial's birthday (March 1, A.D. 40)
7. The date of the Emperor Titus' accession to power (June 23, A.D. 79).
8. The date of the eruption of Mount Vesuvius (August 24, A.D. 79)

Exercise 36d
Using story 36 and the discussion of Roman dates above as guides, give the Latin for:

1. Cornelia received a letter on October 10 that Flavia had written on October 5.
2. On November 3 Cornelia and her mother saw a great fire.
3. On November 4 Eucleides was struck and very seriously wounded by robbers.
4. On November 5 Aurelia bought a very beautiful palla for Cornelia.
5. On November 29 Valerius will arrive at Rome.

ad Kalendās Graecās, *until the Greek Kalends* (Since there were no Kalends in the Greek calendar, this phrase means the event will never happen.)

BUILDING THE MEANING
Translating *quam*

You have now met several uses of **quam**. The following clues should help you choose the correct meaning:

1. In a comparison:
   clue: *comparative adjective or adverb before* **quam**—translate *than*:

   > Marcus est prūdent**ior quam** Sextus.
   > *Marcus is wiser **than** Sextus.*

2. In a phrase with a superlative:
   clue: *superlative adjective or adverb after* **quam**—translate the phrase *as...as possible*:

   > Scrībe **quam** saep**issimē**. (36:25)
   > *Write **as often as possible**.*

3. In an exclamation:
   clue: *adjective or adverb after* **Quam**—translate *How…! or What a…!*

   > **Quam molestus** puer est Sextus!
   > ***What a troublesome*** *boy Sextus is!*

   > **Quam celeriter** tua epistula hūc advēnit! (36:3–4)
   > ***How quickly*** *your letter arrived here!*

4. In a question:
   clue: *adjective or adverb after* **Quam** *and question mark at the end of the sentence*—translate *How…?*

   > **Quam molestus** est Sextus? Sextus est molestior quam Marcus.
   > ***How troublesome*** *is Sextus? Sextus is more troublesome than Marcus.*

5. In a relative clause:
   clue: *singular feminine noun as antecedent of* **quam**—translate *whom, which,* or *that*:

   > <u>Illam epistulam</u> accēpī **quam** tū scrīpsistī Kal. Nov. (36:2–3)
   > *I have received <u>that letter</u>* **that** *you wrote on November 1.*

   > Cornēlia dē <u>Flāviā</u> **quam** Baiīs relīquerat saepe cōgitābat.
   > *Cornelia often used to think about <u>Flavia</u>,* **whom** *she had left behind in Baiae.*

Exercise 36e

Read aloud and translate:

1. Quam pulcher adulēscēns est Valerius! Libentissimē eum accipiēmus.
2. Nihil miserābilius quam illud incendium vīdī.
3. Mulier illa miserrima quam Cornēlia in tertiō tabulātō sitam cōnspexit ex incendiō effugere nōn poterat.
4. Nēmō erat magis ēbrius quam Titus, nam plūs vīnī quam cēterī biberat.
5. Quam pulchra est illa palla quam māter mihi ēmit! Mihi valdē placet.
6. Mīlitēs Rōmānī quī audācissimī erant semper quam fortissimē sē dēfendēbant.
7. Quamquam celerius ambulābat Eucleidēs, praedōnēs eum mox cōnsecūtī sunt.
8. Quam graviter vulnerātus est!
9. Quam celeriter praedōnēs currere possunt? Celerius quam Eucleidēs currere possunt.

audāx, audācis, *bold*

HELGE'S SPINNING

Chapter 6 told how the slave-women in the Cornelius household were spinning wool into strands of yarn at the country house in Baiae, and Cornelia in her letter to Flavia complains of constantly spinning wool at home in Rome. In fact, all women in the ancient world spun and wove, from the humblest peasant to the wife of the emperor. Helge, the Ubian woman you met in previous Frontier Life sections was no exception, having learned the craft as a child from her mother.

The region around Ara Ubiorum was noted for its sheep. The sheep, in fact, was probably one of the very first animals domesticated by man, its fleece used for weaving cloth for clothing and blankets since prehistoric times. The story that follows takes us back to the first year of Helge's marriage to Lucius.

As is done today, the sheep were sheared in the spring so they would not suffer through the summer in their heavy fleeces. Helge's father had sheared sheep, and so had

Greek woman spinning thread. Compare Catullus' description of the Fates spinning the threads of destiny quoted on page 95.
Attic Greek trefoil-mouthed jug, ca. 500–480 B.C.
The British Museum, London

Lucius on the farm in Italy where he was raised. The shears used by both Lucius and Helge's father were identical to those used in modern times until the invention of electric clippers, and it was with a pair of these shears that, in the spring, Lucius and his companions sheared the sheep owned by Numistronius, their centurion, who had a farm near Ara Ubiorum.

Lucius began the shearing with a particularly large ram. With the help of two of his fellow legionaries, he wrestled the ram to the ground and tied its front and back feet so the animal could not run away. Grasping the shears directly above the two blades, Lucius straddled the ram and applying gentle, oblique pressure removed the entire fleece at once, flipping the heavy animal over on one side or the other as necessary. As the lanolin, the natural oil in the sheep's fleece, built up on Lucius' shears, he dipped them into a bucket of water to clean them as he worked.

After all the sheep were sheared, each fleece was spread out and cut apart, and the wool was separated into grades according to its quality. The thickest and strongest fleece came from the sheep's back, and the next thickest came from the sides. The fleece from the belly was soft and airy—just right for tunics. The worst wool came from the legs and tail, where it was apt to be encrusted with dirt. The wool was carefully placed into bags, each marked as to the quality of fleece it contained.

Helge and her friend, Helena Favonia, who also lived in the area surrounding the military camp, were now ready to convert the wool into tunics and cloaks for the legionaries. First, the wool was washed in cold water and beaten with sticks to remove dirt, leaves, and thorns and to detach fibers for easier carding. Then Helge and Helena carded the wool, a task that meant working it through the teeth of flat iron combs with their fingers over and over, separating the fibers from one another.

Finally, after washing the carded wool, this time in warm soapy water, Helge and Helena were ready to dye it. For the cloaks, the wool would be left the natural color of the sheep or dyed brown. However, the tunics had to be a red color by legion order, and it was this color that Helge prepared by filling a pot with water, scraps of iron from the legion armory, and the sour red wine (**posca**) issued to Roman legionaries. To enhance the reddish color, she added some dry stalks of a plant called madder. Letting the pot sit over the fire until just warm, Helge dumped the wool into the mixture and stirred it until it was thoroughly saturated with the dye. Lifting it out, she wrung out the wool and rinsed it in plain water. Wringing it out again, she dipped it into water that had been poured through wood ashes to fix the color. She repeated this process over and over until she had wool of just the right hue.

Helge knew the art of creating good dyes of many bright colors created by using native plants and metals. But the Romans scorned those bright colors for clothing, considering them barbarian.

The washed, correctly colored, and dry wool, placed in baskets, was now ready for spinning. A simple spindle with a circular whorl mounted on it was used throughout the ancient world. The Roman poet Catullus describes how the Fates spun the threads of destiny by twirling this very same instrument with skillful movements of their fingers:

> The right hand lightly drawing out the thread shaped it with fingers turned upwards and then with a twisting movement of the thumb turned downwards twirled the spindle balanced by the circular whorl.

So Helge spun the brick-red wool into strands of yarn.

As the yarn became longer, Helge wound it on the shaft of her spindle. She and Helena continued to spin until the baskets of wool were empty.

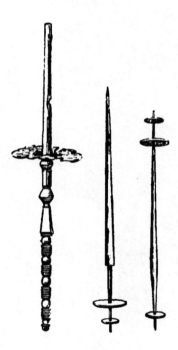

Spindles with circular whorls

Go Online
For: Additional Practice
Visit: PHSchool.com
Web Code: jgd-0010

OFF TO SCHOOL

Māne in urbe fuit strepitus maximus; canēs lātrābant, servī per viās currēbant, sed neque Marcus neque Sextus sē mōvit. Adhūc in lectō iacēbat Sextus et sēcum cōgitābat: "Quis est mē miserior? Cotīdiē ante lūcem mihi necesse est ad lūdum proficīscī. Sed ad lūdum īre vereor. In lūdō numquam laudor; semper castīgor. Illōs versūs Vergiliī memoriā tenēre nōn possum. Ille grammaticus mē experītur, et cotīdiē eadem dīcit: 'Tū,   5
Sexte, nihil scīs quod semper loqueris,' vel 'Es puer pessimus,' vel 'Nisi dīligentius labōrābis, verberāberis.' Itaque domī manēre volō."

Ita cōgitābat Sextus cum Eucleidēs paedagōgus in cubiculum ingressus est. "Surgite, puerī!" inquit. "Nōlīte diūtius in lectō manēre! Est enim tempus ad lūdum proficīscī, ubi Palaemōn, grammaticus ille ērudītissimus, vōs laetus accipiet. Vōs docēbit plūrima quae   10
vōbīs erunt ūtilissima."

Nihil respondērunt puerī; invītī ē lectō surrēxērunt, vestēs induērunt, ē domō ēgressī sunt. Nōndum lūcēbat, sed cum Eucleide in viās urbis profectī sunt. Lanternam eīs praeferēbat Eucleidēs.

Subitō cōnspexit Marcus tabernam quandam. "Ecce, Eucleidēs!" clāmāvit Marcus.   15
"Vidēsne illam tabernam? Est pīstrīnum. Licetne nōbīs aliquid cibī emere?"   *(continued)*

3 **cotīdiē,** adv., *daily, every day*
  lūdus, -ī, m., *school*
  proficīscī, *to set out*
4 **vereor,** *I am afraid*
  castīgō, -āre, –āvī, -ātus, *to rebuke, reprimand*
  Vergilius, -ī, m., *Vergil (Roman poet)*
5 **grammaticus, -ī,** m., *secondary school teacher*
  experītur, *(he) tests*

6 **loqueris,** *you are talking*
  vel, conj., *or*
8 **paedagōgus, -ī,** m., *tutor*
  ingressus est, *(he) entered*
10 **ērudītus, -a, -um,** *learned, scholarly*
11 **ūtilis, -is, -e,** *useful*
12 **ēgressī sunt,** *(they) went out*
13 **profectī sunt,** *(they) set out*
16 **pīstrīnum, -ī,** n., *bakery*

14 **praeferō, praeferre, praetulī, praelātus,** irreg., *to carry X* (acc.)
   in front of Y (dat.)

Exercise 37a
Respondē Latīnē:

1. Cūr miser est Sextus?
2. Quandō necesse est ad lūdum proficīscī?
3. Cūr Sextus in lūdō semper castīgātur?
4. Quālis grammaticus (ut dīcit Eucleidēs) est Palaemōn?
5. Quid Palaemōn puerōs docēbit?
6. Cūr necesse erat Eucleidī lanternam puerīs praeferre?

"Estō," respondit Eucleidēs. "Nōn sērō est. Etiamsī nōs aliquid cibī edēmus, tamen ad tempus ad lūdum perveniēmus."

Puerī igitur scriblītās emunt, Eucleidēs pānem et paulum vīnī. Dum iēntāculum dēvorant, Marcus et Sextus inter sē loquuntur. Tandem iterum profectī mox lūdō 20 appropinquābant.

17 **etiamsī**, conj., *even if*
18 **ad tempus**, *on time*
19 **scriblīta, -ae,** f., *tart or pastry with cheese filling*

paulum, -ī, n., *a small amount, a little*
iēntāculum, -ī, n., *breakfast*
20 **loquuntur,** *(they) talk*

Respondē Latīnē:

1. Ubi Eucleidēs et puerī iēntāculum emunt? 2. Quid emunt puerī? Quid Eucleidēs?

FORMS
Deponent Verbs

Look at these sentences:

Eucleidēs effugere **cōnātus est.**	*Eucleides **tried** to escape.*
Praedōnēs eum **cōnsecūtī sunt.**	*The robbers **overtook** him.*
Sed ad lūdum īre **vereor.**	*But **I am afraid** to go to school.*
Semper **loqueris.**	*You are always **talking**.*
Grammaticus mē **experītur.**	*The teacher **tests** me.*
Brundisiō **proficīscētur.**	*He **will set out** from Brundisium.*
Tempus est **proficīscī.**	*It is time **to set out**.*

In each of the above examples, the Latin verb in boldface has a *passive* ending but its meaning is *active*. Verbs that behave in this way are called *deponent verbs*.

NOTES:
1. Deponent verbs occur in all four conjugations and are conjugated the same as *passive* forms of regular verbs. Deponents are *translated* with *active* meanings:

Regular Verb: Passive
Laudātur. *He is praised.*
Laudārī potest. *He is able to be praised.*

Deponent Verb
Cōnātur. *He tries.*
Cōnārī potest. *He is able to try.*

2. Deponent verbs have only *three* principal parts:
   1st: 1st person singular, present tense: **cōnor,** *I try, I am trying, I do try*
   2nd: present infinitive: **cōnārī,** *to try, to be trying*
   3rd: 1st person singular, perfect tense: **cōnātus sum,** *I tried, I have tried*

	Present	Infinitive	Perfect	Meaning
1st Conj.	cṓnor	cōnā́rī	cōnā́tus sum	*to try*
2nd Conj.	véreor	verḗrī	véritus sum	*to be afraid*
3rd Conj.	lóquor	lóquī	locū́tus sum	*to speak*
(*-iō*)	regrédior	régredī	regréssus sum	*to go back*
4th Conj.	expérior	experī́rī	expértus sum	*to test*

3. The *perfect participle* of a deponent verb, although passive in form, is translated *actively*:

> Puerī in viās urbis **ēgressī** mox lūdō appropinquābant.
> *The boys, **having gone out** into the streets of the city, soon were approaching the school.*

Here is a chart showing sample forms of deponent verbs. Note that the singular imperatives have forms identical to the present active infinitive of non-deponent verbs. In the future and imperfect tenses only the singular forms are shown. In the perfect, pluperfect, and future perfect tenses only the 1st person singular forms are shown.

		1st Conjugation	2nd Conjugation	3rd Conjugation		4th Conjugation
Present Infinitive		cōnā́rī	verḗrī	lóquī	régredī	experī́rī
Imperative		cōnā́re	verére	lóquere	regrédere	experī́re
		cōnā́minī	verḗminī	loquíminī	regredíminī	experī́minī
Present Singular	1	cṓnor	véreor	lóquor	regrédior	expérior
	2	cōnā́ris	verḗris	lóqueris	regréderis	experī́ris
	3	cōnā́tur	verḗtur	lóquitur	regréditur	experī́tur
Plural	1	cōnā́mur	verḗmur	lóquimur	regrédimur	experī́mur
	2	cōnā́minī	verḗminī	loquíminī	regredíminī	experī́minī
	3	cōnā́ntur	verḗntur	loquúntur	regrediúntur	experiúntur
Imperfect Singular	1	cōnā́bar	verḗbar	loquḗbar	regrediḗbar	experiḗbar
	2	cōnābā́ris	verēbā́ris	loquēbā́ris	regrediēbā́ris	experiēbā́ris
	3	cōnābā́tur	verēbā́tur	loquēbā́tur	rebrediēbā́tur	experiēbā́tur
Future Singular	1	cōnā́bor	verḗbor	lóquar	regrédiar	expériar
	2	cōnā́beris	verḗberis	loquéris	regrediéris	experiéris
	3	cōnā́bitur	verḗbitur	loquétur	regrediétur	experiétur
Perfect	1	cōnā́tus sum	véritus sum	locū́tus sum	regréssus sum	expértus sum
Pluperfect	1	cōnā́tus éram	véritus éram	locū́tus éram	regréssus éram	expértus éram
Future Perfect	1	cōnā́tus érō	véritus érō	locū́tus érō	regréssus érō	expértus érō

You have met forms of the following deponent verbs so far (listed by conjugation):

1st: **cōnor, cōnārī, cōnātus sum,** *to try* (36:19)
     moror, morārī, morātus sum, *to delay, remain, stay* (36:8)
2nd: **vereor, verērī, veritus sum,** *to be afraid, fear* (37:4)

3rd:	**collābor, collābī, collāpsus sum**, *to collapse* (34:22)
	cōnsequor, cōnsequī, cōnsecūtus sum, *to catch up to, overtake* (35:18)
	loquor, loquī, locūtus sum, *to speak, talk* (37:6)
	proficīscor, proficīscī, profectus sum, *to set out, leave* (36:9)
	sequor, sequī, secūtus sum, *to follow* (36:18)
(**-iō**)	**ēgredior, ēgredī, ēgressus sum**, *to go out, leave* (37:12)
	ingredior, ingredī, ingressus sum, *to go in, enter* (37:8)
	regredior, regredī, regressus sum, *to go back, return* (36:8)
4th:	**experior, experīrī, expertus sum**, *to test, try* (37:5)

Exercise 37b

Here are some forms of deponent verbs. Translate them into English:

1. proficīscuntur
2. experientur
3. secūtī erāmus
4. morātae sunt
5. verēbimur

6. ēgrederis
7. profectī eritis
8. sequere
9. collābī
10. cōnsequēbātur

Exercise 37c

Refer to the principal parts of the verbs listed above and say the following in Latin:

1. We have tried.
2. You (*sing.*) enter.
3. They had set out.
4. Speak, boys!
5. I will test.
6. She was following.

7. You (*pl.*) collapsed.
8. Don't be afraid, Sextus!
9. They will have returned.
10. We were delaying.
11. He has gone out.
12. I will try to overtake you.

Exercise 37d

Read aloud and translate:

1. Quid puellae facere cōnantur? Puellae pallam facere cōnantur. Quid tū facere cōnāris? Ego labōrāre cōnor. Quid vōs facere cōnāminī? Nōs dormīre cōnāmur.
2. Quandō nōs vīsitāre cōnāberis? Ego mox vōs vīsitāre cōnābor. Amīcī meī quoque vōs vīsitāre cōnābuntur. Nōs omnēs eōdem diē vōs vīsitāre cōnābimur.
3. Quis loquitur? Ego nōn loquēbar. Nōs cum magistrō loquēbāmur.
4. Quō puerī proficīscuntur? Rōmam proficīscuntur. Nōs cum eīs proficīscēmur. Nōnne vōs quoque proficīscī vultis?
5. Quandō puerī ē lūdō ēgredientur? Puerī ē lūdō ēgredientur sextā hōrā. Ēgrediēturne cum puerīs magister? Minimē vērō! Magister in lūdō morābitur.
6. Quandō tū proficīscēris? Ubi māter domum regressa erit, ego proficīscar. Puer prīmā lūce proficīscētur. Servī nunc proficīscī nōn possunt. Mox sequentur.

7. Paulisper in urbe morātī sumus. Cūr morātī estis? Ego morātus sum quod patrem vidēre volēbam. Amīcī meī morātī sunt quod aedificia urbis vidēre volēbant.
8. Prīmā lūce servī Cornēliī in viās ēgressī sunt. Illōs praedōnēs scelestōs sequī cōnātī sunt sed eōs cōnsequī nōn potuērunt.
9. Nōlī in lectō diūtius morārī, Sexte. Cōnāre illōs versūs Vergiliī memoriā tenēre. Fortasse ā grammaticō hodiē laudāberis sī nōn nimis loquēris.
10. Cornēlius convīvīs, "Intrāte, amīcī!" inquit. "Ingrediminī domum meam! Vōs libentissimē excipiō." Convīvae quam celerrimē ingressī inter sē magnō cum strepitū in ātriō colloquēbantur.

sextus, -a, -um, *sixth*   **magister, magistrī,** m., *schoolmaster*

Exercise 37e

In each sentence below, replace the verb in italics with the appropriate form of the deponent verb in parentheses, keeping the same tense, person, and number; then translate the new sentence:

1. Valerius Brundisiō Īdibus Novembribus *discessit*. (proficīscor)
2. Ā grammaticō laudātī sumus quod versūs memoriā tenēre *potuerāmus*. (cōnor)
3. Tabellārius ex urbe quam celerrimē *exībit*. (ēgredior)
4. Māter et Cornēlia in illā tabernā diūtissimē *manēbant*. (moror)
5. "Hīc *sedē*, Marce," inquit Eucleidēs. (moror) "Nōlī mē *vexāre*!" (sequor)
6. Eucleidēs per urbis viās nocte ambulāre *nōn vult*. (vereor)
7. "Ego prīmus," inquit Marcus, "in lūdum *intrāvī*." (ingredior)

Exercise 37f

Using story 37 and the information on deponent verbs as guides, give the Latin for the following. Use deponent verbs whenever possible:

1. Marcus and Sextus were staying in their beds.
2. Marcus and Sextus set out for school before dawn every day.
3. Why are you afraid to go to school, Sextus?
4. The teacher will test Sextus.
5. Sextus always talks in school, never works diligently, and is often beaten by the teacher.

━ ━ ━ ━ ━

Forsan miserōs meliōra sequentur. *For those in misery perhaps better things will follow.* (Vergil, *Aeneid* XII.153)
Multī fāmam, cōnscientiam paucī verentur. *Many fear their reputation, few their conscience.* (Pliny, *Letters* III.20)
Vir sapit quī pauca loquitur. *It is a wise man who speaks little. (Anonymous)*

━ ━ ━ ━ ━

ROMAN EDUCATION I

THE EARLIEST YEARS: EDUCATION IN THE HOME

Little is known about the early training of Roman boys and girls, but certainly the home played the most important part. During the first seven years education was chiefly in the hands of the mother:

> In the good old days, every citizen's son was brought up, not in the chamber of some hired nurse, but in his mother's lap. Thus we are told Cornelia, the mother of the Gracchi, directed their upbringing. The same was true of Aurelia, the mother of Caesar, and of Atia, the mother of Augustus.
>
> Tacitus, *Dialogue* 28

This was not the time of formal instruction; it was the influence of the home on the child that was the greatest at this stage:

> In ancient times it was the established custom that Romans should learn from their elders not only by watching but also by listening. The father of each one served as his teacher.
>
> Pliny, *Letters* VIII.14

The home was always considered the natural place for early training, and the practice of sending children to school away from their home town, although it increased in later years, was looked upon with suspicion by some:

> Surely it is a matter of great importance that your children should study here rather than anywhere else. Where can they live more happily than in their native town, or be more strictly brought up than under their parents' eye, or be educated at less expense than at home? What an easy matter it would be to hire teachers and add to their salaries the money you now spend on lodgings, traveling, and all you have to purchase away from home.
>
> Pliny, *Letters* IV.13

Roman classroom scene

THE PRIMARY SCHOOL

At the age of seven, if their fathers could afford it, children were sent to school—the **lūdus litterārius**—to be taught their "letters" by a schoolmaster, generally called **litterā-tor** or **magister lūdī**. (Note that the Romans used the same word **lūdus** for both *play* and *school*.) The teacher's pay was small, for teaching was not considered very highly as a profession. The curriculum at this stage was limited to three subjects—reading, writing, and arithmetic.

Education at home, however, was not unusual, for there was no state education. It was usually in the hands of a tutor—most often a Greek slave or freedman.

Occasionally, we read of fathers who themselves looked after the education of their sons. This was true of Cato and Aemilius Paulus, but note their different ideas and ideals:

> As soon as Cato's son began to learn with understanding, his father took him in charge and taught him to read, although he had a very good slave, called Chilo, who was a schoolteacher and was already teaching many boys. But Cato did not think it right, as he himself says, that his son should be scolded by a slave or pulled by the ear when slow to learn, nor that such an important thing as education should be left to a slave. He himself therefore taught him reading, law, and gymnastics and also gave him instruction in how to throw a javelin, to fight in armor, to ride and box, to endure both heat and cold, and to swim.
>
> Plutarch, *Cato the Elder* 20

Aemilius Paulus himself looked after the education of his children. He brought them up in the old-fashioned Roman way as he himself had been brought up, but he was even more enthusiastic about Greek education. For this reason their teachers of grammar, logic, and rhetoric, their teachers of sculpture and drawing, those in charge of their dogs and horses, and those who taught them how to hunt, were all Greeks.

Plutarch, *Aemilius Paulus* 6

In schools, discipline was generally very strict. Martial, speaking of one schoolmaster as "a person hated by both girls and boys," continues:

The crested cocks have not yet broken the silence of the night, but you are making a noise by roaring savagely and thrashing your pupils.

Martial, *Epigrams* IX.68

Many Romans followed the Greek custom of sending their children to school accompanied by a slave (**paedagōgus**) to look after their conduct, manners, and morals:

It is the job of the **paedagōgus** to make the boy learn what his teacher has taught him by encouraging and shouting at him, by fetching out the strap, and by using the cane. He makes him do his work by driving every lesson into his head.

Libanius, *Orations* 58.8

REVIEW VIII: CHAPTERS 34–37

Exercise VIIIa: Comparative and Superlative of Adjectives and Adverbs

Supply in the blanks comparative and superlative adjectives or adverbs corresponding to the positive forms in the original statements. Read aloud and translate:

1. Messalla coquum *bonum* habet. Titus coquum ___meliorem___ habet quam Messalla. *
   Cornēlius coquum ___optimum___ omnium habet.
2. Messalla tālōs *dīligenter* iacit. Cornēlius tālōs ___diligentius___ iacit Messallā. Titus tālōs
   ___diligentissime___ omnium iacit.
3. Eucleidēs ad lūdum *lentē* proficīscitur. Marcus ad lūdum ___lentius___ proficīscitur quam
   Eucleides. Sextus ad lūdum ___lentissime___ omnium proficīscitur.
4. Marcus *bene* scrībit. Eucleidēs ___melius___ Marcō scrībit. Grammaticus ___optime___
   omnium scrībit.
5. Messalla ē poculō *pulchrō* bibit. Titus ē poculō ___pulchriore___ bibit quam Messalla. *
   Cornēlius ē poculō omnium ___pulcherrimo___ bibit.
6. Coquus Messallae cēnam *celeriter* parat. Coquus Titī cēnam _____ parat quam
   coquus Messallae. Coquus Cornēliī cenam _____ omnium parat.
7. Eucleidēs ē lectō *sērō* surgit. Marcus ē lectō _____ surgit quam Eucleidēs. Sextus ē
   lectō _____ omnium surgit.
8. Messalla *multum* vīnī bibit. Cornēlius _____ vīnī bibit Messallā. Titus omnium
   _____ vīnī bibit.
9. Cornēlius *magnā* vōce clāmat. Messalla ___miore___ _____ vōce clāmat quam Cornēlius. Titus *
   omnium ___maxima___ vōce clāmat.
10. Praedōnēs tabernārium *ferōciter* verberāvērunt. Praedōnēs lanium _____
    verberāvērunt quam tabernārium. Praedōnēs Eucleidem _____ omnium
    verberāvērunt.

Exercise VIIIb: Forms of Deponent Verbs

Give the requested forms of the following deponent verbs:

	Present	Imperfect	Future	Perfect	Pluperfect	Future Perfect
1. sequor *(3rd sing.)*	___	___	___	___	___	___
2. loquor *(1st pl.)*	___	___	___	___	___	___
3. vereor *(3rd pl.)*	___	___	___	___	___	___
4. cōnor *(1st sing.)*	___	___	___	___	___	___
5. collābor *(2nd sing.)*	___	___	___	___	___	___
6. regredior *(3rd pl.)*	___	___	___	___	___	___
7. moror *(2nd pl.)*	___	___	___	___	___	___
8. experior *(3rd sing.)*	___	___	___	___	___	___

Exercise VIIIc: Imperatives of Deponent Verbs

Give the singular and plural imperatives of the following deponent verbs:

	Singular	Plural
1. cōnor	_____	_____
2. loquor	_____	_____
3. regredior	_____	_____
4. experior	_____	_____
5. vereor	_____	_____

Exercise VIIId: Active Forms of Non-deponent Verbs

Give the requested forms of the following verbs in the active voice:

	Present	Imperfect	Future	Perfect	Pluperfect	Future Perfect
1. vincō (2nd sing.)	____	____	____	____	____	____
2. compleō (1st sing.)	____	____	____	____	____	____
3. hauriō (2nd pl.)	____	____	____	____	____	____
4. excitō (1st pl.)	____	____	____	____	____	____
5. percutiō (3rd pl.)	____	____	____	____	____	____
6. crēdō (3rd sing.)	____	____	____	____	____	____

Exercise VIIIe: Passive Forms of Non-deponent Verbs

Repeat Exercise VIIId, but give the requested forms of the verbs in the passive voice.

Exercise VIIIf: Imperatives of Non-deponent Verbs

Give the singular and plural active imperatives of the verbs in Exercise VIIId.

Exercise VIIIg: Reading Comprehension

Read the following passage and answer the questions below with full sentences in Latin:

THE TROJAN HORSE

Graecī, quī iam decem annōs Troiam obsidēbant, domum regredī valdē cupiēbant. Mussābant igitur, "Quōmodo Troiānī vincentur? Cōnsilium novum et melius capiēmus. Equum ligneum aedificābimus quem extrā mūrōs urbis relinquēmus. In eō pōnentur fortissimī ē mīlitibus nostrīs. Deinde ad īnsulam vīcīnam ipsī proficīscēmur et nōs ibi cēlābimus. Fortasse equus in urbem ā 5 Troiānīs trahētur."

Postquam Graecī abiērunt, laetissimī ex urbe ēgressī sunt Troiānī. Equum ligneum spectant. "Quid est hoc?" rogant. "Cūr equus tantus ē lignō factus est? Cūr Graecī hunc equum relīquērunt?"

Aliī, "Cavēte Graecōs!" inquiunt. "Nōlīte eīs crēdere." Aliī, "Gaudēte!" 10
inquiunt. "Equus, sī intrā mūrōs ductus erit, urbem nostram custōdiet et
dēfendet."

Itaque maximō gaudiō equum intrā mūrōs trahere cōnstituērunt. Nox erat.
Troiānī somnō vīnōque oppressī per tōtam urbem dormiēbant. Ecce! Dē equō
dēscendērunt Graecī. Intereā cēterī ex īnsulā regrediēbantur et urbem quam 15
celerrimē petēbant. Eī quī in equō cēlātī erant portās Graecīs aperuērunt. Magnō
cum strepitū irrūpērunt. Undique clāmor et tumultus, undique incendia et
caedēs. Mātrēs sollicitae cum līberīs per viās currēbant; flammae omnia dēlēbant.
Urbs tandem capta est.

1 **annus, -ī,** m., *year*
2 **cōnsilium capere,** *to form a plan*
3 **ligneus, -a, -um,** *wooden*

18 **caedēs, caedis,** gen. pl., **caedium,** f.,
slaughter

1 **obsideō, obsidēre, obsēdī, obsessus,** *to besiege*
2 **cupiō, cupere, cupīvī, cupītus,** *to desire, want*
18 **dēleō, dēlēre, dēlēvī, dēlētus,** *to destroy*

1. For how many years had the Greeks been besieging Troy?
2. What kind of plan did the Greeks want to adopt?
3. What did they build?
4. Where did they put it?
5. Where did the other Greeks hide?
6. What did the Trojans do after the Greeks left?
7. What were the Trojans saying who did not trust the Greeks?
8. When did the Trojans drag the horse within the walls?
9. Why didn't the Trojans see the Greeks when they descended from the horse?
10. What were the other Greeks doing at this very time?
11. Who opened the gates to the Greeks?

Exercise VIIIh: Discriminating Between Deponent Verbs and Passive Forms of Regular Verbs

The verbs below are taken from the story in Exercise VIIIg. Say whether the verb is
a deponent verb or a passive form of a regular verb. Then give a translation of the verb
that would fit the context in the story.

1. regredī (1)
2. vincentur (2)
3. pōnentur (4)
4. proficīscēmur (5)
5. trahētur (6)
6. ēgressī sunt (7)
7. factus est (8)
8. regrediēbantur (15)
9. cēlātī erant (16)
10. capta est (19)

Go Online

For: Additional Practice
Visit: PHSchool.com
Web Code: jgd-0011

THE LESSONS BEGIN

Omnēs puerī in lūdum vix ingressī erant cum grammaticus ita coepit: "Abhinc trēs mēnsēs prīmus liber Aenēidis ā vōbīs lēctus est. Quis ē vōbīs dē Aenēā mihi nārrāre potest?"

Cui ūnus ē discipulīs respondit: "Urbs Troia ā Graecīs decem annōs obsidēbātur, sed tandem capta et incēnsa est. Effūgit ē ruīnīs illīus urbis Aenēās, et ūnā cum patre fīliōque suō et complūribus amīcīs ex Asiā nāvigāvit, nam terram petēbat quae Hesperia vocāta est. Postquam multa terrā marīque passus est, ad Siciliam vix vēnit. Atque ubi ē Siciliā profectus est, maxima tempestās nāvēs complūrēs dēlēvit. Aenēās ipse, ad Āfricam tempestāte āctus, cum septem modo nāvibus ad urbem quandam advēnit ubi ā rēgīnā Dīdōne cōmiter acceptus ad convīvium invītātus est." *(continued)* 10

1	**coepit,** *(he) began*	6	**nāvigō, -āre, -āvī, -ātus,** *to sail*
2	**mēnsis, mēnsis,** m., *month*		**terra, -ae,** f., *earth, ground, land*
	Aenēis, Aenēidis, f., *the* Aeneid		**Hesperia, -ae,** f., *Hesperia (the land in*
	(an epic poem by Vergil)		*the West, Italy)*
	Aenēās, Aenēae, m., *Aeneas (son of*	7	**mare, maris,** abl. sing., **marī,** gen.
	Venus and Anchises and legendary		pl., **marium,** n., *sea*
	ancestor of the Romans)	8	**tempestās, tempestātis,** f., *storm*
4	**discipulus, -ī,** m., *pupil*		**nāvis, nāvis,** gen. pl., **nāvium,** f., *ship*
	annus, -ī, m., *year*	9	**rēgīna, -ae,** f., *queen*
5	**ruīna, -ae,** f., *collapse, ruin*	10	**Dīdō, Dīdōnis,** f., *Dido (queen of Carthage)*

4 **obsideō, obsidēre, obsēdī, obsessus,** *to besiege*
5 **incendō, incendere, incendī, incēnsus,** *to burn, set on fire*
7 **patior, patī, passus sum,** *to suffer, endure*
8 **dēleō, dēlēre, dēlēvī, dēlētus,** *to destroy*

Exercise 38a
Respondē Latīnē:

1. Quī urbem Troiam obsidēbant?
2. Quis ē ruīnīs urbis effūgit?
3. Quibuscum ex Asiā nāvigāvit?
4. Quam terram petēbat Aenēās?
5. Quid passus est?
6. Quō īnstrūmentō nāvēs complūrēs dēlētae sunt?
7. Quot nāvēs ad terram advēnērunt?
8. Ā quō Aenēās in Āfricā acceptus est?

Tum grammaticus, "Rēs optimē nārrāta est. Sed quid in convīviō factum est?"

Cui alter discipulus, "Rēgīna plūrima rogābat dē urbe Troiā, dē rēbus Troiānīs, dē perīculīs itineris. Tandem omnēs convīvae tacuērunt et Aenēās multa et mīra nārrāre coepit."

Hoc respōnsum grammaticō maximē placuit; quī, "Nunc," inquit, "nōs ipsī audiēmus ea quae ab Aenēā nārrāta sunt. Nunc legēmus aliquōs versūs ē secundō librō Aenēidis. Age, Marce! Mihi recitā illōs versūs!" 15

Marcus igitur ita recitāre coepit:

Conticuēre omnēs intentīque ōra tenēbant.
Inde torō pater Aenēās sīc orsus ab altō: 20
"Īnfandum, rēgīna, iubēs renovāre dolōrem."
They all fell silent and were eager to listen.
Then from his lofty couch Father Aeneas thus began:
"Unspeakable, O Queen, is the grief you bid me revive."

16 **aliquī, -ae, -a,** *some*

━━━━━

Optimum est patī quod ēmendāre nōn possīs. *It is best to endure what you cannot change.* (Seneca, *Moral Epistles* CVII.9)

Caelum, nōn animum, mūtant, quī trāns mare currunt. *Those who run off across the sea change their climate but not their mind.* (Horace, *Epistles* I.II.27)

━━━━━

Like Dido in the *Aeneid* or Ariadne in earlier myth, a woman might help a hero only to be abandoned. *"Ariadne in Naxos," oil on canvas, Evelyn de Morgan, The de Morgan Foundation, London*

FORMS
Numbers in Latin

	Cardinal	Ordinal
I	ūnus, -a, -um, *one*	prīmus, -a, -um, *first*
II	duo, -ae, -o, *two*	secundus, -a, -um, *second*
III	trēs, trēs, tria, *three*	tertius, -a, -um, *third*
IV	quattuor, *four*	quārtus, -a, -um
V	quīnque, *five*	quīntus, -a, -um
VI	sex, *six*	sextus, -a, -um
VII	septem, *seven*	septimus, -a, -um
VIII	octō, *eight*	octāvus, -a, -um
IX	novem, *nine*	nōnus, -a, -um
X	decem, *ten*	decimus, -a, -um
XI	ūndecim, *eleven*	ūndecimus, -a, -um
XII	duodecim, *twelve*	duodecimus, -a, -um
XIII	tredecim, *thirteen*	tertius decimus, -a, -um
XIV	quattuordecim, *fourteen*	quārtus decimus, -a, -um
XV	quīndecim, *fifteen*	quīntus decimus, -a, -um
XVI	sēdecim, *sixteen*	sextus decimus, -a, -um
XVII	septendecim, *seventeen*	septimus decimus, -a, -um
XVIII	duodēvīgintī, *eighteen*	duodēvīcēsimus, -a, -um
XIX	ūndēvīgintī, *nineteen*	ūndēvīcēsimus, -a, -um
XX	vīgintī, *twenty*	vīcēsimus, -a, -um
L	quīnquāgintā, *fifty*	quīnquāgēsimus, -a, -um
C	centum, *a hundred*	centēsimus, -a, -um
D	quīngentī, -ae, -a, *five hundred*	quīngentēsimus, -a, -um
M	mīlle, *a thousand*	mīllēsimus, -a, -um

N.B. The cardinal numbers from **quattuor** to **centum** do not change their form to indicate case and gender.

The question word **Quot...?** requires an answer from the *cardinal* column:

Quot līberōs habēbat lībertus? Septem habēbat.
How many children did the freedman have? He had seven.

The word **Quotus...?** requires an answer from the *ordinal* column:

Quota hōra est? Est nōna hōra.
What time is it? It is the ninth hour.

Exercise 38b

Read aloud and translate:

1. Puerī novem hōrās dormīvērunt. Tempus est eōs excitāre.
2. Convīvae sex hōrās morābantur. Cēna Cornēliī erat optima.
3. Ulixēs multa terrā marīque passus domum decimō annō pervēnit.
4. Quot librī Aenēidis sunt? Duodecim sunt librī Aenēidis.
5. Quota hōra est? Est sexta hōra.
6. Quotus mēnsis annī est Aprīlis? Aprīlis mēnsis annī est quārtus.
7. Ōlim Mārtius mēnsis erat prīmus annī, et septimus vocātus est mēnsis September, octāvus mēnsis Octōber, nōnus mēnsis November, decimus mēnsis December. Nunc mēnsis Iānuārius est prīmus annī.
8. Quot sorōrēs habēbat Dīdō? Ūnam sorōrem Annam nōmine habēbat Dīdō.
9. Marcus ā grammaticō rogātus aliquōs versūs ē secundō librō Aenēidis bene recitāvit.
10. Aenēās, ut in sextō Aenēidis librō legimus, in Plūtōnis rēgnum dēscendit.

Ulixēs, Ulixis, m., *Ulysses, Odysseus (Greek hero of the Trojan War)*

Exercise 38c

Give equivalents for the following in Arabic numerals:

1. XXX
2. XXIV
3. XVII
4. XIX
5. LX
6. CV
7. DXC
8. MDCCLXXVI
9. XLIV
10. CLIX

Exercise 38d

Give the Latin for each of the following questions (each of your questions should expect a numerical answer), and then give an appropriate answer:

1. What hour is it?
2. What month is it?
3. How many months are there in a year?
4. How many brothers and how many sisters do you have?
5. How many books have you read today?

ROMAN EDUCATION II

THE SECONDARY SCHOOL: THE GRAMMATICUS

After five years at a **lūdus litterārius**, children were sent to a **grammaticus**, a grammarian. Secondary education was more restricted, for only the wealthy could send their children to these schools. Here they studied both Latin and Greek literature. In addition, the **grammaticus** would teach mathematics, natural science, astronomy, philosophy, and music, but only in so far as these subjects were relevant to understanding the works of Greek and Latin literature that were read in the schools.

Students had to learn to read aloud books in which there was no punctuation or even spaces between words, and to recite them. They also had to be able to answer very detailed questions on every word of the books they were reading. A favorite author, from the end of the first century B.C. onwards, was Publius Vergilius Maro, whom we call Vergil. He had written a great poem called the *Aeneid* (because its hero was Aeneas) about the origins of the Romans.

We can get some idea of what a lesson in the school of a **grammaticus** might have been like from a grammarian called Priscian who lived in the sixth century A.D. Here is part of a series of questions and answers that he gives on the first line of the second book of Vergil's *Aeneid*.

Conticuēre omnēs intentīque ōra tenēbant.

"Partēs ōrātiōnis quot sunt?"	*"How many parts of speech are there?"*
"Sex."	*"Six."*
"Quot nōmina?"	*"How many nouns?"*
"Duo. *Omnēs* et *ōra*."	*"Two. **omnēs** and **ōra**."*
"Quot verba?"	*"How many verbs?"*
"Duo. *Conticuēre* et *tenēbant*."	*"Two. **conticuēre** and **tenēbant**."*
"Quid aliud habet?"	*"What else does it have?"*
"Participium *intentī* et coniūnctiōnem *-que*."	*"A participle **intentī** and a conjunction **-que**."*
"*Conticuēre* —quae pars ōrātiōnis est?"	*"What part of speech is **conticuēre**?"*
"Verbum."	*"A verb."*
"Quāle?"	*"What tense?"*
"Perfectum"	*"The perfect."*
"Quōmodo dictum?"	*"How is it described?"*
"Indicātīvō coniugātiōnis secundae."	*"Indicative, of the second conjugation."*
"Cuius significātiōnis?"	*"What voice is it?"*
"Actīvae."	*"Active."*
"Dīc passīvum."	*"Tell me the passive."*

And so it goes on for many more questions, each word being treated in the same way.

HIGHER EDUCATION

After assuming the **toga virīlis** at age sixteen, a boy was ready for the most advanced stage of Roman education—that of the teacher of rhetoric (**rhētor**). From the **rhētor** he learned the art of public speaking, a necessary qualification for anyone aspiring to high office in law or politics.

A few favored youths completed their education by further study of rhetoric and philosophy at Athens or some other foreign city.

ATTITUDES TO EDUCATION

Horace's father, though a freedman of moderate means, did not consider it too great a sacrifice to give his son the best possible education. Horace recalls his father's efforts with pride and gratitude:

> My father refused to send me to Flavius' (the local) school where the big sons of the local gentry went, with school-bag and writing-tablets over their left shoulders, bringing their school fees of eight **asses*** on the Ides of each month. He dared to take me to Rome.

Horace, Satires I.6.71–76

Pliny, who showed his interest in a practical way by contributing money to found a school in his native town of Comum, was also concerned that education should be more than book-learning:

> But now the most important thing is who gives him his instruction. Up to the present he has been at home and has had teachers there. At home there is little or no opportunity for going astray. Now his studies must be carried away from home, and we must find a teacher of Latin rhetoric in whose school we shall find a strict training along with good manners and moral standards.

Pliny, Letters III.3

A character in a novel of Petronius deplores the acceptance of lax standards of discipline in schools:

> What's to be done? It's the parents who are to blame for refusing to let their children benefit by severe discipline. But now boys play in school, young men are laughing-stocks in public and, what is worse than either, they refuse to admit in old age the mistakes they learned at school.

Petronius, Satyricon 4

*about 19 cents

Quintilian, a famous "professor" of rhetoric in Rome at the period of our story, has a very different attitude from that of the cruel schoolmaster about whom Martial wrote (see above, page 104):

> The teacher should adopt before all things the attitude of a parent toward his pupils and consider that he is taking the place of those by whom their children have been entrusted to him. He should not have faults himself, nor should he allow his pupils to have any. He should be strict but not harsh, courteous but not lax, lest the former breed hatred, the latter contempt. He should not be bad-tempered, but neither should he pass over what requires correction. When praising the speeches of his pupils, he should be neither grudging nor effusive, for the one will lead to distaste for the work, the other to over-confidence.

Quintilian, Institutio oratoria II.4–8

ST. AUGUSTINE AND PLINY ON EDUCATION

The following passages give two very personal and sharply contrasting views of education. St. Augustine, writing in the late fourth century A.D., looks back on his school days with horror. Pliny, on the other hand, writing in the early second century A.D., remembers his schooling with great fondness:

> Then I was put into school to get learning, in which I (poor wretch) did not know what use there was. And yet, if sluggish in my learning, I was beaten. What miseries and mockeries did I experience then!

St. Augustine, Confessions I.9

> Thanks to you, I am returning to school and (as it were) taking up again the sweetest part of my life; I take my seat, as I used to, with the youngsters and I experience how much respect my learning has among them.

Pliny, Letters II.18

ADDITIONAL READING:
The Romans Speak for Themselves: Book II: "Early Education in Rome,"
pages 41–49.

Go Online
For: Additional Practice
Visit: PHSchool.com
Web Code: jgd-0012

A LESSON FOR SEXTUS

Postquam Marcus fīnem recitandī fēcit, grammaticus, "Illī versūs bene recitātī sunt. Nunc dīc mihi hoc! Quot sunt verba in prīmō versū?" "Quīnque." "Sed quot in secundō versū?" "Octō." "Quid dē verbō *conticuēre* mihi dīcere potes?" "*Conticuēre* est idem ac *conticuērunt*. Sīc verbum saepe scrībunt poētae."

"Bene respondistī. Et tū, Aule, dīc mihi hoc! Quī sunt 'omnēs'?" "Troiānī ūnā cum 5
rēgīnā et comitibus." "Ubi sunt hī omnēs?" "In Āfricā." "Quō in locō?" "Carthāginī." "Unde vēnit Aenēās?" "Troiā." "Quō itinere Troiā nāvigāvit?" "Prīmum ad Siciliam vēnit; deinde tempestāte Carthāginem āctus est."

"Multa tamen dē hāc fābulā omittis, nam Aenēās comitēsque multōs annōs errābant antequam ad Siciliam advēnērunt. Prīmum ad Thrāciam, deinde Dēlum, tum ad Crētam 10
nāvigāvērunt. Cūr nusquam morātus est Aenēās, Marce?" "Monitus ā dīs, Aenēās semper Hesperiam petēbat. Volēbat enim novam condere Troiam."

Omnēs discipulī grammaticum attentē audiēbant—praeter Sextum quī dormitābat. Quem ubi animadvertit grammaticus, "Sexte," clāmāvit, "Expergīscere! Dīc mihi! Ubi est Hesperia?"

(continued) 15

1 **fīnem recitandī fēcit,** *(he) made an end of reciting, (he) stopped reciting*	**Dēlos, Dēlī,** f., *Delos (small island off the eastern coast of Greece)*
2 **verbum, -ī,** n., *word, verb*	**Crēta, -ae,** f., *Crete (large island southeast of Greece)*
3 **idem ac,** *the same as*	11 **nusquam,** adv., *nowhere*
4 **sīc,** adv., *thus, in this way*	**moneō, -ēre, -uī, -itus,** *to advise, warn*
6 **comes, comitis,** m./f., *companion*	**deus, -ī,** nom. pl., **dī,** dat., abl. pl., **dīs,**
8 **Carthāgō, Carthāginis,** f., *Carthage (city on the northern coast of Africa)*	m., *god*
10 **antequam,** conj., *before*	13 **dormitō, -āre, -āvī,** *to be sleepy*
Thrācia, -ae, f., *Thrace (country northeast of Greece)*	

3 **conticēscō, conticēscere, conticuī,** *to become silent*
14 **animadvertō, animadvertere, animadvertī, animadversus,** *to notice*
   expergīscor, expergīscī, experrēctus sum, *to wake up*

Exercise 39a
Respondē Latīnē:

1. Quid Marcus grammaticō dīcit dē verbō *conticuēre*?
2. Quō errābat Aenēās antequam ad Siciliam advēnit?
3. Cūr Aenēās Hesperiam semper petēbat?
4. Quid faciēbat Sextus, dum cēterī discipulī grammaticum audiēbant?

"Hesperia? Nōnne est Graecia?" "Minimē, ō puer abōminande! Hesperia est Italia." "Nīl interest," mussāvit Sextus.

"At maximē interest," respondit grammaticus, īrā maximā commōtus. Ferulam sūmpsit et vōce terribilī, "Extende manum, Sexte!" clāmāvit. Cēterī discipulī conticuērunt. At Sextus grammaticō nōn pāruit. "Nōn extendam," inquit. Stupuit grammaticus. Longum   20
fuit silentium. Tandem, "Abī, puer!" clāmat. "Vocā Eucleidem paedagōgum! Ille tē domum dūcet. Satis procācitātis tuae passus sum. Tē hūc redīre vetō, nisi labōrāre volēs. Nunc abī!"

Cēterī discipulī verbīs grammaticī territī erant. Numquam anteā puer domum missus erat.

17 **interest,** *it is important*   20 **pāreō, -ēre, -uī, -itūrus** + dat., *to obey*
18 **ferula, -ae,** f., *cane*

    19 **extendō, extendere, extendī, extentus,** *to hold out*

Respondē Latīnē:

1. Quid respondit Sextus dē Hesperiā rogātus?
2. Quid sūmpsit grammaticus?
3. Quōmodo grammaticus "Extende manum!" dīcit?
4. Cūr Sextus ā grammaticō domum missus est?

BUILDING THE MEANING
Place Clues

Look at the following sentences:

Ad Forum festīnant.	*They hurry **to the Forum**.*
Rōmam festīnāvit.	*He hurried **to Rome**.*
Ē lūdō venit Eucleidēs.	*Eucleides comes **from the school**.*
Brundisiō discesserat Pūblius.	*Publius had departed **from Brundisium**.*
Cornēlius **in ātriō** amīcōs exspectat.	*Cornelius waits for his friends **in the atrium**.*
Pūblius **Baiīs** morābātur.	*Publius was staying **in Baiae**.*

In the first sentence of each pair, the preposition and the case of the noun give clues to the meaning of the phrase. In the second sentence of each pair, there is no preposition. This is normal with names of cities, towns, and small islands.

NOTES

1. With names of cities, towns, and small islands, the *accusative case* without a preposition indicates place *to which*:

Rōmam festīnāvit.	*He hurried **to Rome**.*
Dēlum nāvigāvit.	*He sailed **to Delos**.*

2. With names of cities, towns, and small islands, the *ablative case* without a preposition may indicate place *from which*:

Brundisiō discesserat Pūblius.	*Publius had gone **from Brundisium**.*
Dēlō abiit.	*He went away **from Delos**.*
Baiīs profectus est.	*He set out **from Baiae**.*

   With names of cities, towns, and small islands, the *locative case* without a preposition indicates place *in which*. The endings of the locative case are as follows:

   a. singular nouns of the 1st and 2nd declensions: identical in spelling to the *genitive*:

Rōm*ae* manēbat.	*He was remaining **in Rome**.*
Brundisi*ī* habitat.	*He lives **in Brundisium**.*

   b. singular nouns of the 3rd declension: same as *ablative* (sometimes *dative*):

Sīdōn*e* multa ēmit.	*He bought many things **in Sidon**.*
Carthāgin*ī* cōmiter acceptus est.	*He was received graciously **at Carthage**.*

   c. plural nouns: same as *ablative*:

Bai*īs* vīllam habet.	*He has a farm **in Baiae**.*
Gād*ibus* morābātur.	*He was staying **at Gades**.*

3. When a noun has the same endings for both place *from which* and place *in which*, the verb will help with the meaning:

Bai*īs* manēbat.	*He was remaining **in Baiae**.*
Bai*īs* profectus est.	*He set out **from Baiae**.*

4. The words **domus**, *home*, and **rūs**, *country, country estate*, behave in a similar way:

   Accusative of place to which:

Domum iit.	*He went **home**.*
Rūs iit.	*He went **to the country/to his country estate**.*

   Ablative of place from which:

Domō profectus est.	*He set out **from home**.*
Rūre rediit.	*He returned **from the country/from his country estate**.*

Locative of place where:

Domī est.

*He is **at home**.*

Rūrī est.

*He is **in the country/on his country estate**.*

The word **rūs, rūris** is a regular 3rd declension neuter noun; its locative is **rūrī**. The feminine noun **domus** appears as a 4th declension noun (see the forms at the left below), but some of its cases have 2nd declension alternatives (at the right below), of which the locative is one:

	Singular		Plural	
Nominative	dom**us**		dom**ūs**	
Genitive	dom**ūs**	dom**ī** (locative)	dom**uum**	dom**ōrum**
Dative	dom**uī**	dom**ō**	dom**ibus**	
Accusative	dom**um**		dom**ūs**	dom**ōs**
Ablative	dom**ū**	dom**ō**	dom**ibus**	
Vocative	dom**us**		dom**ūs**	

Omnia Rōmae cum pretiō. *Everything is available in Rome—for a price!* (Juvenal, *Satires* III.183–184)

Exercise 39b

Use each place name listed below to replace the italicized words in the following sentences. Use the prepositions **ab, in,** or **ad** *only where necessary*:

1. Mox *ad urbem* veniam.
2. Iam *ab urbe* discessī.
3. Diū *in urbe* morābar.

Āfrica, -ae, f.
Athēnae, -ārum, f. pl., *Athens*
Baiae, -ārum, f. pl.
Brundisium, -ī, n.
Carthāgō, Carthāginis, f.

Dēlos, Dēlī, f.
domus, -ūs, f.
Gādēs, Gādium, f. pl.
Gallia, -ae, f., *Gaul*

Philippī, -ōrum, m. pl.
Rōma, -ae, f.
rūs, rūris, n.
Sīdōn, Sīdōnis, f.

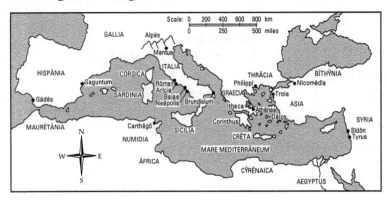

Exercise 39c

Read aloud and translate:

1. Ubi Graecī fīnem bellī fēcērunt, Ulixēs cum comitibus Troiā profectus est.
2. Domum redīre et uxōrem suam vidēre volēbat.
3. Multīs post annīs Ithacam pervēnit.
4. Cornēliī aestāte Baiīs, hieme Rōmae habitant. Nunc autem Cornēliī domī Rōmae sunt.
5. Aestāte Cornēliī domō proficīscuntur; Baiās eunt; rūrī habitant.
6. Aenēās, quī ē Siciliā profectus erat, magnā tempestāte iactātus, Carthāginem tandem advēnit.
7. Carthāginī Aenēās breve modo tempus morābātur; Carthāgine discessit quod novam urbem in Italiā condere volēbat.
8. Hannibal, ubi Saguntum, oppidum Hispāniae, cēpit, iter longum per Galliam et trāns Alpēs in Italiam fēcit.
9. Mox Quīntus Valerius, amīcus Cornēliōrum, ē Bīthȳniā Rōmam regrediētur. Tribus mēnsibus domum perveniet.

bellum, -ī, n., *war*
multīs post annīs, *many years afterward*
hiems, hiemis, f., *winter*
iactō, -āre, -āvī, -ātus, *to toss about, drive to and fro*

oppidum, -ī, *n., town*
Hispānia, -ae, f., *Spain*
trāns, prep. + acc., *across*

Time Clues

1. Prepositions will be found introducing some expressions of time:

   post multōs annōs   *after many years*
   ante prīmam lūcem   *before dawn*

2. Words or phrases in the accusative or ablative cases without prepositions are found expressing other ideas of time:

   a. *Accusative of duration of time:*
   mult**ōs** ann**ōs**   *throughout many years, for many years*
   tōt**um** di**em**   *throughout the whole day, for the whole day*

   b. *Ablative of time when* and *ablative of time within which*:
   aestāt**e**   *in summer*
   e**ō** tempor**e**   *at that time*
   prīm**ā** lūc**e**   *at dawn*
   Īd**ibus** Mārti**īs**   *on the Ides of March*
   brev**ī** tempor**e**   *within a short time, in a short time, soon*
   tr**ibus** mēns**ibus**   *in three months*

3. Adverbs are found in some expressions of time:

a. You have seen adverbs such as the following very frequently (see Chapter 13 of Level I): **crās**, *tomorrow*; **hodiē**, *today*; **iam**, *now, already*; **iterum**, *again, a second time*; **nunc**, *now*; etc. These cause no problems, but note the following:

b. **abhinc**, *back from this point in time*, *ago* + accusative of duration of time:

abhinc trēs diēs   ***back from the present*** *for three days* = *three days* ***ago***

c. **post**, *after(ward)* + ablative
ante, *previously, before* + ablative:

tribus **post** diēbus   ***afterward*** *by three days* = *three days* ***later***
tribus **ante** diēbus   ***previously*** *by three days* = *three days* ***before***

Note that **post** and **ante** may be either prepositions with the accusative or adverbs with the ablative.

Exercise 39d
Select, read aloud, and translate:

1. Puerī ē lūdō (sextā hōrā/paucīs mēnsibus/decem hōrās) rediērunt.
2. Hodiē, Marce, (trēs hōrās/aestāte/ante prīmam lūcem) surrēxistī.
3. Graecī Troiam (quīnque mēnsēs/tribus annīs/decem annōs) obsidēbant.
4. Nōs apud Cornēlium (ūnum mēnsem/nōnā hōrā/tōtum diem) cēnābimus.
5. Ad vīllam (tōtum diem/duōs mēnsēs/aestāte) profectī estis.
6. Ego ad urbem (abhinc trēs diēs/octō mēnsēs/ūnō annō) advēnī.
7. Aenēās comitēsque (duōbus diēbus/multōs annōs/septem annīs) errābant.
8. Sextus iam (ūnō annō/trēs mēnsēs/quīnque hōrīs) in urbe habitat.
9. Discipulī versūs Vergiliī (tōtum diem/brevī tempore/ūnō diē) legēbant.
10. Convīvae ad domum Cornēliānam (brevī tempore/quattuor hōrās/ūnam noctem) advenient.

Exercise 39e
Using story 39 and the information on place and time clues as guides, give the Latin for:

1. When did Aeneas and his companions sail from Troy?
2. Many years later they came to Sicily.
3. They were driven to Carthage by a storm.
4. For many months they remained in Carthage; finally they returned to Sicily.
5. After a long journey they arrived at Hesperia.

Exercise 39f

Read this story of Vergil's life aloud and answer in English the questions that follow:

Pūblius Vergilius Marō, maximus poētārum Rōmānōrum, nātus est Īdibus Octōbribus prope Mantuam, quae est oppidum Italiae septentriōnālis. Puer Cremōnam missus, ab optimīs magistrīs ibi doctus, sextō decimō annō togam virīlem sūmpsit. Paulisper domī in patris fundō morātus, profectus est adulēscēns Mediolānum. Paucōs annōs et litterīs et linguae Graecae dīligentissimē studēbat. 5
Mox tamen, quod pater post bellum ē fundō suō expulsus erat, Vergilius Rōmam cum patre migrāvit. Dum Rōmae habitat, versūs multīs dē rēbus scrīpsit et mox praeclārus factus est poēta. In numerō amīcōrum et poētam Horātium et prīncipem Augustum ipsum habēbat; sed (ēheu!) saepe aegrōtābat et semper īnfirmā erat valētūdine. Interdum Neāpolī in sōlitūdine vīvēbat. Iam 10
quīnquāgintā annōs nātus dum in Graeciā iter facit, prīncipī occurrit Athēnīs. Quī, ad Italiam rediēns, Vergilium sēcum dūxit. Athēnīs profectī ad Italiam nāvigāvērunt. In terram ēgressus Brundisium, Vergilius aegerrimus fīēbat et in eō oppidō mortuus est. Corpus Neāpolim lātum ab amīcīs trīstissimīs est sepultum.

2 **Mantua, -ae,** f., *Mantua* (*town in northern Italy*)
  septentriōnālis, -is, -e, *northern*
3 **Cremōna, -ae,** f., *Cremona* (*town in northern Italy*)
4 **fundus, -ī** m., *farm*
5 **Mediolānum, -ī,** n., *Milan*
  litterae, -ārum, f. pl., *letters, literature*
  lingua, -ae, f., *tongue, language*
  studeō, -ēre, -uī + dat., *to study*
7 **migrō, -āre, -āvī, -ātūrus,** *to move one's home*

8 **Horātius, -ī,** m., *Horace* (*Roman poet*)
9 **Augustus, -ī,** m., *Augustus* (*first Roman emperor*)
  aegrōtō, -āre, -āvī, -ātūrus, *to be ill*
10 **īnfirmā…valētūdine,** *in poor health*
  interdum, adv., *from time to time*
12 **rediēns,** *returning*
13 **in terram ēgressus,** *having disembarked*
  aeger, aegra, aegrum, *ill*

1 **nāscor, nāscī, nātus sum,** *to be born*
6 **expellō, expellere, expulī, expulsus,** *to drive out, expel*
10 **vīvō, vīvere, vīxī, vīctūrus,** *to live*
14 **morior, morī, mortuus sum,** *to die*
  sepeliō, sepelīre, sepelīvī, sepultus, *to bury*

1. When and where was Vergil born?
2. Where was he sent as a boy?
3. At what age did he take up the **toga virīlis?**
4. How long did he stay in Milan?
5. What did he study while in Milan?
6. Why did he move to Rome with his father?
7. Who were among his friends in Rome?
8. At what age did he take his fatal trip to Greece?
9. With whom did he return from Greece?
10. Where did Vergil die and where was he buried?

AUGUSTUS

The assassination of Julius Caesar on the Ides of March, 44 B.C., inaugurated a struggle for power in Rome that took fourteen years of war and intrigue to resolve. The ultimate struggle lay between the consul at the time of Caesar's murder, Marcus Antonius (Mark Antony), and Caesar's principal heir, adopted son, and grandnephew, Octavian. The struggle encompassed such drama and such fervor that subsequent ages have drawn upon it repeatedly for great works of art and literature. Early on in the struggle Cicero fell victim to proscriptions instituted by the Second Triumvirate, a coalition of Octavian, Antony, and Caesar's old lieutenant Lepidus, to fight their common political enemies in the name of avenging Caesar. At Antony's insistence, Cicero's severed head and hands were put on display on the Rostra in the Forum. The conclusion of the struggle was marked by Octavian's victory over Antony at the naval battle of Actium in 31 B.C. and the suicides of Antony and Cleopatra. Octavian was eighteen years old when the struggle began and thirty-two when he finally prevailed. He showed himself to be a ruthless military and political strategist and leader, but his great contributions were to begin when he took the helm in Rome in 30 B.C.

The imposing statue of Augustus from the Villa of Livia at Prima Porta. The figure of Cupid at Augustus' feet alludes to his divine descent from Aeneas, the son of Anchises and Venus; the breastplate is decorated with figures that celebrate Augustus' recovery from the Parthians of the Roman standards lost by Crassus in 53 B.C. Other figures on the breastplate celebrate the new era of peace and prosperity established by Augustus and characterized by contemporary poets as a new golden age (saeculum aureum).

Vatican Museums, Vatican State, Italy

PAX ROMANA

After more than 100 years of political turmoil and civil wars, it seemed that a chance for a lasting peace had come to Rome. In 27 B.C., after adjusting the membership of the Senate and laying other groundwork, Octavian proclaimed the Restoration of the Republic. On the surface he appeared to have put the old constitution back in place: the Senate regained its role of leadership; the popular assemblies met as before to pass laws and elect magistrates to the offices of the **cursus honōrum**. It was in gratitude for this "restoration" that the senators awarded him the title **Augustus**, *Venerable*, by which title he is principally remembered today. In fact, however, it was he who ruled the Empire as its first emperor, and certain powers the Senate granted him assured his authority (**auctoritās**). He had the right to propose legislation in the assemblies as well as decrees in the Senate, where he ranked as senior senator, a position that allowed him to speak first with the consequence of encouraging subsequent speakers to support his proposals. He held guaranteed control over the armies, foreign affairs, and the provinces. The title he preferred for himself, however, was not **imperātor**, *commander*, hence, "emperor," but simply **prīnceps**, *first citizen*, hence, "prince." More important than any titles was his talent for convincing people to do what he wanted without seeming to order their actions.

Later in his life, Augustus personally recorded his accomplishments in his official memoirs, *The Deeds of the Deified Augustus (Res gestae Divi Augusti)*. His account was published on inscriptions that were placed at his tomb in Rome and elsewhere in the empire. One inscription, which survived on the walls of a temple in Ankara, Turkey, is called, because of its location, the **Monumentum Ancyrānum**. In the text Augustus lists the offices and honors he held, his private funding of public works, and his achievements in war and peace. He also stresses that he was just in his treatment of his enemies and always acted within the legal guidelines of the republican constitution that he restored.

The remarkable **auctoritās** that Augustus possessed enabled him to lay the foundation of imperial government. Throughout the empire, professional armies loyal to the emperor enforced the **pāx Rōmāna** that he had established. In the *Res gestae* Augustus indicates his own pride in the peace when he mentions the consecration of the Altar of Augustan Peace (**Āra Pācis Augustae**) on the Campus Martius and the ceremonial closing of the doors of the Shrine of Janus Quirinus three times during his principate, a symbolic gesture of peace for Rome that had occurred only twice before since the founding of the city in 753 B.C.

On those occasions when Augustus did order the doors of the Shrine of Janus opened, the armies under his **imperium** extended the northern frontiers to the Rhine and Danube Rivers, so that communication between the eastern and western provinces was firmly protected. Late in his principate Augustus suffered one military defeat. In A.D. 9, Quinctilius Varus led three legions into a trap in the Teutoberger Forest, where the Germans slaughtered them. Augustus thereupon gave up his attempt to conquer and Romanize Germany. He expressed his displeasure by banging his head against a door in the palace and crying out, "Quinctilius Varus, give me back my legions!"

Augustus realized that he could not direct everything in the empire single-handedly; he therefore created an imperial bureaucracy, staffed by members of the senatorial and equestrian classes, to whom he delegated the responsibility of administering law and order in the provinces and in the city. The **lēgātī** who served as governors in Augustus' proconsular provinces were paid well enough so that they stayed at their posts for years and administered their duties knowledgeably and efficiently. Within the city of Rome **praefectī** and **cūrātōrēs** managed public works and agencies concerned with the citizens' welfare. The superintendent of aqueducts (**cūrātor aquārum**), for example, was in charge of the aqueducts and water supply, and the commander of watchmen (**praefectus vigilum**) commanded the companies of **vigilēs**, who dealt with fire-fighting and minor criminals.

The Roman Empire in the Age of Augustus

Under Augustus' influence, then, the Roman Empire enjoyed a sound economy, marked by increased trade and prosperity and by solvent state finances. To sense that Rome was becoming more prosperous, the citizens of Rome had only to look about them and observe the ambitious building program directed by Augustus and Marcus Agrippa, his right-hand man and son-in-law: the renovation of many old buildings, the completion of the Basilica Julia, and the construction of a new Forum. In addition, to make sure that everyone realized how great Rome, Italy, and their **prīnceps** were, the writers of the Augustan age concentrated on literary themes that glorified the Romans and their nation. Livy's impressive books on the history of Rome supported the idea that Roman character, as displayed by heroes of the past, was the source of Roman greatness. Gaius Maecenas, a wealthy equestrian businessman and a friend of Augustus, was a patron who supported several poets who helped propagandize Augustan nationalism. Horace owed him his Sabine villa and the leisure to explore patriotic themes in his *Odes* as well as the traditional topics of lyric poetry. Vergil dedicated to Maecenas his *Georgics*, poems that praised the Italian landscape and country life, where the Italian peasant farmer flourished.

Even more stirring was Vergil's epic, the *Aeneid*, in which, long before Rome was founded, Jupiter told his daughter Venus that he had granted the Romans "rule without limit" (**imperium sine fīne**) and that a Caesar, descended from the Trojans, would rise to power after many centuries and that the gates of war of the Shrine of Janus would be closed. Later in the epic, when the hero, Aeneas, visits the underworld, his father, Anchises, foretells the future greatness of Rome and specifically points out the spirit of Augustus Caesar, son of a god, who will establish again for Latium a Golden Age (**Aurea Saecula**).

Augustus and Livia
Marble statues, Ephesus Museum, Turkey

At the climax of his predictions, Anchises instructs Aeneas:

> "Tū regere imperiō populōs, Rōmāne, mementō
> (hae tibi erunt artēs) pācisque impōnere mōrem,
> parcere subiectīs et dēbellāre superbōs."

> — *Aeneid* VI.851–853

> "You, Roman, remember to rule nations with power
> (these will be your skills) and to impose the conditions of peace,
> to spare the conquered and to conquer the arrogant."

That, Anchises tells both Aeneas and, through Vergil's epic, the Romans of Augustus' generation, is Rome's mission.

Exercise 39g

Here are the first seven lines of Vergil's *Aeneid*. Read them aloud and translate them:

> Arma virumque canō, Troiae quī prīmus ab ōrīs
> Ītaliam fātō profugus Lāvīniaque vēnit
> lītora, multum ille et terrīs iactātus et altō
> vī superum, saevae memorem Iūnōnis ob īram,
> multa quoque et bellō passus, dum conderet urbem 5
> īnferretque deōs Latiō, genus unde Latīnum
> Albānīque patrēs atque altae moenia Rōmae.

1 **arma, -ōrum,** n. pl., *arms, weapons*
ōra, -ae, f., *shore*
2 **fātum, -ī,** n., *fate*
profugus, -a, -um, *exiled, fugitive*
Lāvīnius, -a, -um, *of Lavinium (name of the town where the Trojans first settled in Italy)*
3 **lītus, lītoris,** n., *shore*
altum, -ī, n., *the deep, the sea*
4 **superī, -ōrum,** m. pl., *the gods above*
superum = superōrum
saevus, -a, -um, *fierce, savage*

memor, memoris, *remembering, mindful, unforgetting*
Iūnō, Iūnōnis, f. *Juno (queen of the gods)*
ob, prep. + acc., *on account of*
5 **dum conderet...īnferretque,** *until he could found...and bring...into*
6 **Latium, -ī,** n., *Latium (the area of central Italy that included Rome)*
genus, generis, n., *race, stock, nation*
7 **Albānus, -a, -um,** *of Alba Longa (city founded by Aeneas' son, Ascanius)*
moenia, moenium, n. pl., *city walls*

1 **canō, canere, cecinī, cantus,** *to sing*

Mantua mē genuit, Calabrī rapuēre, tenet nunc
Parthenopē: cecinī pascua, rūra, ducēs.
Mantua gave me life, Calabria took it away, now
Naples holds me: I sang of pastures, fields, and heroes.
(Inscription on the tomb of Vergil)

Vergil reading the *Aeneid* to Augustus and his sister, Octavia, memorialized here by Ingres.
Legend has it that Octavia fainted when Vergil reached the verses about the death of her son.
Watercolor and graphite drawing, Fogg Art Museum, Harvard University, Cambridge. Bequest of Grenville L. Winthrop

Go Online
For: Additional Practice
Visit: PHSchool.com
Web Code: jgd-0013

TO FATHER FROM SEXTUS

Sextus patrī suō S.P.D.

Avē, mī pater! Sī tū valēs, ego gaudeō. Sed nēmō est mē miserior. Māter mea Pompeiīs mortua est. Tū mē in Italiā relīquistī, cum in Asiam profectus es. O mē miserum!

Prīmō quidem Baiīs habitāre mē dēlectābat. Ibi ad lītus īre, in marī natāre, scaphās 5 spectāre solēbam. In silvīs quoque cum Marcō cotīdiē ambulābam; inde regressus, cum vīlicō Dāvō, quī mē maximē amat, in hortō labōrābam.

Ōlim, dum prope rīvum in silvīs ambulāmus, Cornēliam et Flāviam magnā vōce clāmantēs audīvimus. Statim accurrimus et lupum ingentem puellās petentem cōnspeximus. Tum Marcus, maximō terrōre affectus, arborem ascendit neque dēsilīre 10 ausus est. Ego tamen magnō rāmō lupum reppulī et puellās servāvī sōlus.

At abhinc paucōs mēnsēs nōs omnēs, Baiīs profectī, maximō itinere Rōmam pervēnimus. Dum autem Rōmae habitō, mē dēlectat ad Circum Maximum īre. Russātīs ego faveō quī semper vincunt.

(continued)

2 **Avē!/Avēte!** *Greetings!*
valeō, -ēre, -uī, -itūrus, *to be strong, be well*
5 **prīmō,** adv., *first, at first*

natō, -āre, -āvī, -ātūrus, *to swim*
scapha, -ae, f., *small boat*
6 **inde,** adv., *from there, then*

10 **dēsiliō, dēsilīre, dēsiluī,** *to leap down*
11 **audeō, audēre, ausus sum,** semi-deponent + infin., *to dare (to)*
repellō, repellere, reppulī, repulsus, *to drive off, drive back*

Exercise 40a
Respondē Latīnē:

1. Ubi nunc est Sextī pater?
2. Quid Sextus Baiīs facere solēbat?
3. Quis Sextum maximē amābat?
4. Dīcitne Sextus vēra?
5. Dīcitne Sextus vēram fābulam dē puellīs et lupō?
6. Quid Sextum Rōmae facere dēlectat?
7. Cūr Sextus russātīs favet?

vērus, -a, -um, *true*
vēra dīcere, *to tell the truth*

Nunc tamen miserrimus sum propter īrācundiam Palaemonis magistrī nostrī. Ille 15
enim homō īrācundissimus mē, quamquam discere semper cupiō, saepe ferulā ferōciter
verberat. Cotīdiē dē Aenēae itineribus multa mē rogat. Eī rogantī respondēre semper
cōnor. Cēterōs tamen puerōs semper facillima, mē semper difficillima rogat. Heri
quidem dē Hesperiā loquēbātur, dē quā neque ego neque cēterī puerī quidquam sciunt.
Immō vērō, etiam Aenēās ipse ignōrābat ubi esset Hesperia! Grammaticus tamen, cum 20
ego ignōrārem, īrā commōtus, ferulam rapuit et mē crūdēlissimē verberāvit. Deinde
domum statim ab Eucleide ductus sum. Cum prīmum domum advēnimus, ā Cornēliō
arcessītus sum. Eī rem tōtam explicāre cōnābar, sed mē nē loquī quidem sīvit. Iterum
igitur poenās dedī.

Ō pater, regredere, obsecrō, quam prīmum in Italiam! Ego sum miser et valdē 25
aegrōtō. Amā mē et valē!

15 **īrācundia, -ae,** f., *irritability, bad temper*

19 **neque…neque…quidquam,** *neither…nor…anything*

20 **immō vērō,** adv., *on the contrary, in fact*
   ignōrō, -āre, -āvī, -ātus, *to be ignorant, not to know*
   cum, conj., *since*

21 **crūdēlis, -is, -e,** *cruel*

22 **cum prīmum,** conj., *as soon as*

24 **poena, -ae,** f., *punishment, penalty*
   poenās dare, *to pay the penalty, be punished*

25 **obsecrō, -āre, -āvī, -ātus,** *to beseech, beg*
   quam prīmum, adv., *as soon as possible*

16 **discō, discere, didicī,** *to learn*
   cupiō, cupere, cupīvī, cupītus, *to desire, want*
21 **rapiō, rapere, rapuī, raptus,** *to snatch, seize*
23 **arcessō, arcessere, arcessīvī, arcessītus,** *to summon, send for*

Respondē Latīnē:

1. Estne Palaemōn magister vērō īrācundissimus?
2. Estne rogātiō dē Hesperiā vērō facilis vel difficilis?

3. Aegrōtatne vērō Sextus?

   rogātiō, rogātiōnis, f., *question*

FORMS
Semi-deponent Verbs

Some Latin verbs have regular active forms with active meanings in the present, imperfect, and future tenses but have passive forms with active meanings in the perfect, pluperfect, and future perfect:

   audeō, audēre, ausus sum + infin., *to dare (to)*
   gaudeō, gaudēre, gāvīsus sum, *to be glad, rejoice*
   soleō, solēre, solitus sum + infin., *to be accustomed (to), be in the habit of*

These are called *semi-deponent verbs* because they are deponent (i.e., they have passive forms with active meanings) only in the perfect, pluperfect, and future perfect tenses, those made from the third principal part.

Exercise 40b
Read aloud and translate:

1. audet	9. gaudēmus	17. solent
2. audēbis	10. gāvīsae sumus	18. solitī sumus
3. ausus sum	11. gaudēbāmus	19. solēbāmus
4. audēbāmus	12. gāvīsī eritis	20. solitī eritis
5. ausī erāmus	13. gāvīsus es	21. solētis
6. audētis	14. gāvīsa eris	22. solitae erāmus
7. ausae erunt	15. gaudēbunt	23. solēbam
8. ausī sunt	16. gāvīsus eram	24. solēbitis

BUILDING THE MEANING
Present Participles

Look at the following sentence:

> Cornēliam et Flāviam **clāmantēs** audīvimus. (40:8–9)
> *We heard Cornelia and Flavia **shouting**.*

The word **clāmantēs** is a *present active participle*. As you learned in Chapter 33, participles are *verbal adjectives*, that is, adjectives made from the stems of verbs. The participle **clāmantēs** is a verbal adjective describing **Cornēliam et Flāviam**.

Here are some further examples:

> Cornēliam et Flāviam <u>magnā vōce</u> **clāmantēs** audīvimus. (40:8–9)
> *We heard Cornelia and Flavia **shouting** <u>with a loud voice/loudly</u>.*

> Lupum ingentem <u>puellās</u> **petentem** cōnspeximus. (40:9–10)
> *We caught sight of a huge wolf **attacking** <u>the girls</u>.*

Since participles are *verbal* adjectives, they can be modified by ablatives such as **magnā vōce**, and they can take direct objects such as **puellās**, as seen in the sentences above.

Translating Present Participles:

The present participle describes an action going on *at the same time* as the action of the main verb in the clause. Translation of the participle will vary according to the tense of the main verb:

> Puellās **clāmantēs** audīmus. (main verb present tense)
> *We hear the girls **shouting**.*
> *We hear the girls **who <u>are</u> shouting**.*

(continued)

Puellās **clāmantēs** audīvimus. (main verb perfect tense)
*We heard the girls **shouting**.*
*We heard the girls **who <u>were</u> shouting**.*

Present participles can sometimes best be translated into English as relative clauses (see the examples just above). Sometimes they can best be translated as clauses introduced by subordinating conjunctions:

Puerī **currentēs** dēfessī fīunt.
*The boys **when/while running** become tired.*
*The boys **because/since they are running** become tired.*

Puerī **currentēs** tamen dēfessī nōn fīunt.
*The boys, **although they are running**, nevertheless do not become tired.*

Present Participles as Substantives:

Since participles are adjectives, they can also be used *substantively*, i.e., as words that function as nouns. In Chapter 23 you learned that adjectives may be used substantively, i.e., that **multa et mīra** (neuter plural adjectives) can mean *many wonderful things*. Participles may also be used substantively:

Subitō exclāmāvit ūnus ex **adstantibus**, "Cavēte, omnēs!" (30:18)
*Suddenly one of [those] **standing near** shouted, "Watch out, everyone!"*
*Suddenly one of **the bystanders**....*

Here the participle **adstantibus** is used as a noun meaning *bystanders*.

Exercise 40c

In your reading you have already met these sentences with present participles. The participles are in boldface. Read the sentences aloud and translate them. When participles are being used as adjectives, tell what noun they modify:

1. "Cavēte!" exclāmant **adstantēs**, sed frūstrā.
2. Subitō Cornēlia duōs servōs per viam **festīnantēs** cōnspicit.
3. Nunc Cornēlia cōnspicit poētam versūs **recitantem**, nunc mendīcōs pecūniam **petentēs**. seeking   reciting
4. Convīvae paulisper in ātriō stābant, Cornēlium **exspectantēs**. X praising
5. Titus, ad locum suum lentē **ambulāns**, "Salvēte, amīcī omnēs!" inquit.
6. Ubi īnsulae iam appropinquābāmus, hominēs quōsdam in popīnam **intrantēs** cōnspeximus.
7. Heri vesperī Eucleidēs noster, ab urbe domum **rediēns**, duōs hominēs ē popīnā quādam **exeuntēs** vīdit.

FORMS
Present Participles

Here are the nominative and genitive singular forms of present participles of all four conjugations:

1st: **parāns, parantis,** *preparing*
2nd: **habēns, habentis,** *having*
3rd: **mittēns, mittentis,** *sending*

-iō: **iaciēns, iacientis,** *throwing*
4th: **audiēns, audientis,** *hearing*

The participles of deponent verbs have similar active forms and are active in meaning:

1st: **cōnāns, cōnantis,** *trying*
2nd: **verēns, verentis,** *fearing*
3rd: **loquēns, loquentis,** *speaking*

-iō: **regrediēns, regredientis,** *returning*
4th: **experiēns, experientis,** *testing*

NOTES
1. The nominative ends in *-ns,* and the stem, which is found by dropping the ending from the genitive singular, ends in *-nt-*.
2. The vowel preceding the letters *-ns* is always long.
3. The vowel preceding the letters *-nt-* is always short.

Present participles have 3rd declension endings. Compare the endings of present participles with those of 3rd declension nouns and adjectives and of comparative adjectives:

When the participle is used as a simple *adjective*, the ablative singular ends in *-ī*, just as do 3rd declension adjectives; when the participle is used as a true *verbal adjective* or as a *substantive*, the ablative singular ends in *-e*, just as do 3rd declension nouns, thus:

Number Case	Masc.	Fem.	Neut.
Singular			
Nominative	parāns	parāns	parāns
Genitive	parant*is*	parant*is*	parant*is*
Dative	parant*ī*	parant*ī*	parant*ī*
Accusative	parant*em*	parant*em*	parāns
Ablative	parant*ī/e*	parant*ī/e*	parant*ī/e*
Plural			
Nominative	parant*ēs*	parant*ēs*	parant*ia*
Genitive	parant*ium*	parant*ium*	parant*ium*
Dative	parant*ibus*	parant*ibus*	parant*ibus*
Accusative	parant*ēs*	parant*ēs*	parant*ia*
Ablative	parant*ibus*	parant*ibus*	parant*ibus*

Eucleidēs ā praedōne **currentī** percussus est. (simple adjective)
*Eucleides was struck by the **running** robber.*

Eucleidēs ā praedōne **celerrimē currente** percussus est. (verbal adjective)
*Eucleides was struck by the robber **that was running very quickly**.*

(continued)

Aqua ab **adstante** ad incendium portāta est. (substantive)
*Water was brought to the fire by **a bystander**.*

The present participle of the verb **īre**, *to go*, is **iēns, euntis**. There is no present participle of the verb **esse**, *to be*.

Exercise 40d

Read aloud and translate. Locate three examples of participles used as substantives. Try translating the other participles with relative clauses or with clauses introduced by *when, while,* or *although*:

1. Aenēās Hesperiam petēns Carthāginem advēnit.
2. Marcus patrem epistulās in tablīnō scrībentem invēnit.
3. Adstantēs rogāvī ubi esset incendium.
4. Eucleidēs nocte per viās domum rediēns ā praedōnibus percussus est.
5. Dāvō in hortō labōrantī molestī erant puerī.
6. Mihi rogantī puellae nihil respondērunt.
7. Plūrimī natantium scaphās lītorī appropinquantēs vīdērunt.
8. Audīta est vōx magistrī puerōs reprehendentis.
9. Cornēlius in ātriō Eucleidem exspectāns cēterōs servōs in culīnā colloquentēs audīvit.
10. Cornēliō domō ēgredientī occurrit Titus, frāter eius.
11. Clāmōrēs gaudentium in viīs audītī sunt.
12. Cornēlius servīs fercula in trīclīnium portantibus signum dedit.
13. Cornēliī in caupōnā pernoctantēs mortem timēbant.
14. Mulierēs ad templum prōcēdentēs cōnspeximus.
15. Puellae inter sē colloquentēs multa et mīra dē puerīs nārrābant.
16. Nōs domō ēgredientēs mātrem in ātriō sedentem vīdimus.
17. Sextum arborem ascendentem dēsilīre iussī.

━━━━

Quidquid id est, timeō Danaōs et dōna ferentēs. *Whatever it is, I fear the Greeks, even bearing gifts.* (Vergil, *Aeneid* II.49)
Venientī occurrite morbō! *Meet the malady as it comes!* (Persius, *Satires* III.64)
Rīdentem dīcere vērum quid vetat? *What prevents me from speaking the truth with a smile?* (Horace, *Satires* I.I.24–25)

━━━━

WRITING, LETTERS, AND BOOKS

The letter that Cornelia wrote to Flavia in Chapter 36 and the one that Sextus wrote to his father in Chapter 40 would have been written either on tablets (**tabellae** or **cērae**) or on sheets of material made from papyrus. Tablets made of sheets of wood with the surface hollowed out and filled with wax **(cēra)** were widely used for everyday writing needs and in the schools. Two or more tablets could be fastened together with leather thongs laced through holes, and writing was done on the wax surfaces with a stylus (**stilus**) that was pointed at one end for writing and flat at the other end for erasing mistakes by smoothing the wax.

Letters could also be written on sheets of material made from Egyptian papyrus. This material was manufactured in Egypt and exported throughout the Mediterranean world. It was made from the pith of the triangular stalks of the papyrus plant that grew to be four or five inches thick and up to fourteen feet tall. Strips of the pith were laid out side by side, and another layer of strips was placed over them at right angles. When pressed together the papyrus strips released an adhesive agent that bonded them. The resulting sheets of material were then dried in the sun and smoothed with pumice stone as necessary. Sheets could be glued together as needed, and writing was done with pens (**pennae**) made from reeds or metal with ink made from lamp soot and vegetable gum.

If the letter was written on a pair of tablets, they could be folded together with the writing on the inside and bound with a cord that could be sealed with wax and stamped by the letter writer with his or her signet ring. The papyrus paper could be rolled up, bound, and sealed in the same way.

Books were usually produced by gluing sheets of papyrus side by side into a long strip of material that was then rolled up into what was called a **volūmen**, *roll*. The writing was usually done only on the side of the material that was rolled up inside, and it was done in columns perpendicular to the length of the material. To read a papyrus roll you would hold the roll in your right hand and unroll it with your left, rolling it up again at the left hand as you read the successive columns of text as they appeared from the roll at the right. When finished, one would rewind the material to the right so that it would be ready for the next reader to unroll it. A strip of material called a **titulus** was often attached to the edge of the last sheet of papyrus on the roll and would protrude from the roll. On it would be written the author and title of the book. Knobs might also be attached to the top and bottom of the last sheet of the roll to make it easier to roll it up. Since papyrus rolls were relatively fragile, they were often slipped into cases (**capsae** or **capsulae**) and stored in round wooden boxes or cabinets.

In the third century B.C. great libraries flourished in the centers of Greek civilization in the East, with the most famous one being in Alexandria in Egypt. In the late Republic Romans began to collect books in private libraries in their homes. Cicero, for example, had several libraries, both in his town house and at his country estates. During the reign of Augustus public libraries were established in Rome, and by the time of our story libraries were available in some of the great bathing establishments, where one could also hear recitations of literary works.

Rather than writing themselves, well-to-do Romans would usually have highly trained slaves take dictation. Copies of books could be made by individual slaves copying by sight from an original onto a new papyrus roll or by groups of slaves simultaneously taking dictation from one master reader. The book trade was only loosely organized, but by the time of our story there were book shops in Rome where one could buy books or have copies made. The poet Martial referred to the district in Rome called the Argiletum as a place where his poetry could be bought:

In an age before printing, copies of books were created by a scribe, shown here as later centuries pictured him.

"A Roman Scribe," oil on canvas by Sir Lawrence Alma-Tadema, private collection

> Of course you often go down to the Argiletum. There is a shop opposite Caesar's Forum with its door-posts from top to bottom bearing advertisements, so that you can in a moment read through the list of poets. Look for me in that quarter. No need to ask Atrectus (that is the name of the shopkeeper): out of the first or second pigeon-hole he will offer you Martial smoothed with pumice and smart with purple, for five **dēnāriī**.
>
> Martial, *Epigrams* I.117.9–17

WORD STUDY X

The Present Participial Stem

The stem of the present participle of a Latin verb sometimes becomes an English noun or adjective with a meaning closely related to that of the Latin verb. The stem of the present participle is found by dropping the ending *-is* from the genitive singular, e.g., **laudantis**, stem **laudant-**. The English word *agent* is derived from the Latin **agēns**, **agentis** (stem: **agent-**), the present participle of **agere**, *to do, drive*. Similarly, the English word *vigilant* is derived from **vigilāns**, **vigilantis** (stem: **vigilant-**), the present participle of **vigilāre**, *to stay awake*.

Whether the English word ends in *-ant* or *-ent* usually depends on the spelling of the Latin participle from which it is derived, as the above examples show. There are a few exceptions to this rule: they are words that came from Latin into English through Old French, which regularly changed all Latin present participial stems to *-ant*. Such English words end in *-ant*, regardless of the spelling of the original Latin participle. For example, the English word *dormant*, from Old French *dormant*, is derived from **dormiēns**, **dormientis** (stem: **dormient-**), the present participle of **dormīre**, *to sleep*. To be sure of the correct spelling, always consult an English dictionary.

Exercise 1

Give the English word made from the present participial stem of each of the following Latin verbs. Give the meaning of the English word, and check in a dictionary for its correct spelling:

1. servāre	4. accidere	7. occupāre
2. recipere	5. patī	8. dēfendere
3. exspectāre	6. studēre	9. repellere

Present Participial Stem + Suffix *-ia*

The suffix *-ia* may be added to the stem of the present participle of some Latin verbs. The addition of this suffix forms a first declension noun that designates the *state of*, *quality of*, or *act of* the meaning of the verb:

Latin Verb	Pres. Part.	P. P. Stem	Suffix	Latin Noun
convenīre, *to come together*	**conveniēns**, **convenientis**	**convenient-** +	*-ia*	**convenientia, -ae**, f., *agreement, harmony*
cōnstāre, *to stand firm*	**cōnstāns**, **cōnstantis**	**cōnstant-** +	*-ia*	**cōnstantia, -ae**, f., *steadiness*

When nouns formed in this way come into English, the letters **-tia** become *-ce* or *-cy*, e.g., *convenience, constancy*.

Exercise 2

For each English word below, give the Latin present participle (nom. sing.) and the meaning of the Latin verb from which it is derived. Give the meaning of the English word. Consult an English dictionary, as necessary:

1. audience
2. currency
3. stance
4. cadence
5. science
6. ambulance
7. sequence
8. eloquence
9. credence

Suffixes *-īnus* and *-(i)ānus*

Some Latin adjectives are formed by adding either the suffix *-īnus*, *-a*, *-um* or *-(i)ānus*, *-a*, *-um* to the base of a noun. Such adjectives mean *of* or *pertaining to* the word to which the suffix is attached:

Latin Noun	Base	Suffix	Latin Adjective
Rōma, -ae, f.	**Rōm-** +	*-ānus* =	**Rōmānus, -a, -um**, *Roman, of Rome*
mare, maris, n.	**mar-** +	*-īnus* =	**marīnus, -a, -um**, *marine, of the sea*

English words derived from this kind of Latin adjective generally end in *-ine* or *-an* (occasionally *-ane*), e.g., *marine, Roman*.

Exercise 3

For each Latin word below, give the Latin adjective ending in *-(i)ānus*. Give the English derivative and its meaning:

1. **Āfrica, -ae**, f.
2. **silva, -ae**, f.
3. **merīdiēs, -ēī**, m.
4. **Troia, -ae**, f.
5. **vetus, veteris**
6. **urbs, urbis**, f. (two English words)

The suffix *-īnus* is commonly found on Latin words for animals, e.g., **canīnus, -a, -um**, *of dogs*. The English derivative is *canine*.

Exercise 4

For each of the following animals, give the Latin adjective ending in *-īnus*. Give the English derivative and its meaning:

1. **lupus, -ī**, m.
2. **porcus, -ī**, m.
3. **equus, -ī**, m.
4. **bōs, bovis**, m./f.

Latin in Medicine

The roots of modern medicine go back to ancient Greece and Rome. The Greek physician, Hippocrates, who lived in the fifth century B.C., is considered the "father of medicine." In Roman times it was Galen, doctor to the emperor Marcus Aurelius (ruled A.D. 161–180), who expanded the frontiers of medical knowledge. His writings formed the foundation of medical science for centuries. It is no wonder that Latin and Greek are fundamental to the vocabulary of medicine.

Some Latin medical terms have become common English words, e.g., *abdomen* (belly), *cancer* (crab), *virus* (poison). Others are more obscure, e.g., *angina pectoris* (chest pain), *vena cava* ("hollow vein," vein entering the right *atrium* of the heart). Further evidence of medical Latin may be found in doctors' prescriptions, many of which use Latin abbreviations:

Rx (Recipe)	*Take*
c̄ (cum)	*with*
p.c. (post cibum)	*after eating*
t.i.d. (ter in diē)	*3 times a day*
non rep. (nōn repetātur)	*Do not repeat*

Knowledge of Latin (and Greek) can be very helpful in solving the mystery that often surrounds medical language.

Exercise 5
Replace the italicized words in each sentence with a Latin medical term of equivalent meaning, chosen from the pool below. Consult an English dictionary (or medical dictionary) for the meanings of the terms in the pool.

1. The kick Eucleides received was strong enough to break his *shinbone*.
2. Sometimes a doctor will prescribe a *substance containing no medication* in order to humor a patient whose illness is imaginary.
3. The doctor's prescription read, "Take *at bedtime*."
4. The heartbeat of the *unborn child* was normal.
5. The *small piece of tissue* that hangs down at the back of the throat is a Latin word meaning "little grape."
6. The backbone is made up of several *disk-shaped bones*.
7. The doctor wrote "*before meals*" on the prescription.
8. The *brain* is protected by the skull.
9. The ulcer was located in the *intestine measuring twelve fingers long*.
10. The *outer layer* of the adrenal gland produces important substances.
11. Lifting requires contraction of the *two-headed muscle* of the upper arm.
12. The doctor's abbreviation read, "Take *twice a day*."

biceps	vertebrae	H.S. (hōrā somnī)
cerebrum	placebo	duodenum
tibia	a.c. (ante cibum)	b.i.d. (bis in diē)
fetus	uvula	cortex

Exercise 6
Using reference material from a library or from your science teacher, make a diagram of the human skeleton, and label the bones that have Latin or Greek names.

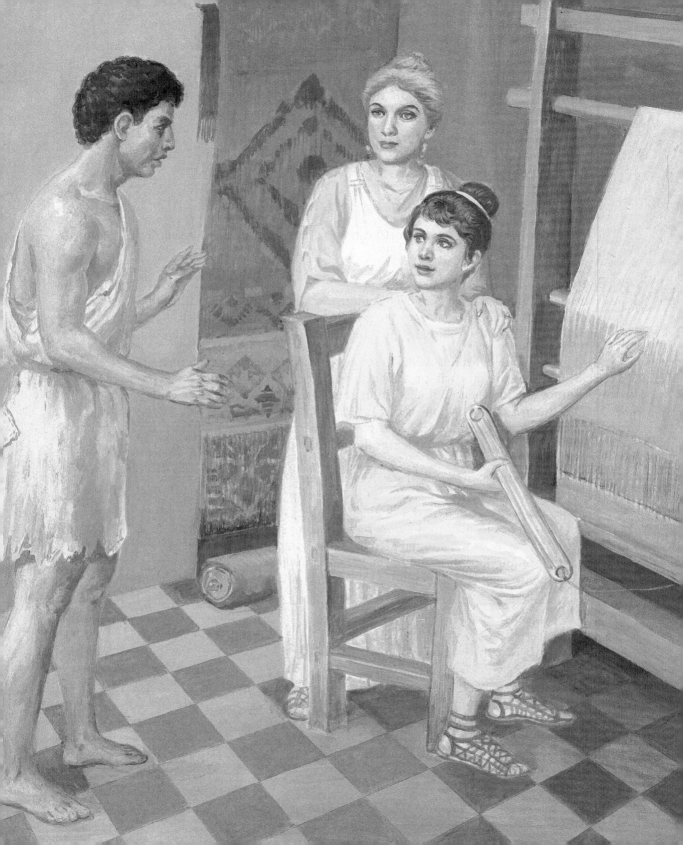

Go Online

For: Additional Practice
Visit: PHSchool.com
Web Code: jgd-0014

DRAMATIC NEWS

Māne erat. Iam puerī ad lūdum profectī erant. Cornēlia sōla in domō sedēns tēlam sine studiō texēbat. Īrācunda erat quod Baiās regredī atque Flāviam amīcam suam vidēre cupiēbat. Dē multīs rēbus cōgitābat trīstis, cum māter ingressa est.

"Trīstis vidēris, Cornēlia. Aegrane es?"

"Urbs Rōma mihi nōn placet, māter," respondit Cornēlia. "Tōtum diem sōla domī 5
maneō. Mihi nōn licet forās īre. Hīc ego labōrō sōla, sed Marcus et Sextus ūnā cum multīs aliīs in lūdō student. Hīc nūllās amīcās habeō. Hīc nē canem quidem habeō. Cūr nōn Baiās regredī licet? Meam enim Flāviam rūrsus vidēre cupiō."

"Cūr Baiās regredī vīs, Cornēlia? Quīntus Valerius, adulēscēns ille optimus, hūc paucīs diēbus veniet. Nōnne eum vidēre vīs? Diū in Bīthȳniā, ut bene scīs, āfuit sed nunc 10
in Italiam regressus est. Nāve ēgressus, paulisper Brundisiī est morātus. Inde abhinc trēs diēs discessisse dīcitur; paucīs diēbus hūc adveniet. Pater tuus diū loquēbātur cum illō servō quī epistulam attulit. Quī ūnā cum dominō suō ē Bīthȳniā profectus, ē multīs itineris perīculīs vix effūgit atque, ut ipse dīcit, dominum ex hīs perīculīs ēripuit."

Cornēlia, cum hoc audīvisset, maximē gaudēbat quod Valerium vidēre valdē cupiēbat. 15
"Quantum mē dēlectat tālia audīre!" inquit. "Arcesse, obsecrō, māter, illum servum! Ipsa cum eō loquī cupiō et dē hīs perīculīs audīre."

Itaque arcessītus servus rem tōtam eīs nārrāvit.

(continued in Chapter 42)

1 **tēla, -ae,** f., *web, fabric*	**dīcitur,** *(he) is said*
2 **studium, -ī,** n., *enthusiasm*	16 **Quantum...!** adv., *How much...!*
6 **forās,** adv., *outside*	**tālia, tālium,** n. pl., *such things*
12 **discessisse,** *to have departed*	

2 **texō, texere, texuī, textus,** *to weave*

Exercise 41a
Respondē Latīnē:

1. Quid faciēbat Cornēlia sōla sedēns?
2. Cūr trīstis Cornēlia vidētur?
3. Ubi tōtum diem manet Cornēlia?
4. Puerīne quoque ibi manent?
5. Habetne in urbe amīcās Cornēlia?
6. Quem Cornēlia rūrsus vidēre cupit?
7. Quō Cornēlia regredī cupit?
8. Quis est Valerius?
9. Quandō Rōmam adveniet Valerius?
10. Ubi morātus est Valerius?
11. Unde in Italiam est Valerius regressus?
12. Quōcum Valerius iter fēcit?
13. Quis epistulam ab hōc servō accēpit?
14. Quid necesse fuit Valeriī servō in itinere facere?
15. Cūr servum Valeriī arcessī Cornēlia vult?

FORMS
Verbs: Perfect Active Infinitive

The form **discessisse**, *to have departed*, which you met in line 12 of story 41, is a *perfect active infinitive*. First look at the principal parts of this verb:

> discēdō, discēdere, discessī, discessūrus

Two clues will help you recognize the perfect active infinitive:

> the perfect stem, **discess-**, formed by dropping the *-ī* from the third principal part

> the ending *-isse*

The perfect active infinitive expresses an action that was completed *before* the action of the main verb:

> Inde abhinc trēs diēs **discessisse** dīcitur. (41:11–12)
> *He is said **to have departed** from there three days ago.*

Exercise 41b
Read aloud and translate (note that the verbs in this exercise and the next are all taken from story 41):

1. trāxisse	4. cōgitāvisse	7. mānsisse
2. fuisse	5. placuisse	8. vīdisse
3. cupīvisse	6. respondisse	9. texuisse

Exercise 41c
Give the Latin for:

1. He is said to have studied diligently.
2. . . . to have had a dog.
3. . . . to have seen Valerius in Brundisium.
4. . . . to have wanted to see him.
5. . . . to have come from Bithynia.
6. . . . to have arrived home.
7. . . . to have brought a letter.
8. . . . to have escaped from many dangers.
9. . . . to have snatched his master from these dangers.
10. . . . to have told the whole thing.

WEAVING THE TUNIC

In the previous Frontier Life section, you read how Helge and her friend Helena spun wool into yarn for weaving. In the story at the beginning of this chapter you saw Cornelia weaving fabric while daydreaming of returning to Baiae and seeing her friend Flavia. We resume our story of frontier life with a description of how Helge wove her yarn into a tunic for her husband Lucius.

To weave the wool into a tunic (Helena was making a cloak), Helge used an upright loom with the warp threads weighted down by stones with holes drilled in them. Before she could string the warp, she had to weave the starting border, which would be attached to the top bar of the loom, for the threads extending from this border would be the warp. Using the pegs of the hand loom, Helge measured off from her strongest, stoutest yarn the exact length she would need for the warp, and she then wove a short border, one finger joint wide.

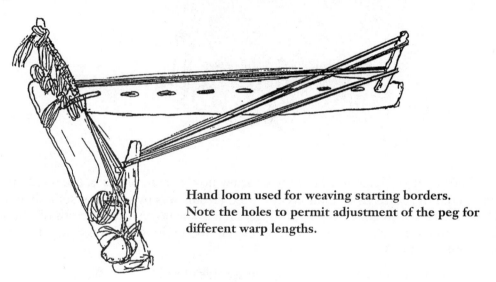

Hand loom used for weaving starting borders. Note the holes to permit adjustment of the peg for different warp lengths.

Her starting border finished, Helge was ready to begin warping her big loom. She attached the border to the round bar that was the top of her loom, taking care that none of the threads became tangled, and she took the warp-weights and arranged them in a row at the base of the loom. She tied the threads to the weights with about six threads to a stone. Weighting all the threads and preparing her loom for the weaving was a painstaking process that took skill and patience. Only then could the weaving of the cloth itself actually begin.

The poet Ovid (*Metamorphoses* VI.55–58) describes the weaving as follows:

A reed separates the threads of the warp, and the woof is inserted through them with sharp shuttles passed quickly by the fingers, and the notched teeth of the comb pound the woof passed through the warp into place.

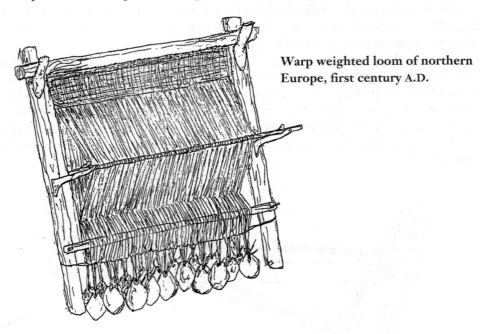

Warp weighted loom of northern Europe, first century A.D.

Since neither Helge nor her mother knew how to read or write, the way that they remembered the patterns of their complicated tartans was by verses of song, handed down from generation to generation. Although Helge was now weaving cloth of a solid color, out of habit she sang a song that told her the instructions and the colors for one of the beautiful clan plaids:

Red, red for the color of the sun, two strands of red.
Blue, blue, twenty strands of blue, the color of my eyes.
Green, five strands of green, the color of the leaves of the oak.
Red, again red, two strands.
Yellow, the color of the sun, five strands of yellow, the color of my hair.

Helge continued singing and weaving until the tunic length was finished.

Taking a bone needle, she threaded it with the same red yarn used for the cloth, and passing it in and out she sewed a border at the bottom. She removed the starting border from the pegs at the top of the loom. Carefully folding the tunic length over her arm, she knelt on the floor and untied the warp weights. Then she repeated the whole process and wove another rectangle of material.

In comparison with the weaving, the actual sewing of the tunic was easy. Helge could not help but notice that the amount of fabric needed was just right for a tunic for her younger brother of thirteen but much, much too small for her father or any other grown man of her people; the Romans were that much smaller than the Ubians and other northern clans. Helge hemmed the two rectangles of fabric together, leaving a neck hole, and at the sides leaving openings for the arms. Looking at the finished tunic, she smiled. "Won't my soldier be pleased with his new tunic," she thought as she carefully folded it.

CHAPTER 42

Go Online

For: Additional Practice
Visit: PHSchool.com
Web Code: jgd-0015

A SLAVE TO THE RESCUE

Quīntus Valerius, dominus meus, abhinc duōs mēnsēs ē Bīthȳniā Rōmam ā patre missus est epistulās ferēns. Ego ūnā cum dominō profectus sum. Cum quattuor diēs nāvigāvissēmus, subitō maxima tempestās coorta est. Nāvis hūc illūc ventīs iactāta in ingentī erat perīculō. Tandem cum undae et ventī nāvem ad īnsulam quandam ēgissent, nōs in terram vix ēvāsimus. Tōtam noctem in lītore morātī, prīmā lūce, quod iam vīs 5 tempestātis cecidisse vidēbātur, in nāvem regressī sumus.

Subitō complūrēs scaphās hominum plēnās cōnspeximus. Magister nāvis nostrae, cum hās scaphās cōnspexisset, "Prō dī immortālēs!" exclāmāvit. "Hī hominēs sunt pīrātae. Ēheu! effugere nōn poterimus."

Cui dominus meus, "Sī mē servāveris," inquit, "pater meus, quī est vir dīves et 10 praeclārus, magnam tibi pecūniam dabit. Haec nāvis est illīs scaphīs celerior. Pīrātae, etiam sī sequentur, nōs nōn capient."

Effugere cōnātī sumus, sed frūstrā. Pīrātae enim, cum nōs effugere cōnantēs cōnspexissent, nāvem nostram adortī sunt. Dominus meus statim gladium strīnxit et mihi clāmāns "Mē sequere!" in scapham dēsiluit. 15

Ego quidem secūtus dominum meum dēfendere coepī, nam vulnus grave accēpisse vidēbātur. Magister nāvis, cum valdē timēret, suōs vetuit nōs adiuvāre. "Sī pīrātīs resistēmus," inquit, "nōs omnēs sine dubiō necābimur." *(continued)*

3 **ventus, -ī,** m., *wind*	**magister, magistrī,** m., *schoolmaster,*
4 **unda, -ae,** f., *wave*	*master, captain*
7 **scapha, -ae,** f., *small boat*	8 **Prō dī immortālēs!** *Good heavens!*
	10 **dīves, dīvitis,** *rich*

3 **coorior, coocorīrī, coortus sum,** *to rise up, arise*
5 **ēvādō, ēvādere, ēvāsī, ēvāsus,** *to escape*
14 **adorior, adorīrī, adortus sum,** *to attack*
18 **resistō, resistere, restitī** + dat., *to resist*

Exercise 42a
Respondē Latīnē:

1. Quis Quīntum Valerium ē Bīthȳniā mīsit?
2. Quot diēs nāvigāverant?
3. Quid nāvem iactāvit?
4. Quem ad locum nāvis ācta est?
5. Quō in locō Valerius et servus noctem morātī sunt?
6. Quid magister nāvis prīmā lūce cōnspexit?
7. Quid pīrātae fēcērunt cum nāvem fugientem cōnspexissent?
8. Quid servus facere coepit cum dominus vulnus accēpisset?

Tum pīrātae, cum nōs superāvissent, arma nōbīs adēmērunt et nōs ad lītus addūxērunt. Cum prīmum in terrā fuimus, pīrātae circum nōs stantēs rogābant quī 20 essēmus, unde vēnissēmus, quō iter facerēmus. Omnēs tacēbant praeter dominum meum. Ille enim, "Sī pecūniam vultis," inquit, "nūllam pecūniam hīc inveniētis. Nōs omnēs pauperēs sumus. At nisi nōs abīre sinētis, vōs omnēs poenās certē dabitis. Cīvis sum Rōmānus."

Rīsērunt pīrātae, et ūnus ex eīs exclāmāvit, "Rōmānōs nōn amō. Sī vōs nūllam 25 pecūniam habētis, vōs certē necābimus." Tum magister nāvis metū commōtus, "Hic adulēscēns," inquit, "vēra nōn dīcit. Pater eius est vir dīvitissimus. Ille magnam vōbīs pecūniam dabit." Itaque pīrātārum aliī dominum meum in casam suam trāxērunt, aliī nōs cēterōs in nāvem redūxērunt et ibi custōdiēbant.

Nocte, cum omnēs dormīrent, ego surrēxī, pūgiōne modo armātus. Clam in mare 30 dēsiluī, ad lītus natāvī, casam pīrātārum summā celeritāte petīvī. Cum casae fūrtim appropinquāvissem, per fenestram vīdī dominum meum in lectō iacentem ac duōs custōdēs vīnum bibentēs. Paulisper nihil faciēbam. Mox tamen alter ē custōdibus ē casā exiit, alter cum dominō meō manēbat. Tum ego silentiō ingressus hunc custōdem pūgiōne percussī. Deinde ē casā ēgressus ad lītus dominum portāvī, nam ille propter 35 vulnus aegrōtābat neque ambulāre poterat. Ibi scapham invēnī quam pīrātae nōn custōdiēbant. Ita ā lītore profectī ex īnsulā ēvāsimus.

Iam multōs diēs in scaphā erāmus cum ā mercātōribus quibusdam inventī sumus. Quoniam neque cibum neque aquam habēbāmus, graviter aegrōtābāmus. Sed mercātōrēs nōs cūrāvērunt et Brundisium attulērunt. Ibi dominus meus multōs diēs morātus iam 40 convaluit et paucīs diēbus aderit.

19 **superō, -āre, -āvī, -ātus,** *to overcome*
23 **pauper, pauperis,** *poor*
28 **casa, -ae,** f., *hut, cottage*

30 **pūgiō, pūgiōnis,** m., *dagger*
clam, adv., *secretly*
39 **quoniam,** conj., *since*

41 **convalēscō, convalēscere, convaluī,** *to grow stronger, get well*

Respondē Latīnē:

1. Quō pīrātae superātōs addūxērunt?
2. Quid pīrātae facient sī Valerius pecūniam nōn habet?
3. Quid servus nocte fēcit?
4. Quōmodo Valerius et servus ex īnsulā ēvāsērunt?

Fortī et fidēlī nihil est difficile. *Nothing is difficult for a brave and trustworthy man.*

BUILDING THE MEANING
Subordinate Clauses with the Subjunctive I

Since Chapter 40 you have been meeting subordinate clauses with their verbs in the *subjunctive*. The subjunctive (Latin, **sub-**, *under* + **iūnct-**, *joined*) is a set of Latin verb forms that are often used in subordinate clauses. Here are examples from the story at the beginning of this chapter:

1. Magister nāvis, cum valdē **timēret**, suōs vetuit nōs adiuvāre. (42:17)
   *The captain of the ship, since/because **he was** very **frightened**, forbade his own men to help us.*

2. Cum quattuor diēs **nāvigāvissēmus**, subitō maxima tempestās coorta est. (42:2–3)
   *When **we had sailed** four days, suddenly a very great storm arose.*

The verb **timēret** in the first sentence above is an *imperfect subjunctive* and is translated *was....*

The verb **nāvigāvissēmus** in the second sentence above is a *pluperfect subjunctive* and is translated *had....*

Exercise 42b
Read aloud and translate these two sentences from story 42, both of which contain verbs in the subjunctive (in boldface):

1. Nocte, cum omnēs **dormīrent**, ego surrēxī, pūgiōne modo armātus.
2. Cum casae fūrtim **appropinquāvissem**, per fenestram vīdī dominum meum in lectō iacentem ac duōs custōdēs vīnum bibentēs.

FORMS
Verbs: Imperfect and Pluperfect Subjunctive Active
Imperfect Subjunctive Active

The imperfect subjunctive active is formed by adding the personal endings to the present active infinitive:

Active Voice

		1st Conjugation	2nd Conjugation	3rd Conjugation		4th Conjugation
Singular	1	portāre*m*	movére*m*	mítterem	iácerem	audíre*m*
	2	portāre*s*	movére*s*	mítterēs	iácerēs	audíre*s*
	3	portāre*t*	movére*t*	mítteret	iáceret	audíret
Plural	1	portāré*mus*	movēré*mus*	mitterémus	iacerémus	audīré*mus*
	2	portāré*tis*	movēré*tis*	mitterétis	iacerétis	audīré*tis*
	3	portāre*nt*	movére*nt*	mítterent	iácerent	audíre*nt*

		ésse
Singular	1	éssem
	2	éssēs
	3	ésset
Plural	1	essémus
	2	essétis
	3	éssent

So also the irregular verbs **posse, velle, nōlle, īre,** and **ferre.**

Be sure to learn these forms thoroughly.

Note that the *e* at the end of the infinitive lengthens to *ē* except before *-m, -t,* and *-nt.*

Pluperfect Subjunctive Active

The pluperfect subjunctive active is formed by adding the personal endings to the perfect active infinitive:

		1st Conjugation	2nd Conjugation	3rd Conjugation		4th Conjugation
Singular	1	portāvíssem	mōvíssem	mīsíssem	iēcíssem	audīvíssem
	2	portāvíssēs	mōvíssēs	mīsíssēs	iēcíssēs	audīvíssēs
	3	portāvísset	mōvísset	mīsísset	iēcísset	audīvísset
Plural	1	portāvissémus	mōvissémus	mīsissémus	iēcissémus	audīvissémus
	2	portāvissétis	mōvissétis	mīsissétis	iēcissétis	audīvissétis
	3	portāvíssent	mōvíssent	mīsíssent	iēcíssent	audīvíssent

		ésse
Singular	1	fuíssem
	2	fuíssēs
	3	fuísset
Plural	1	fuissémus
	2	fuissétis
	3	fuíssent

So also the irregular verbs **posse (potuissem), velle (voluissem), nōlle (nōluissem), īre (īssem),** and **ferre (tulissem).**

Note again that the *e* at the end of the infinitive lengthens to *ē* except before *-m, -t,* and *-nt.* Be sure to learn these forms thoroughly.

Exercise 42c
In story 42, locate four verbs in the imperfect subjunctive and seven in the pluperfect subjunctive.

Exercise 42d
Give the imperfect and pluperfect subjunctives, 3rd person plural, of the following verbs:

1. superō, -āre, -āvī, -ātus

2. ēvādō, ēvādere, ēvāsī, ēvāsus

BUILDING THE MEANING
Subordinate Clauses with the Subjunctive II

1. **Cum** Causal Clauses

   Subordinate clauses that are introduced by the conjunction **cum** may be ***cum causal clauses***; **cum** is translated as *since* or *because*. Such clauses state the reason for the action of the main clause:

   > Magister nāvis, <u>cum valdē **timēret**</u>, suōs vetuit nōs adiuvāre. (42:17)
   > *The captain of the ship, <u>since/because **he was very frightened**</u>, forbade his own men to help us.*

2. **Cum** Circumstantial Clauses

   Subordinate clauses that are introduced by the conjunction **cum** may also be ***cum circumstantial clauses***; **cum** is translated as *when*. Such clauses describe the circumstances that accompanied or preceded the action of the main clause:

   > <u>Cum quattuor diēs **nāvigāvissēmus**</u>, subitō maxima tempestās coorta est. (42:2–3)
   > <u>*When **we had sailed** four days*</u>, *suddenly a very great storm arose.*

   Often only the context and sense will tell you whether **cum** is to be translated *since/because* or *when*.

3. Indirect Questions

   > Pīrātae rogābant <u>quī **essēmus**</u>, <u>unde **vēnissēmus**</u>, <u>quō iter **facerēmus**</u>. (42:20–21)
   > *The pirates were asking <u>who **we were**, from where **we had come**, [and] to where **we were making** a journey</u>.*

   Look at these pairs of sentences:

   a. Direct question: Quī estis?
       Who are you?

   b. Indirect question: Pīrātae rogābant <u>quī **essēmus**.</u>
       *The pirates were asking <u>who **we were**</u>.*

   a. Direct question: Unde vēnistis?
       From where have you come?

   b. Indirect question: Pīrātae rogābant <u>unde **vēnissēmus**</u>.
       *The pirates were asking <u>from where **we had come**</u>.*

(continued)

a. Direct question: Quō iter facitis?
                             To where are you making a journey?

b. Indirect question: Pīrātae rogābant <u>quō iter **facerēmus**</u>.
                             *The pirates were asking <u>to where **we were making a journey**</u>.*

After the introductory words **Pīrātae rogābant**, the direct questions (a) are stated indirectly in subordinate clauses (b, underlined), and their verbs are in the subjunctive. These subordinate clauses are called *indirect questions*.

Exercise 42e

Read aloud and translate; be sure to decide whether **cum** clauses are circumstantial or causal and be sure that your translation reflects the tense of each verb in the subjunctive:

1. Cum prope rīvum ambulārēmus, Cornēliam et Flāviam clāmantēs audīvimus.
2. Grammaticus Marcum rogāvit unde vēnisset Aenēās.
3. Grammaticus Sextum rogāvit ubi esset Hesperia.
4. Grammaticus mē, cum dē Hesperiā ignōrārem, verberāvit.
5. Pīrātae Valerium rogāvērunt quis esset.
6. Magister nāvis, cum pīrātās timēret, dē patre Valeriī vēra dīcere cōnstituit.
7. Servus, cum in mare dēsiluisset, ad lītus celeriter natāvit.
8. Cum casae appropinquāvissem, dominum vīdī.
9. Cum casam intrāvisset, custōdem pūgiōne percussit.
10. Cum neque cibum neque aquam habērent, aegerrimī erant.

Exercise 42f

Using story 42 and the material above on the subjunctive as guides, give the Latin for the following (use subjunctives in all subordinate clauses):

1. When the force of the storm had subsided, we returned onto the ship.
2. Since the men were pirates, we were afraid to resist.
3. When my master had drawn his sword, he leaped down into the boat.
4. We asked why the pirates had captured us poor men.
5. Since my master was ill on account of his wound, he was not able to walk.

PIRACY

Piracy was a constant threat to travel and trade by sea in the ancient world. Merchant ships were often seized by pirates and their goods sold, and sailors and travelers caught by pirates would be sold as slaves at the great slave markets such as that on the island of Delos in the Aegean Sea. Pirates would also attack coastal towns and coastal roads, ruthlessly killing or capturing men, women, and children to ransom or to sell as slaves.

In 74 B.C. Julius Caesar was captured by pirates. The historian Suetonius tells the story:

> While crossing to Rhodes, after the winter season had already begun, he was taken by pirates near the island of Pharmacussa and remained in their custody for nearly forty days in a state of intense vexation, attended only by a single physician and two body-servants; for he had sent off his traveling companions and the rest of his attendants at the outset, to raise money for his ransom. Once he was set on shore on payment of fifty talents, he did not delay then and there to launch a fleet and pursue the departing pirates, and the moment they were in his power to inflict on them the punishment which he had often threatened when joking with them.

> Suetonius, *Julius Caesar* IV.1–2

In 66 B.C., Cicero enumerated the troubles that pirates had caused the Romans in the recent past, claiming that the sea had been virtually closed to Rome's allies, that envoys had been captured, that ransom had been paid for Rome's ambassadors, that the sea had been unsafe for merchants, that Roman lictors had been captured by pirates, that whole cities had fallen into their hands, that the harbors of the Romans and their trading partners had been held by pirates, and that a fleet commanded by a Roman had been captured and destroyed by pirates. Cicero reported that all of these troubles had been ended the previous year, when the Roman general Pompey the Great (**Pompeius Magnus**) was given a fleet and empowered to rid the sea of pirates. Cicero tells what happened:

> Pompeius, though the sea was still unfit for navigation, visited Sicily, explored Africa, sailed to Sardinia and, by means of strong garrisons and fleets, made secure those three sources of our country's grain supply. After that he returned to Italy, secured the two provinces of Spain together with Transalpine Gaul, dispatched ships to the coast of the Illyrian Sea, to Achaea and the whole of Greece, and so provided the two seas of Italy with mighty fleets and strong garrisons; while he himself, within forty-nine days of starting from Brundisium, added all

Cilicia to the Roman Empire. All the pirates, wherever they were, were either captured or put to death; or they surrendered to his power and authority and to his alone.

Cicero, On the Manilian Law 12.34–35

Augustus established a permanent fleet to keep the seas safe from pirates, but the menace remained, and a traveler such as Valerius in our story could easily be captured by pirates while sailing from Asia Minor to Brundisium.

REVIEW IX: CHAPTERS 38–42

Exercise IXa: Place
Select, read aloud, and translate:

1. Mercātōrēs Rōmānī _____ morābantur.   Gādēs/Gādium/Gādibus
2. Cornēliī _____ profectī sunt.   Rōma/Rōmae/Rōmā
3. Cornēliī _____ sērō advēnērunt.   Baiae/Baiārum/Baiās
4. Cornēliī _____ profectī sunt.   domus/domī/domō
5. Mīles Rōmānus _____ discessit.   Carthāginī/Carthāginem/Carthāgine
6. Amīcus mīlitis adhūc _____ habitat.   Carthāginī/Carthāginem/Carthāgō
7. Cornēlia _____ manet.   domī/domum/domō
8. Cornēliī _____ diū manēbant.   Rōmae/Rōmam/Rōmā
9. Cornēliī _____ diū manēbunt.   rūs/rūrī
10. Cornēliī _____ semper aestāte redeunt.   rūs/rūrī

Exercise IXb: Time
Read aloud, supplying the Latin words for the English cues, and translate:

1. Cornēliī in vīllā rūsticā _____ _____ morābantur. (for many months)
2. Ad urbem Rōmam _____ _____ regredientur. (in a few days)
3. Pseudolus _____ _____ _____ porcum ēmit. (three days ago)
4. Cornēliī ad vīllam rūsticam_____ _____ _____ regressī sunt. (after a few months)
5. Puerī in lūdō_____ _____ sedēbant. (for the whole day)
6. Valerius Brundisiō ēgressus Rōmam _____ _____ _____ adveniet. (several days later)

Exercise IXc: Present Participles
Read aloud and translate. Identify all present participles and tell what word they modify, unless they are being used as substantives:

1. Valerius iter ad Italiam faciēns tempestāte ad īnsulam āctus est.
2. Pīrātae celeriter sequentēs nāvem Valeriī cōnsecūtī sunt.
3. Nāvis Valeriī ā sequentibus capta est.
4. Servus Valeriī pīrātās in casā dormientēs adortus est.
5. Custōs ā servō Valeriī in casam ingrediente pugiōne percussus est.
6. Graviter aegrōtantēs ā mercātōribus inveniuntur.

Exercise IXd: Present Participles
Select, read aloud, and translate:

1. Sextum domum _____ audīvit Cornēlius.   intrantī/intrante/intrantem
2. Nāvis Valeriī pīrātās _____ effugere   sequentēs/sequentibus/sequentium
   nōn poterat.
3. Magistrō _____ ūnus ē discipulīs bene   rogantem/rogantī/rogantis
   respondit.
4. Aenēās Hesperiam _____ tempestāte   petentem/petente/petēns
   Carthāginem āctus est.
5. Cornēlius ā frātre nimis vīnī _____   bibentem/bibentis/bibente
   vexātus est.

Exercise IXe: Numbers
Match the cardinal numbers at the left with the corresponding ordinal
numbers at the right and give the meaning of the numbers in each pair:

1. quīnque   a. octāvus
2. octō   b. duodecimus
3. duo   c. quīngentēsimus
4. quīngentī   d. secundus
5. duodecim   e. quīntus
6. centum   f. septimus
7. trēs   g. quīnquāgēsimus
8. novem   h. tertius
9. quīnquāgintā   i. centēsimus
10. septem   j. nōnus

Exercise IXf: Semi-deponent Verbs
Translate into Latin, using semi-deponent verbs:

1. You (sing.) dare.   7. We are accustomed.
2. You (sing.) will be glad.   8. We will dare.
3. You (sing.) were daring.   9. We were daring.
4. You (sing.) dared.   10. We dared.
5. You (sing.) had been glad.   11. We had been accustomed.
6. You (sing.) will have dared.   12. We will have been glad.

Exercise IXg: Perfect Active Infinitives
Give and translate the present and perfect active infinitives of the following verbs:

1. laudō
2. habeō
3. currō
4. iaciō
5. dormiō

Exercise IXh: Imperfect and Pluperfect Subjunctives
Give the imperfect and pluperfect subjunctives of the verbs in Exercise IXg in the following persons and numbers:

1. Second person singular
2. First person plural

Exercise IXi: Subordinate Clauses with the Subjunctive
Read aloud and translate. Identify the tense of each verb in the subjunctive, and identify **cum** causal clauses, **cum** circumstantial clauses, and indirect questions:

1. Cum Vergilius Cremōnam advēnisset, ab optimīs magistrīs doctus est.
2. Scīvistīne ubi Vergilius togam virīlem sūmpsisset?
3. Cum Vergilius Mediolānum vēnisset, litterīs et linguae Graecae dīligentissimē studēbat.
4. Cum mīlitēs patrem Vergiliī ē fundō expulissent, Vergilius et pater Rōmam migrāvērunt.
5. Cum Vergilius Rōmae optimōs versūs scrīberet, poēta praeclārus factus es.
6. Cum Vergilius Rōmae habitāret, saepe aegrōtābat.
7. Cum in Graeciā iter faceret, prīncipī occurrit Athēnīs.
8. Cum prīnceps ad Italiam redīret, Vergilium sēcum dūxit.
9. Cum Brundisium advēnissent, Vergilius aegerrimus factus est.
10. Scīvistīne ubi amīcī Vergilium sepelīvissent?

Read the following passage and answer the questions below in English:

LIFE OF AUGUSTUS

A.d. ix Kal. Oct., M. Cicerōne et C. Antōniō cōnsulibus, nātus est C. Octāvius, quī posteā prīmus prīnceps Rōmānus factus est. Cum quattuor annōs complēvisset, pater mortuus est; Gaius igitur a mātre Atiā alēbātur. Avunculus magnus quoque, C. Iūlius Caesar, eum multa docuisse dīcitur.

Ubi Caesar ā coniūrātīs necātus est, Octāvius iam XVIII annōs nātus aberat in 5 Īllyricō. Rōmam quam celerrimē regressus, hērēs Caesaris testāmentō adoptātus est atque, cum cognōvisset quī Caesarem necāvissent, statim cōnstituit avunculum mortuum, ut patrem, ōlim ulcīscī. Eō tempore tamen, quod nūllum exercitum habēbat, nihil facere poterat.

Intereā, quod M. Antōnius populum Rōmānum excitāverat, coniūrātī ex urbe fugere 10 coāctī sunt. Dum tamen Antōnius coniūrātōs per Italiam persequēbātur, M. Tullius Cicerō, ōrātor ille praeclārissimus, ōrātiōnēs habuit in quibus dīcēbat Antōnium esse hostem reī pūblicae. Tum Octāvius, dīvitiīs ūsus quās testāmentō Caesaris accēperat, senātuī persuāsit ut sē cōnsulem creāret. Eōdem tempore nōminātus est Gaius Iūlius Caesar Octāviānus. Volēbant senātōrēs Octāviānum contrā Antōnium, quem iam 15 timēbant, urbem Rōmam dēfendere. Octāviānus tamen cum Antōniō se coniūnxit.

Prīmō Octāviānus et Antōnius ūnā coniūrātōs in Graeciā cōnsecūtī, proeliō dēbellāvērunt. Deinde, cum coniūrātōs superāvissent, cōnstituērunt Octāviānus et Antōnius imperium Rōmānum inter sē dīvidere. Rōmam regressus est Octāviānus; ad Aegyptum profectus est Antōnius. Rēgīna autem Aegyptiōrum erat Cleopatra, quam 20 pulcherrimam statim amāvit Antōnius. Mox Antōnius et Cleopatra tōtum imperium Rōmānum regere volēbant. Quae cum ita essent, Octāviānō necesse fuit bellum Antōniō īnferre. Proelium ad Actium factum est; Cleopatra Antōniusque victī sē necāvērunt. Octāviānus tōtam Aegyptum bellō captam imperiō Rōmānō addidit. Tum Iānum Quirīnum clausit atque pācem tōtum per imperium prōnūntiāvit. Ipse prīnceps Rōmānōrum factus est. 25

Multa et optima et ūtilissima populō Rōmānō ab eō īnstitūta sunt atque imperium Rōmānum auctum stabilītumque est. Multī etiam poētae—Vergilius, Horātius, Propertius, Ovidius—rēs Rōmānās versibus laudābant. Inter multōs honōrēs quōs senātus eī dedit maximus certē erat cognōmen Augustus, quod eī dēlātum est a.d. XVII Kal. Feb. annō DCCXXVII, A.U.C. Ex hōc tempore mēnsis Sextīlis nōminātus est 30 Augustus.

Bis uxōrem dūxit sed nūllum fīlium habēbat. Generum autem Marcellum in animō habēbat hērēdem adoptāre. Hic tamen annō DCCXXXI A.U.C. trīstissimē morbō mortuus est. Augustus igitur Tiberium, fīlium Līviae uxōris secundae, hērēdem adoptāvit. 35

Cum annum septuāgēsimum sextum paene complēvisset, dum iter in Campāniā facit, trīstissimē morbō a.d. XIV Kal. Sept. mortuus est. Corpus Rōmam relātum ingentī in sepulcrō sepultum est atque ūnō post mēnse senātus, quī Augustum iam dīvīnum esse prōnūntiāverat, eum cum avunculō inter deōs numerāvit.

1 **M.** = Marcus
  C. = Gaius
3 **avunculus, -ī,** m., *maternal uncle*
5 **coniūrātus, -ī,** m., *conspirator*
6 **hērēs, hērēdis,** m., *heir*
8 **ōlim,** adv., *at some future time, one day*
  exercitus, -ūs, m., *army*
10 **populus, -ī,** m., *people*
13 **hostis, hostis,** gen. pl., **hostium,** m.,
  enemy
  rēs pūblica, reī pūblicae, f., *republic, the state*
  dīvitiae, -ārum, f. pl., *riches*
14 **ut sē cōnsulem creāret,** *to make him consul*
15 **contrā,** prep. + acc., *against*
16 **coniungō, coniungere, coniūnxī, coniūnctus,** *to join*

17 **proelium, -ī,** n., *battle*
18 **dēbellō, -āre, -āvī, -ātus,** *to defeat*
19 **imperium, -ī,** n., *power, empire*
20 **Aegyptus, -ī,** f., *Egypt*
22 **bellum īnferre** + dat., *to make war upon*
24 **Iānus Quirīnus, -ī,** m., *shrine of Janus Quirinus*
25 **pāx, pācis,** f., *peace*
  prōnūntiō, -āre, -āvī, -ātus, *to proclaim*
27 **stabiliō, -īre, -īvī, -ītus,** *to steady, make firm*
32 **bis,** adv., *twice*
  uxōrem dūcere, *to marry*
  gener, generī, m., *son-in-law*
33 **morbus, -ī,** m., *illness*
39 **numerō, -āre, -āvī, -ātus,** *to number, include*

2 **compleō, complēre, complēvī, complētus,** *to fill, complete*
3 **alō, alere, aluī, altus,** *to rear*
7 **cognōscō, cognōscere, cognōvī, cognitus,** *to learn*
8 **ulcīscor, ulcīscī, ultus sum,** *to avenge*
11 **cōgō, cōgere, coēgī, coāctus,** *to compel, force*
  persequor, persequī, persecūtus sum, *to pursue*
13 **ūtor, ūtī, ūsus sum** + abl., *to use*
22 **regō, regere, rēxī, rēctus,** *to rule*
26 **īnstituō, īnstituere, īnstituī, īnstitūtus,** *to establish*
27 **augeō, augēre, auxī, auctus,** *to increase*
29 **dēferō, dēferre, dētulī, dēlātus,** irreg., *to award, grant*
37 **referō, referre, retulī, relātus,** irreg., *to bring back*

1. On what day of what month was Gaius Octavius born?
2. How old was he when his father died?
3. Who were responsible for his rearing and education?
4. Where was Octavius when Caesar was assassinated?
5. What did Octavius decide to do when he learned who had assassinated Caesar?
6. Why was he unable to do anything at the time?
7. Why were the conspirators forced to flee from Rome?
8. Who pursued them?
9. What attitude did Cicero take toward Antony?
10. How did Octavius persuade the Senate to make him consul?

(continued)

11. Who overtook the conspirators in Greece and defeated them?
12. Where did the victors go?
13. What were Antony and Cleopatra's plans?
14. Who defeated whom at the battle of Actium?
15. What new province did Octavian add to the Roman empire?
16. What kind of a ruler was Octavian?
17. What was the greatest honor that the Senate gave him?
18. Whom did he want to succeed him as ruler?
19. Why was that not possible?
20. What honor did the Senate confer upon Augustus after his death?

FORMS

The following charts show the forms of typical Latin nouns, adjectives, pronouns, and verbs. As an aid in pronunciation, markings of long vowels and of accents are included.

I. Nouns

Number Case	1st Declension Fem.	2nd Declension Masc.	2nd Declension Masc.	2nd Declension Masc.	2nd Declension Neut.	3rd Declension Masc.	3rd Declension Fem.	3rd Declension Neut.
Singular								
Nominative	puélla	sérvus	púer	áger	báculum	páter	vōx	nómen
Genitive	puéllae	sérvī	púerī	ágrī	báculī	pátris	vócis	nóminis
Dative	puéllae	sérvō	púerō	ágrō	báculō	pátrī	vócī	nóminī
Accusative	puéllam	sérvum	púerum	ágrum	báculum	pátrem	vócem	nómen
Ablative	puéllā	sérvō	púerō	ágrō	báculō	pátre	vóce	nómine
Vocative	puélla	sérve	púer	áger	báculum	páter	vōx	nómen
Plural								
Nominative	puéllae	sérvī	púerī	ágrī	bácula	pátrēs	vócēs	nómina
Genitive	puellárum	servórum	puerórum	agrórum	baculórum	pátrum	vócum	nóminum
Dative	puéllīs	sérvīs	púerīs	ágrīs	báculīs	pátribus	vócibus	nóminibus
Accusative	puéllās	sérvōs	púerōs	ágrōs	bácula	pátrēs	vócēs	nómina
Ablative	puéllīs	sérvīs	púerīs	ágrīs	báculīs	pátribus	vócibus	nóminibus
Vocative	puéllae	sérvī	púerī	ágrī	bácula	pátrēs	vócēs	nómina

Number Case	4th Declension Masc.	4th Declension Neut.	5th Declension Masc.	5th Declension Fem.
Singular				
Nominative	árcus	génū	díēs	rēs
Genitive	árcūs	génūs	diéī	réī
Dative	árcuī	génū	diéī	réī
Accusative	árcum	génū	díem	rem
Ablative	árcū	génū	díē	rē
Vocative	árcus	génū	díēs	rēs
Plural				
Nominative	árcūs	génua	díēs	rēs
Genitive	árcuum	génuum	diérum	rérum
Dative	árcibus	génibus	diébus	rébus
Accusative	árcūs	génua	díēs	rēs
Ablative	árcibus	génibus	diébus	rébus
Vocative	árcūs	génua	díēs	rēs

II. Adjectives

Number Case	1st and 2nd Declension			3rd Declension		
	Masc.	**Fem.**	**Neut.**	**Masc.**	**Fem.**	**Neut.**
Singular						
Nominative	mágn*us*	mágn*a*	mágn*um*	ómn*is*	ómn*is*	ómn*e*
Genitive	mágn*ī*	mágn*ae*	mágn*ī*	ómn*is*	ómn*is*	ómn*is*
Dative	mágn*ō*	mágn*ae*	mágn*ō*	ómn*ī*	ómn*ī*	ómn*ī*
Accusative	mágn*um*	mágn*am*	mágn*um*	ómn*em*	ómn*em*	ómn*e*
Ablative	mágn*ō*	mágn*ā*	mágn*ō*	ómn*ī*	ómn*ī*	ómn*ī*
Vocative	mágn*e*	mágn*a*	mágn*um*	ómn*is*	ómn*is*	ómn*e*
Plural						
Nominative	mágn*ī*	mágn*ae*	mágn*a*	ómn*ēs*	ómn*ēs*	ómn*ia*
Genitive	magn*órum*	magn*árum*	magn*órum*	ómn*ium*	ómn*ium*	ómn*ium*
Dative	mágn*īs*	mágn*īs*	mágn*īs*	ómn*ibus*	ómn*ibus*	ómn*ibus*
Accusative	mágn*ōs*	mágn*ās*	mágn*a*	ómn*ēs*	ómn*ēs*	ómn*ia*
Ablative	mágn*īs*	mágn*īs*	mágn*īs*	ómn*ibus*	ómn*ibus*	ómn*ibus*
Vocative	mágn*ī*	mágn*ae*	mágn*a*	ómn*ēs*	ómn*ēs*	ómn*ia*

III. Comparative Adjectives

Number Case	Masc.	Fem.	Neut.
Singular			
Nominative	púlchrior	púlchrior	púlchrius
Genitive	pulchrió*ris*	pulchrió*ris*	pulchrió*ris*
Dative	pulchrió*rī*	pulchrió*rī*	pulchrió*rī*
Accusative	pulchrió*rem*	pulchrió*rem*	púlchrius
Abative	pulchrió*re*	pulchrió*re*	pulchrió*re*
Vocative	púlchrior	púlchrior	púlchrius
Plural			
Nominative	pulchrió*rēs*	pulchrió*rēs*	pulchrió*ra*
Genitive	pulchrió*rum*	pulchrió*rum*	pulchrió*rum*
Dative	pulchrió*ribus*	pulchrió*ribus*	pulchrió*ribus*
Accusative	pulchrió*rēs*	pulchrió*rēs*	pulchrió*ra*
Ablative	pulchrió*ribus*	pulchrió*ribus*	pulchrió*ribus*
Vocative	pulchrió*rēs*	pulchrió*rēs*	pulchrió*ra*

Adjectives have *positive*, *comparative*, and *superlative* forms. You can usually recognize the comparative by the letters **-ior(-)** and the superlative by **-issimus**, **-errimus**, or **-illimus**:

ignávus, -a, -um, *lazy*	ignávior, ignávius	ignavíssimus, -a, -um
púlcher, púlchra, púlchrum, *beautiful*	púlchrior, púlchrius	pulchérrimus, -a, -um
fácilis, -is, -e, *easy*	facílior, facílius	facíllimus, -a, -um

Some very common adjectives are irregular in the comparative and superlative:

Positive	Comparative	Superlative
bónus, -a, -um, *good*	**mélior, mélius**, *better*	**óptimus, -a, -um**, *best*
málus, -a, -um, *bad*	**péior, péius**, *worse*	**péssimus, -a, -um**, *worst*
mágnus, -a, -um, *big*	**máior, máius**, *bigger*	**máximus, -a, -um**, *biggest*
párvus, -a, -um, *small*	**mínor, mínus**, *smaller*	**mínimus, -a, -um**, *smallest*
múltus, -a, -um, *much*	**plūs,*** *more*	**plúrimus, -a, -um**, *most, very much*
múltī, -ae, -a, *many*	**plúrēs, plúra**, *more*	**plúrimī, -ae, -a**, *most, very many*

*Note that **plūs** is not an adjective but a neuter substantive, usually found with a partitive genitive, e.g., Titus **plūs vīnī** bibit. *Titus drank **more (of the) wine.***

IV. Present Participles

Number / Case	Masc.	Fem.	Neut.
Singular			
Nominative	párāns	párāns	párāns
Genitive	parántis	parántis	parántis
Dative	parántī	parántī	parántī
Accusative	parántem	parántem	párāns
Ablative	parántī/e	parántī/e	parántī/e
Plural			
Nominative	parántēs	parántēs	parántia
Genitive	parántium	parántium	parántium
Dative	parántibus	parántibus	parántibus
Accusative	parántēs	parántēs	parántia
Ablative	parántibus	parántibus	parántibus

V. Numbers

Case	Masc.	Fem.	Neut.	Masc.	Fem.	Neut.	Masc.	Fem.	Neut.
Nom.	únus	úna	únum	dúo	dúae	dúo	trēs	trēs	tría
Gen.	ūníus	ūníus	ūníus	duórum	duárum	duórum	tríum	tríum	tríum
Dat.	únī	únī	únī	duóbus	duábus	duóbus	tríbus	tríbus	tríbus
Acc.	únum	únam	únum	dúōs	dúās	dúo	trēs	trēs	tría
Abl.	únō	únā	únō	duóbus	duábus	duóbus	tríbus	tríbus	tríbus

	Cardinal	**Ordinal**
I	únus, -a, -um, *one*	prímus, -a, -um, *first*
II	dúo, -ae, -o, *two*	secúndus, -a, -um, *second*
III	trēs, trēs, tría, *three*	tértius, -a, -um, *third*
IV	quáttuor, *four*	quártus, -a, -um
V	quínque, *five*	quíntus, -a, -um
VI	sex, *six*	séxtus, -a, -um
VII	séptem, *seven*	séptimus, -a, -um
VIII	óctō, *eight*	octávus, -a, -um
IX	nóvem, *nine*	nónus, -a, -um
X	décem, *ten*	décimus, -a, -um
XI	úndecim, *eleven*	ūndécimus, -a, -um
XII	duódecim, *twelve*	duodécimus, -a, -um
XIII	trédecim, *thirteen*	tértius décimus, -a, -um
XIV	quattuórdecim, *fourteen*	quártus décimus, -a, -um
XV	quíndecim, *fifteen*	quíntus décimus, -a, -um
XVI	sédecim, *sixteen*	séxtus décimus, -a, -um
XVII	septéndecim, *seventeen*	séptimus décimus, -a, -um
XVIII	duodēvīgíntī, *eighteen*	duodēvīcésimus, -a, -um
XIX	ūndēvīgíntī, *nineteen*	ūndēvīcésimus, -a, -um
XX	vīgíntī, *twenty*	vīcésimus, -a, -um
L	quīnquāgíntā, *fifty*	quīnquāgésimus, -a, -um
C	céntum, *a hundred*	centésimus, -a, -um
D	quīngéntī, -ae, -a, *five hundred*	quīngentésimus, -a, -um
M	mílle, *a thousand*	mīllésimus, -a, -um

N.B. The cardinal numbers from **quattuor** to **centum** do not change their form to indicate case and gender.

VI.   Personal Pronouns

Number Case	1st	2nd	3rd Masc.	3rd Fem.	3rd Neut.
Singular					
Nominative	égo	tū	is	éa	id
Genitive	méī	túī	éius	éius	éius
Dative	míhi	tíbi	éī	éī	éī
Accusative	mē	tē	éum	éam	id
Ablative	mē	tē	éō	éā	éō
Plural					
Nominative	nōs	vōs	éī	éae	éa
Genitive	nóstrī	véstrī	eórum	eárum	eórum
	nóstrum	véstrum			
Dative	nóbīs	vóbīs	éīs	éīs	éīs
Accusative	nōs	vōs	éōs	éās	éa
Ablative	nóbīs	vóbīs	éīs	éīs	éīs

Note: The forms of **is, ea, id** may also serve as demonstrative adjectives.

VII.   Reflexive Pronoun

Singular	
Nominative	——
Genitive	súī
Dative	síbi
Accusative	sē
Ablative	sē
Plural	
Nominative	——
Genitive	súī
Dative	síbi
Accusative	sē
Ablative	sē

VIII. Relative Pronoun

Number Case	Masc.	Fem.	Neut.
Singular			
Nominative	quī	quae	quod
Genitive	cúius	cúius	cúius
Dative	cui	cui	cui
Accusative	quem	quam	quod
Ablative	quō	quā	quō
Plural			
Nominative	quī	quae	quae
Genitive	quórum	quárum	quórum
Dative	quíbus	quíbus	quíbus
Accusative	quōs	quās	quae
Ablative	quíbus	quíbus	quíbus

IX. Interrogative Pronoun

Number Case	Masc.	Fem.	Neut.
Singular			
Nominative	quis	quis	quid
Genitive	cúius	cúius	cúius
Dative	cui	cui	cui
Accusative	quem	quem	quid
Ablative	quō	quō	quō
Plural	Same as the plural of the relative pronoun above.		

X. Indefinite Adjective

Number Case	Masc.	Fem.	Neut.
Singular			
Nominative	quídam	quaédam	quóddam
Genitive	cuiúsdam	cuiúsdam	cuiúsdam
Dative	cúidam	cúidam	cúidam
Accusative	quéndam	quándam	quóddam
Ablative	quódam	quádam	quódam
Plural			
Nominative	quídam	quaédam	quaédam
Genitive	quōrúndam	quārúndam	quōrúndam
Dative	quibúsdam	quibúsdam	quibúsdam
Accusative	quósdam	quásdam	quaédam
Ablative	quibúsdam	quibúsdam	quibúsdam

XI. Demonstrative Adjectives and Pronouns

Number Case	Masc.	Fem.	Neut.	Masc.	Fem.	Neut.
Singular						
Nominative	hic	haec	hoc	ílle	ílla	íllud
Genitive	húius	húius	húius	illíus	illíus	illíus
Dative	húic	húic	húic	íllī	íllī	íllī
Accusative	hunc	hanc	hoc	íllum	íllam	íllud
Ablative	hōc	hāc	hōc	íllō	íllā	íllō
Plural						
Nominative	hī	hae	haec	íllī	íllae	ílla
Genitive	hórum	hárum	hórum	illórum	illárum	illórum
Dative	hīs	hīs	hīs	íllīs	íllīs	íllīs
Accusative	hōs	hās	haec	íllōs	íllās	ílla
Ablative	hīs	hīs	hīs	íllīs	íllīs	íllīs

Number Case	Masculine	Feminine	Neuter
Singular			
Nominative	ípse	ípsa	ípsum
Genitive	ipsíus	ipsíus	ipsíus
Dative	ípsī	ípsī	ípsī
Accusative	ípsum	ípsam	ípsum
Ablative	ípsō	ípsā	ípsō
Plural			
Nominative	ípsī	ípsae	ípsa
Genitive	ipsórum	ipsárum	ipsórum
Dative	ípsīs	ípsīs	ípsīs
Accusative	ípsōs	ípsās	ípsa
Ablative	ípsīs	ípsīs	ípsīs

Number Case	Masc.	Fem.	Neut.	Masc.	Fem.	Neut.
Singular						
Nominative	is	éa	id	ídem	éadem	ídem
Genitive	éius	éius	éius	eiúsdem	eiúsdem	eiúsdem
Dative	éī	éī	éī	eídem	eídem	eídem
Accusative	éum	éam	id	eúndem	eándem	ídem
Ablative	éō	éā	éō	eódem	eádem	eódem
Plural						
Nominative	éī	éae	éa	eídem	eaédem	éadem
Genitive	eórum	eárum	eórum	eōrúndem	eārúndem	eōrúndem
Dative	éīs	éīs	éīs	eísdem	eísdem	eísdem
Accusative	éōs	éās	éa	eósdem	eásdem	éadem
Ablative	éīs	éīs	éīs	eísdem	eísdem	eísdem

XII. Adverbs

Latin adverbs may be formed from adjectives of the 1st and 2nd declensions by adding *-ē* to the base of the adjective, e.g., **strēnuē**, *strenuously*, from **strēnuus, -a, -um.** To form an adverb from a 3rd declension adjective, add *-iter* to the base of the adjective or *-er* to bases ending in **-nt-**, e.g., <u>brev*iter*</u>, *briefly*, from **brevis, -is, -e,** and **prūdent*er*,** *wisely*, from **prūdēns, prūdentis.**

laét*ē*, *happily*	laét*ius*	laet*íssimē*
fēlíc*iter*, *luckily*	fēlíc*ius*	fēlíc*íssimē*
celér*iter*, *quickly*	celér*ius*	celér*rimē*
prūdént*er*, *wisely*	prūdént*ius*	prūdent*íssimē*

Note the following as well:

díū, *for a long time*	diút*ius*	diūt*íssimē*
saépe, *often*	saép*ius*	saep*íssimē*
sérō, *late*	sér*ius*	sēr*íssimē*

Some adverbs are irregular:

béne, *well*	**mélius,** *better*	**óptimē,** *best*
mále, *badly*	**péius,** *worse*	**péssimē,** *worst*
fácile, *easily*	**facílius,** *more easily*	**facíllimē,** *most easily*
magnópere, *greatly*	**mágis,** *more*	**máximē,** *most*
paúlum, *little*	**mínus,** *less*	**mínimē,** *least*
múltum, *much*	**plūs,** *more*	**plúrimum,** *most*

XIII. Regular Verbs Active: Infinitive, Imperative, Indicative

				1st Conjugation	2nd Conjugation	3rd Conjugation		4th Conjugation
Infinitive				par*áre*	hab*ére*	mítt*ere*	iác*ere (-iō)*	aud*íre*
Imperative				pár*ā*	háb*ē*	mítt*e*	iác*e*	aúd*ī*
				par*áte*	hab*éte*	mítt*ite*	iác*ite*	aud*íte*
Present	Singular		1	pár*ō*	háb*eō*	mítt*ō*	iáci*ō*	aúd*iō*
			2	pár*ās*	háb*ēs*	mítt*is*	iáci*s*	aúd*īs*
			3	pár*at*	háb*et*	mítt*it*	iáci*t*	aúd*it*
	Plural		1	par*ámus*	hab*émus*	mítt*imus*	iáci*mus*	aud*ímus*
			2	par*átis*	hab*étis*	mítt*itis*	iáci*tis*	aud*ítis*
			3	pár*ant*	háb*ent*	mítt*unt*	iáci*unt*	aúd*iunt*
Imperfect	Singular		1	par*ábam*	hab*ébam*	mitt*ébam*	iaci*ébam*	audi*ébam*
			2	par*ábās*	hab*ébās*	mitt*ébās*	iaci*ébās*	audi*ébās*
			3	par*ábat*	hab*ébat*	mitt*ébat*	iaci*ébat*	audi*ébat*
	Plural		1	par*ābámus*	hab*ēbámus*	mitt*ēbámus*	iaci*ēbámus*	audi*ēbámus*
			2	par*ābátis*	hab*ēbátis*	mitt*ēbátis*	iaci*ēbátis*	audi*ēbátis*
			3	par*ábant*	hab*ébant*	mitt*ébant*	iaci*ébant*	audi*ébant*
Future	Singular		1	par*ábō*	hab*ébō*	mítt*am*	iáci*am*	aúdi*am*
			2	par*ábis*	hab*ébis*	mítt*ēs*	iáci*ēs*	aúdi*ēs*
			3	par*ábit*	hab*ébit*	mítt*et*	iáci*et*	aúdi*et*
	Plural		1	par*ábimus*	hab*ébimus*	mitt*émus*	iaci*émus*	audi*émus*
			2	par*ábitis*	hab*ébitis*	mitt*étis*	iaci*étis*	audi*étis*
			3	par*ábunt*	hab*ébunt*	mítt*ent*	iáci*ent*	aúdi*ent*
Perfect	Singular		1	par*ávī*	háb*uī*	mís*ī*	iéc*ī*	aud*ívī*
			2	par*ávístī*	hab*uístī*	mis*ístī*	iēc*ístī*	audi*vístī*
			3	par*ávit*	háb*uit*	mís*it*	iéc*it*	aud*ívit*
	Plural		1	par*ávimus*	hab*úimus*	mís*imus*	iéc*imus*	aud*ívimus*
			2	par*ávistis*	hab*uístis*	mis*ístis*	iēc*ístis*	audi*vístis*
			3	par*āvérunt*	hab*uérunt*	mis*érunt*	iēc*érunt*	audi*vérunt*
Pluperfect	Singular		1	par*áveram*	hab*úeram*	mís*eram*	iéc*eram*	aud*íveram*
			2	par*áverās*	hab*úerās*	mís*erās*	iéc*erās*	aud*éverās*
			3	par*áverat*	hab*úerat*	mís*erat*	iéc*erat*	aud*íverat*
	Plural		1	par*āverámus*	hab*uerámus*	mis*erámus*	iēc*erámus*	audiv*erámus*
			2	par*āverátis*	hab*uerátis*	mis*erátis*	iēc*erátis*	audiv*erátis*
			3	par*áverant*	hab*úerant*	mís*erant*	iéc*erant*	aud*íverant*
Future Perfect	Singular		1	par*áverō*	hab*úerō*	mís*erō*	iéc*erō*	aud*íverō*
			2	par*áveris*	hab*úeris*	mís*eris*	iéc*eris*	aud*íveris*
			3	par*áverit*	hab*úerit*	mís*erit*	iéc*erit*	aud*íverit*
	Plural		1	par*āvérimus*	hab*uérimus*	mis*érimus*	iēc*érimus*	audiv*érimus*
			2	par*āvéritis*	hab*uéritis*	mis*éritis*	iēc*éritis*	audiv*éritis*
			3	par*áverint*	hab*úerint*	mís*erint*	iéc*erint*	aud*íverint*

XIV. Regular Verbs Passive: Infinitive, Imperative, Indicative

			1st Conjugation	2nd Conjugation	3rd Conjugation		4th Conjugation
Infinitive			port*ári*	mov*éri*	mítt*í*	iác*í*	aud*íri*
Imperative			port*áre*	mov*ére*	mítt*ere*	iác*ere*	aud*íre*
			port*áminí*	mov*éminí*	mitt*íminí*	iac*íminí*	aud*íminí*
Present	Singular	1	pórto*r*	móveo*r*	mítto*r*	iácio*r*	aúdio*r*
		2	portá*ris*	mové*ris*	mítte*ris*	iáce*ris*	audí*ris*
		3	portá*tur*	mové*tur*	mítti*tur*	iáci*tur*	audí*tur*
	Plural	1	portá*mur*	mové*mur*	mítti*mur*	iáci*mur*	audí*mur*
		2	portá*miní*	mové*miní*	mittí*miní*	iací*miní*	audí*miní*
		3	portá*ntur*	mové*ntur*	mittú*ntur*	iaciú*ntur*	audiú*ntur*
Imperfect	Singular	1	portā*bar*	mové*bar*	mittē*bar*	iacié*bar*	audié*bar*
		2	portā*báris*	mové*báris*	mittē*báris*	iacié*báris*	audiē*báris*
		3	portā*bátur*	mové*bátur*	mittē*bátur*	iacié*bátur*	audiē*bátur*
	Plural	1	portā*bámur*	mové*bámur*	mittē*bámur*	iacié*bámur*	audiē*bámur*
		2	portā*bámíní*	mové*bámíní*	mittē*bámíní*	iacié*bámíní*	audiē*bámíní*
		3	portā*bántur*	mové*bántur*	mittē*bántur*	iacié*bántur*	audiē*bántur*
Future	Singular	1	portá*bor*	mové*bor*	mítt*ar*	iáci*ar*	aúdi*ar*
		2	portá*beris*	mové*beris*	mitt*éris*	iaci*éris*	audi*éris*
		3	portá*bitur*	mové*bitur*	mitt*étur*	iaci*étur*	audi*étur*
	Plural	1	portá*bimur*	mové*bimur*	mitt*émur*	iaci*émur*	audi*émur*
		2	portá*bímíní*	mové*bímíní*	mitt*émíní*	iaci*émíní*	audi*émíní*
		3	portā*búntur*	mové*búntur*	mitt*éntur*	iaci*éntur*	audi*éntur*

		Perfect Passive		Pluperfect Passive		Future Perfect Passive	
Singular	1	portátus, -a	sum	portátus, -a	éram	portátus, -a	érō
	2	portátus, -a	es	portátus, -a	érās	portátus, -a	éris
	3	portátus, -a, -um	est	portátus, -a, -um	érat	portátus, -a, -um	érit
Plural	1	portátí, -ae	súmus	portátí, -ae	erámus	portátí, -ae	érimus
	2	portátí, -ae	éstis	portátí, -ae	erátis	portátí, -ae	éritis
	3	portátí, -ae, -a	sunt	portátí, -ae, -a	érant	portátí, -ae, -a	érunt

XV. Regular Verbs: Infinitives

	Present		Perfect
	Active	Passive	Active
1	portáre	portári	portāvísse
2	movére	movéri	mōvísse
3	míttere	míttí	mísísse
iō	iácere	iácí	iēcísse
4	audíre	audíri	audīvísse

XVI. Deponent Verbs: Infinitive, Imperative, Indicative

			1st Conjugation	2nd Conjugation	3rd Conjugation		4th Conjugation
Present Infinitive			cōnā́rī	verḗrī	lóquī	régredī	experī́rī
Imperative			cōnā́re	verḗre	lóquere	regrédere	experī́re
			cōnā́minī	verḗminī	loquíminī	regredíminī	experī́minī
Present	Singular	1	cṓnor	véreor	lóquor	regrédior	expérior
		2	cōnā́ris	verḗris	lóqueris	regréderis	experī́ris
		3	cōnā́tur	verḗtur	lóquitur	regréditur	experī́tur
	Plural	1	cōnā́mur	verḗmur	lóquimur	regrédimur	experī́mur
		2	cōnā́minī	verḗminī	loquíminī	regredíminī	experī́minī
		3	cōnā́ntur	verḗntur	loquúntur	regrediúntur	experiúntur
Imperfect	Singular	1	cōnā́bar	verḗbar	loquḗbar	regrediḗbar	experiḗbar
		2	cōnābā́ris	verēbā́ris	loquēbā́ris	regrediēbā́ris	experiēbā́ris
		3	cōnābā́tur	verēbā́tur	loquēbā́tur	regrediēbā́tur	experiēbā́tur
Future	Singular	1	cōnā́bor	verḗbor	lóquar	regrédiar	expériar
		2	cōnā́beris	verḗberis	loquḗris	regrediḗris	experiḗris
		3	cōnā́bitur	verḗbitur	loquḗtur	regrediḗtur	experiḗtur
Perfect		1	cōnā́tus sum	véritus sum	locū́tus sum	regréssus sum	expértus sum
Pluperfect		1	cōnā́tus éram	véritus éram	locū́tus éram	regréssus éram	expértus éram
Future Perfect		1	cōnā́tus érō	véritus érō	locū́tus érō	regréssus érō	expértus érō

XVII. Regular and Irregular Verbs Active: Subjunctive

Imperfect

Active Voice							
			1st Conjugation	2nd Conjugation	3rd Conjugation		4th Conjugation
Singular	1		portā́rem	movḗrem	mítterem	iácerem	audī́rem
	2		portā́rēs	movḗrēs	mítterēs	iácerēs	audī́rēs
	3		portā́ret	movḗret	mítteret	iáceret	audī́ret
Plural	1		portārḗmus	movērḗmus	mitterḗmus	iacerḗmus	audīrḗmus
	2		portārḗtis	movērḗtis	mitterḗtis	iacerḗtis	audīrḗtis
	3		portā́rent	movḗrent	mítterent	iácerent	audī́rent

		esse
Singular	1	éssem
	2	éssēs
	3	ésset
Plural	1	essḗmus
	2	essḗtis
	3	éssent

So also the irregular verbs **posse, velle, nōlle, īre,** and **ferre.**

Pluperfect

			1st Conjugation	2nd Conjugation	3rd Conjugation		4th Conjugation
Pluperfect	Singular	1	portāvíssem	mōvíssem	mīsíssem	iēcíssem	audīvíssem
		2	portāvíssēs	mōvíssēs	mīsíssēs	iēcíssēs	audīvíssēs
		3	portāvísset	mōvísset	mīsísset	iēcísset	audīvísset
	Plural	1	portāvissémus	mōvissémus	mīsissémus	iēcissémus	audīvissémus
		2	portāvissétis	mōvissétis	mīsissétis	iēcissétis	audīvissétis
		3	portāvíssent	mōvíssent	mīsíssent	iēcíssent	audīvíssent

			esse
	Singular	1	fuíssem
		2	fuíssēs
		3	fuísset
	Plural	1	fuissémus
		2	fuissétis
		3	fuíssent

So also the irregular verbs **posse (potuissem)**,
velle (voluissem), **nōlle (nōluissem)**, **īre
(īssem)**, and **ferre (tulissem)**.

XVIII. Irregular Verbs: Infinitive, Imperative, Indicative

			Infinitive ésse	pósse	vélle	nólle
			Imperative es	—	—	nólī
			éste	—	—	nolíte
Present	Singular	1	sum	póssum	vólō	nólō
		2	es	pótes	vīs	nōn vīs
		3	est	pótest	vult	nōn vult
	Plural	1	súmus	póssumus	vólumus	nólumus
		2	éstis	potéstis	vúltis	nōn vúltis
		3	sunt	póssunt	vólunt	nólunt
Imperfect	Singular	1	éram	póteram	volébam	nōlébam
		2	érās	póterās	volébās	nōlébās
		3	érat	póterat	volébat	nōlébat
	Plural	1	erámus	poterámus	volēbámus	nōlēbámus
		2	erátis	poterátis	volēbátis	nōlēbátis
		3	érant	póterant	volébant	nōlébant
Future	Singular	1	érō	póterō	vólam	nólam
		2	éris	póteris	vólēs	nólēs
		3	érit	póterit	vólet	nólet
	Plural	1	érimus	potérimus	volémus	nōlémus
		2	éritis	potéritis	volétis	nōlétis
		3	érunt	póterunt	vólent	nólent

			Infinitive	férre	férrī	íre
			Imperative	fer / férte	férre / féríminī	ī / íte
Present	Singular	1		férō	féror	éō
		2		fers	férris	īs
		3		fert	fértur	it
	Plural	1		férimus	férimur	ímus
		2		fértis	feríminī	ítis
		3		férunt	ferúntur	éunt
Imperfect	Singular	1		ferébam	ferébar	íbam
		2		ferébās	ferēbáris	íbās
		3		ferébat	ferēbátur	íbat
	Plural	1		ferēbámus	ferēbámur	ībámus
		2		ferēbátis	ferēbámini	ībátis
		3		ferébant	ferēbántur	íbant
Future	Singular	1		féram	férar	íbō
		2		férēs	feréris	íbis
		3		féret	ferétur	íbit
	Plural	1		ferémus	ferémur	íbimus
		2		ferétis	ferémini	íbitis
		3		férent	feréntur	íbunt

XIX. Irregular Verbs: Perfect, Pluperfect, Future Perfect Indicative

Full charts are not supplied for these forms because (except for the perfect of **eō**, for which see below) they are not irregular in any way. They are made in the same way as the perfect, pluperfect, and future perfect tenses of regular verbs, by adding the perfect, pluperfect, and future perfect endings to the perfect stem. The perfect stem is found by dropping the *-ī* from the third principal part. The first three principal parts of the irregular verbs are as follows (the perfect stem is underlined):

sum, esse, <u>fuī</u>   volō, velle, <u>voluī</u>   ferō, ferre, <u>tulī</u>

possum, posse, <u>potuī</u>   nōlō, nōlle, <u>nōluī</u>   eō, īre, <u>iī</u> or <u>īvī</u>

Examples:

Perfect: fuistī, voluērunt, tulimus
Pluperfect: fueram, potuerant, nōluerāmus
Future Perfect: fuerō, volueris, tulerimus

The perfect forms of **eō** made from the stem **i-** are as follows:

Singular: iī, īstī, iit   Plural: iimus, īstis, iērunt

Note that the stem vowel (**i-**) contracts with the *-i* of the endings *-istī* and *-istis* to give **ī-** (**īstī, īstis**). Thus also the perfect infinitive: **īsse** (for **iisse**).

The perfect forms of **eō** made from the stem **īv-** are regular, as follows:

Singular: īvī, īvistī, īvit   Plural: īvimus, īvistis, īvērunt

REFERENCE GRAMMAR

I. NOUNS

A. Nominative Case

1. Subject

A noun or pronoun in the nominative case may be the subject of a verb:

In pictūrā est **puella**.... (1:1)
*A **girl** is in the picture....*

2. Complement

A linking verb may be accompanied by a complement in the nominative case:

Cornēlia est **puella**.... (1:1)	Cornēlia est **laeta**.... (1:2–3)
*Cornelia is a **girl**....*	*Cornelia is **happy**....*

While the verb **esse** is the most common linking verb, the verbs in the following sentences are also classed as linking verbs and have complements in the nominative case:

"Quam **scelestus** ille caupō <u>vidētur</u>!" (21:22)
*"How **wicked** that innkeeper <u>seems</u>!"*

"'Nōn sine causā tū <u>vocāris</u> **Pseudolus**.'" (31:23)
*"'Not without reason <u>are</u> you <u>called</u> **Pseudolus**.'"*

"Quis <u>creābitur</u> **arbiter** bibendī?" (34:4)
*"Who <u>will be chosen</u> **master** of the drinking?"*

<u>Fit</u> in diēs **molestior**. (34h:16)
*"He <u>becomes</u> **more troublesome** every day."*

B. Genitive Case (see Book I-A, page 80)

The genitive case usually relates or attaches one noun to another.

1. Genitive of Possession

...vīlicus ipse <u>vīllam</u> **dominī** cūrat. (11:3)
*...the overseer himself looks after the <u>country house</u> **of the master**.*

2. Genitive with Adjectives

Words or phrases in the genitive case may be found with certain adjectives, especially those having to do with fullness:

Brevī tempore ārea est <u>plēna</u> **servōrum** et **ancillārum**.... (11:4)
*In a short time the threshing-floor is <u>full</u> **of slaves** and **slave-women**....*

3. Partitive Genitive

A word or phrase in the genitive case may indicate the whole of which something is a part (see Book I-B, page 95):

"Nihil **malī**," inquit. (21:7)
"*Nothing of a bad thing*," *he said.*
"*Nothing bad*" or "*There is nothing wrong.*"

Crās satis **temporis** habēbimus. (23f:14)
Tomorrow we will have enough (of) time.

With numbers and the words **paucī**, *a few*, **quīdam**, *a certain*, and **nūllus**, *no, no one*, the preposition **ex** or **dē** with the ablative is used:

ūnus **ē praedōnibus** (26:24)   *one of the robbers*

The partitive genitive is used with superlative adjectives and adverbs (see Book II-A, pages 64 and 76):

Titus erat bibendī arbiter pessimus **omnium**. (34:24)
Titus was the worst master of the drinking of all.

Hic puer optimē **omnium** scrībit. (35h:2)
This boy writes best of all.

4. Genitive of Indefinite Value

The genitive case may be found in statements or questions of the general value of something (compare this with the ablative of price, below):

"'**Quantī**,' inquit Pseudolus, 'est illa perna?'" (31:7–8)
"'*How much*,' *says Pseudolus*, '*is that ham?*'"

C. Dative Case

1. Indirect Object of Transitive Verbs

A word or phrase in the dative case may indicate the indirect object of transitive verbs, especially verbs of "giving," "telling," or "showing" (see Book I-B, pages 52–53 and 55 and Exercise 22c):

…servī cistās Cornēliōrum **raedāriō** trādidērunt. (22:2)
…*the slaves handed the chests of the Cornelii over to the coachman.*

2. Dative with Intransitive Verbs

Intransitive verbs and verbs that may be transitive but are used without a direct object may be accompanied by words or phrases in the dative case (see Book I-B, page 55):

Aulus **Septimō** clāmāvit. (21:8–9) *Aulus shouted to Septimus.*

3. Dative with Intransitive Compound Verbs
   Many intransitive compound verbs are accompanied by words or phrases in the dative case (see Book I-B, pages 78–79):

   Iam **urbī** appropinquābant. (22:12)
   *Already they were coming near to/approaching **the city**.*

4. Dative with Special Intransitive Verbs (see Book I-B, page 119)
   The dative case is used with special intransitive verbs such as **cōnfīdere**, *to trust*, **favēre**, *to (give) favor (to)*, *to (give) support (to)*, **nocēre**, *to do harm (to)*, and **placēre**, *to please*:

   Ego **russātīs** favēbō. (27:25)
   *I will give favor **to the reds**.*   *I will favor **the reds**.*

5. Dative with Impersonal Verbal Phrases and Impersonal Verbs
   The dative case is found with impersonal verbal phrases such as **necesse est** and with impersonal verbs (see Book I-B, page 56):

   "**Nōbīs** necesse est statim discēdere." (9:13–14)
   "*It is necessary **for us** to leave immediately.*"

   "Licetne **nōbīs**," inquit Marcus, "hīc cēnāre?" (20:7)
   "*Is it allowed **for us**,*" *said Marcus,* "*to eat here?*"
   "*May we eat here?*"

6. Dative with Verbs of Taking Away or Depriving
   A word in the dative case sometimes denotes the person or thing from which something is taken:

   Mihi est adēmptum baculum.... (35:20)
   *(My) stick was taken away **from me**....*

7. Dative of Possession
   When found with a form of the verb **esse,** the dative case may indicate possession; the thing possessed is the subject of the clause and the person who possesses it is in the dative:

   ...servus quīdam **cui** nōmen est Pseudolus. (31:5–6)
   *...a certain slave, **to whom** the name is Pseudolus.*
   ...whose name is Pseudolus.
   ...who has the name Pseudolus.

D. Accusative Case
   1. Direct Object
      A word or phrase in the accusative case may be the direct object of a transitive verb (see Book I-A, pages 20 and 40–41):

      Sextus...semper **Cornēliam** vexat. (4:1)   *Sextus...is always annoying **Cornelia**.*

2. Double or Predicate Accusative
Verbs of naming, electing, making, and asking often take two accusatives, the first the direct object and the second a predicate to that object:

Cēterōs...puerōs semper **facillima, mē** semper **difficillima** rogat. (40:18)

He always (asks) the other boys very easy things, me he always asks very difficult things.

3. Accusative with Prepositions
The accusative case is used with certain prepositions, especially those expressing motion toward or into or through (see Book I-A, page 64):

ad **vīllam**, *to/toward the country house* (2:7)
in **piscīnam**, *into the fishpond* (3:8)
per **agrōs**, *through the fields* (9:1)

Prepositional phrases with the accusative case may also indicate the vicinity in which someone or something is located:

prope **rīvum** (5:3)
near the stream
...iānitor ad **iānuam** vīllae dormit. (9:3)
...the doorkeeper sleeps near/at the door of the country house.

4. Accusative of Place to Which without a Preposition
With names of cities, towns, small islands, and the words **domus** and **rūs**, the idea of place to which is expressed by the accusative case without a preposition (see Book II-A, pages 118–120):

Rōmam festīnāvit.
He hurried to Rome.

Domum iit.
He went home.

Rūs proficīscitur.
He sets out for the country.

5. Accusative of Duration of Time
Words or phrases in the accusative case without a preposition may indicate duration of time (see Book II-A, page 121):

Iam **multōs diēs** in scaphā erāmus.... (42:38)
We had already been in the boat for many days....

6. Adverbial Accusative
   A word in the accusative case may be used as an adverb:

   Multum et diū clāmat Ianius, sed Pseudolus **nihil**
   respondet. (31:25)
   *The butcher shouts **a lot** and for a long time, but Pseudolus makes
   no reply.*

7. Exclamatory Accusative
   The accusative case is used in exclamations:

   "Ō **mē miseram!**" (9:18)
   "Poor me!"

8. For the accusative and infinitive, see IX.D below.

E. Ablative Case
   1. Ablative of Respect
      A noun or phrase in the ablative may denote that with respect to
      which something is or is done:

      In pictūrā est puella, **nōmine** Cornēlia. (1:1)
      *In the picture is a girl, Cornelia **with respect to her name**.*
      *In the picture is a girl, Cornelia **by name/called** Cornelia.*

   2. Ablative of Time When
      A noun or phrase in the ablative case without a preposition may
      indicate time when:

      Etiam in pictūrā est vīlla rūstica ubi Cornēlia **aestāte**
      habitat. (1:2)
      *Also in the picture is the country house and farm where Cornelia lives
      in summer.*

   3. Ablative of Time within Which
      A noun or phrase in the ablative case without a preposition may
      indicate time within which:

      Brevī tempore Cornēlia est dēfessa. (2:4–5)
      ***In/Within a short time** Cornelia is tired.*

   4. Ablative of Instrument, Means, or Cause
      A word or phrase in the ablative case without a preposition may
      indicate the means by which, the instrument with which, or the
      cause on account of which an action is carried out or a person or
      thing is in a certain state (see Book I-A, page 91, Book I-B, page
      79, and Book II-A, pages 34–35):

Dāvus eum **tunicā** <u>arripit</u> et **baculō** <u>verberat</u>. (means, instrument, 12:17–18)
*Davus <u>grabs hold of</u> him **by the tunic** and <u>beats</u> him **with his stick**.*

Tuā culpā raeda <u>est in fossā</u>. (cause, 14:7)
***Because of your fault** the carriage <u>is in the ditch</u>.*
It's your fault that the carriage is in the ditch.

The ablative of instrument, means, or cause is often used with passive verbs (see Book II-A, page 35):

…nam interdiū nihil intrā urbem **vehiculō** <u>portātur</u>. (29:3–4)
*…for during the day nothing <u>is carried</u> **by a vehicle** within the city.*

5. Ablative of Agent
   If the action of a passive verb is carried out by a person, the ablative of agent is used, consisting of the preposition **ā** or **ab** with the ablative case (see Book II-A, page 35):

   …māter et fīlia **ā servīs** per urbem <u>ferēbantur</u>. (29:1–2)
   *…the mother and her daughter <u>were being carried</u> through the city **by slaves**.*

6. Ablative of Manner
   A phrase consisting of a noun and adjective in the ablative case may be used with or without the preposition **cum** to indicate how something happens or is done (see Book II-A, page 34):

   Tum venit Dāvus ipse et, "Tacēte, omnēs!" **magnā vōce/magnā cum vōce** <u>clāmat</u>. (11:6)
   *Then Davus himself comes, and <u>he shouts</u> **in a loud voice**, "Be quiet, everyone!"*

   The ablative of manner may consist of a single noun with **cum**:

   Caupō iam **cum rīsū** <u>clāmāvit</u>…. (19:17)
   *Now **with a laugh/jokingly** the innkeeper <u>shouted</u>….*

   Occasionally the ablative of manner may consist of a noun in the ablative case without an accompanying adjective or **cum**:

   Tum ego **silentiō** ingressus…. (42:34)
   *Then I having entered **silently**….*

7. Ablative of Price
   The ablative case is used to refer to the specific price of something (compare this with the genitive of indefinite value, above):

   "Itaque tibi **decem dēnāriīs** eum vēndam." (31:17–18)
   *"Therefore I will sell it to you **for ten denarii**."*

8. Ablative of Comparison

The ablative of comparison may be found with comparative adjectives and adverbs (see Book II-A, pages 72 and 76):

Mārtiālis **Eucleide** est multō <u>prūdentior</u>. (35d:4)
*Mārtial is much <u>wiser</u> **than** Eucleides.*

Sextus paulō <u>celerius</u> **Marcō** currere potest. (35h:4)
*Sextus can run a little <u>faster</u> **than** Marcus.*

9. Ablative of Degree of Difference

The ablative case is used to express the degree of difference with comparative adjectives, adverbs, and other words implying comparison (see Book II-A, pages 72 and 76):

"Quam libenter eum rūrsus vidēbō! Sānē tamen **multō** <u>libentius</u> tē vidēbō ubi tū Rōmam veniēs!" (36:10–11)
*"How gladly I will see him again! But of course I will see you **much** <u>more gladly/more gladly</u> **by much** when you come to Rome!"*

Multīs <u>post</u> **annīs**...pervēnit. (39c:3)
*"He arrived...**many years** <u>later/later</u> **by many years**.*

10. Ablative of Separation

Verbs or adjectives implying separation are often accompanied by words or phrases in the ablative, sometimes with **ab** or **ex** and sometimes without a preposition, to express the thing from which something is separated or free:

...vir **vīnō** <u>abstinentissimus!</u> (34h:28) ...*a man <u>most abstinent</u> from wine!*

11. Ablative with Prepositions

The ablative case is used with certain prepositions, especially those expressing motion from or out of, place where, and accompaniment (see Book I-A, pages 64 and 90):

<u>ab</u> **urbe**, <u>*from*</u> ***the city*** (13:12)   <u>in</u> **pictūrā**, <u>*in*</u> ***the picture*** (1:1)
<u>ē</u> **silvā**, <u>*out of*</u> ***the woods*** (5:12)   <u>sub</u> **arbore**, <u>*under*</u> ***the tree*** (1:3)
<u>ex</u> **agrīs**, <u>*out of*</u> ***the fields*** (2:7)   <u>cum</u> **canibus**, <u>*with*</u> ***dogs*** (12:9)

12. Ablative of Place from Which without a Preposition

With names of cities, towns, small islands, and the words **domus** and **rūs**, the idea of place from which is expressed by the ablative case without a preposition (see Book II-A, page 119):

Brundisiō...proficīscētur.... (36:8–9)
*He will set out **from Brundisium**....*

Domō/Rūre profectus est.
*He set out **from home/from the country**.*

13. Ablative of Description

A noun and adjective in the ablative case may be used without a preposition to describe another noun:

[Vergilius] semper **īnfirmā** erat **valētūdine**. (39f: 9–10)
*[Vergil] was always **of weak health**.*

F. Vocative Case

The vocative case is used when addressing a person or persons directly (see Book I-A, page 56):

"Dēscende, **Sexte**!" (4:6)
*"Come down, **Sextus**!"*

"Abīte, **molestī**!" (3:8–9)
*"Go away, **pests**!"*

G. Locative Case

The locative case is used to indicate place where with names of cities, towns, and small islands and with the words **domus** and **rūs** (see Book II-A, pages 119–120):

Rōmae *at Rome*, **Brundisiī** *at Brundisium*, **Carthāginī** *at Carthage*, **Baiīs** *at Baiae*, **domī** *at home*, and **rūrī** *in the country*

II. ADJECTIVES

A. Agreement

Adjectives agree with the nouns they modify in gender, number, and case (see Book I-B, pages 5–6)

B. Adjectives Translated as Adverbs

Adjectives may sometimes best be translated as adverbs:

Brevī tempore, ubi Marcus advenit, eum **laetae** excipiunt. (5:12–13)
*In a short time, when Marcus arrives, they welcome him **happily**.*

C. Adjectives as Substantives

Adjectives may be used as substantives, i.e., as nouns (see Book I-B, page 66):

"Abīte, **molestī**!" (3:8–9)
*"Go away, **pests**!"*

Multa et **mīra** vidēbunt puerī. (23:12)
*The boys will see **many** (and) **wonderful (things)**.*

D. Comparison of Adjectives

Adjectives occur in positive, comparative, and superlative degrees (see Book II-A, pages 64 and 65). For an example of a comparative adjective, see **prūdentior** in I.E.8 above, and for an example of a superlative adjective, see **pessimus** in I.B.3 above.

Instead of following the rules given in Book II-A, page 65, a few adjectives form their comparative and superlative degrees with the adverbs **magis** and **maximē:**

Paulātim igitur fiēbat **magis ēbrius?** (34h:21)
*Did he therefore gradually become **more drunk?***

Statim factus est **maximē ēbrius**.... (34h:22)
*Suddenly he became **very drunk**.*

Comparative adjectives may be used with **quam** or with the ablative case to express the comparison (see Book II-A, pages 64 and 72):

"Quis enim est prūdentior **quam** Gaius?" (34:7)
"Quis enim est prūdentior **Gaiō**?"
*"For who is wiser **than** Gaius?"*

Mārtiālis est multō prūdentior **quam** Eucleidēs.
Mārtiālis **Eucleide** est multō prūdentior. (35d:4)
*Martial is much wiser **than** Eucleides.*

Superlative adjectives may be used with the partitive genitive, see I.B.3 above.

III. ADVERBS

A. Adverbs may modify verbs, other adverbs, or adjectives (see Book I-A, pages 100–101):

Laeta est Flāvia quod Cornēlia **iam** in vīllā <u>habitat</u>. (1:5)
*Flavia is happy because Cornelia <u>is</u> **now** <u>living</u> in the country house.*

Scrībe **quam** <u>saepissimē</u>. (36:25)
*Write **as** <u>often</u> **as possible**.*

"**Valdē** <u>dēfessī</u>," respondit Cornēlius. (23:9)
*"**Very** <u>tired</u>," replied Cornelius.*

B. Comparison of Adverbs

Adverbs occur in positive, comparative, and superlative degrees (see Book II-A, pages 74–76). For an example of a comparative adverb, see **celerius** in I.E.8 above, and for an example of a superlative adverb, see **optimē** in I.B.3 above.

The comparative adverb may be used with **quam** or with the ablative case:

Nēmō celerius **quam** frāter meus currere potest. (35h:3)
*No one is able to run faster **than** my brother.*

Sextus celerius **Marcō** currere potest. (35h:4)
*Sextus is able to run faster **than** Marcus.*

The superlative adverb may be used with a partitive genitive, see I.B.3 above.

IV. VERBS

A. Function
Verbs may be divided into three types according to their function in the sentence or clause:
1. Linking verbs connect a subject with a predicate noun or adjective:

Cornēlia **est** puella Rōmāna. (1:1)   *Cornelia **is** a Roman girl.*

For other examples, see I.A.2 above.

2. Intransitive verbs describe actions that do not take direct objects:

Cornēlia...in Italiā **habitat**. (1:1–2)   *Cornelia **lives** in Italy.*

3. Transitive verbs describe actions that take direct objects:

Sextus...semper Cornēliam **vexat**. (4:1)
*Sextus...always **annoys** Cornelia.*

B. Voice
1. Active and Passive
Verbs may be either active or passive in voice. In the active voice the subject performs the action of the verb; in the passive voice the subject receives the action of the verb (see Book II-A, pages 23–24, 33, and 42–43):

Incolae omnia **agunt**. (active, Book II-A, page 23)
*The tenants **are doing** everything.*

Ab incolīs omnia **aguntur**. (passive, Book II-A, page 23)
*Everything **is being done** by the tenants.*

2. Deponent Verbs
Some verbs, called deponent, are passive in form but active in meaning (see Book II-A, pages 98–100):

Subitō **collāpsus est**. (34:22)   *Suddenly **he collapsed**.*

3. Semi-deponent Verbs
Some verbs, such as **audeō**, **audēre**, **ausus sum**, have regular active forms with active meanings in the present, imperfect, and future tenses but have passive forms with active meanings in the perfect, pluperfect, and future perfect tenses (see Book II-A, pages 132–133):

Tum Marcus arborem ascendit neque dēsilīre **ausus est**. (40:10–11)
Then Marcus climbed a tree and **did** *not* **dare** *jump down.*

4. Impersonal Verbs
See IX, Uses of the Infinitive, below.

C. Tenses of the Indicative
1. Present
The present tense describe an action or a state of being in present time (see Book I-A, page 73):

In pictūrā **est** puella...quae in Italiā **habitat**. (1:1–2)
In the picture **is** *a girl...who* **lives** *in Italy.*

2. Vivid or Historic Present
Sometimes a writer will switch to the present tense while describing past events; this is called the vivid or historic present and helps make the reader feel personally involved in the narrative (see Book II-A, page 23).

3. Imperfect
The imperfect tense (see Book I-A, page 106) describes a continuing, repeated, or habitual action or state of being in past time:

Ego et Marcus **spectābāmus** cisium. (continuing action, 14:10)
Marcus and I **were watching** *the carriage.*

Cornēlius...Syrum identidem **iubēbat** equōs incitāre. (repeated action, 13:1–2)
Cornelius **kept ordering** *Syrus again and again to spur on the horses.*

Dāvus in Britanniā **habitābat**. (habitual action)
Davus **used to live** *in Britain.*

The imperfect tense may also indicate the beginning of an action in past time (see Book I-A, page 107):

Equōs ad raedam nostram **dēvertēbat**. (14:11)
He **began to turn** *the horses* **aside** *in the direction of our carriage.*

The imperfect tense with **iam** and an expression of duration of time is often best translated in English with a pluperfect:

Iam <u>multōs diēs</u> in scaphā **erāmus** cum ā mercātōribus quibusdam inventī sumus. (42:38)
*We **had already been** in the boat <u>for many days</u> when we were found by certain merchants.*

4. Future
The future tense indicates an action that will take place at some time subsequent to the present (see Book I-B, page 67):

"Brevī tempore ad Portam Capēnam **adveniēmus**...." (22:26)
*"In a short time **we will arrive** at the Porta Capena...."*

5. Perfect System
The perfect, pluperfect, and future perfect tenses are formed from the perfect stem, which is derived from the third principal part of the verb.

a. The perfect tense refers to an action that happened or that someone did in past time or to an action completed as of present time (see Book I-B, pages 16–17):

Eō ipsō tempore ad iānuam caupōnae **appāruit** homō obēsus.... (18:12)
*At that very moment a fat man **appeared** at the door of the inn....*

"Servī meī alium lectum tibi **parāvērunt**." (19:17–18)
*"My slaves **have prepared** another bed for you."*

b. The pluperfect tense describes an action that was completed prior to some other action in the past (see Book I-B, page 79):

Titus in itinere mōnstrāvit puerīs mīra aedificia quae prīncipēs in Palātīnō **aedificāverant**. (24:19–20)
*Along the way Titus showed the boys the wonderful buildings that the emperors **had built** on the Palatine.*

c. The future perfect tense describes an action that will have been completed before another action in future time begins (see Book I-B, page 84):

"Cum **intrāverimus**, tandem aurīgās ipsōs spectābimus." (26:17–18)
*"When we **enter/will have entered**, we will finally watch the charioteers themselves."*

D. Mood

1. **Indicative Mood**

   The term *indicative mood* refers to a set of verb forms that are used to express statements or questions of fact in main clauses and statements of fact in many subordinate clauses:

   "Cum **intrāverimus**, tandem aurīgās ipsōs **spectābimus**." (26:17–18)
   "When we enter/will have entered, we will finally watch the charioteers themselves."

2. **Imperative Mood**

   The imperative mood is used to express a command (see Book I-A, page 74):

   "**Abīte**, molestī!" (3:8–9)
   "Go away, pests!"

   A negative command is expressed by **nōlī/nōlīte** and the infinitive:

   "**Nōlī** servōs **excitāre**!" (9:9)
   "Don't wake up the slaves!"

3. **Subjunctive Mood**

   The term *subjunctive mood* refers to a set of verb forms that you have seen used in certain types of subordinate clauses: **cum** causal clauses, **cum** circumstantial clauses, and indirect questions (see below). This mood gets its name from the Latin elements **sub-**, *under*, and **iūnct-**, *joined*, because verbs in this mood are often found in subordinate clauses, i.e., clauses that are "joined under" the main clause. In such clauses the subjunctive is often not translated any differently from the way a verb in the corresponding tense of the indicative would be translated. (For examples, see below.)

V. PARTICIPLES

A. Present Participles (see Book II-A, pages 133–134)

1. **Participles as Verbal Adjectives**

   Participles are verbal adjectives and may modify nouns:

   Nunc cōnspicit <u>poētam</u> versūs **recitantem**. (29:5)
   Now she catches sight of a <u>poet</u> reciting verses.

   Since the participle is a verbal adjective, it may take a direct object of its own; in the sentence above **versūs** is the object of the participle **recitantem**.

2. Participles as Substantives
Present active participles are frequently used as substantives (nouns) (see Book II-A, page 134):

"Cavēte!" exclāmant **adstantēs**.... (29:9–10)
*"Watch out!" shout **the bystanders**....*

B. Perfect Participles as Adjectives
Perfect participles often modify the subject of the verb of the clause (see Book II-A, pages 50–51):

Itaque coquus **vocātus** ab omnibus laudātus est. (33:26)
*Therefore the cook, **having been summoned**, was praised by everyone.*
See Book II-A, page 51 for alternative translations.

...inde **regressus**...in hortō labōrābam. (40:6–7)
*...**having returned** from there...I worked in the garden.*

VI.   GERUNDS
The gerund is a neuter verbal noun that appears in the genitive, dative, accusative, and ablative singular only. It will be formally introduced in Book III. Gerunds are translated as verbal nouns in English:

"Quis creābitur arbiter **bibendī**?" (34:4)
*"Who will be made master **of the drinking**?"*

VII.   SENTENCES

A. Agreement
The subject and verb of a sentence must agree in number; a singular subject takes a singular verb, and a plural subject, a plural verb:

Cornēlia est puella Rōmāna.... (1:1)   ***Cornelia** is a Roman girl....*

Cornēlia et Flāvia sunt puellae Rōmānae.... (2:1–2)
***Cornelia and Flavia** are Roman girls....*

B. Questions
1. Questions may be introduced by many interrogative words:

   Quid facit Cornēlia?   ***What** is Cornelia doing?*

2. Questions may also be introduced by the particle **-ne** attached to the end of the first word (often the verb) of the question:

   Est**ne** puer ignāvus? (5:4)   *Is the boy cowardly?*

3. Questions that expect the answer "yes" are introduced with **nōnne**:

   "**Nōnne** cēnāre vultis?" (19:2)   *"**Surely** you want to eat, **don't you?**"*

C. Coordinating Conjunctions

Conjunctions are words that join together (Latin **con-,** *together* + **iungere,** *to join*) sentences or elements within a sentence. Coordinating conjunctions join elements that are simply added to one another and are of equal grammatical importance (Latin **co-,** *together, same* + **ōrdō,** *order, rank*):

Cornēlia sedet **et** legit. (1:3)   *Cornelia sits **and** reads.*

Etiam Sextus dormit **neque** Cornēliam vexat. (6:2)
*Even Sextus is sleeping **and** is **not** annoying Cornelia.*

Marcus **neque** ignāvus **neque** temerārius est. (5:5–6)
*Marcus is **neither** cowardly **nor** rash.*

Hodiē puellae nōn sedent **sed** in agrīs ambulant. (2:2–3)
*Today the girls are not sitting **but** are walking in the fields.*

Servī in vīllā sedent, **nam** dēfessī sunt. (8c:8)
*The slaves are sitting in the country house, **for** they are tired.*

Sextus est puer molestus quī semper Cornēliam vexat. Cornēlia **igitur** Sextum nōn amat. (4:1–2)
*Sextus is an annoying boy who always annoys Cornelia. Cornelia, **therefore**, does not like Sextus.*

VIII.   SUBORDINATE CLAUSES

A clause is a group of words containing a verb. The following sentence contains two clauses, each of which is said to be a main clause because each could stand by itself as a complete sentence:

Rīdent Marcus et Cornēlia, sed nōn rīdet Sextus. (4:10–11)
Marcus and Cornelia laugh, but Sextus does not laugh.

Subordinate (Latin **sub-,** *below* + **ōrdō,** *order, rank*) clauses are clauses that are of less grammatical importance than the main clause in a sentence. They are sometimes called dependent (Latin **dē-,** *down from* + **pendēre,** *to hang*) clauses because they hang down from the main clause and cannot stand by themselves. They are joined to the main clause by pronouns, adverbs, or subordinating conjunctions.

A. Adjectival Subordinate Clauses with Verbs in the Indicative

Subordinate clauses are modifiers. They may be descriptive, like adjectives, and modify nouns:

Cornēlia est puella Rōmāna **quae** in Italiā habitat. (1:1–2)
*Cornelia is a Roman girl, **who lives in Italy.***

Etiam in pictūrā est vīlla rūstica **ubi** Cornēlia aestāte habitat. (1:2)
*Also in the picture is a country house and farm **where Cornelia lives in the summer.***

The relative pronoun (**quī, quae, quod**) introduces relative clauses, as in the first example above, and agrees with its antecedent in number and gender; its case depends on its use in its own clause (see Book II-A, pages 4–5):

Deinde īrā commōtus servum petit <u>ā **quō** porcus aufūgit</u>. (29:11–12)
*Then in a rage he goes after the slave <u>from **whom** the pig escaped</u>.*

The relative pronoun **quō** is masculine and singular because of the gender and number of its antecedent, **servus**; it is ablative because of its use with the preposition **ā** in its own clause.

Omnia <u>**quae** videt Cornēlia</u> eam dēlectant. (29:5)
*Everything <u>**that** Cornelia sees</u> pleases her.*

The relative pronoun **quae** is neuter and plural because of the gender and number of its antecedent, **omnia**; it is accusative because of its use as the direct object of **videt** in its own clause.

"…īre ad mercātōrem quendam <u>**cuius** taberna nōn procul abest</u>…." (28:10)
*"…to go to a certain merchant <u>**whose** shop is not far away</u>…."*

The relative pronoun **cuius** is masculine and singular because of the gender and number of its antecedent, **mercātōrem quendam**; it is genitive because of its use as a possessive within its own clause (*whose shop*).

B. Adverbial Subordinate Clauses with Verbs in the Indicative
In contrast to adjectival subordinate clauses described above, most subordinate clauses are adverbial, that is, they modify the verb of the main clause or the action of the main clause as a whole and are introduced by subordinating conjunctions that express ideas such as the following:

sī, condition:

> <u>**Sī** tū puer strēnuus es</u>, ascende arborem!
> *<u>**If** you are an energetic boy</u>, climb a tree!*

quamquam, concession:

> <u>**Quamquam** dominus abest</u>, necesse est nōbīs strēnuē labōrāre. (11:7)
> *<u>**Although** the master is away</u>, it is necessary for us to work hard.*

dum, ubi, cum, etc., time:

> <u>**Dum** Cornēlia legit</u>, Flāvia scrībit. (1:4–5)
> *<u>**While** Cornelia reads</u>, Flavia writes.*

Dum per viam ībant, Aurēlia et Cornēlia spectābant rūstīcōs quī in agrīs labōrābant. (13:3–4)
(**Dum** with the imperfect tense = *while/as long as.*)
While/As long as they were going along the road, Aurelia and Cornelia were looking at the peasants who were working in the fields.

Dum puerī cibum dēvorant, subitō intrāvit mīles quīdam. (20:13)
***While** the boys were devouring their food, a certain soldier suddenly entered.*
(Here the present tense verb in the **dum** clause is to be translated with the English past tense that describes ongoing action.) (See Book I-B, page 27.)

Puerī, **ubi** clāmōrem audiunt, statim ad puellās currunt. (5:10)
*The boys, **when** they hear the shout, immediately run to the girls.*

Crās, **ubi surgētis**, puerī, clāmōrem et strepitum audiētis.
*Tomorrow, **when** you get up/will get up, boys, you will hear shouting and noise.*

Cum intrāverimus, tandem aurīgās ipsōs spectābimus. (26:17–18)
***When** we enter/will have entered, we will finally watch the charioteers themselves.*

(While the verbs of the subordinate clauses are in the future, **surgētis,** and future perfect, **intrāverimus,** we translate them into English as presents; see Book I-B, page 84. The use of the tenses is more exact in Latin.)

quod, cause:

Cornēlia est laeta **quod** iam in vīllā habitat. (1:2–3)
*Cornelia is happy **because** she now lives in the country house.*

Conjunctions you have met that may introduce adverbial subordinate clauses with their verbs in the indicative are:

dum, *as long as* (15:1)
dum, *while* (20:13)
nisi, *if not, unless* (18:16)
postquam, *after* (21:10)
quamquam, *although* (11:7)
quod, *because* (1:3)
simulac, *as soon as* (24:1)
sī, *if* (5:1)
ubi, *when* (5:10)
ut, *as* (16:17)

C. Adverbial Subordinate Clauses with Verbs in the Subjunctive

1. **Cum** Causal Clauses

Subordinate clauses that are introduced by the conjunction **cum** and have their verbs in the subjunctive may be **cum** causal clauses; **cum** is translated as *since* or *because*. Such clauses are adverbial and state the reason for the action of the main clause (see Book II-A, page 153):

Magister nāvis, **cum** <u>valdē</u> **timēret**, suōs vetuit nōs adiuvāre. (42:17)
*The captain of the ship, **<u>since/because</u> <u>he was very</u> frightened**, forbade his own men to help us.*

2. **Cum** Circumstantial Clauses

Subordinate clauses that are introduced by the conjunction **cum** and have their verbs in the subjunctive may also be **cum** circumstantial clauses; **cum** is translated as *when*. Such clauses are adverbial and describe the circumstances that prevailed at the time of the action of the main clause (see Book II-A, page 153):

Cum <u>quattuor diēs</u> **nāvigāvissēmus**, subitō maxima tempestās coorta est. (42:2–3)
***When we had sailed** <u>four days</u>, suddenly a very great storm arose.*

Often only the context and sense will tell you whether **cum** is to be translated *since/because* or *when*.

D. Substantive Subordinate Clauses with Verbs in the Subjunctive

a. Indirect Questions (see Book II-A, pages 153–154)

Indirect questions are substantive or noun clauses that may serve as the object of the main verb of the sentence; their verbs are in the subjunctive.

Pīrātae rogābant <u>quī</u> **essēmus**, <u>unde</u> **vēnissēmus**, <u>quō iter</u> **facerēmus**. (42:20–21)
*The pirates were asking <u>who **we were**, from where **we had come**, [and] to where **we were making** a journey</u>.*

IX. USES OF THE INFINITIVE

A. Complementary Infinitive

The meaning of verbs and verbal phrases such as **velle, nōlle, posse, parāre, solēre, timēre**, and **in amimō habēre** is often completed by a complementary infinitive (see Book I-A, page 26):

Cūr Marcus arborēs **ascendere** <u>nōn vult</u>? (5:4)
*Why <u>does Marcus not want</u> **to climb** trees?*

B. Infinitive as Subject

The infinitive may be used as the subject of the verb **est**, with a neuter singular complement (see Book I-B, page 28):

"Etiam in caupōnā **pernoctāre** saepe <u>est</u> <u>perīculōsum</u>." (20:19)
"***To spend the night** in an inn <u>is</u> also often <u>dangerous</u>.*"
"*<u>It is</u> also often <u>dangerous</u> **to spend the night** in an inn.*"

C. Infinitive with Impersonal Verbal Phrases and Impersonal Verbs

Impersonal verbal phrases and impersonal verbs are often used with infinitives (see Book I-B, page 28):

Nōbīs igitur <u>necesse est</u> statim **discēdere**. (9:13–14)
***To leave** immediately <u>is necessary</u> for us.*
*<u>It is necessary</u> for us **to leave** immediately.*

"<u>Licet</u>ne nōbīs," inquit Marcus, "hīc **cēnāre**?" (20:7)
"*<u>Is it allowed</u> for us,*" *Marcus said,* "***to dine** here?*"
"*May we dine here?*"

Strictly speaking, the infinitive is the subject of the impersonal verbal phrase or impersonal verb, but we usually supply *it* as the subject in English and translate the infinitive after the verb.

D. Accusative and Infinitive (see Book I-A, page 72, and Book I-B, page 28):

The verbs **docēre**, *to teach*, **iubēre**, *to order*, and **vetāre**, *to forbid*, are used with an accusative and infinitive:

Aurēlia **Cornēliam** <u>docet</u> vīllam **cūrāre**. (6:11)
*Aurelia <u>teaches</u> **Cornelia** (how) **to take care of** the country house.*

Ancillam <u>iubet</u> aliās tunicās et stolās et pallās in cistam **pōnere**. (10:2)
*<u>She orders</u> **the slave woman to put** other tunics and stolas and pallas into a chest.*

Cūr pater meus **nōs exīre** <u>vetat</u>? (26:12)
*Why <u>does</u> my father <u>forbid</u> **us to go out**?*

LATIN TO ENGLISH VOCABULARY

Numbers in parentheses at the end of entries refer to the chapters in which the words appear in vocabulary entries or in Building the Meaning or Forms sections. Roman numerals refer to Review chapters.

A

ā or **ab**, prep. + abl., *from, by* (13, 29, 31)

ábeō, abíre, ábiī or **abívī, abitúrus**, irreg., *to go away* (3, 9)

abhínc, adv., *ago, previously* (25, 39)

abōminándus, -a, -um, *detestable, horrible* (39)

ábstinēns, abstinéntis + abl., *refraining from* (34)

ábstulī (see **aúferō**)

ábsum, abésse, áfuī, āfutúrus, irreg., *to be away, be absent, be distant* (11, 25)

ac, conj., *and* (30)

  ídem ac, *the same as* (39)

áccidit, accídere, áccidit, *it happens* (14, 26)

accípiō, accípere, accḗpī, accéptus, *to receive, get, welcome* (31)

accúmbō, accúmbere, accúbuī, accubitúrus, *to recline (at table)* (32)

accúrrō, accúrrere, accúrrī, accursúrus, *to run toward/up to* (29)

accúsō, -áre, -ávī, -átus, *to accuse* (21)

ácer, ácris, ácre, *keen* (34)

ad, prep. + acc., *to, toward, at, near* (2, 9)

  ad témpus, *on time* (37)

áddō, áddere, áddidī, ádditus, *to add* (31)

addúcō, addúcere, addúxī, addúctus, *to lead on, bring* (29)

adhúc, adv., *still, as yet* (5, 13)

ádimō, adímere, adḗmī, adémptus + dat., *to take away (from)* (35)

ádiuvō, adiuváre, adiúvī, adiútus, *to help* (6, 21)

admóveō, admovḗre, admóvī, admótus, *to move toward* (22)

adóptō, -áre, -ávī, -átus, *to adopt* (IX)

adórior, adorírī, adórtus sum, *to attack* (42)

adstántēs, adstántium, m. pl., *bystanders* (29)

ádsum, adésse, ádfuī, adfutúrus, irreg., *to be present, be near* (26)

aduléscēns, adulēscéntis, m., *young man, youth* (36)

advéniō, adveníre, advḗnī, adventúrus, *to reach, arrive (at)* (5, 23)

advesperáscit, advesperáscere, advesperávit, *it gets dark* (17)

aedifícium, -ī, n., *building* (17)

aedíficō, -áre, -ávī, -átus, *to build* (24)

aéger, aégra, aégrum, *ill* (39)

aegrótō, -áre, -ávī, -átúrus, *to be ill* (39)

Aenḗās, Aenḗae, m., *Aeneas (son of Venus and Anchises and legendary ancestor of the Romans)* (38)

Aenéis, Aenḗidis, f., *the Aeneid* (38)

aéstās, aestátis, f., *summer* (1, 12)

aéstus, -ūs, m., *heat* (24, 25)

afféctus, -a, -um, *affected, overcome* (35)

áfferō, afférre, áttulī, allátus, irreg., *to bring, bring to, bring in* (29, 32)

África, -ae, f., *Africa* (38)

áger, ágrī, m., *field, territory, land* (2)

agnóscō, agnóscere, agnóvī, ágnitus, *to recognize* (18)

ágō, ágere, ḗgī, áctus, *to do, drive* (8, 14, 23)

  Áge!/Ágite! Come on! (8)

  Grátiās tíbi ágō! *I thank you! Thank you!* (26)

  Quid ágis? *How are you?* (18)

Albánus, -a, -um, *of Alba Longa (city founded by Aeneas' son, Ascanius)* (39)

albátus, -a, -um, *white* (27)

áliquī, -ae, -a, *some* (38)

áliquid, *something* (25)

áliter, adv., *otherwise* (26)

álius, ália, áliud, *another, other, one... another* (10)

  áliī... áliī..., *some...others...* (9)

Álpēs, Álpium, f. pl., *the Alps* (39)

álter, áltera, álterum, *a/the second, one (of two), the other (of two), another* (1)

    álter...álter, *the one...the other* (16)

áltus, -a, -um, *tall, high, deep* (38)

    áltum, -ī, n., *the deep, the sea* (39)

ámbulō, -áre, -ávī, -átúrus, *to walk* (2)

amíca, -ae, f., *friend* (2)

amícus, -ī, m., *friend* (3)

ámō, -áre, -ávī, -átus, *to like, love* (4)

ámor, amóris, m., *love* (34)

amphitheátrum, -ī, n., *amphitheater* (25)

ancílla, -ae, f., *slave-woman* (6)

ánima, -ae, f., *soul, "heart"* (33)

animadvértō, animadvértere, animadvértī, animadvérsus, *to notice* (39)

ánimus, -ī, m., *mind* (16)

    ánimum recuperáre, *to regain one's senses, be fully awake* (21)

    Bónō ánimō es!/éste! *Be of good mind! Cheer up!* (32)

    in ánimō habére, *to intend* (16)

ánnus, -ī, m., *year* (38)

    múltīs post ánnīs, *many years afterward* (39)

ánte, prep. + acc., *before, in front of* (36, 39)

ánte, adv., *previously, before* (39)

ánteā, adv., *previously, before* (20)

ántequam, conj., *before* (39)

antíquus, -a, -um, *ancient* (26)

apériō, aperíre, apéruī, apértus, *to open* (16, 26)

ápium, -ī, n., *parsley* (34)

appáreō, -ére, -uī, -itúrus, *to appear* (15, 18)

appéllō, -áre, -ávī, -átus, *to call, name* (21)

appropínquō, -áre, -ávī, -átúrus + dat. or **ad** + acc., *to approach, come near (to)* (4, 22)

Aprílis, -is, -e, *April* (36)

ápud, prep. + acc., *with, at the house of, in front of, before* (16, 26)

áqua, -ae, f., *water* (6)

aquaedúctus, -ūs, m., *aqueduct* (23, 25)

aránea, -ae, f., *cobweb* (34)

árbiter, árbitrī, m., *master* (34)

    árbiter bibéndī, *master of the drinking* (34)

árbor, árboris, f., *tree* (1)

arcéssō, arcéssere, arcessívī, arcessítus, *to summon, send for* (40)

árcus, -ūs, m., *arch* (24, 25)

área, -ae, f., *open space, threshing-floor* (11)

árma, -órum, n. pl., *arms, weapons* (39)

armátus, -a, -um, *armed* (42)

arrípiō, arrípere, arrípuī, arréptus, *to grab hold of, snatch, seize* (5, 19, 26)

ars, ártis, gen. pl., **ártium,** f., *skill* (14)

ascéndō, ascéndere, ascéndī, ascénsus, *to climb, climb into (a carriage)* (4, 22)

Ásia, -ae, f., *Asia (Roman province in western Asia Minor)* (21)

aspáragus, -ī, m., *asparagus* (33)

aspérsus, -a, -um, *sprinkled* (33)

at, conj., *but* (23)

Athénae, -árum, f. pl., *Athens* (39)

átque, conj., *and, also* (22)

átrium, -ī, n., *atrium, main room* (26)

atténtē, adv., *attentively, closely* (20)

attónitus, -a, -um, *astonished, astounded* (24)

audāx, audácis, *bold* (36)

aúdeō, audére, aúsus sum, semi-deponent + infin., *to dare (to)* (40)

aúdiō, -íre, -ívī, -ítus, *to hear, listen to* (4, 20)

aúferō, auférre, ábstulī, ablátus, irreg., *to carry away, take away* (29, 32)

aufúgiō, aufúgere, aufúgī, *to run away, escape* (29)

Augústus, -a, -um, *August* (36)

Augústus, -ī, m., *Augustus (first Roman emperor)* (39)

aúreus, -a, -um, *golden* (25)

auríga, -ae, m., *charioteer* (13)

aúrum, -ī, n., *gold* (21)

aut, conj., *or* (26)

    aut...aut, conj., *either...or* (26)

aútem, conj., *however, but, moreover* (31)

auxílium, -ī, n., *help* (5, 15)

    Fer/Férte auxílium! *Bring help! Help!* (5)

Ávē!/Avéte! *Hail! Greetings!* (40)

B

báculum, -ī, n., *stick, staff* (10, 15)

báiger, -árum, f. pl., *Baige*

béllum, -ī, n., *war* (39)

béne, adv., *well* (22, 35)

bíbō, bíbere, bíbī, *to drink* (31)

Bīthýnia, -ae, f., *Bithynia (province in Asia Minor)* (39)

bōlétus, -ī, m., *mushroom* (33)

bónus, -a, -um, *good* (12, 34)

    bóna, -órum, n. pl., *goods, possessions* (26)

    Bónō ánimō es!/éste! *Be of good mind!*
        Cheer up! (32)

bōs, bóvis, m./f., *ox, cow* (15)

brévis, -is, -e, *short* (2, 34)

    bréviter, adv., *briefly* (35)

Británnia, -ae, f., *Britain* (8)

Británnicus, -a, -um, *British* (3)

Brundísium, -ī, n., *Brundisium* (36)

    Brundísiī, *at Brundisium* (36)

    Brundísiō, *from Brundisium* (36)

    Brundísium, *to Brundisium* (36)

C

cachínnus, -ī, m., *laughter* (30)

cádō, cádere, cécidī, cāsū́rus, *to fall* (3, 22)

caélum, -ī, n., *sky, heaven* (17)

Caésar, Caésaris, m., *Caesar, emperor* (27)

cálidus, -a, -um, *warm* (5)

Calígula, -ae, m., *Caligula (emperor, A.D. 37–41)* (27)

candēlábrum, -ī, n., *candelabrum, lamp-stand* (32)

cándidus, -a, -um, *white, fair-skinned, beautiful* (34)

cánis, cánis, m./f., *dog, the lowest throw of the*
    knucklebones (12, 34)

cánō, cánere, cécinī, cántus, *to sing* (39)

cántō, -áre, -ávī, -átus, *to sing* (21)

cápiō, cápere, cḗpī, cáptus, *to take, catch,*
    capture (21)

captívus, -ī, m., *captive, prisoner* (26)

cáput, cápitis, n., *head* (25)

cáreō, carére, cáruī, caritū́rus + abl., *to need,*
    lack (33)

cāríssimus, -a, -um, *dearest* (16)

cárō, cárnis, gen. pl., **cárnium**, f., *meat, flesh* (31)

Carthágō, Cartháginis, f., *Carthage (city on the*
    northern coast of Africa) (39)

cása, -ae, f., *hut, cottage* (42)

castígō, -áre, -ávī, -átus, *to rebuke, reprimand* (37)

cásū, *by chance, accidentally* (32)

caúda, -ae, f., *tail* (18)

caúpō, caupónis, m., *innkeeper* (17)

caupóna, -ae, f., *inn* (17, 20)

caúsa, -ae, f., *reason* (25)

    quā dē caúsā, *for this reason* (32)

    Quam ob caúsam...? *For what reason...?* (28)

cáveō, cavére, cā́vī, caútus, *to be careful, watch out*
    for, beware (4, 13, 23)

céleber, célebris, célebre, *famous* (31)

céler, céleris, célere, *swift* (34)

    celériter, adv., *quickly* (8, 13, 35)

    celérius, adv., *more quickly* (35)

    celérrimē, adv., *very fast, very quickly* (14)

    celérrimus, -a, -um, *fastest, very fast* (29)

    quam celérrimē, adv., *as quickly as possible* (34)

celéritās, celeritátis, f., *speed* (29)

    súmmā celeritáte, *with the greatest speed, as fast*
        as possible (29)

célō, -áre, -ávī, -átus, *to hide, conceal* (11)

céna, -ae, f., *dinner* (19)

cénō, -áre, -ávī, -átus, *to dine, eat dinner* (19)

centésimus, -a, -um, *hundredth* (38)

céntum, *a hundred* (15, 38)

Cérberus,-ī, m., *Cerberus (three-headed dog guard-*
    ing the underworld) (32)

cértus, -a, -um, *certain* (35)

    cértē, adv., *certainly* (19, 35)

céssō, -áre, -ávī, -ātū́rus, *to be idle, do nothing,*
    delay (14)

céterī, -ae, -a, *the rest, the others* (33)

Chárōn, Charónis, m., *Charon (ferryman in the*
    underworld) (32)

cíbus, -ī, m., *food* (6)

circénsis, -is, -e, *in the circus* (27)

    lúdī circénsēs, lūdórum circénsium, m. pl.,
        chariot-racing (27)

círcum, prep. + acc., *around* (32)

circúmeō, circumíre, circúmiī or **circumívī,**
    circúmitus, irreg., *to go around* (24)

Círcus Máximus, -ī, m., *Circus Maximus (a*
    stadium in Rome) (23)

císium, -ī, n., *light two-wheeled carriage* (14, 15)

císta, -ae, f., *trunk, chest* (10)

cívis, cívis, gen. pl., **cívium**, m./f., *citizen* (13)

clam, adv., *secretly* (42)

clámō, -áre, -ávī, -átúrus, *to shout* (3)

clámor, clāmóris, m., *shout, shouting* (5)

claúdō, claúdere, claúsī, claúsus, *to shut* (26)
   claúsus, -a, -um, *shut, closed* (24)

clíēns, cliéntis, gen. pl., **cliéntium**, m., *client, dependent* (25)

coépī, *I began* (38)

cógitō, -áre, -ávī, -átus, *to think* (21)

cognómen, cognóminis, n., *surname (third or fourth name of a Roman)* (IX)

collábor, collábī, collápsus sum, *to collapse* (34, 37)

cóllis, cóllis, gen. pl., **cóllium**, m., *hill* (35)

collóquium, -ī, n., *conversation* (26)

cólloquor, cólloquī, collocútus sum, *to converse, speak together* (37)

cólō, cólere, cóluī, cúltus, *to cultivate* (23)

cómes, cómitis, m./f., *companion* (39)

cómiter, adv., *courteously, graciously, in a friendly way* (32)

commissátiō, commissātiónis, f., *drinking party* (34)

commóveō, commovére, commóvī, commótus, *to move, upset* (29, 30)
   commótus, -a, -um, *moved* (14)

cómparō, -áre, -ávī, -átus, *to buy, obtain, get ready* (32)

cómpleō, complére, complévī, complétus, *to fill, complete* (33)

compléxus, -ūs, m., *embrace* (9, 25)

complúrēs, -ēs, -a, *several* (32)

cóncidō, concídere, cóncidī, *to fall down* (14)

concúrrō, concúrrere, concúrrī, concursúrus, *to run together, rush up* (35)

concúrsō, -áre, -ávī, -átus, *to run to and fro, run about* (29)

cóndō, cóndere, cóndidī, cónditus, *to found, establish* (36, 39)

condúcō, condúcere, condúxī, condúctus, *to hire* (23)

cōnfíciō, cōnfícere, cōnfécī, cōnféctus, *to accomplish, finish* (25, 32)

cōnfídō, cōnfídere, cōnfísus sum + dat., *to give trust (to), trust* (26)

coníciō, conícere, coniécī, coniéctus, *to throw* (21)

cóniūnx, cóniugis, m./f., *husband, wife* (26)

cónor, -árī, -átus sum, *to try* (36, 37)

cónsequor, cónsequī, cōnsecútus sum, *to catch up to, overtake* (35, 37)

cōnsídō, cōnsídere, cōnsédī, *to sit down* (23)

cōnspíciō, cōnspícere, cōnspéxī, cōnspéctus, *to catch sight of* (4, 21)

cōnstítuō, cōnstitúere, cōnstítuī, cōnstitútus, *to decide* (23)

cónsul, cónsulis, m., *consul* (36)

cónsulō, cōnsúlere, cōnsúluī, cōnsúltus, *to consult* (7)

conticéscō, conticéscere, contícuī, *to become silent* (38, 39)

cóntrā, adv., *in return* (34)

convaléscō, convaléscere, conváluī, *to grow stronger, get well* (42)

convíva, -ae, m., *guest (at a banquet)* (31)

convívium, -ī, n., *feast, banquet* (34)

cónvocō, -áre, -ávī, -átus, *to call together* (12)

coórior, coorírī, coórtus sum, *to rise up, arise* (42)

cóquō, cóquere, cóxī, cóctus, *to cook* (6, 32)

cóquus, -ī, m., *cook* (33)

Cornēliánus, -a, -um, *belonging to Cornelius* (10)

Cornéliī, -órum, m. pl., *the members of the family of Cornelius* (22)

coróna, -ae, f., *garland, crown* (34)

corónō, -áre, -ávī, -átus, *to crown* (34)

córpus, córporis, n., *body* (21)

corrípiō, corrípere, corrípuī, corréptus, *to seize, grab* (35)

cotídiē, adv., *daily, every day* (37)

crās, adv., *tomorrow* (10, 13)

crédō, crédere, crédidī, créditus + dat., *to trust, believe* (35)

Cremóna, -ae, f., *Cremona (town in northern Italy)* (39)

créō, -áre, -ávī, -átus, *to appoint* (34)

Créta, -ae, f., *Crete (large island southeast of Greece)* (39)

crínēs, crínium, m. pl., *hair* (28)

crótalum, -ī, n., *castanet* (21)

crūdélis, -is, -e, *cruel* (40)

cubículum, -ī, n., *room, bedroom* (8, 15)

cúbitum íre, *to go to bed* (19)

Cúius...? *Whose...?* (22)

culína, -ae, f., *kitchen* (21)

cúlpa, -ae, f., *fault, blame* (14)

cum, prep. + abl., *with* (12)

cum, conj., *when, since* (22, 40)

  cum prímum, *as soon as* (40)

cúnctī, -ae, -a, *all* (14)

Cupídō, Cupídinis, m., *Cupid (the son of Venus)* (34)

cúpiō, cúpere, cupívī, cupítus, *to desire, want* (40)

Cūr...? *Why...?* (1)

cúra, -ae, f., *care* (34)

Cúria, -ae, f., *Senate House* (23)

cúrō, -áre, -ávī, -átus, *to look after, take care of* (6)

currículum, -ī, n., *race track* (27)

cúrrō, cúrrere, cucúrrī, cursúrus, *to run* (2, 23)

custódiō, -íre, -ívī, -ítus, *to guard* (17)

cústōs, custódis, m., *guard* (26)

cýathus, -ī, m., *small ladle, measure (of wine)* (34)

D

dē, prep. + abl., *down from, concerning, about* (16)

débeō, -ére, -uī, -itus, *to owe;* + infin., *ought* (26)

décem, *ten* (15, 38)

Decémber, Decémbris, Decémbre, *December* (36)

décimus, -a, -um, *tenth* (38)

dédicō, -áre, -ávī, -átus, *to dedicate* (33)

dēféndō, dēféndere, dēféndī, dēfénsus, *to defend* (I, 35)

dēféssus, -a, -um, *tired* (2)

dēíciō, dēícere, dēiḗcī, dēiéctus, *to throw down;* pass., *to fall* (32)

deínde, adv., *then, next* (8, 13)

dēléctō, -áre, -ávī, -átus, *to delight, amuse* (29)

déleō, dēlére, dēlévī, dēlétus, *to destroy* (38)

Délos, -ī, f., *Delos (small island off the eastern coast of Greece)* (39)

dēmónstrō, -áre, -ávī, -átus, *to show* (24)

dēnárius, -ī, m., *denarius (silver coin)* (31)

dēpónō, dēpónere, dēpósuī, dēpósitus, *to lay down, put aside, set down* (31)

dērídeō, dērīdére, dērísī, dērísus, *to laugh at, get the last laugh* (33)

dēscéndō, dēscéndere, dēscéndī, dēscēnsúrus, *to come/go down, climb down* (4, 23)

dēsíderō, -áre, -ávī, -átus, *to long for, desire, miss* (26)

dēsíliō, dēsilíre, dēsíluī, *to leap down* (40)

déus, -ī, nom. pl., **dī,** dat., abl. pl., **dīs,** m., *god* (35, 39)

  Dī immortálēs! *Immortal Gods! Good heavens!* (33)

  Prō dī immortálēs! *Good heavens!* (42)

dēvértō, dēvértere, dēvértī, dēvérsus, *to turn aside* (14, 27)

dévorō, -áre, -ávī, -átus, *to devour* (20)

dī (nom. pl. of **déus**) (33, 39)

dícō, dícere, díxī, díctus, *to say, tell* (20, 21)

  dícitur, *(he/she/it) is said* (41)

  salútem dícere, *to send greetings* (36)

  véra dícere, *to tell the truth* (40)

Dídō, Dīdónis, f., *Dido (queen of Carthage)* (38)

díēs, diḗī, m., *day* (5, 13, 25)

  in díēs, *every day, day by day* (34)

difficilis, -is, -e, *difficult* (34)

difficúltās, difficultátis, f., *difficulty* (35)

díligēns, dīligéntis, *diligent, painstaking, thorough* (35)

dīligénter, adv., *carefully* (19)

discédō, discédere, discéssī, discessúrus, *to go away, depart* (9, 22, 41)

discípulus, -ī, m., *pupil* (38)

díscō, díscere, dídicī, *to learn* (40)

dissímilis, -is, -e, *dissimilar* (34)

díū, adv., *for a long time* (15, 35)

  diūtíssimē, adv., *longest* (35)

  diútius, adv., *longer* (35)

díves, dívitis, *rich* (42)

dívidō, dīvídere, dīvísī, dīvísus, *to divide* (IX)

dīvínus, -a, -um, *divine* (IX)

dō, dáre, dédī, dátus, *to give* (21)

  poénās dáre, *to pay the penalty, be punished* (40)

  sē quiétī dáre, *to rest* (23)

dóceō, docére, dócuī, dóctus, *to teach* (6, 21)

dóleō, -ére, -uī, -itúrus, *to be sorry, be sad* (18)

dólor, dolóris, m., *grief* (38)

dómina, -ae, f., *mistress, lady of the house* (17)

dóminus, -ī, m., *master, owner* (11)

dómus, -ūs, f., *home* (23, 25, 39)

   dómī, *at home* (26, 39)

   dómō, *from home* (23, 39)

   dómum, *homeward, home* (23, 39)

dónec, conj., *until* (33)

dónō, -áre, -ávī, -átus, *to give* (34)

dórmiō, -íre, -ívī, -ītúrus, *to sleep* (4)

dórmitō, -áre, -ávī, *to be sleepy* (39)

dúbium, -ī, n., *doubt* (30)

dúcō, dúcere, dúxī, dúctus, *to lead, take, bring* (7, 19, 20)

dum, conj., *while, as long as* (1)

dúo, dúae, dúo, *two* (15, 38)

duódecim, *twelve* (38)

duodécimus, -a, -um, *twelfth* (38)

duodēvīgíntī, *eighteen* (38)

duodēvīcésimus, -a, -um, *eighteenth* (38)

E

ē or **ex**, prep. + abl., *from, out of* (2, 5, 9)

ébrius, -a, -um, *drunk* (34)

Écce! *Look! Look at…!* (1)

édō, ésse, édī, ésus, irreg., *to eat* (33)

éfferō, efférre, éxtulī, ēlátus, irreg., *to carry out, bring out* (30)

effúgiō, effúgere, effúgī, *to flee, run away, escape* (11, 21, 29)

effúndō, effúndere, effúdī, effúsus, *to pour out;* pass., *to spill* (32)

égo, *I* (5, 27)

ēgrédior, égredī, ēgréssus sum, *to go out, leave* (37, 39)

Éheu! *Alas!* (7)

Ého! *Hey!* (25)

ēíciō, ēícere, ēiécī, ēiéctus, *to throw out, wash overboard* (30)

élegāns, ēlegántis, *elegant, tasteful* (29)

ēmíttō, ēmíttere, ēmísī, ēmíssus, *to send out* (30)

émō, émere, émī, émptus, *to buy* (21, 31)

énim, conj., *for* (20)

éō, íre, íī or **ívī, itúrus**, irreg., *to go* (7, 17, 19, 20, 21)

   cúbitum íre, *to go to bed* (19)

éō, adv., *there, to that place* (23)

epístula, -ae, f., *letter* (7)

équus, -ī, m., *horse* (10)

ērípiō, ērípere, ērípuī, ēréptus, *to snatch (from), rescue* (29)

érrō, -áre, -ávī, -ātúrus, *to wander, be mistaken* (5, 18)

ērudítus, -a, -um, *learned, scholarly* (37)

ērúptiō, ēruptiónis, f., *eruption* (26)

ésse (see **sum**)

Éstō! *All right! So be it!* (20)

ēsúriō, -íre, -ívī, -ītúrus, *to be hungry* (19)

et, conj., *and, also* (1)

   et…et, conj., *both… and*

étiam, adv., *also, even* (1, 6, 13)

etiámsī, conj., *even if* (37)

Eúge! *Hurray!* (33)

Eúgepae! *Hurray!* (7)

Eurýdicē, -ēs, f., *Eurydice (wife of Orpheus)* (VII)

ēvádō, ēvádere, ēvásī, ēvásus, *to escape* (42)

ēvértō, ēvértere, ēvértī, ēvérsus, *to overturn, upset* (32)

ex or **ē**, prep. + abl., *from, out of* (2, 5, 9)

excípiō, excípere, excépī, excéptus, *to welcome, receive, catch* (5, 16, 22)

éxcitō, -áre, -ávī, -átus, *to rouse, wake (someone) up* (8)

   excitátus, -a, -um, *wakened, aroused* (25)

exclámō, -áre, -ávī, -átus, *to exclaim, shout out* (10)

excúsō, -áre, -ávī, -átus, *to forgive, excuse* (33)

   sē excūsáre, *to apologize* (33)

éxeō, exíre, éxiī or **exívī, exitúrus**, irreg., *to go out* (5, 23)

expéllō, expéllere, expulī, expúlsus, *to drive out, expel* (39)

expergíscor, expergíscī, experréctus sum, *to wake up* (39)

expérior, experírī, expértus sum, *to test, try* (37)

éxplicō, -áre, -ávī, -átus, *to explain* (19)

   rem explicáre, *to explain the situation* (19)

exspéctō, -áre, -ávī, -átus, *to look out for, wait for* (15)

éxstāns, exstántis, *standing out, towering* (23)

exstínguō, exstínguere, exstínxī, exstínctus, *to put out, extinguish* (30)

exténdō, exténdere, exténdī, exténtus, *to hold out* (18, 39)

éxtrā, prep. + acc., *outside* (23)

éxtrahō, extráhere, extráxī, extráctus, *to drag out, take out* (14, 21)

éxuō, exúere, éxuī, exútus, *to take off* (33)

F

fábula, -ae, f., *story* (20)

fácilis, -is, -e, *easy* (34)
  fácile, adv., *easily* (35)

fáciō, fácere, fécī, fáctus, *to make, do* (1, 23)
  íter fácere, *to travel* (13)

fáctiō, factiónis, f., *company (of charioteers)* (27)

fátum, -ī, n., *fate* (39)

fátuus, -a, -um, *stupid* (13)

fáveō, favére, fávī, fautúrus + dat., *to give favor (to), favor, support* (27)

Februárius, -a, -um, *February* (36)

félēs, félis, gen. pl., **félium**, f., *cat* (21)

félīx, fēlícis, *lucky* (34)
  fēlíciter, adv., *well, happily, luckily* (35)

fémina, -ae, f., *woman* (3)

fenéstra, -ae, f., *window* (30)

férculum, -ī, n., *dish, tray* (33)

fēriátus, -a, -um, *celebrating a holiday* (27)

fériō, -íre, -ívī, -ítus, *to hit, strike* (16)

férō, férre, túlī, látus, irreg., *to bring, carry, bear* (5, 12, 17, 21)
  Fer/Férte auxílium! *Bring help! Help!* (5)

férōx, ferócis, *fierce* (35)
  feróciter, adv., *fiercely* (13)

férula, -ae, f., *cane* (39)

festínō, -áre, -ávī, -atúrus, *to hurry* (9)

fidélis, -is, -e, *faithful* (31, 34)

fília, -ae, f., *daughter* (11)

fílius, -ī, m., *son* (11)

fíniō, -íre, -ívī, -ítus, *to finish* (21)

fínis, fínis, gen. pl., **fínium**, m., *end* (29)

fíō, fíerī, fáctus sum, irreg., *to become, be made, be done, happen* (34)

flámma, -ae, f., *flame* (29)

flōs, flóris, m., *flower* (34)

foédus, -a, -um, *filthy, disgusting* (34)

fórās, adv., *outside* (41)

fortásse, adv., *perhaps* (15)

fórte, adv., *by chance* (33)

fórtis, -is, -e, *brave, strong* (18)
  fortíssimē, adv., *most/very bravely* (35)
  fórtiter, adv., *bravely* (35)

Fórum, -ī, n., *the Forum (town center of Rome)* (25)

fóssa, -ae, f., *ditch* (12)

frágor, fragóris, m., *crash, noise, din* (4)

fráter, frátris, m., *brother* (11)

frígidus, -a, -um, *cool, cold* (5)

fritíllus, -ī, m., *cylindrical box* (34)

frōns, fróntis, gen. pl., **fróntium**, f., *forehead* (12)

frústrā, adv., *in vain* (14)

frústum, -ī, n., *scrap* (33)

fúgiō, fúgere, fúgī, fugitúrus, *to flee* (18, 25)

fúī (see **sum**)

fúmus, -ī, m., *smoke* (29)

fúndus, -ī, m., *farm* (39)

fúrtim, adv., *stealthily* (4, 13)

fústis, fústis, gen. pl., **fústium**, m., *club, cudgel* (35)

G

Gádēs, Gádium, f. pl., *Gades (Cadiz, a town in Spain)* (21)

Gállia, -ae, f., *Gaul* (39)

gaúdeō, gaudére, gāvísus sum, *to be glad, rejoice* (14, 40)

gaúdium, -ī, n., *joy* (23)

gémō, gémere, gémuī, gémitus, *to groan* (3)

génus, géneris, n., *race, stock, nation* (39)

gérō, gérere, géssī, géstus, *to wear* (10)

gládius, -ī, m., *sword* (21, 26)
  gládium stríngere, *to draw a sword* (26)

glīs, glíris, m., *dormouse* (28)

glória, -ae, f., *fame, glory* (27)

grácilis, -is, -e, *slender* (34)

Graécia, -ae, f., *Greece* (21)

Graécus, -a, -um, *Greek* (17)
  Graécī, -órum, m. pl., *the Greeks* (I)

grammáticus, -ī, m., *secondary school teacher* (37)

grátia, -ae, f., *gratitude, thanks* (26)

    Grátiās tíbi ágō, *I thank you! Thank you!* (26)

grátīs, adv., *free, for nothing* (31)

grávis, -is, -e, *heavy, serious* (35)

grúnniō, -íre, *to grunt* (29)

gustátiō, gustātiónis, f., *hors d'oeuvre, first course* (33)

H

habénae, -árum, f. pl., *reins* (22)

hábeō, -ére, -uī, -itus, *to have, hold* (10, 20, 26)

    in ánimō habére, *to intend* (16)

    ōrātiónem habére, *to deliver a speech* (26)

hábitō, -áre, -ávī, -átus, *to live, dwell* (1)

haéreō, haerére, haésī, haesúrus, *to stick* (14)

haúriō, hauríre, haúsī, haústus, *to drain* (34)

hédera, -ae, f., *ivy* (34)

Hérculēs, Hérculis, m., *Hercules (Greek hero)* (34)

héri, adv., *yesterday* (20)

Hespéria, -ae, f., *Hesperia (the land in the West, Italy)* (39)

hīc, adv., *here* (9, 13)

hic, haec, hoc, *this, the latter* (18, 19, 20, 25, 26, 31)

híems, híemis, f., *winter* (39)

Hispánia, -ae, f., *Spain* (39)

hódiē, adv., *today* (2, 13)

hólus, hóleris, n., *vegetable* (32)

hómō, hóminis, m., *man* (18)

    hóminēs, hóminum, m. pl., *people* (15, 36)

hónor, honóris, m., *honor* (IX)

hóra, -ae, f., *hour* (9)

    Quóta hóra est? *What time is it?* (38)

Horátius, -ī, m., *Horace (Roman poet)* (39)

hórtus, -ī, m., *garden* (3)

hóspes, hóspitis, m., *guest, host, friend, a person related to one of another city by ties of hospitality* (16)

hūc, adv., *here, to here* (36)

    hūc illúc, adv., *here and there, this way and that* (23)

húmī, *on the ground* (27)

húmilis, -is, -e, *humble* (34)

I

iáceō, -ére, -uī, -itúrus, *to lie, be lying down* (26)

iáciō, iácere, iécī, iáctus, *to throw* (10, 20)

iáctō, -áre, -ávī, -átus, *to toss about, drive to and fro* (39)

iam, adv., *now, already* (1, 8, 13)

    nōn iam, adv., *no longer* (2, 13)

iánitor, iānitóris, m., *doorkeeper* (9)

iánua, -ae, f., *door* (9)

Iānuárius, -a, -um, *January* (36)

íbi, adv., *there* (5, 13)

id (see **is**)

ídem, éadem, ídem, *the same* (3, 31)

    ídem ac, *the same as* (39)

idéntidem, adv., *again and again, repeatedly* (13)

Īdūs, Īduum, f. pl., *the Ides* (36)

iēntáculum, -ī, n., *breakfast* (37)

ígitur, conj., *therefore* (4)

ignávus, -a, -um, *cowardly, lazy* (5)

ígnis, ígnis, gen. pl., **ígnium**, m., *fire* (32)

ignórō, -áre, -ávī, -átus, *to be ignorant, not to know* (40)

ílle, ílla, íllud, *that; he, she, it; the former; that famous* (11, 15, 16, 20, 22, 25, 26, 31)

illúc, adv., *there, to that place* (23)

    hūc illúc, adv., *here and there, this way and that* (23)

ímber, ímbris, gen. pl., **ímbrium**, m., *rain* (23)

ímmemor, immémoris + gen., *forgetful* (22)

ímmō, adv., *rather, on the contrary* (31)

    ímmō vérō, adv., *on the contrary, in fact* (40)

immóbilis, -is, -e, *motionless* (12)

immortális, -is, -e, *immortal* (27)

    Dī immortálēs! *Immortal Gods! Good heavens!* (33)

    Prō dī immortálēs! *Good heavens!* (42)

impédiō, -íre, -ívī, -ítus, *to hinder, prevent* (11)

in, prep. + abl., *in, on, among* (1, 9, 28)

    in ánimō habére, *to intend* (16)

in, prep. + acc., *into, against* (3, 9)

    in díēs, *every day, day by day* (34)

    in quíbus, *among whom* (28)

incéndium, -ī, n., *fire* (30)

incéndō, incéndere, incéndī, incénsus, *to burn, set on fire* (38)

íncitō, -áre, -ávī, -átus, *to spur on, urge on, drive* (10)

íncola, -ae, m./f., *inhabitant, tenant* (30)

incólumis, -is, -e, *unhurt, safe and sound* (14)

índe, adv., *from there, then* (38, 40)

índuō, indúere, índuī, indútus, *to put on* (8, 23)

íneō, iníre, íniī or **inívī, ínitus**, irreg., *to go into, enter* (28)

īnfándus, -a, -um, *unspeakable* (38)

īnfāns, īnfántis, m./f., *infant, young child* (30)

ínferī, -órum, m. pl., *the underworld* (32)

ínferō, īnférre, íntulī, illátus, irreg., *to bring in* (39)

īnfírmus, -a, -um, *weak, shaky, frail* (4, 30)

íngēns, ingéntis, *huge* (22)

ingrédior, íngredī, ingréssus sum, *to go in, enter* (37)

innocéntia, -ae, f., *innocence* (21)

ínquit, *(he/she) says, said* (7)

īnspíciō, īnspícere, īnspéxī, īnspéctus, *to examine* (21)

ínsula, -ae, f., *island, apartment building* (30)

inténtus, -a, -um, *intent, eager* (38)

ínter, prep. + acc., *between, among* (33)

intérdiū, adv., *during the day, by day* (23)

intérdum, adv., *from time to time* (39)

intéreā, adv., *meanwhile* (10, 13)

ínterest, *it is important* (39)

interpéllō, -áre, -ávī, -átus, *to interrupt* (14)

íntrā, prep. + acc., *inside* (22)

íntrō, -áre, -ávī, -átus, *to enter, go into* (8, 19)

inúrō, inúrere, inússī, inústus, *to brand* (12)

invéniō, inveníre, invénī, invéntus, *to come upon, find* (12, 21)

invítō, -áre, -ávī, -átus, *to invite* (28, 32)

invítus, -a, -um, *unwilling* (21)

ínvocō, -áre, -ávī, -átus, *to invoke, call upon* (34)

iócus, -ī, m., *joke, funny story, prank* (16)

    per iócum, *as a prank/joke* (16)

ípse, ípsa, ípsum, *himself, herself, itself, themselves, very* (6, 10, 29, 31)

íra, -ae, f., *anger* (11)

īrācúndia, -ae, f., *irritability, bad temper* (40)

īrācúndus, -a, -um, *irritable, in a bad mood* (40)

īrátus, -a, -um, *angry* (3, 33)

íre (see **éō**) (7, 17)

irrúmpō, irrúmpere, irrúpī, irrúptus, *to burst in* (33)

is, éa, id, *he, she, it; this, that* (27, 31)

íta, adv., *thus, so, in this way* (3, 13, 21)

    Íta vérō! adv., *Yes! Indeed!* (3, 13)

Itália, -ae, f., *Italy* (1)

ítaque, adv., *and so, therefore* (16)

íter, itíneris, n., *journey, route* (10, 13, 15)

    íter fácere, *to travel* (13)

íterum, adv., *again, a second time* (8, 13)

Íthaca, -ae, f., *Ithaca (island home of Ulysses)* (39)

iúbeō, iubére, iússī, iússus, *to order, bid* (10, 19, 21)

Iúlius, -a, -um, *July* (36)

Iúnius, -a, -um, *June* (36)

Iúnō, Iūnónis, f., *Juno (queen of the gods)* (39)

iússa, -órum, n. pl., *commands, orders* (32)

K

Kaléndae, -árum, f. pl., *the Kalends (first day in the month)* (36)

L

lábor, labóris, m., *work, toil* (24)

labórō, -áre, -ávī, -átus, *to work* (3)

lácrimō, -áre, -ávī, -átus, *to weep, cry* (9)

laétus, -a, -um, *happy, glad* (1)

    laétē, adv., *happily* (35)

lána, -ae, f., *wool* (6)

    lánam tráhere, *to spin wool* (6)

lánius, -ī, m., *butcher* (31)

lantérna, -ae, f., *lantern* (37)

lapídeus, -a, -um, *of stone, stony* (33)

lápis, lápidis, m., *stone* (25)

Latínus, -a, -um, *Latin* (39)

Látium, -ī, n., *Latium (the area of central Italy that included Rome)* (39)

lātrátus, -ūs, m., *a bark, barking* (25)

látrō, -áre, -ávī, -átúrus, *to bark* (12)

laúdō, -áre, -ávī, -átus, *to praise* (18)

Lāvínius, -a, -um, *of Lavinium (name of the town where the Trojans first settled in Italy)* (39)

lávō, lavắre, lắvī, laútus, *to wash* (20)

lectíca, -ae, f., *litter* (23)

lectīcắrius, -ī, m., *litter-bearer* (23)

léctus, -ī, m., *bed, couch* (19)

lēgắtus, -ī, m., *envoy* (18)

légō, légere, légī, léctus, *to read* (1, 24)

léntus, -a, -um, *slow* (35)

   léntē, adv., *slowly* (2, 13)

lépus, léporis, m., *hare* (31)

libénter, adv., *gladly* (36)

líber, líbrī, m., *book* (24)

líberī, -ốrum, m. pl., *children* (10, 11)

lībértās, līberắtis, f., *freedom* (21)

lībértus, -ī, m., *freedman* (29)

lícet, licḗre, lícuit + dat., *it is allowed* (20, 24, 52)

   lícet nóbīs, *we are allowed, we may* (20)

lígō, -ắre, -ắvī, -ắtus, *to bind up* (35)

língua, -ae, f., *tongue, language* (39)

liquắmen, liquắminis, n., *garum (a sauce made from fish, used to season food)* (33)

líttera, -ae, f., *letter (of the alphabet)* (12)

   lítterae, -ắrum, f. pl., *letter, epistle, letters, literature* (39)

lítus, lítoris, n., *shore* (39)

lócus, -ī, m., *place* (33)

lóngus, -a, -um, *long* (15)

   lóngē, adv., *far* (35)

lóquor, lóquī, locútus sum, *to speak, talk* (37)

lúcet, lūcḗre, lúxit, *it is light, it is day* (6)

lúdō, lúdere, lúsī, lūsúrus, *to play* (16)

   pílā lúdere, *to play ball* (16)

lúdus, -ī, m., *game, school* (26, 37)

   lúdī, -ốrum, m. pl., *games* (24)

   lúdī circénsēs, lūdốrum circénsium, m. pl., *chariot-racing* (27)

lúna, -ae, f., *moon* (33)

lúpa, -ae, f., *she-wolf* (II)

lúpus, -ī, m., *wolf* (5)

lútum, -ī, n., *mud* (26)

lūx, lúcis, f., *light* (21)

   príma lúce, *at dawn* (21)

M

mágis, adv., *more* (34, 35)

magíster, magístrī, m., *schoolmaster, master, captain* (37, 42)

magníficus, -a, -um, *magnificent* (24)

magnópere, adv., *greatly* (31, 35)

mágnus, -a, -um, *big, great, large, loud (voice, laugh)* (4, 34)

máior, máior, máius, gen., **maiốris,** *bigger* (34)

Máius, -a, um, *May* (36)

málum, -ī, n., *apple* (32)

málus, -a, -um, *bad, evil* (21, 34)

   mále, adv., *badly* (35)

mandắtum, -ī, n., *order, instruction* (22)

mắne, adv., *early in the day, in the morning* (21)

máneō, manḗre, mắnsī, mānsúrus, *to remain, stay, wait* (9, 20, 23)

Mántua, -ae, f., *Mantua (town in northern Italy)* (39)

mánus, -ūs, f., *hand* (18, 25)

máppa, -ae, f., *napkin* (27)

máre, máris, gen. pl., **márium,** n., *sea* (38)

Mártius, -a, -um, *March* (36)

máter, mátris, f., *mother* (6, 11)

máximus, -a, -um, *biggest, greatest, very great, very large* (23, 34)

   máximē, adv., *most, very much, very* (34, 35)

mē, *me* (4)

   mécum, *with me* (9)

médicus, -ī, m., *doctor* (33)

Mediolánum, -ī, n., *Milan* (39)

médius, -a, -um, *mid-, middle of* (20)

   média nox, médiae nóctis, f., *midnight* (20)

Mégara, -ae, f., *Megara (a city in Greece)* (21)

Mehércule! *By Hercules! Goodness me!* (18)

mélior, mélior, mélius, gen., **meliốris,** *better* (19, 34)

   mélius, adv., *better* (35)

mémor, mémoris, *remembering, mindful, unforgetting* (39)

memória, -ae, f., *memory* (30)

   memóriā tenḗre, *to remember* (37)

mendícus, -ī, m., *beggar* (29)

ménsa, -ae, f., *table* (29)

  secúndae ménsae, -árum, f. pl., *second course,*
    dessert (33)

ménsis, ménsis, m., *month* (38)

mercátor, mercatóris, m., *merchant* (22)

Mercúrius, -ī, m., *Mercury (messenger god)* (32)

merídiē, adv., *at noon* (33)

mérus, -a, -um, *pure* (34)

  mérum, -ī, n., *undiluted wine* (34)

méta, -ae, f., *mark, goal, turning post* (27)

métus, -ūs, m., *fear* (26)

méus, -a, -um, *my, mine* (7)

mígrō, -áre, -ávī, -átúrus, *to move one's home* (39)

míles, mílitis, m., *soldier* (20)

mílle, *a thousand* (15, 38)

míllésimus, -a, -um, *thousandth* (38)

mínimus, -a, -um, *very small, smallest* (34)

  minímē, adv., *least* (35)

  Mínimē (vérō)! adv., *No! Not at all! No indeed!*
    (3, 13)

mínor, mínor, mínus, gen., minóris, *smaller* (34)

  mínus, adv., *less* (35)

mínuō, minúere, mínuī, minútus, *to lessen, reduce,*
  decrease (31)

mírus, -a, -um, *wonderful, marvelous, strange* (23)

mísceō, miscére, míscuī, míxtus, *to mix* (34)

míser, mísera, míserum, *unhappy, miserable,*
  wretched (9)

miserábilis, -is, -e, *miserable, wretched* (30)

míttō, míttere, mísī, míssus, *to send* (9, 20, 31)

módo, adv., *only* (18)

módus, -ī, m., *way, method* (34)

moénia, moénium, n. pl., *walls* (39)

mólēs, mólis, gen. pl., mólium, f., *mass, huge*
  bulk (24)

moléstus, -a, -um, *troublesome, annoying* (4)

  moléstus, -ī, m., *pest* (3)

móneō, -ére, -uī, -itus, *to advise, warn* (39)

mōns, móntis, gen. pl., móntium, m., *mountain,*
  hill (24)

  Mōns Vesúvius, Móntis Vesúviī, m., *Mount*
    Vesuvius (a volcano in southern Italy) (26)

mónstrō, -áre, -ávī, -átus, *to show* (22)

mórior, mórī, mórtuus sum, *to die* (39)

móror, -árī, -átus sum, *to delay, remain, stay*
  (36, 37)

mors, mórtis, gen. pl., mórtium, f., *death* (21)

mórtuus, -a, -um, *dead* (16)

móveō, movére, móvī, mótus, *to move* (14, 24)

mox, adv., *soon, presently* (6, 13)

múlier, mulíeris, f., *woman* (27)

múlsum, -ī, n., *wine sweetened with honey* (33)

multitúdō, multitúdinis, f., *crowd* (23)

múltus, -a, -um, *much* (31, 34)

  múltum, adv., *greatly, much* (31, 35)

  múltī, -ae, -a, *many* (3, 34)

  múltīs post ánnīs, *many years afterward* (39)

múrmur, múrmuris, n., *murmur, rumble* (15)

múrus, -ī, m., *wall* (23)

mūs, múris, m., *mouse* (21)

Músa, -ae, f., *Muse (goddess of song and poetry)* (VII)

mússō, -áre, -ávī, -átúrus, *to mutter* (11)

N

nam, conj., *for* (8)

nārrátor, nārrātóris, m., *narrator* (8)

nárrō, -áre, -ávī, -átus, *to tell (a story)* (20)

  nārrátus, -a, -um, *told* (20)

náscor, náscī, nátus sum, *to be born* (39)

násus, -ī, m., *nose* (33)

nátō, -áre, -ávī, -átúrus, *to swim* (40)

návigō, -áre, -ávī, -átus, *to sail* (38)

návis, návis, gen. pl., návium, f., *ship* (38)

-ne (indicates a question) (3)

nē…quídem, adv., *not even* (34)

Neápolis, Neápolis, acc., Neápolim, f., *Naples* (15)

necésse, adv. or indecl. adj., *necessary* (6, 13)

nécō, -áre, -ávī, -átus, *to kill* (20)

néglegēns, neglegéntis, *careless* (28)

  neglegénter, adv., *carelessly* (28)

neglegéntia, -ae, f., *carelessness* (28)

némō, néminis, m./f., *no one* (9)

néque, conj., *and…not* (6)

  néque…néque, conj., *neither…nor* (5)

  néque…néque…quídquam, *neither…nor…*
    anything (40)

nésciō, -íre, -ívī, -ítus *to be ignorant, not to know* (9)

níger, nígra, nígrum, *black* (33)

níhil, *nothing* (4)

nīl, *nothing* (34)

nímis, adv., *too much* (34)

nísi, conj., *unless, if…not, except* (18, 26)

nóceō, -ére, -uī, -itúrus + dat., *to do harm (to), harm* (26)

noctúrnus, -a, -um, *happening during the night* (22)

nólō, nólle, nóluī, irreg., *to be unwilling, not to wish, refuse* (5, 17, 21)

Nólī/Nolíte + infin., *Don't…!* (9)

nómen, nóminis, n., *name* (1, 15)

nōn, adv., *not* (2, 13)

nōn iam, adv., *no longer* (2, 13)

Nónae, -árum, f. pl., *Nones* (36)

nóndum, adv., *not yet* (6, 13)

Nónne…? (introduces a question that expects the answer "yes") (19)

nōnnúmquam, adv., *sometimes* (26)

nónus, -a, -um, *ninth* (16, 38)

nōs, *we, us* (8, 27)

nóster, nóstra, nóstrum, *our* (14, 27)

nótus, -a, -um, *known* (31)

nóvem, *nine* (15, 38)

Novémber, Novémbris, Novémbre, *November* (36)

nóvus, -a, -um, *new* (16)

nox, nóctis, gen. pl., **nóctium**, f., *night* (11)

média nox, médiae nóctis, f., *midnight* (20)

núbēs, núbis, gen. pl., **núbium**, f., *cloud* (15)

núllus, -a, -um, *no, none* (9)

númerō, -áre, -ávī, -átus, *to count* (33)

númerus, -ī, m., *number* (11)

númquam, adv., *never* (20)

nunc, adv., *now* (6, 13)

núntius, -ī, m., *messenger* (7)

núsquam, adv., *nowhere* (39)

O

ō (used with vocative and in exclamations) (9)

ob, prep. + acc., *on account of* (39)

obdórmiō, -íre, -ívī, -ītúrus, *to go to sleep* (21)

obésus, -a, -um, *fat* (18)

obscúrō, -áre, -ávī, -átus, *to hide* (30)

óbsecrō, -áre, -ávī, -átus, *to beseech, beg* (40)

obsérvō, -áre, -ávī, -átus, *to watch* (6)

obsídeō, obsidére, obsédī, obséssus, *to besiege* (38)

occupátus, -a, -um, *busy* (7)

occúrrō, occúrrere, occúrrī, occursúrus + dat., *to meet* (24)

octávus, -a, -um, *eighth* (36, 38)

óctō, *eight* (15, 38)

Octóber, Octóbris, Octóbre, *October* (36)

óculus, -ī, m., *eye* (26)

óleum, -ī, n., *oil* (32)

olfáciō, olfácere, olfécī, olfáctus, *to catch the scent of, smell, sniff* (12, 18)

ólim, adv., *once (upon a time)* (18)

olíva, -ae, f., *olive* (33)

olīvétum, -ī, n., *olive grove* (14, 15)

omíttō, omíttere, omísī, omíssus, *to leave out, omit* (39)

ómnis, -is, -e, *all, the whole, every, each* (6, 18)

ónus, óneris, n., *load, burden* (15)

óppidum, -ī, n., *town* (39)

ópprimō, opprímere, oppréssī, oppréssus, *to overwhelm* (30)

oppréssus, -a, -um, *crushed* (25)

óptimus, -a, -um, *best, very good, excellent* (20, 31, 34)

óptimē, adv., *best, very well, excellently* (34, 35)

vir óptime, *sir* (20)

óra, -ae, f., *shore* (39)

ōrátiō, ōrātiónis, f., *oration, speech* (26)

ōrātiónem habére, *to deliver a speech* (26)

ōrátor, ōrātóris, m., *orator, speaker* (22)

órdior, ōrdírī, órsus sum, *to begin* (38)

ōrnāméntum, -ī, n., *decoration*; pl., *furnishings* (30)

ōrnátus, -a, -um, *decorated* (32)

Órpheus, -ī, m., *Orpheus (legendary singer and husband of Euryudice)* (VII)

ōs, óris, n., *mouth, face, expression* (38)

óvum, -ī, n., *egg* (32)

P

paedagógus, -ī, m., *tutor* (37)

paéne, adv., *almost* (30)

Palātínus, -a, -um, *on/belonging to the Palatine Hill* (24) pálla, -ae, f., *palla* (10)

pállium, -ī, n., *cloak* (32)

pánis, pánis, gen. pl., pánium, m., *bread* (32)

párēns, paréntis, m./f., *parent* (11)

páreō, -ére, -uī, -itúrus + dat., *to obey* (39)

páriēs, paríetis, m., *wall (of a house or room)* (30)

párō, -áre, -ávī, -átus, *to prepare, get ready* (5, 20)

    parátus, -a, -um, *ready, prepared* (10)

    sē paráre, *to prepare oneself, get ready* (22)

pars, pártis, gen. pl., pártium, f., *part, direction, region* (13)

párvulus, -a, -um, *small, little* (26)

párvus, -a, -um, *small* (30, 34)

páscō, páscere, pávī, pástus, *to feed, pasture* (31)

pássum, -ī, n., *raisin-wine* (33)

páter, pátris, m., *father* (6, 11)

pátior, pátī, pássus sum, *to suffer, endure* (38)

patrónus, -ī, m., *patron* (25)

pátruus, -ī, m., *uncle* (22)

paúcī, -ae, -a, *few* (34)

paulátim, adv., *gradually, little by little* (34)

paulísper, adv., *for a short time* (20)

paúlum, adv., *little* (35)

paúlum, -ī, n., *a small amount, a little* (37)

paúper, paúperis, *poor* (42)

péctō, péctere, péxī, péxus, *to comb* (28)

pecúnia, -ae, f., *money* (21)

pécus, pécoris, n., *livestock, sheep and cattle* (33)

péior, péior, péius, gen., peióris, *worse* (34)

    péius, adv., *worse* (35)

per, prep. + acc., *through, along* (6, 9)

    per iócum, *as a prank/joke* (16)

percútiō, percútere, percússī, percússus, *to strike* (35)

perículósus, -a, -um, *dangerous* (17)

perículum, -ī, n., *danger* (14, 15)

pérna, -ae, f., *ham* (31)

pernóctō, -áre, -ávī, -átúrus, *to spend the night* (17)

persuádeō, persuādére, persuásī, persuásus, *to make something* (acc.) *agreeable to someone* (dat.), *persuade someone of something; to persuade someone* (dat.) (36)

pertérritus, -a, -um, *frightened, terrified* (5)

pervéniō, perveníre, pervénī, perventúrus + ad + acc., *to arrive (at), reach* (25)

pēs, pédis, m., *foot* (13)

péssimus, -a, -um, *worst* (34)

    péssimē, adv., *worst* (35)

pestiléntia, -ae, f., *plague* (33)

pétō, pétere, petívī, petítus, *to look for, seek, head for, aim at, attack* (5, 21)

pictúra, -ae, f., *picture* (1)

píla, -ae, f., *ball* (16)

    pílā lúdere, *to play ball* (16)

pínguis, -is, -e, *fat, rich* (31)

pīráta, -ae, m., *pirate* (21)

pírum, -ī, n., *pear* (33)

piscína, -ae, f., *fishpond* (3)

pīstrínum, -ī, n., *bakery* (37)

pláceō, -ére, -uī + dat., *to please* (34)

plácidē, adv., *gently, peacefully* (14)

plaústrum, -ī, n., *wagon, cart* (15)

plénus, -a, -um, *full* (11)

plúit, plúere, plúit, *it rains, is raining* (23)

plúrēs, plúrēs, plúra, gen., plúrium, *more* (34)

plúrimus, -a, -um, *most, very much* (34)

    plúrimī, -ae, -a, *most, very many* (34)

    plúrimum, adv., *most* (35)

plūs, plúris, n., *more* (35)

    plūs vínī, *more wine* (34)

plūs, adv., *more* (35)

Plútō, Plūtónis, m., *Pluto (king of the underworld)* (32)

póculum, -ī, n., *cup, goblet* (33)

poéna, -ae, f., *punishment, penalty* (40)

    poénās dáre, *to pay the penalty, be punished* (40)

poéta, -ae, m., *poet* (25)

Pompéiī, -órum, m. pl., *Pompeii*

pónō, pónere, pósuī, pósitus, *to put, place* (10, 21)

pōns, póntis, gen. pl., póntium, m., *bridge* (23)

popína, -ae, f., *eating-house, bar* (33)

pórcus, -ī, m., *pig, pork* (28, 33)

pórta, -ae, f., *gate* (11)

pórtō, -áre, -ávī, -átus, *to carry* (6)

póscō, póscere, popóscī, *to demand, ask for* (34)

póssum, pósse, pótuī, irreg., *to be able; I can* (5, 14, 21)

post, prep. + acc., *after* (20)

post, adv., *after(ward)* (39)

   múltīs post ánnīs, *many years afterward* (39)

pósteā, adv., *afterward* (33)

póstis, póstis, gen. pl., **póstium**, m., *door-post* (25)

póstquam, conj., *after* (20)

postrídiē, adv., *on the following day* (26)

praecípitō, -áre, -ávī, -átus, *to hurl* (18)

   sē praecipitáre, *to hurl oneself, rush* (18)

praeclárus, -a, -um, *distinguished, famous* (13)

praecúrrō, praecúrrere, praecúrrī, praecursúrus, *to run ahead* (18)

praédō, praedónis, m., *robber* (26)

praéferō, praeférre, praétulī, praelátus, irreg. + acc. and dat., *to carry X* (acc.) *in front of Y* (dat.) (37)

praéter, prep. + acc., *except* (21)

praetéreā, adv., *besides, too, moreover* (15)

praetéreō, praeteríre, praetérii or **praeterívī, praetéritus**, irreg., *to go past* (15)

praetéxta, tóga, -ae, f., *toga with purple border* (10)

prásinus, -a, -um, *green* (27)

prétium, -ī, n., *price* (31)

prídiē, adv. + acc., *on the day before* (36)

prímus, -a, -um, *first* (21, 38)

   prímā lúce, *at dawn* (21)

   prímō, adv., *first, at first* (40)

   prímum, adv., *first, at first* (23)

   cum prímum, conj., *as soon as* (40)

   quam prímum, adv., *as soon as possible* (40)

prínceps, príncipis, m., *emperor* (7)

príus, adv., *earlier, previously* (33)

procácitās, procācitátis, f., *insolence* (39)

prócāx, procácis, *insolent;* as slang, *pushy* (31)

prōcédō, prōcédere, prōcéssī, prōcessúrus, *to go forward* (33)

prócul, adv., *in the distance, far off, far* (15)

Prō dī immortálēs! *Good heavens!* (42)

proficíscor, proficíscī, proféctus sum, *to set out, leave* (36, 37)

prófugus, -a, -um, *exiled, fugitive* (39)

prōmíttō, prōmíttere, prōmísī, prōmíssus, *to promise* (9)

prónus, -a, -um, *face down* (35)

própe, prep. + acc., *near* (5, 9)

própter, prep. + acc., *on account of, because of* (26)

próximus, -a, -um, *nearby* (33)

prúdēns, prūdéntis, *wise, sensible* (34)

   prūdénter, adv., *wisely, sensibly* (34, 35)

puélla, -ae, f., *girl* (1)

púer, púerī, m., *boy* (3)

púgiō, pūgiónis, m., *dagger* (42)

púlcher, púlchra, púlchrum, *beautiful, pretty, handsome* (28)

   pulchérrimus, -a, -um, *most/very beautiful* (32)

   púlchrē, adv., *finely, excellently* (35)

púllus, -ī, m., *chicken* (32)

púlvis, púlveris, m., *dust* (15)

púniō, -íre, -ívī, -ítus, *to punish* (21)

púrgō, -áre, -ávī, -átus, *to clean* (6)

Q

quā dē caúsā, *for this reason* (32)

quadrátus, -a, -um, *squared* (25)

quaérō, quaérere, quaesívī, quaesítus, *to seek, look for, ask (for)* (30)

Quális...? Quális...? Quále...? *What sort of...?* (4)

Quam...! adv., *How...! What a...!* (13, 29, 36)

Quam...? adv., *How...?* (36)

quam, adv., *than, as* (34, 36)

   quam, adv. + superlative adj. or adv., *as...as possible* (35, 36)

   quam celérrimē, adv., *as quickly as possible* (34)

   quam prímum, adv., *as soon as possible* (40)

Quam ob caúsam...? *For what reason...?* (28)

quámquam, conj., *although* (11)

Quándō...? adv., *When...?* (12, 21)

Quántus, -a, -um...? *How big...? How much...?* (41)

   Quántī...? *How much (in price)...?* (31)

   Quántum...! adv., *How much...!* (41)

quártus, -a, -um, *fourth* (38)

quártus décimus, -a, -um, *fourteenth* (38)

quáttuor, *four* (15, 38)

quattuórdecim, *fourteen* (38)

-que, enclitic conj., *and* (36)

quī, quae, quod, *who, which, that* (1, 3, 14, 28, 29, 36)

Quī...? Quae...? Quod...? interrog. adj., *What...? Which...?* (29)

Quid ágis? *How are you?* (18)

quídam, quaédam, quóddam, *a certain* (10, 29)

quídem, adv., *indeed* (31)

nē...quídem, adv., *not even* (34)

quiēs, quiétis, f., *rest* (23)

sē quiétī dáre, *to rest* (23)

quiéscō, quiéscere, quiévī, quiētúrus, *to rest, keep quiet* (13, 23)

quíndecim, *fifteen* (38)

quīngentésimus, -a, -um, *five-hundredth* (38)

quīngéntī, -ae, -a, *five hundred* (15, 38)

quīnquāgésimus, -a, -um, *fiftieth* (38)

quīnquāgíntā, *fifty* (15, 38)

quínque, *five* (15, 38)

quíntus, -a, -um, *fifth* (26, 38)

quíntus décimus, -a, -um, *fifteenth* (38)

Quirīnális, -is, -e, *Quirinal (Hill)* (35)

Quis...? Quid...? *Who...? What...?* (1, 4, 29)

Quid ágis? *How are you?* (18)

Quō...? adv., *Where...to?* (4)

quō...eō..., *the (more)...the (more)...* (36)

Quócum...? *With whom...?* (12, 26)

quod (see quī, quae, quod)

quod, conj., *because;* with verbs of feeling, *that* (1, 13, 29)

Quō īnstrūméntō...? *With what instrument...? By what means...? How...?* (12)

Quómodo...? adv., *In what manner...? In what way...? How...?* (12)

quóniam, conj., *since* (42)

quóque, adv., *also* (2, 13)

Quot...? *How many...?* (15, 38)

Quótus, -a, -um...? *What/Which (in numerical order)...?* (38)

Quóta hóra est? *What time is it?* (38)

R

raéda, -ae, f., *carriage* (10)

raedárius, -ī, m., *coachman, driver* (10)

rámus, -ī, m., *branch* (4)

rápiō, rápere, rápuī, ráptus, *to snatch, seize* (40)

récitō, -áre, -ávī, -átus, *to read aloud, recite* (29)

recitándī, *of reciting* (39)

réctus, -a, -um, *right, proper* (35)

réctē, adv., *rightly, properly* (31, 35)

recúmbō, recúmbere, recúbuī, *to recline, lie down* (29)

recúperō, -áre, -ávī, -átus, *to recover* (21)

ánimum recuperáre, *to regain one's senses, be fully awake* (21)

réddō, réddere, réddidī, rédditus, *to give back, return* (29)

rédeō, redíre, rédiī or redívī, reditúrus, irreg., *to return, go back* (7, 23)

rédiēns, redeúntis, *returning* (39)

réditus, -ūs, m., *return* (25)

redúcō, redúcere, redúxī, redúctus, *to lead back, take back* (42)

refíciō, refícere, refécī, reféctus, *to remake, redo, restore* (32)

rēgína, -ae, f., *queen* (38)

régnum, -ī, n., *kingdom* (32)

regrédior, régredī, regréssus sum, *to go back, return* (36, 37)

relínquō, relínquere, relíquī, relíctus, *to leave behind* (16, 21)

remóveō, removére, remóvī, remótus, *to remove, move aside* (21)

rénovō, -áre, -ávī, -átus, *to renew, revive* (38)

repéllō, repéllere, réppulī, repúlsus, *to drive off, drive back* (5, 40)

reprehéndō, reprehéndere, reprehéndī, reprehénsus, *to blame, scold* (6, 31)

rēs, réī, f., *thing, matter, situation, affair* (19, 25)

rem explicáre, *to explain the situation* (19)

rēs urbánae, rérum urbānárum, f. pl., *affairs of the city/town* (33)

resístō, resístere, réstitī + dat., *to resist* (42)

respóndeō, respondére, respóndī, respōnsúrus, *to reply* (5, 21)

respónsum, -ī, n., *reply* (38)

retíneō, retinére, retínuī, reténtus, *to hold back, keep* (31)

révocō, -áre, -ávī, -átus, *to recall, call back* (7)

rídeō, rīdére, rísī, rísus, *to laugh (at), smile* (3, 21)

rīmósus, -a, -um, *full of cracks, leaky* (23)

rísus, -ūs, m., *smile, laugh* (13, 25)

rívus, -ī, m., *stream* (5)

ríxa, -ae, f., *quarrel* (29)

rogátiō, rogātiónis, f., *question* (40)

rógō, -áre, -ávī, -átus, *to ask* (12)

   sē rogáre, *to ask oneself, wonder* (21)

Róma, -ae, f., *Rome* (7)

   Rómae, *in Rome* (39)

   Rómam, *to Rome* (7)

Rōmánus, -a, -um, *Roman* (1)

   Rōmánī, -órum, m. pl., *the Romans* (III)

rósa, -ae, f., *rose* (34)

róta, -ae, f., *wheel* (15)

ruína, -ae, f., *collapse, ruin* (38)

rúmpō, rúmpere, rúpī, rúptus, *to burst* (29)

rúrsus, adv., *again* (36)

rūs, rúris, n., *country, country estate* (39)

   rúre, *from the country* (39)

   rúrī, *in the country* (39)

   rūs, *to the country* (39)

russátus, -a, -um, *red* (27)

rústica, vílla, -ae, f., *country house and farm* (1)

rústicus, -ī, m., *peasant* (13)

S

sácculus, -ī, m., *small bag (used for holding money)* (34)

saépe, adv., *often* (2, 13, 35)

   saépius, adv., *more often* (35)

   saepíssimē, adv., *most often* (35)

saévus, -a, -um, *fierce, savage* (39)

sal, sális, m., *salt, wit* (34)

saltátrīx, saltātrícis, f., *dancer* (21)

sáltō, -áre, -ávī, -atúrus *to dance* (21)

sálūs, salútis, f., *greetings* (36)

   salútem dícere, *to send greetings* (36)

   salútem plúrimam dícere, *to send fondest greetings* (36)

salútō, -áre, -ávī, -átus, *to greet, welcome* (7)

Sálvē!/Salvéte! *Greetings! Hello!* (7)

sálvus, -a, -um, *safe* (5)

sánē, adv., *certainly, of course* (36)

sánguis, sánguinis, m., *blood* (33)

sátis, adv., *enough* (23)

   sátis témporis, *enough time* (23)

scápha, -ae, f., *small boat, ship's boat* (40, 42)

sceléstus, -a, -um, *wicked* (10)

scíndō, scíndere, scídī, scíssus, *to cut, split, carve* (33)

scíō, -íre, -ívī, -ítus, *to know* (16)

scriblíta, -ae, f., *tart or pastry with cheese filling* (37)

scríbō, scríbere, scrípsī, scríptus, *to write* (1, 24)

sē, *himself, herself, oneself, itself, themselves* (11)

secúndus, -a, -um, *second* (9, 38)

   secúndae ménsae, -árum, f. pl., *second course, dessert* (33)

secúrus, -a, -um, *carefree, unconcerned* (35)

sed, conj., *but* (2)

sédecim, *sixteen* (38)

sédeō, sedére, sédī, sessúrus, *to sit* (1, 21)

sélla, -ae, f., *sedan chair, seat, chair* (28)

sēmisómnus, -a, -um, *half-asleep* (9)

sémper, adv., *always* (4, 13)

senátor, senātóris, m., *senator* (7)

senátus, -ūs, m., *Senate* (25)

sénex, sénis, m., *old man* (I)

séniō, sēniónis, m., *the six (in throwing knucklebones)* (34)

sepéliō, sepelíre, sepelívī, sepúltus, *to bury* (39)

séptem, *seven* (15, 38)

Septémber, Septémbris, Septémbre, *September* (36)

septéndecim, *seventeen* (38)

septentriōnális, -is, -e, *northern* (39)

séptimus, -a, -um, *seventh* (13, 38)

séptimus décimus, -a, -um, *seventeenth* (38)

septuāgésimus, -a, -um, *seventieth* (IX)

sepúlcrum, -ī, n., *tomb* (22)

séquor, séquī, secútus sum, *to follow* (36, 37)

 séquēns, sequéntis, *following* (25)

sérō, adv., *late* (21, 35)

 sérius, adv., *later* (35)

 sēríssimē, adv., *latest* (35)

sérvō, -áre, -ávī, -átus, *to save* (26, 30)

sérvus, -ī, m., *slave* (3)

seu = síve, conj., *or if* (34)

sex, *six* (15, 38)

séxtus, -a, -um, *sixth* (37, 38)

séxtus décimus, *sixteenth* (38)

sī, conj., *if* (5)

 sī vīs, *if you wish, please* (26)

sīc, adv., *thus, in this way* (38, 39)

Sicília, -ae, f., *Sicily* (38)

sígnum, -ī, n., *signal* (27)

siléntium, -ī, n., *silence* (15)

sílva, -ae f., *woods, forest* (5)

símilis, -is, -e, *similar* (34)

símul, adv., *together, at the same time* (9, 13)

símulac, conj., *as soon as* (24)

símulō, -áre, -ávī, -átus, *to pretend* (21)

síne, prep. + abl., *without* (26)

sínō, sínere, sívī, sítus, *to allow* (34)

sīs = sī vīs, *if you wish, please* (36)

sítus, -a, -um, *located, situated* (33)

sólea, -ae, f., *sandal* (32)

sóleō, solére, sólitus sum + infin., *to be accustomed (to), be in the habit of* (10, 40)

sōlitúdō, sōlitúdinis, f., *solitude* (39)

sollícitus, -a, -um, *anxious, worried* (4)

sólus, -a, -um, *alone* (3)

sómnium, -ī, n., *dream* (21)

sómnus, -ī, m., *sleep* (21)

sónitus, -ūs, m., *sound* (21, 25)

sórdidus, -a, -um, *dirty* (19)

sóror, soróris, f., *sister* (11)

S.P.D. = salútem plúrimam dícit (36)

spectáculum, -ī, n., *sight, spectacle* (30)

spectátor, spectatóris, m., *spectator* (27)

spéctō, -áre, -ávī, -átus, *to watch, look at* (7)

spéculum, -ī, n., *mirror* (28)

státim, adv., *immediately* (5, 13)

státua, -ae, f., *statue* (3)

stéla, -ae, f., *tombstone* (33)

stércus, stércoris, n., *dung, manure* (21)

stértō, stértere, stértuī, *to snore* (25)

stílus, -ī, m., *pen* (25)

stō, stáre, stétī, statúrus, *to stand* (10, 22)

stóla, -ae, f., *stola (a woman's outer garment)* (10)

strátum, -ī, n., *sheet, covering* (32)

strénuus, -a, -um, *active, energetic* (2)

 strénuē, adv., *strenuously, hard* (6, 13, 35)

strépitus, -ūs, m., *noise, clattering* (23, 25)

stríngō, stríngere, strínxī, stríctus, *to draw* (26)

 gládium stríngere, *to draw a sword* (26)

stúdeō, -ére, -uī + dat., *to study* (39)

stúdium, -ī, n., *enthusiasm, study* (41)

stúltus, -a, -um, *stupid, foolish* (23)

stúpeō, -ére, -uī, *to be amazed, gape* (23)

suávis, -is, -e, *sweet, delightful* (34)

sub, prep. + abl., *under, beneath* (1, 9)

súbitō, adv., *suddenly* (3, 13)

Subúra, -ae, f., *Subura (a section of Rome off the Forum, known for its night life)* (35)

súī (see **sē**)

sum, ésse, fúī, futúrus, irreg., *to be* (1, 14, 20, 21)

súmmus, -a, -um, *greatest, very great, the top of…*(35)

 súmmā celeritáte, *with the greatest speed, as fast as possible* (29)

súmō, súmere, súmpsī, súmptus, *to take, take up, pick out* (22)

súperī, -órum, m. pl., *the gods above* (39)

súperō, -áre, -ávī, -átus, *to overcome* (42)

súprā, prep. + acc., *above* (23)

súprā, adv., *above, on top* (21)

súrgō, súrgere, surréxī, surrēctúrus, *to get up, rise* (6, 21)

súus, -a, -um, *his, her, one's, its, their (own)* (9, 27)

T

tabellárius, -ī, m., *courier* (13)

tabérna, -ae, f., *shop* (25)

tablínum, -ī, n., *study* (26)

tabulátum, -ī, n., *story, floor* (30)

táceō, -ére, -uī, -itus, *to be quiet* (9)

tácitē, adv., *silently* (9, 13)

taédet, taedére, taésum est, *it bores* (16)

tálī, -órum, m. pl., *knucklebones* (34)

tális, -is, -e, *such, like this, of this kind* (23)

   tália, tálium, n. pl., *such things* (41)

tam, adv., *so* (30)

támen, adv., *however, nevertheless* (6, 13)

támquam, conj., *just as if* (33)

tándem, adv., *at last, at length* (2, 13)

tántus, -a, -um, *so great, such a big* (24)

   tántum, adv., *only* (15)

tárdus, -a, -um, *slow* (15)

tē (from tū) (4)

téla, -ae, f., *web, fabric* (41)

temerárius, -a, -um, *rash, reckless, bold* (5)

tempéstās, tempestátis, f., *storm* (38)

témplum, -ī, n., *temple* (40)

témptō, -áre, -ávī, -átus, *to try* (9)

témpus, témporis, n., *time* (2, 8, 12, 15)

   ad témpus, *on time* (37)

téneō, tenére, ténuī, téntus, *to hold* (9, 25)

   memóriā tenére, *to remember* (37)

térgum, -ī, n., *back, rear* (35)

térra, -ae, f., *earth, ground, land* (26, 38)

térreō, -ére, -uī, -itus, *to frighten, terrify* (4)

terríbilis, -is, -e, *frightening* (39)

térritus, -a, -um, *frightened* (39)

térror, terróris, m., *terror, fear* (22)

tértius, -a, -um, *third* (25, 36, 38)

tértius décimus, -a, -um, *thirteenth* (38)

testāméntum, -ī, n., *will, testament* (IX)

téxō, téxere, téxuī, téxtus, *to weave* (41)

Thrácia, -ae, f., *Thrace (country northeast of Greece)* (39)

tímeō, -ére, -uī, *to fear, be afraid (to/of)* (5)

tímidus, -a, -um, *afraid, fearful, timid* (21)

tímor, timóris, m., *fear* (35)

tóga, -ae, f., *toga* (8)

   tóga praetéxta, -ae, f., *toga with purple border* (10)

   tóga virílis, tógae virílis, f., *toga of manhood, plain white toga* (10)

tórus, -ī, m., *couch* (38)

tótus, -a, -um, *all, the whole* (21)

trádō, trádere, trádidī, tráditus, *to hand over* (7, 22)

tráhō, tráhere, tráxī, tráctus, *to drag, pull* (6, 12, 25)

   lánam tráhere, *to spin wool* (6)

trāns, prep. + acc., *across* (39)

trédecim, *thirteen* (38)

trémō, trémere, trémuī, *to tremble* (21)

trēs, trēs, tría, *three* (13, 15, 38)

trīclínium, -ī, n., *dining room* (31)

trístis, -is, -e, *sad* (36)

Tróia, -ae, f., *Troy* (I, 38)

Troiánus, -a, -um, *Trojan* (I)

   Troiánī, -órum, m. pl., *the Trojans* (I)

tū, *you* (sing.) (4, 27)

túlī (see férō)

tum, adv., *at that moment, then* (4, 13)

tumúltus, -ūs, m., *uproar, commotion* (25)

túnica, -ae, f., *tunic* (8)

túrba, -ae, f., *crowd, mob* (23)

túus, -a, -um, *your* (sing.) (9, 27)

U

Úbi...? adv., *Where...?* (10, 12)

úbi, adv., conj., *where, when* (1, 5, 13)

Ulíxēs, Ulíxis, m., *Ulysses, Odysseus (Greek hero of the Trojan War)* (38)

úlulō, -áre, -ávī, -átus, *to howl* (33)

úmbra, -ae, f., *shadow, shade (of the dead)* (31, 33)

úmquam, adv., *ever* (31)

únā, adv., *together* (33)

únda, -ae, f., *wave* (42)

Únde...? *From where...?* (12)

úndecim, *eleven* (38)

ūndécimus, -a, -um, *eleventh* (17, 38)

ūndēvīcésimus, -a, -um, *nineteenth* (38)

ūndēvīgíntī, *nineteen* (38)

úndique, adv., *on all sides, from all sides* (23)

unguéntum, -ī, n., *ointment, perfume* (34)

únus, -a, -um, *one* (15, 38)

   únā, adv., *together* (33)

urbánus, -a, -um, *of the city/town* (33)

   rēs urbánae, rérum urbānárum, f. pl., *affairs of the city/town* (33)

urbs, úrbis, gen. pl., **úrbium**, f., *city* (7)
ut, conj., *as* (16)
útilis, -is, -e, *useful* (37)
úva, -ae, f., *grape, bunch of grapes* (33)
úxor, uxóris, f., *wife* (11)

V

váldē, adv., *very, very much, exceedingly* (19)
váleō, -ére, -uī, -itúrus, *to be strong, be well* (40)
  Válē!/Valéte! *Goodbye!* (9)
valētúdō, valētúdinis, f., *health (good or bad)* (39)
-ve, enclitic conj., *or* (34)
véhemēns, veheméntis, *violent* (35)
  veheménter, adv., *very much, violently, hard* (19)
vehículum, -ī, n., *vehicle* (13, 15)
vel, conj., *or* (37)
vélle (see **vólō**)
véndō, véndere, véndidī, vénditus, *to sell* (28)
vénetus, -a, -um, *blue* (27)
véniō, veníre, vénī, ventúrus, *to come* (7, 20)
véntus, -ī, m., *wind* (42)
Vénus, Véneris, f., *Venus (the goddess of love); the highest throw of the knucklebones* (34)
venústus, -a, -um, *charming* (34)
vérberō, -áre, -ávī, -átus, *to beat, whip* (11)
verbósus, -a, -um, *talkative* (26)
vérbum, -ī, n., *word, verb* (39)
véreor, verérī, véritus sum, *to be afraid, fear* (37)
Vergílius, -ī, m., *Vergil (Roman poet)* (37)
versipéllis, versipéllis, gen. pl., **versipéllium**, m., *werewolf* (33)
vérsus, -ūs, m., *verse, line (of poetry)* (29)
vértō, vértere, vértī, vérsus, *to turn* (16)
vérus, -a, -um, *true* (40)
  Íta vérō! *Yes! Indeed!* (3, 13)
  Mínimē vérō! *No indeed! Not at all!* (31)
  véra dícere, *to tell the truth* (40)
  vérō, adv., *truly, really, indeed* (31)
vésperī, *in the evening* (18)
véster, véstra, véstrum, *your* (pl.) (22, 27)
vēstígium, -ī, n., *track, footprint, trace* (12, 15)
vestiméntum, -ī, n., *clothing;* pl., *clothes* (33)

véstis, véstis, gen. pl., **véstium**, f., *clothing, garment* (29)
vétō, vetáre, vétuī, vétitus, *to forbid, tell not to* (26)
vétus, véteris, *old* (34)
véxō, -áre, -ávī, -átus, *to annoy* (3)
  vexátus, -a, -um, *annoyed* (28)
vía, -ae, f., *road, street* (10)
  Vía Áppia, -ae, f., *Appian Way* (11)
viátor, viātóris, m., *traveler* (18)
vīcésimus, -a, -um, *twentieth* (38)
vīcínus, -a, -um, *neighboring, adjacent* (1)
víctor, victóris, m., *conqueror, victor* (27)
vídeō, vidére, vídī, vísus, *to see* (4, 21)
  vidétur, *(he/she/it) seems* (21)
vígilō, -áre, -ávī, -ātúrus, *to stay awake* (19)
vīgíntī, *twenty* (36, 38)
vílicus, -ī, m., *overseer, farm manager* (11)
vílla, -ae, f., *country house* (1)
  vílla rústica, -ae, f., *country house and farm* (1)
víncō, víncere, vícī, víctus, *to conquer, win* (27)
vínea, -ae, f., *vineyard* (12)
vínum, -ī, n., *wine* (25)
  vínō ábstinēns, *refraining from wine, abstemious* (34)
vir, vírī, m., *man, husband* (3, 11)
  vir óptime, *sir* (20)
vírga, -ae, f., *stick, rod, switch* (13)
virílis, -is, -e, *of manhood* (23)
  tóga virílis, tógae virílis, f., *toga of manhood, plain white toga* (10)
vīs, acc., **vim**, abl., **vī**, f., *force, amount* (30)
vísitō, -áre, -ávī, -átus, *to visit* (23)
vítō, -áre, -ávī, -átus, *to avoid* (13)
vívō, vívere, víxī, victúrus, *to live* (39)
vix, adv., *scarcely, with difficulty, only just* (24)
vócō, -áre, -ávī, -átus, *to call, invite* (28)
vólō, vélle, vóluī, irreg., *to wish, want, be willing* (5, 17, 20, 21)
  sī vīs, *if you wish, please* (36)
vōs, *you* (pl.) (8, 27)
vōx, vócis, f., *voice* (4)
vúlnerō, -áre, -ávī, -átus, *to wound* (33)
vúlnus, vúlneris, n., *wound* (35)
vult (from **vólō**) (5, 17)

ENGLISH TO LATIN VOCABULARY

Verbs are usually cited in their infinitive form. For further information about the Latin words in this list, please consult the Latin to English Vocabulary list.

A

able, to be, **pósse**
about, **dē**
above, **súprā**
absent, to be, **abésse**
abstemious, **vīnō ábstinēns**
accidentally, **cásū**
accomplish, to, **cōnfícere**
accuse, to, **accūsáre**
accustomed (to), to be, **solére**
across, **trāns**
active, **strénuus**
add, to, **áddere**
adjacent, **vīcínus**
adopt, to, **adoptáre**
advise, to, **monére**
Aeneas, **Aenéās**
Aeneid, the, **Aenéis**
affair, **rēs**
affairs of the city/town, **rēs urbánae**
affected, **afféctus**
afraid, **tímidus**
afraid, to be, **verérī**
afraid (to/of), to be, **timére**
Africa, **África**
after, **póstquam**
after(ward), **post**
afterward, **pósteā**
again, **íterum, rúrsus**
again and again, **idéntidem**
against, **in**
ago, **abhínc**
aim at, to, **pétere**

Alas! **Éheu!**
Alba Longa, of, **Albánus**
all, **cúnctī, ómnis, tótus**
All right! **Éstō!**
allow, to, **sínere**
allowed, it is, **lícet**
allowed, we are, **lícet nóbīs**
almost, **paéne**
alone, **sólus**
along, **per**
Alps, the, **Álpēs**
already, **iam**
also, **átque, étiam, quóque**
although, **quámquam**
always, **sémper**
amazed, to be, **stupére**
among, **in, ínter**
amount, **vīs**
amphitheater, **amphitheátrum**
amuse, to, **dēlectáre**
ancient, **antíquus**
and, **ac, átque, et, -que**
and...not, **néque**
and so, **ítaque**
anger, **íra**
angry, **īrátus**
annoy, to, **vexáre**
annoyed, **vexátus**
annoying, **moléstus**
another, **álius, álter**
anxious, **sollícitus**
apartment building, **ínsula**
apologize, to, **sē excūsáre**
appear, to, **appārére**
Appian Way, **Vía Áppia**
apple, **málum**
appoint, to, **creáre**
approach, to, **appropinquáre**
April, **Aprílis**

aqueduct, **aquaedúctus**
arch, **árcus**
arise, to, **cooríri**
armed, **armátus**
arms, **árma**
around, **círcum**
aroused, **excitátus**
arrive (at), to, **adveníre, pervenire**
as, **quam, ut**
as…as possible, **quam** + superl. adj. or adv.
as fast as possible, **súmmā celeritáte**
as long as, **dum**
as quickly as possible, **quam celérrimē**
as soon as, **cum prímum, símulac**
as soon as possible, **quam prímum**
as yet, **adhúc**
Asia Minor, **Ásia**
ask, to, **rogáre**
ask (for), to, **póscere, quaérere**
ask oneself, to, **sē rogáre**
asparagus, **aspáragus**
astonished, **attónitus**
astounded, **attónitus**
at, **ad**
at the house of, **ápud**
Athens, **Athénae**
atrium, **átrium**
attack, to, **adoríri, pétere**
attentively, **atténtē**
August, **Augústus**
Augustus, **Augústus**
avoid, to, **vītáre**
awake, to be fully, **ánimum recuperáre**
away, to be, **abésse**

B

back, **térgum**
bad, **málus**
badly, **mále**
bag (used for holding money), small, **sácculus**
bakery, **pīstrínum**
ball, **píla**

banquet, **convívium**
bar, **popína**
bark, a, **lātrátus**
bark, to, **lātráre**
barking, **lātrátus**
be, to, **ésse**
be done, to, **fíeri**
be made, to, **fíeri**
Be of good mind! **Bónō ánimō es!/éste!**
bear, to, **férre**
beat, to, **verberáre**
beautiful, **cándidus, púlcher**
beautiful, most/very, **pulchérrimus**
because, **quod**
because of, **própter**
become, to, **fíeri**
bed, **léctus**
bed, to go to, **cúbitum íre**
bedroom, **cubículum**
before, **ánte, ánteā, ántequam, ápud**
beg, to, **obsecráre**
began, I, **coépī**
beggar, **mendícus**
begin, to, **ōrdíri**
believe, to, **crédere**
beneath, **sub**
beseech, to, **obsecráre**
besides, **praetéreā**
besiege, to, **obsidére**
best, **óptimē, óptimus**
better, **mélior, mélius**
between, **ínter**
beware, to, **cavére**
bid, to, **iubére**
big, **mágnus**
big, such a, **tántus**
bigger, **máior**
biggest, **máximus**
bind up, to, **ligáre**
Bithynia, **Bīthýnia**
black, **níger**
blame, **cúlpa**
blame, to, **reprehéndere**
blood, **sánguis**

blue, **vénetus**
boat, small/ship's, **scápha**
body, **córpus**
bold, **aúdāx**, **temerárius**
book, **líber**
bores, it, **taédet**
born, to be, **náscī**
both…and, **et…et**
box, cylindrical, **fritíllus**
boy, **púer**
branch, **rámus**
brand, to, **inúrere**
brave, **fórtis**
bravely, **fórtiter**
bravely, most/very, **fortíssimē**
bread, **pánis**
breakfast, **iēntáculum**
bridge, **pōns**
briefly, **bréviter**
bring, to, **addúcere**, **afférre**,
     dúcere, **férre**
Bring help! **Fer/Férte auxílium!**
bring in, to, **afférre**, **īnférre**
bring out, to, **efférre**
bring to, to, **afférre**
Britain, **Británnia**
British, **Británnicus**
brother, **fráter**
Brundisium, **Brundísium**
Brundisium, at, **Brundísiī**
Brundisium, from, **Brundísiō**
Brundisium, to, **Brundísium**
build, to, **aedificáre**
building, **aedifícium**
bulk, huge, **mólēs**
bunch of grapes, **úva**
burden, **ónus**
burn, to, **incéndere**
burst, to, **rúmpere**
burst in, to, **irrúmpere**
bury, to, **sepelíre**
busy, **occupátus**
but, **at**, **aútem**, **sed**
butcher, **lánius**

buy, to, **comparáre**, **émere**
by, **ā** or **ab**
By Hercules! **Mehércule!**
bystanders, **adstántēs**

C

Caesar, **Caésar**
Caligula, **Calígula**
call, to, **appelláre**, **vocáre**
call back, to, **revocáre**
call together, to, **convocáre**
call upon, to, **invocáre**
can, I, **póssum**
candelabrum, **candēlábrum**
cane, **férula**
captain, **magíster**
captive, **captívus**
capture, to, **cápere**
care, **cúra**
carefree, **sēcúrus**
careful, to be, **cavére**
carefully, **dīligénter**
careless, **néglegēns**
carelessly, **neglegénter**
carelessness, **neglegéntia**
carriage, **raéda**
carriage, light two-wheeled, **císium**
carry, to, **férre**, **portáre**
carry away, to, **auférre**
carry out, to, **efférre**
carry X in front of Y, to, **praeférre**
cart, **plaústrum**
Carthage, **Carthágō**
carve, to, **scíndere**
castanet, **crótalum**
cat, **félēs**
catch, to, **cápere**, **excípere**
catch sight of, to, **cōnspícere**
catch up to, to, **cónsequī**
Cerberus, **Cérberus**
certain, **cértus**
certain, a, **quídam**

certainly, **cértē**, **sā́nē**
chair, **sélla**
chance, by, **cásū**, **fórte**
chariot-racing, **lū́dī circénsēs**
charioteer, **aurī́ga**
charming, **venústus**
Charon, **Chárōn**
Cheer up! **Bónō ánimō es!/éste!**
chest, **císta**
chicken, **púllus**
child, young, **ínfāns**
children, **lī́berī**
circus, in the, **circénsis**
Circus Maximus, **Círcus Máximus**
citizen, **cī́vis**
city, **urbs**
city, of the, **urbā́nus**
clattering, **strépitus**
clean, to, **pūrgā́re**
client, **clī́ēns**
climb, to, **ascéndere**
climb down, to, **dēscéndere**
climb into (a carriage), to, **ascéndere**
cloak, **pállium**
closed, **claúsus**
closely, **atténtē**
clothes, **vestīménta**
clothing, **vestīméntum**, **véstis**
cloud, **nū́bēs**
club, **fū́stis**
coachman, **raedā́rius**
cobweb, **arā́nea**
cold, **frī́gidus**
collapse, **ruī́na**
collapse, to, **collā́bī**
comb, to, **péctere**
come, to, **venī́re**
come down, to, **dēscéndere**
come near (to), to, **appropinquā́re**
Come on! **Áge!/Ágite!**
come upon, to, **invenī́re**
commands, **iússa**
commotion, **tumúltus**
companion, **cómes**

company (of charioteers), **fáctiō**
complete, to, **complére**
conceal, to, **cēlā́re**
concerning, **dē**
conquer, to, **víncere**
conqueror, **víctor**
consul, **cṓnsul**
consult, to, **cōnsúlere**
contrary, on the, **ímmō vḗrō**
conversation, **collóquium**
converse, to, **cólloquī**
cook, **cóquus**
cook, to, **cóquere**
cool, **frī́gidus**
Cornelius, belonging to, **Cornēliā́nus**
cottage, **cása**
couch, **léctus**, **tórus**
count, to, **numerā́re**
country, **rūs**
country, from the, **rū́re**
country, in the, **rū́rī**
country, to the, **rūs**
country estate, **rūs**
country house, **vī́lla**
country house and farm, **vī́lla rústica**
courier, **tabellā́rius**
course, first, **gustā́tiō**
course, second, **secúndae ménsae**
courteously, **cṓmiter**
covered, **aspérsus**
covering, **strā́tum**
cow, **bōs**
cowardly, **ignā́vus**
cracks, full of, **rīmṓsus**
crash, **frágor**
Cremona, **Cremṓna**
Crete, **Créta**
crowd, **multitū́dō**, **túrba**
crown, **corṓna**
crown, to, **corōnā́re**
cruel, **crūdḗlis**
crushed, **oppréssus**
cry, to, **lacrimā́re**
cudgel, **fū́stis**

cultivate, to, **cólere**
cup, **póculum**
Cupid, **Cupídō**
cut, to, **scíndere**

D

dagger, **púgiō**
daily, **cotídiē**
dance, to, **saltáre**
dancer, **saltátrīx**
danger, **perículum**
dangerous, **perīculósus**
dare (to), to, **audére**
dark, it gets, **advesperáscit**
daughter, **fília**
dawn, at, **prímā lúce**
day, **díēs**
day, by, **intérdiū**
day, during the, **intérdiū**
day, early in the, **máne**
day, every, **in díēs**
day, it is, **lúcet**
day before, on the, **prídiē**
day by day, **in díēs**
dead, **mórtuus**
dearest, **cāríssimus**
death, **mors**
December, **Decémber**
decide, to, **cōnstitúere**
decorated, **ōrnátus**
decoration, **ōrnāméntum**
decrease, to, **minúere**
dedicate, to, **dēdicáre**
deep, **áltus**
deep, the, **áltum**
defend, to, **dēféndere**
delay, to, **cessáre**, **morárī**
delight, to, **dēlectáre**
delightful, **suávis**
deliver a speech, to, **ōrātiónem habére**
Delos, **Délos**
demand, to, **póscere**
denarius (silver coin), **dēnárius**

depart, to, **discédere**
dependent, **clíēns**
desire, to, **cúpere**, **dēsīderáre**
dessert, **secúndae ménsae**
destroy, to, **dēlére**
detestable, **abōminándus**
devour, to, **dēvoráre**
Dido, **Dídō**
die, to, **mórī**
difficult, **diffícilis**
difficulty, **difficúltās**
difficulty, with, **vix**
diligent, **díligēns**
din, **frágor**
dine, to, **cēnáre**
dining room, **trīclínium**
dinner, **céna**
dinner, to eat, **cēnáre**
direction, **pars**
dirty, **sórdidus**
disgusting, **foédus**
dish, **férculum**
dissimilar, **dissímilis**
distance, in the, **prócul**
distant, to be, **abésse**
distinguished, **praeclárus**
ditch, **fóssa**
divide, to, **dīvídere**
divine, **dīvínus**
do, to, **ágere**, **fácere**
do harm (to), to, **nocére**
doctor, **médicus**
dog, **cánis**
done, to be, **fíerī**
Don't…! **Nōlī/Nōlíte** + infinitive
door, **iánua**
doorkeeper, **iánitor**
door-post, **póstis**
dormouse, **glīs**
doubt, **dúbium**
down from, **dē**
drag, to, **tráhere**
drag out, to, **extráhere**
drain, to, **hauríre**

draw, to, **stríngere**
draw a sword, to, **gládium stríngere**
dream, **sómnium**
drink, to, **bíbere**
drinking party, **commissátiō**
drive, to, **ágere, incitáre**
drive back, to, **repéllere**
drive off, to, **repéllere**
drive out, to, **expéllere**
drive to and fro, to, **iactáre**
driver, **raedárius**
drunk, **ébrius**
dung, **stércus**
dust, **púlvis**
dwell, to, **habitáre**

E

each, **ómnis**
eager, **inténtus**
earlier, **príus**
early in the day, **máne**
earth, **térra**
easily, **fácile**
easy, **fácilis**
eat, to, **ésse**
eat dinner, to, **cēnáre**
eating-house, **popína**
egg, **óvum**
eight, **óctō**
eighteen, **duodēvīgíntī**
eighteenth, **duodēvīcésimus**
eighth, **octávus**
either…or, **aut…aut**
elegant, **élegāns**
eleven, **úndecim**
eleventh, **ūndécimus**
embrace, **compléxus**
emperor, **Caésar, prínceps**
end, **fínis**
endure, to, **pátī**
energetic, **strénuus**
enough, **sátis**
enough time, **sátis témporis**

enter, to, **íngredī, iníre, intráre**
enthusiasm, **stúdium**
envoy, **lēgátus**
epistle, **lítterae**
eruption, **ērúptiō**
escape, to, **aufúgere, effúgere, ēvádere**
establish, to, **cóndere**
Eurydice, **Eurýdicē**
even, **étiam**
even if, **etiámsī**
evening, in the, **vésperī**
ever, **úmquam**
every, **ómnis**
every day, **cotídiē, in díēs**
evil, **málus**
examine, to, **īnspícere**
exceedingly, **váldē**
excellent, **óptimus**
excellently, **óptimē, púlchrē**
except, **nísi, praéter**
exclaim, to, **exclāmáre**
excuse, to, **excūsáre**
exiled, **prófugus**
expel, to, **expéllere**
explain, to, **explicáre**
explain the situation, to, **rem explicáre**
expression, **ōs**
extinguish, to, **exstínguere**
eye, **óculus**

F

fabric, **téla**
face, **ōs**
face down, **prónus**
fact, in, **ímmō vérō**
fair-skinned, **cándidus**
faithful, **fidélis**
fall, to, **cádere**
fall down, to, **concídere**
fame, **glória**
famous, **céleber, praeclárus**
famous, that, **ílle**
far, **lóngē, prócul**

far off, **prócul**
farm, **fúndus**
farm manager, **vílicus**
fast, very, **celérrimē, celérrimus**
fast as possible, as, **súmmā celeritáte**
fastest, **celérrimus**
fat, **obésus, pínguis**
fate, **fátum**
father, **páter**
fault, **cúlpa**
favor, to, **favére**
fear, **métus, térror, tímor**
fear, to, **timére, veréri**
fearful, **tímidus**
feast, **convívium**
February, **Februárius**
feed, to, **páscere**
few, **paúci**
field, **áger**
fierce, **férōx, saévus**
fiercely, **feróciter**
fifteen, **quíndecim**
fifteenth, **quíntus décimus**
fifth, **quíntus**
fiftieth, **quinquāgésimus**
fifty, **quīnguāgíntā**
fill, to, **complére**
filthy, **foédus**
find, to, **inveníre**
finely, **púlchrē**
finish, to, **cōnfícere, finíre**
fire, **ígnis, incéndium**
fire, to set on, **incéndere**
first, **prímus**
first, (at), **prímō, prímum**
first course, **gustátiō**
first day in the month, **Kaléndae**
fishpond, **piscína**
five, **quínque**
five hundred, **quīngéntī**
five-hundredth, **quīngentésimus**
flame, **flámma**
flee, to, **effúgere, fúgere**
flesh, **cárō**

floor, **tabulátum**
flower, **flōs**
follow, to, **séqui**
following, **séquēns**
following day, on the, **postrídiē**
food, **cíbus**
foolish, **stúltus**
foot, **pēs**
footprint, **vēstígium**
for, **énim, nam**
for a short time, **paulísper**
forbid, to, **vetáre**
force, **vīs**
forehead, **frōns**
forest, **sílva**
forgetful, **ímmemor**
forgive, to, **excūsáre**
former, the, **ílle**
Forum, the, **Fórum**
found, to, **cóndere**
four, **quáttuor**
fourteen, **quattuórdecim**
fourteenth, **quártus décimus**
fourth, **quártus**
frail, **īnfírmus**
free, **grátīs**
freedman, **lībértus**
freedom, **lībértās**
friend, **amíca, amícus, hóspes**
friendly way, in a, **cómiter**
frighten, to, **terrére**
frightened, **pertérritus, térritus**
frightening, **terríbilis**
from, **ā, ab, ē, ex**
front of, in, **ánte, ápud**
fugitive, **prófugus**
full, **plénus**
furnishings, **ōrnāménta**

G

Gades, **Gádēs**
game, **lúdus**
games, **lúdī**

gape, to, **stupḗre**
garden, **hórtus**
garland, **corṓna**
garment, **véstis**
garum, **liquā́men**
gate, **pórta**
Gaul, **Gállia**
gently, **plácidē**
get, to, **accípere**
get ready, to, **parā́re**
get up, to, **súrgere**
get well, to, **convalḗscere**
girl, **puélla**
give, to, **dáre, dōnā́re**
give back, to, **réddere**
give favor (to), to, **favḗre**
give trust (to), to, **cōnfī́dere**
glad, **laétus**
glad, to be, **gaudḗre**
gladly, **libénter**
glory, **glṓria**
go, to, **íre**
go around, to, **circumī́re**
go away, to, **abī́re, discḗdere**
go back, to, **redī́re, régredī**
go down, to, **dēscéndere**
go forward, to, **prōcḗdere**
go in, to, **íngredī**
go into, to, **iníre, intrā́re**
go out, to, **égredī, exī́re**
go past, to, **praeterī́re**
goal, **mḗta**
goblet, **póculum**
god, **déus**
gods above, the, **súperī**
gold, **aúrum**
golden, **aúreus**
good, **bónus**
good, very, **óptimus**
Good heavens! **Dī immortā́lēs! Prō dī immortā́lēs!**
Goodbye! **Válē/Valḗte!**
Goodness me! **Mehércule!**
goods, **bóna**

grab, to, **corrípere**
grab hold of, to, **arrípere**
graciously, **cṓmiter**
gradually, **paulā́tim**
grape, **ū́va**
gratitude, **grā́tia**
great, **mágnus**
great, so, **tántus**
great, very, **máximus, súmmus**
greater, **máior**
greatest, **máximus, súmmus**
greatest speed, with the, **súmmā celeritā́te**
greatly, **magnópere, múltum**
Greece, **Graécia**
Greek, **Graécus**
Greeks, the, **Graécī**
green, **prásinus**
greet, to, **salū́tāre**
greetings, **sálūs**
Greetings! **Ā́vē!/Avḗte! Sálvē!/Salvḗte!**
greetings, to send, **salū́tem dī́cere**
grief, **dólor**
groan, to, **gémere**
ground, **térra**
ground, on the, **húmī**
grunt, to, **grunnī́re**
guard, **cústōs**
guard, to, **custōdī́re**
guest, **hóspes**
guest (at a banquet), **convī́va**

H

habit of, to be in the, **solḗre**
Hail! **Ā́vē!/Avḗte!**
hair, **crī́nēs**
half-asleep, **sēmisómnus**
ham, **pérna**
hand, **mánus**
hand over, to, **trā́dere**
handsome, **púlcher**
happen, to, **fī́erī**
happens, it, **áccidit**
happily, **fēlī́citer, laétē**

happy, **laétus**
hard, **strénuē**
hare, **lépus**
harm, to, **nocére**
have, to, **habére**
he, is, **ílle**
head, **cáput**
head for, to, **pétere**
health (good or bad), **valētúdō**
hear, to, **audíre**
"heart," **ánima**
heat, **aéstus**
heaven, **caélum**
heavy, **grávis**
Hello! **Sálvē!/Salvéte!**
help, **auxílium**
Help! **Fer/Férte auxílium!**
help, to, **adiuváre**
her (own), **súus**
Hercules, **Hércūlēs**
here, **hīc, hūc**
here, to, **hūc**
here and there, **hūc illúc**
herself, **ípsa, sē**
Hesperia, **Hespéria**
Hey! **Ého!**
hide, to, **cēláre, obscūráre**
high, **áltus**
highest throw of the knucklebones, the, **Vénus**
hill, **cóllis, mōns**
himself, **ípse, sē**
hinder, to, **impedíre**
hire, to, **condúcere**
his (own), **súus**
hit, to, **feríre**
hold, to, **habére, tenére**
hold back, to, **retinére**
hold out, to, **exténdere**
holiday, celebrating a, **fēriátus**
home, **dómum, dómus**
home, at, **dómī**
home, from, **dómō**
homeward, **dómum**
honor, **hónor**

Horace, **Horátius**
horrible, **abōminándus**
hors d'oeuvre, **gustátiō**
horse, **équus**
host, **hóspes**
hour, **hóra**
house, **dómus**
house of, at the, **ápud**
How…! **Quam…!**
How…? **Quam…?, Quō īnstrūméntō…?, Quómodo…?**
How are you? **Quid ágis?**
How big…? **Quántus…?**
How many…? **Quot…?**
How much…? **Quántus…?**
How much…! **Quántum…!**
How much (in price)…? **Quántī…?**
however, **aútem, támen**
howl, to, **ululáre**
huge, **íngēns**
humble, **húmilis**
hundred, a, **céntum**
hundredth, **centésimus**
hungry, to be, **ēsuríre**
hurl, to, **praecipitáre**
hurl oneself, to, **sē praecipitáre**
Hurray! **Eúge!/Eúgepae!**
hurry, to, **festináre**
husband, **cóniūnx, vir**
hut, **cása**

I

I, **égo**
Ides, the, **Ídūs**
idle, to be, **cessáre**
if, **sī**
if…not, **nísi**
ignorant, to be, **ignōráre, nescíre**
ill, **aéger**
ill, to be, **aegrōtáre**
immediately, **státim**
immortal, **immortális**
Immortal Gods! **Dī immortálēs!**

important, it is, **ínterest**
in, **in**
in front of, **ápud**
in return, **cóntrā**
in vain, **frústrā**
Indeed! **Íta vérō!**
indeed, **quídem, vérō**
infant, **ínfāns**
inhabitant, **íncola**
inn, **caupóna**
innkeeper, **caúpō**
innocence, **innocéntia**
inside, **íntrā**
insolence, **procácitās**
insolent, **prócāx**
instruction, **mandátum**
instrument…, With what, **Quō īnstrūméntō…?**
intend, to, **in ánimō habére**
intent, **inténtus**
interrupt, to, **interpelláre**
into, **in**
invite, to, **invītáre, vocáre**
invoke, to, **invocáre**
irritability, **īrācúndia**
irritable, **īrācúndus**
island, **ínsula**
it, **ílle, is**
Italy, **Itália**
Ithaca, **Íthaca**
its (own), **súus**
itself, **ípse, sē**
ivy, **hédera**

J

January, **Iānuárius**
joke, **iócus**
joke, as a, **per iócum**
journey, **íter**
joy, **gaúdium**
July, **Iúlius**
June, **Iúnius**
Juno, **Iúnō**
just as if, **támquam**

K

Kalends, the, **Kaléndae**
keen, **ácer**
keep, to, **retinére**
kill, to, **necáre**
kind, of this, **tális**
kingdom, **régnum**
kitchen, **culína**
know, not to, **ignōráre, nescíre**
know, to, **scíre**
known, **nótus**
knucklebones, **tálī**

L

lack, to, **carére**
ladle, small, **cýathus**
lady of the house, **dómina**
lamp-stand, **candēlábrum**
land, **áger, térra**
language, **língua**
lantern, **lantérna**
large, **mágnus**
large, very, **máximus**
last, at, **tándem**
last laugh, to get the, **dērīdére**
late, **sérō**
later, **sérius**
latest, **sēríssimē**
Latin, **Latínus**
Latium, **Látium**
latter, the, **hic**
laugh, **rísus**
laugh (at), to, **dērīdére, rīdére**
laughter, **cachínnus**
Lavinium, of, **Lāvínius**
lay down, to, **dēpónere**
lazy, **ignávus**
lead, to, **dúcere**
lead back, to, **redúcere**
lead on, to, **addúcere**
leaky, **rīmósus**
leap down, to, **dēsilíre**

learn, to, **díscere**
learned, **ērudítus**
least, **mínimē**
leave, to, **égredī, profícíscī**
leave behind, to, **relínquere**
leave out, to, **omíttere**
length, at, **tándem**
less, **mínus**
lessen, to, **minúere**
letter, **epístula, lítterae**
letter (of the alphabet), **líttera**
letters, **lítterae**
lie, to, **iacére**
lie down, to, **recúmbere**
light, **lūx**
light, it is, **lúcet**
like, **símilis**
like, to, **amáre**
like this, **tális**
line (of poetry), **vérsus**
listen to, to, **audíre**
literature, **lítterae**
litter, **lectíca**
litter-bearer, **lectīcárius**
little, **párvulus**
little, a, **paúlum**
little by little, **paulátim**
live, to, **habitáre, vívere**
livestock, **pécus**
load, **ónus**
located, **sítus**
long, **lóngus**
long for, to, **dēsīderáre**
long time, for a, **díū**
longer, **diútius**
longest, **diūtíssimē**
Look (at)...! **Écce...!**
look after, to, **cūráre**
look at, to, **spectáre**
look for, to, **pétere, quaérere**
look out for, to, **exspectáre**
loud (voice, laugh), **mágnus**
love, **ámor**
love, to, **amáre**

luckily, **fēlíciter**
lucky, **félīx**
lying down, to be, **iacére**

M

made, to be, **fíerī**
magnificent, **magníficus**
main room in a house, **átrium**
make, to, **fácere**
make something (acc.) agreeable to someone (dat.),
    to, **persuādére**
man, **hómō, vir**
manhood, of, **virílis**
manner...?, In what, **Quómodo...?**
Mantua, **Mántua**
manure, **stércus**
many, **múltī**
many, very, **plúrimī**
many years afterward, **múltīs post ánnīs**
March, **Mártius**
mark, **méta**
marvelous, **mírus**
mass, **mólēs**
master, **árbiter, dóminus, magíster**
master of the drinking, **árbiter bibéndī**
matter, **rēs**
may, we, **lícet nóbīs**
me, **mē**
me, with, **mécum**
means...?, By what, **Quō īnstrūméntō...?**
meanwhile, **intéreā**
measure (of wine), **cýathus**
meat, **cárō**
meet, to, **occúrrere**
Megara, **Mégara**
members of the family of Cornelius,
    the, **Cornéliī**
memory, **memória**
merchant, **mercátor**
Mercury, **Mercúrius**
messenger, **núntius**
method, **módus**
mid-, **médius**

middle of, **médius**
midnight, **média nox**
Milan, **Mediolánum**
mind, **ánimus**
mindful, **mémor**
mine, **méus**
mirror, **spéculum**
miserable, **míser, miserábilis**
miss, to, **dēsīderáre**
mistaken, to be, **erráre**
mistress, **dómina**
mix, to, **miscére**
mob, **túrba**
moment, at that, **tum**
money, **pecúnia**
month, **ménsis**
mood, in a bad, **īrācúndus**
moon, **lúna**
more, **mágis, plúrēs, plūs**
more wine, **plūs vínī**
moreover, **aútem, praetéreā**
morning, in the, **máne**
most, **máximē, plúrimī, plúrimum,
    plúrimus**
mother, **máter**
motionless, **immóbilis**
Mount Vesuvius, **Mōns Vesúvius**
mountain, **mōns**
mouse, **mūs**
mouth, **ōs**
move, to, **commovére, movére**
move aside, to, **removére**
move one's home, to, **migráre**
move toward, to, **admovére**
moved, **commótus**
much, **múltum, múltus**
much, too, **nímis**
much, very, **máximē, plúrimus**
mud, **lútum**
murmur, **múrmur**
Muse, **Músa**
mushroom, **bōlétus**
mutter, to, **mussáre**
my, **méus**

N

name, **nómen**
name, to, **appelláre**
napkin, **máppa**
Naples, **Neápolis**
narrator, **nārrátor**
nation, **génus**
near, **ad, própe**
near, to be, **adésse**
nearby, **próximus**
necessary, **necésse**
need, to, **carére**
neighboring, **vīcínus**
neither…nor, **néque…néque**
neither…nor…anything,
    néque…néque…quídquam
never, **númquam**
nevertheless, **támen**
new, **nóvus**
next, **deínde**
night, **nox**
night, happening during the, **noctúrnus**
nine, **nóvem**
nineteen, **ūndēvīgíntī**
nineteenth, **ūndēvīcésimus**
ninth, **nónus**
no, **núllus**
No! **Mínimē (vérō)!**
No indeed! **Mínimē vérō!**
no longer, **nōn iam**
no one, **némō**
noise, **frágor, strépitus**
none, **núllus**
Nones, **Nónae**
noon, at, **merídiē**
northern, **septentriōnális**
nose, **násus**
not, **nōn**
Not at all! **Mínimē vérō!**
not even, **nē…quídem**
not yet, **nóndum**
nothing, **níhil, nīl**
nothing, for, **grátīs**

nothing, to do, **cessáre**
notice, to, **animadvértere**
November, **Novémber**
now, **iam, nunc**
nowhere, **núsquam**
number, **númerus**

O

obey, to, **pārére**
obtain, to, **comparáre**
October, **Octóber**
Odysseus, **Ulíxēs**
of course, **sáne**
often, **saépe**
often, more, **saépius**
often, most, **saepíssime**
oil, **óleum**
ointment, **unguéntum**
old, **vétus**
old man, **sénex**
olive, **olíva**
olive grove, **olīvétum**
omit, to, **omíttere**
on, **in**
on account of, **ob, própter**
on time, **ad témpus**
once (upon a time), **ólim**
one, **únus**
one (of two), **álter**
one…another, **álius…álius**
one…the other, the, **álter…álter**
oneself, **sē**
only, **módo, tántum**
only just, **vix**
open, to, **aperíre**
open space, **área**
or, **aut, -ve, vel**
or if, **seu**
oration, **ōrátiō**
orator, **ōrátor**
order, **mandátum**
order, to, **iubére**
orders, **iússa**

Orpheus, **Órpheus**
other, **álius**
other (of two), the, **álter**
others, the, **céterī**
otherwise, **áliter**
ought, **debére**
our, **nóster**
out of, **ē, ex**
outside, **éxtrā, fórās**
overcome, **afféctus**
overcome, to **superáre**
overseer, **vílicus**
overtake, to, **cónsequī**
overturn, to, **ēvértere**
overwhelm, to, **opprímere**
owe, to, **debére**
owner, **dóminus**
ox, **bōs**

P

painstaking, **díligēns**
Palatine Hill, belonging to the, **Palātínus**
palla, **pálla**
parent, **párēns**
parsley, **ápium**
part, **pars**
pastry with cheese filling, **scriblíta**
pasture, to, **páscere**
patron, **patrónus**
pay the penalty, to, **poénās dáre**
peacefully, **plácidē**
pear, **pírum**
peasant, **rústicus**
pen, **stílus**
penalty, **poéna**
people, **hóminēs**
perfume, **unguéntum**
perhaps, **fortásse**
person related to one of another city by ties of
    hospitality, **hóspes**
persuade, to, **persuādére**
persuade someone of something, to, **persuādére**
pest, **moléstus**

pick out, to, **súmere**
picture, **pictúra**
pig, **pórcus**
pirate, **pīráta**
place, **lócus**
place, to, **pónere**
place, to that, **illúc**
plague, **pestiléntia**
play, to, **lúdere**
play ball, to, **pílā lúdere**
please, **sī vīs, sīs**
please, to, **placére**
pleasing to someone to do something, it is, **líbet**
Pluto, **Plútō**
poet, **poéta**
Pompeii, **Pompéiī**
poor, **paúper**
pork, **pórcus**
possessions, **bóna**
pour out, to, **effúndere**
praise, to, **laudáre**
prank, **iócus**
prank/joke, as a, **per iócum**
prepare, to, **paráre**
prepare oneself, to, **sē paráre**
prepared, **parátus**
present, to be, **adésse**
presently, **mox**
pretend, to, **simuláre**
pretty, **púlcher**
prevent, to, **impedíre**
previously, **abhínc, ánte, ánteā**
price, **prétium**
prisoner, **captívus**
promise, to, **prōmíttere**
proper, **réctus**
properly, **réctē**
pull, to, **tráhere**
punish, to, **pūníre**
punished, to be, **poénās dáre**
punishment, **poéna**
pupil, **discípulus**
pure, **mérus**
pushy, **prócāx**

put, to, **pónere**
put aside, to, **dēpónere**
put on, to, **indúere**
put out, to, **exstínguere**

Q

quarrel, **ríxa**
queen, **rēgína**
question, **rogátiō**
quickly, **celériter**
quickly, more, **celérius**
quickly, very, **celérrimē**
quiet, to be, **tacére**
quiet, to keep, **quiéscere**
Quirinal (Hill), **Quirīnális**

R

race, **génus**
race track, **currículum**
rain, **ímber**
raining, it is, **plúit**
rains, it, **plúit**
raisin-wine, **pássum**
rash, **temerárius**
rather, **ímmō**
reach, to, **adveníre, perveníre**
read, to, **légere**
read aloud, to, **recitáre**
ready, **parátus**
ready, to get, **comparáre, sē paráre**
really, **vérō**
rear, **térgum**
reason, **caúsa**
reason, for this, **quā dē caúsā**
reason…?, For what, **Quam ob caúsam…?**
rebuke, to, **castīgáre**
recall, to, **revocáre**
receive, to, **accípere, excípere**
recite, to, **recitáre**
reciting, of, **recitándī**
reckless, **temerárius**
recline, to, **recúmbere**

recline (at table), to, **accúmbere**
recognize, to, **agnóscere**
recover, to, **recuperáre**
red, **russátus**
redo, to, **refícere**
reduce, to, **minúere**
refraining from, **ábstinēns**
refraining from wine, **vīnō ábstinēns**
refuse, to, **nólle**
regain one's senses, to, **ánimum recuperáre**
region, **pars**
reins, **habénae**
rejoice, to, **gaudére**
remain, to, **manére, morárī**
remake, to, **refícere**
remember, to, **memóriā tenére**
remembering, **mémor**
remove, to, **removére**
renew, to, **renováre**
repeatedly, **idéntidem**
reply, **respónsum**
reply, to, **respondére**
reprimand, to, **castīgáre**
rescue, to, **ērípere**
resist, to, **resístere**
rest, **quíēs**
rest, the, **céterī**
rest, to, **sē quiétī dáre, quiéscere**
restore, to, **refícere**
return, **réditus**
return, to, **réddere, redíre, régredī**
returning, **rédiēns**
revive, to, **renováre**
rich, **díves, pínguis**
right, **réctus**
rightly, **réctē**
rise, to, **súrgere**
rise up, to, **coorírī**
road, **vía**
robber, **praédō**
rod, **vírga**
Roman, **Rōmánus**
Romans, the, **Rōmánī**
Rome, **Róma**

Rome, in, **Rómae**
Rome, to, **Rómam**
room, **cubículum**
rose, **rósa**
rouse, to, **excitáre**
route, **íter**
ruin, **ruína**
rumble, **múrmur**
run, to, **cúrrere**
run about, to, **concursáre**
run ahead, to, **praecúrrere**
run away, to, **aufúgere, effúgere**
run to and fro, to, **concursáre**
run together, to, **concúrrere**
run toward/up to, to, **accúrrere**
rush, to, **sē praecipitáre**
rush up, to, **concúrrere**

S

sad, **trístis**
sad, to be, **dolére**
safe, **sálvus**
safe and sound, **incólumis**
said, (he/she), **ínquit**
said, (he/she/it) is, **dícitur**
sail, to, **nāvigáre**
salt, **sal**
same, the, **ídem**
same as, the, **ídem ac**
same time, at the, **símul**
sandal, **sólea**
savage, **saévus**
save, to, **serváre**
say, to, **dícere**
says, (he/she), **ínquit**
scarcely, **vix**
scent of, to catch the, **olfácere**
scholarly, **ērudítus**
school, **lúdus**
schoolmaster, **magíster**
scold, to, **reprehéndere**
scrap, **frústum**
sea, **áltum, máre**

seat, **sélla**
second, **secúndus**
second, a/the, **álter**
second time, a, **íterum**
secretly, **clam**
sedan chair, **sélla**
see, to, **vidére**
seek, to, **pétere, quaérere**
seems, (he/she/it), **vidétur**
seize, to, **arrípere, corrípere, occupáre, rápere**
-self, **ípse**
sell, to, **véndere**
Senate, **senátus**
Senate House, **Cúria**
senator, **senátor**
send, to, **míttere**
send fondest greetings, to, **salútem plúrimam
    dícere**
send for, to, **arcéssere**
send greetings, to, **salútem dícere**
send out, to, **ēmíttere**
sensible, **prúdēns**
sensibly, **prūdénter**
September, **Septémber**
serious, **grávis**
set down, to, **dēpónere**
set out, to, **proficíscī**
seven, **séptem**
seventeen, **septéndecim**
seventeenth, **séptimus décimus**
seventh, **séptimus**
seventieth, **septuāgésimus**
several, **complúrēs**
shade (of the dead), **úmbra**
shadow, **úmbra**
shaky, **īnfírmus**
she, **éa, ílla**
she-wolf, **lúpa**
sheep and cattle, **pécus**
sheet, **strátum**
ship, **návis**
ships's boat, **scápha**
shop, **tabérna**
shore, **lítus, óra**

short, **brévis**
short time, for a, **paulísper**
shout, **clámor**
shout, to, **clāmáre**
shout out, to, **exclāmáre**
shouting, **clámor**
show, to, **dēmōnstráre, mōnstráre**
shut, **claúsus**
shut, to, **claúdere**
Sicily, **Sicília**
sides, from/on all, **úndique**
sight, **spectáculum**
signal, **sígnum**
silence, **siléntium**
silent, to become, **conticéscere**
silently, **tácitē**
similar, **símilis**
since, **cum, quóniam**
sing, to, **cánere, cantáre**
sir, **vir óptime**
sister, **sóror**
sit, to, **sedére**
sit down, to, **cōnsídere**
situated, **sítus**
situation, **rēs**
six, **sex**
sixteen, **sédecim**
six (in throwing knucklebones), the, **sénio**
sixteenth, **séxtus décimus**
sixth, **séxtus**
skill, **ars**
sky, **caélum**
slave, **sérvus**
slave-woman, **ancílla**
sleep, **sómnus**
sleep, to, **dormíre**
sleep, to go to, **obdormíre**
sleepy, to be, **dormitáre**
slender, **grácilis**
slow, **léntus, tárdus**
slowly, **léntē**
small, **párvulus, párvus**
small, very, **mínimus**
small amount, a, **paúlum**

small boat, **scápha**
smaller, **mínor**
smallest, **mínimus**
smell, to, **olfácere**
smile, **rísus**
smile, to, **rīdére**
smoke, **fúmus**
snatch, to, **arrípere, rápere**
snatch from, to, **ērípere**
snore, to, **stértere**
so, **íta, tam**
So be it! **Éstō!**
soldier, **míles**
solitude, **sōlitúdō**
some, **áliquī**
some...others..., **áliī...áliī...**
something, **áliquid**
sometimes, **nōnnúmquam**
son, **fílius**
soon, **mox**
sorry, to be, **dolére**
sort of...?, What, **Quális...?**
soul, **ánima**
sound, **sónitus**
space, open, **área**
Spain, **Hispánia**
speak, to, **lóquī**
speak together, to, **cólloquī**
speaker, **ōrátor**
spectacle, **spectáculum**
spectator, **spectátor**
speech, **ōrátiō**
speed, **celéritās**
speed, with the greatest, **súmmā celeritáte**
spend the night, to, **pernoctáre**
spill, to, **effúndere**
spin wool, to, **lánam tráhere**
split, to, **scíndere**
spur on, to, **incitáre**
squared, **quadrátus**
staff, **báculum**
stand, to, **stáre**
standing out, **éxstāns**
statue, **státua**

stay, to, **manére, morárī**
stay awake, to, **vigiláre**
stealthily, **fúrtim**
stick, **báculum, vírga**
stick, to, **haerére**
still, **adhúc**
stock, **génus**
stola, **stóla**
stone, **lápis**
stone, of, **lapídeus**
stony, **lapídeus**
storm, **tempéstās**
story, **fábula, tabulátum**
story, funny, **iócus**
strange, **mírus**
stream, **rívus**
street, **vía**
strenuously, **strénuē**
strike, to, **feríre, percútere**
strong, to be, **valére**
stronger, to grow, **convaléscere**
study, **stúdium**
study (room), **tablínum**
study, to, **studére**
stupid, **fátuus, stúltus**
Subura, **Subúra**
such, **tális**
such things, **tália**
suddenly, **súbitō**
suffer, to, **pátī**
summer, **aéstās**
summon, to, **arcéssere**
support, to, **favére**
surname, **cognómen**
sweet, **suávis**
swift, **céler**
swim, to, **natáre**
switch, **vírga**
sword, **gládius**

T

table, **ménsa**
tail, **caúda**

take, to, **cápere, dúcere, súmere**
take away (from), to, **adímere, auférre**
take back, to, **redúcere**
take care of, to, **cūráre**
take off, to, **exúere**
take out, to, **extráhere**
take up, to, **súmere**
talk, to, **lóquī**
talkative, **verbósus**
tall, **áltus**
tart with cheese filling, **scriblíta**
tasteful, **élegāns**
teach, to, **docére**
teacher, secondary school, **grammáticus**
tell, to, **dícere**
tell (a story), to, **nārráre**
tell not to, to, **vetáre**
tell the truth, to, **véra dícere**
temper, bad, **īrācúndia**
temple, **témplum**
ten, **décem**
tenant, **íncola**
tenth, **décimus**
terrified, **pertérritus**
terrify, to, **terrére**
territory, **áger**
terror, **térror**
test, to, **experírī**
testament, **testāméntum**
than, **quam**
thanks, **grátia**
Thank you! **Grátiās tíbi ágō!**
that, **is, ílle, quī, quod**
that famous, **ílle**
that place, to, **éō**
the (more)…the (more), **quō…éō…**
their (own), **súus**
themselves, **ípsī, sē**
then, **deínde, índe, tum**
there, **éō, íbi, illúc**
there, from, **índe**
therefore, **ígitur, ítaque**
thing, **rēs**
think, to, **cōgitáre**

third, **tértius**
thirteen, **trédecim**
thirteenth, **tértius décimus**
this, **hic, is**
this way and that, **hūc illúc**
thorough, **díligēns**
thousand, a, **mílle**
thousandth, **mīllésimus**
Thrace, **Thrácia**
three, **trēs**
threshing-floor, **área**
through, **per**
throw, to, **conícere, iácere**
throw down, to, **dēícere**
throw of the knucklebones, the highest, **Vénus**
throw of the knucklebones, the lowest, **cánis**
throw out, to, **ēícere**
thus, **íta, sīc**
time, **témpus**
time, on, **ad témpus**
time to time, from, **intérdum**
timid, **tímidus**
tired, **dēféssus**
to, **ad**
today, **hódiē**
toga, **tóga**
toga, plain white, **tóga virílis**
toga of manhood, **tóga virílis**
toga with purple border, **tóga praetéxta**
together, **símul, únā**
toil, **lábor**
told, **nārrátus**
tomb, **sepúlcrum**
tombstone, **stéla**
tomorrow, **crās**
tongue, **língua**
too, **praetéreā**
top, on, **súprā**
top of, the, **súmmus**
toss about, to, **iactáre**
toward, **ad**
towering, **éxstāns**
town, **óppidum**
town, of the, **urbánus**

trace, **vēstīgium**
track, **vēstīgium**
travel, to, **íter fácere**
traveler, **viátor**
tray, **férculum**
tree, **árbor**
tremble, to, **trémere**
Trojan, **Troiánus**
Trojans, the, **Troiánī**
troublesome, **moléstus**
Troy, **Tróia**
true, **vérus**
truly, **vérō**
trunk, **císta**
trust, to, **cōnfídere**, **crédere**
try, to, **cōnárī**, **experírī**, **temptáre**
tunic, **túnica**
turn, to, **vértere**
turn aside, to, **dēvértere**
turning post, **méta**
tutor, **paedagógus**
twelfth, **duodécimus**
twelve, **duódecim**
twentieth, **vīcésimus**
twenty, **vīgíntī**
two, **dúo**
two-wheeled carriage, light, **císium**

U

Ulysses, **Ulíxēs**
uncle, **pátruus**
unconcerned, **sēcúrus**
under, **sub**
underworld, the, **ínferī**
unforgetting, **mémor**
unhappy, **míser**
unhurt, **incólumis**
unless, **nísi**
unspeakable, **īnfándus**
until, **dónec**, **dum**
unwilling, **invítus**
unwilling, to be, **nólle**
uproar, **tumúltus**

upset, to, **commovére**, **ēvértere**
urge on, to, **incitáre**
us, **nōs**
useful, **útilis**

V

vegetable, **hólus**
vehicle, **vehículum**
Venus, **Vénus**
verb, **vérbum**
Vergil, **Vergílius**
verse, **vérsus**
very, **ípse**, **máximē**, **váldē**
very much, **váldē**, **veheménter**
victor, **víctor**
vineyard, **vínea**
violent, **véhemēns**
violently, **veheménter**
visit, to, **vīsitáre**
voice, **vōx**

W

wagon, **plaústrum**
wait, to, **manére**
wait for, to, **exspectáre**
wake (someone) up, to, **excitáre**, **expergíscī**
wakened, **excitátus**
walk, to, **ambuláre**
wall, **múrus**, **páriēs**
walls, **moénia**
wander, to, **erráre**
want, to, **cúpere**, **vélle**
war, **béllum**
warm, **cálidus**
warn, to, **monére**
wash, to, **laváre**
wash overboard, to, **ēícere**
watch, to, **observáre**, **spectáre**
watch out for, to, **cavére**
water, **áqua**
wave, **únda**
way, **módus**

way, in this, **íta, sīc**
way...?, In what, **Quómodo...?**
way and that, this, **hūc illūc**
we, **nōs**
weak, **īnfírmus**
weapons, **árma**
wear, to, **gérere**
weave, to, **téxere**
web, **téla**
weep, to, **lacrimáre**
welcome, to, **accípere, excípere, salūtáre**
well, **béne, fēlíciter**
well, to be, **valére**
well, very, **óptimē**
werewolf, **versipéllis**
What...? **Quī...?, Quid...?**
What a...! **Quam...!**
What time is it? **Quóta hóra est?**
What/Which (in numerical order)...? **Quótus...?**
wheel, **róta**
When...? **Quándō...?**
when, **cum, úbi**
where, **úbi**
Where...? **Úbi...?**
where...?, From, **Únde...?**
Where...to? **Quō...?**
which, **quī**
Which...? **Quī...?**
which (in numerical order)...? **Quótus...?**
while, **dum**
whip, to, **verberáre**
white, **albátus, cándidus**
who, **quī**
Who...? **Quis...?**
whole, the, **ómnis, tótus**
whom...?, With, **Quócum...?**
Whose...? **Cúius...?**
Why...? **Cūr...?**
wicked, **sceléstus**
wife, **cóniūnx, úxor**
will, **testāméntum**
willing, to be, **vélle**
win, to, **víncere**

wind, **véntus**
window, **fenéstra**
wine, **vínum**
wine, undiluted, **mérum**
wine sweetened with honey, **múlsum**
winter, **híems**
wise, **prúdēns**
wisely, **prūdénter**
wish, to, **vélle**
wish, if you, **sī vīs, sīs**
wish, not to, **nólle**
wit, **sal**
with, **ápud, cum**
with difficulty, **vix**
without, **síne**
wolf, **lúpus**
woman, **fémina, múlier**
woman's outer garment, **stóla**
wonder, to, **sē rogáre**
wonderful, **mírus**
woods, **sílva**
wool, **lána**
word, **vérbum**
work, **lábor**
work, to, **labōráre**
worried, **sollícitus**
worse, **péior, péius**
worst, **péssimē, péssimus**
wound, **vúlnus**
wound, to, **vulneráre**
wretched, **míser, miserábilis**
write, to, **scríbere**

Y

year, **ánnus**
Yes! **Íta vérō!**
yesterday, **héri**
you, (sing.) **tū**, (pl.) **vōs**
young man, **aduléscēns**
your, (sing.) **túus**, (pl.) **véster**
youth, **aduléscēns**

INDEX OF GRAMMAR

INDEX OF CULTURAL INFORMATION

Maecenas, Gaius, 127
Magister lūdī, 103
Magna taberna, 17
Mall, shopping, 17
Manilian Law, On the (Cicero), 155–156
Manners, of children, 104
Mappae, 39
Marius, Gaius, 27–29
Maro, Publius Vergilius, 113
Martial, 17
  Epigrams, 9, 104, 138
Martial law, 27
Mathematics, 113
Meals, midday, 39
Medicine
  roots, 140
  vocabulary, Latin origins, 140–141
Mediterranean Sea, 29, 137
Menus, 54
Merchants, 17
Metamorphoses (Ovid), 146
Mirrors, 7
Mission, under Augustus, 127
Mithridates, King, 28–29
Mobs, 79
Monarchy, 81
Monumentum Ancyrānum, 125
Morals, of children, 104
Mulsum, 54
Murderers, 29
Music, 113

Napkins, 39
Nationalism, Augustan, 127
Natural science, 113
Needles, 147
Nero, Emperor, 17, 22
News, 52
Novus homō, 27, 78

Octavian, 124, 125
Odes (Horace), 127
Olympic Games, motto, 77
Optimātēs, 26, 28–29, 79, 81

Orations (Libanius), 104
Ōrnātrīcēs, 7
Outlaws, 29
Ovid
  Art of Love, 8
  Metamorphoses, 146

Paedagōgus, 104
Papyrus
  export of, 137
  manufacture of, 137
Parades, 80
Parthian Empire, 79
Patron, 37
Patrōnus, 37
Pāx Rōmāna, 125–128
Peasants, 26
Penelope, 93
Pennae, 137
Pens, 137
Pensions, 27
Peristȳlium, 16
Petronius, *Satyricon*, 52, 55, 114
Pharnaces, 80
Pharsalus plain, 80
Philosophy, 113
Piracy, 155–156
Pirates, 29
Plaids, woven, 146
Pliny, *Letters*, 102, 114–115
Plutarch
  Aemilius Paulus, 104
  Cato the Elder, 104
Politics, 114
Pompeius, Gnaeus (Pompey, the Great), 29,
  79–80, 155
Populārēs, 26, 28, 79
Populāris, 27
Populus Rōmānus, 26
Posca, 94
Poverty, 26
Power, tribunes, 29
Power base, 27
Praefectī, 126

▪▪▪▪▪ CREDITS ▪▪▪▪▪

Special gratitude is extended to Jenny Page of The Bridgeman Art Library, London, for her invaluable assistance in locating illustrative materials sought for *ECCE ROMANI*.

The publisher gratefully acknowledges the contributions of the agencies, institutions, and photographers listed below:

Chapter 28
(p. 6)   (a) Bronze head of a Roman woman, first quarter 2nd Century A.D., Louvre, Paris/Bridgeman Art Library, London; Bronze head of a Roman man, 1st–2nd Century A.D., Louvre, Paris/ Bridgeman Art Library, London

(b) Sardonyx cameo thought to be of Emperor Julian and his wife (361– 363 A.D.), British Museum, London/Bridgeman Art Library, London

(p. 7) Bas relief sculpture of a hair-dresser, circa 50 A.D., Landesmuseum, Hesse/Bridgeman Art Library, London

(p. 8) "A Roman Boat Race" by Sir Edward John Poynter (1836–1919), The Maas Gallery, London/Bridgeman Art Library, London

(p. 9) Woman Having Her Hair Dressed by a Maidservant, South West corner of South Wall, Oecus 5, 60–50 B.C. (fresco) Villa dei Misteri, Pompeii/ Bridgeman Art Library, London

Chapter 30
(p. 27) "Marius Triumphing Over the Cimbri" by Saverio Altamura (1826–1897), Museo e Gallerie Nazionali di Capodimonte, Naples/Bridgeman Art Library, London

(p. 28) "Caius Marius Amid the Ruins of Carthage" by John Vanderlyn, The Albany Institute of History and Art, Albany

Chapter 31
(p. 32) Roman butcher's, stone frieze, 2nd Century B.C., Musée de la Civilisation, Paris/Bridgeman Art Library, London

Chapter 32
(p. 39) Preparations for a banquet: fragment of marble, limestone, and glass mosaic pavement from Carthage, Roman c. 180–190 A.D., Louvre, Paris/Bridgeman Art Library, London

(p. 45) "Psyche and Charon" by John Roddam Spencer-Stanhope (1829–1908), Roy Miles Gallery, London/Bridgeman Art Library, London

Chapter 33
(p. 53) Roman tableware. Photograph courtesy Elizabeth Lyding Will

(p. 58) "Orpheus Charming the Animals," Roman mosaic, Blanzy, Musée Municipal, Laon, France/Giraudon/ Bridgeman Art Library, London

Chapter 34
(p. 61) Counters and dice, Gallo-Roman, second half of 1st Century B.C., Musée Alesia, Alise-Sainte-Reine/ Giraudon/Bridgeman Art Library, London

(p. 64) Dionysiac Mystery Cult, c. 60–50 B.C. (fresco) Villa dei Misteri, Pompeii/Bridgeman Art Library, London

Chapter 35
(p. 78) "Cicero and the Magistrates Discovering the Tomb of Archimedes" by Benjamin West (1738–1820), Christie's, London/Bridgeman Art Library, London

(p. 81) Statue of Julius Caesar of the Trajan Era, Campidoglio, Rome/Bridgeman Art Library, London

Chapter 36
(p. 90) "Neaera Reading a Letter from Catullus" by Henry J. Hudson, Bradford Art Galleries & Museums/ Bridgeman Art Library, London

(p. 93) Woman spinning. Attic trefoil-mouthed jug, c. 500–480 B.C. The Granger Collection, New York

Chapter 37
(p. 103) Stone relief of Roman classroom scene, photograph courtesy The Mansell Collection

Chapter 38
(p. 110) "Ariadne in Naxos" by Evelyn de Morgan (1850–1919), The de Morgan Foundation, London/Bridgeman Art Library, London

Chapter 39
(p. 124) Augustus of Prima Porta. Braccio Nuovo, Vatican Museums, Vatican State. Scala/Art Resource, New York

(p. 127) Augustus (63 B.C.–A.D. 14) and his wife Livia (39 B.C.–A.D. 14) seated classical marble statues, Ephesus Museum, Turkey/Bridgeman Art Library, London

(p. 129) Detail from "Vergil Reading the *Aeneid* to Augustus," by J.A.D. Ingres (1780–1867), courtesy of the Fogg Art Museum, Harvard University Art Museums, Cambridge; bequest of Grenville L. Winthrop

Chapter 40
(p. 138) "A Roman Scribe" by Sir Lawrence Alma-Tadema (1836–1912), private collection/Bridgeman Art Library, London

Chapter 41
(pp. 145–146) Drawings by Mary O. Minshall